POTTERY AND PORCELAIN MARKS

POTTERY AND PORCELAIN MARKS

EUROPEAN, ORIENTAL AND U.S.A.

IN CHRONOLOGICAL ORDER

Compiled by

E. George Perrott B.A.

Marks drawn by J.W. Perrott

Gemini Publications Ltd.

Published by Gemini Publications Ltd.
31 Newbridge Road, Bath, BA1 3HE, England.

Publishing Consultant Lisa H. Disney.
Jacket Design by Dylan Channon.

ISBN 0 9530637 0 4

Printed and Bound in England by
The Bath Press
Lower Bristol Road
Bath, England.

CONTENTS

Acknowledgements and Credits

Wendy Perrott (my wife) For her unstinting work on the mark and back-stamp illustrations, and her persistent encouragement when at times I felt like giving it all up.

Maggie Battson, of Battson Translations, 17 Laxton Gardens, Baldock, Herts. For her help translating information from the German factories.

Franz Feeberger, an Austrian who lives in Ramsgate, Kent, and is an agent for a number of Continental ceramic factories, who also kindly translated some of the German and French information.

Ramsgate Local Lending Library, whose staff ordered and supplied books from throughout the British lending system.

Hanley Reference Library and Museum, Stoke-on-Trent, Staffordshire, England. For the staff's helpful assistance carrying and fetching various volumes of books on the occasions that I visited them.

Gladstone Pottery Museum, Uttoxeter Road, Longton, Stoke-on-Trent, ST3 1PQ, England.

The British Library, London, England.

International Trade Publications Limited. For the valuable information I gleaned from their publication Tableware International and their earlier publication Pottery Gazette.

For all the Factories and potters and ceramic clubs who kindly answered my request for information, of which, some I list below who were especially helpful.

Babbacombe Pottery and Toni-Raymond Pottery Ltd., Torquay, Devon, England.
Belleek Pottery Ltd., (Fergus Cleary, Head of Design) Belleek,, Co. Fermanaugh, Ireland.
BodaNova-Höganäs Keramik AB, Box 23, S-263, 21 Höganäs, Sweden.
Bretby Art Pottery, Tooth & Co.Ltd., Woodville, Burton-on-Trent, England.
Buchan, A.W.,& Co., 14 Comrie Street, Crieff, Perthshire, Scotland.
Burgess & Leigh Ltd., Burslem, Stoke-on-Trent, England.
Cauldon Potteries Ltd., Ferrybridge, W. Yorkshire, England.
My appreciation to Mr. John E. Perks, Managing Director of `Royal Cauldon` and other Companies in this Group who helped me immensely with this project.
Chessell Pottery (I.O.W.) Ltd., Yarmouth, Isle of Wight, England.
Chittlehampton Pottery, (Roger Cockram) Chittlehampton, Nth.Devon, England.
Connoisseur Ltd., Lower Road, Ledbury, Herefordshire, England.
Coquet, Jean Louis, Limoges, France.
Crich Pottery, (Diana and David Worthy) Market Place, Crich, Derbyshire, England.
Crochendy Crefftau`r Cantref Tywyn Pottery, (Peter Roberts) Gwynedd, Wales.
Crown Trent China Ltd., Spring Garden Road, Longton, England.
Dartmouth Pottery Ltd., Cobden Works, Leopold Street, Birmingham, England.
Denby Pottery Co. Ltd., (Linda Salt, Museum Curator) Denby, Derbyshire, England.
Dudson Group, The, (I.J.Dudson, Man. Director) Scotia Road, Tunstall, Stoke-on-Trent, England.
Special thanks to Mr. I.J. Dudson for his generous help with this project.
Eigen Arts (Barbara Eigen) 150 Bay Street, Jersey City, NJ 07302, U.S.A.
FAIART Faiancas e Porcelanas, S.A.,AP.94 Pinheiros, 2441 Batalha Codex, Portugal.
Fulham Pottery, The, Ingate Place, London, SW8 3NS, England.
Gien France, (Stephanie Ferre) Place de la Victoire, 45500 Gien, France.
Goebel Porzellanfabrik, W., (Dieter E. Schneider) Coburger Strasse 7, D-96472 Rodental, Germany.
Grayshott Pottery, Surrey Ceramic Co. Ltd., School Road, Grayshott, Surrey, England.

Acknowledgements and Credits (Cont`)

Green, T.G.Ltd., Church Gresley, Burton-on-Trent, Staffordshire, DE11 8EF, England.
Haviland Limoges, c/o Haviland UK Limited (Brian Williams,Director) Plantation Road,
Newstead Trading Estate, Trentham, Stoke-on-Trent, ST4 8HX, England.
Honiton Art Potteries Ltd., (P. Redvers, Man. Director) 30-32 The High St., Devon, EX14 8PU, England.
Special thanks to Carl Rosen, Chairman of Honiton Pottery Collectors Society.
Hornsea Pottery Ltd. (David Leather, Man. Director) Hornsea, Humberside, HU18 1UD, England.
Hutschenreuther AG, Porzellanfabriken, Postfach 1340, D-95087 Selb, Germany.
Special thanks to Norbert Westphal and Andrea Täuber and the Hutschenreuther Museum for information they supplied of the Hutschenreuther Group of Companies.
Jersey Pottery Ltd., Gorey Village, Jersey, Channel Islands.
Johnson Brothers Ltd., (A Wedgwood Company) Barlaston, Stoke-on-Trent, ST12 9ES, England.
Johnson Tiles Ltd., H.& R., Highgate Tile Works, Tunstall, Stoke-on-Trent, ST6 4JX, England.
Kahla/Thüringen Porzellan GmbH, Christian-Eckardt-Strasse 38, 07768 Kahla, Germany.
Kaiser-Porzellan, Alboth & Kaiser GmbH & Co.KG, Postfach 1160, 8623 Staffelstein, Germany.
Kent (1989), James, Old Foley Pottery, King Street, Fenton, ST4 EDH, England.
KPM-Königliche Porzellan-Manufaktur Berlin GmbH, Wegelystrasse 1, D-10623 Berlin, Germany.
Koninklijke Mosa B.V., Royal Mosa, (C.H.van der Wiel, President) Meerssenerweg 358, 6224 AL,
Maastricht, Holland.
Koninklijke Porceleyne Fles, Royal Delft, Rotterdamsewg 196, PO Box 11, NL-2600 Delft, Holland.
Langenthal Swiss China Works Ltd., (Gabriela Kunzli) Bleienbachstrasse,CH-4900 Langenthal,Switzerland.
Leach, David, Lowerdown Pottery, Bovey Tracey, Devon, TQ13 9LE, England.
Leach, Janet, Leach Pottery, St. Ives, Cornwall, England.
Leach, John, Muchelney Pottery, Langport, Somerset, TA10 ODW, England.
Lindner Porzellan KG Postfach 1180, D-96324 Kups, Germany.
Lladro Comercial SA. (Marta Licer, Communication Dept.) Tavernes Blanques, 46016 Valencia, Spain.
Marioni Paolo s.r.l., Via G. Giusti 199, 50041 Calenzano-F1, Italy.
Mason Cash & Co.Ltd., (John E.Perks, Man.Director) Pool Street, Church Gresley, Derbyshire, England.
Mason's Ironstone, (A Wedgwood Company) Broad Street, Hanley, Stoke-on-Trent, ST1 4HH, England.
Meakin, J.&G., Ltd., (A Wedgwood Company) Barlaston, Stoke-on-Trent, ST12 9ES, England.
Meissen GmbH, Staatliche Porzellan-Manufaktur, D-01662 Meissen, Talstrasse 9, Germany.
Special thanks to Paul Prem, Sales Director, for the help and information he supplied.
Melba-Wain (England) Ltd., Corwell Road, Longton, Stoke-on-Trent, ST3 2JV, England.
Merkelbach Manufaktur GmbH, (Judith Engelmann) Postfach 1346, D-56194 Höhr-Grenhausen, Germany.
Monaco, Manufacture De, (Joram Rozewicz, Marketing Dir.) 4, quai Antoine 1er, MC 98000 Monaco.
Principaute De Monaco.
Moorland Pottery Ltd., Chelsea Works, 72a Moorland Road, Burslem, Stoke-on-Trent, ST6 1DY, England.
Moorcroft, W., P.L.C., Sandbach Road, Burslem, Stoke-on-Trent, ST6 2DQ, England.
My appreciation to Mr. W .John S. Moorctroft, (Man. Director) for the help he gave me.
Naturecraft Ltd., (Peter A. Tomlins, Man.Dir.) Havannah Street, Congleton, Cheshire, CW12 2AQ, England.
Noritake (U.K.) Ltd., (M. Tomori, Man.Dir.) 19 Heathfield, Stacey Bushes, Milton Keynes,
MK12 6HP, England.
Park Rose Ltd., Carnaby Covert Lane, Bridlington, Yorkshire, YO15 3QF, England.
Poole Pottery Ltd., The Quay, Poole, Dorset, BH15 1RF, England.
My appreciation to Leslie Hayward author of Poole Pottery and archivist for the Poole Pottery Collectors Club, and my thanks to Gloria Peek (Secretary).
Porcelaine de Paris, 8, rue de la Pierre-Levee, 75543 Paris Cedex 11, France.
Porcelanas Nou, C.B., Ctra.Cheste, Km.1`5, 46191 Villamarchante, Valencia, Spain.
Porcellane Principe, Vicenza, Italy. c/o The Alexander Collections Ltd.,No.1 The Broadway, Old Amersham,
Bucks, HP7 OHL, England.
Pordamsa-Porcelanas del Ampurden SA. Apdo 36, La Bisbal, E-17100 Gerona, Spain.
Porsgrunds Porselaensfabrik A/S, N-3901 Porsgrunn, Box 100, Norway.
Portmeirion Potteries Ltd., (Anwyl Cooper-Willis) London Road, Stoke-on-Trent, ST4 7QQ, England.

Acknowledgements and Credits (Cont`)

Price & Kensington Potteries Ltd., Trubshaw Cross, Longport, Stoke-on-Trent, ST6 4LR , England.
Prinknash Pottery, Prinknash Abbey, Cranham, Gloucestershire, England.
Purbeck Pottery Ltd., 5 Eldon Place, Westbourne, Bournemouth, BH4 9AZ, England.
ÖSPAG, A-1015 Wien, Goethegasse 3, Postfach 128, Austria.
Oxford (Ireland) Ltd., Carrigaline, Co.Cork, Ireland.
Rossware, Leighton Court, Lower Eggleton, Ledbury, Herefordshire, HR8 2UN, England.
Royal Daulton plc., Minton House, London Road, Stoke-on-Trent, England.
And especially Valerie Baynton, Museums Manager and Alexander Clement, Curator, Sir Henry Doulton Gallery for their particular assistance of the Royal Doulton Group of Companies, including: Royal Crown Derby, Minton, Royal Albert, and the many others in the Group.
Royal Grafton Ltd., Grafton Works, Marlborough Road, Longton, Stoke-on-Trent, ST3 1ED, England.
Royal Limoges, 28, rue Donzelot, 87000 Limoges, France.
Royal Winton, Norfolk Street, Shelton, Stoke-on-Trent, ST1 4PA, England.
Royal Worcester Ltd., Severn Street, Worcester, WR1 2NE, England.
My appreciation to The Dyson Perrins Museum Trust, for sending the various information of `Worcester`s` history and marks.
Sadler, James & Sons Ltd., Market Place, Burslem, Stoke-on-Trent, ST6 4AZ, England.
Seltmann GmbH, Porzellanfabriken Christian, Postfach 2040, 92610 Weiden/Opf. Germany.
My appreciation to this Company for the amount of time and information they gave me in order to cover the various other factories in this substantial Group of Companies.
Søholm Keramik A/S, Lillevangsvej 6, DK-3700 Røenne, Denmark.
Spode (Part of the Royal Worcester Group) Church St., Stoke-on-Trent, ST4 1BX, England.
Springfield China Ltd., Greendock Street, Longton, Stoke-on-Trent, ST3 2NA, England.
Staffordshire Tableware Ltd., Meir Park, Stoke-on-Trent, ST3 7AA, England.
Steelite International plc., Orme Street, Stoke-on-Trent, ST6 3RB, England.
Tams Group PLC, John, Longton, Stoke-on-Trent, ST3 2PG, England.
Thewalt GmbH, Gartenstr 20, PO Box 1449, D-56195 Hoehr-Grenhausen, Germany.
Villeroy & Boch AG, Rieffstrasse 46, D-66663 Merzig, Germany.
My thanks to Adolf Scholtes, Isabel Eck and the Villeroy & Boch Ceramic Museum for the help and information they supplied.
Wade Collectors Club, Royal Victoria Pottery, Westport Road, Burslem, Stoke-on-Trent, ST6 4AG, England.
Watson's Potteries Ltd., Henry, Wattisfield, Suffolk, IP22 1NH, England.
Weatherby & Sons Ltd., J.H., Falcon Pottery, Old Town Road, Hanley, Stoke-on-Trent, ST1 2LB, England.
Wedgwood & Sons Ltd., Josiah, Barlaston, Stoke-on-Trent, ST12 9ES, England.
My thanks to Miss Gaye Blake Roberts, Curator of the Wedgwood Museum for her helpful suggestions and information she provided of the Companies that comprise The Wedgwood Group.
Wenford Bridge Pottery, (Seth & Ara Cardew) St.Breward, Bodmin, Cornwall, PL30 3PN, England.
Winchcombe Pottery, (Raymond Finch) Winchcombe, Gloucestershire, England.
Winterling Porzellan AG. Postfach 9, 8686 Kirchenlamitz, Germany.
Wood & Son (Longport) P.L.C., Arthur, Davenport Street, Longport, Stoke-on-Trent, ST6 4LL, England.

And finally to our family and friends and our colleagues in the antiques trade, too many to mention here, who gave both my wife and myself lots of help and encouragement throughout this project.

My apologies for any errors or omissions within this book, and should any reader know of any significant marks that I may have left out or misinterpreted, or any Pottery or Porcelain Manufacture that would like their marks/backstamps included in the next revised edition please let me know through the Publisher.

Thank you
E.G.P.

INTRODUCTION

The introduction to many reference books usually consists of a list of information and technical jargon that most readers tend not to look at. Therefore, all I intend to refer to here is how this book can work for the reader and what information can be gleaned from it. It has, first of all, a comprehensive selection of approximately 10,000 marks and backstamps.

It consists of marks from the most important regions throughout the ceramic history of the world. It commences in 1368 with the Ming Dynasty of China and takes the reader through the `Maiolica` marks of the 15th Century Italian Renaissance, the German `Stoneware` and French `Faïence` of the 16th Century and continues through to the great factories of Europe including Meissen, Sèvres, and the English factories of Wedgwood, Derby, Minton, Doulton, etc. It shows how in the late 18th century North America came on the scene and during the second half of the 19th century distinguished themselves with celebrated wares from factories such as Rookwood. It concludes in relatively modern times with, amongst others, Noritake of Japan, Moorcroft of England and Lladro from Spain.

The one positive difference from other books on marks is that this one has been compiled in date order and includes factories and potters up to the present day. The reader can research any date within a particular period of history and find the marks of all the important factories and potters which existed or started their production during that specific time. He can look up the year 1650 for instance, and discover that the great `Kutani` porcelain of Kaga, Japan, were producing their wares at the same time as Nicholas Hubble of Wrotham in England was incising a recognised mark on his slip glazed earthenware. Amongst others in that year were the French potters of Toulouse and Rennes. During this era the tin-glazed factories of Delft in Holland were capturing Europe with their Chinese style, blue and white ware. One of these pot-works was De Porceleyne Fles (The Porcelain Jar) which was founded in 1653 by David Anthonisz V.D. Pieth. The factory is still producing today, but of course with different production methods and materials.
The big breakthrough in European ceramics was in 1709 when Johann Friedrich Böttger produced the first hard-paste porcelain body, and in the following year, 1710, The Royal Saxon Porcelain Factory of Meissen, Germany, was established.

The aim throughout this work is to allow the collector to date a piece by the means of a mark. However, the mark alone does not preclude a piece is valuable, but to all intents and purposes, a marked example must be more desirable than a similar unmarked one.

E.G.P.

The terms used throughout this work are explained as follows:-

Pottery and Earthenware includes all forms of earthenware made from clays usually covered with lead glaze.

Faïence, Fayence, Maiolica and Delft includes all forms of earthenware coated with a tin enamel glaze.

Stoneware is a hard, non-porous vitrifield earthenware.

Porcelain (hard-paste) is a translucent hard white form of ceramics originally produced and exported from China, and first produced in Europe at Meissen, Germany, in 1710.

Porcelain (soft-paste) was produced in Europe as an alternative, because the formula of hard-paste was not known until the early 18th Century.

The lay-out of this book is very simple but it is worth explaining to the reader how it works.

The area or region (i.e. **FORLI**, Italy. or **BRUSSELS,** Belgium.) is printed in **BOLD** capital letters. If there are only a few factories within a main area they will all be listed together as in Example 1. **BRUSSELS**. If it is a large region like **LIMOGES** or **BURSLEM** the individual factories and potters are listed separately under their own dates and marks and printed as in Example 2.

Example 1.

1705 BRUSSELS, Belgium, - - ***`A Bruxelles`***

FAÏENCE AND HARD-PASTE PORCELAIN

1705- Witsenburg and Mombaers, FAÏENCE -

1724- Mombaers, Phillipe, - - - - -

1766- Antoisenet, Jaques, - - - - -

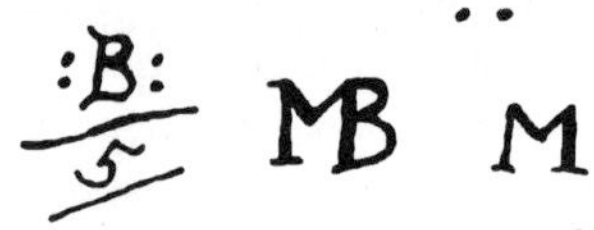

1786-90 Schaerbeek. HARD-PASTE PORCELAIN.
Red or blue-

c.1787-1803 Etterbeek. HARD-PASTE PORCELAIN.
Red or purple-

c.1791-1803 Louis Cretté. - - - - - - ***`L. Cretté Bruxelles rue d`Aremberg 1791`***

Example 2.

1651 Simpson, Ralph, BURSLEM, Staffordshire, England.
1651-c.1724 SLIPWARE - - - *RALPH SIMPSON.*

Sometimes there are families or groups of potters that continue working a factory over a number of years, or even over centuries like Wedgwood or Doulton of England. These groups are shown under the original date the factory first opened, then each subsequent change is listed in date order. See 1815 Royal Doulton plc. for instance.

Example 3.

Where a potter or decorater or a change of ownership is listed in the main grouping like BRUSSELS above, the entry will be cross-referenced in date order and entered as follows:-

---

1787 Etterbeek, Belgium. - - - see 1705 BRUSSELS.

Useful information for recognising and dating British ceramics.

1. (1800) The incorporation of the Royal Arms into a mark indicates a date after 1800.
2. (1810) A pattern number or name usually indicates a date after 1810.
3. (1850) Where the word `Royal` is added to a manufacturer`s name it usually indicates a piece after 1850.
4. (1862) The Trade Mark Act became law in 1862 so any piece bearing the word `Trade Mark` usually means it was made after 1862.
5. (1880) `Ltd` incorporated in a mark means that the wares were made after 1880.
6. (1891) From 1891 the American McKinley Tariff Act was introduced and it became necessary to mark export wares with the country of origin hence `ENGLAND` or any other country shown on a piece, means it was made after 1891.
7. `MADE IN ENGLAND` as with other countries usually means 20th Century pieces.
8. `English Bone China` or simply `Bone China` indicates a product of the 20th Century.

British Patent Office Registration mark.

A diamond-shaped mark appears on Victorian ceramics from 1842 to 1883. This mark shows that the design was registered with the British Patent Office. The date of the diamond mark only indicates the time the patent was registered; the actual design could still be produced ten years later but would still bear the original diamond mark. Nevertheless, it is still a reasonable indication of age. Illustrated below are the two forms of diamond marks used for particular years, showing the initials for dating and registering designs.

(a) Category IV = Ceramics.
(b) Year
(c) Month
(d) Day
(e) Batch number.

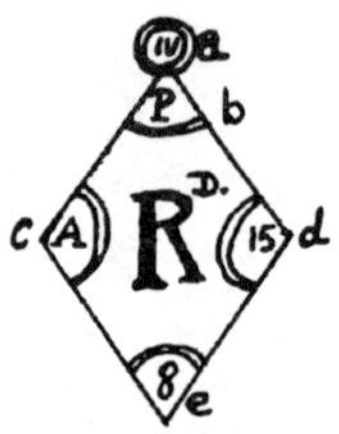

1842-67

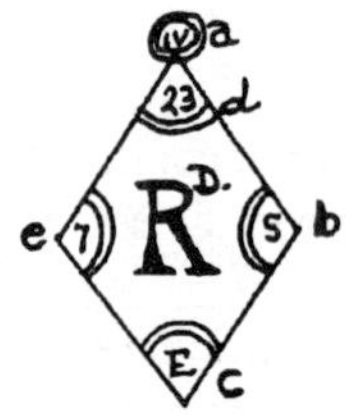

1868-83

The left-hand diamond was used between 1842 and 1867 after which the right-hand diamond was employed 1868 and 1883.

Index to year and month letters:-

1842 to 1867 (Year letter on top)

1842 = X	1855 = E
1843 = H	1856 = L
1844 = C	1857 = K
1845 = A	1858 = B
1846 = I	1859 = M
1847 = F	1860 = Z
1848 = U	1861 = R
1849 = S	1862 = O
1850 = V	1863 = G
1851 = P	1864 = N
1852 = D	1865 = W
1853 = Y	1866 = Q
1854 = J	1867 = T

1868 to 1883 (Year letter to the right)

1868 = X	1876 = V
1869 = H	1877 = P
1870 = C	1878 = D
1871 = A	1879 = Y
1872 = I	1880 = J
1873 = F	1881 = E
1874 = U	1882 = L
1875 = S	1883 = K

Month (Both periods)

A = December	H = April
B = October	I = July
C or O = January	K = November (and December 1860)
D = September	M = June
E = May	R = August (and 1st to 19th Sept. 1857)
G = February	W = March

British Patent Office Registration Mark (Cont`)

From 1884 the method of using the diamond mark discontinued and the designs were numbered consecutively with an `Rd` number. In the following table are the approximate numbers shown for each year up to and including 1983.

All numbers were registered from January in each year.

1884 = 1	1909 = 535200	1934 = 789000	1959 = 891700
1885 = 19700	1910 = 552000	1935 = 799100	1960 = 895000
1886 = 40500	1911 = 574800	1936 = 808800	1961 = 899900
1887 = 64500	1912 = 594200	1937 = 817300	1962 = 904600
1888 = 90500	1913 = 612400	1938 = 825200	1963 = 909400
1889 = 116600	1914 = 630200	1939 = 832600	1964 = 914500
1890 = 141300	1915 = 644900	1940 = 837500	1965 = 919600
1891 = 163800	1916 = 653500	1941 = 838600	1966 = 924500
1892 = 185700	1917 = 659000	1942 = 839200	1967 = 929300
1893 = 205200	1918 = 662900	1943 = 840000	1968 = 934500
1894 = 224700	1919 = 666100	1944 = 841000	1969 = 939900
1895 = 247000	1920 = 673700	1945 = 842700	1970 = 944900
1896 = 268400	1921 = 680100	1946 = 845500	1971 = 950000
1897 = 291200	1922 = 687100	1947 = 849700	1972 = 955300
1898 = 311700	1923 = 695000	1948 = 853300	1973 = 960700
1899 = 331700	1924 = 702700	1949 = 857000	1974 = 965200
1900 = 351200	1925 = 710200	1950 = 860900	1975 = 969200
1901 = 368200	1926 = 718100	1951 = 863100	1976 = 973800
1902 = 385200	1927 = 726300	1952 = 866300	1977 = 978400
1903 = 402200	1928 = 734400	1953 = 869300	1978 = 982800
1904 = 424400	1929 = 742700	1954 = 872500	1979 = 987900
1905 = 447800	1930 = 751200	1955 = 876100	1980 = 993000
1906 = 471800	1931 = 760600	1956 = 879300	1981 = 998300
1907 = 494000	1932 = 769700	1957 = 882900	1982 = 1004500
1908 = 518600	1933 = 779300	1958 = 887100	1983 = 1010600

1368 MING DYNASTY, CHINA.

Hard-paste porcelain.

1368-98 **Hung-wu** - - - 洪武年製

1399-1402 **Chien-wên** - - - 建文

1403-24 **Yung-lo** - - - 永樂年製

1425- **Hung-hsi** - - - 洪熙

1426-35 **Hsüan-tê** - - - 大明宣德年製

1436-49 **Chêng-t`ung** - - - 正統

1450-57 **Ching-t`ai** - - - 景泰

1457-64 **T`ien-shun** - - - 天順

1465-87 **Ch`êng-hua** - - -

成化年製

大明成化年製

1488-1505 **Hung-chih** - - - 大明弘治年製

1506-21 **Cheng-tê** - - - 大明正德年製

Continued over -

1368 MING DYNASTY, China. (Cont`)

1522-66	Chia-ching	大明嘉靖年製
1567-72	Lung-ch`ing	大明隆慶年製
1573-1619	Wan-li	大明萬曆年製
1620-	T`ai-ch`ang	泰 昌
1621-27	T`ien-ch`i	大明天啟年製
1628-43	Ch`ung-chêng	崇禎年製

Chinese marks usually consist of six characters and read downward from right to left as follows:-

Example: 1621-27 T`ien-ch`i period.

4. = ch`i (ch`i)	1. = Ta (Great)	啟 大
5. = Nien (period)	2. = Ming (Ming)	年 明
6. = Chih (made)	3. = T`ien (T`ien)	製 天

Sometimes only 4 characters are used, Ta (1) and Ming (2) being omitted.

1450 SIENA, Tuscany, Italy.
15th & 16th Century MAIOLICA. -

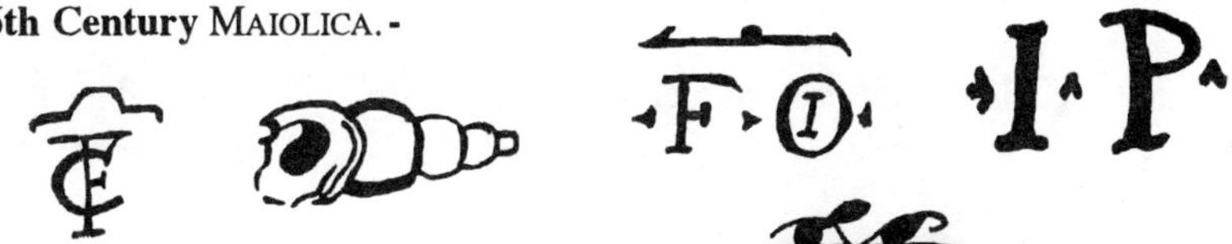

c.1515-20 Maestro Benedetto - -

1451 FAENZA, Emilia, Italy.
14th & 15th Century MAIOLICA.

1451- Andrea di Bono - -

1477- Nicolo Orsini - -

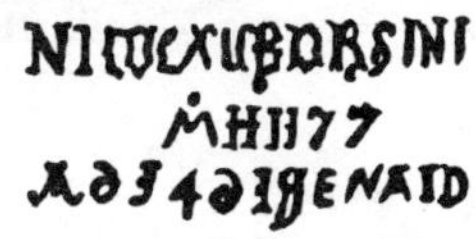

1475 Mark on maiolica plate. -

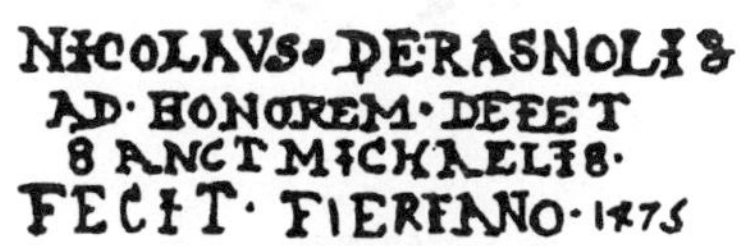

1485- Don Giorgio - - -

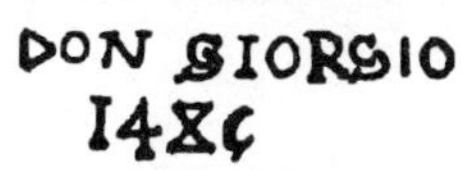

1487- Betini - - -

c.1490-1530 Casa Pirota Factory -

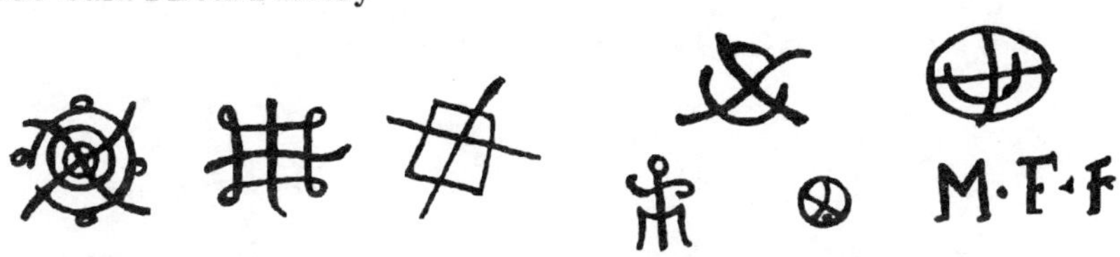

1510 Mark on dated tiles - -

1510-15- - - -

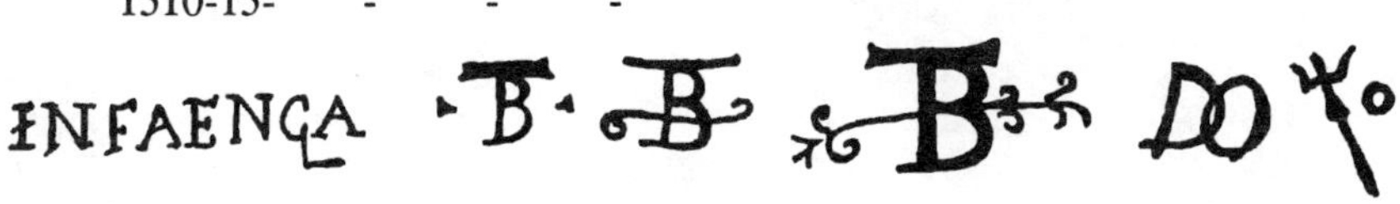

Continued over -

1451

1451 FAENZA, Emilia, Italy. (Cont`)

c.1530 Mark on Commemorative plate for Charles V.

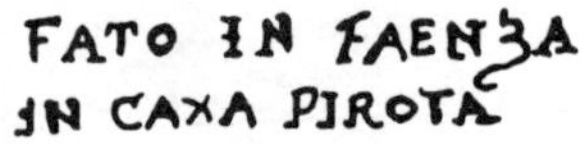

c.1530-35 Baldassare Manara. -

1549 (dated) mark on drug pot-

1546 (dated) Giovanni Brame - - -

c.1560 - Maestro Virgiliotto Calamelli. -

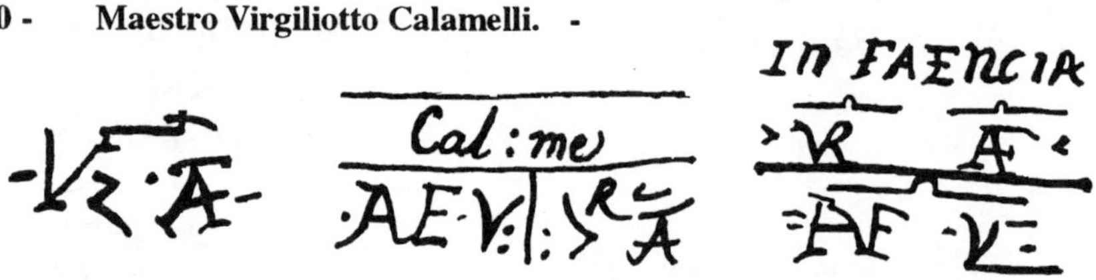

1575 - Rainerio - - -

1651 (dated) mark on a white tazza -

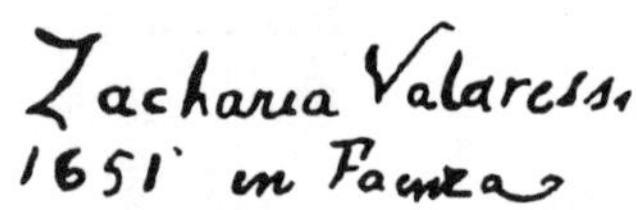

c.1750 Antonio Maria Regoli. - -

18th century marks:- Ferniani and descendants.

Francesco Ballanti - - -

1777 (dated) Benini Fabrique. - - - - -

1850-78 A. Farini - -

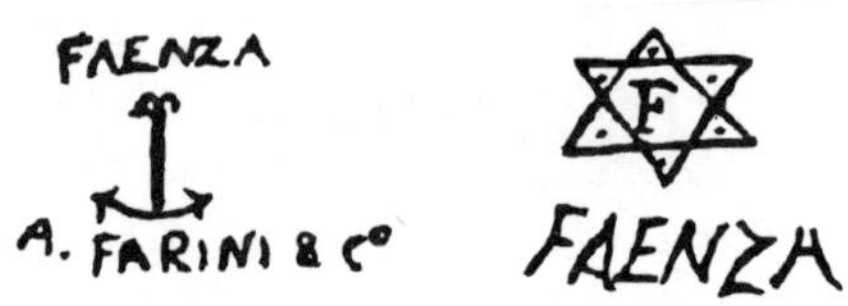

1457	T`ien-shun, China.	-	-	-	see 1368 MING.
1465	Ch`êng-hua, China.	-	-	-	see 1368 MING.
1477	Orsini, Nicolo, Italy.	-	-	-	see 1451 FAENZA
1485	Giorgio, Don. Italy.	-	-	-	see 1451 FAENZA
1487	Betini, Italy.-	-	-	-	see 1451 FAENZA
1488	Hung-chih, China.	-	-	-	see 1368 MING
1490	Pirota, Casa, Italy.	-	-	-	see 1451 FAENZA

1495 DERUTA, Umbria, Italy.

15th & 16th century MAIOLICA -

1525 (dated) mark on a plate -

1537-54 Francesco Urbini

1539 (dated) mark on a plate, (Victoria and Albert Museum) -

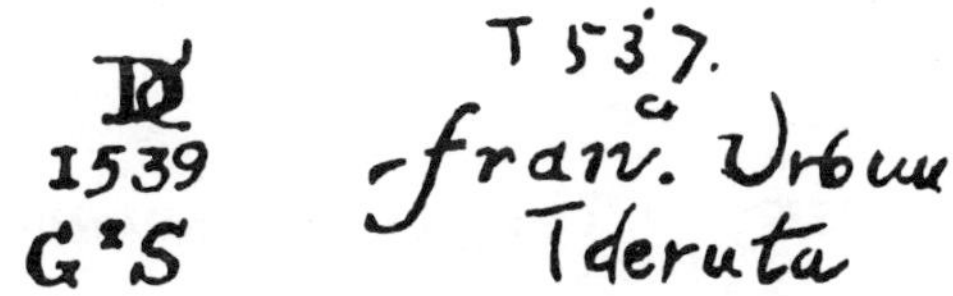

1544 (dated) mark on a plate, (Victoria and Albert Museum) - - -

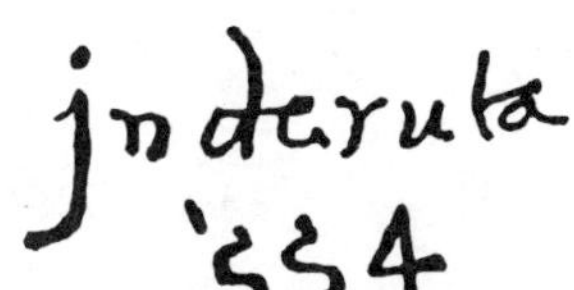

1545 (dated) mark on a plateau, (Victoria and Albert Museum) - - -

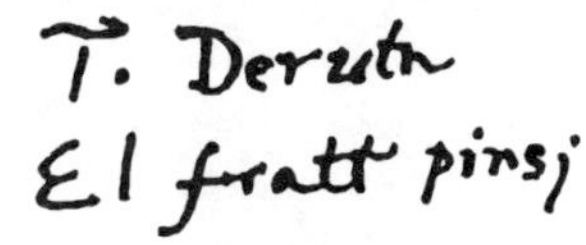

1579 (dated) mark - -

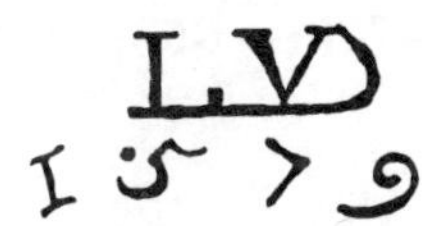

1630- Petrus Paulus. - - - ***PETRUS PAULUS MANCINUS DE DIRUTA***

1771 - - ***1771 Fabrico di Maiolica fina di Gregorio Caselli in Deruta***

1495 GUBBIO, Duchy of Urbino, Italy.

MAIOLICA ESPECIALLY RUBY METALLIC LUSTRE.

c.1518-41 Maestro Giorgio Andreoli.-

1519 (dated) mark on a plate, (Victoria and Albert Museum) - - -

1536 **Maestro Perestino.** - -

1535-40 **Maestro `N` probably Cencio, son of Giorgio Andreoli.** - - -

1537 **Cencio or Vincentio Andreoli (son)**

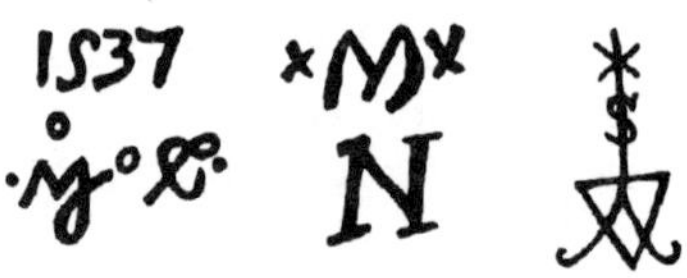

1541 **Maestro Gilleo** - -

c.1857-81 **Giovanni Spinaci** - - - -

1862 **International Exhibition. Messrs Carocci, Fabbri & Co. exhibited reproductions of 15th and 16th maiolica in metallic lustre. M.Pietro Gay the director received an award for the pieces.**

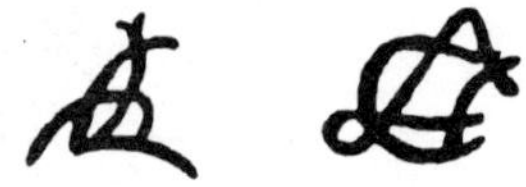

1506 CAFAGGIOLO, nr.Florence, Italy.

EARLY 16TH CENTURY TO MID 18TH CENTURY MAIOLICA -

`SPR` (Semper) motto of Medici family.

1509- Giovanni Acole. -

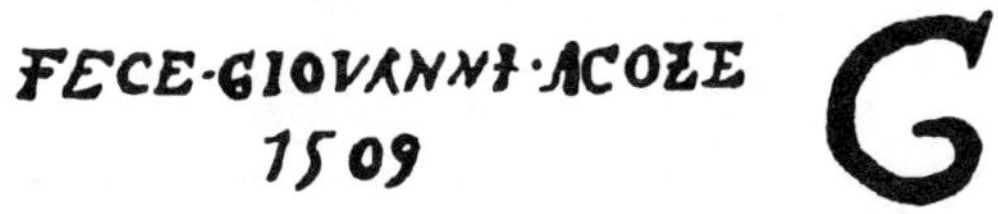

1516- Medici, Giuliano de third son of Lorenzo. -

G L O
V 1
S

1570 Mark on large dish. - -

IN CHAFAGGIOLO
FATO ADI 21 DI JUNIO, 1570

1506	Chêng-tê, China. - - - -	see 1368 MING
1509	Acole,Giovanni, Italy. - - - -	see 1506 CAFAGGIOLO
1515	Benedetto,Maestro, Italy. - - - -	see 1450 SIENA
1516	Medici, Guiliano de`, Italy. - - -	see 1506 CAFAGGIOLO
1518	Andreoli, Giorgio, Maestro, Italy.- - -	see 1495 GUBBIO

1520 CASTEL DURANTE, Italy (renamed URBANIA in 1635) see 1520 URBINO.

16TH CENTURY MAIOLICA

Urbino marks

1519 (dated) marks on a pharmacy vase,
(British Museum) -

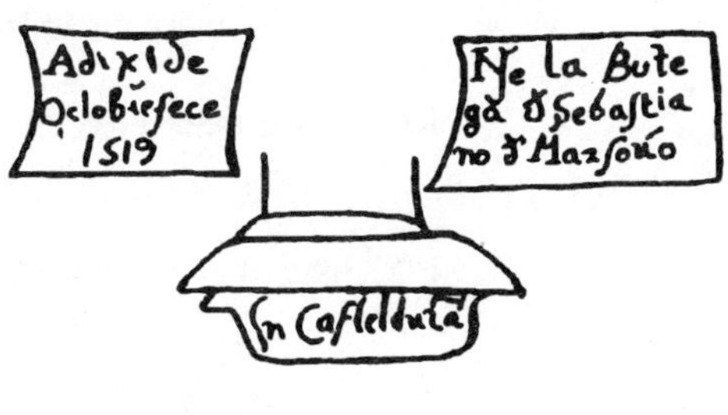

1521-28 Nicola Pellipario (painter) -

Continued over -

1520

1520 CASTEL DURANTE, Italy. (Cont`)

1524 (dated) mark on a plate. -

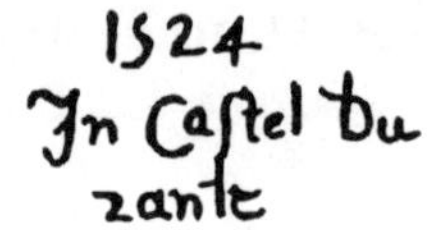

c.1543 Francesco Durantino.

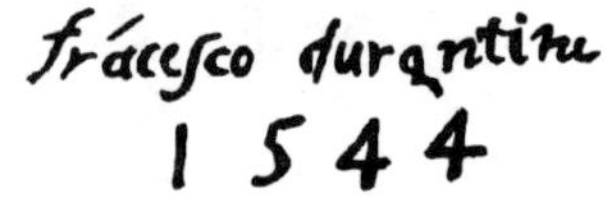

1555 (dated) inscription on a pharmacy vase *IN CASTELLO DURANTI. APRESO A URBINO. MIGLIE 7. 1555.*

1635 Renamed URBANIA.

1520 NUREMBERG, Bavaria, Germany.

16th century FAÏENCE..

Due to their number, the individual factories and potters of NUREMBERG have been listed under their own dates and marks within this book.

1520 PESARO, nr. Urbino, Italy.

15th and 16th century MAIOLICA.

Giambattista Passeri. - - -

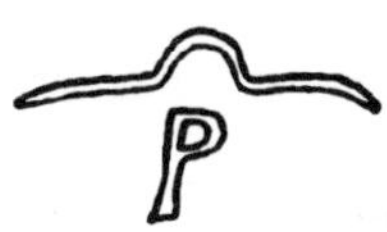

Potters of Pesaro:-

c.1542-52 Mo. Bernardino Gagliardino, Girolamo Lanfranchi, Rinaldo. -

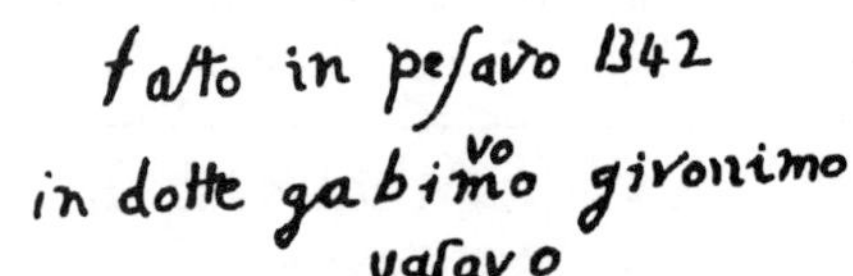

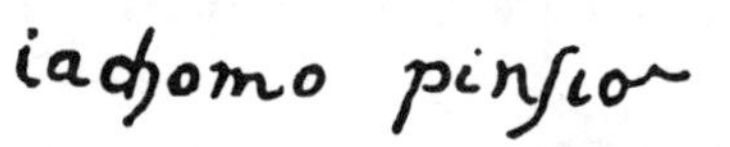

1542 Maestro Girolamo (dated) - - - *`in la botega di maestro Girolame de le Gabice`*

1566 (dated) mark on a plate- - -

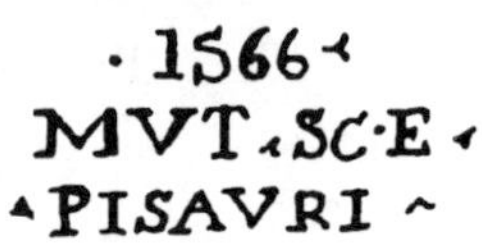

1582 Dated mark -

1757 (dated) mark on a medicine vase- -

1763 Casali and Callegari - -

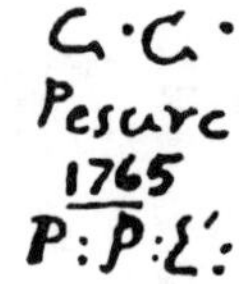

Continued over -

1520 PESARO, nr. Urbino, Italy. (Cont`)

`Fillippo Antonio Callegari, Pesaro` - - *F.A.C.*
P.
Callegari
Pesaro

1771 (dated) mark on a maiolica jug -

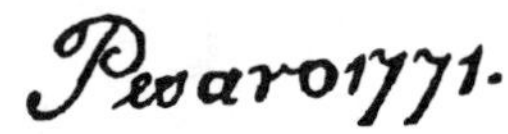

c.1870 **Magrini & Co.** - - - - -

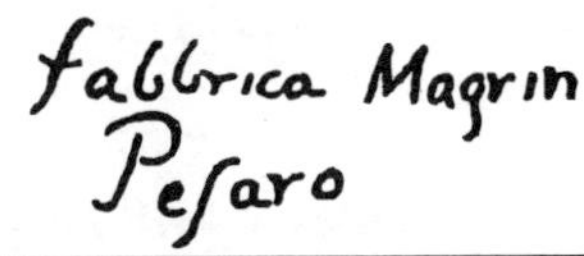

1520 URBINO, Italy.

see 1520 CASTEL DURANTE.

16th to 18th century MAIOLICA.

c.1520- **Nicola da Urbino, painter.** -
(Nicola Pellipario)

c.1530- **Artists of Urbino:-**
Federigo di Giannantonio,
Nicola di Gabriele,
Gian Maria Mariani,

1530-44 **Francesco Xanto Avelli of Rovigo.** -

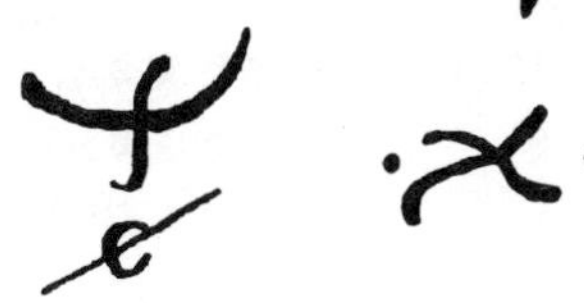

1531 (dated) Mark on a plate - - - -
(Victoria and Albert Museum)

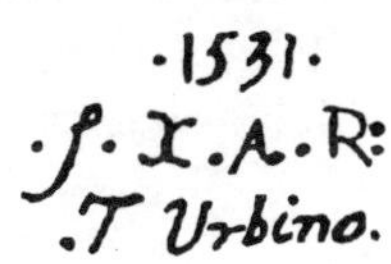

1543- **Fontana, Guido,** Dated mark -

1544 (dated) Mark on the border of a plate. - -

Continued over -

1520-26

1520 URBINO, Italy. (Cont`)

1544- Orazio Fontana and family (Pellipario) - -

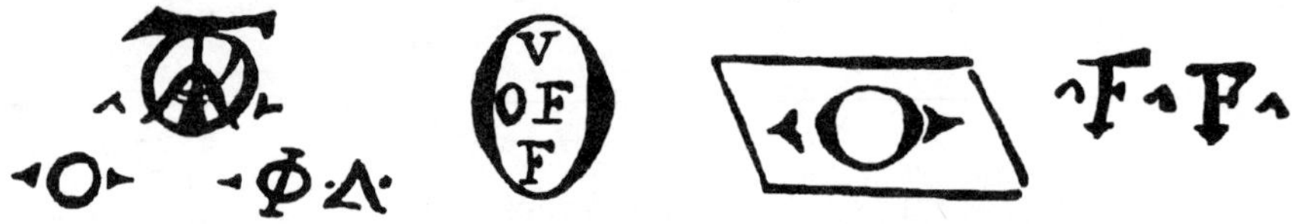

1544 (dated) Mark on a plate, (British Museum)
Orazio Fontana - -

c.1584- Alfonzo Patanazzi and family - -

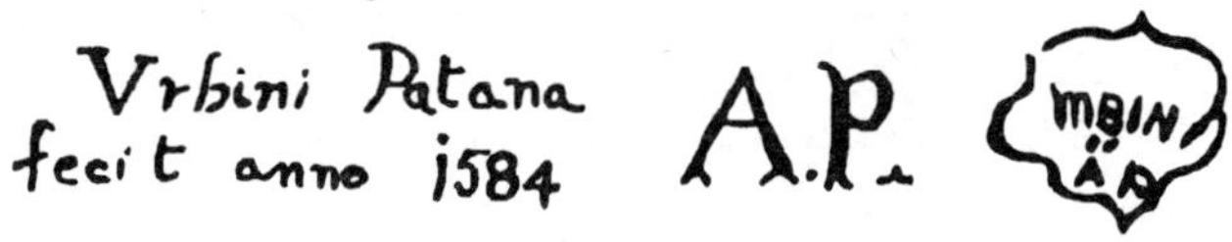

1606 (dated) Alfonzo Patanazzi.
Mark on a large dish (Victoria and Albert Museum)

1617 (dated) Francesco Patanazzi. mark on a plate. -

1773 (dated) M. Rolet.
This inscription on a lamp
(Victoria and Albert Museum) - -

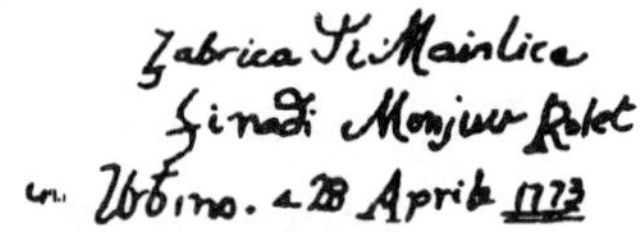

1521 Pellipario, Nicola, (painter) Italy. - - see 1520 CASTEL DURANTE.
1522 Chia-ching, China. - - - - - see 1368 MING.

1525 SAINT-PORCHAIRE, nr.Bressieure, France.

There are reputed to be only 65 pieces of this faïence in existence.
It is also referred to as `Henry Deux`.

1526 Reinhard, NUREMBERG, Bavaria, Germany.

16th Century Faïence. -

1526 ROUEN, Seine-Inférieure, France.

c.1526- MAIOLICA OR FAÏENCE IN ITALIAN STYLE

1542 (dated) Inscription on tiles - - ***A ROUEN 1542.***

c.1640- Marks found on faïence - -

Due to their numbers, the individual factories and potters of ROUEN have been listed under their own dates and marks within this book.

1527 FABRIANO, Duchy of Urbino, Italy.

16TH CENTURY MAIOLICA.

1527 (dated) mark on a tazza. Exhibited in the Paris Exhibition in 1867. - - -

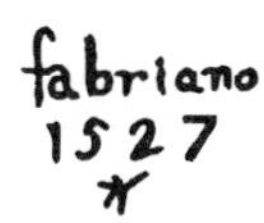

1527 YAMASHIRO, Japan.

1527- Kio or Kiyoto, formerly called Miaco.

KIOTO

Due to their numbers, the individual factories and potters of YAMASHIRO have been listed under their own dates and marks within this book.

1528 Raku Ware, YAMASHIRO, Japan.

C.1528 RAKU WARE

A Corean, named Ameya introduced Raku ware into Japan for making tea bowls. Teinim, his wife, continued after his death.

1588- Chojiro (son) Studio name `Tamaka`

c.1840- Raku Tanniu. - - -

1530-47

1530 Gabriele, Nicola di, Italy. - - - - see 1520 URBINO
1530 Giannantonio, Federigo di, Italy - - - see 1520 URBINO.
1530 Manara, Baldassare, Italy. - - - - see 1451 FAENZA.
1530 Mariani, Gian Maria, Italy. - - - see 1520 URBINO.
1530 Xanto, Avelli Francesco, Italy. - - - see 1520 URBINO.

1535 RIMINI, Italy.

15TH AND 16TH CENTURY MAIOLICA.

1536 Perestino, Maestro, Italy. - - - - see 1495 GUBBIO.
1537 Cencio/Vincentio Andreoli, Italy. - - - see 1495 GUBBIO.
1537 Urbini, Fracesco, Italy. - - - - see 1495 DERUTA.

1542 FORLI, Italy.

16TH CENTURY MAIOLICA.

1542- `fata in forli` mark - - *`fata in forli`*

1545- `Fu Fata in Forli` mark. - - *`FU FATA IN FORLI`* (in monogram)

1541 Gilleo, Maestro, Italy. - - - - see 1495 GUBBIO.
1542 Gagliardino, Bernardino, (Potter) Italy. - - see 1520 PESARO.
1542 Lanfranchi, Girolamo, (Potter) Italy. - - see 1520 PESARO.
1542 Rinaldo, Maestro, (Potter) Italy. - - - see 1520 PESARO.
1543 Durantino, Francesco, Italy. - - - see 1520 CASTLE DURANTE.
1543 Fontana, Guido, Italy. - - - - see 1520 URBINO.

1544 VITERBO, Roma, Italy.

16TH CENTURY MAIOLICA.

1544 Fontana, Orazio, Italy. - - - - see 1520 URBINO.
1545 `Fu Fata in Forli`, Italy - - - - see 1542 FORLI.
1546 Brame, Giovanni, Italy. - - - - see 1451 FAENZA.

1547 VERONA, Italy.

16TH CENTURY MAIOLICA.

Franco Giovani Batista - -

`Gio Giovanni Batista da Faenza In Verona M.....

1548 NIMES, Gard, France.

c.1548- MADE IN THE MANNER OF ITALIAN MAIOLICA.

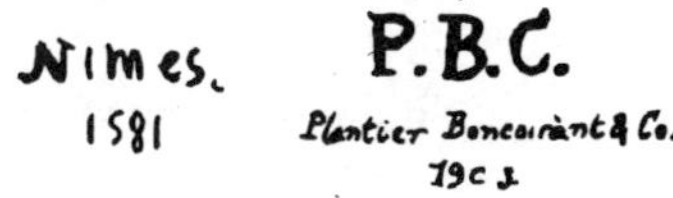

1548 PADUA, ITALY.

MAIOLICA AND LEAD-GLAZED `SGRAFFIATO` EARTHENWARE.

1548 (dated) Mark on a maiolica plate, Victoria and Albert Museum. — *PADVA. 1548.*

1555 - 1563- marks-

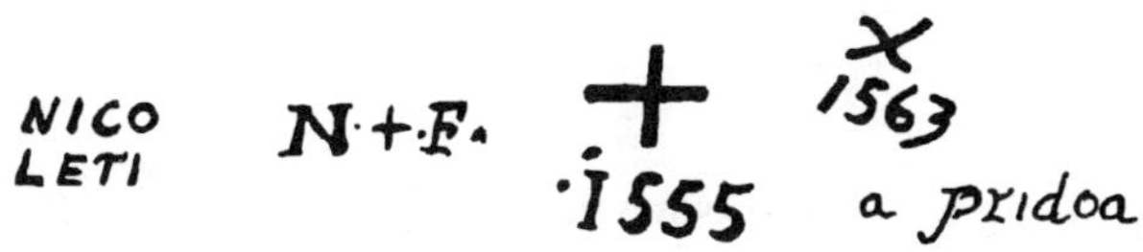

1564 (dated) Mark on a plate, British Museum. - *A. PADOA+ 1564.*

1550 KREUSSEN, nr.Bayreuth, Germany.

16TH CENTURY STONEWARE.

Vest family house-marks - - -

1600- Hans Christoph Vest - -	*HANS CHRISTOPH VEST*
1603- Georgius Vest - -	*GEORGIUS VEST*
Caspar Vest - - -	*CASPAR VEST*
1628- Initial marks - -	*G.L.M.E.L.* *M.M.C.* *M.J.W.C.*
1644- Adam Scharf - - -	*ADAM SCHARF*

Sachsen, Johann Georg Herzog von, Duke and Elector of Saxony. - - -

1550 SAVONA, nr.Genoa, Liguria, Italy.

16TH - 18TH CENTURY MAIOLICA.

Shield of arms of Savona - -

Cross from the arms of Savoy -

c.1620 **Guidobono, G. A. - -**

Fortress marks - -

c.1650 **Salomini, Girolamo:- -**

Rubatto, S. - -

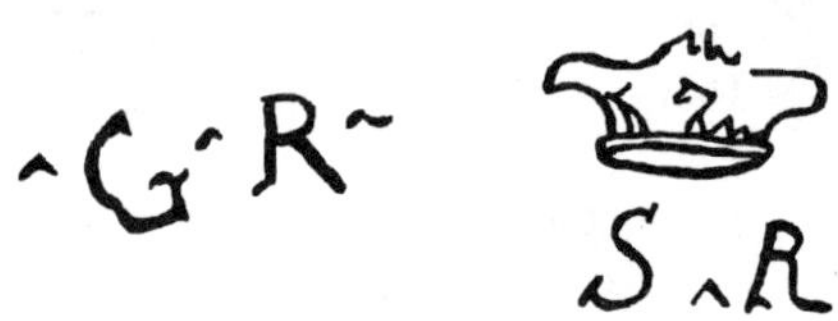

Rubatto and Boselli- - -

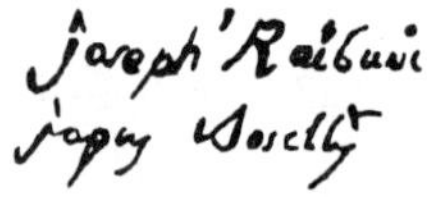

c.1665- **Levantino (mark of beacon from Genoa harbour) - -**

Mark of Chiodo (potter) - - -

Continued over -

1550 SAVONA, nr. Genoa, Liguria, Italy. (Cont`)

c.1665- Levantino (Cont`)

Levantino, Luigi - -
Agostino - - -
Giordano - - -

c.1675- Pescetto - -
(Also mark with 3 fishes)

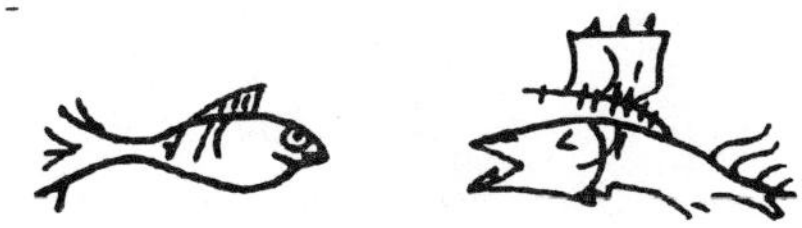

c.1720- Ratti, Agostino. - - -

AGOSTINO RATTI
SAVONA. 1720.

1735 (dated) Borrelli,M. (Mark on a jar)

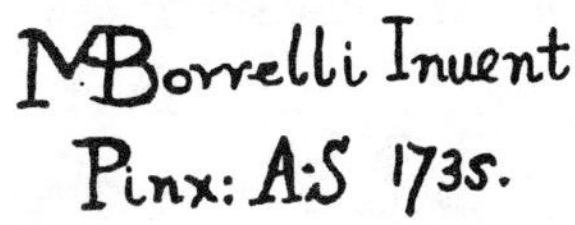

c.1750 Folco, Sebastiano. - -

c.1775 Boselli, Giacomo. - - -

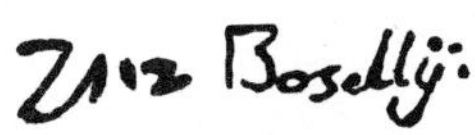

c.1850 Marcenaro - - - -

19th century creamware makers:-

1852- Ferro, Francesco, - Impressed-

1856 Folco, Antonio, (creamware) -

c.1860- Ricci, Sebastiano, (creamware) -

1550 VENICE, Italy.

16TH CENTURY MAIOLICA.

c.1550- Pieragnolo, Francesco/Cecio di - -

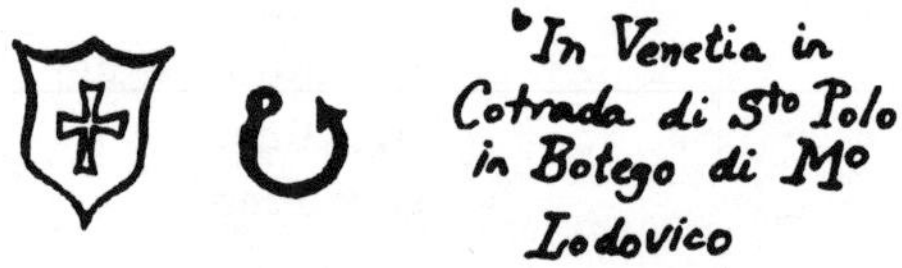

Bertolini - -

<u>Late 17th and early 18th century marks:</u> -

<u>18th century hard-paste porcelain:</u> -

c.1720-27 Vessi Factory `Casa Eccelma Vessi` -

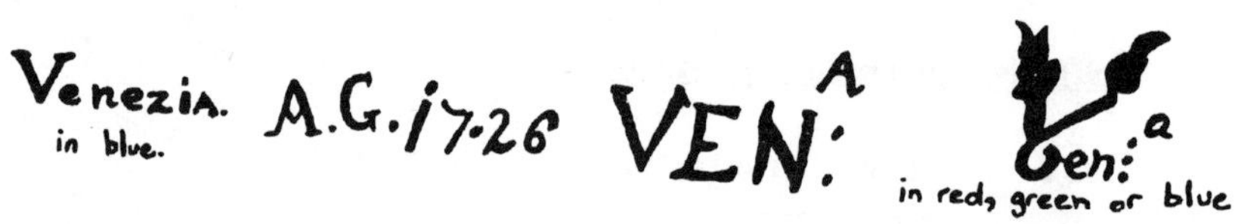

1758-63 Hewelcke,Nathaniel Friedrich, -
(HARD-PASTE PORCELAIN)

c.1764-1812 Cozzi, Geminiano, (HYBRID SOFT-PASTE) -

`1765 Venezia
Faba Geminiano
Cozzi`

1552 ANTWERP, Belgium.
16TH AND 17TH CENTURY MAIOLICA.
Italian type pottery produced - - - -

1560 Calamelli, Maestro Virgiliotto, Italy. - - see 1451 FAENZA

1565 RAEREN, nr.Aix-la-Chapelle, Rhineland, Germany.
STONEWARE.

1566-94 Emens, Jan, - - - - -

c.1570- Kran, Engel, - - - - -

1576- Mennicken, Jan, - - - - *`I M 1576`*

1577(dated)Mennicken, Baldem (Baldwin) - *WAN . GOT . WIL . SO . IST MEIN . ZILL . MESTER BALDEM . MENNICKEN POTTENBECKER . WONEDE ZO . DEN . RORREN . IN LEIDEN . GEDOLT . 1577*

1583- Mennicken der Alte - - - *`M.der A 1583`*

1590- Emens, Georg, - - - - *G.E. 1590*

1591- Pitz, D., - - - - - *D.P. 1591*
R

1595- Higler, Hans,- - - - - *H.H. 1595*

c.1630-50 Wolf, Tilman, - - - - *T.W.*
Kannenbacker, Tilman Wolf, - - *T.W.K.*

1880- Schiffer, Hubert, - - - **H.S.**

1566 Emens, Jan,.Germany. - - - - - see 1565 RAEREN
1567 Lung Ch`ing, China. - - - - - - see 1368 MING
1570 Kran, Engel,.Germany. - - - - - see 1565 RAEREN

1573 OWARI, Japan.

Owari is the province where the most important manufacturers of porcelain are based, second only to Hizen; Okasaki being the principal one.

1573-1592 **Oribe-Yaki. Furna Oribe started a factory at Narumi.**

1640- **Gempin-Yaki made at Nogoya - - -**

c.1730 Gempin reproduction mark -

c.1670- **Ofuke or Mifukai-Yaki. Made at Akuza -**
c.1820 mark - - -

c.1675- **Shuntai-Yaki. Akuza ware. - -**
c.1830 mark - -

Shuntai

1752 **Inuyama-Yaki. Made at Inaki - - -**
1810- Factory moved to Maruyama

c.1806- **Seto-Yaki.** Made at Seto in Great Japan. Kato-Tamikichi studied the method of making porcelain in Arita, and returned to Seto to produce `Sometsuke` Modern wares by Kawamote-Hansuke and Masukichi.

1876- `Made by Hansuke of Great Japan. - -

Made by Hokuham at the Kito House. -

c.1820- **Toyosuke-Yaki. Haraku factory - in Nagoya.-**

c1876- **Nagoya-Yaki. The Shippo Kuwaisha factory made cloisonne enamel.**
1876- Philadelphia Exhibition. -

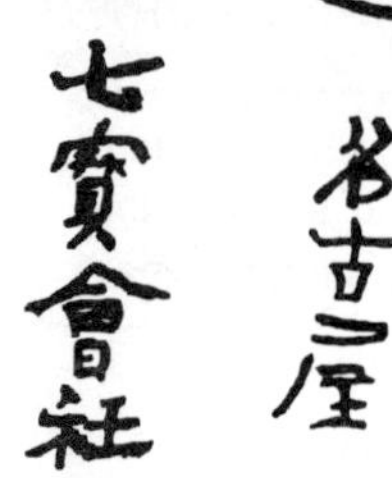

1573	Wan Li, China. - - - - -	see 1368 MING

1575 FLORENCE, Italy.

SOFT-PASTE PORCELAIN.

c.1580- Francesco I. (de` Medici) Grand Duke of Tuscany; reputed to be the first known manufacturer of artificial porcelain in Europe. He called on the help of the celebrated Bernard Buontalenti.

c.1587- Mark on a porcelain hunting-bottle. Probably a trial piece.

Arms of the Medici family which reads: `Franciscus Medici Magnus Etruriae Dux Secundus`

1878- Ulysse Cantagalli (d.1901) Maiolica reproductions .

1575 PALERMO. Sicily, Italy.

LATE 16TH - 17TH CENTURY MAIOLICA. - - - *FATTO IN PALERMA 1606.*

1607- Cono Sarerond - - - -

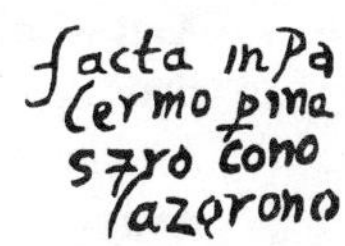

1575	Rainerio, Italy. - - - - -	see 1451 FAENZA.
1576	Mennicken, Jan,. Germany. - - -	see 1565 RAEREN

1577 TURIN, Piedmont, Italy.

16TH CENTURY MAIOLICA. - - - - *`Fatta in Torino adi 12 d Setebre 1577.*

Shield of Savoy - - - - - -

Continued over -

1577-80

1577 TURIN, Piedmont, Italy (Cont`)

1725-c.45 **Giorgio Rossetti di Macello** - -

c.1750 **Gioanetti, Vittorio Amedeo (Vineuf)** -

c.1765 **Ardizzone, G.A.,** - - -

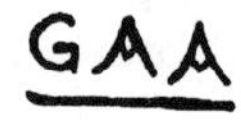

1776 (dated) Mark on an oblong china tray -

c.1823 **Borgano. Mark on a service** - - ***`Borgano`***

1846-63 **Luigi Richard e C.** Mark of factory making porcelain and earthenware in English fashion. ***Luigi Richard e C.***

1580 HIZEN (Island of Kiushiu) Japan.

Potters marks do not appear on wares from Hizen, or any of the Arita porcelains made before the 19th century, but marks of good omen are sometimes found.

1590- **Karatzu-Yaki.** Dates back to 11th century. Most of the wares were made for tea ceremonies.

1895 **Nakazato Keizo ceased work making sophisticated figures.**

c.1610- **Arita-Yaki. Celebrated for its well-produced porcelain. A Corean named Risampei discovered native materials to manufacture porcelain.**

Arita 17th century marks:- - - -

Fu ki cho shun

Arita 18th century marks:- - - -

Ho tai no takaru

Continued over -

1580 HIZEN (Island of Kiushiu) Japan. (Cont`)

<u>Arita 19th century marks:-</u>

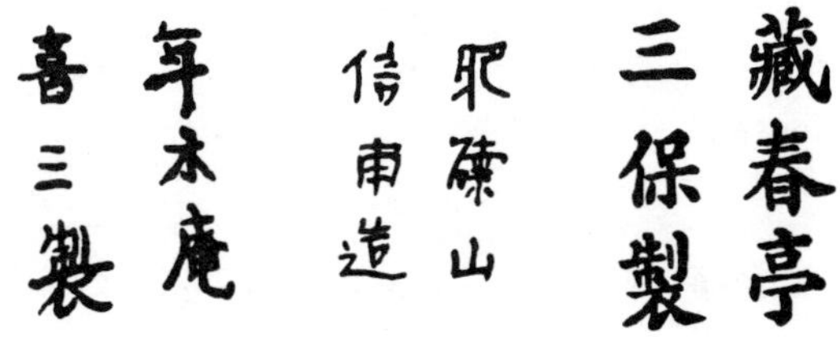

Zoshun-tei Sam-po sei

c1620- **Kakiemon Ware.** Regarded as the most beautiful enamelled porcelain made in Japan.

c.1650- **Imari-Yaki.** Designed mainly for the European market, a strong coarse porcelain imported from the port of Amari by the Dutch in the 17th cen.

c.1660- **Kutani-Yaki.** `Fuku` (Happiness) frequently found on this ware.

c.1660 **Okawaji or Nabeshima-Yaki.** - -
Early Nabeshima porcelain was made specifically for the Prince of Nabeshima.

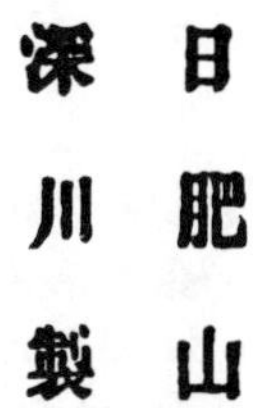

18th and 19th Century mark -

1712- **Mikawaji or Hirado-Yaki.** - -
1751- Matsura, the Prince of Hirado, acquired the factory. - -

1803-64 **Kameyama-Yaki.** Blue and white Chinese style porcelain. - -

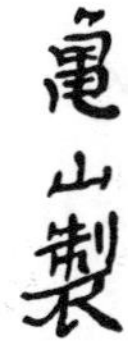

1580 Francesco I. Grand Duke of Tuscany, Italy. - - see 1575 FLORENCE.

1583 BIZEN, Japan.

From 1583 Bizen potters made finely modelled figures in a place called Imbe. Early wares are called `Ko Bizen`

Ko Bisen
Imbe Yaki

c.1680 Ka ichi - - - - - -

c.1750 (18th century) K`wa-bo - -

1780-1830 Kimura Uji - - - - - -

c.1840- Yoshida tsukuru- (Made by Yoshida) - -

c.1850- Kiyo-chika - - -

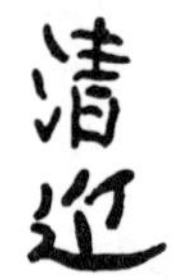

c.1850- Terami - - -

c1860- Imbe pottery of Great Japan. - - - -
`Dia Ni-pon Im-be to`-

1583 CHIKUZEN, Japan.

Potteries existed here from the 9th century, but its importance dated from the 16th century.

c.1583 Two Coreans, Shinkuro and Hachizo, set up kilns around 1580. The wares are known as - Takatori-Yaki.

c.1770- Takatori Pottery - - - - -

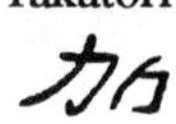

c.1780- Ka - - - - - - - - -

c.1780- Shun (for Shunzan) in Suo - -

c.1800- Yamaka- - - - - - - -

c.1820- Takatori Ki - - - - -

1827- Soshichi at Hakata - - - - -

c.1850- Teiten - - - - - -

19th Cen. Taka (for Takatori) - - - - - -

1583 Mennicken, der Alte, Germany. - - - see 1565 RAEREN.
1584 Patanazzi, Alfonzo and family, Italy. - - see 1520 URBINO

1585 HAARLEM, Holland.

TIN-GLAZED EARTHENWARE (DELFTWARE)

1585- Hendrick C. Vroom. - -

1630- Abraham de Kooge. - -

1585 NAGATO, Japan.

c.1585- Hagi-Yaki ware was first made by a Corean named Rikei, who took the name of Koraizaemon.

Foot rim usually had a triangular nick.

c.1650- Matsumoto. A factory was opened here by a potter named Kimsetsu.

c.1716- Toyo-Ura-Yama. - - -
1846- Mark on a terra-cotta ash-bowl.

1587 PISA, Tuscany, Italy.

Mark on a large vase. - *PISA*

19th Cen. Devers, J., - - -

1588 Chojiro, Japan. - - - - - see 1528 Raku Ware.

1589 NEVERS, Nievre, France.

16TH CENTURY FAÏENCE.

Domenique Conrade, from Savona,Italy, founded his fabrique at Nevers in and around 1578. His brothers, Baptiste and Augustin were also associated with him.

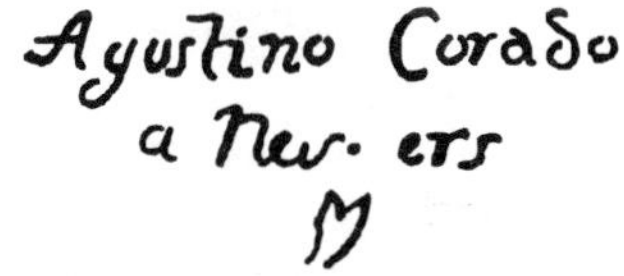

1602-60 Custode, Jehan.,- - - - - -

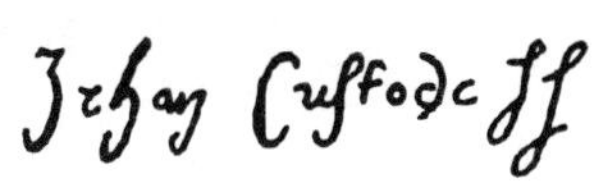

Continued over -

1589

1589 NEVERS, Nievre, France. (Cont`)

1622 (dated) Boulard, J., - - - - *J Boulard a Nevers 1622.*

17th Cen. Bourdu, Jaques, - - -

c.1629-49 Lefebvre, Denis, (attributed) - -

1632- Bourcier, Barthélémy,

1644- Conrade, Antoine, (2nd.Generation)

1652- Custode, Pierre, and family - -

c.1660- Conrade, Dominique, (3rd.Generation) -

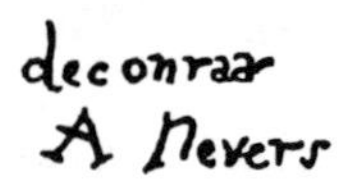

1689(dated)Borne, Henri, (probably) - -

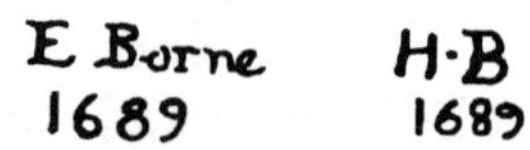

1726 Seigne, Jaques, - - - - -

1738 (dated) Mark on a dish with the four seasons. -

Borne
Pinxit
Anno 1738

1764 (dated)Bigourat, Claude, - - - *Claude Bigourat 1764*

1860 Ristori, T., - - - - -

1870 Signoret - - - - -

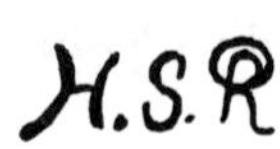

c.1890 Montagnon, M., Reproductions of earlier styles. - - - -

1590 BASSANO, Venezia, Italy.

16TH - 18TH CENTURY MAIOLICA. - -

1595- Marinoni, S., - -

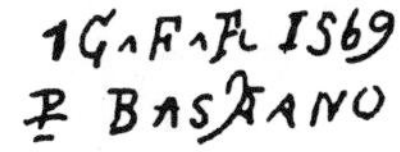

1602- Marnard - - -

Roman artists at Bassano:-

c.1725- Terchi, Antonio,. - -

c.1725- Terchi, Bartolomeo,- -

1590 Emens, Georg, Germany. - - - - see 1565 RAEREN.
1590 Karatzu-Yaki, Japan. - - - - see 1580 HIZEN.
1591 Pitz, D., Germany. - - - - see 1565 RAEREN
1595 Higler, Hans, Germany. - - - - see 1565 RAEREN.

1596 SATSUMA, Japan.

c.1596 Shimazu Yoshihiro, Prince of Satsuma established a factory using Corean potters.

1780-1800 Hoju - - -

Satsuma ware was buff-coloured stoneware brightly coloured and gilded.

c.1800-c.60 Various marks used. - -

In the 19th century, an ivory white lustred ware with crackled glaze was produced.
Wholesale imitations of this ware is produced elsewhere in Japan.

1820-40 Hohei. - - - -

1830- Seikozan - - - -

c.1840- Tatsumonji (Hoyu) - - - -

1597-1607

1597 HÖHR-GRENZHAUSEN, in Nassau, Germany.
STONEWARE PRODUCED HERE FROM THE 15TH CENTURY.

Various marks- - - - IM 1E LB 1C

PR WR 1EM FC BG LM 1K

18th Century mark - - - *K B L Höhr*

1790- **Johannes Mennechen mark** - *Johannes Mennechen Höhr 1790*

1873- **Merkelbach & Wick-** - - - 

1599 Jansz, Thomes, (Delft Artist) DELFT, Holland.
TIN-GLAZED EARTHENWARE (DELFTWARE)

TOME
ZWA

1600 ROME, Italy.
16TH - 17TH CENTURY MAIOLICA. - - - *`FATTO . IN . BOTEGA DE . M . DIOMEDE DURANTE . IN . ROMA`*

1623 (dated) - - - *`ALMA ROMA 1623`*

`FATTO . IN . ROMA DA . GIO . PAULO SAVONO . MDC`

c.1736- **Terchi, Bartolomeo,-** - *ROMA MAG 1769`* (incised)

1761-84 **Cuccumos, Filippo,** (PORCELAIN) - - - - 

1785-1831 **Volpato, Giovanni,** PORCELAIN AND EARTHENWARE. Impressed - *G. VOLPATO ROMA*

1602 Custode, Johann, France. - - - - - - see 1589 NEVERS.
1602 Marnard, Italy. - - - - - - - see 1590 BASSANO.
1603 Vest, Georgius, Han Christoph and Caspar, Germany - see 1550 KREUSSEN.
1606 Patanazzi, Alfonzo, Italy. - - - - - - see 1520 URBINO.
1607 Sarerond,Cono, Italy. - - - - - - see 1575 PALERMO.

1610 AVON, Seine-et-Marne, France.
LEAD-GLAZED EARTHENWARE IN PALISSY STYLE.
Barthélémy Blemont (probably) Incised - 

1610 CANDIANA, nr. Padua, Italy.
Early 17th century MAIOLICA AND PORCELLANOUS WARE.
Noted for its Turkish designs. - *CANDIANA 1620*

S. F. C.

P. A. CROSA.

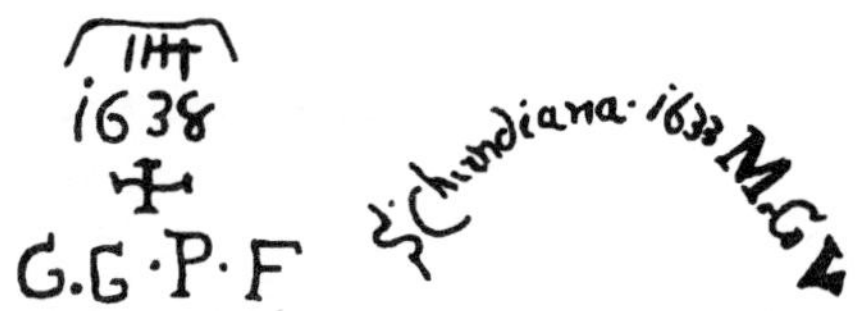

1610 MANISES, Valencia, Spain.

1941 **Ceramicas Hispania.** - -
HARD-PASTE PORCELAIN

1610 Arita-Yaki, Japan. - - - - see 1580 HIZEN.

1612 DELFT, nr. Rotterdam, Holland.
17th century FAÏENCE KNOWN THROUGHOUT THE WORLD PURELY AS `DELFT`
The individual factories and potters of DELFT have been
listed under their own dates and marks within this book.

1612 Livermore, John, WROTHAM, Kent, England.
c.1612-58 SLIPWARE. - - - - *I. L.*

1612 WROTHAM, Kent, England.
ONE OF THE EARLIEST AREAS OF POTTERY MANUFACTURE IN ENGLAND. MAINLY SLIPWARE.
The indiviual factories and potters of WROTHAM have been listed
under their own dates and marks within this book.

1615 Hermansz, Cornelis, (Delft Artist) DELFT, Holland.
TIN-GLAZED EARTHENWARE (DELFTWARE) - -

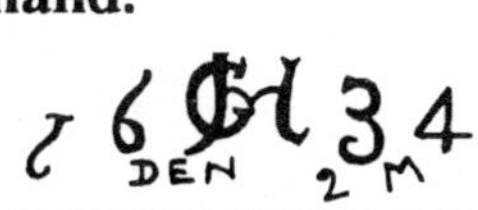

1617 Patanazzi, Francesco, Italy- - - - see 1520 URBIN

1620-30

1620 Ifield, Thomas, WROTHAM, Kent, England.

c.1620-c.75. SLIPWARES. - - - - - *T. I.*

1620 Guidobono, G.A., Italy. - - - - see 1550 SAVONA.
1620 Kakiemon Ware, Japan. - - - - see 1580 HIZEN.
1620 T`ai Ch`ang, China. - - - - see 1368 MING.
1621 T`ien Ch`i, China. - - - - see 1368 MING.
1622 Boulard, J, France. - - - - see 1589 NEVERS.

1625 HAMBURG, Germany.

c.1625 FAÏENCE. -
c.1640-55 - - - 

1756- **Lessel, Johann Otto,** - -
Johann Otto Lessel sculpsit et Pinxit Hamburg 1756

1627 MONTELUPO, Tuscany, Italy.

MAIOLICA.
1627 (dated) - - - 

1639 (dated) Raffaello Girolamo. - - 

1628 Schipper, Cornelis, (Delft Artist) DELFT, Holland.

TIN-GLAZED EARTHENWARE (DELFTWARE) - - 

1628 Ch`ung Chêng, China. - - - - see 1368 MING
1629 Lefebvre, Denis, France. - - - - see 1589 NEVERS.

1630 HIGO, Japan.

c.1630- **Yatsushiro-Yaki.** Agano Kizo, a Corean set up a kiln at Koda making what is generally known as Yatsushiro ware. 

1720 "Yatsu-Shiro" - - 

Sogen - - 

c.1797 `Amidayama` - - - - - 

c.1840 `Shodai` - - - 

Shofu - - - 

19th Century `Ya = Yatsushiro` mark - - - - 

1630 OMI, Japan.

c.1630- **Shigaraki-Yaki.** A rough pottery called Ko-Shigaraki dates back to the 13th Century.

17th Century. Shigaraki Uichu (potter) - - - - - -

19th Century (early) `Koto` PORCELAIN - - -

`Meiho` Signature on `Koto` ware - - - -

1815-40 `Takuzan` (made at Yedo) - -

c.1850 `Yuko` - - -

1630 ROTTERDAM, Holland.

1630- TIN-GLAZED EARTHENWARE (DELFTWARE)

1630- **Sachtieven, C.,** - - -

1700- **Luffneu, Adriaen,** - - -

1715- **Boumeester, Cornelis,** -

1739- **Aalmis, Jan, (Jun)** - - -

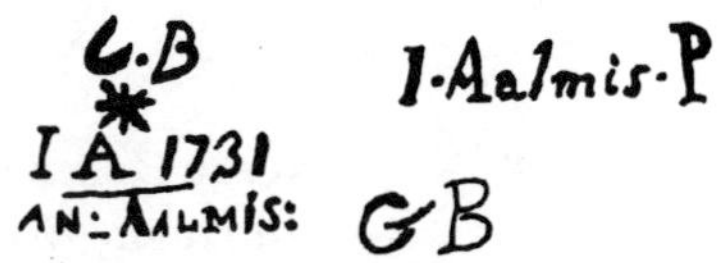

1741- **Backhuyzen, -** - - - - -

1759- **Govert, Henderick,** - -

1786- **van der Vliet, J.,** - - -

1630	Kooge, Abraham de, Holland. - - -	see 1585 HAARLEM.
1630	Petrus Paulus, Italy. - - - -	see 1495 DERUTA
1630	Wolf, Tilman, Germany. - - - -	see 1565 RAEREN.
1632	Bourcier, Barthélémy, France. - - -	see 1589 NEVERS.
1635	Urbania, Italy. - - - - -	see 1520 CASTLE DURANTE

1639 De metale Pot (The Metal Pot) DELFT, Holland.

1639-	TIN-GLAZED EARTHENWARE (DELFTWARE)	
1667-	**L. Cleffius.** - - - - -	
1691-	**Lambert van Eenhorn** - -	
1738-	**Pieter Paree** - - -	

1639 Raffaello Girolamo, Italy. - - - - - see 1627 MONTELUPO

1640 Junius, Isaac, (Delft Artist) DELFT, Holland.

TIN-GLAZED EARTHENWARE (DELFTWARE)

1640 Zengoro Family, YAMASHIRO, Japan.

c.1640- **Tenkaichi Soshiro (4th Generation)** - - -
Ryozen (10th Generation)

c.1810 mark - -

1825-53 Eiraku mark - - -

c.1853 `Omuro` mark - -

c.1800- **Zengoro Hozen (son)** - -
Studio name `Eiraku`
Eiraku Wazen (son)
Eiraku Tokuzen (grandson)

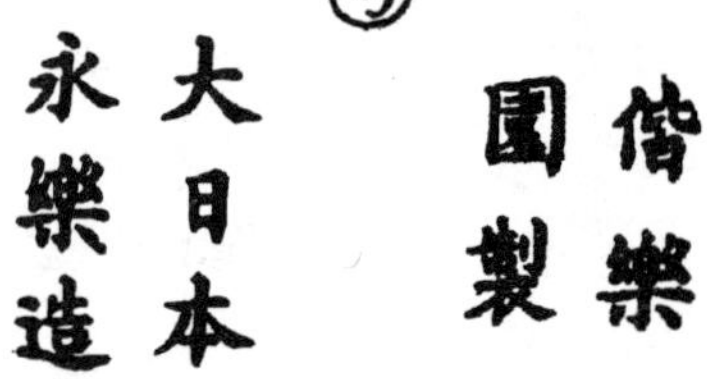

1640 Gempin-Yaki, Nogoya, Japan. - - - - see 1573 OWARI.

1642 De twee Scheepjes (The Two Little Ships) DELFT, Holland.

1668-	**Cornelis Keiser.** - - - - - - - -	
1707-25	**Jan Gaal.** - - - -	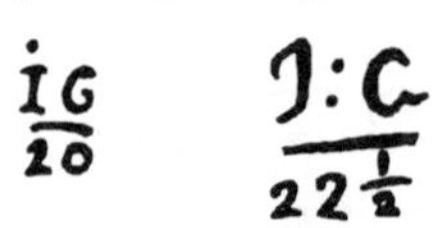
1759-70	**A. Pennis.** - - - - - - - -	
1764-	**Anthony Pennis (reg. mark)**	

1642 Keiser, de Aelbregt, (Delft Artist) DELFT, Holland.

TIN-GLAZED EARTHENWARE (DELFTWARE)

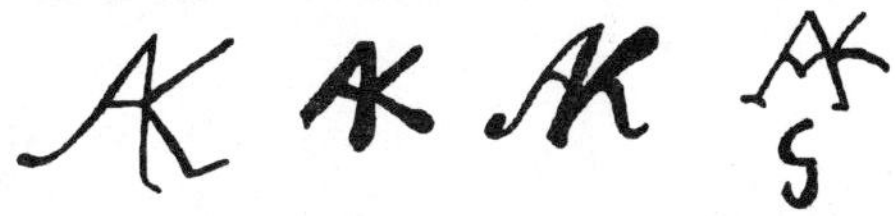

1642 Richardson, George, WROTHAM, Kent, England.

1642-77 SLIPWARES. - - - - - *G. R.*

1644 Asahi, YAMASHIRO, Japan.

1644-1730 ASAHI IS A DULL RED, BUFF, STONEWARE

1852- **Revived by Chobei (potter) descendant of original potters.**

1644 CH`ING DYNASTY, China.

1644-1661 Shun-chih. - 大清順治年製

1662-1722 K`ang-hsi. - 大清康熙年製

1723-1735 Yung-chêng. - 大清雍正年製

1736-1795 Ch`ien-lung. - 大清乾隆年製

1796-1821 Chia-ch`ing. - 嘉慶年製

1821-1850 Tao-kuang. - 大清道光年製

Continued over -

1644

1644 CH`ING DYNASTY, China, (Cont`)

1851-1861 Hsien-fêng. - 大清咸豐年製

1862-1875 T`ung-chih. - 大清同治年製

1875-1909 Kuang-hsü - 大清光緒年製

1909-1912 Hsüan-t`ung.- - - 大清宣統年製

1916- Hung-hsien. (Yüan Shih-kai) - 洪憲年製

Chinese marks usually consists of six characters and read downward from right to left as follows:-

<u>Example: 1736-1795 Ch`ien-lung period:</u>

4.=lung	**(Lung)**	**1.=Ta**	**(Great)**
5.=Nien	**(period)**	**2.=Ch`ing**	**(Ch`ing)**
6.=Chih	**(made)**	**3.=Ch`ien**	**(Ch`ien)**

大清乾隆年製

Sometimes only 4 characters are used, Ta (1) and Ch`ing (2) being omitted.

1644 TOTOMI, Japan.

c.1644- SHIDORO-YAKI

Wares first made in a village called Shidoro-mura.

SHIDORO

18th and 19th Century mark- - -

1644 Conrade, Antoine, France. - - - - see 1589 NEVERS.
1644 Scharf, Adam, Germany. - - - - see 1550 KREUSSEN.
1644 Shun-chih, China. - - - - see 1644 CH`ING.

1645 De Griekse A. (The Greek A.) DELFT, Holland.

1645- TIN-GLAZED EARTHENWARE. (DELFTWARE)

1645- **G.L. Kruyk** - - - - -

1674- **Eenhorn, Samuel van,** - - -

S.v E.

1687- **Korks, Adrianus,** - - - - -

1759- **Dextra, Jan Theunis-**

1765 **Adriaens, J. Halder,** - -

1645 Schaper, Johann, NUREMBERG, Germany.

(B. 1621; D. 1670) ALSO WORKED WITH GLASS. - -

1648 De dubbelde Schenkkan (The Double Tankard) DELFT, Holland.

1648- TIN-GLAZED EARTHENWARE. (DELFTWARE)

1670- **Cuyst, Gerrit,** - - -

1675- **Kessel, Amerensie van,** - -

1721- **Gillis et Hendrick de Koning** -

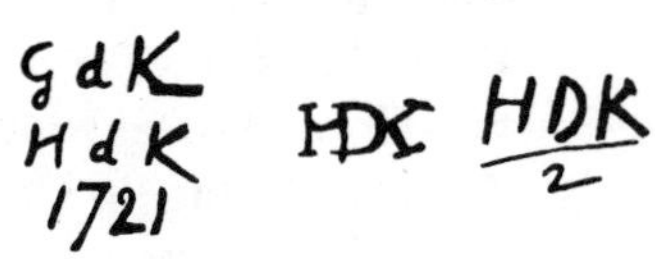

1764- **Spaandonck, T.,** - - -

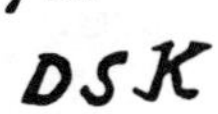

1648-50

1648 De oud Moriaans hooft (The Old Moor`s Head) DELFT, Holland.

1648 TIN-GLAZED EARTHENWARE. (DELFTWARE)

1661- Hoppestein, J.W., - - -

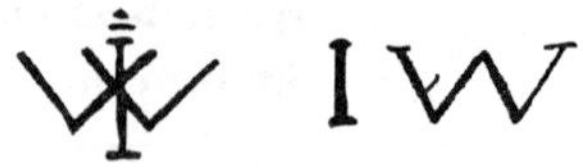

1680- Hoppestein, Rochus, - -

1714- Kool, Jac., - - - - -

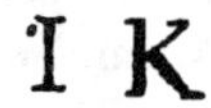

1759- Kruisweg, Anthone, - - -

1764- Verstelle, Geertruy, - - - -

1649 Hoeven, J.G.van d., (Delft Artist) DELFT, Holland.

TIN-GLAZED EARTHENWARE (DELFTWARE)

1650 BRISTOL, Avon, England.

c.1650- TIN-GLAZED EARTHENWARE (DELFT) AND 18TH CENTURY PORCELAIN.
The individual factories and potters of BRISTOL have been listed under their own dates and marks within this book.

1650 Hubble, Nicholas, WROTHAM, Kent, England.

c.1650-c.87. SLIPWARES. - - - *N. H.*

1650 KAGA, Japan.

Materials for making porcelain were found near the village of Kutani-mura, but it did not become a success until Goto Saijiro returned from Arita in 1664 with his secrets of the HIZEN potters.

1650-1750 Kutani factories.
1779 Honda Teikichi, (d.1822) - -
1809- Yoshida Danemon, (Kutani revival)
1840- Iida Hachiroemon. - -
Up to 1850 the `Kutani` mark was the only one apparently used. - -

1850- The names of potters and the full mark `Dai Nippon Kutani tsukurn` (Made at Kutani in Great Japan) have been marked on wares.

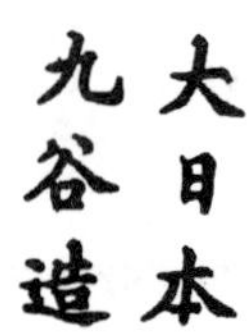

Continued over -

1650 KAGA, Japan. (Cont`)

<u>Pottery marks:-</u>

c.1807 Kinju (Mark of Mokubei in Kaga) -

c.1810 Yamamoto - - -

1858-64 Zengora Wazen (son of Eiraku)

1875- KAGA-YAKI. Seal of Tozan on a pair of flower vases by Kichizo Uchiumi at Kutani in 1875. - - -

1666-Ohi-Machi-Yaki. Raku-type ware.
Haji Chozaemon (founder) -
1827- Gembei and successors of Eda-machi, Kanazawa,

1650 MARSEILLES, Bouches-du-Rhône, France.

17th century FAÏENCE.
The individual factories and potters of MARSEILLES have been listed under their own dates and marks within this book.

1650 MINO, Japan.

c.1650-1810Mino-Yaki. Earthenware made in several villages in the province up to 1810. -
1810- Real porcelain, called `Shin-sei` (new thing) was made. - - - - -

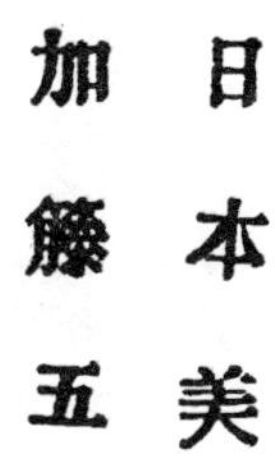

1830- Ichi-no-Kura Factory - - -

19th Century. Yamato sei = made at Yamato on eggshell porcelain. -

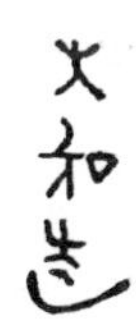

1875- Kato Gosuke of Tajimimura. - -

Togi-yoku (Jade pottery garden)

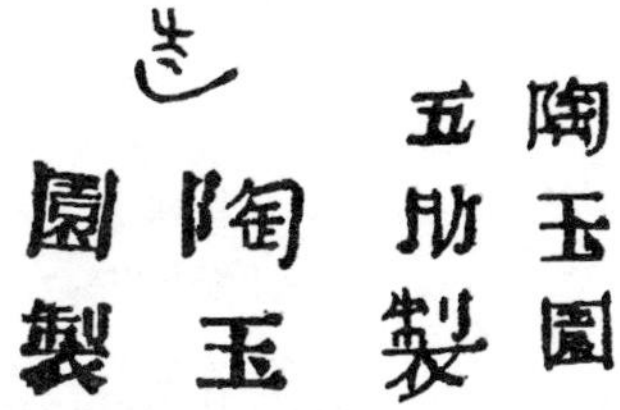

1650

1650 ORLÉANS, Loiret, France.

17th Century Faïence.

1753-70 Soft-paste porcelain. - - 

1770- Hard-paste porcelain. Printed in blue -
(also found on `Fine faïence`)

c.1756-60 **Jean Louis, (modeller)** - - - 

c.1756-60 **Pierre Renault (or Renard)** incised- 

c.1790- **Molier-Bardin** (porcelain)- - - 

c.1800- **Barlois and Dabot.** stencilled red - - 

1806-12 **Benoist Le Brun.** - **impressed** *GRAMMONT*
Agate and marbled earthenware - *LAINE FABOT*
at later dates. *A ORLÉANS*

ORLÉANS

Red with blue dot - - 

1650 RENNES, Ille-et-Vilaine, France.

16th and 17th century lead-glazed ware.

c.1750-c.95. Faïence. - - - 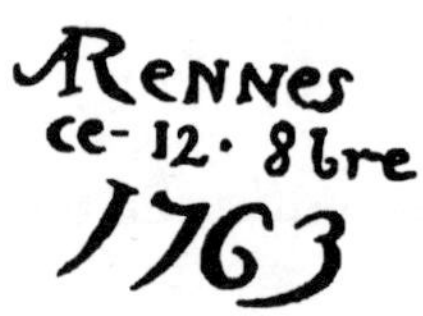

1749- **Factory started by Tutrel:**
Michel Derennes (painter at Tutrel`s)

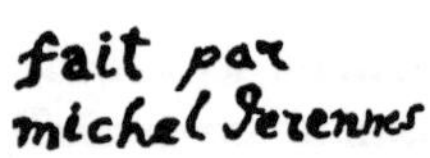

1756 **Jean-Baptiste-Alexis Bourgoin** (painter and modeller)- - - - 

1772 **Jean Baron** (painter) - - 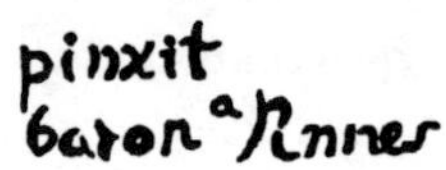

Continued over -

1650 RENNES, Ille-et-Vilaine, France. (Cont`)

1767 **Hirel de Choisy** (painter) later at Sèvres-

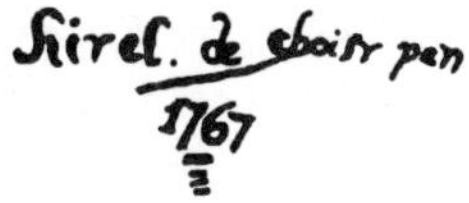

1771 **Derennes, Michel,** - - - *Michel Derennes*

1780 **Bouchereau, Luc,** - - - *Luc Bouchereau*

1834 **Le Duc, Pierre,** - - - *Pierre Le Duc*

1650 TOULOUSE, Haute-Garonne, France.

c.1650-1849 LEAD-GLAZED EARTHENWARE. FAÏENCE AND CREAMWARE.

1657 (dated) SLIPWARE - - - *`Mathieu de Benque*
Sleur de Fustinac
1657`

1756 (dated) Inscription on faïence pilgrim bottle. - *`Laurens Basso*
A Toulouza
Le 14th May 1756`

1797 **Fouque, Joseph-Jacques and**
Arnoux, Antoine (CREAMWARE) - - - -
1829 **François and Antoine Fouque**
with Arnoux. - -

1650 Salomini, Girolama, Italy. - - - - see 1550 SAVONA.
1650 Imari-Yaki, Japan. - - - - see 1580 HIZEN.
1650 Matsumoto, Japan. - - - - see 1585 NAGATO.

1651 BURSLEM, Staffordshire, England.

A renowned region in Staffordshire well known for its many factories producing quality wares like Wedgwood.

The individual factories and potters of BURSLEM have been listed under their own dates and marks within this book.

1651 Simpson, Ralph, BURSLEM, Staffordshire, England.

1651-c.1724. SLIPWARE. - - -

RALPH SIMPSON

1652/53

1652 De Paauw (The Peacock) DELFT, Holland.

1652- TIN-GLAZED EARTHENWARE (DELFTWARE)

1652- **C.J. Messchert / A.G. van Noorden** -

1697- **Kam, David, -** - -

1759- **Jac. de Milde** - - -

1652 YAMATO, Japan.

c.1652- Akahada-Yaki. 17TH CENTURY TEA WARE WITH A PINKISH GREY GLAZE.

1761- A BUFF GLAZED WARE.

1840- Dated mark on incense-box impressed-

19th Century. Akahada-Yama. Mark on a stoneware tea-bowl.- - - - - - - -

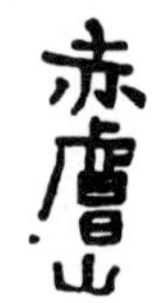

1850-70 Bokuhaku. - - -

1652 Custode, Pierre, France. - - - - see 1589 NEVERS

1653 De Porceleyne Fles (The Porcelain Jar) DELFT, Holland.

1653-55 **David Anthonisz V.D. Pieth (Founder)**

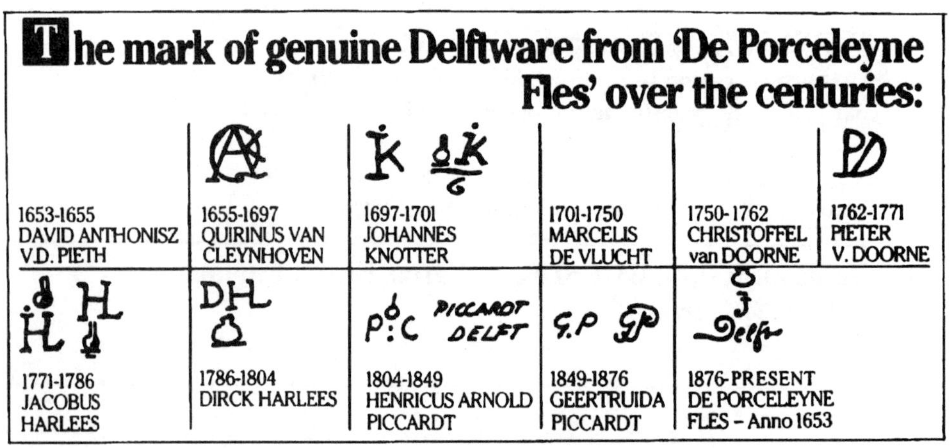

The mark of genuine Delftware from 'De Porceleyne Fles' over the centuries:
1653-1655 DAVID ANTHONISZ V.D. PIETH
1655-1697 QUIRINUS VAN CLEYNHOVEN
1697-1701 JOHANNES KNOTTER
1701-1750 MARCELIS DE VLUCHT
1750-1762 CHRISTOFFEL van DOORNE
1762-1771 PIETER V. DOORNE
1771-1786 JACOBUS HARLEES
1786-1804 DIRCK HARLEES
PICCARDT DELFT
1804-1849 HENRICUS ARNOLD PICCARDT
1849-1876 GEERTRUIDA PICCARDT
1876-PRESENT DE PORCELEYNE FLES – Anno 1653

Continued over -

1653 De Porceleyne Fles, (The Porcelain Jar) DELFT, Holland. (Cont`)

By the middle of the 17th century there were more than thirty small potteries in Delft alone. Over the years all of them have gone out of business with the exception of `De Porceleyne Fles` which continues to the present day.

1876- Joost Thooft and associate Mr. Labouchere formed the company called `De Porceleyne Fles. Firma Joost Thooft & Labouchere` Between them they made a new type of blue Delft with the white and hard body of English stoneware. Joost Thooft died at the age of 44.

1904- Limited Company formed. Shares auctioned at the Amsterdam stock-market. Name changed to:- N.V. Delftsch Aardewerkfabriek De Porceleyne Fles, late Joost Thooft and Labouchere.

1919- Company was granted the title `Royal` for their efforts to bring back the fame of `Delftware` to the ceramic industry in the Netherlands.

Since 1879 De Porceleyne Fles has marked their wares with a year code which you will find on the bottom or back of every article produced.

Yearcode

A - 1879	T - 1898	AM - 1917	BF - 1936	BY - 1954	CR - 1972
B - 1880	U - 1899	AN - 1918	BG - 1937	BZ - 1955	CS - 1973
C - 1881	V - 1900	AO - 1919	BH - 1938	CA - 1956	CT - 1974
D - 1882	W- 1901	AP - 1920	BI - 1939	CB - 1957	CU - 1975
E - 1883	X - 1902	AQ - 1921	BJ - 1940	CC - 1958	CV - 1976
F - 1884	Y - 1903	AR - 1922	BK - 1941	CD - 1959	CW- 1977
G- 1885	Z - 1904	AS - 1923	BL - 1942	CE - 1960	CX - 1978
H- 1886	AA- 1905	AT - 1924	BM- 1943	CF - 1961	CY - 1979
I - 1887	AB- 1906	AU - 1925	BN - 1944	CG - 1962	CZ - 1980
J - 1888	AC- 1907	AV - 1926	BO - 1945	CH - 1963	DA - 1981
K- 1889	AD- 1908	AW- 1927	BP - 1946	CI - 1964	DB - 1982
L - 1890	AE- 1909	AX- 1928	BQ -	CJ - 1965	DC - 1983
M- 1891	AF- 1910	AY - 1929	BR - 1947	CK - 1966	DD - 1984
N - 1892	AG-1911	AZ - 1930	BS - 1948	CL - 1967	DE - 1985
O - 1893	AH-1912	BA - 1931	BT - 1949	CM- 1968	DF - 1986
P - 1894	AI - 1913	BB - 1932	BU - 1950	CN - 1969	DG - 1987
Q - 1895	AJ - 1914	BC - 1933	BV - 1951	CO - 1970	DH - 1988
R - 1896	AK- 1915	BD - 1934	BW- 1952	CP - 1971	DI - 1989
S - 1897	AL- 1916	BE - 1935	BX - 1953	CQ-	DJ - 1990

(Courtesy of Koninklijke Porceleyne Fles, Royal Delft, Netherlands)

1655

1655 de 3 Astonne (The Three Ashbarrels) DELFT, Holland.

1655 TIN-GLAZED EARTHENWARE (DELFTWARE)

1655- **Jer. Pieter van Kessel** - -

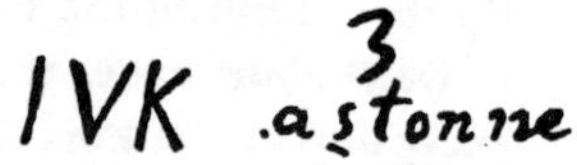

1674- **G.P. Kam** - - - -

1712- **Zacharias Dextra (manager)** -

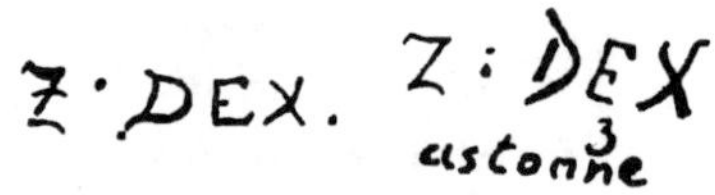

1759- **Hendrik van Hoorn (manager)** -

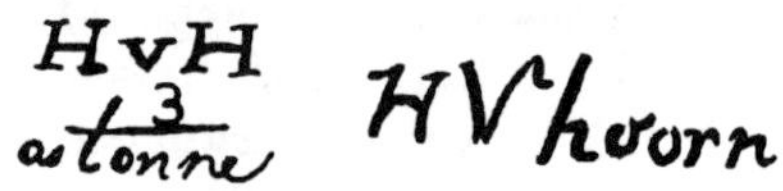

1655 De Klaeuw (The Claw) DELFT, Holland.

1655- TIN-GLAZED EARTHENWARE. (DELFTWARE)

1662- **Cornelisz van der Hoeve** - - -

1668- **Cornelia van Schoonhoven** - -

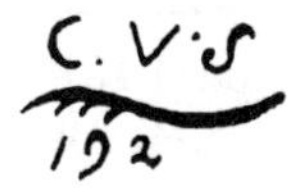

1702- **Lysbet van Schoonhoven** - - -

1739- **C. van Dyck** - - - - - -

1768- **L. Sanders** - - - - - -

1830- **Van Putten & Cie.** - - - - -

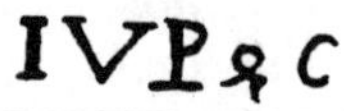

1655 IWAMI, Japan.

1655- **Naka -mura,** GREY STONEWARE.
Factory started by Toshiro for the Prince of Soma. Soma-Yaki. Badge of the Prince of Soma found in relief on some Soma ware.- - - -

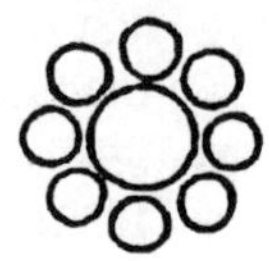

Various marks found on Soma-Yaki -

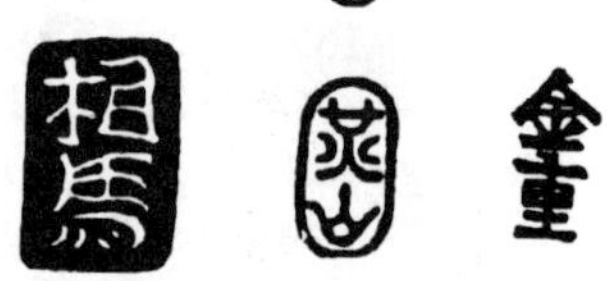

c.1840 **Nag-ami (potter)** - - - - -

1655 Ninsei (Enamelled faïence) YAMASHIRO, Japan.

Nomura Seisuke (potter) Studio name Ninsei.
Creamy or Grey stoneware with crackled glaze and enamelled decoration known as `Awata` ware.

17th Century Awata marks `Onike`

c.1685-c.1850 `Gobosatsu` - - -

1846 Tanzam (at Awata)- -

c.1710 `Hozan` Art name given to Yasubei 1865. Tai Hei. - - - -

c.1720- Tokuro Yohei and family. `Dai Nipon Taizan Sei` - - - - - - -

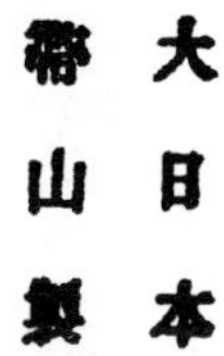

1756- `Kinkozan` Kagiya (potter) and family. -

1820- `Bizan` Hasegawa Kumenosuke and family.

c.1820- `Kozan` on Awatafayence.- - -

1655 Quiring A. Kleynoven (Delft Artist) DELFT, Holland.

TIN-GLAZED EARTHENWARE (DELFTWARE) - - - -

1655	Cleynhoven, Quirinus Van, DELFT, Holland. -	see 1653 De Porceleyne Fles.
1657	Mathieu de Benque, France. - - -	see 1650 TOULOUSE.
1657	Sleur de Fustinac, France. - - - -	see 1650 TOULOUSE.

1658 Delft Red Stoneware, DELFT, Holland.

1658- Ary de Milde - - -

M. de Milde - - - -

Continued over -

1658/61

1658 Delft Red Stoneware, DELFT, Holland. (Cont`)

1691- **Lamberus van Eenhorn** -

Imitation Chinese marks-

1706 **Jacobus de Caluwe** - -

1658 Frytom, Frederick v., (Delft Artist) DELFT, Holland.

TIN-GLAZED EARTHENWARE (DELFTWARE) - - -

1659 J. van den Houk (Delft Artist) DELFT, Holland.

TIN-GLAZED EARTHENWARE (DELFTWARE) - - -

1660 J. Groenland (Delft Artist) DELFT, Holland.

TIN-GLAZED EARTHENWARE (DELFTWARE) - -

1660 HANLEY, Staffordshire, England.

c.1660- A major area for ceramics where many factories are still producing.

The individual factories and potters of HANLEY have been listed under their own dates and marks within this book.

1660 Toft, James, Ralph and Thomas, HANLEY, Staffordshire, England.

c.1660-EARTHENWARES, SLIP-DECORATED.

James (b.1673) Ralph (b.1638) Thomas (d.1689)

James Toft
Ralph Toft
Thomas Toft

1660 Conrade, Dominique, France. - - - see 1589 NEVERS.
1660 Kutani-Yaki, Japan. - - - see 1580 HIZEN.
1660 Okawaji or Nabeshima-Yaki, Japan. - - see 1580 HIZEN.

1661 J.A. van Hammen (Delft Artist) DELFT, Holland.

TIN-GLAZED EARTHENWARE (DELFTWARE) - - -

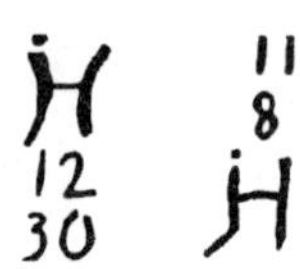

1661 HANAU, Frankfurt-am-Main, Germany.

1661-1806 FAÏENCE. - - -

1680-90 **Bally, H.,** - - -

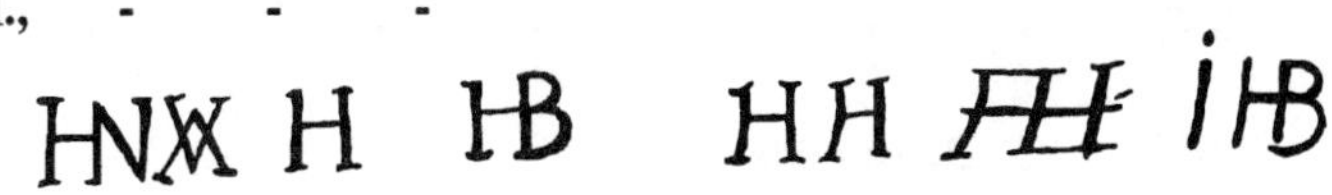

1694-1712 marks - - - 

1740-86 **Hieronymus von Alphen** - -

1793- Dated mark. - - 

1661 `t Hart` (The Heart) DELFT, Holland.

1661- TIN-GLAZED EARTHENWARE (DELFTWARE)

1661- **J. Mesoris** - - - -

1679- Symon Mes - - - 

1661- **Joris Mes.** - - - - 

1714- **M.v.d. Bogaert** - - - 

1760- **Hendrik van Middeldijk** - - 

1661 Hoppestein, J.W., DELFT, Holland. - - see 1648 De oud Moriaans hooft

1662 J. Kulick, (Delft Artists) DELFT, Holland.

TIN-GLAZED EARTHENWARE (DELFTWARE) - - - 

J. Kruijck. - - - - - - - 

J.C. van d. Burgh. - - - - - - 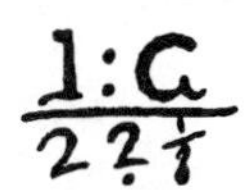

1662 Hoeve, Cornelisz van der, DELFT, Holland. - see 1655 De Klaeuw.

1662 K`ang-hsi, China. - - - - - see 1644 CH`ING.

1663-68

1663 de Boot. (The Boat) DELFT, Holland.

1663- TIN-GLAZED EARTHENWARE (DELFTWARE)

1663- **A. Reygens.** - - - - - 

1675- **D. van der Kest.** - - - - 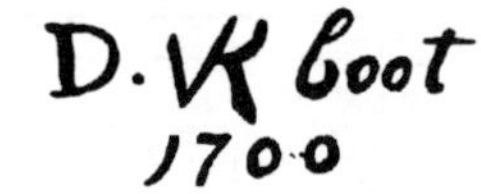

1707- **Willem van Dale.** - - - 

1759- **Johannes van den Appel.** - - 

1663 J. de Weert, (Delft Artists) DELFT, Holland.

TIN-GLAZED EARTHENWARE (DELFTWARE) - - - - 

Willem Kleffyus. - - - - - 

1664 Goto Saijiro, Japan. - - - - see 1650 KAGA.
1665 Levantino, Italy. - - - - - see 1550 SAVONA.

1666 FRANKFURT-AM-MAIN, Germany.

1666 - c.1770 FAÏENCE.

1666 Haji Chozaemon, Japan. - - - - see 1650 KAGA.
1666 Ohi-Machi-Yaki, Japan. - - - - see 1650 KAGA.

1667 T. Mesch (Delft Artists) DELFT, Holland.

TIN-GLAZED EARTHENWARE (DELFTWARE) 

P. Kam. - - - - 

1667 L. Cleffius, DELFT, Holland. - - - see 1639 De metale Pot.

1668 Corn. de Keizer (Delft Artists) DELFT, Holland.

TIN-GLAZED EARTHENWARE (DELFTWARE) - - - - - 

Jan Pieters. - - - - - - - - - 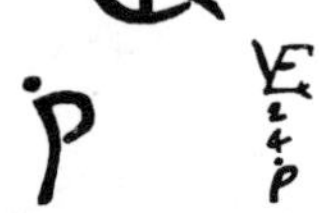

1668 Cornelia van Schoonhoven, DELFT, Holland. - see 1655 De Klaeuw.
1668 Keiser, Cornelis, DELFT, Holland. - - see 1642 De twee Scheepjes.

1669 DIJON, Côte-d`Or, France.

1669-c.1854 FAÏENCE. - - -

1669 Flyt M. Byckloh (Delft Artist) DELFT, Holland.

TIN-GLAZED EARTHENWARE (DELFTWARE) - -

1670 John Greene, (d.1686) WROTHAM, Kent, England.

17th century SLIPWARES. - - - *I. G.*

1670 Hendrick van Swanenburgh (Delft Artist) DELFT, Holland.

TIN-GLAZED EARTHENWARE (DELFTWARE)

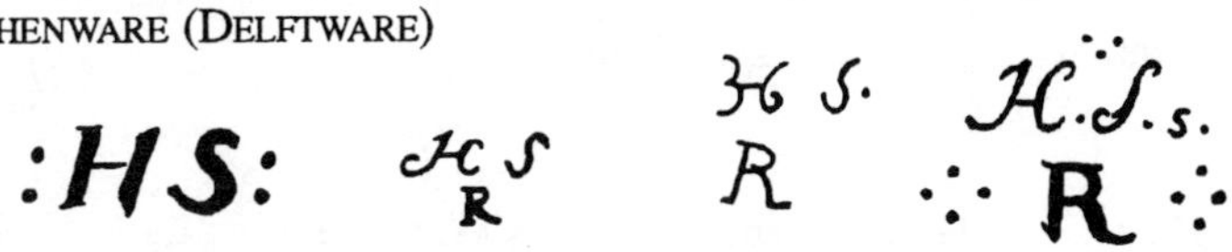

1670 SAINT-CLOUD, Seine-et-Oise, France.

FAÏENCE.

c.1670- **Pierre Chicaneau (d.c.1678)** -
widow married Henri Trou Blue -

1722- Henri Trou (after being shown the porcelain secret) - -

Underglaze blue or red
or sometimes incised- -

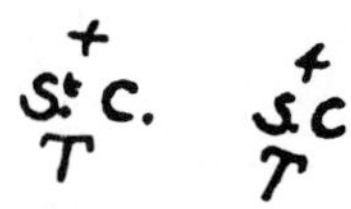

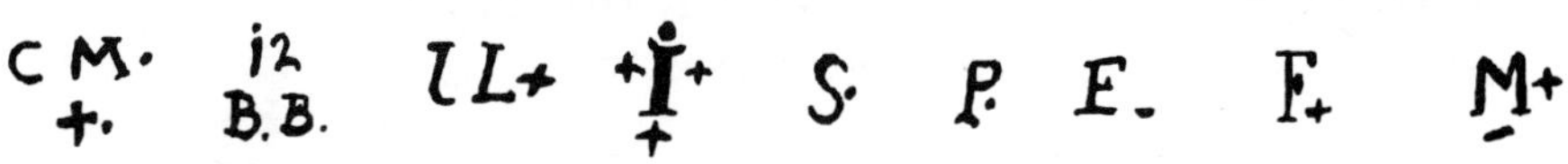

c.1678-1766 SOFT-PASTE PORCELAIN. incised-

Sun-face marks (in blue) - -

1670 Cuyst, Gerrit, DELFT, Holland. - - - see 1648 De dubbelde Schenkkan
1670 Ofuke or Mifukai-Yaki, Japan. - - - see 1573 OWARI.

1671

1671 De trie Klokken (The 3 Bells) DELFT, Holland.

1671- TIN-GLAZED EARTHENWARE (DELFTWARE)

1671- **Rottewel, Barbara,** - - - -

1675- **Rottewel, B, / Laen, J. van der,** - -

1675- **Laen, Jan Janzs van der,** - - -

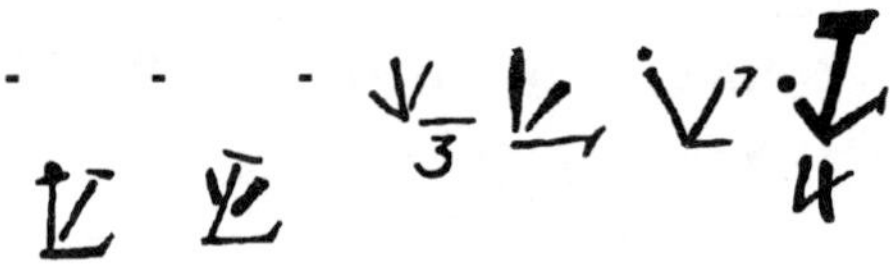

1700- **Mesch, Pieter Simon,** - - -

1759- **Gaal, Cornelia, / Does, W. van der,** -

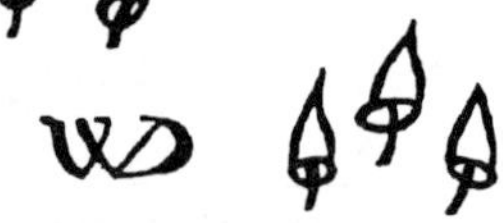

1830- **Putten, J. van, & Cie.** - - -

1671 FULHAM, London, England.

1671- John Dwight. Early English potter produced SALT-GLAZED STONEWARE.
The individual factories and potters of FULHAM have been
listed under their own dates and marks within this book.

1671 de Romeyn (The Rummer) DELFT, Holland.

1671- TIN-GLAZED EARTHENWARE (DELFTWARE)

1671- **Gouda, Martinus,** - - - -

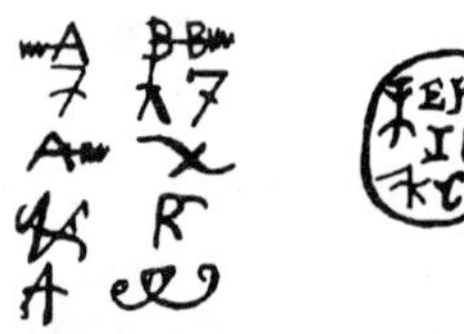

1696- **Reinier Hey** - - - - -

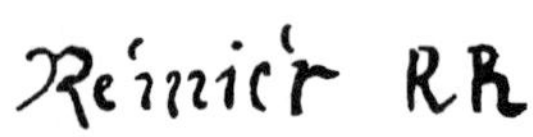

1759- **Marum, Petrus van,** -

1764- **Kloot, J. van der,** - - -

1672 de trie Porceleyne Flessjes (The Three Porcelain Scent-Bottles)
DELFT, Holland.

1672- TIN-GLAZED EARTHENWARE (DELFTWARE)

1672- **Pynacker, Jacobus,** - - - -

1676- **Kool, Jacobus,** - - - -

1690- **Pynacker, Adriaen,** - - - -

1697- **Kool, W.,** - - - - -

1764- **Brouwer, Hugo,** - - - -

1674 Eenhorn, Samuel van, DELFT, Holland. - - see 1645 De Griekse A.
1674 Kam, G.P., DELFT, Holland. - - - see 1655 de 3 Astonne.

1675 de Roos (The Rose) DELFT, Holland.

1675- TIN-GLAZED EARTHENWARE (DELFTWARE)

1675- **Cosyn, Arendt,** -

1759- **Does, Dirck van der,** - - -

1803- **Bosch, H. van der, / Mandele, P. van der,-**
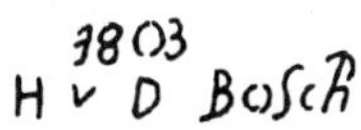

1830- **Putten, J. van & Cie,** - - -

1675 Helmback, Abraham, NUREMBERG, Germany.

c.1675-1700. - - - - - -

1675 Laen, Jan Janzs, DELFT, Holland. - - see 1671 de trie Klokken.
1675 Kessel, Amerensie van, DELFT, Holland. - see 1648 De dubbelde Schenkkan.
1675 Kest, D. van der, DELFT, Holland. - - see 1663 de boot.
1675 Pescetto, Italy. - - - - - - see 1550 SAVONA.
1675 Rottewel, B, / Laen, J, van der, DELFT, Holland. see 1671 de trie Klokken.
1675 Shuntai-Yaki, Akuza ware, Japan. - - see 1573 OWARI.

1676-79

1676 PAVIA, nr. Milan, Lombardy, Italy.

c.1676 GLAZED EARTHENWARE (SGRAFFIATO)

c.1676-1694 Cuzio family - - - *IOHANNES. ANTONIUS,*

Some members of the *BARNABAS. CUTIUS.*

Cusio family - *PAPLAENSIS*

1708 Maiolica marks - - - -

c.1710 Fratelli Cantu - - - -

1676 Kool, Jacobus, DELFT, Holland. - - see 1672 de trie Porceleyne Flessjes.

1677 IZUMO, Japan.

c.1677-1720 Gombei of Rakuzan made tea ware.
Hagi and Seto style.

1750-1860 Zen and Zenshiro family. - -

1764-1868 Fujina Factory founded by Funaki Yajibei.
Earthenware. Prince Fumai (Patron)
1875- Factory re-opened by Jakuzan

1780-1840 Rakuzan at Matsuye - -

c.1830 Unyei. Fujina ware.- - - -

19th Century Wakayama - - - -

1679 CASTELLI, Abruzzi, Italy.

17TH AND 18TH CENTURY MAIOLICA.

1686-1746 Dr.Francesco Antonio Grue. -

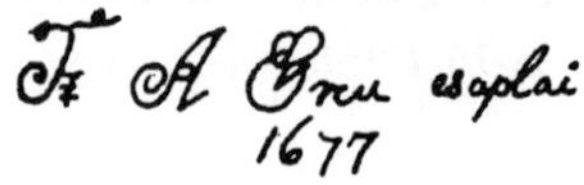

1670 Gentile, Benardino - - -

1718 Dr. Franc Anton Grue. - - ***Dr Franc Anton Grue 1718***

Continued over -

1679 CASTELLI, Abruzzi, Italy. (Cont`)
17th and 18th Century MAIOLICA.

1732- G. Rocco di Castelli - -

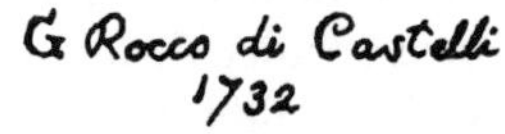

Fuina, Gesualde, - - - -

1735 D.Francisci Antonti Xaveri Grue. *D. Francisci Antonii Xarerii Grue*

c.1776 Liborio Grue. - - -

Carmine Gentile. (b.1678,d.1763) - -

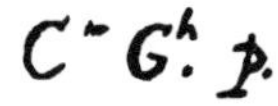

Gentili - - - - - - *P G*

Bernardino Gentili. (b.1727,d.1813) *Bernardino Gent.p.*

c.1796 Saverio Grue. - - -

1679 Clérissy, Pierre, MOUSTIERS, France.
1679-1728.
1728-36 Antoine II, (son)
1736-83 Pierre II, (grandson)
1783- Sold to Joseph Fouque

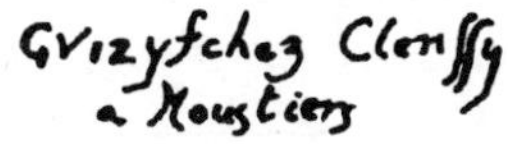

1679 Dirk J. v. Schie (Delft Artist) DELFT, Holland.
TIN-GLAZED EARTHENWARE (DELFTWARE) - -

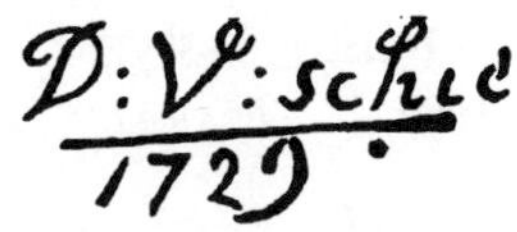

1679 Het Bijltje (The Hatchet) DELFT, Holland.
1679- TIN-GLAZED EARTHENWARE (DELFTWARE)

1679- Huibrecht Brouwer - -
1697- Joris van Torenburg -

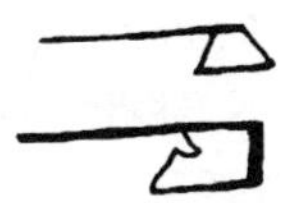

1759- Joost Brouwer - -

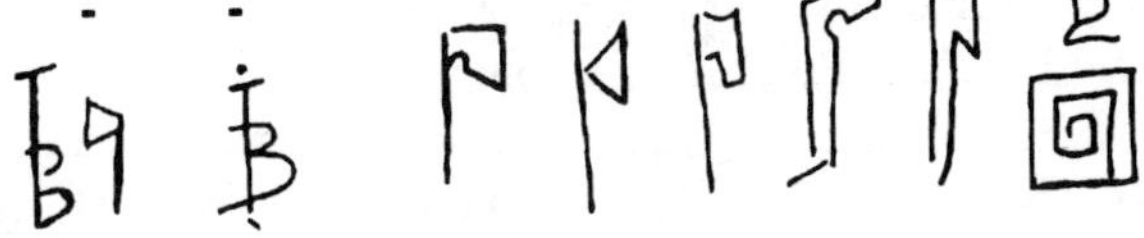

1679-87

1679 MOUSTIERS, Basses-Alpes, France.
1679-19th century FAÏENCE.
The individual factories and potters of MOUSTIERS have been listed under thier own dates and marks within this book.

1679 Mes, Symon, DELFT, Holland. - - - - see 1661 t`hart.

1680 CASSEL, (KASSEL) Hesse-Nassau, Germany.
1680-1788 FAÏENCE.
1724-35 **Johann Christoph Gilze** - - **`Hessen-Land`**

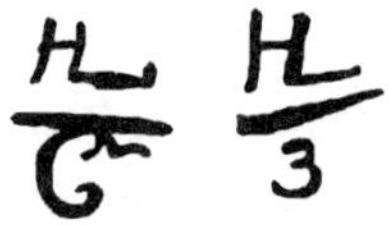

1740-64 marks -

1766-88 HARD-PASTE PORCELAIN, **mark of the Hessian lion `Hessen-Cassel`** - **(similar to Frankenthal mark)**

1680 TUNSTALL, Staffordshire, England.
A large Staffordshire region producing all types of ceramics from their many factories.
The individual factories and potters of TUNSTALL have been listed under their own dates and marks within this book.

1680 Ka ichi, Japan. - - - - - - - see 1583 BIZEN.

1683 Groen, Joh., (Delft Artist) DELFT, Holland.
TIN-GLAZED EARTHENWARE (DELFTWARE) - -

1684 NAPLES, Italy.
c.1684- MAIOLICA. - - - -

The individual factories and potters of NAPLES have been listed under their own dates and marks within this book.

1685 William Simpson, TUNSTALL, Staffordshire, England.
c.1685-c.1715. SLIPWARES.- - - *WILLIAM SIMPSON*
This name is also mentioned at Burslem and Hanley.

1685 `Gobosatsu` YAMASHIRO, Japan. - - see 1655 Ninsei.
1686 Dr. Grue, Francesco Antonio, Italy. - - see 1679 CASTELLI.

1687 Nieutlet, Guillaume, (Delft Artist) DELFT, Holland.
TIN-GLAZED EARTHENWARE (DELFTWARE) - -

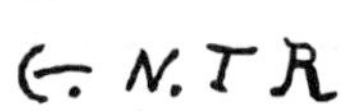

1687 Korks, Adriaenus, DELFT, Holland. - - see 1645 De Grieksche A.

1689 de Star (The Star) DELFT, Holland.

1689- TIN-GLAZED EARTHENWARE (DELFTWARE)

1689- **Witsenburgh, T.,** - - -

1694- **Lange, J. der,** - - -

1720- **Berg, Cornelis der,**

1759- **Berg, Justus de,** -

1764- **Kiel, Albertus,** -

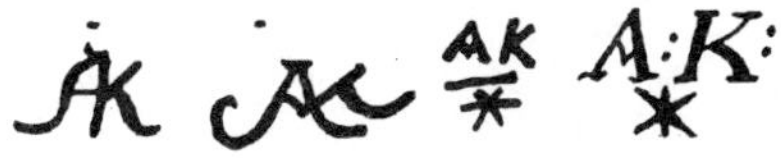

1689 Bourne, Henri, France. - - - - SEE 1589 NEVERS.

1690 IZUMI, Japan.

Late 17th century Kichizaemon, Ueda of Sakai

Minato-Yaki. THIN MOTTLED CHINA OF YELLOW TINT SOMETIMES CLARET COLOUR.

c.1800- **19th Century. Minato yaki** -

1828-29 **(Bunsei period) Kichizaemon the fifth copied Raku ware and Chinese `Kochi-yaki`**

Kwan-kei - - - -

1690 Meir, Richard, SHELTON, Staffordshire, England.

Late 17th-Early 18th century. SLIPWARE. Sliptrailed- *RICHARD MEIR*

1690 Poulisse, Pieter, (Delft Artist) DELFT, Holland.

TIN-GLAZED EARTHENWARE (DELFTWARE) - -

Wal, J. van der, - - -

1690-93

1690 QUIMPER, Finistere, France.

1690- FAÏENCE.
1743-82 **Pierre-Paul Caussy.-** - - 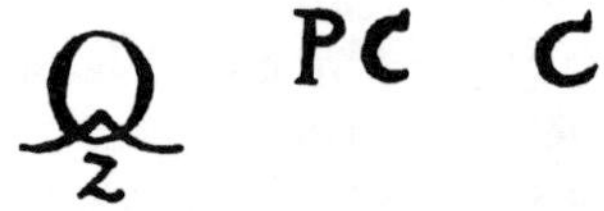

1782- **Antoine de la Hubaudiere.** STONEWARE AND FAÏENCE. - - - - 

1872- **Fougeray-** IMITATION OF 18TH CENTURY FAÏENCE. - 

1690 VARAGES, Var, France.

c.1690-1800 FAÏENCE IN MOUSTIERS AND MARSEILLES STYLES.

1698 (dated) - - - ***`Fait par moi E. armand a` varages 1698.***

1690 SHELTON, Staffordshire, England.

A well known Staffordshire region with many factories still producing wares today (1996)
The individual factories and potters of SHELTON have been listed under their own dates and marks within this book.

1690	Pynacker, Adriaen, DELFT, Holland. -	see 1672 de trie Porceleyne Flessjes
1691	Eenhoorn,Lambertus van, DELFT, Holland.	see 1639 De metale Pot.
1691	Eenhoorn, Lambertus van, DELFT, Holland.	see 1658 Delft Red Stoneware.

1692 de Fortuyn (The Fortune) DELFT, Holland.

1692- TIN-GLAZED EARTHENWARE (DELFTWARE)
1692- **L. van Dale.** - - - 

1706- **Oosterwijek, Joris,** - - 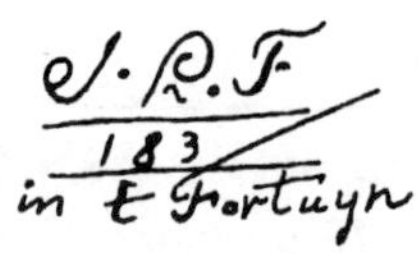

1759- **P.van den Briel / Elisabeth Elling.** 

1693 de vergulde Bloempot (The Golden Flowerpot) DELFT, Holland.

1693- TIN-GLAZED EARTHENWARE (DELFTWARE)
1693- **Stroom, P. van der,** - - - 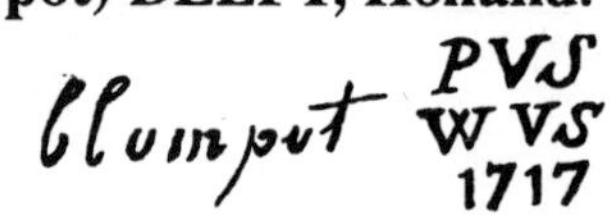

1698- **Broeckerhoff, S. van,** - - 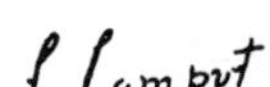

1759- **Burch, Paulus van der,** - - 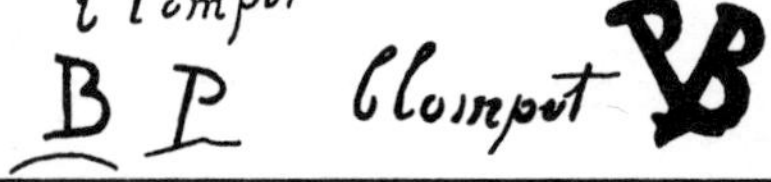

1693 **SAN QUIRICO D`ORCIA, nr. Siena, Italy.**

1693-18th century. MAIOLICA.

1723 (dated) Arms of Cardinal Chigi (founder) -

Bartolommeo Terchi (painter) - - ***`Bar. Terchi Romano in S. Quirico`***

1694 **Meir, John, SHELTON, Staffordshire, England.**

Late 17th - Early 18th Century. SLIPWARE. - - *John Meir 1708*

1694 **Schagen, Cornelius van, (Delft Artist) DELFT, Holland.**

TIN-GLAZED EARTHENWARE (DELFTWARE) - - C.V:S

1694 Lange, J. der, DELFT, Holland. - - - see 1689 de Star.

1695 **Kloot, Corn. van d., (Delft Artist) DELFT, Holland.**

TIN-GLAZED EARTHENWARE (DELFTWARE) C VK 1729

Verburg, J., - - - -

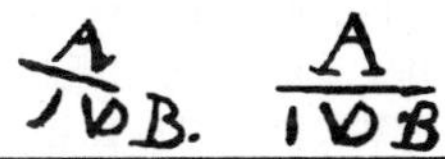

1696 **de Dissel (The Pole) DELFT, Holland.**

1696- TIN-GLAZED EARTHENWARE (DELFTWARE)

IN· DE·DELFSE. VIN·KEL,

1696- **Hurck, Pieter van,** - .I.D.

1696 **LILLE, France.**

1696-1802 FAÏENCE.

Veuve Februrier and Boussemart -

1711-30 SOFT-PASTE PORCELAIN - -

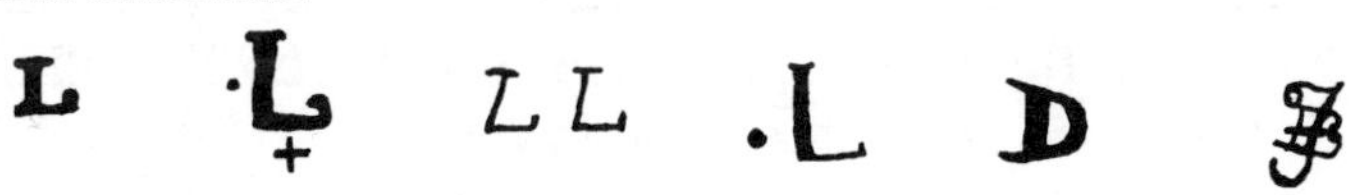

1711-55 **Barthélémy Dorez** - - -

FAÏENCE AND SOFT-PASTE PORCELAIN.

1716- `F.& B. DOREZ`

Continued over -

1696-1700

1696 LILLE, France. (Cont`)

1729-73 **Joseph-François Boussemaert.** -
FAÏENCE.

1773-1802 **Phillippe Auguste Petit** -

1784-1817 **Leperre-Durot (under protection of the Dauphin)** HARD-PASTE PORCELAIN. -

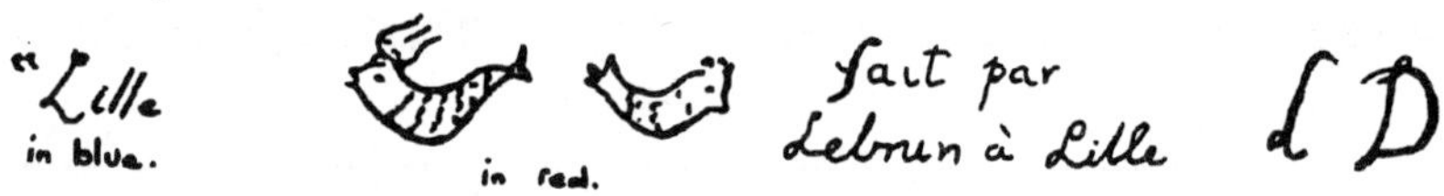

1696 Witsenburg,C, (Delft Artist) DELFT, Holland.
TIN-GLAZED EARTHENWARE (DELFTWARE)

1696 Reinier Hey, DELFT, Holland. - - see 1671 de Romeyn.
1697 Kam, David, DELFT, Holland. - - see 1652 De Paauw.
1697 Knotter, Johannes, DELFT, Holland. - see 1653 De Porceleyne Fles.
1697 Kool, W., DELFT, Holland. - - see 1672 de trie Porceleyne Flessjes.
1697 Torenburg, Joris van, DELFT, Holland. - see 1679 Het Bijltje.

1698 Baans, Dirck, (Delft Artist) DELFT, Holland.
TIN-GLAZED EARTHENWARE (DELFTWARE)

A. Brouwer - - - - -

1698 Heugue, H, ROUEN, France.
1698-c.1800 A family of potters producing faïence.

1698 Broekerhoff, S. van, DELFT, Holland. - see 1693 de vergulde Bloempot

---

1699 Kloot, Bart van d, (Delft Artist) DELFT, Holland.
TIN-GLAZED EARTHENWARE (DELFTWARE) - -

1700 Ball, Izaac, BURSLEM, Staffordshire, England.
17th-18th century SLIPWARE. - - - *I. B.*

1700 Glass, Joseph, HANLEY, Staffordshire, England.
17th-18th century SLIPWARES. - - - *JOSEPH GLASS*

1700 Kuick, Michiel van, (Delft Artist) DELFT, Holland.
TIN-GLAZED EARTHENWARE (DELFTWARE) - -

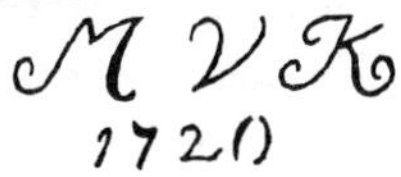

1700 Levavasseur, Jean-Marie, ROUEN, France.
c.1700- FAMILY POTTERS. - - -

1700 STOKE, Staffordshire, England.
c.1700 One of the famous Staffordshire regions with many factories including the renowned `Minton`
The individual factories and potters of STOKE have been listed under their own dates and marks within this book.

1700 Luffneu, Adriaen, Holland. - - - see 1630 ROTTERDAM.
1700 Mesch, Pieter Simon, DELFT, Holland. - - see 1671 de trie Klokken.

1701 de porceleyne Schotel (The Porcelain Dish) DELFT, Holland.
1701- TIN-GLAZED EARTHENWARE (DELFTWARE)
1725- **Pennis, Joh,** - - -

1764- **Duyn, Johannes van,-**

1701 Houten, Jacob van, (Delft Artist) DELFT, Holland.
TIN-GLAZED EARTHENWARE (DELFTWARE) - -

1701 De Vlucht, Marcelis, DELFT, Holland. - - see 1653 De Porceleyne Fles.

1702 Heath, Job, STOKE, Staffordshire, England.
Early 18th century EARTHENWARE. Sliptrailed- ***JOB HEATH***

1702 Schoonhove, Lysbet van, DELFT, Holland. - - see 1655 De Klaeuw.

1705 BRUSSELS, Belgium. - - ***`A Bruxelles`***
FAÏENCE AND HARD-PASTE PORCELAIN

1705- **Witsenburg and Mombaers,** FAÏENCE -

1724- **Mombaers, Phillipe,** - - -

1766- **Antoisenet, Jaques,** - - - -

Continued over -

1705-08

1705 BRUSSELS, Belgium. (Cont`)

1786-90 **Schaerbeek,** HARD-PASTE PORCELAIN. red or blue- -

c.1787-1803 Etterbeek. HARD-PASTE PORCELAIN. - red or purple-

c.1791-1803 Louis Cretté- - - ***`L. CrettéBruxelles rue d`Aremberg 1791`***

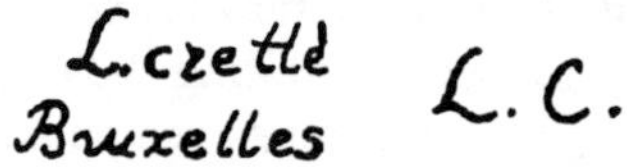

1705 Sand, S. van der, (Delft Artist) DELFT, Holland.

TIN-GLAZED EARTHENWARE (DELFTWARE) - -

1706 Caluwe, Jacobus de, DELFT, Holland. - - see 1658 Delft Red Stoneware.
1706 Oosterwijek, Joris, DELFT, Holland. - - see 1692 de Fortuyn.

1707 BRUNSWICK, Germany.

1707-1807 FAÏENCE. **Duke Anton Ulrich of Brunswick.**
The individual factories and potters of BRUNSWICK have been listed under their own dates and marks within this book.

1707 Caussy, Paul, ROUEN, France.

1707- **Son and grandson.** FAÏENCE.

1707 Gaal, Joh, (Delft Artist) DELFT, Holland.

TIN-GLAZED EARTHENWARE (DELFTWARE) - -

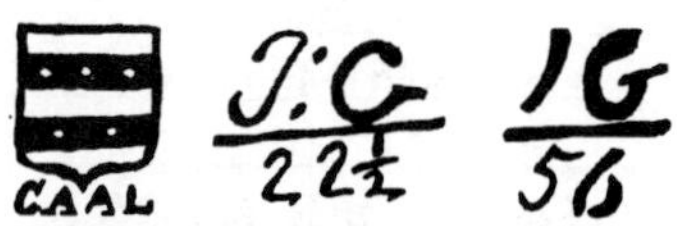

1707 Dale, Willem van, DELFT, Holland. - - see 1663 de boot.
1707 Gaal, Jan, DELFT, Holland. - - - see 1642 De twee Scheepjes.

1708 Broeckerhoff, Jac. van, (Delft Artist) DELFT, Holland.

TIN-GLAZED EARTHENWARE (DELFTWARE) - -

1708 DRESDEN, Saxony, Germany.

1708-84 **Cristiane Hörisch,** FAÏENCE.
The individual factories and potters of DRESDEN have been listed under thier own dates and marks within this book.

1710 MEISSEN, nr. Dresden, Saxony, Germany.

1710 - HARD-PASTE PORCELAIN.

1706- Jasper porcelain and fine red stoneware.

1706-c.35 Böettger`s red stoneware, the forerunner of European porcelain.

1711 Throwers and moulders marks, impressed

Early stoneware unexplained marks- incised-

c.1720s Crossed swords on red stoneware- -

1707-08 The secret of hard-paste porcelain, as made by the Chinese, was discovered by the Alchemist, J.F. Böttger and a number of dedicated assistants at Venus Tower, Dresden.

1710- Foundation of Meissen Porcelain Manufactory.
In 1710 the Manufactory was established in the Albrechtsburg Fortress in Meissen by the Elector of Saxony (Frederick Augustus I.) and King of Poland (Augustus II.) called Augustus the Strong.

1710-63 Royal and Electoral Porcelain Manufactory.
1710-19 Böttger period.
1722- Steinbrueck, Johann Melchior (administrator) suggested the crossed-swords of the Elector of Saxony should be used as the Meissen mark.

1709 - 40 Augustus Rex monogram,
(pieces for Royal use) - underglaze blue- -
1709-26 Registered as a trademark in Germany in 1875, but it is believed that this mark went well beyond 1726.

1717- Blue mark under the glaze was first used.

1720-56 and 1763-65 Höroldt, Johann Gregorius.
Porcelain painter, decorator, colour chemist.

Johan Gregorius
Höroldt Inven
Meissen den 22
Janu. ano 1727

Continued over -

1710

1710 MEISSEN, nr. Dresden, Saxony, Germany. (Cont`)

1720-30 `Kite` and `Caduceus` underglaze blue- known as whip mark or Mercurus` rod. Meissen date these marks between 1712-19 in 1875 trademark registration, but blue underglaze mark was not available until 1717.

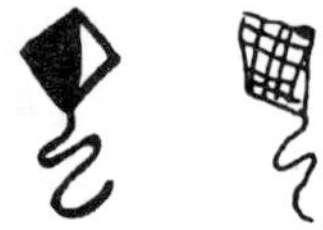

Early 18th century imitation Chinese and Japanese marks in underglaze blue. (Mainly used for exports to Turkey)
It is thought that these marks were also used during Count Marcolini directorship (1774-1814)

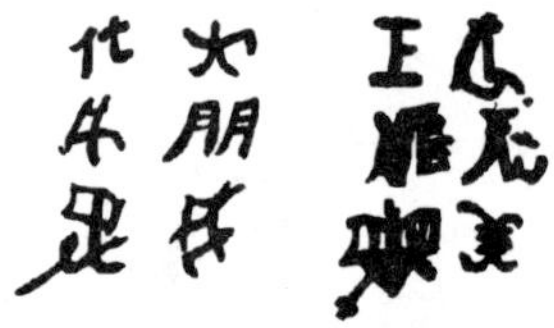

1722- Meissener Porzellan Manufaktur
Sometimes with crossed swords.
underglaze blue - - - -

1722- Königliche Porzellan Manufaktur
underglaze blue - - - -

1722- Königliche Porcelaine Fabrique
underglaze blue - - - -

c.1725 Palace marks:-

`Königliche Hof-Conditorie` (Royal Court Confectionery)

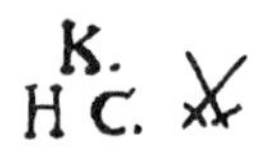

`Königliche Hof-Conditorie Warschau` (Royal Court Confectionery in Warsaw) - - - - - -

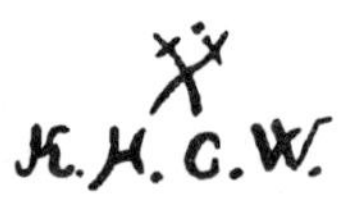

`Churfurstliche Hof-Conditorie` (Prince-Electoral Court Confectionery) - - - - - - - -

`Königliche Hof-Kuche` (Royal Court Kitchen) -

18th Century Royal Russian Collection at St. Petersburg, Russia. - - - - - -

Continued over -

1710 MEISSEN, nr. Dresden, Saxony, Germany. (Cont`)

c.1725-30 Known as the `Cosel` mark after Countess Cozel, but this has been unsubstantiated by recent research. Gold overglaze -

c.1725-c.30 Early crossed-swords marks.
In the beginning the swords were usually painted by apprentices and every mark was different. underglaze blue -

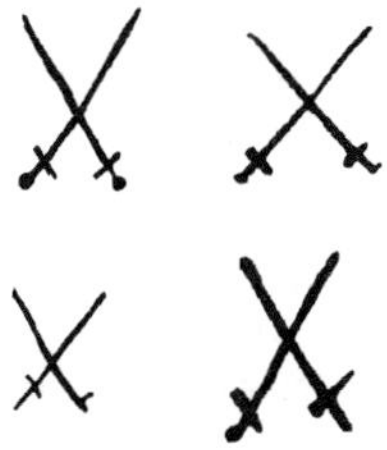

1727-28 and 1730-33 Kirchner, Johann Gottlieb,
Sculptor.
1731-75 Kaendler, Johann Joachim, - - ***J.J. Kaendler***
Sculptor and modeller.
1735-49 Eberlein, Johann Friedrich,
Sculptor and modeller.

1733-63 `Production Period` Registered dot mark by Meissen in 1875. underglaze blue -

1763-74 `Production Period` Registered by Meissen in 1875. underglaze blue - -

1748-61 Meyer, Friedrich Elias,
Sculptor and modeller.

c.1764-1938 Marks on wares sold in white. - -

1938-present - -

1763-1806 Electoral Saxon Porcelain Manufactory.

1764-80 Acier, Michel Victor,
Sculptor and modeller.
1769-1812 Jüchtzer, Christian Gottfried,
Sculptor.

1774-1815 Camillo Count Marcolini (Director)
Two dot period only lasted a few months before Marcolini changed the mark to include a star. The `star` mark was probably used well beyond Marcolini`s period. Crossed-swords (star period) - - -

Continued over -

1710

1710 MEISSEN, nr. Dresden, Saxony, Germany. (Cont`)

c.1800 Late Marcolini period marks -

Marks used on biscuit porcelain figures -

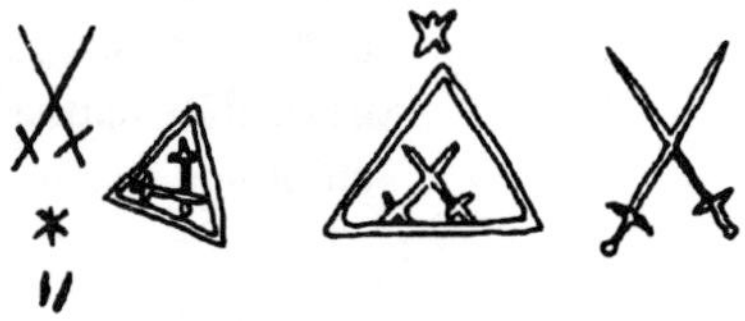

1814-33 **von Oppel`s directorship.**

1817-24 Crossed swords with Roman numerals. - (To identify grades of paste)

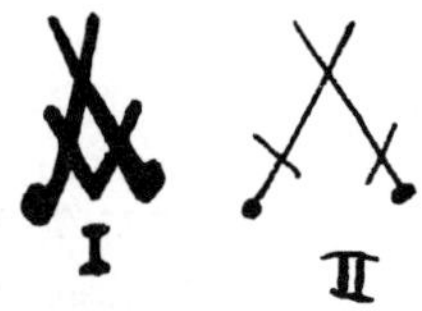

1824-50. During von Oppel`s period many 18th century pieces were re-introduced. The mark of the crossed swords were very badly painted on the wares, probably to give the impression that they were old pieces.- -

1833-70 **Kuhn, Hienrich Gottlieb, (Director)**
1836-86 Leuteritz, Ernst August,
Sculptor and modeller.

1850-1924 Crossed swords with `pommel` marks were introduced. (Similar marks were used in the 18th century with the blades straight) These marks had curved blades and did not cross in the middle of the blades. Sometimes one blade was shorter than the other.

1850-c.69 Marks used for quality control.
1850-late 19th Century. Marks on groups, figurines and vases. - - -

1852-69 Marks on tableware.
2 incisions = Substandard.
3 incisions = Brac (defective)
4 incisions = Insignificant.

Quality marks for the English market continued beyond these dates.

Continued over -

1710 MEISSEN, nr. Dresden, Saxony, Germany. **(Cont`)**

1858-1906 Braunsdorf, Eduard Julius,
Porcelain painter.

1865- **Site of production transferred to Triebischtal.**

1890-1907 Hentschel, Julius Konrad,
Sculptor and modeller.
1891-1933 Walther, Paul, Sculptor.
1903-29 Hösel, Erich, Sculptor.
1911-37 Börner, Emil Paul, (Freelance 1959-60)
Sculptor, modeller and decorator.
1912-13 Münch-Khe, Willi, (Freelance 1925-32 and 56)
Sculptor, modeller and painter.
1912-39 Oehme, Erich, (Freelance after 1954 until he died in 1970) Sculptor and modeller.
1917-68 Struck, Alexander, Sculptor.

1918- **Renamed State Porcelain Manufactory**

1918- Scheurich, Paul, (Freelance after 1918 until he died in 1945) Sculptor and modeller.
1919- `Jasper porcelain` (red fine stoneware)
Re-introduced with a new formula.

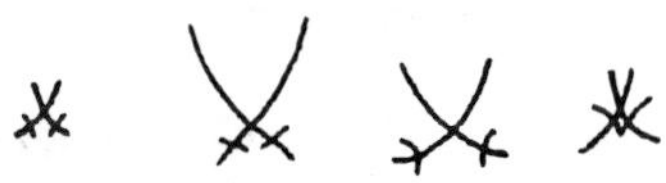

Registered mark.`Böttgersteinzeug` imprinted with crossed-swords - -

1920- Esser, Max, (Freelance after 1920 until he died in 1943) Sculptor and modeller.

1924-33 **Max Adolf Pfeiffer (Director)**
1933 Pfeiffer forced to resign by Nazis.
1924-34 Crossed-swords (Dot beween blades) -

1934- Dot removed from mark -

1938 Mark used occasionally - Royal Dresden China

1943- Werner, Heinz,
Porcelain painter and decorator.
1944- Bretschneider, Volkmar,
Modeller, decorator and painter.

1945-46 **Small arc was added beneath hilts signifying joining of the swords after the war.** -

Continued over -

1710

1710 MEISSEN, nr. Dresden, Saxony, Germany. (Cont`)

1946-50 **Property of The Soviet Government.**
1950- **After the Soviets handed back the factory to the German Democratic Republic Meissen introduced additional marks (away from the crossed swords) in underglaze blue near the footring.**

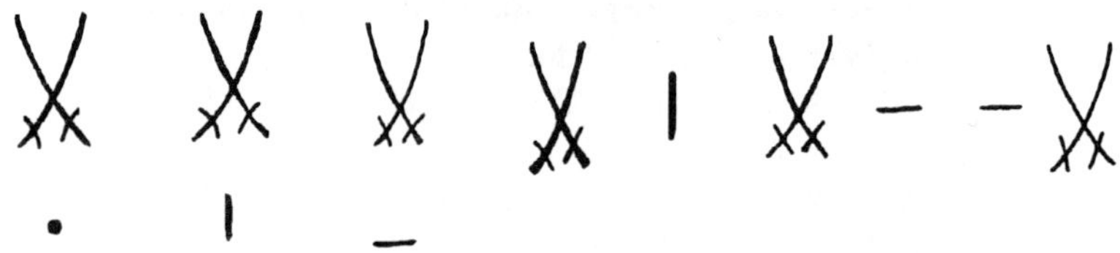

1951-53 1953-57 1957-72 1972-80 1980 1980

1947- Stolle, Rudi, Porcelain painter.
1948- Zepner, Ludwig, Modeller.

1948 Year Signs

1948 - △	1949 - O	1950 - □	1951 - —	1952 - V
1953 - ⊥	1954 - ˥	1955 - >	1956 - :	1957 - ◇
1958 - ⊣	1959 - D	1960 - ∩	1961 - ♀	1962 - N
1963 - =	1964 - [	1965 - Λ	1966 - •	1967 - <
1968 - Y	1969 - /	1970 - ⊢	1971 - ∇	1972 - ⅄
1973 - o	1974 -)(	1975 - ⊂	1976 -]	1977 - ✕
1978 - Σ	1979 - X	1980 - *A*	1981 - *B*	1982 - *C*
1983 - *D*	1984 - *E*	And so on.		

1950- Strang, Peter, Sculptor.

1963-73 Mark -

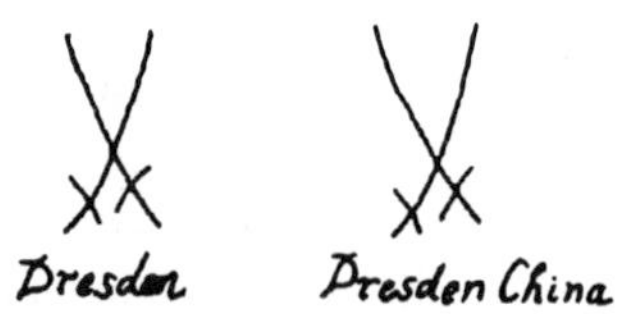

1969- Danielczyk, Jorg, Sculptor and modeller.

1971-81 Mark registered in the U.S.A.- -

Continued over -

1710 MEISSEN, Saxony, Germany. (Cont`)

1972 `Meissen` marks used on special items since 1972 - -

1973- Klöde, Sylvia, Sculptor and modeller.
1986- Wachs, Sabine, Modeller and decorator.

1990- Private enterprise (GmbH)
1991- Property of Saxon state government.

(For further information see Robert E. Röntgen`s *The Book of Meissen)*
(By Courtesy of Staatliche Porzellan-Manufaktur Meissen GmbH, Saxony, Germany.)

1710 Simpson, John, BURSLEM, Staffordshire, England.

Early 18th century. SLIPWARES. - *JOHN SIMPSON*
I. S.

1710 `Hozan` (Yasubei) Japan. - - - - see 1655 Ninsei.

1711 ANSBACH, Bavaria, Germany.

FAÏENCE AND EARTHENWARE, AND LATER, PORCELAIN. -

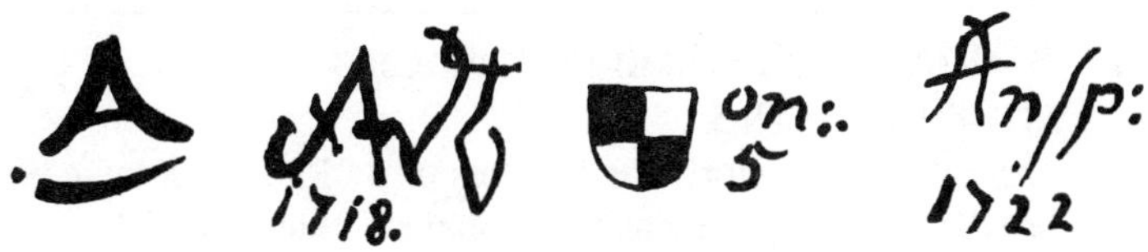

Painters` marks:-

1711-12 Johann Caspar Ripp. - -

1711-33 George Christian Oswald. - -

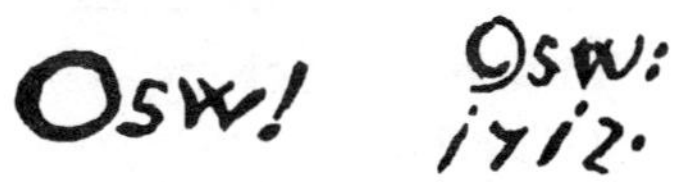

1715- (d.1786) Johann Georg Christoph Popp.-

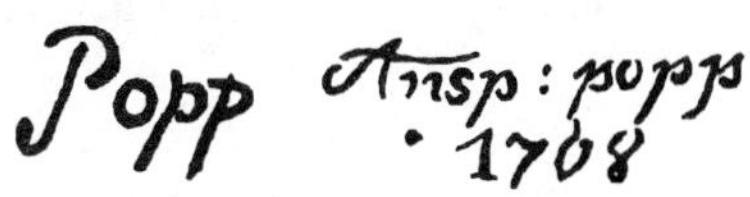

1716-19 Johann Heinrich Wackenfeld. - -

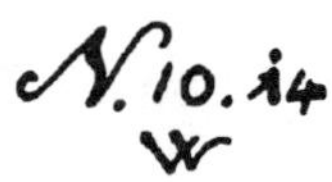

1718—30 Kruckenberger, Christian Emanuel. -

Continued over -

1711

1711 ANSBACH, Bavaria, Germany. (Cont`)

1723-50 **Johann Leonard Uz.** - - - 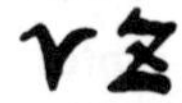

1724-56 **Johann Wolfgang Meyerhöfer** - - 

1726-30 **Joachim Leonhard Wolf.** - - - 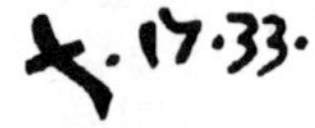

1732-44 **Johann Leonhard Förster.** - - - 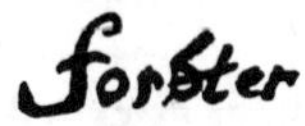

1732-38 **Georg Nicolaus Hofmann.** - - - 

1746-66 **Mathias Carl Rosa.** - - - - 

c.1758- HARD-PASTE PORCELAIN:-
The eagle of Brandenberg to which the Margraves family belong.
Kandler, Johann Friedrich (artistic director)

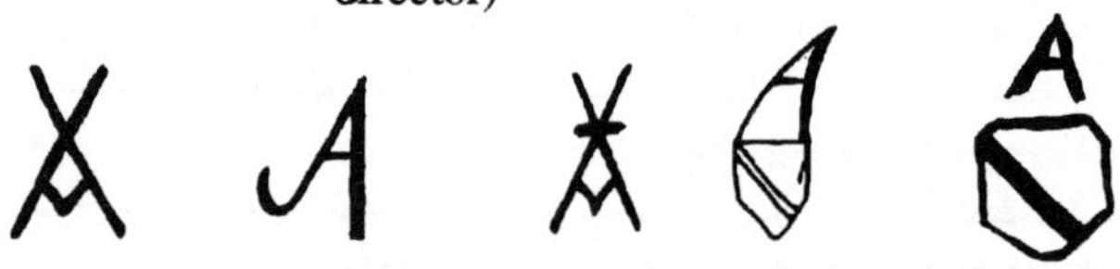

1764- **Factory transferred to Bruckberg.**

1711 BORDEAUX, Gironde, France.

1711-c.1855 FAÏENCE.
The individual factories and potters of BORDEAUX have been listed under their own dates and marks within this book.

1711 Dakin, Thomas, SHELTON, Staffordshire, England.

Early 18th century EARTHENWARES. Sliptrailed- *THOMAS DAKIN*

1711 Fauchier Factory, MARSEILLES, France.

1711-c.94.

1711- **Joseph Fauchier (d.1751)** - - 

1751- **Joseph Fauchier (son) (d.1789)** - 

1711 Horn, Heinrich Christoph von, & Hantelmann, Werner von, BRUNSWICK, Germany.

1711-49 FAÏENCE. - - - - 

1711 Malkin, Samuel, BURSLEM, Staffordshire, England.

Early 18th century. SLIPWARES. - - - - - *S. M.*

1711 Dorez, Barthélémy, France. - - - see 1696 LILLE.
1712 Caduceus mark, Germany. - - - - see 1710 MEISSEN.
1712 Dextra, Zacharias, DELFT, Holland. - - see 1655 de 3 Astonne.
1712- Mikawaji or Hirado-Yaki, Japan. - - - see 1580 HIZEN.

1713 BAYREUTH, Bavaria, Germany.

c.1713- FAÏENCE.- - -

The individual factories and potters of BAYREUTH have been listed under their own dates and marks within this book.

1713 de Vier Helden van Roome (The Four Roman Heroes) DELFT, Holland.

1713-TIN-GLAZED EARTHENWARE (DELFTWARE)

Boender, Mathijs, - - -

1714 Bogaert, M. v.d. DELFT, Holland. - - see 1661 t`hart.
1714 Kool, Jac, DELFT, Holland. - - - see 1648 De oud Moriaans hooft.

1715 AUGSBURG, Swabia, Germany.

18TH CENTURY. PORCELAIN. GOLD CHINOISERIES PAINTED ON CHINESE AND EARLY MEISSEN PORCELAINS.

Aufenwerth, Johann, (d.1728) Hausmaler. - -

c.1720 **Seuter, Bartholomaus, (b.1678, d.1754)** - -

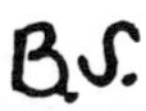

1715 Mark, Johann Andreas, NUREMBERG, Germany.

c.1715-70 FAÏENCE. - - -

1715 Rossbach, Johann, NUREMBERG, Germany.

Painter. - - - -

1715 Ralph Wood, BURSLEM, Staffordshire, England.

1715-72 EARTHENWARE, FIGURES. - - - - - *R. WOOD.*
1748-95 **Ralph Wood (son)** - - - - *Ra. WOOD.*
1781-1801 **Ralph Wood (grandson)** - - - *Ra. WOOD.*
BURSLEM
Ralph Wood

c.1770-90 **Rebus trees (very rare)** - - -

1715-18

1715	Boumeester, Cornelis, Holland. - - -	see 1630 ROTTERDAM.
1715-	Popp, Johann Georg Christoph, Germany. -	see 1711 ANSBACH.

1716 DOROTHEENTHAL, nr.Arnstadt, Thuringia, Germany.

c.1716-c.1806. Faïence.

\`Augustenburg\` - - - - 

1726- Alex, Johann Christoph (Painter) - - 

Rasslender,Johann Michel, (painter) - - 

Franz, Johann Martin, (painter) - - - 

Meiselbach, Johann Martin, (painter) - - 

1716	Dorez, F.& B., France. - - - - -	see 1696 LILLE.
1716	Toyo-Ura-Yama, Japan. - - - -	see 1585 NAGATO.
1716	Wackenfeld, Johann Heinrich, Germany. - -	see 1711 ANSBACH.

1717 ERFURT, Thuringia, Germany.

c.1717-92 Faïence.

1720- **Michael Grantz.** (painter) - - - 

J.J. Wunderlich (painter) - - - 

Georg Matthäus Schmidt. - - - 

1738-52 **Christian Andreas Vogel.** - - - 

1717 Grebner, G.F., NUREMBERG, Germany.

1717-30 Painter. - - -

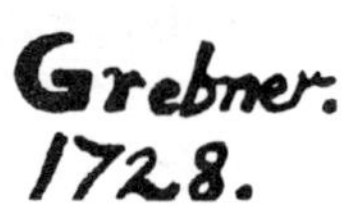

1718 Ferrat, Jean-Baptiste, MOUSTIERS, France.

1718-91 Faïence. - - -

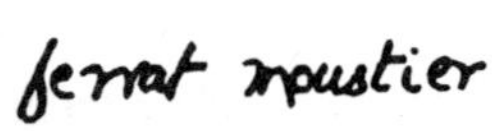

1718 SAINT-AMAND-LES-EAUX, Nord, France.

1718-1882 FAÏENCE AND CREAMWARES. - -

1740- - -

1740-93 **Pierre Fauquez and family** -

Mark on creamware-
underglaze blue - - - -

1771-78 **Jean-Baptiste-Joseph Fauquez.**
SOFT-PASTE PORCELAIN - - -
Mark painted in underglaze blue-

1773- - - -

1773- Gilot. - - - - - - -

1780- -

c.1800-82 **Bettignies,Maximilien-Joseph** - -
REPRODUCTIONS. SÈVRES AND OTHERS.

1815 Painter`s mark-

20th century- -

1718 Grue, Dr. Franc Anton, Italy. - - - see 1679 CASTELLI.
1718 Kruckenberger,Christian Emanuel, Germany. - see 1711 ANSBACH.

1719 VIENNA, Austria.

1719-1864 HARD-PASTE PORCELAIN.

1719-44 **Paquier, Claudius Innocentius Du, factory.**
c.1720-30 Chinese style pieces. blue

1730- **Bottengruber, A.,** -

1744-84 State period:

1744-49 overglazed in red or other colours impressed -

1747-58 **Grunbuhel, Maierhoffer de** (director)

1747- **Niedermeyer,Joseph** (master modeller) made figures.

1749-80 Shield marks in blue - -

1750-80 Court use in blue - - -

1755- **Anreiter, Antonius** (painter) -

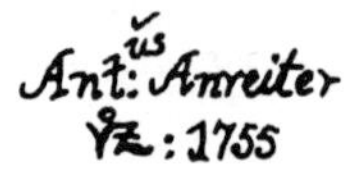

1758-70 **Wolf, Joseph,** (director)

1768- **Jünger, Christopher** (decorator) - ***Ch: v. Junger`***

1784-1864 **Sorgenthal period:**

1820-27 - blue - -

c.1827-50 - impressed - -

1829- **Böck, Josef,** (decorator) - - -

c.1850-64 - - blue - -

Cancellation marks on white wares. Blue -

Mark in blue, the `A` in red or green - -

1783 - Onwards Additional marks were added:-

The 18th century showed the last two numbers of the year (i.e:- 1794 were marked `94`) The 19th century shows the last three numbers (i.e:- 1840 were marked `840`)

1880 - Dorfl, Franz, (decorator) - - -

c.1885 Vater, Josef, (decorator) - - -

1720 Bourne, Samuel, HANLEY, Staffordshire, England.
EARLY 18TH CENTURY FIGURES. - impressed- *S. BOURNE*

1720 BRESLAU, Silesia, Germany.
c.1720- HARD-PASTE PORCELAIN.
c.1720-30 **Bottengruber, Ignaz,** (also at Vienna) -

c.1732-40 **Bressler, Hans Gottlieb von,** - - H. G. v B. 1732

20th Century Stoneware mark - - - -

1720 de jonge Moriaans hooft, (The Young Moor`s Head) DELFT, Holland.
1720- TIN-GLAZED EARTHENWARE (DELFTWARE)
1759- **Verhagen, Joh.,** - - - I VH 1728 IVH 1729
1764- **Strale, Hestera,** - - - C∴B:S.

1720 Gebhard, Johann Melchior, NUREMBERG, Germany.
c.1720- HAUSMALER. - - - IMG

1720 Guillibaud Factory, ROUEN, France.
c.1720-50 MAIOLICA/FAÏENCE. - -

Guillibaud
GB Mrs Guillibeaux

1720 RUDOLSTADT, Thuringia, Germany.
1720-91 FAÏENCE. - - -

R Rudolstad

The individual factories and potters of RUDOLSTADT have been listed under their own dates and marks within this book.

1720/21

1720 ZERBST, Anhalt, Germany.

1720-1861 FAÏENCE.

1721-96 Factory mark. -

1722-23 **Langendorf, Christian** (artist) - -

1761-82 **Langendorf, Christian Andreas** (son) -

1724- **Koch, Joh Heinrich** (painter) - -

1793-1861 Impressed mark - ***ZERBST***

c.1795 **Late 18th century (Sandkull)** - ***L S***
Z

1720	Berg, Cornelis d., DELFT, Holland. - - -	see 1689 de Star.
1720	Grantz, Michael,.Germany. - - - -	see 1717 ERFURT.
1720	Höroldt, Johann Gregor, Germany. - - -	see 1710 MEISSEN.
1720	Ratti, Agostino, Italy. - - - - -	see 1550 SAVONA.
1720	Seuter,Bartholomaus, Germany. - - - -	see 1715 AUGSBURG.
1720	Tokuro Yohei and family, YAMASHIRO, Japan. -	see 1655 Ninsei.
1720	Vessi Factory, Italy. - - - - -	see 1550 VENICE.
1720	\`Yatsu-Shiro\` Japan. - - - - -	see 1630 HIGO.

1721 Amsterdam, Leonard van, (Delft Artist) DELFT, Holland.

TIN-GLAZED EARTHENWARE (DELFTWARE) - -

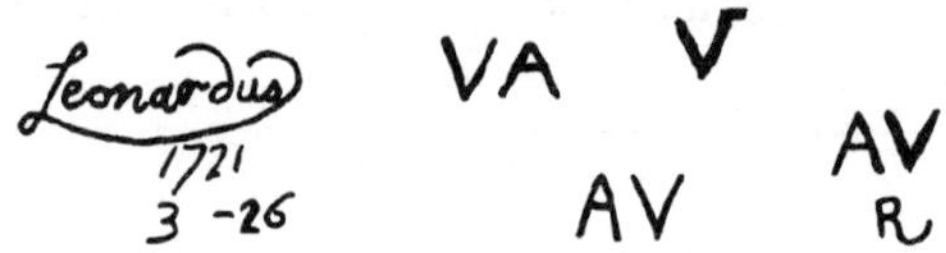

1721 STRASBOURG, Alsace, France.

1721-81 FAÏENCE.
1752-55 PORCELAIN (transferred to Frankenthal)
1721-39 **Hannong, Charles-François**

Wackenfeld, Jean-Henri (Helped to develop both porcelain and faïence)

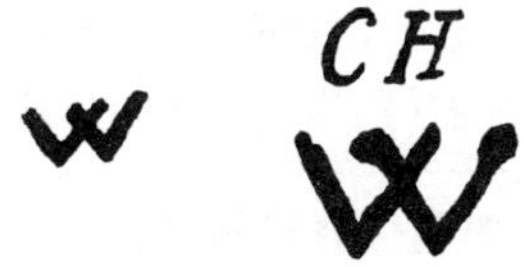

c.1721-40 Painters:-
Mittmann, Nicholas, - - -

Montoson, Henri, - - - -

Herman, Jean, or Hannsmann, Joseph,-

c.1740-60 **Hannong, Paul,** (FAÏENCE) - -

1762-81 **Hannong, Joseph,.** - -

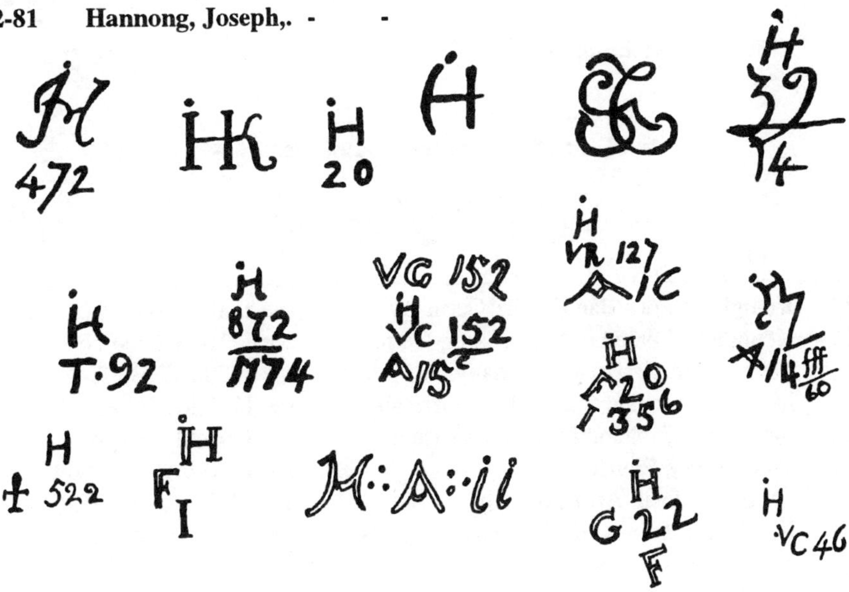

1721-23

1721 Gillis et Hendrick de Koning, DELFT, Holland.- see 1648 De dubbelde Schenkkan.

1722 COPENHAGEN, Denmark.

1722 - c.1770 The Store Kongensgade Factory. FAÏENCE.
The individual factories and potters of COPENHAGEN have been listed under their own dates and marks within this book.

1722 DURLACH, Baden, Germany.

1722-1840 FAÏENCE AND CREAMWARES.

1722-26 **Wachenfeld, Johann Heinrich.** - -

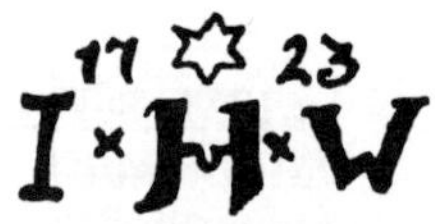

1764-90 **Pfalzgraf, Johann Valentin.**(painter) -

1818- **Marks on creamwares.** impressed- ***`DURLACH`***

1722 Glüer, Justus (painter) NUREMBERG, Germany.

1722-23 MAIOLICA. - - -

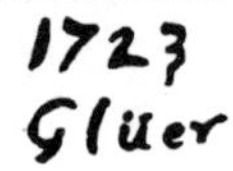

1722 LA ROCHELLE, Charente-Inférieure, France.

1722-89 FAÏENCE.

1743- **Briqueville, J.** - - -

1749-89 **Roussencq.** - - - -

Fouques, Arnoux & Cie - -

1780- **Roland, Jean,** - - -

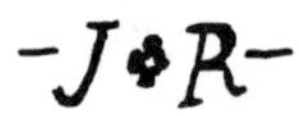

2nd Half 18th Century. Various marks -

1722 Königliche Porzellan Fabrik, Germany. - see 1710 MEISSEN.
1722 Königliche Porzellan Manufaktur, Germany. see 1710 MEISSEN.
1722 Langendorf, Christian, Germany. - - see 1720 ZERBST.
1722 Meissen Porzellan Manufaktur, Germany. see 1710 MEISSEN.
1722 Steinbrueck, Johann Melchior, Germany. see 1710 MEISSEN.
1722 Trou, Henry, France. - - - see 1670 SAINT-CLOUD.
1723 Chigi, Cardinal, Arius, of Italy. - - see 1693 SAN QUIRICO D`ORCIA.
1723 Uz, Johann Leonhard, Germany. - - see 1710 ASBACH
1723 Yung-chêng, China. - - - see 1644 CH`ING.

1724 Wanderer, J.W.G. BAYREUTH, Bavaria, Germany.

And family. - - - - - 

Marks of the family- - - 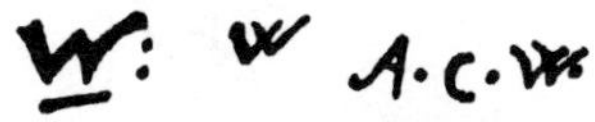

1724 Gilze, Johann Christoph, Germany. - - see 1680 CASSEL
1724 Koch, Joh Heinrich, Germany. - - - see 1720 ZERBST.
1724 Meyerhofer, Johann Wolfgang, Germany. - see 1711 ANSBACH.
1724 Monbaers, Phillipe, Belgium. - - - see 1705 BRUSSELS.

1725 BERNBURG, Thuringia, Germany.

18th century FAÏENCE.

c.1725- **Ripp, Johann Kaspar.** (probable founder) - 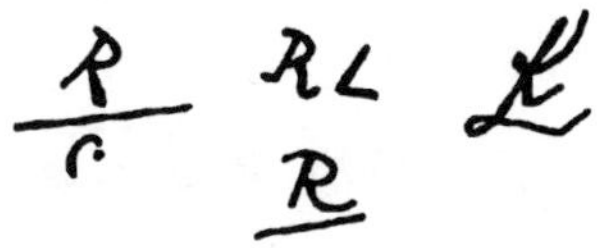

1725- **Duke Victor Friedrich.** monogram- 

1725 BERNE, Switzerland.

18th century FAÏENCE.

1758-63 **Willading, Augustin.** - blue- 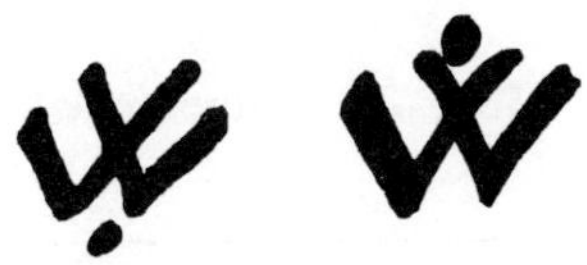

1760-76 **Frisching, Franz Rudolf.** - - 

1767-98 **Früting, Emanuel Jacob.** - black- 

1725 CHANTILLY, Oise, France.

SOFT-PASTE PORCELAIN.

1725-1800 **Cirou, Ciquaire (Founder) (d.1751)**
Louis-Henri de Bourbon, Prince de Condé
1751-c.89 **Peyrard Aran and Antheaume de Surval.**

rare mark- - -

Marks of workmen - - -

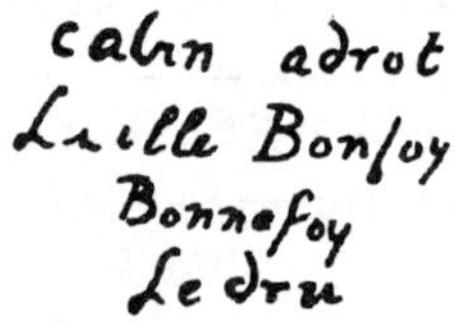

1796 - Beginning 19th century. - -

1803-12 **Pigory (mayor of Chantilly)**
HARD-PASTE PORCELAIN - blue-

c.1818 **Bougon and Chalot** - -

1845-70 **Aaron, Michel-Isaac** - blue-

1725 LODI, Lombardy, Italy.

18th century FAÏENCE. - - - - - -

c.1725- **Ferreti, Simpliciano.** - - -

c.1750- **Morsenchio-Capelletti.** - - -

1764 (dated) On Faïence dish. - -

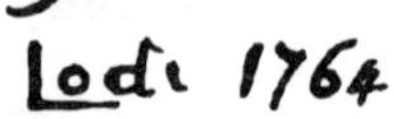

Rosetti mark- - - -

1767 **Crevani, Felix,** - - -

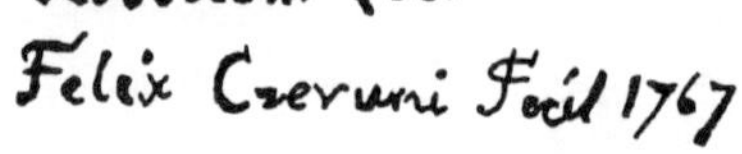

1725 MILAN, Italy.
18th century FAÏENCE.

1747- **Clerici, Felice** (date on a dinner service) -

1756- **Rubati, Pasquale,** - - -

F.
Pasquale Rubati
Milo.

1765- Fabbrica di Pasquale Rubati
Milano- - -

1770-75 **Confalonieri, Cesare,** - -

1775-82 **Fabbrica di Santa Cristana** -

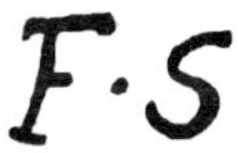

1833-73 **Julius Richard & Co., at San Cristoforo,**
(EARTHENWARE) -

c.1895-20th Cen. Società Ceramica Lombarda. -

1873-20th Cen. Richard-Ginori, Società Ceramica. -

Cacciapuoti (artist)

1725

1725 Pössinger, N.,(painter) NUREMBERG, Germany.
1725-30 - - -

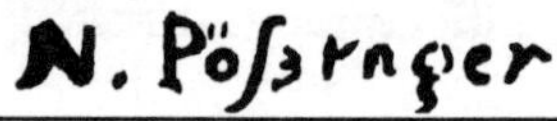

1725 RÖRSTRAND, nr.Stockholm, Sweden.
1725- FAIENCE, PORCELAIN. - -

1726-onwards. Various dated factory marks:-

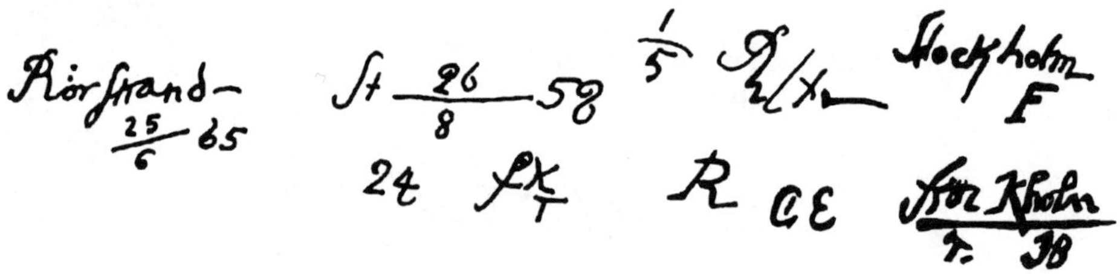

1763-82 Ohrn, Jacob,.CREAM-COLOURED WARES. -

RÖRSTRAND
impressed

1797- Bengt Reinhold Gejer acquired the Factory.
HARD-PASTE PORCELAIN;-
Early 19th century marks:-

1850- - -

1852- - - - -

1884- - -

Modern mark -

1725 Stroom, P. van der, (Delft Artist) DELFT, Holland.
TIN-GLAZED EARTHENWARE (DELFTWARE)

1725 Ferreti, Simpliciano, Italy. - - - - see 1725 LODI.
1725 Macello, Giorgio Rossetti, di, Italy. - - see 1577 TURIN.
1725 Pennis, Joh., DELFT, Holland. - - - see 1701 de porceleyne Schotel.
1725 Terchi, Bartolomeo & Antonio, Italy. - - see 1590 BASSANO.

1726 ALCORA, Valencia, Spain.
c.1726 - c.1785 FAÏENCE.

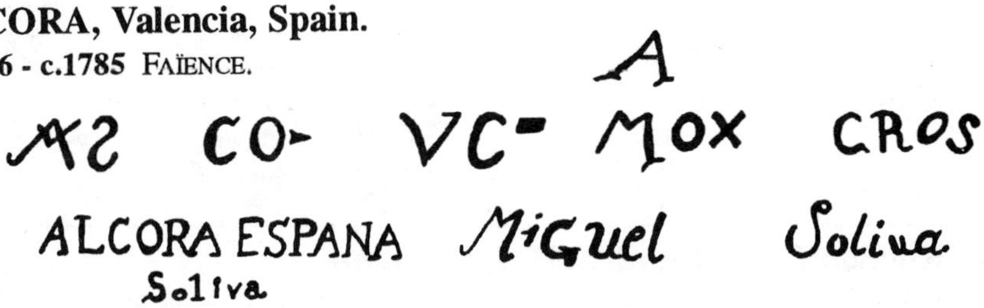

1727-43 **Ferrer, Vincente** (painter) - -
1735-50 **Cros, Vincente** (painter) - -

c.1775- HARD-PASTE PORCELAIN. - -
c.1775- CREAMWARES.- - - -
1784-onwards - - -

c.1805. (19th century) - - - -

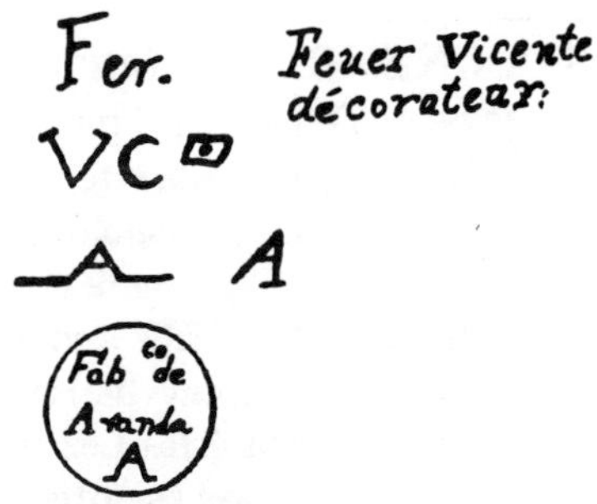

1726 Kordenbusch, Andreas, (painter) NURENBERG, Germany.

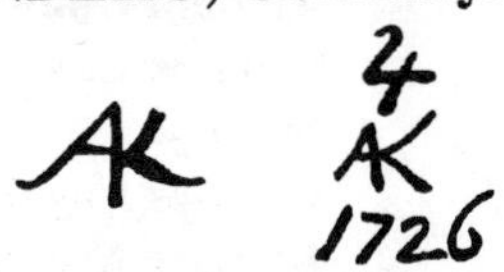

1726 Alex, Johann Christoph, Germany. - - see 1716 DOROTHEENTHAL.
1726 Seigne, Jaques, France. - - - - see 1589 NEVERS.
1726 Wolf, Joachim Leonhard, Germany. - - see 1711 ANSBACH.

1727 Pfau, Johann Ernst, COPENHAGEN, Denmark.
1727-48 FAÏENCE. - - -

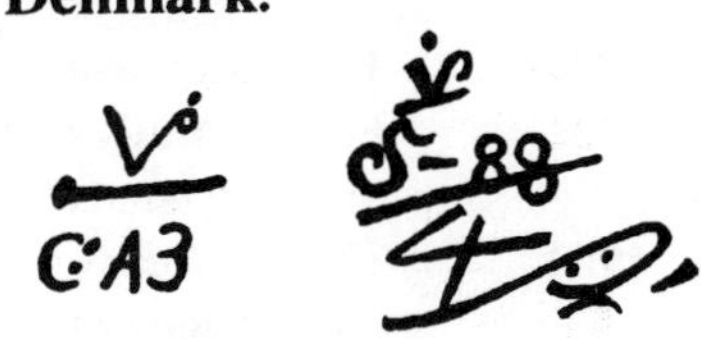

1727 Ferrer, Vincente, Spain. - - - - see 1726 ALCORA.

1728

1728 APT, Vaucluse, France.

1728-1852 FAÏENCE AND EARTHENWARES. - - *La Bergère dans l'inquiétude au départ de son amant à Castelet parmoy César Moulin fils ex`*

Moulin, César at Le Castelet. -

c.1790-1802 Arnoux, Veuve. impressed- VA

c.1795- Sagy, L., - Leon Sagy Apt 37 — L. Sagy Apt

1728 Knoller, G.W., BAYREUTH, Germany.

1728-44 - - - - blue - BK ·B·K·

1728 LUNÉVILLE, Meurthe-et-Moselle, France.

1728- FAÏENCE, `TERRE DE PIPE` — `Chambrette Lunéville`

1728- **Chambrette, Jacques,** (founder)
Duc Leopold. (sponser)
1748- `terre de pipe` introduced.

1749- **Lunéville and Saint-Clement (a branch of Lunéville) was given permission by Stanislas Lezcinski (father-in-law of Louis XV) to use the title `Manufacture Royal`** see 1758 SAINT-CLEMENT. G N

1758- **Chambrette, Jacques, died.**
Madam Chambrette and Gabriel (son) with Charles Loyal (son-in-law) took over the factory. — Manufacture de Saint Clement

1763- **Charles Loyal took into partnership, Richard Mique and Paul Louis Cyfflé.** — S. Clement
1763- Paul Louis Cyfflé left the business. and opened his own factory modelling groups of figures called `terre de Lorraine` see 1763 Cyfflé, Paul-Louis,

1794-1824 **Keller and Guerin took over the factory.**

1824- **Thomas & Sons, Germain, took over the factory.**

1922- **Fenal Family of Bandonviller became the majority shareholders in the business.**

1962- **The Factories of Lunéville, Badonviller and Saint-Clement were amalgamated.**

1978- **Sarrequemines Vaisselle acquired.** see 1784 Sarrequimines.

(By kind permission of Sarrequemines Vaisselle, PARIS, France.)

1728 NOVE, Venezia, Italy.
FAÏENCE AND CREAMWARE
1762-1835 SOFT-PASTE PORCELAIN.
1728 Antonibon, Giovanni Battista

1738 Antonibon, Pasqual (son)

1755 (dated) `Antonibon`s Fabrique` - - *Della fabrica di Gio Batta Antonibon nelle nove di Decen 1755.*

1762 Pasqual took his son, Giovanni Battista into partnership making - - - maiolica, terraglia or terre de pipe as well as porcelain.

c.1780- Baccin, Giovanni Maria (creamware) -

1781-1802 Parolini, Signor,.Partnership. -

1802-1824 Baroni, Giovanni,. - -

1802-1810 (dated) on a vase - - ***Faba Baroni Nove.***

1825- Antonibon, Giovanni Battista took possession again. - -
1835 Discontinued porcelain production.

<u>19th century creamware</u>

`Bernardi - - - -

Cecchetto, G.M. - - -

Viero, G.B. - - - -

1728	Clérissy, Antoine II (son) MOUSTIERS, France. -	see 1679 Pierre Clérissy.
1729	Boussemaert, Joseph-François, France. - - -	see 1696 LILLE.

1730

1730 AIRE, Pas-de-Calais, France.

c.1730-90 FAÏENCE.

c.1730-55 Prudhomme, Pierre-Joseph. - -

1755-c.90 Dumetz, François. - - - - - - -

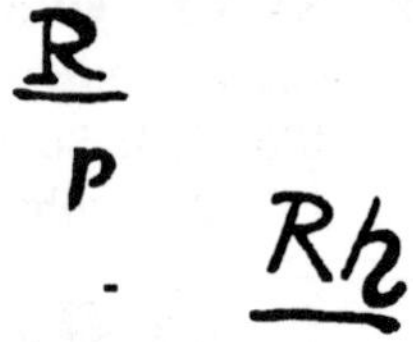

1730 CLERMONT-FERRAND, Puy-de-Dôme, France.

c.1730-43 FAÏENCE. - - -

Perrot and Sèves.

1733- Savignot. - - -

c.1774-c.84 Verdier, Donnat and Morel. - -

c.1790- Launche, Pierre and Perrier. - -

PATRIOTIC FAÏENCE.

1730 Hess, Fred. v., (Delft Artist) DELFT, Holland.

TIN-GLAZED EARTHENWARE (DELFTWARE) - -

1730 Ken-zan, YAMASHIRO, Japan.

1730- Mark on dated bowl - - -

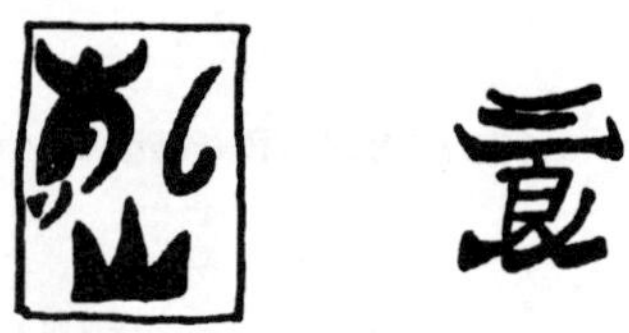

1750- Mark on dated fire-pan - -

c.1810- Snadai Kensan (3rd generation)- -

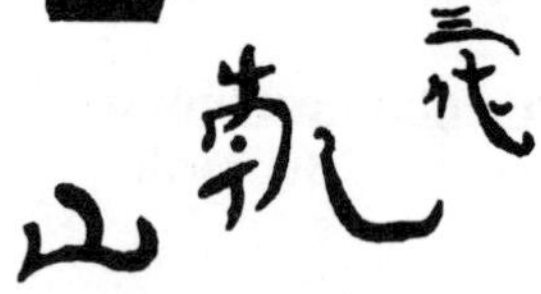

1730 Kordenbusch, Georg Friedrich, NUREMBERG, Germany.

c.1730 (d.1763) - - - - - -

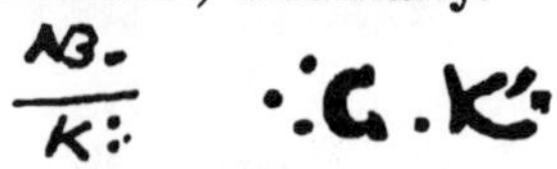

1730 LA FOREST, Savoie, France.

1730-1810 FAÏENCE.

Bouchard, Noel - - -

1730 MOULINS, Allier, France.
c.1730-c.1810 FAÏENCE.

1741- - -

1793-1800 -

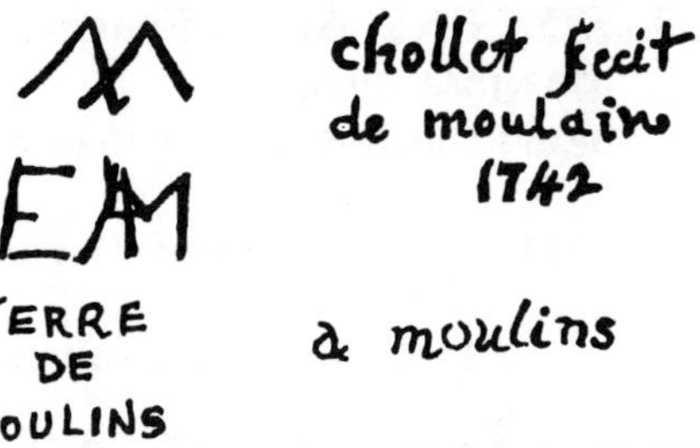

1730 WINCANTON, Somerset, England.
c.1730-67 Ireson, Nathaniel. - -
TIN-GLAZED EARTHENWARE

WINCANTON
Nathaniel Ireson
1748

1730 Bottengruber, A., Austria. - - - - - see 1719 VIENNA.

1731 Chambrette, Jacques, LUNÉVILLE, France.
1731-58 FAÏENCE. - - -

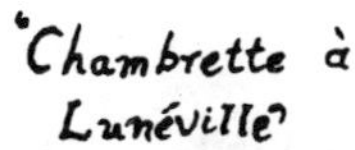

1758-88 Chambrette, Gabriel and Charles Loyal, see 1728 LUNÈVILLE.

1731 Kaendler, Johann Joachim, Germany. - - - see 1710 MEISSEN

1732 BOISETTE, Seine-et-Marne, France.
1732- FAÏENCE. - - -
1778-c.92 HARD-PASTE PORCELAIN.
Vermonet Jacques and son.

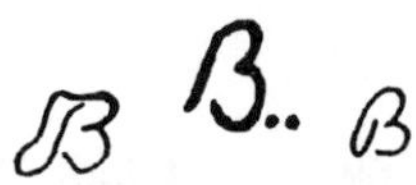

1732 DESVRES, Pas-de-Calais, France.
1732- FAÏENCE. - - -

Poulaine, Dupre, - -

1764- Sta, Jean-François. - -

1899- Fourmaintraux, Gabriel, -
HARD-PASTE PORCELAIN.

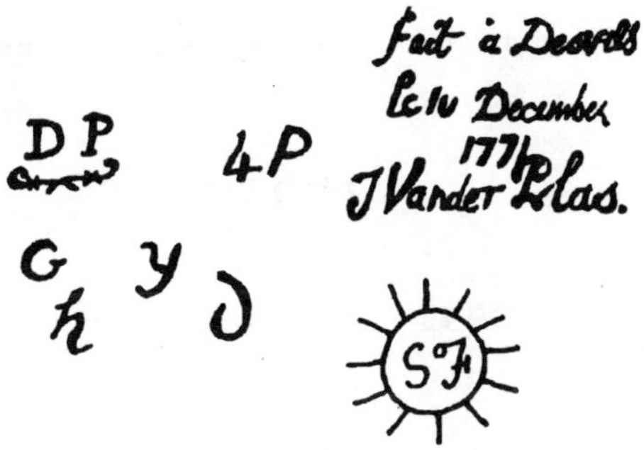

1732 SAMADET, Landes, France.
1732-19th century. FAÏENCE. - - -

1732 Bressler, Hans Gottlieb von, Germany. - - see 1720 BRESLAU.
1732 Forster, Johann Leonhard, Germany. - - see 1711 ANSBACH.
1732 Hofmann, Georg Nicolaus, Germany. - - see 1711 ANSBACH.
1732 G. Rocco di Castelli, Italy.- - - - see 1679 CASTELLI.

1733 SINCENY, Aisne, France.

1733-1864 FAÏENCE.

Jean Baptiste de Fayard (founder) - -

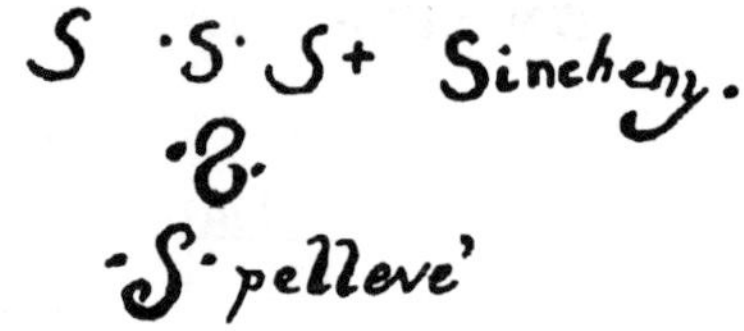

1733-37 **Pierre Pellevé(1st director)** -

c.1735-95 Various letter marks - -

1737-75 **Malériat, Leopold,** painter. - -

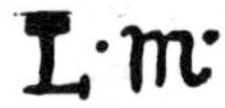

c.1740 **Jeannot, Pierre,** painter. - -

c.1750 **Bedeaux, Joseph,** painter. - -

c.1750-c.75 **Bertrand, Pierre,** painter. - -

c.1750 **Daussy, Alexandré,** painter. -

1769 **Ghåil, François-Joseph.** - -

c.1773 **Le Cerf, Joseph, painter.** -

Early marks.- - -

1775-95 **Second period.** - -

1824- **Lecomte and Dantier.** - - - *L. et D.*

Mandois. - - - - -

1733 Savignat, France. - - - see 1730 CLERMONT-FERRAND.

1734 Bowen, John, (apprenticed painter) BRISTOL, England.

1734- ENGLISH DELFTWARE - - -

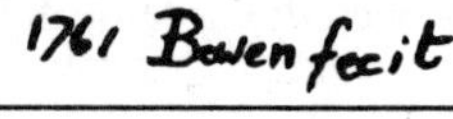

1734 Franks, Richard, Redcliffe Backs, BRISTOL, England.

c.1734- DELFTWARE, PLATES, DISHES AND DUTCH TILES.
Thomas Franks (son) taken into partnership.
1777- Works moved to Water Lane.
1784- **Ring, Joseph, purchased the works.** *RING & CO.*
1788- **Ring & Taylor. Mr Taylor and Mr Carter taken into partnership. Delftware discontinued.**

(see Ceramic Art of Great Britain by Jewitt)

1734 MENNECY-VILLEROY, Ile-de-France, France.

1734-1806 SOFT-PASTE PORCELAIN, FAÏENCE AND CREAMWARE.
Louis-François de Neufville duc de Villeroy.(protector)

1734-48 **Paris**
1748-73 **Mennecy** - - -

1773-1806 **Bourg-la-Reine**

1738 (dated) Mark on faïence - blue

Japanese style wares. Early marks. - -

Middle and late period marks. - -

1756- **Simon, Mathieu,** Incised - -
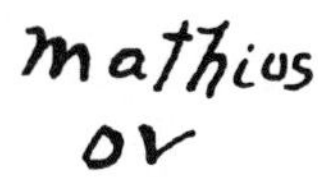

1767- **Mô, Christophe,** (modeller) - -

1767- **Mô, Jean.** - - - - - -
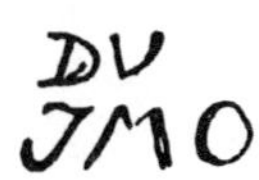

1774-1806 **Bourg-la-Reine** - - - - -
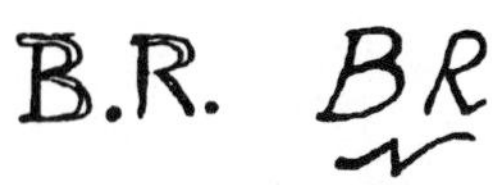

1735 DOCCIA, nr.Florence, Italy.

1735- SOFT-PASTE AND LATER, HARD-PASTE PORCELAIN.

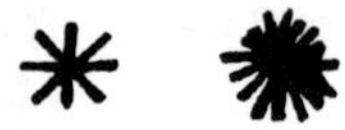

1735- **Marchese Carlo Ginori (founder) d.1757.**
Carlo Wandhelien (chemist) director of works.

Niccolo Sebastiano - - - -

1757- **Senator Lorenzo Ginori (son)**
Carlo Leopoldo Ginori (g.son)
Lorenzo Ginori Lisci (g.g.son)
PORCELAIN WITH TIN-GLAZE. -

In blue, red or purple -

In red or green - -

c.1792- **Fanciullacci, Pietro,** (chemist and painter)-

1821- **Capo di Monte early moulds transferred to Doccia.**
Imitations of Capodimonte and Naples.

19th century marks:

c.1810- - - - - -

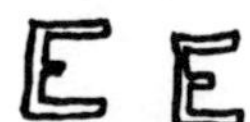

1847-73 - - - - -

1873-1903 - - -

1874-88 - - - - -

1884-91 - impressed- *Ginori*
GIN

Late 19th century - Richard Ginori -

1735 Metzsch, Johann Friedrich, BAYREUTH, Germany.

1735-51 HAUSMALER. FAÏENCE. - -

1735 Remmey & Crolius, Potters Hill, NEW YORK, N.Y., U.S.A.

c.1735- POTTERY. - - -

1798 Dated mark on spouted jug. - ***New York, Feby 17th, 1798***
Flowered by
Mr. Clarkson Crolius.

1735 VALENCIENNES, Nord, France.

1735-c.80 FAÏENCE (UNIDENTIFIED)

Dorez, F.L., - - -

1785-1810 Fauques, J-B, & Lamoninary - - ***VALENCIEN***

HARD-PASTE PORCELAIN AND BISCUIT FIGURES

Underglaze blue -

1862- Benard, V., - - - - -

1735 WRISBERGHOLZEN, Hanover, Germany.

1735-1834 FAÏENCE. - - -

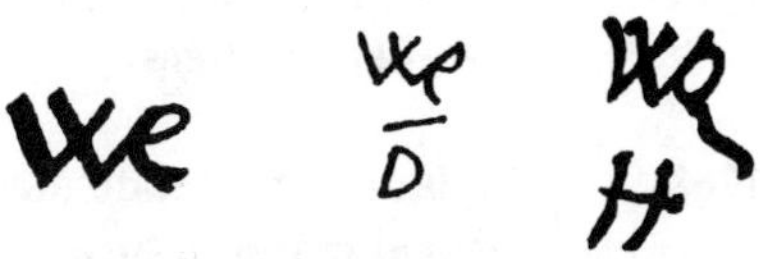

1735 Borrelli, M., Italy. - - - - see 1550 SAVONA.
1735 Cros, Vincente, Spain. - - - - see 1726 ALCORA.
1735 Grue, D-Francisci Antonti Xaveri, Italy. - - see 1679 CASTELLI.

1736 Borne, Claude,(painter) ROUEN, France.

1736- FAÏENCE. - - -

1736 ISE, Japan.

1736-95 **Gozaemon, Numanami, of Kuwana Banko-Yaki. Ko-Banko ware** - -

Banko and Fuyeki mark-

c.1810- Isawa. - - - - -

1830 **Yusetsu, Mori,** used the Banko seal producing Ko-Banko style ware. 19th century factories produced Yusetsu ware and it is often called Banko ware. Banko-marks-

Ni-pon Yu-setsu - -

c.1850- Akoji. - - - - -

1875 **Ise-Banko-**YAKI. RED BISCUIT WARE. Nippon Banko- Impressed seals-

1736 LIMOGES, Haute-Vienne, France.

1736- FAÏENCE - - -

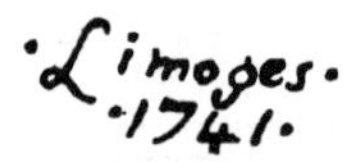

1771- HARD-PASTE PORCELAIN. - -
Grellet brothers

1788- **Alluaud, M. Made director of the Royal manufacture.** - -
1799- succeeded by his son François.

1784- **Factory aquired by the King to make white wares for decoration at Sèvres.**

The individual factories and potters of LIMOGES have been listed under their own dates and marks within this book.

1736	Ch`ien-lung, China. - - - - - -	see 1644 CH`ING.
1736	Clérissy, Pierre II. (grandson) MOUSTIERS, France. -	see 1679 Clérissy, Pierre.
1736	Terchi, Bartolomeo, Italy. - - - - - -	see 1600 ROME.

1737 LES ISLETTES, Meuse, France.
c.1737- FAÏENCE.
1785- Bernard, François,

FABRIQUE DE CIT BERNARD, AUX ISLETTES`

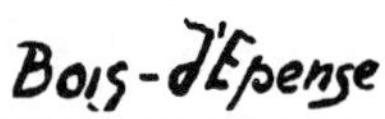

1737 MÜNDEN, Hanover, Germany.
1737-1854 FAÏENCE AND EARTHENWARE.
1737-93 **F. von Hanstein.** - -

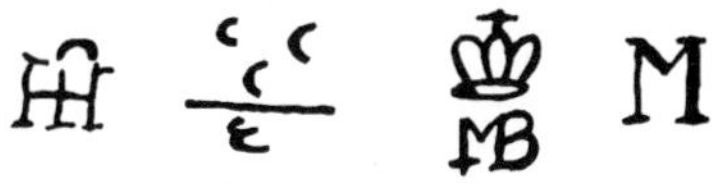

1737 Maériat, Leopold, France. - - - - see 1733 SINCENY.

1738 COBURG, Thuringia, Germany
1738-86 FAÏENCE. - -
1860- **Riemann, Albert,**
HARD-PASTE PORCELAIN. -

1738 Olerys, Joseph, and Langier, Jean-Baptiste, MOUSTIERS, France.
1738-c.90 Faïence. - - -

1738 VINCENNES, France.
1738- SOFT-PASTE PORCELAIN.

Dubois, Robert and Gilles (brothers)
Louis XV gave permission for the Dubois brothers to open a factory close to the Chateau of Vincennes. After three years they were dismissed for misconduct.

c.1741- **Charles Adam** directed the factory from this point in time.
1745- **A new company was formed under the protection of the King**
1756 **Factory moved to more suitable premises at Sèvres.**

c.1765 A hard-paste porcelain factory was set up by Pierre Antoine Hannong but closed in 1788.

1738 Antonibon, Pasqual, (son) Italy. - - - see 1728 NOVE.
1738 Pieter, Paree, DELFT, Holland. - - - see 1639 De Metale Pot.
1738 Vogel, Christian Andreas, Germany. - - see 1717 ERFURT.

1739/40

1739 OFFENBACH, nr.Frankfurt-am-Main, Germany.
1739-c.1805 FAÏENCE. - - -

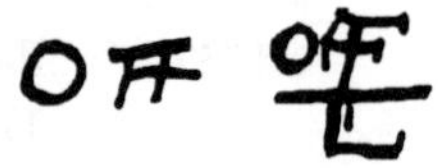

1739 POTSDAM, nr. Berlin, Germany.
1739-1800 FAÏENCE.
Rewend, Christian Friedrich.

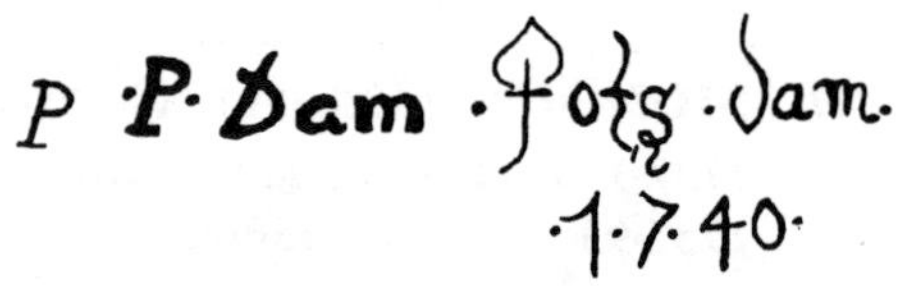

1739 Aalmis, Jan, (Jun) Holland. - - - see 1630 ROTTERDAM
1739 Dyck, C. van, DELFT, Holland. - - - see 1655 De Klaeuw.

1740 CHESTERFIELD, Derbyshire, England.
The individual factories and potters of CHESTERFIELD have been listed under their own dates and marks within this book.

1740 COBRIDGE, Staffordshire, England.
The individual factories and potters of COBRIDGE have been listed under their own dates and marks within this book.

1740 Fossé and widow, (potters) ROUEN, France.
c.1740-c.58 - - - -

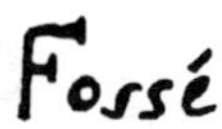

1740 Heath, Joshua, HANLEY, Staffordshire, England.
1st half 18th century. EARTHENWARE. - - *JOSHUA HEATH*

1740 HILDESHEIM, Hanover, Germany.
18th century. HARD-PASTE PORCELAIN DECORATORS.

c.1749-75 **Busch, Canon of Hildesheim** (engraver) - (b.1704 d.1779) ***Busch`***

c.1776- **Kratzberg, Canon of Hildesheim.** (engraver) -

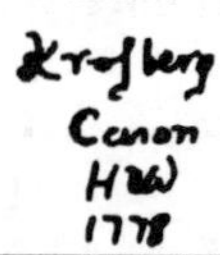

1740 MARANS, Charente-inférieure, France.
1740- FAÏENCE.

Roussencq, Pierre, (founder) monogram-

1756 Transferred to La Rochelle.

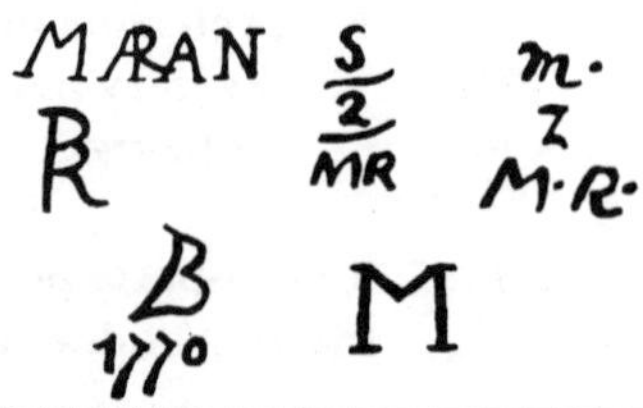

1740 Mouchard, Pierre and family, (potters) ROUEN, France.

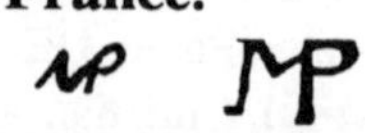

1740 NOTTINGHAM, England.

c.1740-80 Lockett, William. STONEWARE. Incised ***Wm. Lockett***

1740 Perrin, Veuve, factory. MARSEILLES, France.

c.1740-c.95 FAÏENCE. - - - V.P vp.

1740 Shaw, Ralph, COBRIDGE, Staffordshire, England.

Early 18th century EARTHENWARE. - - ***Made by Ralph Shaw October 31. Cobridge gate***

1740 Whieldon, Thomas, Little Fenton, FENTON, Staffordshire, England.

c.1740-c.80 EARTHENWARE, AGATEWARE, SALT-GLAZED STONEWARE.

Thomas Whieldon is regarded as one of the most important men in the history of English pottery. Among his workers, he employed and taught such names as Spode, Astbury, Garner, Greatbach, and many more. Josiah Wedgwood was his partner at an early age, who went on to build, what we know today to be one of the greatest pottery and porcelain manufacturing companies in the world. Whieldon`s early productions were knife-hafts and snuff-boxes in agateware. He progressed to producing tableware in cauliflower, melon, shapes, etc. He is best known for his cauliflower teapot and his tortoiseshell-type tablewares. Thomas Whieldon made a substantial fortune from his endeavours and in 1786 became High Sheriff of the County. In 1798 he died at the age of 86.

Whieldon did not mark his wares, they can only be recognised by their glazes and shapes.

(For further information see `Jewitt`s` Ceramic Art inGreat Britain*)*

1740	Alphen, Hieronymus von, Germany.	-	see 1661 HANAU.
1740	Fauquez, Pierre, and family, France.	-	see 1718 ST.AMAND-LES-EAUX.
1740	Hannong, Paul, France.	- - -	see 1721 STRASBOURG.
1740	Jeannot, Pierre, France.	- - -	see 1733 SINCENY.

1741/42

1741 FULDA, Hesse, Germany.

1741-58 FAÏENCE.

Arms of Fulda. -

Löwenfinck, Adam Friedrich von.

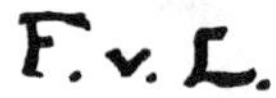

Factory marks:- - -

1764-90 HARD-PASTE PORCELAIN - -

1768-88 **`Fürstlich-Fuldaisch`** - - -
Heinrich von Bibra, Prince-Bishop of Fulda. - -

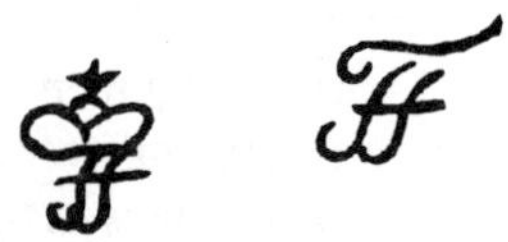

1788-1803 **Adalbert III von Harstall, Prince-Bishop.** - -

1741 GÖPPINGEN, Wurtemberg, Germany.

1741-78 FAÏENCE.

Arms of Wurtemberg (stags horn) -

Pliederhauser, Johann Mathias, - -

1741 HAGUENAU, Alsace, France.

1741-81.

A branch of the Hannong factory at Strasbourg. see 1721 STRASBOURG.

1741 Adams, Charles, France. - - - - see 1738 VINCENNES.
1741 Backhuyzen, Holland. - - - - see 1630 ROTTERDAM.
1741 Thévenet, Père, (decorator) France. - - see 1745 SÈVRES.

1742 Flower, Joseph, 2, The Quay, BRISTOL, England.

c.1742- DELFTWARE. Most pieces are unmarked.-
1777- **Moved premises to Corn Street.**

1742 PARIS, France.

The individual factories, potters and decorators of PARIS have been listed under their own dates and marks within this book.

1743 CAPODIMONTE, Italy.

1743-59 SOFT-PASTE PORCELAIN.

King Charles III of Spain established the factory.

impressed-

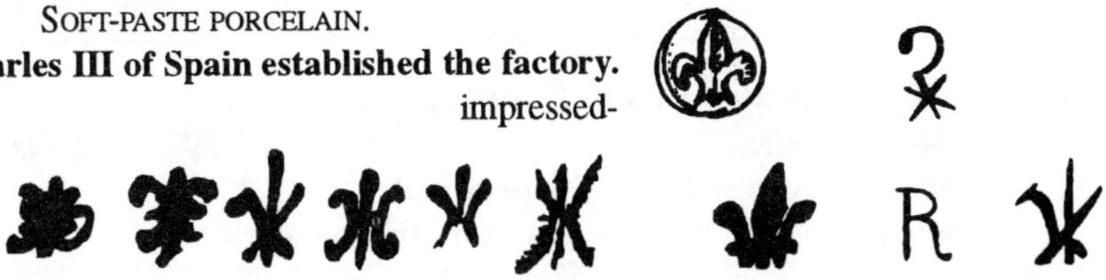

1743 Gérin, Claude-Humbert, Pont-aux-Chou, PARIS, France.

c.1743-85 EARTHENWARE, SALT-GLAZED STONEWARE AND CREAMWARE.

gold-

1777 Mignon mark.

HARD-PASTE PORCELAIN. - underglaze blue-

1743 HOLITSCH, Hungary.

1743-1826 FAÏENCE AND EARTHENWARE.

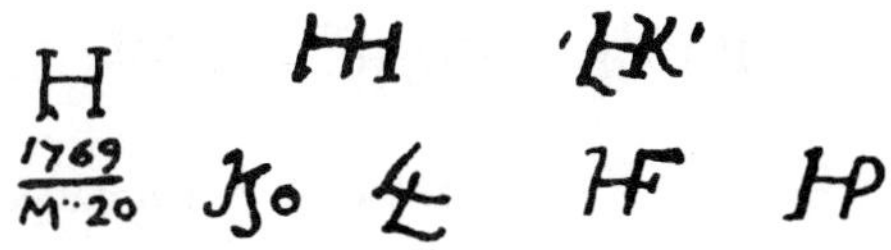

1743 LIVERPOOL, Merseyside, England.

Although pottery was obviously made at a very early date, `Jewitt` says that the first mention of it being made in Liverpool was in 1674 when pottery items appeared in a list of town dues.
Shaw`s Delft Ware Works is the earliest delft works known to be recorded in the Liverpool area. `Shaw`s Brow` which takes its name from the pot-works became a centre crammed full of potters producing delftware, earthenware, and eventually in the mid 18th century, porcelain.
Among the many pot-works that existed in Liverpool during the 18th century, below are a few of the more important ones. Hardly any of these marked their wares with a backstamp.

1752-65 **Chaffers, Richard,** DELFTWARE AND PORCELAIN.
1755/56 CHINA WARE.

c.1753- **Reid, William, (Liverpool China Manufactury)**
CHINA WARE AND BLUE AND WHITE EARTHENWARE.

1760-70 **Pennington, Seth, Shaw`s Brow.**
FINE EARTHENWARE. Probable marks used - -

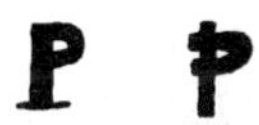

1760- **Deare & Co., Thomas, Patrick`s Hill Pot-House.**
EARTHENWARE (BLUE AND WHITE)

c.1760-73 **The Flint Pot Works was carried on by a Mr Okel**
MAKING BLUE AND WHITE EARTHENWARE.
c.1773- Rigg and Peacock took over the pottery on the death of Mr Okel.

The other individual factories and potters of LIVERPOOL have been listed under their own dates and marks elsewhere within this book.

1743/44

1743 Briquville, J. France. - - - - see 1722 LA ROCHELLE.
1743 Caussy, Pierre-Paul, France. - - - see 1690 QUIMPER.

1744 APREY, Haute-Marne, France.

c.1744-1860 FAÏENCE.
Lallemant, Jacques, Baron d`Aprey and Lallemant, Joseph, de Villehaut, were the founders.

1772 and earlier marks generally. 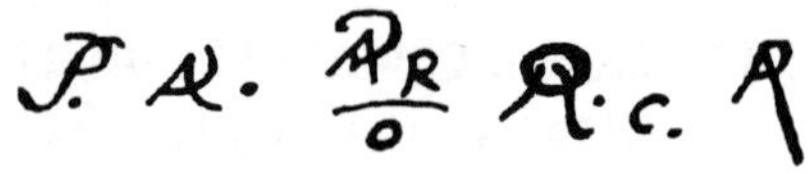

Rare marks. - 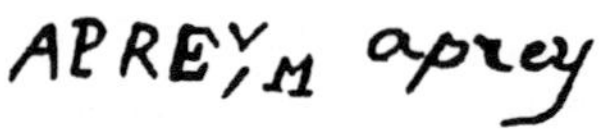

1832-78 **Girard, Abel,** (Old moulds and marks used)- 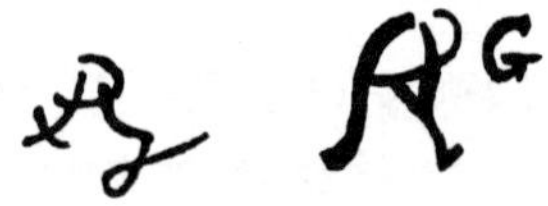

c.1890- **Unglazed red pottery.** impressed- ***APREY***

1744 Bow China Manufactury, Stratford-le-Bow, LONDON, England.

c.1744- PORCELAIN.
The date when this factory first produced wares is not known, but on the 6th December 1744, Edward Heylyn and Thomas Frye took out a patent whose specification was that of china or porcelain.

Most wares were unmarked

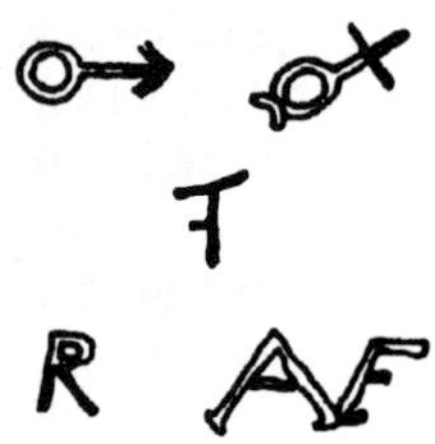

1750- **Weatherby and Crowther acquired the works,** which at that time were called `New Canton`. According to `Jewitt`, a Mr Binns F.S.A. owned an inkstand decorated in blue, which bore the words:- `MADE AT NEW CANTON 1750`. Another is marked `1751`.

MADE AT NEW CANTON 1750

1753- **Bow China Warehouse opened near the Royal Exchange, Cornhill, London.**
1762- Mr Weatherby died.
1763- John Crowther declared bankrupt.

1763- **John Crowther (son) carried on the factory at Bow.**
1770- Warehouse opened in St. Pauls Churchyard.

1775- **William Duesbury, Derby China Works, acquired the factory.**

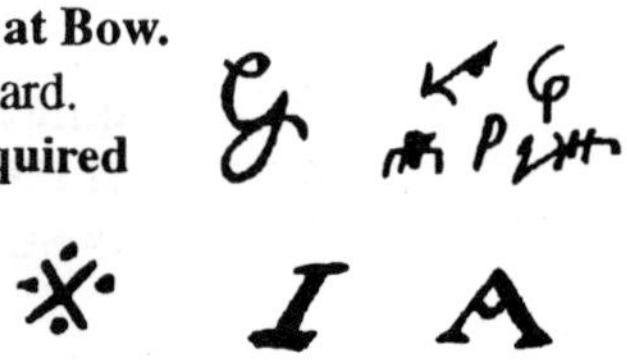

Marks are either incised or usually painted blue.
There are many marks that have been attributed to this factory but most of them are doubtful, however, the few shown here, most compilers tend to agree on.

1744 ST. PETERSBURG, Russia.

1744 A HARD-PASTE PORCELAIN
Factory was established by the Empress Elizabeth Petrowna. Catherine II. patronised the factory.

1744-62 **Russian Imperial Porcelain Factory**

Directors mark. -

1762-96 **Catherine II.** mark. in blue-

1796-1801 **Paul I.** - - - -

1801-25 **Alexander I.** - - - -

1825-55 **Nicholas I.** - - -

1855-81 **Alexander II.** - - -

1881-94 **Alexander III.** - - -

1894-1917 **Nicholas II.** - - - -

1917- **Soviet regime** - - - - -

St. Petersburg became known as Petrograd.
Staatliche Porcelain Works, Petrogad.
Factory renamed:-

1924- **Staatliche Porcelain Factory, Leningrad.**

Some various marks used:-

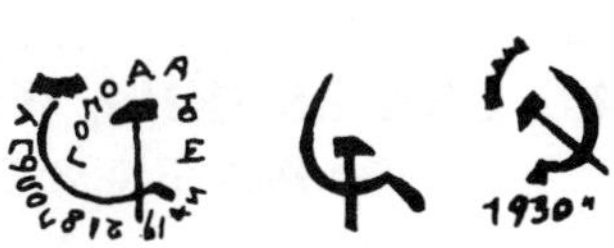

1745

1745 Chelsea China Works, LONDON, England.

c.1745-84 SOFT-PASTE PORCELAIN.

The history of the Chelsea China Works is very vague, the founder is not recorded, but by 1745 it had quite a reputation as being one of the best porcelain manufacturers in Europe. George II. gave it his support and the Duke of Cumberland actually gave an annual subscription to the works.

No marks on early wares.

c.1745-c.50 Incised mark -

Triangle mark -

1750-69 **M. Nicholas Spremont (or Sprimont) owned the works at this stage and did much to establish its already fine reputation.**

c.1749-52 Raised anchor mark on pad (Gold or red) -

Two anchors side by side were sometimes used -

1750-69 Various marks used according to `Jewitt` (in red, blue, brown and gold)

1769- Mr Spremont retired.

c.1769- **Mr James Cox became owner, who engaged Francis Thomas, who previously worked under Mr Spremont as overseer.**

1770- Francis Thomas died.

1769- **Mr Duesbury of Derby China Works became new owner and made Richard Barton manager.** see 1749 Royal Derby.

1784- **Chelsea Works closed.**

c.1769-84 Chelsea/Derby mark. (gold or enamel) -

1745 Chely, Rudolph Anton, BRUNSWICK, Germany.

1745-57 FAÏENCE. manganese purple-

1745 CRAILSHEIM, Würtemberg, Germany.

c.1745-c.1840 FAÏENCE. - - - -

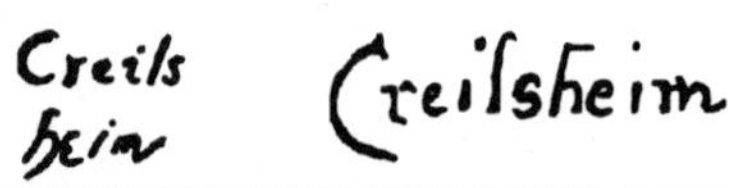

1745 Fränkel, Adolf, and Schreck, Johann Veit, BAYREUTH, Germany.

1745-47 PROPRIETORS. - - -

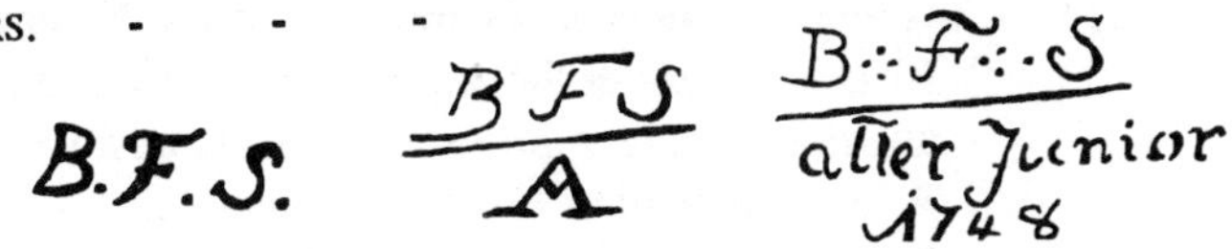

1745 KÜNERSBERG, nr. Memmingen, Germany.

1745-c.1790 FAÏENCE. - - - - -

1745-48 **Conradi, Johann Georg,** - -

1745-58 **Espen-Müller, Johannes,** - - - - - -

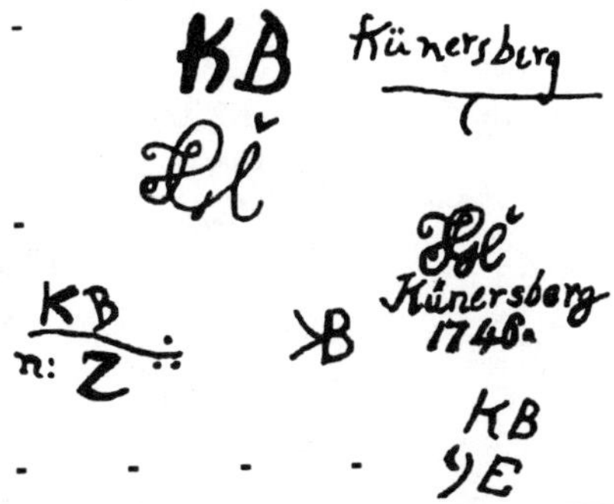

1745 ROCKINGHAM, Nr. Swinton, Yorkshire, England.

1745-1842 EARTHENWARE, HARD BROWN WARE, ETC.

c.1826- PORCELAIN. ***EARLY WARES NOT MARKED***

c.1745 **Edward Butler** established a tile-yard and pot-works for common earthenware on the estate of Charles, Marquis of Rockingham Swinton Common.

1765- **William Malpass in partnership with John Brameld and his son William.**

1778- **Thomas Bingley & Co.**

c.1778-87 impressed mark (rare) ***BINGLEY***

Thomas Bingley became principal proprietor with partners, John and William Brameld and a Mr. Sharpe.

Brown and Yellow wares, good quality blue and white tableware, etc., were made.

1787-1806 **Greens, Bingley & Co., Swinton Pottery.** The `Greens` from the `Leeds Pottery` took an active interest in Swinton.

c.1795- **`Rockingham Ware`** A fine reddish-brown china was first produced here and lends its name to similar wares made by other factories. Especially in the U.S.A. The famous `Cadogan Pot` was made in Rockingham Ware.

1806- **Brameld & Co.**

1806-42 impressed mark- ***BRAMELD***

John and William Brameld acquired the factory after the dissolvement of Greens, Bingley & Co.

Continued over -

1745

1745 ROCKINGHAM, Nr. Swinton, Yorkshire, England. (Cont`)

c.1813- **George Frederick, Thomas and John Wager Brameld,** sons of the old proprietors, succeeded and made many improvements to the business. A high standard of excellence was achieved.

c.1826-30 marks-

ROCKINGHAM
BRAMELD

ROCKINGHAM
WORKS
BRAMELD

1825 **Earl Fitzwilliam, owner of the property at Swinton, became financially involved in the works.**

c.1826-30 Griffin mark from the crest of the Earl Fitzwilliam Marquis of Rockingham. -

c.1830-42 mark -

ROYAL
ROCKINGHAM
WORKS
BRAMELD

1842 **Rockingham works was closed and sold off. Isaac Baguley (painter) carried on his own business in a small way, still using the `Griffin` mark.** c.1842- Baguley mark -

1745 SÈVRES, France.

SOFT-PASTE PORCELAIN. see 1738 VINCENNES.

The factory was first established at Vincennes in 1738, and transferred to more suitable premises at Sèvres in1756.

1738-c.1800 SOFT-PASTE PORCELAIN.

c.1770-present HARD-PASTE PORCELAIN.

1745-53 **The company was directed by Charles Adam at the Chateau de Vincennes under the special patronage of the King.**

1753- **Eloy Richard, purchased from Charles Adam his special right at Vincennes. King Louis XV took a third share and it became a Royal factory Madame de Pompadour took a great personal interest in the company.**

c.1745-93 **Louis XV and Louis XVI.**

Continued over -

1745 SÈVRES, France. (Cont`)

1741-1752 Period.

Marks and monograms of Painters, Decorators and gilders at the Royal Sèvres Factory:-

1741-77 **Thévenet père,** Flowers. - - - - 

1746-1800 **Capelle.** landscapes. 

1746-85 **Armand,Pierre, Louis, Philippe.** birds, flowers, etc. - - 

1747-55 **Houry,** flowers.- - - 

1748-62 **Fourè** flowers. - - - 

1748-65 **Becquet.** flowers - - 

1748-93 **Caton.** pastorals, children's - portraits. - - 

1749-70 **Grison.** gilder. - - - 

1749-86 **Cardin.** bouquets. - - (1793 chief of painters.) 

1749-96 **Le Guay, père,** gilder, noted for his work in blue at Vincennes. - 

1750-75 **Binet.** detached bouquets. - 

1750-75 **Xhrouet.** landscapes. (Probably inventor of rose-coloured ground) 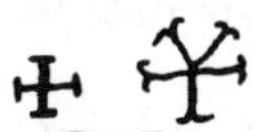

1750-80 **Baudouin.** gilder. - - 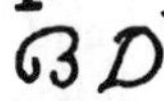

1750-1800 **Bertrand.** bouquets. - - 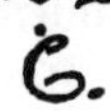

1751-1800 **Barbet.** flowers. - - 

1751-59 **Pajou,** figures. - - - 

1752-93 **Evans.** birds, butterflies, landscapes. - - - 

1752-1807 **Fontaine.** flowers, ornaments. - - - 

1752-57 **Carrié** flowers. - - - 

1752-58 **Anteaume,Jean-Jacques.** landscapes and animals. - 

1752-59 **Thévenet, fils,** - - - flowers, ornaments. - - 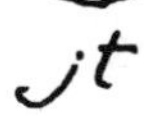

Continued over -

1745

1745 SÈVRES, France. (Cont`)

1752-92 **Sioux, aîné**
bouquets, garlands. - - -  R

1752-59 **Sioux, jeune,**
flowers, garlands. - - - O

1752-89 **Genest, figures, etc.,** - - - G
(Chief of painters) -

1752-90 **Vieillard, emblems,** ornaments. - 

1753-93 **DATE LETTERS were used to indicate the year of manufacture, They were set within or alongside the crossed `L`s` A mark shown below the `L`s`, usually indicates the painter.**

A - 1753	**L - 1764**	**V - 1774**	**GG - 1784**
B - 1754	**M - 1765**	**X - 1775**	**HH - 1785**
C - 1755	**N - 1766**	**Y - 1776**	**II - 1786**
D - 1756	**O - 1767**	**Z - 1777**	**JJ - 1787**
E - 1757	**P - 1768**	**AA - 1778**	**KK - 1788**
F - 1758	**Q - 1769**	**BB - 1779**	**LL - 1789**
G - 1759	**R - 1770**	**CC - 1780**	**MM - 1790**
H - 1760	**S - 1771**	**DD - 1781**	**NN - 1791**
I - 1761	**T - 1772**	**EE - 1782**	**OO - 1792**
J - 1762	**U - 1773**	**FF - 1783**	**PP - 1793**
K- 1763.			

1753 Mark with date letter - - blue enamel-

1753- Period **Marks and monograms of Painters, Decorators and Gilders at the Royal Sèvres Factory.**

1753-1803 **Vincent,** gilder. - - 2000

1753-54 **Fontelliau, A.** gilder. - 

1753-61 **Ledoux. birds,** landscapes. - 

1753-70 **Vavasseur.** arabesque, - W
flowers. - -

1753-79 **Vandé,** gilder. - - 

1753-88 **Chauvaux, aîné** - - 
Gilder of first class. -

1753-90 **Taillandier.** bouquets.
- - - - 

1753-93 **Rosset.** landscapes,
flowers, animals. - - 

Continued over -

1745 SÈVRES, France. (Cont`)

1754 **Mark with date letter-** - blue enamel- - 

1754 Period **Marks and monograms of Painters, Decorators and Gilders at the Royal Sèvres Factory.** (Cont`)

1754-1803 **Dodin,** figures, portraits. 

1754-1805 **Levé, Denis.** flowers, ornaments. - 

1754-55 **Tabary,** birds. - - 

1754-58 **Aubert, aîné,** flowers. 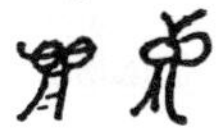

1754-59 **Prévost,** gilder. - - 

1754-62 **Boucher,** flowers. - - 

1754-64 **Mongenot,** flowers.- - 

1754-73 **Mutel,** landscapes.- - 

1754-1800 **Boulanger, père,** flowers. - 

1754-80 **Morin,** Marine and military subjects. - - 

1754-91 **Mérault, aîné** decorator. - 

1755- **Mark with date letter.** blue enamel- - - 

1755-59 Period **Marks and monograms of Painters, Decorators and Gilders at the Royal Sèvres Factory.** (Cont`)

1755-1800 **Chulot,** flowers, emblems. 

1755-93 **Cornaille,** flowers. - 

1755-93 **Noël,** flowers, ornaments. 

1755-93 **Parpette, Philippe,** flowers and gilding.- 

1755-57 **Chevalier, Pierre François,** flowers, bouquets. - - 

1755-75 **Héricourt,** flowers. - - 

1756-1806 **Petit, Nicholas,aîné,** flowers. 

Continued over -

1745

1745 SÈVRES, France. (Cont`)

1756-59 Marks and monograms (Cont`)

1756-57	**Dubois, Jean René** flowers and garlands.	
1756-58	**Genin, Charles,** flowers.	+
1756-58	**Gomery,** birds, flowers	
1756-60	**Tandart,** flowers.	• • •
1756-62	**Bienfait,** gilding.	✡
1756-86	**Buteux père,** flowers.	
1756-88	**Chapuis aîné** flowers, birds.	Cp
1757-1807	**Weydinger père,** flowers.	W
1757-95	**Tardi.** bouquets.	
1757-80	**Michaud,** flowers bouquets and medallions.	X
1757-93	**Bouchet, Jean,** landscapes animals, ornaments.	
1757-75	**Catrice.** flowers.	
1757-90	**Pithou aîné,** figures.	Pt.
1758-59	**Rocher.** figures.	xx
1758-75	**Rousell.** flowers.	RL
1758-81	**Aloncle, François,** birds, flowers, emblems.	N
1758-1802	**La Roche.** flowers.	LR
1759-75	**Pierre aîné** gilder.	pe
1759-79	**Mérault jeune,** flowers.	9
1759-66	**Buteaux jeune,** flowers.	9.

1760- **King became sole owner of the Sèvres factory M. Boileau was made director.**

Continued over -

1745 SÈVRES, France. (Cont`)

1760-1769 Marks and monograms. (Cont`)

1760-95 **Pithou jeune,** flowers, figures. - 

1763-1800 **Pierre jeune,Jean Jacques,** Bouquets, garlands. - - - 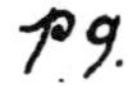

1763-65 **Fritsch.** figures children. - - - 

1763-92 **Bulidon.** bouquets. - - - 

1763-93 **Lecot,** chinese subjects. - - 

1764-1803 **Asselin.** Portraits, miniatures. - 

1764-80 **Drand,** chinese subjects and gilding. - - - - 

1764-80 **Falot,** Arabesque, birds, butterflies. - - - - 

1764-91 **Nicquet.** painter, gilder. - - 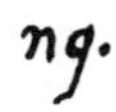

1765-78 **Théodore.** painter, gilder. - - 

1765-87 **Chabry.** Miniatures, pastorals. - 

1765-93 **Commelin,** garlands, bouquets. - 

1766-78 **Joyau.** bouquets. - - - 

1766-75 **Le bel aîné** figures, flowers. - 

1766-79 **Raux, aîné,** bouquets. - - 

1768-74 **Dusolle,** flowers. - - - 

1769-73 **Hilken,** figures. - - - 

1769-80 **Grémont.** garlands, bouquets. - 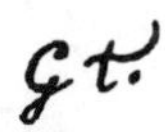

1769-91 **Barrat.** fruit and flowers. - - 

c.1770-93 **Mark with crown usually used on hard-paste.** - - - - - - 

1770-1777 Period **Marks and monograms of Painters, Decorators and Gilders at the Royal Sèvres Factory.**

1770-1812 **Choisy, de,** flowers, ornaments. - - 

Continued over -

1745

1745 SÈVRES, France. (Cont`)

Marks and monograms (Cont`)

1770-84	**Henrion,** bouquets.	
1771-93	**Girard.** Arabesque, chinese subjects.	
1771-1800	**Pfeiffer,** bouquets.	
1771-1825	**Gérard, Claud Charles,** Pastorals, miniatures.-	
1772-1817	**Leguay, Pierre Andre.** Miniatures.	
1772-75	**Jubin,** gilder.	
1772-77	**Chapuis jeune,** flowers.	
1772-80	**Michel,** bouquets.	
1772-97	**Castel.** landscapes, hunting birds.	
1773-78	**Pouillot,** flowers.	
1773-83	**Chauveaux fils,** bouquets.	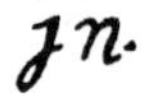
1773-86	**Schradre.** landscapes, birds.	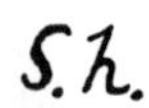
1773-1822	**Buteux fils cadet,** landscapes.	
1773-94	**Le Bel jeune,** flowers.	
1773-95	**Sinsson, Nicholas,** Flowers, groups and garlands.-	
1776-1817	**Le Grand,** gilder.	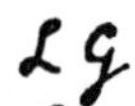
1777-1801	**Fumez,** bouquets.	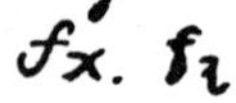
1777-90	**Dieu.** Chinese subjects, flowers, gilding.	
1777-79	**Levé, Felix,** Chinese, Flowers.	
1777-1805	**Le Bel Dame.** flowers.	
1777-95	**Noualhier Dame, née Durosey, Sophie,** flowers.	

1778 **Double letter mark.-**

Continued over -

1745 SÈVRES, France. (Cont`)

1778-1780 Period — **Marks and monograms of Painters, Decorators and Gilders at the Royal Sèvres Factory.**

1778-1817	**Bunel Marie-Barbe,** flowers-	MB
1778-1824	**Weydinger, Joseph,** Gilder and painter. - -	W
1778-1823	**Philippine aînè,** - - Child subjects.	·P:H.
1778-1840	**Le Gay,** Figures and portraits. - - -	L G
1778-81	**Le Guay, E.C.** Figures. -	L G
1778-81	**Boulanger fils,** Pastorals and children. - - -	
1779-1800	**Chanou Dame,** Gilder. -	JD
1779-98	**Chanou,** Flowers. - -	Sc
1779-1806	**Massy.** Flowers and emblems. - - -	M
1779-1822	**Vandé, P.J.B.** Gilder. -	VD
1779-85	**Léandre,** Children and emblems. - - -	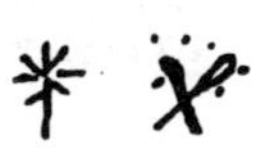
1780-1801	**Dutanda,** Bouquets, garlands. - - -	DT
1780-91	**Barre,** Detached bouquets.-	B

1780 — **Jewelled porcelain was introduced.**
The mark was sometimes decorated as shown. - -

1780 — **Hard-paste porcelain with date letter.-**
blue or red enamel - -

1781-1790 Period. — **Marks and monograms of Painters, Decorators and Gilders at the Royal Sèvres Factory.**

1781-1802	**Gérard Dame, (née Vautrin)** Flowers. - - -	
1781-1815	**Weydinger, Pierre,** Painter and Gilder. - -	
1783-	**Couturier.** Gilding. - -	C E.
1783-1836	**Philippine Jun.** Flowers - and animals.	Ph.

Continued over -

1745

1745 SÈVRES, France, (Cont`)

Marks and monograms (Cont`)

1784-93 **Lamprecht, George,** - Animals and figures. - 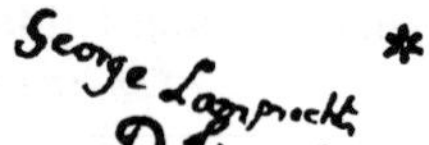

1785-1825 **Drouet.** Flowers and birds.- 

1785-91 **Boucot, P.** Flowers, - - arabesque and garlands. 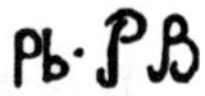

1785-93 **Bouillat fils,** Flowers - and landscapes. 

1786-1822 **Buteux, Theodore,** - - Painter. 

1787-91 **Gauthier,** Landscapes. - 

1788-98 **Parpette aînée,** Flowers. - 

1790-91 **Moiron,** Flowers. - - 

1792-1804 **First Republic.** - in blue- -

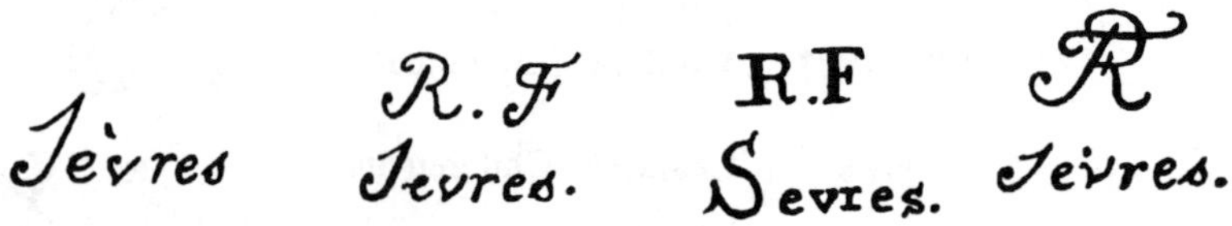

1792-1794 Period **Marks and monograms of Painters, Decorators and Gilders at the Royal Sèvres Factory.**

1792-1830 **Godin.** Gilder and Painter. - - - 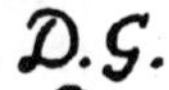

1794-1816 **Parpette jeune,** Flowers. - 

1794-1822 **Despèrais, C.** Decorator. - 

1795 (dated) On a cup and saucer. Victoria and Albert Museum. - - - - 

1795-1802 Period **Marks and monograms of Painters, Decorators and Gilders at the Royal Sèvres Factory.**

1795-1832 **Michaud, Pierre Louis,** Painter and Gilder. - - 

1795-1843 **Sinsson, Jacques Nicholas, père,** Flowers. - - 

1796-1820 **Maqueret Mme.,(née Bouillat)-** Flowers. 

Continued over -

1745 SÈVRES, France. (Cont`)

Marks and monograms (Cont`)

1797-1822	**Boitel.** Gilding. - -	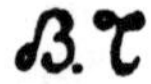
1801-17	**Troyon,** Painter and-Gilder.- -	
1801-23	**Georget.** Figures. - -	
1802-13	**Swebach,** Military subjects. -	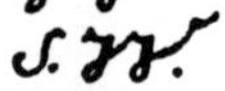
1802-27	**Durosey.** Gilding. - -	
1802-40	**Boullemier, Antoine Gabriel,** - Gilder.	

1793-1800 Letters denoting the year were rarely used during the Revolution period and they were replaced by the following signs:-

1801-17 <u>**Key signs for year:-**</u>

1801	**Year IX denotes -**	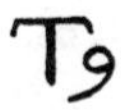	**1807 Denotes -**	**7**
			1808 "	**8**
1802	**" X "**		**1809 "**	**9**
			1810 "	**10**
1803	**" XI "**		**1811(onze)**	**oz**
			1812(douze)	**dz**
1804	**" XII "**		**1813(treize)**	**tz**
			1814(quatorze)	**qz**
1805	**" XIII "**	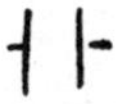	**1815(quinze)**	**qn**
			1816(seize)	**sz**
1806	**" XIV "**		**1817(dix sept)**	**ds**

1818 - onwards. The year is indicated by the last two figures i.e. 18 indicates 1818 and so on.

1803-04 **Consular period.** - printed red -

1804-14 **First Empire:-**
1804-1809 - stencilled red- -
Mark used by Napoleon.

1810-14 - printed in red- -

Continued over -

1745

1745 SÈVRES, France. (Cont`)

1803-1808 Period. **Marks and monograms of Painters, Decorators and Gilders at the Royal Sèvres Factory.**

1803-19 **Deutsch.** Ornaments and flowers. - - - - - Dh

1803-40 **Constant.** Gilder. - - - - C.C.

1804-15 **Delafosse, Denis.** Figures. - - - - - DF

1806-38 **Boullemier, François-Antoine,** Gilder.- - - - - - FB

1806-12 **Robert, J. F.** Landscapes. - - RB

1807-12 **Davignon, Jean-François,** - - D.F. Figures.

1807-14 **Langlacé.** Landscapes. - - L.G.

1807-15 **Moreau.** Gilder. - - - MR

1807-46 **Béranger, Antoine,** - - - BG Figures.

1808-17 **Degault, J.M.** Figures. - - De Gault

c.1810-20 **Wedgwood style, cameo relief.** - impressed- - Sevres,

1811-1813 Period **Marks and monograms of Painters, Decorators and Gilders at the Royal Sèvres Factory.**

1811-46 **Huard. Decorator,** Ornaments. - h.d.

1811-19 **Capronnier, François,** Gilder. - C.P

1813-30 **Ganeau fils,** Gilder. - - - Gu

1813-30 **Robert, P-R.** Ornaments. - - PR

1813-48 **Develly, Jean-Charles,** - - CD animals.

1813-50 **Boullemier fils,** - - - Bh Gilder.

1814-24 **Louis XVIII** - - -

1821 mark- - - - printed blue- - -

1822 mark - - - printed blue- - -

Continued over -

1745 SÈVRES, France. (Cont`)

1814-1823 Period. **Marks and monograms of Painters, Decorators and Gilders at the Royal Sévres Factory.**

1814-26 **Charrin, Fanny,** Figures. - - - J.C.

1814-42 **Boullemier fils,** Gilder. - D^N.B

1815-45 **Poupart.** Landscapes. - P

1815-39 **Barbin, François-Hubert,** Ornaments.- - - - B

1818-48 **Ducluzeau, Mme.,** Figures, etc. - - - A.D

1818-46 **Sinsson, P.** Flowers. - - SSp

1818-55 **Schilt, Louis Pierre.** Flowers. - LS

1819-48 **Didier, Charles-Antoine.** Ornaments. - D.I

1820-66 **Régnier, F.,** Figures. - - R

1823-45 **Constantin,** Figures. - C.C.

1824-30 **Charles X** - - - -

1824 mark - - - printed blue-

1825 marks - - - blue-

1830 marks - - blue-

1830 mark (used from August to December) -

Continued over -

1745

1745 SÈVRES, France, (Cont`)

1824-1830 Period. **Marks and monograms of Painters, Decorators and Gilders at the Royal Sèvres Factory.**

1825-57 **Fontaine, Jean Joseph.** - Flowers. 

1825-63 **Régnier, Hyacinthe,-** - Figures etc. 

1830-47 **Sinsson, L.** Flowers. - - 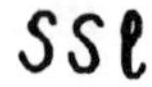

1830-48 **Moriot.** Figures. - - 

1830-48 **Louis-Philippe** - - -

1831-34 - - - blue or gold- 

1833 onwards. Mark used for white porcelain. - chrome green- 

1834-45 - - - blue or gold- 

1837 The Chateau d`Eu white and gold services have this additional mark- - 

1845-48 Mark, usually on white wares -
1.chrome green- - 

2. blue or gold- - 

Destination marks added - red- -  

1831-1847 Period **Marks and monograms of Painters, Decorators and Gilders at the Royal Sèvres Factory.**

1831-70 **Richard, Joseph,.** Decorations. - - - 

1832-78 **Richard, François Gervais** Decorations. - - - 

1833-72 **Richard, Eugène,.** - - Flowers. 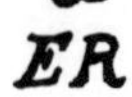

1841-73 **Trager, J.** Flowers, birds. - 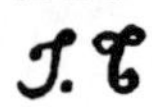

Continued over -

1745 SÈVRES, France, (Cont`)

Marks and monograms (Cont`)

1843-69 **André, Jules.** - - 
Landscapes.

1844-81 **Barré, Louis Desiré** - - 
Flowers.
(1881- Chief of painters).

1844-81 **David, Alexandre.**
Ornaments. - - - 

1847-84 **Cabau, Eugène-Charles.**
Flowers. - - - 

1848-51 **Second Republic** - - -  

Destination mark red- 

c.1850. Emile Lessore (d.1876) - - 

1848-51 Period **Marks and monograms of Painters, Decorators and Gilders at the Royal Sèvres Factory.**

1848-84 **Mérigot,** Decorator.- - 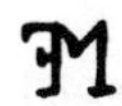

1849-90 **Gobert,** Figures. - - 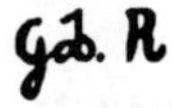

1850-71 **Roussel,** Figures. - - 

1851-70 **Humbert,** Figures. - - 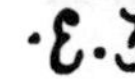

1851-88 **Gély, J.** Ornaments,- - 
Pâte-sur-pâte. -

1852-70 **Second Empire** - - - -
1852 mark - - 

1854 **Monogram mark of the Emperor Napoleon III.**
Revival of soft-paste - 

Destination mark red- 

Continued over -

1745

1745 SÈVRES, France. (Cont`)

1860-99 Biscuit figures. - impressed- -

1861 White wares issued without decorations. - stencilled green- -

1852-1870 Period. **Marks and monograms of Painters, Decorators and Gilders at the Royal Sèvres Factory.**

1852-79	**Charpentier,** Gilder. -	
1852-83	**Barriat, Charles,.** Figures and ornaments. -	
1852-80	**Dammouse, Pierre-Adolphe,** Figures and ornaments. - Pâte-sur-pâte. -	
1852-80	**Renard, Emile,** - - Decorator.	
1854-70	**Pline,** Decorator. - -	
1855-83	**Bulot, Eugène,** - - Flowers.	
1856-70	**Faraguet, Mme.,** - - Figures.	
1858-84	**Derichsweiler, G.** - - Decorator.	
1858-71	**Meyer.** Figures. - -	
1858-92	**Réjoux, Emile,** - - Decorator.	
1858-1904	**Bonnuit, Achile,** - - Decorations.	
1860-70	**Maussion,** Figures. - - -	
1862-76	**Milet, Optat,** - - - Decorator.	
1863-79	**Goupil,** Figures. - -	
1864-81	**Ficquenet, Charles,** - - Flowers and ornaments. Pâte-sur-pâte. -	
1864-85	**Guillemain,** Decorator. -	
1864-96	**Lambert,** Flowers. - -	
1865-1902	**Archelais,** Decorator. -	

Continued over -

1745 SÈVRES, France. (Cont`)

1865-1879 Marks and monograms, (Cont`)

1865-94 **Célos,** Decorator. - - Pâte-sur-pâte. 

1866-95 **Hallion, François,** - - Gilder. 

1866-95 **Legay.** Pâte-sur-pâte. - - 

1870-90 **Hallion, Eugène,** - - Landscapes. 

1871-onwards. Third Republic. - - - - - 

1872-99 marks. red - - -  

1874-88 **Escallier, Mme.,** - Decorator. 

1877- **Auvillain,** - - Ground colour. 

1877- **Bieuville,** - - Decorator. 

1878- **Fournier,** - - Decorator. 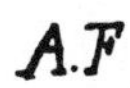

1878-1900 **Belet, E.,** - - Flowers, etc. 

1878-1900 **Blanchard, Alexandre,-** Decorator and modeller. 

1878-1905 **Doat, T. M.** Sculptor,- Pâte-sur-pâte. 

1879- **Belet, L.,** - - Decorator. 

1879- **Drouet,** - - Decorator. 

1879-82 **Ouint, Ch.,** - - Decorator. 

1879-82 **Tristan,** - - Decorator. 

1880-89 mark. - red- - 

1880-1887 Marks and monograms, (Cont`)

1880- **Brécy,** - - Decorator. 

1880- **Devicq,** - - Decorator. 

1880- **Peluche,** - - Decorator. 

Continued over -

1745

1745 SÈVRES, France. (Cont`)

1881-1889 Marks and monograms, (Cont`)

1881- **Renard, H.,** - - Decorator. 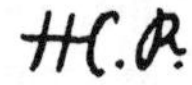

1881-86 **Maugendre,** - - Sculptor. 

1882-88 **Paillet,** - - Figures. 

1883- **Ligné,** - - Decorator. 

1883- **Simard,** - - Decorator. 

1883-88 **Sieffert,** - - Figures. 

1884- **Hallion, E.,** - - Landscapes. 

1886- **Jardel,** - - Decorator. 

1887- **Trager, H.,** - - Decorator. 

1888-91 stamped in relief- 

1888- **Morin,** - - Gilder. 

1888- **Pihan,** - - Decorator. 

1888- **Trager, L.,** - - Decorator. 

1888-93 **Ouint, E.,** - - Coloured grounds. 

1889-1904 **Ulrich,** - - Decorator. 

1890-1904 (no date) red- 

1890-1904 Marks and monograms, (Cont`)

1890- **Sandoz,** - - Decorator. 

1896- **Lasserre,** - - Decorator. 

1902- **Ballanger,** - - Decorator. 

1902- **Bocquet,** - - Decorator. 

1902- **Gobled,** - - Decorator. 

Continued over -

1745 SÈVRES, France. (Cont`)

Marks and monograms (Cont`)

1902- **Quennoy,** - - 
Decorator.

1902- **Richard, L.,** - - 

Decorator.

1902-04 **Catteau,** - - 
Decorator.

1903- **Fournerie,** - - 
Decorator.

1904- **Eaubonne, d`,** - 
Decorator.

1900-04 Year mark.Chrome green-

1900-02 Decoration dates.
1902-04 - - - -

1900-02 Gilding dates - -
1902-04 - - - -

1900- **Large decorated specimens-** - -

Various later marks:- - - -

1926

1928-40

1941

1971

1745 Zieremans, Hendrick, (Delft Artist) DELFT, Holland.

TIN-GLAZED EARTHENWARE (DELFTWARE) - -

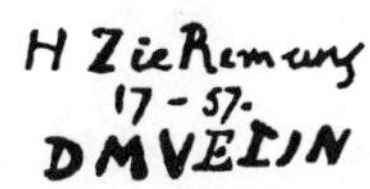

1745 Louis XV and Louis XVI, France. - - see 1745 SÈVRES.

1746

1746 HÖCHST, nr. Mayence, Germany.

1746-58 FAÏENCE.

1750-96 HARD-PASTE PORCELAIN.

Marks are that of Archbishop of Mayence protector of the fabrique. (a wheel of six spokes from the arms) -

Various painters marks:- - - -

1746-49 **Löwenfinck, Adam Friedrich von,** (technical director) see 1746 Löwenfinck.

1746- Hess, Georg Friedrich (painter) -

1747-51 **Dannhofer, Joseph Philipp,** - - see 1747 Dannhofer.

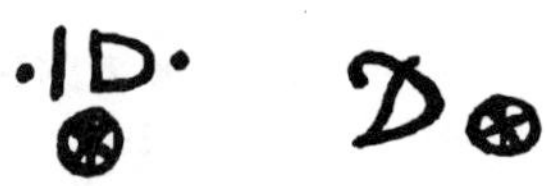

1749-53 **Benckgraff, Johannes,** (technical director)

c.1749- Adam, Ludwig, (decorator) -

c.1750- Hess, Ignaz, (painter) - - see 1750 Hess, Ignaz,

c.1750- **Zeschinger, Johannes,** - - - see 1750 Zeschinger.

c.1750-53 **Feilner, Simon,** - - - - see 1750 Feilner, Simon.

1753- Diefenbach, (painter) - -

1765-78 **Melchior, Johann Peter,** - - -

1746 Löwenfinck, Adam Friedrich von, HÖCHST, Germany.

1746-53 PAINTER. Also worked at various other factories including Meissen and Bayreuth.

F. v. L.
v. Löwenf. peint
de Löwenfincken pinx.

1746 Mortlock, John, (Retailer) Oxford Street, LONDON, England.

1746-c.1930 In the early years John Mortlock was agent for the Rockingham works and on some wares had his own mark as a backstamp. - - ***MORTLOCK***

C.1810- **Mortlock also became agents for Nantgarw, Coalport, Swansea and Minton. - -** Many marks of various designs were found printed with Mortlock`s name included.

MORTLOCKS
OXFORD STREET

1746	Armand, P.L.P., (birds/flowers) France. - - -	see 1745 SÈVRES.
1746	Capelle, (landscapes) France. - - - -	see 1745 SÈVRES.
1746	Rosa, Mathias Carl, Germany. - - - -	see 1711 ANSBACH.

1747 Dannhofer, Joseph Philipp, HÖCHST, Germany.

1747-51 FAÏENCE. Also worked at various other factories, including Vienna, Bayreuth and Ludwigsburg.

1747 Pfeiffer & Fränkel, (widow) BAYREUTH, Germany.

1747-60 PROPRIETORS. - - -

1760-67 **Pfeiffer, Johann Georg.** - - PROPRIETOR.

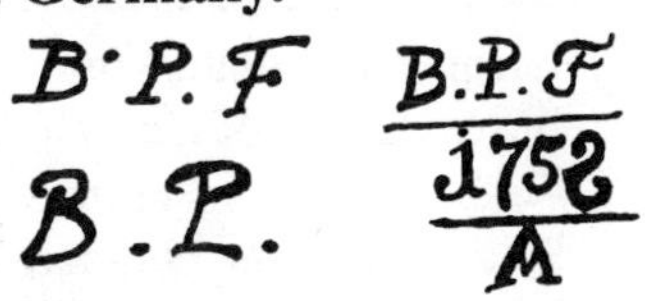

Oswald, Johann Martin Anton. - PAINTER.

1747	Clerici, Felice, Italy. - - - - - -	see 1725 MILAN.
1747	Grunbuhel, Maierhoffer de (director) Austria. - -	see 1719 VIENNA.
1747	Houry, decorator. France. - - - - - -	see 1745 SÈVRES.
1747	Niedermeyer, Joseph, modeller, Austria. - - -	see 1719 VIENNA.

1748 ANGOULÊME, Charente, France.

1748-c.1890 FAÏENCE. - - -

ANGOULÊME
anno; 1770

1748 GÖGGINGEN, nr. Augsburg, Germany.

1748-52 FAÏENCE. - - -

Simon, H., (painter) - - -

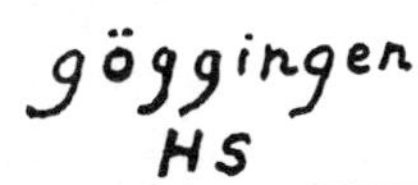

1748 Lund & Miller`s Factory, BRISTOL, England.

1748-52 SOFT-PASTE (SOAPSTONE) PORCELAIN. - ***BRISTOL***

c.1752. Transferred to Worcester. - - ***BRISTOLL***

1748 MONTEREAU, Seine-et-Marne, France.

1748-19th century. SALT-GLAZED STONEWARE, CREAMWARE.

Mazois, John Hill & Warburton. - - **MONTEREAU M^{AU} NO 1**

Leboeuf & Thibaut - - - - - L. L. et T.

1748 SCEAUX, Seine, France.

c.1748-19th century. FAÏENCE.

c.1748-1813 `Sceaux Penthièvre` - - -

Patronage of the High Admiral

Duc de Penthièvre.

Stencilled marks- -

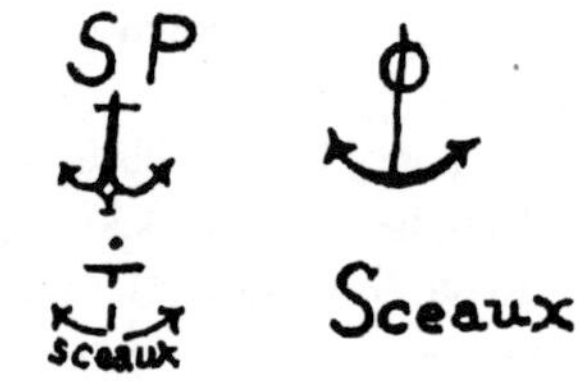

SOFT-PASTE PORCELAIN - - -

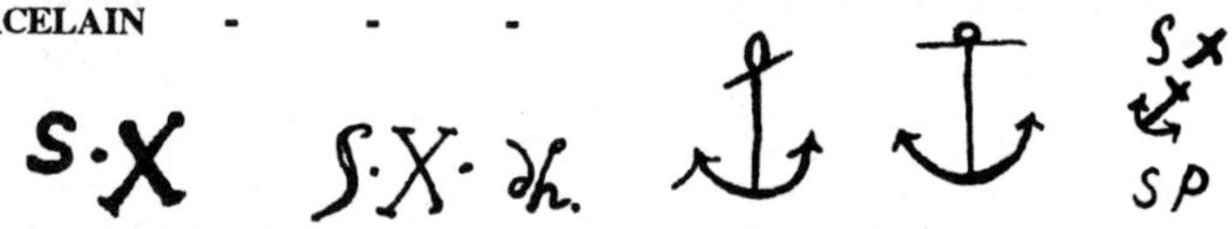

1748 Becquet, (decorator) France. - - - see 1745 SÈVRES.
1748 Busch, Canon of Hildesheim, Germany. - - see 1740 HILDESHEIM.
1748 Caton, (decorator) France. - - - - - see 1745 SÈVRES.
1748 Fourè, (decorator) France. - - - - - see 1745 SÈVRES.
1748 Wood, Ralph, (son) BURSLEM, England. - see 1715 Ralph Wood.

1749 Fouque, Joseph (d.1800) MOUSTIERS, France.

1749-1852 FAÏENCE. - - -

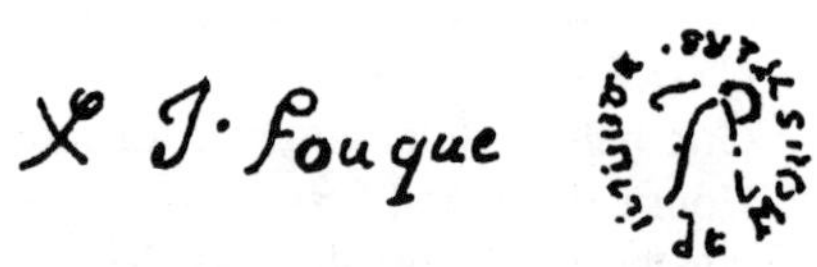

Pelloquin, Jean-François, - -

1749 Leroy Factory, MARSEILLES, France.

1749-c.1793 Leroy, Louis (d.1788)

Leroy, Antoine (son)

Continued by Sauze, Jean-Baptiste

1749 LONGTON-HALL, Staffordshire, England.

c.1749-60 PORCELAIN.

Rare marks in underglaze blue-

Most wares are un-marked.

1749 Reichard, Johann Heinrich, BRUNSWICK, Germany.

1749-56 **Behling, Johann Erich,** -

FAÏENCE.

B & R

R & B

1749 Royal Crown Derby Porcelain Co. Ltd., DERBY, England.

c.1748-56 The Planche Period.

Andre Planche, a Huguenot, completed his apprenticeship to a London goldsmith in 1747. It is known that a china works existed near St. Mary`s bridge in 1752 and it was probably there that Planche first made his `dry edge` figures. The dates of the figures range from 1751 to 1754` and some of the finest are those representing the five `Senses` and the four `Elements`

No marks worth noting were recorded during this period except those on three small jugs marked: `Derby` `D1750` and `D

1756-86 William Duesbury I. Period

A partnership between Andre Planche (potter) John Heath (banker) and William Duesbury (enameller) resulted in the opening of the Nottingham Road Factory. A far greater range of both tableware and ornamental wares were made. It was about this time that patch marks left on the bases of figures, made during firing, first appeared. These marks continued through to the Chelsea-Derby period.

Derby had no factory marks before Duesbury purchased the Chelsea works. Patch marks on figures caused during firing, first appeared.

Planche left the factory eventually and William Duesbury became the dominant partner.

1769 Chelsea Factory acquired

see 1745 Chelsea

Duesbury operated both works for a time but he transferred some of the extremely skilled craftsmen from Chelsea to Derby. It was about this time that numbers started to appear on the bases of figures. According to Jewitt, ` The figures and groups were numbered and registered for re-production`

c.1769 First mark used on wares incised or painted sometimes accompanied by a gold anchor -

1770- Biscuit or unglazed porcelain figures first appeared.

c.1770-80 Marks normally in gold - -

Continued over -

1749

1749 Royal Crown Derby Porcelain Co. Ltd., DERBY, England. (Cont`)

1773- London showroom at No.1, Bedford Street in Covent Garden opened, and Royal patronage was obtained.

c.1780-84 Marks normally in blue or puce -

1776 Bow China Works aquired see 1744 Bow.

1784 Chelsea Factory closed. Most of the painters and craftsmen had already moved to Derby.

1786 William Duesbury died.

1786-95 William Duesbury II. Period.

During this period Derby was to become the most important porcelain factory in Britain and among the finest in Europe. The Derby pattern books (begun around 1780) shows the remarkable range of fine products during this period. They give all the known painters, patterns and shapes.

c.1784-1806 Mark normally in blue or puce
until 1806 usually red -

Unfortunately, the amount of work created from this success, caused a decline in Mr Duesbury`s health and he was induced to take into partnerership a Mr Michael Kean, an Irish miniature painter.

1795-1811 Duesbury and Kean.

c.1795 Duesbury and Kean mark very rarely used -

1795 William Duesbury dies at the early age of 34.

Michael Kean marries Duesbury`s widow.

This new ownership marked a temporary decline in the factory. Many of the craftsmen could not work with Kean and within a short period they left the Derby works. Kean, however, continued production with the help of those workers that stayed, but the wares declined in standards and eventually Kean was forced to sell his interest and the Duesbury family entered into an agreement to lease the factory to a Mr Robert Bloor.

1811-48 Robert Bloor Period.

Robert Bloor eventually purchased the works.

1811-c.20 Continues with old `Duesbury mark in red- -

Although he had little experience in china manufacture, nevertheless, Robert Bloor employed some great artists and a lot of fine wares were produced during this period.

Continued over -

1749 Royal Crown Derby Porcelain Co. Ltd., DERBY, England.

1811-48 Robert Bloor Period (Cont`)

The `Imari` patterns became very popular during Bloor`s reign which incidentally are still made today (1995) at Osmaston Road.

From 1812 to 1826 the factory remodelled a set of Paris Street Cries, a figure of Napoleon, a bust of Nelson, and fourteen figures illustrating the adventures of Dr Syntax.

c.1820-25 Mark carelessly drawn in red- - -

c.1825
printed

c.1835

c.1840
red normally

1846 Robert Bloor dies. After a long illness, the factory passed into the hands of a Mr Thomas Clarke, husband to a grand-daughter of Robert Bloor who closed the works and sold the models to a number of Staffordshire factorys, in particular a Mr Boyle of Fenton.

1848-1935 King Street Period.

On the closure of the Nottingham Road Factory, a group of men that worked there, **William Locker, Samuel Fearn (potter) John Henson (potter) Samuel Sharpe (potter) Sampson Hancock and James Hill (painters and gilders)** began the production of china at King Street. under the name of **Locker & Co.**

1848-59

1859 William Locker died. Shortly afterwards the works changed to Stevenson & Co., and then Stevenson, Sharp & Co.

1859-63

1866 Mr Stevenson died. and from then, the style changed to Hancock & Co., after which it became :-

1866-1935 Sampson Hancock.

1935 Merged into Derby Crown Porcelain Co.

The type of production at King Street was mostly traditional, and moulds from Nottingham Road were used. Nevertheless, this small factory helped to carry on the skills and traditions of `Derby` china.

1863-1935

Continued over -

1749

1749 Royal Crown Derby Porcelain Co. Ltd., DERBY, England. (Cont`)

1877- Derby Crown Porcelain Company, Osmaston Road.

Principal directors were Edward Phillips and William Litherland. Phillips was a practical potter and Litherland was the head of a family of china and glass retailers in Liverpool. A factory was built in the Arboretum in Osmaston Road. As in the past, the factory once more attracted many talented artists.

1877-90

1890 The company was appointed `Manufacturers of porcelain to Her Majesty`

1890-1963 mark

1890-The Royal Crown Derby Porcelain Company.

Today, the company is part of Royal Doulton Limited, England`s leading group of bone china and hand-made full lead crystal manufacturers.

1963-76 mark -

Derby Year Cyphers.

The `V` mark of 1904 is accompanied by the word `England` and that of 1942 with the words `Made in England`
The same applies to the `X` of 1901 and 1947.

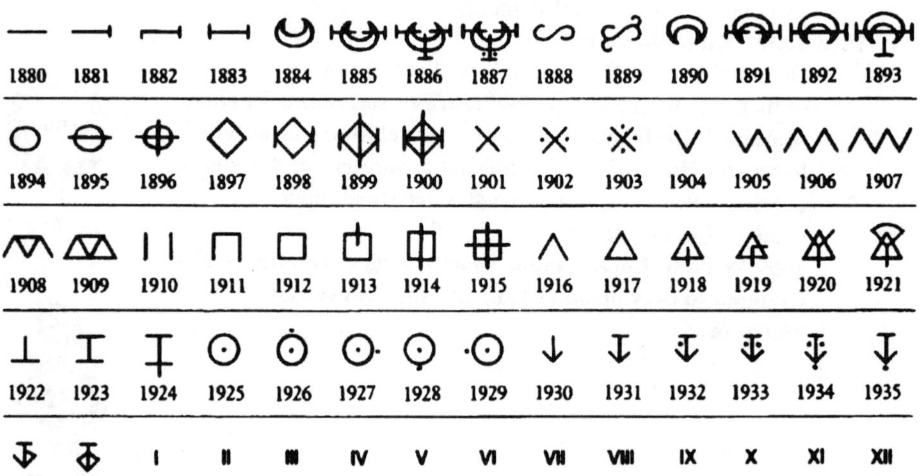

		I	II	III	IV	V	VI	VII	VIII	IX	X	XI	XII
1936	1937	1938	1939	1940	1941	1942	1943	1944	1945	1946	1947	1948	1949
XIII	XIV	XV	XVI	XVII	XVIII	XIX	XX	XXI	XXII	XXIII	XXIV	XXV	XXVI
1950	1951	1952	1953	1954	1955	1956	1957	1958	1959	1960	1961	1962	1963

XXVII	XXVIII	XXIX	XXX	XXXI	XXXII	XXXIII	XXXIV	XXXV	XXXVI	XXXVII	XXXVIII
1964	1965	1966	1967	1968	1969	1970	1971	1972	1973	1974	1975

Continued over -

1749 Royal Crown Derby Porcelain Co.Ltd.,DERBY, England, (Cont`)

Derby Year Cyphers (Cont`)

XXXIX	**XL**	**XLI**	**XLII**	**XLIII**	**XLIV**	**XLV**	**XLVI**	**XLVII**	**XLVIII**	**XLIX**
1976	**1977**	**1978**	**1979**	**1980**	**1981**	**1982**	**1983**	**1984**	**1985**	**1986**
L	**LI**	**LII**	**LIII**	**LIV**	**LV**	**LVI**	**LVII**	**LVIII**	**LIX**	
1987	**1988**	**1989**	**1990**	**1991**	**1992**	**1993**	**1994**	**1995**	**1996**	

Note. The year of production can be achieved by adding the value of the Roman numeral to the year, 1937

(These backstamps and information are published with kind permission of the trademark and copyright owner. This publication has been produced independently and neither the author nor the publisher have any connection with the company)
(By kind permission of Royal Doulton plc., Minton House, Stoke-on-Trent)

1749 Benckgraff, Johannes, Germany. - - - see 1746 HÖCHST.
1749 Cardin, (decorator) France. - - - see 1745 SÈVRES.
1749 Derrenes, Michel, France. - - - - see 1650 RENNES.
1749 Grison, (gilder) France. - - - - see 1745 SÈVRES.
1749 Le Guay père, E.A., (gilder) France. - - see 1745 SÈVRES.
1749 Ludwig, Adam, Germany. - - - - see 1746 HÖCHST.
1749 Raised Anchor mark, England. - - - see 1745 CHELSEA.
1749 Roussencq, France. - - - - see 1722 LA ROCHELLE.
1749 Tutrel, France. - - - - - see 1650 RENNES.

1750 ABTSBESSINGEN, Thuringia, Germany.

Mid 18th century FAÏENCE. - - - -

1766-77 **Muth, Heinrich Christoph,** - -

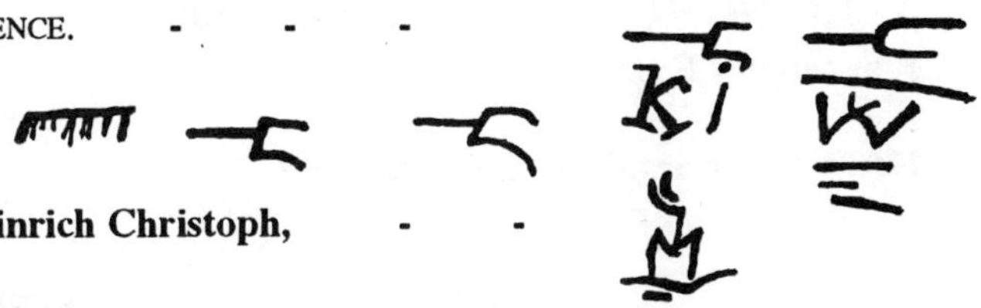

1750 Astbury, SHELTON, Staffordshire, England.

Mid 18th century. RED EARTHENWARE. incised or impressed- ***ASTBURY***

1750 Baddeley, Ralph and John, SHELTON, Staffordshire, England.

1750-95 EARTHENWARE. - impressed- ***BADDELEY***

R & J BADDELEY

1750 COIMBRA, Portugal.

18th - 19th century FAÏENCE. - - - -

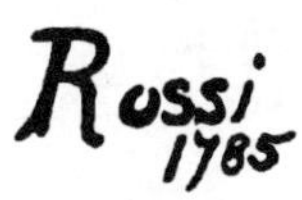

1750

1750 Derby Pot Works, Derbyshire, England.

c.1750-80 CREAMWARES.

Thomas Radford, engraver. or Richard Holdship. - - *T. RADFORD SC DERBY*

RADFORD fecit DERBY POT WORKS

1750 Dohachi, Takahashi, YAMASHIRO, Japan.

1750-93 (d 1804)

c.1840-75 Dohachi III.

Dohachi II. Died 1856

1840 `Kachu tei Dohachi` (Made by Dohachi in the Kachu house) Kioto. - - -

1875- Dohachi IV. at Kiyomizu.

1750 Feilner, Simon, HÖCHST, Germany.

1750-53 Also worked at various other factories including Paris and Furstenberg.

1750 Hess, Ignatz, HÖCHST, Germany.

c.1750- FAÏENCE. - - -

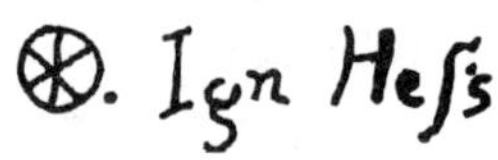

1750 KELLINGHUSEN, Holstein, Germany.

18th century FAÏENCE.

1763-82 Carsten Behren`s factory. -

1785-95 Moeller, Joachim, - -

1795-1820 Grauer, Dr. Sebastian, -

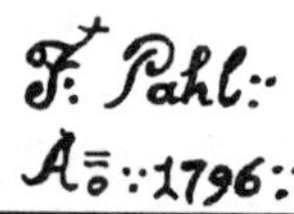

1750 KII or KISHIU, Japan.

c.1750 KISHIU-YAKI.

Waka-yama. of Kii. Eiraku-Hozen was sent there by Prince of Kii to promote the art. Kairakuyen sei (made by Kairakuyen). A name given to Eiraku Hozen by Prince Harunori.

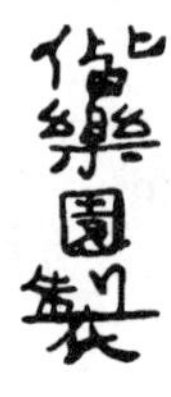

Continued over -

1750 KII or KISHIU, Japan. (Cont`)

c.1790 **Zuishi. A ware made at Meppotani.** -

1828-68 **Kairakuyen Factory at Nishiyama.** -

c.1840 **Seinei. Raku Tannin mark-** -

1847-66 **Nan-ki Otokoyama (Made at Otoko-yama in Southern Kii)**

嘉永元年
南紀男山製

1850 **SANRAKUYEN-YAKI. Kishiu porcelain.**

Jui (Long life) -

JUI

三樂
園製

1750 Kitei, YAMASHIRO, Japan.

18TH CENTURY POTTERS. Four generations
Studio name Wake Heikichi.

Kitei at Kiyomizu. - - -
(Kitei at tortoise house)

Ki for Kitei- - -

1800 **Kentei.** Unglazed faïence with designs in gold or enamels. - - -

`Otowa` mark of Otowaya Sozaemon.
Succeeded by second Kentei.- -

1750

1750 NEWCASTLE UPON TYNE, Tyne and Wear, England.
The individual factories and potters of NEWCASTLE UPON TYNE have been listed uder their own dates and marks within this book.

1750 Robert`s Factory, MARSEILLES, France.
c.1750-c.92 FAÏENCE.

1773- **Robert, Joseph-Gaspard.** HARD-PASTE PORCELAIN.

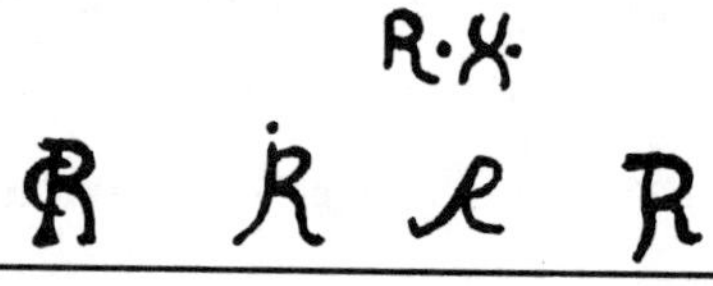

1750 rue de la Roquette, PARIS, France.
c.1750-c.90 FAÏENCE AND PORCELAIN.
c.1750- Ollivier. - - OLLIVIER A PARIS — ollivier a paris

1750 TOURS, Indre-et-Loire, France.
c.1750 **Epron, Mathurin,** FAÏENCE. - - *`Fait a Tours ce 21 mars 1782*
1770 **Sailly, Thomas,** FAÏENCE AND EARTHENWARE.

1776-83 **Sailly & Son.** HARD-PASTE PORCELAIN. incised- *A Tours 1782`*
1782- Sailly, Noël, (son)
1842-c.61 **Avisseau, Charles,** - -
1862- Avisseau, M.E., (son)

a Visseau atour 1855

Landais, M., Reproductions of Palissy and Henri II. wares. - -

1750 Warburton, John, Carr`s Hill Pottery, NEWCASTLE, England.
c.1750-1817 EARTHENWARE. - - - *J. WARBURTON N. ON TYNE*

1750 Watson`s Pottery, PRESTONPANS, Lothian, Scotland.
c.1750-1840 EARTHENWARE - Impressed- *WATSON*
1800-40 Printed- *WATSON & CO.*

1750 White, William J., Fulham Pottery, LONDON, England.
c.1750-1850 STONEWARE. Same site as John Dwight`s early pottery *W. W.* (date)
Incised- *W.J. WHITE* (date)

1750 Zeschinger, Johannes, HÖCHST, Germany.
c.1750- FAÏENCE. Also worked at Furstenberg.

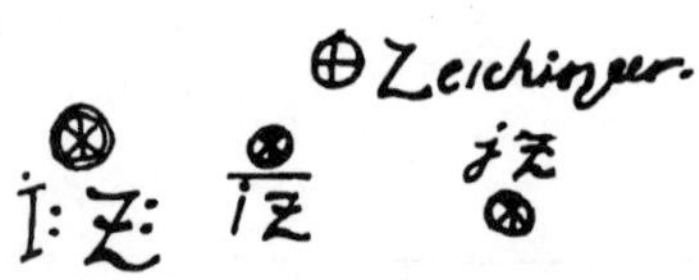

1750 Baudouin, père, (gilder) France. - - - see 1745 SÈVRES.
1750 Bedeaux, Joseph, (painter) France. - - see 1733 SINCENY.
1750 Bertrand, (decorator) France. - - - see 1745 SÈVRES.
1750 Bertrand, Pierre, (painter) France. - - see 1733 SINCENY.
1750 Binet, (painter) France. - - - - see 1745 SÈVRES.
1750 Daussy, Alexandé, (painter) France. - - see 1733 SINCENY.
1750 Doorne, Christoffel van, DELFT, Holland. - see 1653 De Porceleyne Fles.
1750 Folco, Sebastiano, Italy. - - - - see 1550 SAVONA.
1750 Gionetti, Vittorio Amedeo, Italy. - - - see 1577 TURIN.
1750 `K`wa-bo` Japan. - - - - see 1583 BIZEN.
1750 Morsenchio-Capelletti, Italy. - - - see 1725 LODI.
1750 Regoli, Antonio Maria, Italy. - - - see 1451 FAENZA.
1750 Spremont, M. Nicholas, England.- - - see 1745 Chelsea China Works.
1750 Xhrouet, (decorator) France. - - - see 1745 SÈVRES.

1751 AUMUND, nr.Vegesack, Bremem, Germany.

1751-61 FAÏENCE.

1751-57 **Mülhausen, Johann Christoph, - Terhellen, Wilhelm and Diederich.** - -

1751-57 Terhellen, D.& W. - - -

1757-61 **Erberfeld, Albrecht von,** - - - -

1751 BERLIN, Prussia, Germany.

1751- HARD-PASTE PORCELAIN.
Wegely, Wilhelm Caspar, is granted permission by the King of Prussia, Frederick II to open porcelain factory in Berlin.

Marks in underglaze blue- - -

1753- Reichard, Ernst Heinrich, appointed master model maker.
1754- Clauce, Jakob, is put in charge of painting department.
1757- Wegely closes his factory and sells the stocks, tools and materials.

1761- **Gotzkowsky, Johann Ernst,** buys secret porcelain formular from E.H. Reichard who stays on as Arkanist and head of department.

Marks in underglaze blue-

Continued over -

1751

1751 BERLIN, Prussia, Germany. (Cont`)

1763- **King purchased factory from Gotzkowsky for 225,000 Reichsthalers.**

1763-80 Marks in underglaze blue-

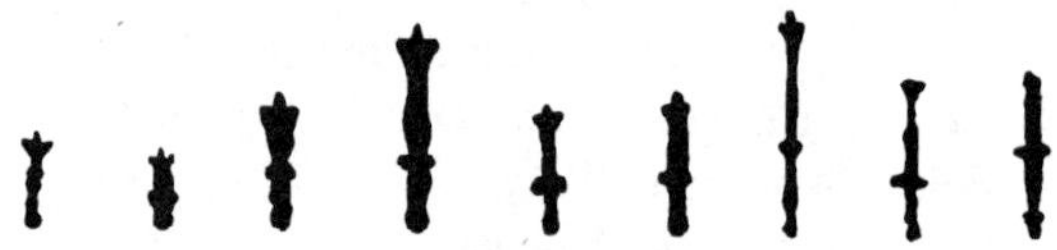

Name changed to KÖNIGLICHE PORZELLAN-MANUFAKTUR (KPM) or Royal Porcelain Manufactory, and used the `sceptre` as its symbol on the base of all pieces.

1780-1800 Marks in uderglaze blue-

1786- **Frederick William II, successor to Frederick the Great.**

c.1800 and c.1810 marks-

c.1800 c.1810

1803-13 Painters marks in blue-

1807/08 **Napoleon`s troops occupy Berlin and confiscate KPM`s money for the benefit of the French authorities.**

1814- **Frick, Christoph Georg, KPM`s Arkanist,** developes a brilliant and stylish green colour scale based on chromium oxide and a new grey-black combination based on iridium.

1815-20 mark- -

1817-23 Painters marks in red- -

1820-30 marks, blue- - -

1823-32 mark in red- -
and 1844-47 in blue- -

c.1825 impressed mark- - - -

1832 mark in red- - -

Continued over -

1751 BERLIN, Prussia, Germany. (Cont`)

1837 mark- - -

1837-44 mark- - -

1844-47 mark- -

1847-49 mark- - -

1849-70 mark -

1870- mark- - - - -

1878- **Seger, Hermann,** joins the company and begins to develope new soft porcelain and delicate glazes: oxblood, celedon, etc.,

1882 Seger marks-

1902- Schmuz-Baudiss, Theo, Artistic Director
KPM`s Art Nouveau porcelain becomes a leading influence in porcelain design.

1911 mark blue- -

1913 mark green- - -

1913 Memorial mark-

1914- Patriotic porcelain becomes the `in` subject.
1943- KPM building in Berlin-Tiergarten is bombed and destroyed.

1944-57 Selb mark- -

1945- **KPM`s factory moves to emergency quarters in Selb. whilst the Berlin factory is being rebuilt.**

1945 Berlin - - - - -

Continued over -

1751

1751 BERLIN, Prussia, Germany. (Cont`)

1957- **KPM reunite at the old rebuilt Berlin premises.**

1962-92 - - - 

1988- **KPM becomes a limited company, with a new, but old name: KPM - Königliche Pozellan-Manufaktur Berlin GmbH.**

1988 Memorial mark- - 

1992 mark - - 

1993 mark - - - - 

(Courtesy of Königliche Porzellan Manufaktur, Berlin, Germany)

1751 MARTRES, Haute-Garonne, France.

Mid 18th century FAÏENCE. - - - ***Fait a Martres 1751`***

1751 SAINT-OMER, Pas-de-Calais, France.

1751-95 FAÏENCE.

Saladin, Louis,

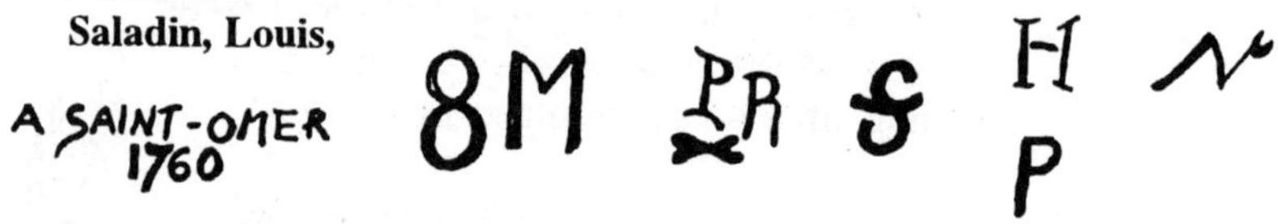

1751 TOURNAY, Belgium.

1751- SOFT-PASTE PORCELAIN.

1751-96 **Peterinck, F. J.**

Early marks in blue, gold, crimson, etc.

1756-81 - in various colours-

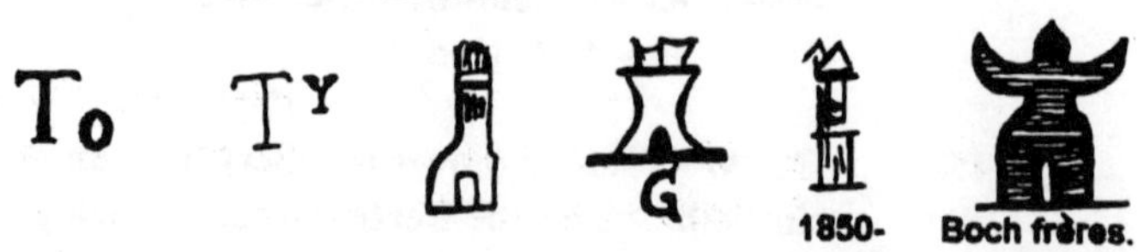

1850- **Boch frères.** 

1751 WORCESTER, Warmstry House, Worcestershire, England.

1751-1793 Dr. Wall period.

The company was established by a group of fifteen men who were headed by Dr. John Wall (physician), William Davis (apothecary), Richard and Josiah Holdship, and Edward Cave.

Soft-paste porcelain was produced from a method used by Miller and Lund, a failing porcelain factory in Bristol.

1751-65 Workmans` marks, painted underglaze blue
Similar marks were found on various wares from other factories making porcelain.

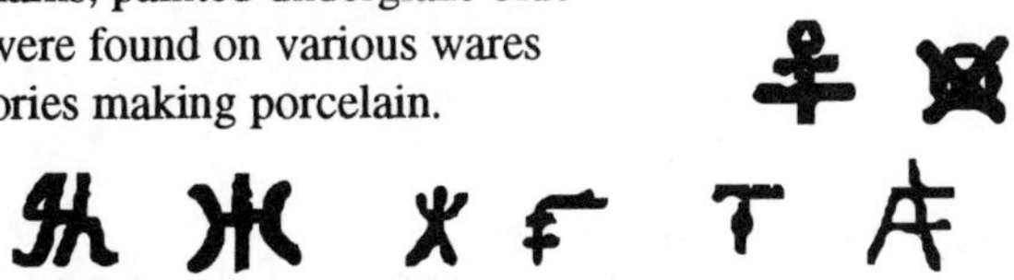

c.1755-75 `W` marks. painted underglaze blue-

c.1755-75 Square marks, in blue.

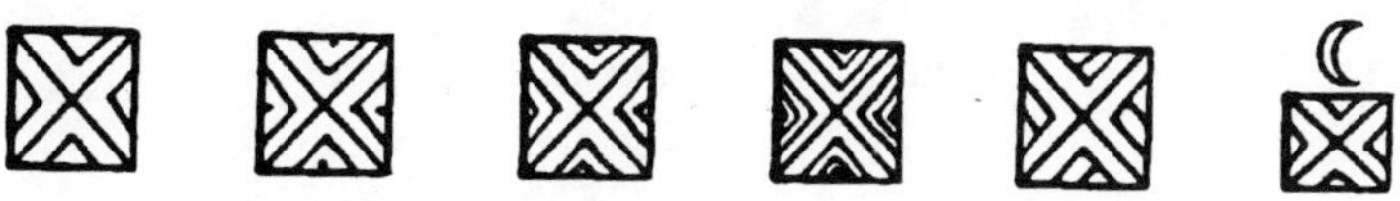

c.1755-90 Crescent marks, painted underglaze blue-

Robert Hancock (also worked at Bow) joined the firm and by 1756 had perfected a transfer printing process which was to open up a whole new field of decoration.

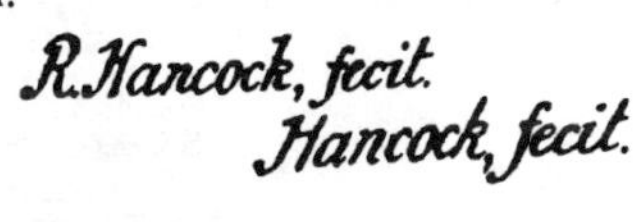

Richard Holdship, mark with an anchor (indicating `Holdship`)

1760-70 The work of several excellent painters were seen around during this period, especially:- J.H. O`Neale and John Donaldson.

Continued over -

1751

1751 WORCESTER, Warmstry House, England. (Cont`)

c.1760-70 Copies of other factory marks were used on rare occasions. Sèvres, Chantilly and Meissen.

c.1760-75 Imitation Japanese decoration. Marks in blue-

1776- Dr. John Wall died.
1783- William Davis died.

1783-92 **Flight period.**
Thomas Flight purchased the business for his two sons, Joseph and John, to run.
1789 Royal Warrant granted.

1791 John Flight died.
Martin Barr appointed as new partner.

1792-1804 **Flight & Barr period.**
Flight & Barr marks are infrequent.

`Barr` mark-

1804-13 **Barr, Flight & Barr period.**
Martin Barr Junior was taken into the partnership.

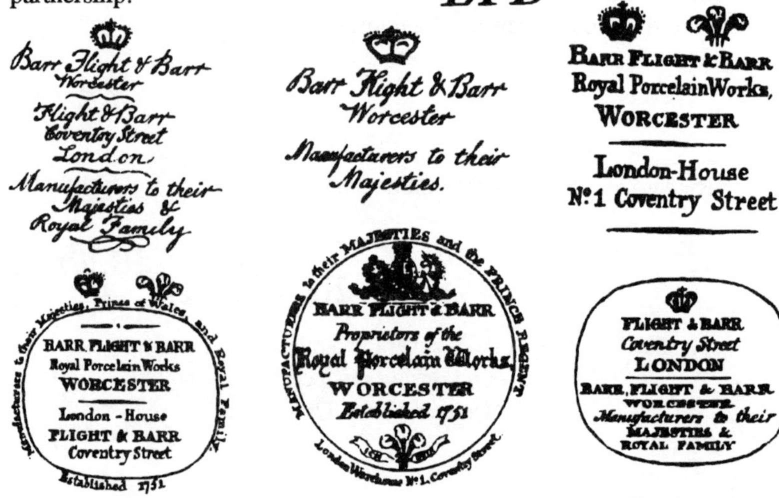

Continued over -

1751 WORCESTER, Warmstry House, England. (Cont`)

1813- Martin Barr Senior died.

1813-40 **Flight, Barr & Barr period.**
George Barr taken into partnership.

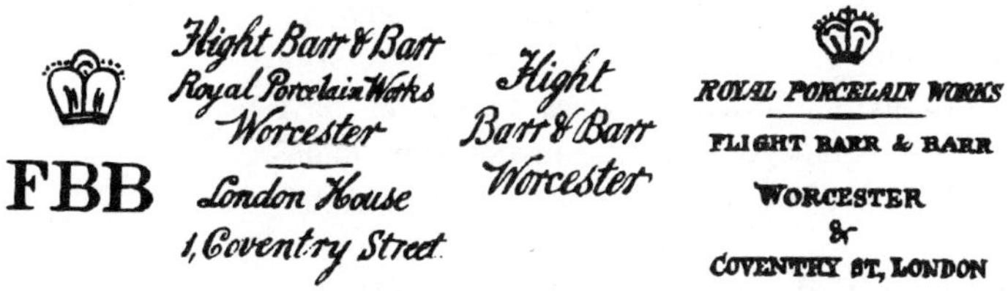

1840-52 **Chamberlain & Co. amalgamates with Flight, Barr & Barr, Worcester.** see 1786 Chamberlains.
1848 Walter Chamberlain and John Lilly became owners of the business.

1852-62 **Kerr & Binns period.**
Many new young designers employed during this period, such as, W.B. Kirk, T.Brock, T. Bott, and the Callowhill brothers.

1862-1900 **R. Binns formed a new stock company. Worcester Royal Porcelain Co. Ltd. (Royal Worcester)**

1862-67 Standard printed mark. Last two numbers of the year when present, indicate the date. i.e. `65` = 1865.

From 1867 a letter system was used to indicate the year of manufacture.
From 1876 the crown sits down onto the circle :-

A = 1867	K = 1875	U = 1883
B = 1868	L = 1876	V = 1884
C = 1869	M = 1877	W= 1885
D = 1870	N = 1878	X = 1886
E = 1871	P = 1879	Y = 1887
G = 1872	R = 1880	Z = 1888
H = 1873	S = 1881	O = 1889
I = 1874	T = 1882	a = 1890

Continued over -

1751

1751 WORCESTER, Warmstry House, England. (Cont`)

1889- **G. Grainger & Co. acquired.** see 1801 Grainger, Wood,
1902- Workforce of Grainger intergrated into Royal Worcester.

Royal Worcester was awarded many prizes for their products during this period especially at the Exhibitions in London, Paris, Melbourne and Vienna. In 1893 at the Chicago World Fair, Royal Worcester exhibited the largest vessel they have ever produced. The `Chicago Vase` was modelled by James Hadley, gilded by Josiah Davis and painted by Edward Raby.

From 1891 pieces were coded with a system of dots and/or symbols below the standard mark.

1892

1891 `Royal Worcester England` added.
1892 One dot. 1893 Two dots. 1894 Three dots.
Continued until 1915 when 24 dots are arranged around the standard mark.

1916

1916 * (star mark) below the backstamp.
1917 * and one dot. 1918 * and two dots.
Continued until 1927 when 11 dots are arranged around the standard mark.

c.1900 **E.P. Evans and C.W. Dyson-Perrins take over Company.**
1905- **James Hadley & Sons Ltd. acquired** see 1896 Hadley & Sons.
Hadley workforce absorbed into Royal Worcester.

1938

1928	▭	and the words `made in England`		
1929	◇	"	"	"
1930	÷	"	"	"
1931	∞	"	"	"
1932	ooo	"	"	"
1933	ooo•	"	"	"
1934	•ooo•	"	"	"

Continued until 1941 when there were 9 dots and the triple circle mark.

1930 Company went into the receivers hands. Mr. Dyson-Perrins took over the company and Joseph Gimson became Works Manager. Many freelance modellers were employed such as, Stella Crofts, Gwendoline Parnell, Fred Doughty and Doris Lindner, etc.
1935 Gwendoline Parnell`s figures of George V. and Queen Mary were issued as the first Limited Edition models.

Continued over -

1751 WORCESTER, Warmstry House, England. (Cont`)

1942-48 No dating system used.
1949 V
1950 W

1951 W. (With one dot)
1952 .W.
1953 .W. .

Continued until 1963 when 13 dots are arranged around the standard mark. After 1956 the letter `W` was nearly always substituted with the letter `R` in a circle. i.e. 1960 = R or W with 10 dots.
From 1963 all new marks have the year in full.

1956

1954-	**Worcester became a Public Company.**	
1958-	**Palissy Pottery Ltd. acquired.** - -	see 1905 Jones (Longton)
1976-	**Spode Ltd.,Josiah, acquired.** - -	see 1770 Spode, Josiah,
1976-	**Royal Worcester Spode Ltd. (Company re-named)**	

Dyson-Perrins Museum holds the finest collection of Worcester porcelain and china in the world and many thousands of visitors go there every year.
(By courtesy of Royal Worcester Spode Ltd., Severn St., Worcester.)

1751	Aran, Payrard, and Antheaume de Surval, France. -	see 1725 CHANTILLY.
1751	Barbet (decorator) France. - - - - - -	see 1745 SÈVRES.
1751	Fauchier, Joseph II. MARSEILLES, France. - -	see 1711 Fauchier Factory.
1751	Matsura, Prince of Hirado, Japan.- - - -	see 1580 HIZEN.
1751	Pajou (figures) France. - - - - - -	see 1745 SÈVRES.

1752 DUBLIN, Ireland.

1752-c.71 **Delamain, Captain Henry,**
TIN-GLAZED EARTHENWARE (DELFTWARE)

Most wares were unmarked

Mark on delft ware probably earlier than `Delamain`

c.1752-57 Rare mark - ***H.D.***

1770-1829 **Donovan & Son, John,** - - ***DONOVAN***
Decorator of English pottery and porcelain. Painted - ***DONOVAN DUBLIN***

1872-85 **Vodrey`s Pottery.** EARTHENWARE.
Impressed- ***VODREY DUBLIN POTTERY***

1752

1752 GERA, Thuringia, Germany.

c.1752-c.80 Faïence. - -

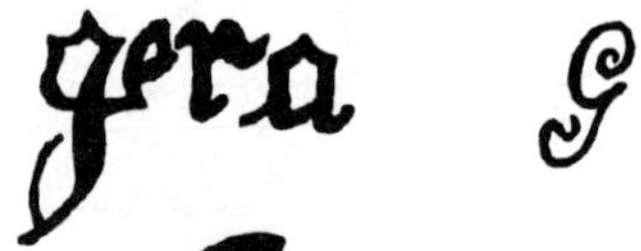

c.1752- Matthias Eichelroth, (painter) - -

1752 LIÈGE, Belgium.

1752-1811 Faïence. -

c.1770- Joseph Boussemaert-

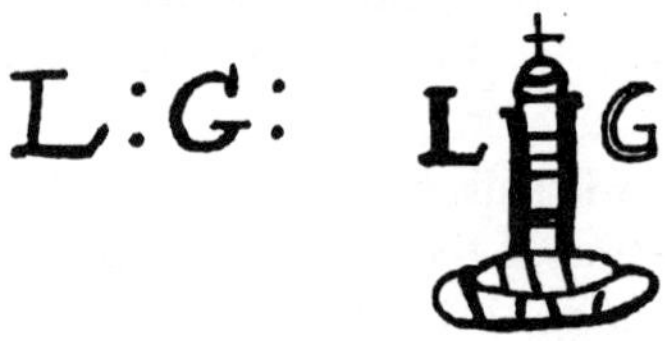

1775-1800 - - -

1752 POITIERS, Haute-Vienne, France.

1752 (dated) Morreine - - -

1776- Faïence.

Pierre Pasquier & Felix Faulcon- - -

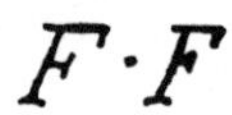

1752 SCHREZHEIM, Wurtemberg, Germany.

1752- Faïence. **(Founded by Wintergurt)**

c.1776-84 Joseph Jaumann, (painter) - -

1752 Vizeer, P., (Delft Artist) DELFT, Holland.

Tin-glazed earthenware (Delftware) - -

1752	Anteaume, Jean-Jacques (decorator) France. -	see 1745 SÈVRES.
1752	Carrié (decorator) France. - - - -	see 1745 SÈVRES.
1752	Chaffers, Richard, England. - - -	see 1743 LIVERPOOL.
1752	Evans, (decorator) France. - - - -	see 1745 SÈVRES.
1752	Genest, (figures) France. - - -	see 1745 SÈVRES.
1752	Fontaine, (decorator) France. - - -	see 1745 SÈVRES.
1752	Inuyama-Yaki, Japan. - - - -	see 1573 OWARI.
1752	Red Anchor, England. - - - -	see 1745 CHELSEA.
1752	Sioux aîné, (decorator) France. - - -	see 1745 SÈVRES.
1753	Sioux jeune, (decorator) France. - - -	see 1745 SÈVRES.
1752	Thévenet fils, (decorator) France. - - -	see 1745 SÈVRES.
1752	Vieillard, (painter) France. - - - -	see 1745 SÈVRES.

1753 FÜRSTENBERG, Brunswick, Germany.

1753-present day. HARD-PASTE PORCELAIN.

Duke Carl I of Brunswick.

Early marks- - in blue-

c.1790-c.1845 - - in blue-

Horse of Brunswick- Impressed-

Reproduction marks of old models

Modern marks. - - -

1753 GLIENITZ, Silesia, Germany.

1753- FAÏENCE AND GLAZED EARTHENWARE.

1767-c.1780 Countess Anna Barbara von Gaschin.

`Gaschin-Glienitz` - - -

1825-68 Cream and white earthenware-

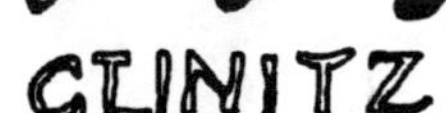

1830-70 - Mittelstadt. Impressed-

1753 GROSS-STIETEN, Mecklenberg, Germany.

c.1753 FAÏENCE.

von Hagen, (proprietor) - - -

Chely, Christoph Rudolph, - -

1753

1753 LA TOUR D'AIGUES, Vaucluse, France.

1753- FAÏENCE.

1773- Probably also made porcelain.

1753 NYMPHENBURG, nr.Munich, Bavaria, Germany.

1753- HARD-PASTE PORCELAIN.
Elector Maximilian III Joseph.
The wares are usually made in white and decorated elsewhere. This is why sometimes the shield will be impressed and the name of a Factory painted.

1753-57 Ringler, Josef Joachim, (technical director)

1754-64 Bustelli, Franz Anton, (Modellmeister) - F·B

1754-55 Ponnhauser, Josef, (modeller)

1756-58 Willand (decorator) - - J.W:

1757- Hartl, Johann Paul Rupert, (chemist)

1758-60 Georg Christoph Lindemann (painter) - - GCL 1758

Mark on a porcelain cup and saucer- *C.G. LINDEMAN Pinxit.*

1758-68 J.A. Huber (gilder) - -
With Arms of Bavaria -

.J765.
.JAH.

1758-1813 Kajetan Purtscher (painter) - C· Pulsher

c.1760 mark - -

1764-97 Auliczek, Dominikus, (Modellmeister)
1773- Appointed factory inspector.
1797- Dismissed as incompetent.

Continued over -

1753 NYMPHENBURG, nr. Munich, BavariaGermany. (Cont`)

1764-97 **Auliczek, Dominikus,** (Modellmeister) **(Cont`)**

1765-71 Johann Klein (painter) -

c.1765 Franz Jezinger (painter) -

1795-1814 Anton Auer (painter) -

1770 Maximilian III Josef died.

1770 **Karl Theodor of the Palatinate** Court of the Elector, who owned the Frankenthal factory, succeeded Maximilian.

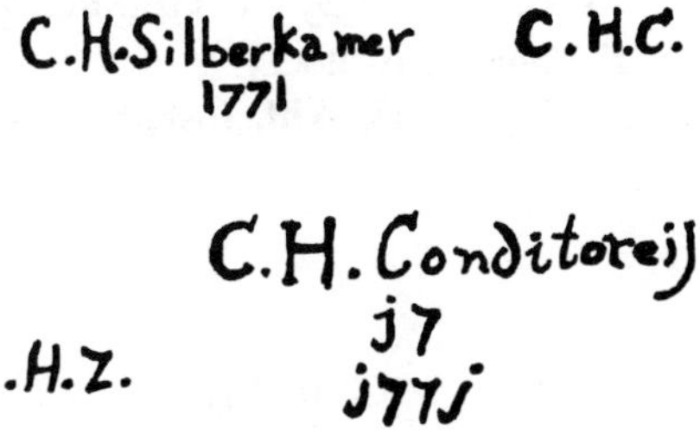

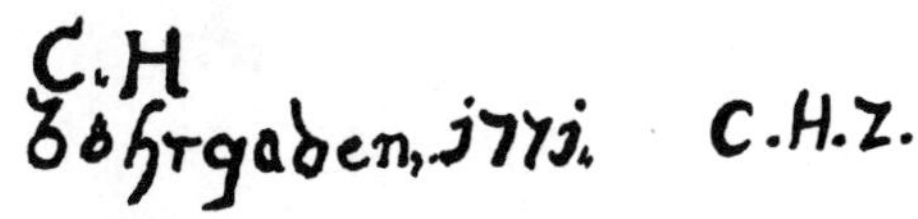

1799 Frankenthal closed and moulds were transferred to Nymphenburg. Moulds are still used today for reproducing old Frankenthal figures and groups.

1796-1810 **Melchior, Johann Peter,** (Modellmeister) -

1800-29 Adam Clair, (repairer) - - -

Modern marks. - - -

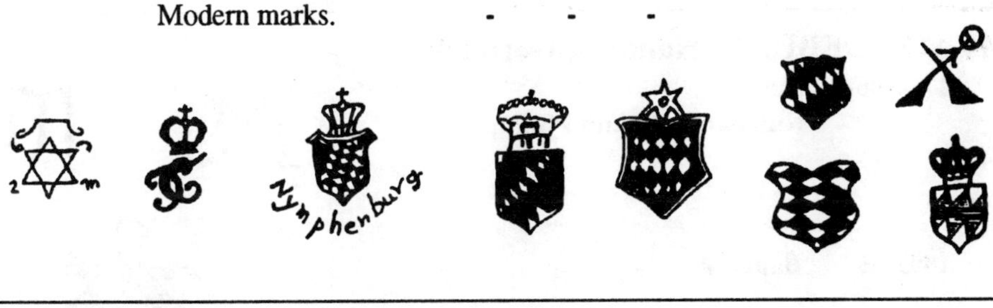

1753 SCHWERIN, Mecklenberg, Germany.

1753 FAÏENCE. - -

Apfelstädt, Johann Adam,-

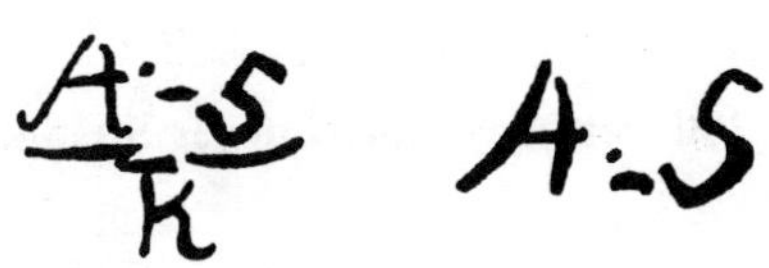

1753/54

1753 Chauveaux aîné, (gilder/painter) France. - - - see 1745 SÈVRES.
1753 Diefenbach (painter) Germany. - - - - see 1746 HÖCHST.
1753 Fontelliau, A. (gilder/colour maker) France. - - see 1745 SÈVRES.
1753 Ledoux, (decorator) France. - - - - see 1745 SÈVRES.
1753 Reid, William, England. - - - - - see 1743 LIVERPOOL.
1753 Rosset, (flowers/landscapes) France. - - - see 1745 SÈVRES.
1753 Taillandier, (flowers) France. - - - - see 1745 SÈVRES.
1753 Vavasseur aîné, (flowers) France. - - - - see 1745 SÈVRES.
1753 Vandé père, (gilder) France. - - - - see 1745 SÈVRES.
1753 Vincent aîné, (gilder) France. - - - - see 1745 SÈVRES.

1754 FRIEDBERG, nr.Augsburg, Bavaria, Germany.

1754-68 Faïence.

Hackhl, Joseph, - - -

`Chur-Bayen` - - - -

1754 Kastrup, COPENHAGEN, Denmark.

c.1754-1814 Faïence.

1754-62 **Fortling, Jacob,** - - -

1781-94 **Mantzius, Jacob C.L.,** - -

1754 MAGDEBURG, Hanover, Germany.

1754-86 Faïence.

Guichard, Johann Philipp.

1802-65 **Bauer, A.** - - -

20th century- Annaburger Steingutfabrik, - -

1754 NIDERVILLER, France.

1754- Faïence. **1765-** Porcelain.

1754-70 **Baron Jean-Louis de Beyerlé** - -
(Founder) In manganese brown or black-

Porcelain mark in blue-

1759-c.1808 Charles-Gabriel Sauvage,
(modeller) Also called`Lemire` Incised-

1770-93 **Comte de Custine** - -
Lanfrey, Claude-François (painter) blue-

In brown or black-

Porcelain mark usually blue or brown- -

1780- Paul-Louis Cyfflé`s moulds were aquired and used by the Factory.

1793-1827 **Claude-François Lanfrey.**
Became proprietor after the execution of the Count. Stencilled- -

c.1794 Mark on figures,
Impressed on applied label-

Late 18th century marks. black-

1754	Aubert aîné, (Flowers(France.	- - -	see 1745 SÈVRES.
1754	Boucher,(Flowers/garlands) France.	- -	see 1745 SÈVRES.
1754	Boulanger père, (gilder) France.	- - -	see 1745 SÈVRES.
1754	Bustelli, Franze, Germany.	- - -	see 1753 NYMPHENBURG.
1754	Gallimor, Shropshire, England.	- - -	see 1775 CAUGHLEY.
1754	Levé, Denis, (flowers/ornaments) France.	-	see 1745 SÈVRES.
1754	Méreault aîné, (flowers/borders) France.	- -	see 1745 SÈVRES.
1754	Mongenot, (Flowers) France.	- - -	see 1745 SÈVRES.
1754	Morin, (Military/seascapes) France.	- -	see 1745 SÈVRES.
1754	Mutel, (landscapes/birds) France.	- - -	see 1745 SÈVRES.
1754	Ponnhauser, Josef, Germany.	- - -	see 1753 NYMPHENBURG.
1754	Prévost aîné, (gilder) France.	- - -	see 1745 SÈVRES.
1754	Tabary, (birds) France.	- - - -	see 1745 SÈVRES.

1755

1755 ARNHEM, Holland.

1755-73 FAÏENCE. - - -
Kerckhoff, Joh. van,

1755 BONN, Rhineland, Germany.

1755- **Mehlem, Franz A.** POTTERY. -

1755 FRANKENTHAL, Palatinate, Germany.

1755-99 HARD-PASTE PORCELAIN AND SOME FAÏENCE.

Elector Palatine Karl Theodor in blue-

1755-c59 **Hannong, Paul Anton.** Impressed-

18th century faïence marks -

1756-75 **Luck, Karl Gottlieb,** modeller (1766 Modellmeister.)

1758-62 **Hannong, Joseph,** Incised- -

1759-62 **Hannong, Joseph-Adam.**(son) - -

1762- **Elector Palatine, Karl Theodore von der Pfalz aquired the factory.**
1762-66 **Linck, Franz Konrad,** (modellmeister.)

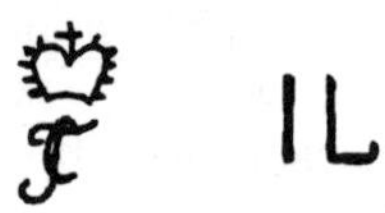

1762-70 **Bergdoll, Adam,** in blue- - -

1762-99 **Glöckel,** painter, enamel- - -

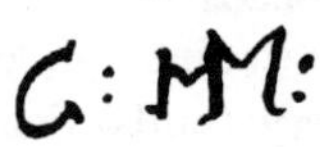

Continued over -

1755 FRANKENTHAL, Palatinate, Germany. (Cont`)

1765-84 **Appel,** painter. enamel-

1769-70 **Berthevin, Pierre,** Experimented with transfer printing.

1770- **Feilner, Simon,** Appointed inspector.
1775- Appointed director.

c.1770-88 Mark with last two numerals to indicate the year - -

1787-99 **Clair, Adam,** repairer. -

1795- **Recum, Peter van,** blue-

1797-98 **Recum, Johann Nepomuk van** Potter. in blue- -

1800 **Factory closed.** Moulds distributed between Grunstadt and Nymphenburg.

1755 LESUM, nr.Bremen, Germany.

1755-present day. FAÏENCE AND EARTHENWARE.

1755-94 Vielstich, Johann Christoph, -

Grote, PAINTER. - -

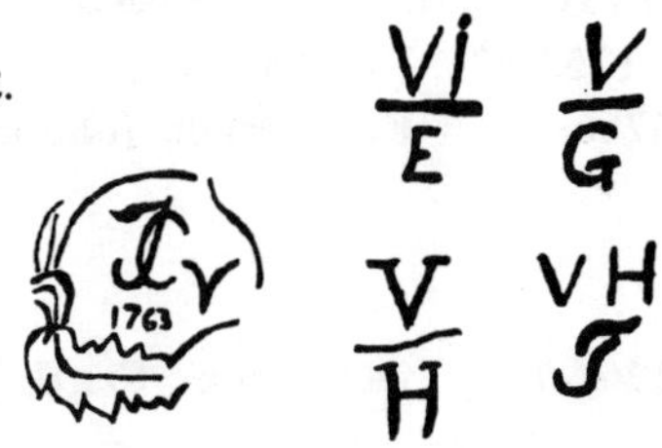

1755 POPPELSDORF, Bonn, Germany.

1755-present day. FAÏENCE AND EARTHENWARE.

1825- **Wessel, Ludwig.** - - -

c.1890- -

1755

1755 SCHLESWIG, Germany.

1755-1814 FAÏENCE.
Ludwig von Lücke, Otto, Burgomaster, and Johann Rambusch. - - -

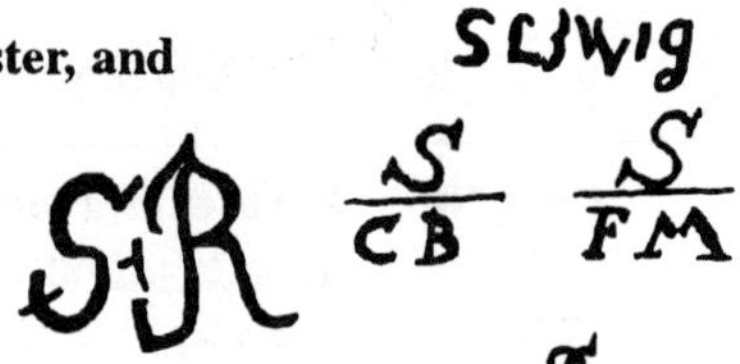

1755-56 **Otte & Lücke** - - - - - - -

1758- **Rambusch took over the factory.** - -

1760-65 **Ewald, Johann Cornelius,** painter. - - -

1761-65 **Odewald, Boerre,** painter. - - -

1764-91 **Conrade Bade,** painter. - - -

1773 **Rambusch died.** Factory passed to his son.
1800-03 **Lachmann and Wolff**
1814- **Factory closed.**

1755 STRALSUND, Pomerania, Germany.

c.1755-92 FAÏENCE.
1766- **Ehrenreich, Johann Eberhardt Ludwig,**

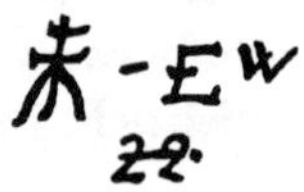

1767-79 **Oehrstrom, Friedrich Christian,**- -

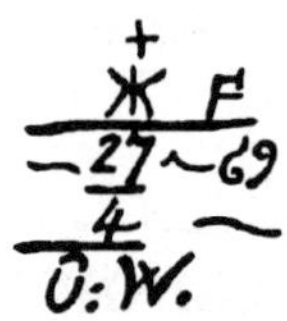

1770 (dated) Factory mark - - -

Frantzen, Johann Otto, painter. - -

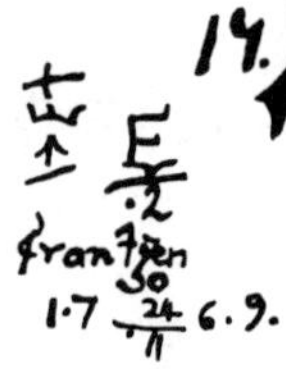

Dettloff, Christian Adam, painter. -

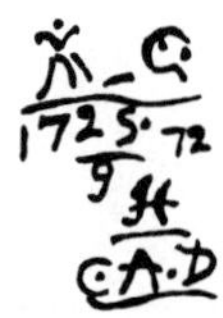

1755 Anreiter, Antonius, Austria. - - - see 1719 VIENNA.
1755 Antonibon's Fabrique, Italy. - - - see 1728 NOVE.
1755 Chaffers, Richard, England. - - - see 1743 LIVERPOOL.
1755 Chevalier, (flowers) France. - - - see 1745 SÈVRES.
1755 Chulot,(flowers/emblems) France. - - see 1745 SÈVRES.
1755 Cornailles, Antoine-Toussaint, France. - - see 1745 SÈVRES.
1755 Dumetz, François, France. - - - - see 1730 AIRE.
1755 Héricourt,(flowers) France. - - - see 1745 SÈVRES.
1755 Noël, (figures) France. - - - - see 1745 SÈVRES.
1755 Parpette,(flowers) France. - - - - see 1745 SÈVRES.

1756 Dieul, (painter) ROUEN, France.

c.1756 FAÏENCE. - - -

1756 Hancock, Robert, WORCESTER, England.

c.1756-65 Engraver of transfer prints. Worked for Caughley and other factories. -

1756 LUDWIGSBURG, Wurtemberg, Germany.

1756-1824 HARD-PASTE PORCELAIN.
1756- B.C. Hackher first attempted to make porcelain.

1758-93 **Duke Karl Eugen acquired factory. (Duke of Wurtemberg)**
1759-99 **J.G. Ringer, Director.**

G.F. Riedel, Obermaler.

1760-70 Marks usually on figures -

1760-89 J.G. Heinzenmann, painter - enamel colours-
1760-1802 D.C. Sausenhofer,painter- enamel colours-

1761- **Johann Martin Frantz**

Marks similar to Niderviller and Brunswick. -

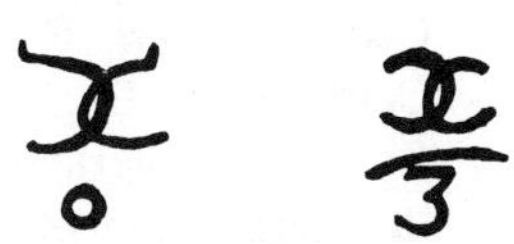

1762-72 **Jean-Jacob Louis,** Modellmeister.
1763- FAÏENCE. **Pieces are exceptionally rare.**
1764-67 **Domenico Feretti (Court Sculptor)**

Continued over -

1756

1756 LUDWIGSBURG, Wurtemberg, Germany. (Cont`)

1764-70 Johann Michael Burckhardt, Painter.

c.1765- J.J. Grothe, painter, enamel colours- 

c.1785- **P.J. Scheffauer.**

J.H. Dannecker.

c.1785- Stag`s horns from arms of Wurtemberg.-  

1793-95 **Duke Ludwig.** - - - 

1806-16 **King Friedrich.** - - - -  

1806-18 Mark used during this period. -

1816-24 **King Wilhelm.** - - - 

1818 Mark used after this date - - 

1948- **Modern marks** -    

1756 Sadler, John, & Green, Guy, LIVERPOOL, England.

PRINTING ON CERAMICS. Wedgwood and other factories used their printing process.

Green, Liverpool

J. Sadler, Liverpool

1756 Bienfait, Jean-Baptiste, (gilder) France. - - - see 1745 SÈVRES.
1756 Bourgoin, Jean-Baptiste-Alexis, France. - - - see 1650 RENNES.
1756 Buteux, (figures) France. - - - - - see 1745 SÈVRES.
1756 Chappuis aîné, (flowers) France. - - - - see 1745 SÈVRES.
1756 Derby Porcelain Works, England.- - - - see 1749 DERBY.
1756 Dubois, Jean-René, (flowers) France. - - - see 1745 SÈVRES.
1756 Duesbury, William, England. - - - - see 1749 DERBY.
1756 Genin, (flowers) France. - - - - - see 1745 SÈVRES.
1756 Gold Anchor, England. - - - - - see 1745 CHELSEA.
1756 Gomery, (birds/flowers) France. - - - - see 1745 SÈVRES.
1756 `Kinkozan` Kagiya and family, YAMASHIRO, Japan. - see 1655 Ninsei.
1756 Laurens Basso A. Toulouza, France. - - - see 1650 TOULOUSE.
1756 Lessel, Johann Otto, Germany. - - - - see 1625 HAMBURG.

Continued over -

1756	Louis, Jean, (modeller) France. - -	see 1650 ORLEANS.
1756	Luck, Karl Gottlieb, (modeller) Germany.	see 1755 FRANKENTHAL.
1756	Mathieu, Simon, France. - - -	see 1734 MENNECY-VILLEROY.
1756	Petit aîné, (gilder) France. - - -	see 1745 SÈVRES.
1756	Renault, Pierre, France. - - -	see 1650 ORLEANS.
1756	Rubati, Pasquale, Italy, - - -	see 1725 MILAN.
1756	Tandart, (flowers) France. - - -	see 1745 SÈVRES.
1756	Willand, (decorator) Germany. - -	see 1753 NYMPHENBERG.

1757 de twee Wildemans (The Two Wild Men) DELFT, Holland.

1757- TIN-GLAZED EARTHENWARE (DELFTWARE)

1757- **Bogaert, Matheus van der,** - -

1764- **Beek, Willem van,** - - -

1757 GOTHA, Thuringia, Germany.

1757-present day. HARD-PASTE PORCELAIN.

c.1757-1795 Wilhelm von Rotberg (Founder) -

1795-1802 widow sold 1802.

1772- **Gabel,** painter.
Schulz and Brehm.
Ruger, painter.
Frey, painter.

1802 Prince August von Gotha - -
Gabel, Schulz and Brehm,
Directed the factory with Henneberg.

1813-34 **Egidius Henneberg** (proprietor)
1834-81 Family continued.

c.1850- `Hennebergsche Porzellan -
Manufaktur`
On lithophanies.

1866- **Morgenroth & Co.,** - -

1883- **Gebr. Simson.** - - -

1892- **Fr. Pfeffer,** FAIENCE AND PORCELAIN. - -
FIGURES AND DOLLS` HEADS.

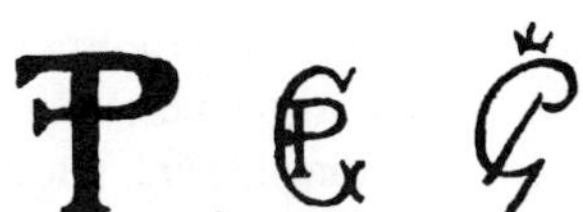

20th century mark. - -

1757/58

1757 HERREBØE, nr. Friedrichshald, Norway.

1757-c.72 FAÏENCE.

c.1758- **Peter Hofnagel** (Founder) - -

Joseph Large. Signature mark-

c.1760- **H.C.F. Hosenfeller,** painter- -

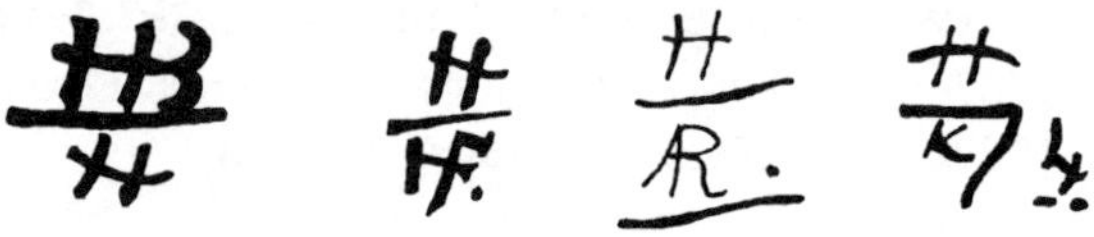

1757 LOWESTOFT, Suffolk, England.

c.1757-1802 SOFT-PASTE PORCELAIN.

Founders were Philip Walker, Robert Browne, Obed Aldred and John Richman.

1757- Robert Allen entered the firm at 12 years of age and eventually became manager. After the closure of the factory, he opened a retail shop, with a kiln out the back where he decorated wares.

c.1760-75 Early workman`s marks. - -
Painted in underglaze blue, usually on inner wall of foot rim.

1770 **Robert Browne & Co.,**
c.1775-90 Meissen crossed swords and the crescent of Worcester imitations.-

1757 Michel Vallet (potter) ROUEN, France.

1757- POTTERS. - - - - - - -

1757	Bouchet, Jean,(landscapes) France. - -	see 1745 SÈVRES.
1757	Catrice, (flowers) France. - - - - -	see 1745 SÈVRES.
1757	Erberfield, Albrecht von, Germany. - -	see 1751 AUMUND.
1757	Ginori, Senator Lorenzo, Italy. - - -	see 1735 DOCCIA.
1757	Hartl, Johann Paul Rupert, Germany. - -	see 1753 NYMPHENBURG.
1757	Micaud, Jacques, (flowers/ornaments) France. -	see 1745 SÈVRES.
1757	Pithou aîné, (figures) France. - - -	see 1745 SÈVRES.
1757	Tardi, (bouquets) France. - - - -	see 1745 SÈVRES.
1757	Weydinger père, (flowers/gilding) France. -	see 1745 SÈVRES.

1758 ELLWANGEN, Würtemberg, Germany.

c.1758- HARD-PASTE PORCELAIN. underglaze blue-

1758 KELSTERBACH, Hesse Darmstadt, Germany.

1758-c.1823 FAIENCE AND CREAMWARES. - -

1758- Frede, Johann Christian and Maritz, Kaspar, FAÏENCE.

1761-c.95 Porcelain Factory.

Landgrave, Ludwig VIII. - -

1761-64 Busch, Christian Daniel, of Meissen (director)

Vogelmann, Karl, modeller.

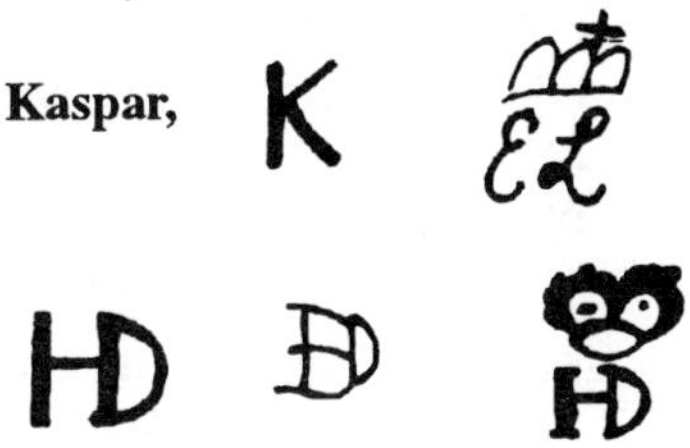

Seefried, Peter Antonius, modeller. - **S**

1758- MARIEBERG, nr. Stockholm, Sweden.

1758- FAÏENCE. **1766-** PORCELAIN.

The individual factories and potters of MARIEBERG have been listed under their own dates and marks within this book.

1758 SAINT-CLÉMENT, Meurthe-et-Moselle, France.

FAÏENCE, and a branch of Lunéville producing white biscuit figures. - `SC`

see 1728 LUNÉVILLE

1758. Jacques Chambrette died.

1758-63 Charles Loyal and Paul-Louis Cyfflé -

19th Century marks - - *`St.Clement`* *`St. Ct`*

1758 Thion, Jean-François, MOUSTIERS, France.

1758-88 FAÏENCE. - - -

1758	Aloncle, Françios, France. - - - - -	see 1745 SÈVRES.
1758	Chambrette, G. and Loyal, C., LUNÉVILLE, France.	see 1731 Chambrette, Jacques,
1758	Eugen, Duke Karl, Germany. - - -	see 1756 LUDWIGSBURG.
1758	Hannong, Joseph, Germany. - - -	see 1755 FRANKENTHAL.
1758	Hewelcke, Nathaniel Friedrich, Italy. - -	see 1550 VENICE.
1758	Hofnagel, Peter, Norway. - - - -	see 1757 HERREBOW.
1758	Huber, J.A., (gilder) Germany. - - -	see 1753 NYMPHENBURG.
1758	Kandler, Johann Friedrich, Germany. - -	see 1711 ANSBACH.
1758	La Roche, (flowers) France. - - -	see 1745 SÈVRES.
1758	Lindemann, George Christoph, Germany. -	see 1753 NYMPHENBURG.
1758	Purtscher, Kajetan, Germany. - - -	see 1753 NYMPHENBURG.
1758	Rambusch, Germany. - - - -	see 1755 SCHLESWIG.
1758	Rocher, (figures) France. - - - -	see 1745 SÈVRES.
1758	Rouselle, (flowers) France. - - -	see 1745 SÈVRES.
1758	Willading, Augustin, Switzerland. - -	see 1725 BERNE.
1758	Wolf, Joseph, (director) Austria. - - -	see 1719 VIENNA.

1759

1759 AMBERG, Bavaria, Germany.

1759-1910 EARTHENWARE. FAÏENCE.
1790- STONEWARE BEGUN.
1836- **Mayer, Stephan, and Son,**
1850- **Kick, Eduard.**

CREAMWARES, HARD-PASTE PORCELAIN, and reproductions of Ludwigsburg porcelain models. - ***AMBERG***

1759 de Lampetkan (The Ewer) DELFT, Holland.

1759- TIN-GLAZED EARTHENWARE (DELFTWARE)

1759- **Gerrit Brouwer** - -

1780- **Abraham van der Keel** -

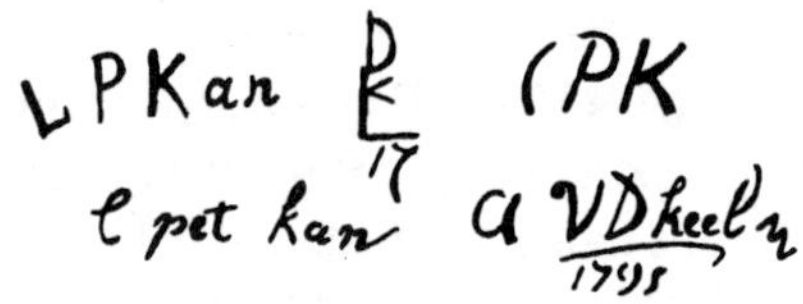

1759 Hoetem, Phillippus, (Delft Artist) DELFT, Holland.

TIN-GLAZES EARTHENWARE (DELFTWARE) - -

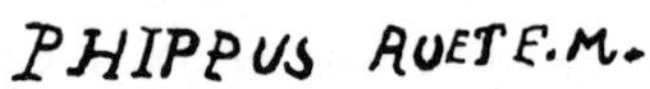

1759 Kyomizu, YAMASHIRO, Japan.

1759- Rokubei, potter (died) - -
1811- Rokubei Seisai (son)
1860- Sho-un (grandson)

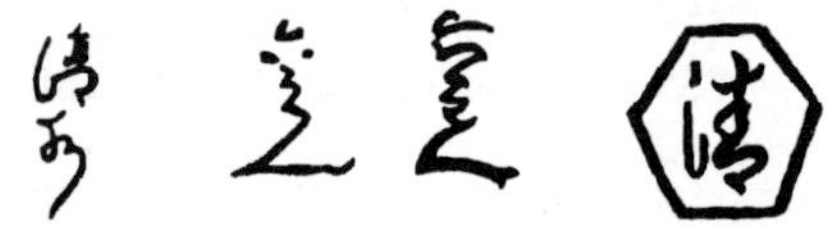

1759 Wedgwood, Josiah & Sons Ltd.,Barlaston, Staffordshire, England.

c.1759- **Burslem Factory.** GENERAL CERAMICS.
c.1759-c.69 impressed mark -

c.1759- These marks sometimes appear in a curve, this is due to the letters being individually impressed-

1762- Creamware introduced known as Queen`s ware by royal consent of Queen Charlotte.

c.1769-80 **Wedgwood & Bentley .** impressed Marks on Ornamental wares. The addition of `Etruria` is rare.

WEDGWOOD & BENTLEY

WEDGWOOD & BENTLEY ETRURIA

impressed- - **W. & B.**

1769- **Etruria Factory opened 13th June.**
1769-80 Mark used on useful wares-
1780 onwards, used on all wares- - **WEDGWOOD**

c.1769-80 Earliest form of the Wedgwood & Bentley mark. Used on ornamental wares only. -

Continued over -

1759 Wedgwood, Josiah & Sons Ltd., Barlaston, England. (Cont`)

1769-80 Impressed or raised mark found on the inside corner of plinths of early Black Basalt vases, and sometimes on the pedestals of busts and large figures. Sometimes appears without the word `Etruria`

1769-80 Mark found around the screw - on Black Basalt, granite and Etruscan vases.

1769-80 Marks impressed on small cameos and intaglios. Sometimes bear catalogue numbers. — **Wedgwood & Bentley 356** — **W. & B.**

1780- (November) Thomas Bentley died

1780-c.95 `Upper and lower case` mark Used on all types of wares. Impressed- — **Wedgwood.**

c.1790- Wedgwood & Sons
Rare impressed mark- — **WEDGWOOD & SONS**

1795- Josiah Wedgwood died, and is remembered as `The Father of English Potters`

c.1805 Used by Josiah Wedgwood II on lustre wares, Black Basalt, and Jasper pieces. (Very rare) — **JOSIAH WEDGWOOD Feb. 2nd. 1805**

c.1812-29 Printed on bone china in red, blue or gold- — **WEDGWOOD**

c.1827-61 Rare printed mark on stone - china. - - — **WEDGWOOD`S STONE CHINA**

c.1840-45 Impressed- — **WEDGWOOD ETRURIA**

c.1840-68 `Pearlware` Impressed- — **PEARL**
1868- Impressed- — **P**

Continued over -

1759

1759 Wedgwood, Josiah & Sons Ltd., Barlaston, England. (Cont`)

1860 - In addition to the normal Wedgwood mark, a system of three letter date marks were used. The first letter indicated the month, the second the potter, and the third the year.

First letter for the month:-

January -	J	July	V (1860-63)
February-	F		L (1864-1907)
March -	M (1860-63)	Aug	W
-	R (1864-1907)	Sept.	S
April -	A	Oct	O
May -	Y (1860-63)	Nov.	N
-	M (1864-1907)	Dec.	D
June -	T		

Third letter for the year:-

A	-	1872 -	1898
B	-	1873 -	1899
C	-	1874 -	1900
D	-	1875 -	1901
E	-	1876 -	1902
F	-	1877 -	1903
G	-	1878 -	1904
H	-	1879 -	1905
I	-	1880 -	1906
J	-	1881	
K	-	1882	
L	-	1883	
M	-	1884	
N	-	1885	
O	1860	1886	
P	1861	1887	
Q	1862	1888	
R	1863	1889	
S	1864	1890	
T	1865	1891	
U	1866	1892	
V	1867	1893	
W	1868	1894	
X	1869	1895	
Y	1870	1896	
Z	1871	1897	

The years 1860-64 and 1886-90 indicate two possible dates. (i.e. JBS could be January 1864 or 1890)
From 1891 the words `England` appeared on wares.

Continued over -

1759 Wedgwood, Josiah & Sons Ltd., Barlaston, England. (Cont`)

From 1907 the figure 3 was substituted for the first (month) letter.
From 1924 the figure 4 was used. The last letter continued to indicate the year, as shown below:-

(3) J	1907	(3) V	1919
K	1908	W	1920
L	1909	X	1921
M	1910	Y	1922
N	1911	Z	1923
O	1912	(4) A	1924
P	1913	B	1925
Q	1914	C	1926
R	1915	D	1927
S	1916	E	1928
T	1917	F	1929
U	1918		

(Examples 3BS = 1916, 4BD = 1927)

The following potters` marks can help to date `Pearl Ware` and cream-ware of the 19th Century. In some cases, it can also identify the potter responsible for a particular item.

1812-16	Mark used on Bone China - -	G G
1817-20	" " " " - -	T
1818-21	Small squares usually on plates- Various sizes-	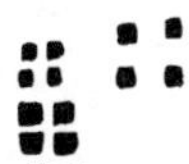
1821-30	Mark on soup plates. - -	8 8
1826-35	Mark. - - - -	0 0
1830-	Mark. - - - -	H H
1834-	Mark used on plates.- - -	K4
c.1845-	John Travis (plate and dishmaker) -	
1853-83	John Travis (plates and certain Majolica wares) -	●

<u>**Marks used by hollow ware pressers-**</u>

1852-	Thomas Tooth. - - -	D E
1852-	Robert Williamson. - - -	T U
1853-	William Morgan. - - -	( )
1854-	Herbert Bell. - - - -	T T
1854-	Hensleigh Bowers. - - -	♡ ♡
1854-	Edward Finney. - - -	X X
1854-	James Smith. - - - -	G^tG^t
1855-	John Steele. - - - -	25
1860	Henry Kerry. - - - -	X
1860-	Henry Parker.- - - -	Q

Continued over -

1759

1759 Wedgwood, Josiah & Sons Ltd., Barlaston, England. (Cont`)

Marks used by various potters.

1850-55	Mark in use. - - - -	**S S**
1852-	Eli Till (dish maker) - - -	**C**
1853-	William Dawson (plate maker) -	**C D**
1855-	George Platt and Henry Parker. -	**5 5**
1855-	John Keel (comport maker) - -	**2 5**
1859-	Thomas Adams (dish maker) -	*****
1859-	Thomas Horwell (plate maker) -	**O**
1859-	Joseph Johnson (plate maker) -	**H**

From 1930 the actual date was applied on the wares, first as the last two figures of a mark sequence which included the month and the potter` Example: 3B35 = March 1935, and later simply as two figures, Example: 57 = 1957. Sometimes workmen`s errors occur, and also the letters are not always legible.

c.1858-76 **Lessore, Emile,** (decorator) - -

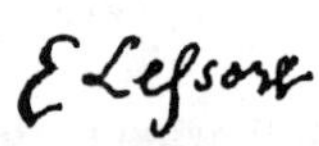

c.1878- **Portland vase mark,** printed on bone-china - - -

1891 - `England` added.

c.1910 - `Made in England` added -

c.1920 - `Bone China` added. -

1929 - Sans serif type mark - **WEDGWOOD**

1940- **Barlaston Factory established**

c.1940 Printed mark on Queen`s ware -

c.1950-62 `Rejafix` machine-printed mark used on bone-china. - -
(1962 Normal version printed mark)

1952- Printed on engraved patterns - **ENGRAVED BY WEDGWOOD STUDIO**

Continued over -

1759 Wedgwood, Josiah & Sons Ltd., Barlaston, England. (Cont`)

1967- `Oven-to-Tableware` mark -

1967- `Georgetown Collection` mark -

Modern marks in use today (1995) :-

WEDGWOOD®

(By kind permission of Josiah Wedgwood & Sons Ltd., Stoke-on-Trent, England.)

1759 WEESP, Holland.

1759-71 HARD-PASTE PORCELAIN. underglaze blue-
1771 Moved to Oude Loosdrecht.

1759	Appel, Johannes van den, DELFT, Holland. -	see 1663 de boot.
1759	Berg, Justus de, DELFT, Holland. - -	see 1689 de Star.
1759	Brouwer, Joost, DELFT, Holland.- - -	see 1679 Het Bijltje.
1759	Burch, Paulus van der, DELFT, Holland.- -	see 1693 de vergulde Bloempot.
1759	Buteux père, (flowers) France. - - -	see 1745 SÈVRES.
1759	Briel, P.van den,/Elling, Elisabeth, DELFT, Holland.	see 1692 de Fortuyn.
1759	Dextra, Jan Theunis, DELFT, Holland. - -	see 1645 De Grieksche A.
1759	Does, Dirck van der, DELFT, Holland. - -	see 1675 de Roos.
1759	Does, W. van der, DELFT, Holland. - -	see 1671 de trie Klokken
1759	Gaal, Cornelia, DELFT, Holland. - - -	see 1671 de trie Klokken.
1759	Govert, Henderick, Holland. - - -	see 1630 ROTTERDAM.
1759	Hannong, Joseph-Adam, Germany. - -	see 1755 FRANKENTHAL.
1759	Hoorn, Hendrik van, DELFT, Holland. - -	see 1655 De 3 Astonne.
1759	Kruisweg, Anthone, DELFT, Holland. - -	see 1648 De oud Moriaanshooft.
1759	`Lemire` France.- - - - -	see 1754 NIDERVILLER.
1759	Marum, Petrus van, DELFT, Holland. - -	see 1671 De Romeyn.
1759	Mérault jeune, (flowers) France. - - -	see 1745 SÈVRES.
1759	Milde, Jac.de, DELFT, Holland. - - -	see 1651 De Paauw.
1759	Pennis, A.,DELFT, Holland. - - -	see 1642 De twee Scheepjes.
1759	Pierre aîné, gilder, France. - - - -	see 1745 SÈVRES.
1759	Ringer, J.G. Germany. - - - -	see 1756 LUDWIGSBURG.
1759	Sauvage, Charles-Gabriel, France. - -	see 1754 NIDERVILLER.
1759	Verhagen, Joh., DELFT, Holland. - - -	see 1720 de jonge Moriaans hooft.

1760 Billinge, Thomas, LIVERPOOL, England. - - *Billinge Sculp*

c.1760-80 ENGRAVER. - Signature mark - *Liverpool*

1760

1760 BUEN RETIRO, Madrid, Spain.

1760-1804 SOFT-PASTE PORCELAIN.
1804-1808 HARD-PASTE PORCELAIN.
1760-1808 **Charles III Bourbon, King of Naples.**
Continuation of Capo-di-monte of Italy.

1760-70 **Gricci, from Capo-de-Monte,** -
Chief modeller.

1775- **Nofri, Salvador,** - - - - -

1804-1808 Hard-paste porcelain mark. - -

1760 Coade`s Artificial Stone Works, LAMBETH, London England.

c.1760- TERRA-COTTA, ARTIFICIAL STONE, ETC.
Mr.& Mrs. Coade (founders) - - ***COADE LAMBETH***
1769 Mr. Sealy (nephew) taken into partnership.
1811- **Coade & Sealy (new partnership)**

1760 Eberhard, Johann & Ehrenreich, Ludwig, MARIEBERG, Sweden.

1760-66 FAÏENCE - - -

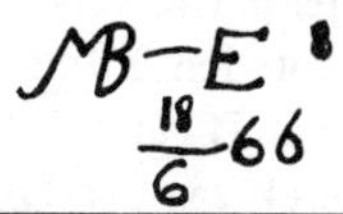

1760 Edkins, Michael and Betty, BRISTOL, England.

c.1760- DELFT WARE PAINTER - - -
Mark on dated blue plate-

(see Ceramic Art of Great Britain by Jewitt)

1760 ÉPINAL, Vosges, France.

c1760- FAIENCE AND CREAMWARES. Impressed- ***ÉPINAL***
François Vautrin
Stanlislas, King of Poland (protector)
1766- **Le Bon, brothers.**

1760 FENTON, Staffordshire, England.

Situated between Stoke and Longton. Several factories have managed their businesses from this well known region of Staffordshire.
The individual factories and potters of FENTON have been listed under their own dates and marks within this book.

1760 Fournier, Louis, COPENHAGEN, Denmark.

1760-66 SOFT-PASTE PORCELAIN. blue enamel-
Frederik V of Denmark.

1760 Giustiniani, Nicola, NAPLES, Italy.

1760 CREAMWARES AND PORCELAIN.

c.1790 Giustiniani, Biagio, (son) - ***BG N***

Fabbrica Michele Giustiniani - ***FMG***
Napoli. - ***N***
Giustiniani, Antonio and Salvatore,
\`Fratelli Giustiniani Napoli\` - ***FG N***

1760 Greatbatch, William, FENTON, Staffordshire, England.

c.1760-80 EARTHENWARE. MODELLER AND POTTER. Printed- ***GREATBATCH***
Colleague of Josiah Wedgwood.

1760 Guichard, Antony, MOUSTIERS, France.

c.1760 FAÏENCE. - - -

1760 JEVER, Oldenburg, Germany.

1760-76 FAÏENCE. - - -
Johann Friedrich Samuel Tännich.

1760 KLOSTER-VEILSDORF, Thuringia, Germany.

c.1760-95 **Prince Wilhelm Eugen von Hildburhausen** (Founder)
Friedrich Doll (Court Sculptor) made Director.
HARD-PASTE PORCELAIN.

c.1777-83 Kotta, Franz, modeller.

1789- Greiner,Wilhelm Heinrich, -

1797-1822 Greiner family acquired the factory. -

Modern factory marks- - -

1760

1760 LENZBURG, Switzerland.

18th century FAÏENCE.

c.1767 **Hunerwadel, Marcus**

Klug, A.H. & H.C.,-

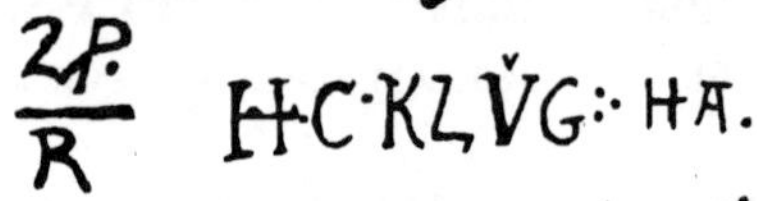

1774-96 **Frey, Hans Jacob,** - - -

1760 LEEDS POTTERY, Yorkshire, England.

c.1760- EARTHENWARES, CREAM-WARES, BASALT, ETC. — **MOST WARES WERE UNMARKED**

c.1760- **Records seem to suggest that the two Green brothers were the first notable proprietors of the Leeds Pottery.**

c.1770- impressed mark - **LEEDS * POTTERY**

1773- **Humble, Green & Co.** - - - **LEEDS POTTERY**

Impressed mark (rare) - **L P**

1783- **Hartley, Greens & Co.**

1783- Book of designs issued in English French and German.

1794- 2nd. edition of catalogue and pattern book was produced.

Greens, Hartley & Co.

LEEDS. POTTERY

Impressed marks:-

1825- **Samuel Wainwright & Co.**

1832 Samuel Wainwright died.

1832- **Leeds Pottery Company,**

Trustees carried on the business.

HARTLEY GREENS & Co.
LEEDS POTTERY

1840-47 **Stephen and James Chappell.**

1850- **Samuel Warburton,**

Warburton and Britton,

1863- Mr Warburton died

1863- **Richard Britton (sole proprietor)**

1872 John and Alfred (sons) join the business.

Impressed mark -

1872-78 **Richard Britton & Sons.**

Initials printed within marks of various designs- **R. B.& S.**

(For further information see `Jewitts` Ceramic art in Great Britain)

1760 MOSCOW, Russia.

c.1760 HARD-PASTE PORCELAIN.

The individual factories and potters of MOSCOW have been listed under their own dates and marks within this book.

1760 Palmer, Humphrey, HANLEY, Staffordshire, England.

c.1760-78 EARTHENWARES, STONEWARES. impressed -

Wedgwood type.

1760 Shore, Joseph, Isleworth, LONDON, England.

1760-1800 PORCELAIN. - - - ***SHORE & CO***

S. & CO.

S. & G.

Richard Goulding (painter) was a partner. ***ISLEWORTH***

William Goulding (son) assisted in the factory.

Mark on dated piece - ***Wm. GOULDING***

June 20th, 1770

1760 TAVERNES, nr.Moustiers, France.

1760-80 **Gaze,** Faïence. - -

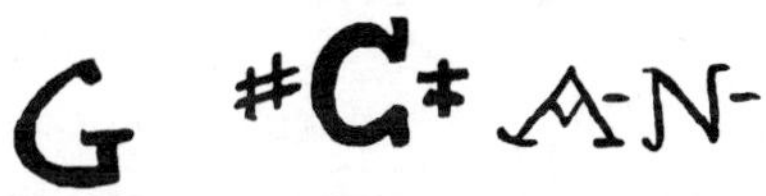

1760 Verhaast, Gysbert, (Delft Artist) DELFT, Holland.

TIN-GLAZED EARTHENWARE (DELFTWARE) - -

1760	Boileau, M., France. - - - -	see 1745 SÈVRES.
1760	Deare & Co., Thomas, England. - - -	see 1743 LIVERPOOL.
1760	Ewald, Johann Cornelius, Germany. - -	see 1755 SCHLESWIG.
1760	Flint Pot Works, England. - - - -	see 1743 LIVERPOOL.
1760	Frisching, Franz Rudolf, Switzerland, - -	see 1725 BERNE.
1760	Heinzenmann, J.G., Germany. - - -	see 1756 LUDWIGSBURG.
1760	Hosenfeller, H.C.F. painter, Norway. - -	see 1757 HERREBOE.
1760	Pennington, Seth, England. - - -	see 1743 LIVERPOOL.
1760	Pfeiffer, Johann Georg, BAYREUTH, Germany.	see 1747 Pfeiffer & Fränkel
1760	Pithou jeune, (flowers/ornaments) France. -	see 1745 SÈVRES.
1760	Sausenhofer, D.C. (painter) Germany. - -	see 1756 LUDWIGSBURG.

1761 MONTAUBAN, in Quercy, Tarn-et-Garonne, France.

1761-c.1810 FAÏENCE. - - *`Montauban en Quercy 1799`*

1778- **Lestrade, D.,**

1761/62

1761	Buckwald, Johann, Germany. - - -	see 1765 ECKERNFÖRDE.
1761	Busch, Christian Daniel, Germany. - -	see 1758 KELSTERBACH.
1761	Cuccumos, Filippo, Italy. - - - -	see 1600 ROME.
1761	Frantz, Johann Martin, Germany. - - -	see 1756 LUDWIGSBURG.
1761	Gotzkowsky, Johann Ernst, Germany. - -	see 1751 BERLIN.
1761	Landgrave, Ludwig VIII., Germany. - -	see 1758 KELSTERBACH.
1761	Langendorf, Christian Andreas(son) Germany -	see 1720 ZERBST.
1761	Odewald, Boerre, (painter) Germany. - -	see 1755 SCHLESWIG.

1762 Bonnefoy`s Factory, MARSEILLES, France.

1762-c.1827 Bonnefoy, Antoine, (d.1793) FAÏENCE.

1803- HARD-PASTE PORCELAIN.

1762 CRÉPY-EN-VALOIS, Oise, France.

1762-70 SOFT-PASTE PORCELAIN. incised-

Gaignepain, Louis-François.

1762 Gros Caillou, or Vaugirand-lès-Paris, PARIS, France.

c.1762 **Broillet, Jacques-Louis,** HARD-PASTE PORCELAIN-

1773- **Advenier and Lamare.** - -

1762 KATZHÜTTE, Thuringia, Germany.

1864- Hertwig & Co., HARD-PASTE PORCELAIN. -

1762 KIEL, Holstein, Germany.

1762-c.93 FAÏENCE. - - - -

c.1762-66 **J.S.F. Tännich.** - -

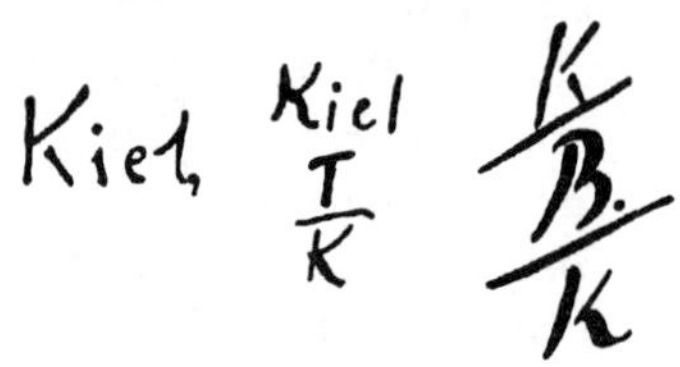

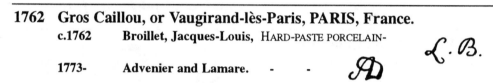

1766- **Renners and Newman** (proprietors) -
Jean Buchwald (master potter)
c.1768 Made director.
Abraham Leihamer (painter) -

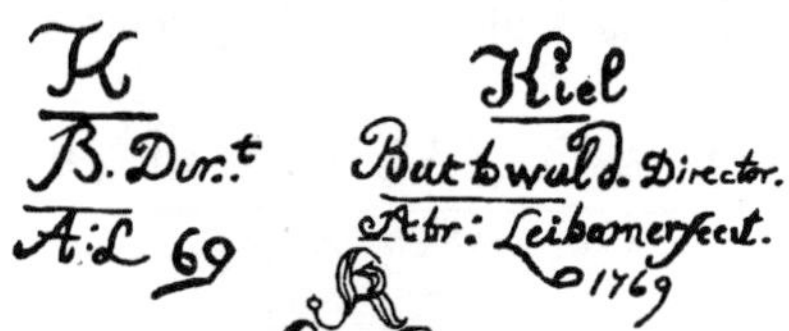

c.1900-c24 **Kieler Kunst-Keramik** - -

1762 LANE END, Longton,Staffordshire, England.

A Staffordshire region where many factories are still producing.
The individual factories and potters of LANE END have been listed under their own dates and marks within this book.

1762 LONGTON, Staffordshire, England.

Yet another Staffordshire region that produced some of the best earthenware and still producing it today.
The individual factories and potters of LONGTON have been listed under their own dates and marks within this book.

1762 Maling, William, North Hylton Pottery, SUNDERLAND, England.

1762-67 EARTHENWARES. impressed- ***MALING***
Continued by Family until 1815
Transferred to Ouseburn Pottery. see 1817 Robert Maling

1815-67 **Phillips, John,** Continued this pottery together with the Sunderland or `Garrison` pottery. see 1807 Sunderland Pottery

Various marks with printed designs including the factory`s name. ***JOHN PHILLIPS HYLTON POTTERY***

1762 RHEINSBERG, Brandenburg, Germany.

1762-1866 ***FAIENCE, CREAMWARES ETC.,*** - -
Lüdicke, Karl Friedrich, `Rheinsberg-Lüdicke`

L. R. B. G.

1786- EARTHENWARES - - impressed- ***R.***

1762 SUNDERLAND, Tyne and Wear, England.

Several factories were established here producing mainly transfer printed cream-coloured wares noted for a pink lustre.
The individual factories and potters of SUNDERLAND have been listed under their own dates and marks within this book.

1762 Turner, John, LANE END, Longton, Staffordshire, England.

c.1762-1806 EARTHENWARES, WEDGWOOD-TYPE WARES, ETC.

c.1770- - impressed- **TURNER**
c.1770-87 - - impressed- **I. TURNER**
c.1780-86 - - impressed- **TURNER & CO.**
and 1803-06 - -

1784- Appointed potter to the Prince of Wales- printed or impressed-

1800-05 **Stoneware patent.** painted- Turner's-Patent.
1805 **Patent sold to Spode.**

1762

1762 Aelteste Volkstedter Porzellan.` GmbH, RUDOLSTADT, Germany.

1760- **Macheleit, Georg Heinrich, (founder)**
Discovered also the secret of porcelain paste.

1760-67 Porcelain figures, etc.
Under patronage of Prince J. Fr. von Schwarzberg Rudolstadt.

Hayfork marks -

1767- **Nonne, Christian,** dominated the company for 3 decades, producing coffee, chocolate and tea services, centrepieces, candlesticks, etc. and especially lace figures.
Meissen sword type marks brought a protest from the Meissen Factory in 1772 - -

c.1788 a stroke was added to the swords -

1797-99 **Prince Ernst Constantin von Hessen Philippstal.**

1799- **Greiner,W.,& Holzapfel,K.,**
c.1800- Marks in blue -

1815-60 **Greiner, Stauch & Co.,**

1861- **Karl Ens, sr. becomes co-owner, and his sons, Eduard and Karl, jr. took charge and switched production to ornamental porcelain.**

20th century produced some of the best wares. Miniature models by Ernst Barlach, Gerhard Marcks, Max Esser, Etha Richter and Professor Paul Scheurich.
20th century marks - -

c.1920s **The heyday of the factory with artists such as Arthur Storch, Hugo Meisel and Gustav Oppel, and especially the figures and groups produced by Carl Fuchs.**

1945- The extensive range of models was enriched after the 2nd World War by Gustav Oppel, Otto Kramer and Gustav Theile in the traditional Volkstedt style.

1990 **German reunification.**

1990- **Königlich priv. Porzellanfabrik Tettau, (part of Seltmann Group) acquire factory.** see 1794 Tettau GmbH.

1995 modern mark -

(By kind permission of Porzellanfabriken Christian Seltmann Gmbh. Germany)

1762 Bergdoll, Adam, Germany. - - - see 1755 FRANKENTHAL.
1762 Catherine II., Russia. - - - - see 1744 ST. PETERSBURG.
1762 Doorne, Pieter V., DELFT, Holland. - - see 1653 De Porceleyne Fles.
1762 Glöckel, (painter) Germany. - - - see 1755 FRANKENTHAL.
1762 Hannong, Joseph, France. - - - - - see 1721 STRASBOURG.
1762 Karl Theodor, Elector Palatine, Germany. - see 1755 FRANKENTHAL.
1762 Linck, Franz Konrad, Germany. - - - see 1755 FRANKENTHAL.
1762 Louis, Jean-Jacob, (Modellmeister) Germany. - see 1756 LUDWIGSBURG.

1763 Child, Smith, TUNSTALL, Staffordshire, England.

1763-90 EARTHENWARES. - impressed- ***CHILD***

1763 Cyfflé Paul-Louis, LUNÉVILLE, France.

1763- Modeller of figures and groups called `*terre de Lorraine*` impressed-

1769 Cyfflé acquired his own factory.
1780- Moulds sent to Niderviller and Bellevue.

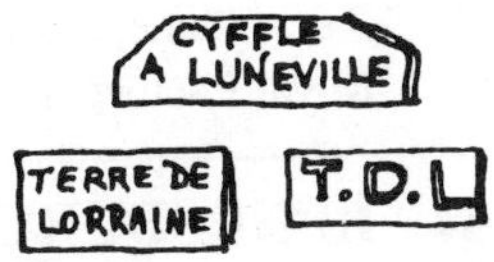

1763 FRANKFURT-AN-DER-ODER, Brandenburg, Germany.

1763-19th century. FAÏENCE AND EARTHENWARE.

Heinrich, Karl. (Frankfurt-Heinrich) -

20th century Theodor Paetsch. - - - - - -

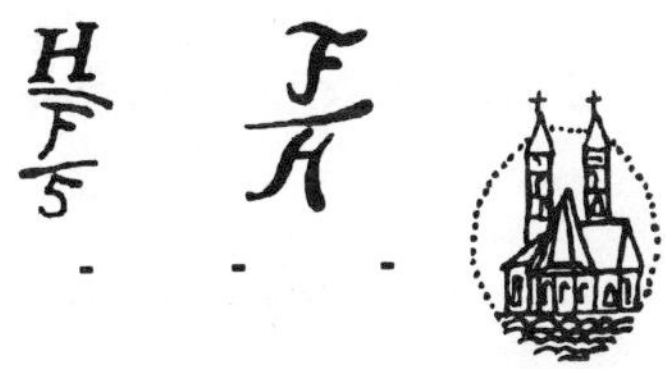

1763 Østerbro, COPENHAGEN, Denmark.

1763-69 **Øster Bro Fabrik,** FAÏENCE. -
Hasrisz, J. (painter)

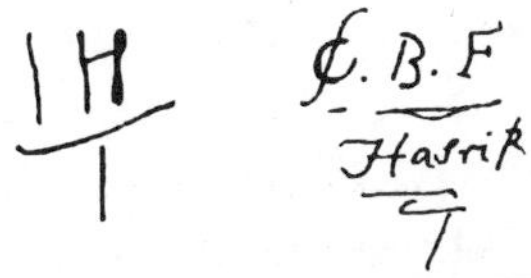

1763 OTTWEILER, Rhineland, Germany.

1763-94 FAÏENCE AND HARD-PASTE PORCELAIN.
1784-94 EARTHENWARE GLAZED. - - - -
Prince Wilhelm Heinrich (patron)
1763-67 Pellevé, Etienne-Dominique,
1766 dated mark on figure (Hamburg)

1763 PROSKAU, Silesia, Germany.

1763-93 FAÏENCE. **1763-1850** EARTHENWARE.
1763-69 **Count Leopold von Proskau** - -

1770-83 Dietrichstein - -
1783-93 Leopold - - - - -

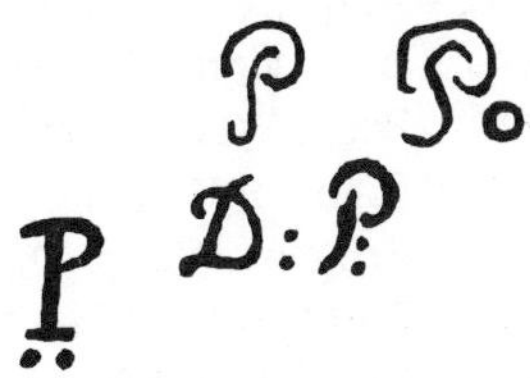

1788-1850 EARTHENWARE Impressed- - ***PROSKAU***

1763/64

1763 ZÜRICH, Switzerland.

1763-1897 PORCELAIN, FAIENCE.
1778- EARTHENWARES

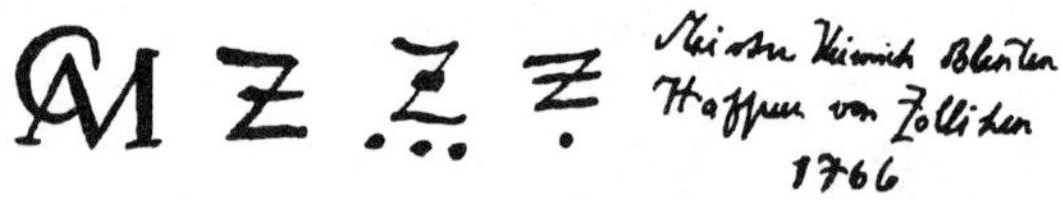

1763 Acier, Michel Victor, Germany. - - - see 1710 MEISSEN.
1763 Bulidon, (flowers) France. - - - - see 1745 SÈVRES.
1763 Carsten Behren`s Factory, Germany. - - see 1750 KELLINGHUSEN.
1763 Casali and Callegari, Italy. - - - - see 1520 PESARO.
1763 Crowther, John, LONDON, England. - - see 1744 Bow China.
1763 Electoral Saxon Porcelain Manufactory, Germany. see 1710 MEISSEN.
1763 Fritsch, (Figures/children) France. - - see 1745 SÈVRES.
1763 Lecot, (chinese subjects) France. - - - see 1745 SÈVRES.
1763 Ohrn, Jacob, Sweden. - - - - - see 1725 RORSTRAND.
1763 Pierre jeune, Jean-Jacques, (flowers) France. - see 1745 SÈVRES.
1763 Royal Factory, Prussia, Germany. - - - see 1751 BERLIN.

1764 RENDSBURG, Holstein, Germany.

1764-72 FAÏENCE
Burgesses, Clar and Lorentzen. -

1764-c.84 **Christian Friedrich Clar.** - -

1765-66 **Joachim Friedrich Duve** - -

1772-1818 CREAMWARES - - **REN. I.** **RF**

1764 WALLENDORF, Thuringia, Germany.

1764 HARD-PASTE PORCELAIN.
Imitation Meissen mark - - -

1778 - - -

c1890 **Kaempfe & Heubach** - -

1764 Asselin, (figures/portraits) France. - see 1745 SÈVRES.
1764 Auliczek, Dominikus, Germany. - - see 1753 NYMPHENBURG.
1764 Bade, Conrade, (painter) Germany. - see 1755 SCHLESWIG.
1764 Beek, Willem van, DELFT, Holland. - see 1757 de twee Wildemans.
1764 Bigourat, Claude, France. - - - see 1589 NEVERS.
1764 Brouwer, Hugo, DELFT, Holland. - see 1672 De 3 porceleyne Flessies.
1764 Burkhardt, Johann Michael, Germany. - see 1756 LUDWIGSBURG.
1764 Cozzi, Geminiano, Italy. - - - see 1550 VENICE.

Continued over -

1764	Drand, (chinoiseries/gilding) France. - -	see 1745 SÈVRES.
1764	Duyn, van J., DELFT, Holland. - - -	see 1701 De porceleyn Schotel.
1764	Falot, (birds, etc.) France. - - - -	see 1745 SÈVRES.
1764	Ferretti, Domenico, Germany. - - -	see 1756 LUDWIGSBURG.
1764	Fujina Factory, Funaki Yajibei, Japan. - -	see 1677 IZUMO.
1764	Kiel, Albertus, DELFT, Holland. - - -	see 1689 de Star.
1764	Kloot, Johannes van der, DELFT, Holland. -	see 1671 De Romeyn.
1764	Nicquet, (flowers) France. - - - -	see 1745 SÈVRES.
1764	Pfalzgraf, Johann Valentin, (painter) Germany. -	see 1722 DURLACH.
1764	Spaandonck, T., DELFT, Holland. - -	see 1648 De dubbelde Schenkkan.
1764	Strale, Hestera, DELFT, Holland. - - -	see 1720 `t Jonge Moriaenshooft.
1764	Sta, Jean-François, France. - - -	see 1732 DESVRES.
1764	Verstelle, Geertruy, DELFT, Holland. - -	see 1648 De oud Moriaans hooft.

1765 Christian, Philip, LIVERPOOL, England. Impressed- *CHRISTIAN*

1765 ECKERNFÖRDE, Schleswig, Germany.

1765-85 FAÏENCE. (Factory begun in 1759 at Criseby)

1761-68 **Johann Buckwald,** (director, modeller and potter)

1765 **Otte, Johann Nicolaus** (founder) -

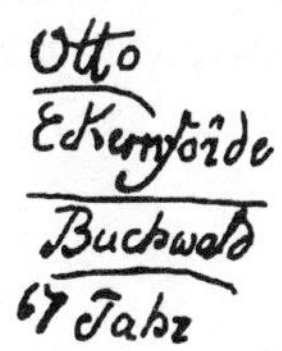

c.1765-68 **Buckwald, Johann,** - - -

Leihamer, Abraham, (painter) - - - -

1767-69 **Ewald, Johann Cornelius** (painter) -

1765 FLÖRSHEIM, nr. Frankfurt-am-Main, Germany.

1765-present. FAÏENCE. -

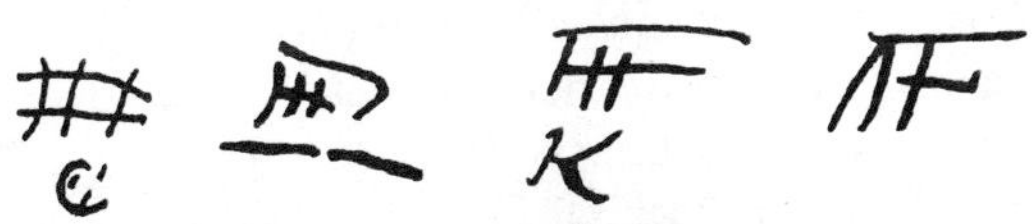

1765-73 **Müller, Georg Ludwig (founder)**

1769 (dated) Diehl, Nicolaus (painter) -

1771 (dated) Baumann, Johann Peter, - - - -

Continued over -

1765

1765 FLÖRSHEIM, nr. Frankfurt-am-Main, Germany. (Cont`)

1773- **Carthusian Monastery, Mainz.**
Kaspar Dreste (manager)
1784 (dated) `Chur-Mainz` - -

1781-93 Weingartner, Mathias Joseph
FAÏENCE-FINE. Impressed- - -

1765 Gardner, Francis, MOSCOW, Russia.

c.1765-1891 HARD-PASTE PORCELAIN. - blue-

c.1810 - impressed-

c.1850 - Printed red-

1765 Kuik, Michiel v., (Delft Artist) DELFT, Holland.

TIN-GLAZED EARTHENWARE (DELFTWARE) - -

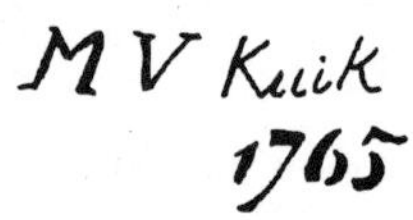

1765 PALSJÖ, nr. Helsingborg, Sweden.

1765-74 FAÏENCE.
1774 (dated) Palsjö Fabrik
blue or manganese-

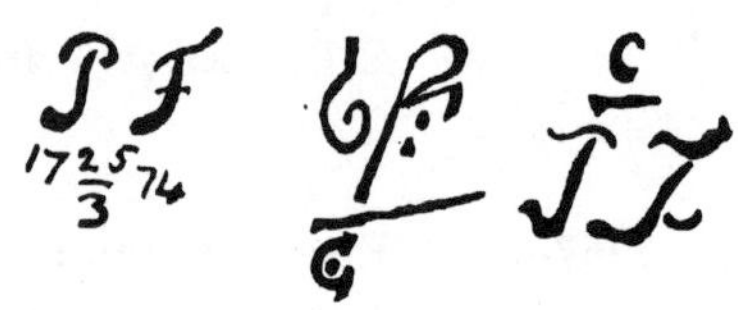

1765	Appel, (painter) Germany. - - - -	see 1755 FRANKENTHAL.
1765	Ardizzone, G.A., Italy. - - - -	see 1577 TURIN.
1765	Chabry fils, (pastorals) France. - - -	see 1745 SÈVRES.
1765	Commelin, (flowers/garlands) France. - -	see 1745 SÈVRES.
1765	Duve, Joachim Friedrich, Germany. - -	see 1764 RENDSBURG.
1765	Grothe, J.J. (painter) Germany. - - -	see 1756 LUDWIGSBURG.
1765	Adriaens, J. Halder, DELFT, Holland. - -	see 1645 De Grieksche A.
1765	Hannong, Pierre Antoine, France.- - -	see 1738 VINCENNES.
1765	Jezinger, Franz, Germany. - - - -	see 1753 NYMPHENBURG.
1765	Klein, Johann, Germany. - - - -	see 1753 NYMPHENBURG.
1765	Malpass, William, England. - - -	see 1745 ROCKINGHAM.
1765	Melchior, Johann Peter, Germany. - -	see 1746 HÖCHST.
1765	Theodor, (painter/gilder) France. - - -	see 1745 SÈVRES.

1766 Berthevin, Pierre, MARIEBERG, Sweden.

1766-69 FAÏENCE AND SOFT-PASTE PORCELAIN -

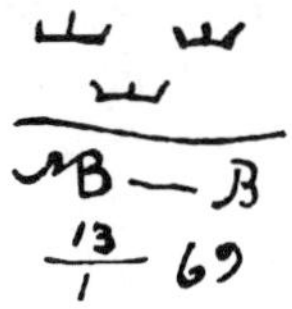

Frantzen, J.O. (painter) Enamel -

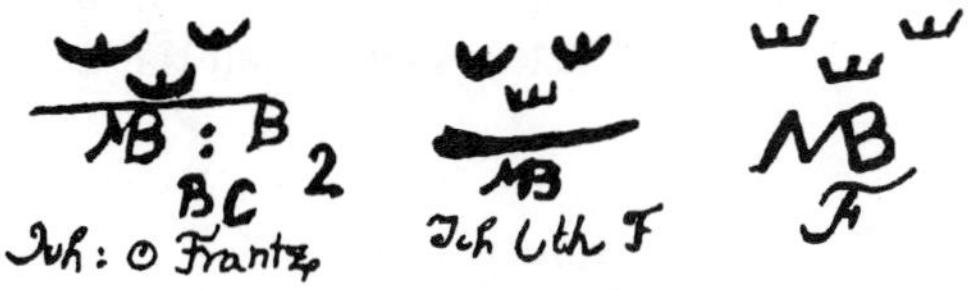

SOFT-PASTE PORCELAIN MARK. Impressed-

1766 HAGUE, THE, Holland.

c.1766-90 HARD-PASTE PORCELAIN. -
Factory was originally used for decorating German porcelain.

Ansbach mark in blue- -

1885- **Rozenburg factory** - -
W.W. von Gudenberg (founder)
Theodorus Colenbrander (director)

1766 Schol, S. v.d., (Delft Artist) DELFT, Holland.

TIN-GLAZED EARTHENWARE (DELFTWARE) - -

1766	Antoisenet, Jaques, Belgium. - - -	see 1705 BRUSSELS.
1766	Buchwald and Leihamer, Germany. - -	see 1762 KIEL.
1766	Ehrenreich, Johann Eberhardt Ludwig, Germany.	see 1755 STRALSUND.
1766	`Hessian lion` Germany. - - - - -	see 1680 CASSEL.
1766	Joyau, (flowers) France. - - - - -	see 1745 SÈVRES.
1766	Le Bel aîné, (figures/flowers) France. - -	see 1745 SÈVRES.
1766	Le Bon brothers, France. - - - - -	see 1760 ÉPINAL.
1766	Muth, Heinrich Christoph, Germany. - -	see 1750 ABTSBESSINGEN.
1766	Raux âiné, (flowers) France. - - -	see 1745 SÈVRES.
1766	Renners & Newmann, Germany. - - -	see 1762 KIEL.

1767 LIMBACH, Thuringia, Germany.

1772- HARD-PASTE PORCELAIN. - - 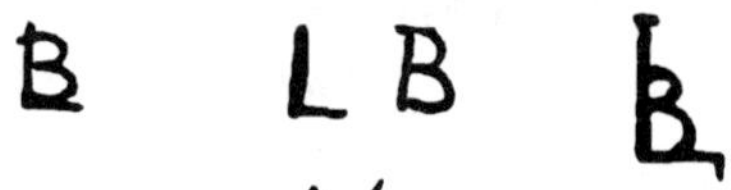

1772-88 Meissen imitation marks- 

1767-c.1800 Haag, Johann Jacob Heinrich -
(Factory painter and Hausmaler) 

1772-97 Greiner, Gotthelf, - -
1797- Gotthelf Greiner Sohne -
These marks were also used at
Groszbreitenbach a branch of Limbach.

1767 Mokubei, Kiyoto, Japan.
Potter (b.1767, d.1833) Imitated Kochi-yaki
(a Chinese Ming pottery)

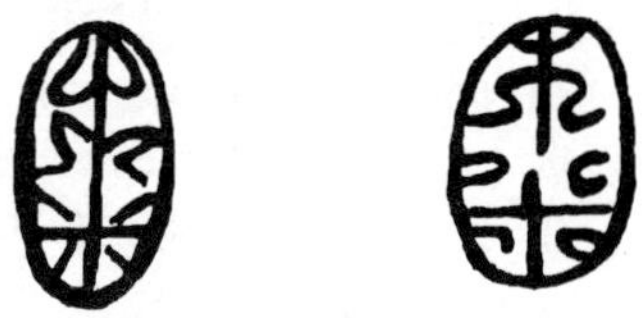

`Koki Kwan Mokubei tsukuru`
(made by Mokubei connoisseur of antique pots)-

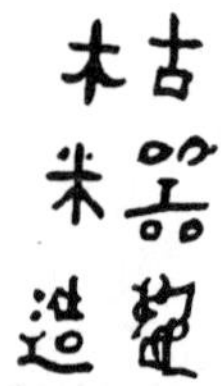

1767 RATO, nr. Lisbon, Portugal.
1767-19th century. FAÏENCE.

1767-71 T. Brunetto - - 

1771-c.1814 S. de Almeida- - - - - 

1767 Smith Pottery, Joseph, BUCKS COUNTY, Pennsylvania, U.S.A.
c.1767-19th century, EARTHENWARES. incised-

1767 Villeroy & Boch AG., METTLACH, Rhineland, Germany.

1767- This company has developed from the beginnings of a small tableware manufacturer in 1748 to the modern multi-ceramic business it is today (1996)

1748 François Boch established a pottery which remained in the family until 1835.
1754 François Boch died.

1767- François Boch`s sons Jean-François, Dominique and Pierre-Joseph establish a faïence factory in Septfontaines, Eich, Luxembourg.

1786 Various marks, usually printed blue:-

1775- Boch brothers purchase a warehouse in Brussels to supply the northern part of Austrian Netherlands, now Belgium.

1787-1812 marks- B.L B·L

1792- François Boch`s estate is divided between the sons. Dominique and Jean-François.

1792- Pierre-Joseph Boch became sole proprietor of Audun-le-Tiche and Septfontaines. This is why he was accepted as the founder.

1796- The Septfontaines factory is severely damaged by the French revolutionary army during the occupation of Luxembourg.

1813-25 Luxembourg marks-

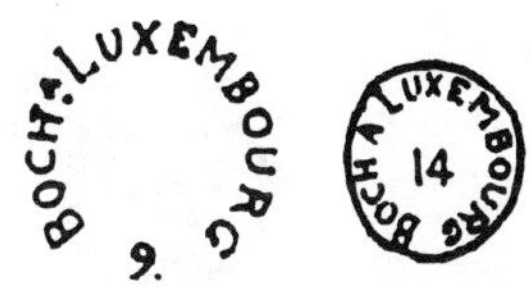

1823-55 various mark: -

1809- Mettlach factory established by Jean-François, son of Pierre-Joseph Boch. It produced tableware and is the seat of the company`s headquarters today (1995)

J.F.B.Cie

Continued over -

1767

1767 Villeroy & Boch AG., METTLACH, Rhineland, Germany. (Cont`)

1809- **Mettlach Factory (Cont`)**

1813-25 Various marks: -

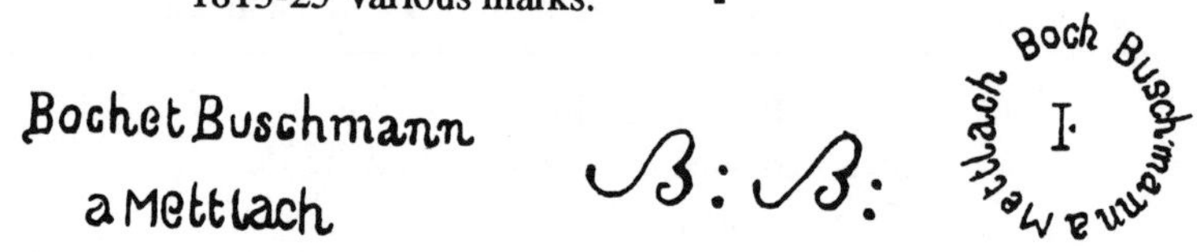

1836- **Villeroy & Boch group established by the merger of the three factories by Jean-François Boch and Nicolas Villeroy.-** see 1791 Villeroy, Nicolas,

1836-76 Villeroy & Boch marks: -

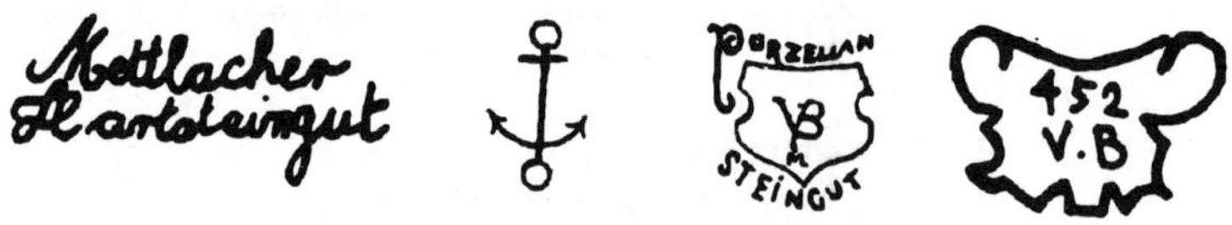

1855-74 Villeroy & Boch marks: -

1874-1900 marks:- - -

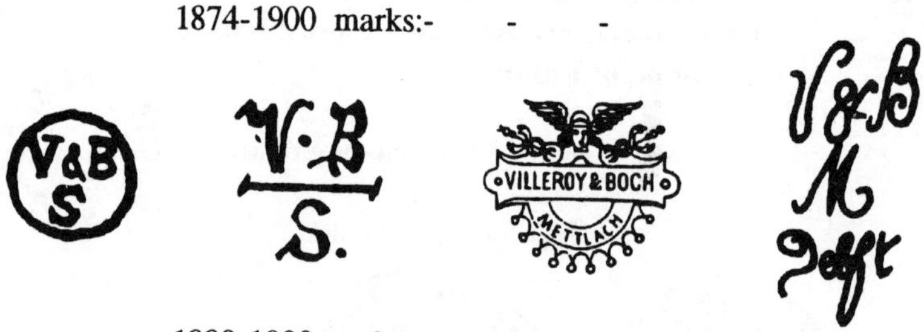

1880-1900 marks:- - -

Continued over -

1767 Villeroy & Boch AG., METTLACH, Rhineland, Germany (Cont`)

1841- **Eugen and Victor, sons of Jean-François Boch, and their brother-in-law J-B Nothomb, establish the faïence factory `Boch Freres Keramis` in La Louviere, Belgium, which still operates today.**

1843- Villeroy & Boch establish a crystal factory in Wadgassen on the river Saar.

1856- **Dresden Factory established** to produce high quality tableware. Later architecturally applied ceramics, sanitary ware and tiles are added.

1874

1900

1869- The Mosaikfabrik, a factory for the production of mosaic work, was built in Mettlach.

1879- Thonwaarenfabrik Fellenberg & Cie, Merzig. acquired. Specializes in bricks and drainpipes.

1883-1912 **Majolika-Fabrik, Schramberg in the Black Forest.** which manufacture tableware, decorative ceramics, and insulating ceramics. Factory closed 1912.

c.1874 Schramberg marks-

1874

1890-1912

1904- Bolshoi Theatre in Moscow. Floor laid with tiles produced in Mettlach.

1912- Merzig and Dresden factories teach the Mettlach factory how to produce sanitary ware from faïence, and later porcelain.

1919-31 **Mehlem Faience Factory in Bonn acquired.** Closed in 1931.

1926- **Tableware factory in Torgau, near Leipzig established to support the Dresden factory.** Expropriated in 1948 but reincorporated in 1990 after the reunification of Germany.

1939-45 Most of the factories are irreparably damaged during the war.

1948-86 **Pabst Tiles Factory in Hamburg acquired.**

1948 In the east, the factories in Dresden, Deutsch-Lissa and Torgau are expropriated without compensation.

Continued over -

1767/68

1767 Villeroy & Boch AG., METTLACH, Rhineland, Germany. (Cont`)

1956-	**SGC group in France, which produce tiles, was acquired.**
1957-	Wall tiles and sanitary ware factory built in La Ferte-Gaucher, France.
1976-	**Hienrich Porzellan Factory, Selb, acquired.**
1986-	`Gallo Design` brand name acquired.
1987-	**Villeroy & Boch becomes a Public Limited Company.**
1990-	**Villeroy & Boch go public by offering preferential shares on the stock exchange.**
1990-	Torgau faïence factory in East Germany is reincorporated into the group. and is known as Faiencerie Torgau.
1990-	**Longchamp faïence factory, France, acquired. to serve as an ancillary to the Luxembourg plant.**

Logo used since 1990- Villeroy&Boch

1991-	**Merzig Tableware Factory built to supplement the nearby Mettlach Factory where market demand has outstripped production.**

(By kind permission of Villeroy & Boch, Mettlach, Germany.)

1767	Choisy, Hirel de, France. - - -	see 1650 RENNES.
1767	Crevani, Felix, Italy. - - -	see 1725 LODI.
1767	Ewald, Johann Cornelius,, Germany. -	see 1765 ECKERNFÖRDE.
1767	Früting, Emanuel Jacob, Switzerland. -	see 1725 BERNE.
1767	Gaschin, Countess Anna Barbara von, Ger.	see 1753 GLIENITZ.
1767	Hunerwadel, Marcus, Switzerland. -	see 1760 LENZBURG.
1767	Klug, A.H. & H.C. Switzerland. - -	see 1760 LENZBURG.
1767	Mô, Christophe, France. - - -	see 1734 MENNECY-VILLEROY.
1767	Mô, Jean, France. - - -	see 1734 MENNECY-VILLEROY.
1767	Nonne, Christian, Germany. - -	see 1762 Aelteste Volkstedter.
1767	Oehrstrom, Friedrich Christian, Germany.	see 1755 STRALSUND.

1768 ETIOLLES, Seine-et-Oise, France.

c.1768- HARD, AND SOFT-PASTE PORCELAIN.

c1768 **Dominique Pellevé** Incised-

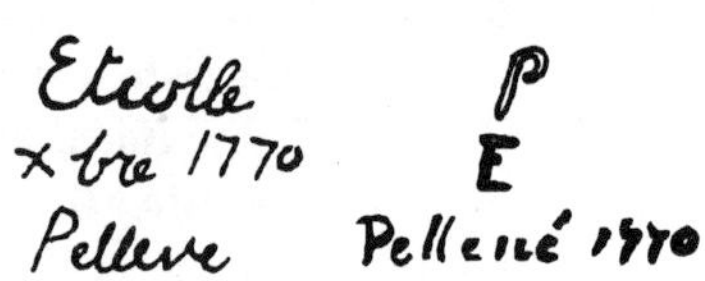

Jean-Baptiste Monier Incised-

1768 Cookworthy, William, PLYMOUTH, Devonshire, England.

1768-HARD-PASTE PORCELAIN.

William Cookworthy founded the first English hard-paste porcelain factory where the products were made purely from English ingredients. He tried to make his porcelain equal to that of Sèvres and Dresden. To achieve this he engaged the services of Mon. Saqui (or Soqui) from Sèvres and Henry Bone from Plymouth. They were principally employed in painting high-class birds and flowers. The wares consisted of dinner, coffee and tea services, figures and animal groups, etc.

Marks are usually painted in red or blue. Below are a selection found on various pieces. Workmans marks sometimes occur.

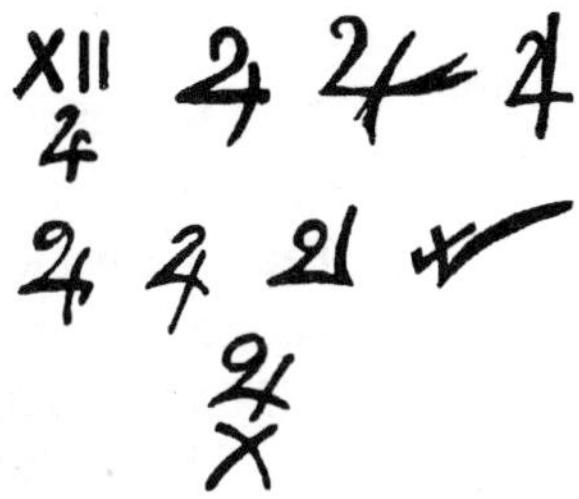

c.1770 Factory moved to Bristol. Richard Champion was part of the overall set-up at Bristol and probably became manager.

1770 Marks on a pair of small sauce boats-

Mr.
Wm. Cookworthy`s
Factory, Plymouth
1770

1774-Richard Champion bought the business and the porcelain patent rights and continued the manufacture under the name of `W. Cookworthy & Co` see 1774 W. Cookworthy.

1768	Dusolle, (flowers) France. - - - - - -	see 1745 SÈVRES.
1768	Fürstlich-Fuldaisch, Germany. - - - - -	see 1741 FULDA.
1768	Jünger, Christopher, decorator, Austria. - - -	see 1719 VIENNA.
1768	Sanders, L., DELFT, Holland. - - - - -	see 1655 De Klaeuw.

1769 Adams, William & Sons (Potters) Ltd., TUNSTALL, England.

1769- EARTHENWARES, JASPERS, PARIAN, ETC.

1769-1800 impressed- **ADAMS & CO.**

1787-1864 impressed- **ADAMS**

1804-40 Blue printed earthenwares. Printed-

1810-25 Earthenwares. Impressed- - - -

c.1815 Rare mark. Impressed- **W. ADAMS & CO**

Continued over -

1769

1769 Adams, William & Sons (Potters) Ltd., TUNSTALL, Eng. (Cont`)

1819-64 W. Adams & Sons. Printed- **W. A. & S.**

Factory`s name and initials printed within marks of various patterns and designs. - **W. ADAMS & SON**

1845-64 Parian figures and groups.

Impressed- **ADAMS**

Factory`s name printed within marks of various patterns and designs. - - **W. ADAMS**

1879- Printed mark of various designs. -

1891- `England` added

1879 Mark introduced. - -

1891 `England` added- - -

1890-1914 Printed mark on Ironstone wares-

1896 `TUNSTALL` is added - - - -

1893-1917 Mark with various printed designs- **W. A. & CO.**

1891-`England` added - -

1896-20th century, Printed marks-

1896-20th century, Used on Jasper wares-

1914-18 - - Printed mark-

1950-62 `CALYX WARE` with various printed and impressed designs. **CALYX WARE**

1963- `MICRATEX` Trade-name of new body with various other designs. **MICRATEX**

(William Adams are now situated at Barlaston, Stoke-on-Trent, Staffordshire)

1769 BERO-MÜNSTER, Switzerland.
c.1769-80 FAÏENCE. **Dolder, Andreas,-**
c.1780 Transferred to Lucerne.

1769 Neale & Palmer, HANLEY, England.
c.1769-76 EARTHENWARES in the style of Wedgwood. ***NEALE & PALMER***

1769 Sten, Henrik, MARIEBERG, Sweden.
1769-88 FAÏENCE AND PORCELAIN. - -

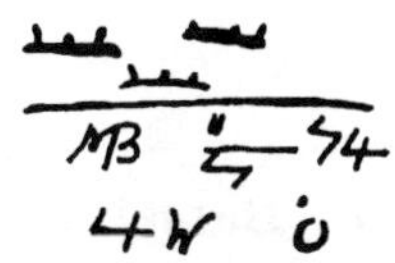

Impressed- **Sten**
M B

Porcelain- Impressed-

1769 VAUX, Seine-et-Oise, France.
1769- HARD-PASTE PORCELAIN. - -
Laborde & Hocquart - -

1769	Barrat, (fruit/flowers) France. - - -	see 1745 SÈVRES.
1769	Berthevin, Pierre, Germany. - - -	see 1755 FRANKENTHAL.
1769	Chelsea/Derby mark, England. - - -	see 1745 CHELSEA.
1769	Cox, James, England. - - - -	see 1745 CHELSEA.
1769	Diehl, Nicolaus, (painter) Germany. - -	see 1765 FLÖRSHIEM.
1769	Etruria Factory opened, BURSLEM, England. -	see 1759 Wedgwood, Josiah,
1769	Ghåil, François-Joseph, France. - - -	see 1733 SINCENY.
1769	Grémont jeune, (flowers) France. - - -	see 1745 SÈVRES.
1769	Hileken, (figures) France. - - - -	see 1745 SÈVRES.
1769	Wedgwood & Bentley, BURSLEM, England. -	see 1759 Wedgwood Ltd.

1770 ARRAS, Pas-de-Calais, France.
1770-90 SOFT-PASTE PORCELAIN. -
Joseph-François Boussemart (Founder)

1771-90 **Dlles Delemer,** Underglaze blue-

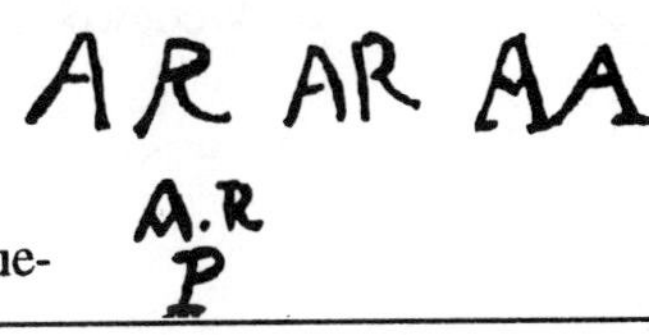

1770 BADEN-BADEN, Germany.
1770- FAÏENCE, PORCELAIN AND EARTHENWARES.
1770-78 **Zacharias Pfalzer,**
Porcelain, Underglaze blue-

Late 18th century. Painted in gold-

Faïence, Printed black or in colour-

1770

1770 Bonnin & Morris, Southwark, PHILADELPHIA, U.S.A.
c.1770- Mark on cream-ware fruit dish.
Underglaze blue- - - **P**

1770 COLOGNE, Rhineland, Germany.
c.1770-c.1910 FAÏENCE AND HARD-PASTE PORCELAIN. -
Impressed- **KÖLN**

Painted black- 

1770 Daniel, John, COBRIDGE, Staffordshire, England.
c.1770-c.86 EARTHENWARES. Incised signature- ***JOHN DANIEL***

1770 Heath, J., HANLEY, Staffordshire, England. - ***I. H.***
c.1770-1800 EARTHENWARE, CREAMWARE, Impressed- ***HEATH***

1770 HUBERTUSBURG, Saxony, Germany.
1770-1848 Tännich, Johann Samuel Friedrich.
c.1775 Count Marcolini of Meissen (director)
FAÏENCE, AND THEN WEDGWOOD TYPE CREAMWARES. -

1770-74 -

1818-35
Wedgwood mark imitation- impressed- -

1818-38 mark-

1840-50 Weigel and Messerschmidt - - **W & M**

1770 LEEDS, West Yorkshire, England.
The individual factories and potters of LEEDS have been listed under their own dates and marks within this book.

1770 MOSBACH, Baden, Germany.

1770-72 **Berthevin, Pierre,** FAÏENCE AND CREAMWARES.

Carl Theodor, Elector-Palatine (patron)
(also at Frankenthal) - - - -

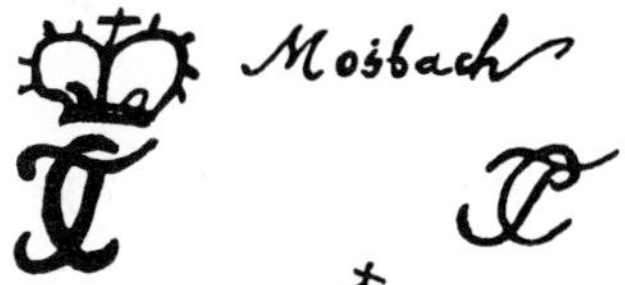

1770-81 **Tännich, Joh. Samuel Friedrich, from Meissen, Strasburg and Kiel. 1774 made manager.**

1774 Sax (painter) - - - -

c.1780 **List, J.G.F., made director.**

1818- CREAMWARES - Impressed- ***M*** ***MOSBACH***

1770 Savy`s Factory, MARSEILLES, France.

c.1770- **Savy, Honoré, (d.c.1793)** -
Previously partner to Veuve Perrin.

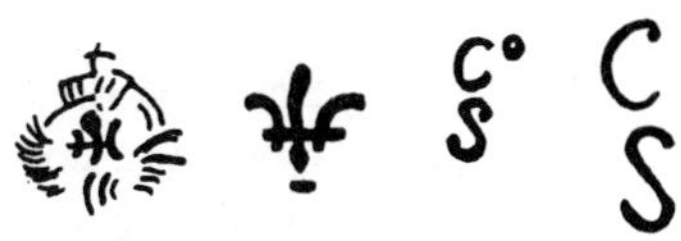

1770 Spode, Josiah, STOKE-0n-Trent, Staffordshire, England.

1770- EARTHENWARES, BONE-CHINA, STONE-CHINA, ETC.

c.1770

1770-97 **Josiah Spode (Founder)** learnt his trade as an apprentice to Thomas Whieldon in 1749.

1776- Spode completes the purchase of his factory.

1778- **London premises at 29 Fore Street, Cripplegate, opened for marketing Spode wares.**

c.1784- William Copeland is sent to London to assist Josiah Spode II (son)

1789- Larger premises at 45 Fore Street, taken over.

1796- **Spode acquires even larger premises in London at 5 Portugal Street, Lincoln`s Inn Fields, which he re-names `Staffordshire Warehouse`**

1797- Josiah Spode I dies. 17th August.

c.1800

c.1800- Bone-china introduced, and is an immediate success.

1805- **Spode II and William Copeland become partners in London business.**

1806- The Prince of Wales appoints Josiah Spode `Potter and English Porcelain Manufacture to His Royal Highness`

1806

Continued over -

1770

1770 Spode, Josiah, STOKE-on-Trent, England. (Cont`)

c.1813- Stone-China body introduced.

c.1813 c.1822

1813- **Spode and Copeland enter into second partnership-**

c.1812

1821- Felspar Porcelain introduced- -

c.1825

1826- **William Copeland died, 20th January. Spode II and William Taylor Copeland enter into a 7 year partnership.**

1827- **Spode II died, 16th July,**
Copeland and Spode III run the business.

1829- **Spode III died, 6th October. Copeland runs the business for the trustees of the Spode estate.**

c.1830

1833- **Copeland acquires the Spode business. Thomas Garrett joins the company which becomes, Copeland & Garrett.**

c.1833 c.1833 c.1840

1842- Parian body (a very fine porcelain) introduced-

1847- **Copeland and Garrett partnership dissolved.**
W.T. Copeland purchases Chelsea and Chelsea/Derby moulds.

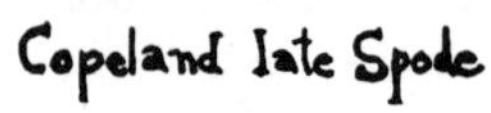

c.1850 c.1860

1851- Crystal Palace Exhibition. Bronze Medal awarded.

1868- **William Taylor Copeland dies, 12th April.**

c.1888 1894 c.1890 c.1900

Continued over -

1770 Spode, Josiah, STOKE-on-Trent, Staffordshire, England, (Cont`)

1913- **Richard Pirie Copeland died.**
Ronald and Gresham Copeland (sons)
run the business.

c.1920

c.1920

1932- **W.T. Copeland & Sons Ltd. Incorporated.**
1966- **Company joins the Carborundum Group of Companies.**

c.1940

1970- **Bicentenary of the founding firm. Name of Company changed to Spode Limited.**
All backstamps re-designed to achieve a uniform identity.

1970

1970

1970

1976- **Company merges with the Worcester Royal Porcelain Company.**
1978- **Royal Worcester Ltd., buys the Carborundum Ltd. shares and becomes sole owner of the Royal Worcester Spode Ltd.**

(By kind permission of Spode (Royal Worcester Spode Ltd.) Stoke-on-Trent, England)

1770 VRON, Somme, France.

1770- FAÏENCE. - - -

Verlingue - - -

MANUFACTURE DE
VRON 25 AVRIL
DELAHODDE-VERLINGUE
1815

1815 **Delahodde** - - Impressed-

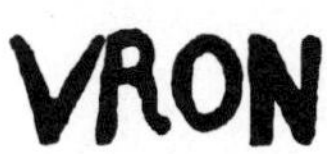

1770

1770 WIESBADEN, Nassau, Germany.

1770-95 Faïence and creamwares. - -

Wiesbaden-Dreste - - - -

Nassau-Usingen - - - -

1770	Boussemaert, Joseph, Belgium. - - -	see 1752 LIÈGE.
1770	Browne & Co., Robert, England. - - -	see 1757 LOWESTOFT.
1770	Chelsea/Derby mark, England. - - -	see 1749 DERBY.
1770	Choisy, (flowers/ornaments) France. - -	see 1745 SÈVRES.
1770	Comte de Custine, France.- - - -	see 1754 NIDERVILLER.
1770	Confalonieri, Cesare, Italy. - - -	see 1725 MILAN.
1770	Dietrichstein, Germany. - - - -	see 1763 PROSKAU.
1770	Donovan & Son, John, Ireland. - - -	see 1752 DUBLIN.
1770	Feilner, Simon, Germany. - - - -	see 1755 FRANKENTHAL.
1770	Henrion, (flowers) France.- - - -	see 1745 SÈVRES.
1770	Karl Theodor, Germany. - - - -	see 1753 NYMPHENBURG.
1770	Lanfrey, Claude-François, (painter) France. -	see 1754 NIDERVILLER.
1770	Sailly, Thomas, France. - - - -	see 1750 TOURS.
1770	Takatori Pottery, Japan. - - - -	see 1583 CHIKUZEN.

1771 Clignacourt, Montmartre, PARIS, France.

1771-c.98 HARD AND SOFT PASTE PORCELAIN.

Registered mark blue or gold- - - 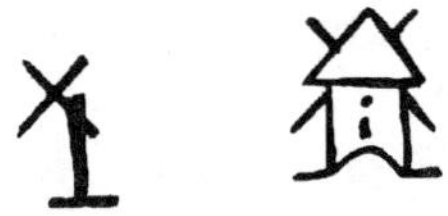

1775-91 **Deruelle, Pierre,** - - - - - 

1775-93 **Louis-Stanislas-Xavier (protector)** - 

Stencilled in red-

`Porcelaine de Monsieur` - - - 

1791-98 **Moitte,** (modeller) - - *Moitte*

1771 Faubourg Saint-Denis, PARIS, France.

1771-76 **Hannong, Pierre Antoine.**

HARD-PASTE PORCELAIN. - - 

1773 Registered mark - 

1779- **Stahn, registered mark for Charles-Philippe, Comte d`Artois, protector of the factory.** red, blue or gold- - 

c.1800-10 **Marc Schoelcher** - - - - - 

1771 Naples Royal Porcelain Factory, NAPLES, Italy.

MAIOLICA AND PORCELAIN

1654- **F. Brandi Produced maiolica in Naples in 1654.** - - - - 

1784- **Carlo Coccore** - - - - - 

19th Century- Del Vecchio - - - - - 

Continued over -

1771

1771 Naples Royal Porcelain Factory, NAPLES, Italy. (Cont`)

1771-1806 Ferdinand IV. Porcelain.

1773-87 `Fabbrica Reale Ferdinandea` -

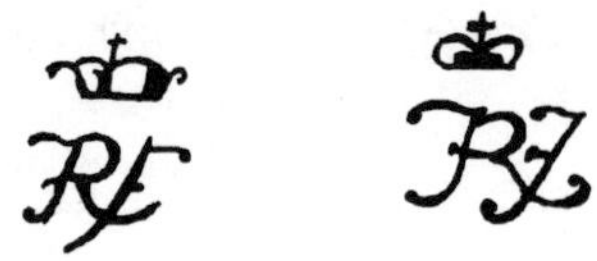

Late 18th century marks -

Incised- -

blue or red- -

c.1790 Giordano (modeller) incised-

1771 OUDE LOOSDRECHT, Holland.

1771-84 HARD-PASTE PORCELAIN.

Mol, Johannes de, incised-

Marks in various enamel colours-

1771 Royal Copenhagen Factory, COPENHAGEN, Denmark.

c.1771- **Müller, F.H.,** (Founder)
HARD-PASTE PORCELAIN.
Painters employed at the factory:-
Gylding, Seipslus, and Ruch.

1775- **Became Royal Copenhagen Factory.**
1775-1820 Wave type marks underglaze blue.-
This mark was used again between 1850-70.

1820-50 - -

1870-90 - -

Continued over -

1771 Royal Copenhagen Factory, COPENHAGEN, Denmark. (Cont`)

1889 & c.1892 -

1894-1900
and 1894-1922 -

1905 - - -

1922 & c.1923 -

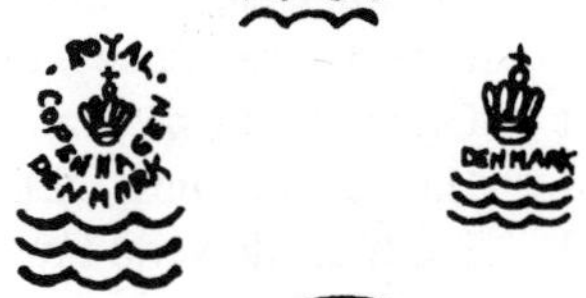

1929-50 - -

1835- Copyright on Biscuit ware - - **E N E R E T**

c.1863- Marks on earthenwares - -

1868-1922 - -

1872-1930 Best quality-

1903-69 Multi-coloured
decorations underglazed

(Information by courtesy of Royal Copenhagen Porcelain & Georg Jensen Silver Ltd. Denmark.)

1771/72

1771 STOCKELSDORF, nr. Lübeck, Germany.

1771-19th Century. FAÏENCE.

Buckwald and Leihamer
Modeller and painter.

Creuzfeldt (painter) -

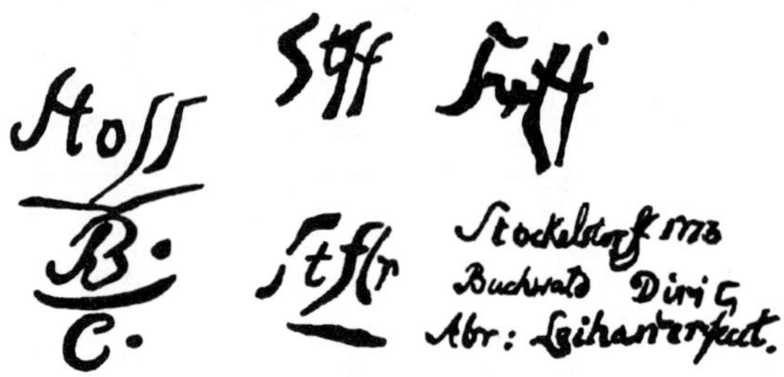

1771	Almeida, S. de, Portugal. - - -	see 1767 RATO.
1771	Baumann, Johann Peter, Germany. -	see 1765 FLÖRSHEIM.
1771	Caselli, Gregorie, Italy. - - -	see 1495 DERUTA.
1771	Delemer, Dlles, France. - - -	see 1770 ARRAS.
1771	Fauquez, Jean-Baptiste-Joseph, France. -	see 1718 ST-AMAND-LES-EAUX.
1771	Gérard, Claude-Charles, (pastorals) France	see 1745 SÈVRES.
1771	Girard, (arabesques) France. - -	see 1745 SÈVRES.
1771	Grellet brothers, France. - - -	see 1736 LIMOGES.
1771	Harlees, Jacobus, DELFT, Holland. -	see 1653 DePorceleyne Fles.
1771	Pfeiffer, (flowers) France. - - -	see 1745 SÈVRES.

1772 KÖNIGSBERG, East Prussia, Germany.

1772-1810 FAÏENCE AND EARTHENWARES.

1772-88 **Ehrenreich, Johann Eberhard Ludwig**

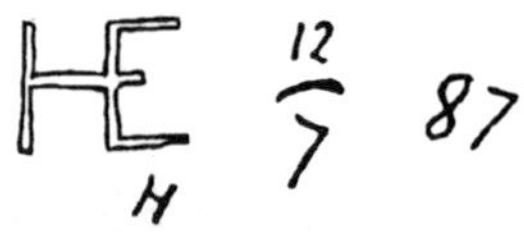

1775-85 **Collin, Paul Heinrich,** - - - ***`freres Collin***
Wedgwood style wares ***a` Konigsberg`***

1780-1810 Lead-glazed wares impressed- - **K**

1772 ROTHERHAM, S. Yorkshire, England.

The individual factories and potters of ROTHERHAM have been listed under their own dates and marks within this book.

1772 Walker & Son, ROTHERHAM, England.

c.1772- EARTHENWARE. - - ***WALKER***

1772	Castel, (landscapes/birds) France.- - -	see 1745 SÈVRES.
1772	Chappuis jeune, (flowers) France. - -	see 1745 SÈVRES.
1772	Frey (painter) Germany. - - - -	see 1757 GOTHA.
1772	Gabel, (painter) Germany. - - - -	see 1757 GOTHA.
1772	Greiner, Gotthelf, Germany. - - -	see 1767 LIMBACH.

Continued over -

1772 Jubin, (gilder) France. - - - - see 1745 SÈVRES.
1772 Le Guay, Pierre-André, (figures) France.- - see 1745 SÈVRES.
1772 Michel, Ambroise, France. - - - see 1745 SÈVRES.
1772 Ruger, (painter) Germany. - - - - see 1757 GOTHA.
1772 Schulz and Brehm, Germany. - - - see 1757 GOTHA.
1772 Turner, Thomas, Shropshire, England. - - see 1775 CAUGHLEY.

1773 Abbey, Richard, LIVERPOOL, England. — ***ABBEY***

1773-80 ENGRAVER AND PRINTER. - - — ***LIVERPOOL***

1790 Became a potter — ***R. Abbey, Sculp.***

1773 Faubourg Saint-Antoine, PARIS, France.

1773- **Morelle** - - - — M.A.P

1773 LISBON, Portugal.

1773- HARD-PASTE PORCELAIN. — LISBOA 1793 — IAG 

Figueireido (sculptor)

IOÃO DE FIG^{DO} — J. M PEREIRA

1773 Porcelaine de Paris, rue de la Pierre-Levee, PARIS, France.

1773- **Locre, Jean-Baptiste,** registered his trade-mark. He set up business in Rue de la Fontaine au Roi. Laurent Russinger, from Saxony ran his factory and later became a partner.

c.1773-1820
underglaze blue

1787-c.97 **Russinger became sole owner.** — RUSSINGER et LOCRE

c.1797-1820 **Pouyat, François, acquired the factory.** c.1817 Pouyat`s two sons obtained the backing of the Duc de Berry and relaunched production in the tradition of `Locre` The Duc de Berry was assassinated and the kilns ceased to work. — Pouyat x Russinger

1829-46 **Clauss, Jean-Marx, took on Pouyat`s workforce** and opened up the present factory at the newly-built Rue de la Pierre-Levee. — NO MARKS WERE USED DURING CLAUSS 1 & 2 PERIODS

1846-69 **Clauss, Alphonse-Marx (son)** Large quantities of heavy style tableware, vases, etc., were made during Clauss 1 & 2 periods.

Continued over -

1773

1773 Porcelaine de Paris, rue de la Pierre-Levee, PARIS, France. (Cont`)

1869-87 **Clauss, Eugène-Marx (grandson)**
Produced late 18th century style Vases with ormolu gilded fittings, mantle-piece clocks, figures and groups, etc.,
Clauss 3 used trade-marks of famous factories at the request of his clients. Sometimes he would slip in his initials.

c.1870-90
underglaze blue
(Meissen type mark)

1887- **Bloch, Achille, and Bourdois, Leon, bought the Rue de la Pierre-Levee works. Bloch changed the name to `Porcelaine de Paris.`**

1880-1920
Blue or red

c.1880-1970
Blue
(Capo di Monte type mark)

1890-1920
Blue

c.1890-1900
underglaze blue,gold,red.

1900- **Leon Bourdois leaves the company, and the Bloch family becomes the sole owners.**

1925- Art Deco Exhibition. Robert Bloch (son) shows innovating insight in his choice of artists. Edouard-Marcel Sandoz created is `Poisson-chat` vase for the company.

1900-14
(Meissen)

1900
(Augustus Rex)

c.1900-40
Blue and gold in relief.

1939-45 Factory struggled to survive during the war.

1945 **Robert Bloch and Paul Molho set about putting the company back on its feet.**

1946-72

1949- **Michel Bloit** Decision to open a transfer workshop.

1973-

Continued over -

1773 Porcelaine de Paris, rue de la Pierre-Levee, PARIS, France. (Cont`)

c.1980 Patrick Molho takes over from Michel Bloit.

This particular design is printed within marks of various patterns. - -

1982

1991- Luc Doublet acquires the company.
Many Porcelaine-de-Paris products are on display in the Louvre Museum and the Museum of Decorative Arts.

Modern mark (1995)-
(Blue and gold)

For further information see <u>Trois siecles de Porcelaine de Paris</u> by Michel Bloit.
(By kind permission of Porcelaine de Paris, Rue de la Pierre Levee, Paris)

1773 Rabe & Co., BRUNSWICK, Germany.

1773-76 FAÏENCE. - - -

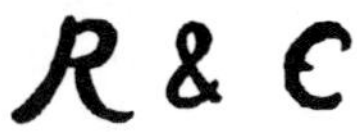

1773 SÖLVESBORG, Sweden.

1773-93 FAÏENCE. - - -

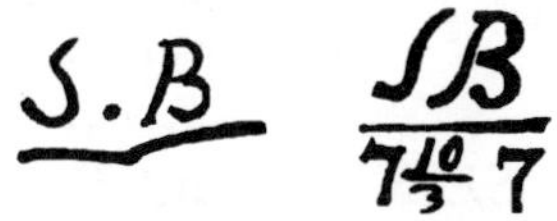

1773 Souroux, rue de la Roquette, PARIS, France.

1773-84 HARD-PASTE PORCELAIN. - -

1773	Advenier and Lamare, PARIS, France. -	see 1762 Gros Caillou.
1773	Bourge-la-Reine, France. - - -	see 1734 MENNECY-VILLEROY.
1773	Buteux fils cadet (flowers/landscapes) France.	see 1745 SÈVRES.
1773	Carthusian Monastery, Mainz, Germany.-	see 1765 FLORSHEIM.
1773	Chauveaux fils (bouquets) France. -	see 1745 SÈVRES.
1773	`Fabbrica Reale Ferdinandea` NAPLES, Italy.	see 1771 Naples Royal Factory.
1773	Gilot, France. - - - -	see ST.AMAND-LES-EAUX.
1773	Humble, Green & Co., England. - -	see 1760 LEEDS POTTERY.
1773	Le Bel jeune (flowers) France. - -	see 1745 SÈVRES.
1773	Le Cerf, Joseph, (painter) France.- -	see 1733 SINCENY.
1773	Petit, Phillipe Auguste, France. - -	see 1696 LILLE.
1773	Pouillot, (flowers) France. - - -	see 1745 SÈVRES.
1773	Rigg & Peacock, England.- - -	see 1743 LIVERPOOL.
1773	Robert, Joseph-Gospard, MARSEILLES, Fra.	see 1750 Roberts Factory.
1773	Rolet, M., Italy. - - - -	see 1520 URBINO.
1773	Schradre, (birds/landscapes) France. -	see 1745 SÈVRES.
1773	Sinsson, N., (flowers) France. - -	see 1745 SÈVRES.

1774

1774 Dubois, Jerome-Vincent, Rue de la Roquette, PARIS, France.

1774-87 HARD-PASTE PORCELAIN.

Underglaze blue-

1774 Wm. Cookworthy & Co., BRISTOL, Avon, England.

1774- HARD-PASTE PORCELAIN.

Marks painted blue -

Richard Champion bought the factory and the rights of the porcelain patent from William Cookworthy having been involved with the business since 1770. see 1768 Wm. Cookworthy, Plymouth.

Marks painted blue, numbers in gold-

1775 **Richard Champion renewed his porcelain patent,** against strong opposition from Josiah Wedgwood as leader of the Staffordshire Potteries.

1781 **Champion eventually sold his rights to the Society of the Staffordshire Potteries.**

1774 LA SEINIE, Saint-Yrieix, Haute-Vienne, France.

1774-1856 Hard-paste porcelain - red-

1774 MORS, Denmark.

1774-c.84 FAÏENCE AND STONEWARE.

Thomas Lund (owner) - -

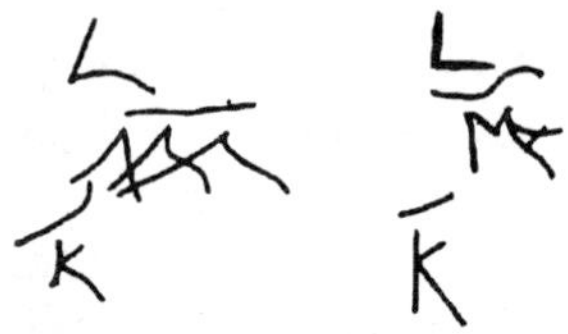

1774 rue de Petit Carrousel, PARIS, France.

1774-1800 **Guy, Charles-Bartélémy (decorator)**

Stencilled in red -

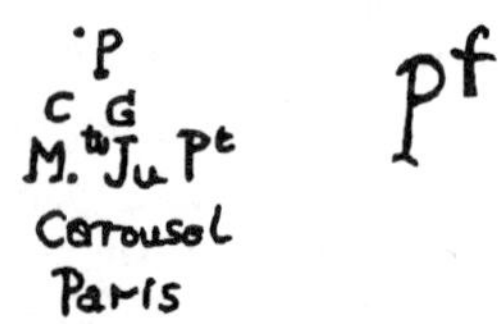

1774 rue de Reuilly, PARIS, France.

c.1774-87 HARD-PASTE PORCELAIN. Colours or gold-

Lassia, Jean-Joseph.

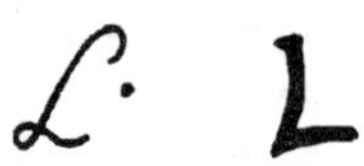

1774 Usinger, Heinrich, HÖCHST, Germany.

1774-84 DECORATOR. - - -

1774 VIANNA DO CASTELLO, Darque, Portugal.

1774- FAÏENCE. - - -

1774 WARSAW, Poland.

1774- Faïence. - - -

1774-93 **Belveder manufactory** - -

1783- **Wolff manufactory** - -

1774	Champion, Richard, BRISTOL, England.	see 1768 Cookworthy, Wm.,
1774	Frey, Hans Jacob, Switzerland. - -	see 1760 LENZBURG.
1774	`Marcolini Period` Germany. - -	see 1710 MEISSEN.
1774	Palsjö Fabrik, Sweden. - - -	see 1765 PALSJÖ.
1774	Sax, (painter) Germany. - - -	see 1770 MOSBACH.
1774	Verdier, Donnat and Morel, France. -	see 1730 CLERMONT-FERRAND.

1775 CAUGHLEY, Shropshire, (Salopian) England.

1775- PORCELAIN.

The site of the first works was begun by a Mr Browne where he produced earthenware.

1754- Mr Gallimore (after the death of Mr Browne) obtained a lease on the works for a term of 62 years.

1772- Thomas Turner married Mr Gallimore`s daughter and became the proprietor.

Early marks not known

1775- **Thomas Turner established the porcelain works.**

Early mark impressed in a circle- **TURNER - GALLIMORE SALOPIAN**

`C` or crescent marks in blue- (Similar to Worcester)

`S` marks printed in blue-

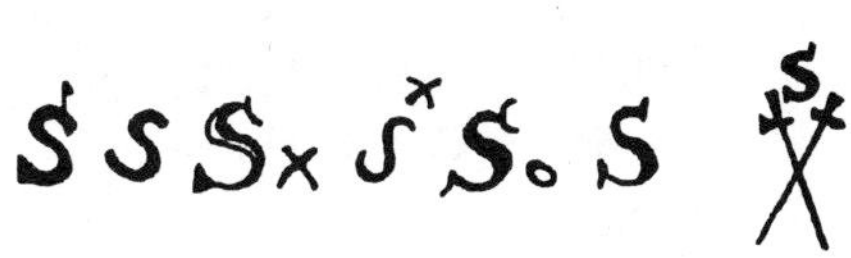

Continued over -

1775

1775 CAUGHLEY, Shropshire, (Salopian) England. (Cont`)

Thomas Turner and a partner named Shaw opened a retail outlet in London and named it the Salopian China Warehouse and from time to time held sales there.

SALOPIAN
Salopian
impressed marks

1780- `Willow Pattern` First made in England.
1788- Both Robert Chamberlain and Graingers of Worcester purchased Caughley china and painted and finished it at Worcester.
(According to Miss Gaye Blake Roberts, Curator of Wedgwood Museum (1995) The Chinese-type marks intertwined around numbers, which are shown in some marks books are not Caughley but Worcester during William Davis`s period.)
1799- Business sold to John Rose & Co. Coalport.
c.1815 Works closed and removed to Coalport.

1775 CHATILLON, Seine, France.

c.1775- HARD-PASTE PORCELAIN red-

D V
chatillon Chatillon

1775 Coombes, BRISTOL, Avon, England.

c.1775-1805 REPAIRER OF CHINA,
Brown lustre -

Coombes
Queen St
Bristol

1775 Gordon`s Pottery, PRESTONPANS, Lothians, Scotland.

c.1775-1832 EARTHENWARES. - impressed- **GORDON**
c.1805- Initials of George Gordon printed within various patterns and designs- **G. G.**

1775 Klos, A., SCHIEDAM, Holland.

TIN-GLAZED EARTHENWARE. (DELFTWARE)- -

Schiedam
A:klos

1775 rue Thiroux, PARIS, France.

c.1775-19th century. HARD-PASTE PORCELAIN.
underglaze blue-

Leboeuf, André-Marie, Stencilled in red - A
(Protected by Queen Marie-Antoinette)

1794- Leboeuf & Housel - - -
1797-98 Guy & Housel. - - -

Gh
Rue Thirou
a Paris

Gh

1775 TREVISO, Venezia, Italy.

c.1775-c.1835 SOFT-PASTE PORCELAIN.

Giuseppe and Andrea Fontebasso.

1799 **Fratelli Fontebasso -**

20th century Societa` Ceramica Andrea Fontebasso. (S.C.A.F.T.)

1775 WÜRZBURG, Lower Franconia, Germany.

c.1775-80 HARD-PASTE PORCELAIN.

Johann Kaspar Geyger (founder) - - C · G W

1775	Boselli, Giacomo. Italy. - - - -	see 1550 SAVONA.
1775	Collin, Paul Heinrich, Germany. - - -	see 1772 KONIGSBERG
1775	Count Marcolini, Germany. - - -	see 1770 HUBERTUSBURG.
1775	Cristana, Fabbrica di Santa, Italy. - - -	see 1725 MILAN.
1775	Deruelle, Pierre, PARIS, France. - - -	see 1771 Clignacourt.
1775	Xavier, Louis-Stanislas, PARIS, France. - -	see 1771 Clignacourt.

1776 Neale & Co., James, HANLEY, Staffordshire, England.

c.1776-86 EARTHENWARES, WEDGWOOD TYPE.

c.1776-78 Impressed- **N NEALE**

Mark within a circle - **I. NEALE**
I. NEALE. HANLEY

c.1778-86 Impressed- **NEALE & CO.**

1776 TRIESTE, Italy.

1776 MAIOLICA

1780 **Filipuzzi & Co.,** - - - -

1776-78

1776 VINOVO, nr. Turin, Italy.

1776-1820 HYBRID SOFT-PASTE PORCELAIN. -

1780-1815 **Dr. Gioanetti, Vittorio Amadeo,-**

Fornario - -

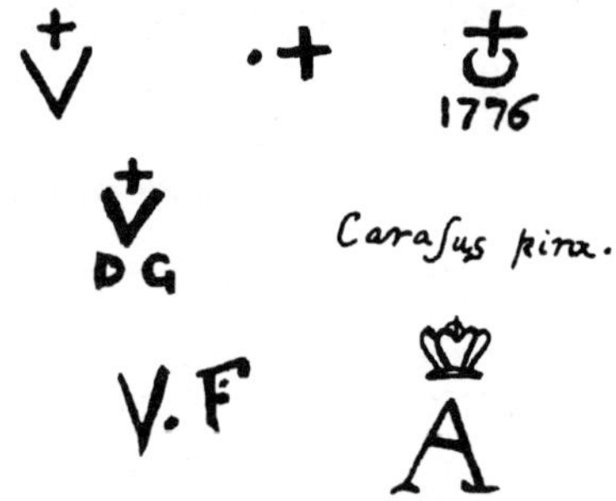

1776 Grue, Liborie, Italy. - - - see 1679 CASTELLI.
1776 Jaumann, Joseph, (painter) Germany. - - see 1752 SCHREZHEIM.
1776 Kratzberg, Canon of Hildesheim, Germany. - see 1740 HILDESHEIM.
1776 Le Grand, (painter/gilder) France. - - see 1745 SÈVRES.
1776 Pasquier, Pierre, & Faulcon, Felix, France. - see 1752 POITIERS.
1776 Sailly & Son, France. - - - - see 1750 TOURS.

1777 Dortu, Jacob, MARIEBERG, nr. Stockholm, Sweden.

1777-78 HARD-PASTE PORCELAIN. - -

Blue or red-

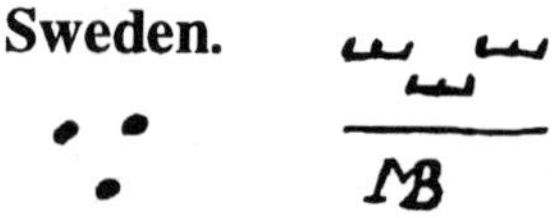

1777 ILMENAU, Thuringia, Germany.

Hard-paste porcelain. Christian Zacharias Grabner (founder)
Duke Karl August of Weimar. (sponsor)
The individual factories and potters of ILMENAU have been listed under their own dates and marks within this book.

1777 Benini Fabrique, Italy. - - - see 1451 FAENZA.
1777 Dieu, (painter/gilder) France. - - see 1745 SÈVRES.
1777 Fumez, (flowers) France. - - - see 1745 SÈVRES.
1777 Kotta, Franz, (modeller) Germany. - see 1760 KLOSTER-VEILSDORF.
1777 Le Bel, Dame, (flowers) France. - - see 1745 SÈVRES.
1777 Levé, Felix, (flowers/chinoiseries) France. see 1745 SÈVRES.
1777 Mignon, PARIS, France. - - - see 1743 Gerin, Claude-Humbert.
1777 Noualhier, Dame, (flowers) France. - see 1745 SÈVRES.

1778 Bingley & Co., Thomas, SWINTON, Yorkshire, England.

1778-87 EARTHENWARES. - - Impressed- **BINGLEY**

1778 Fonteyn, Cornelis J., (Delft Artist) DELFT, Holland.

TIN-GLAZED EARTHENWARE (DELFTWARE) - - - -

1778 DIRMSTEIN, nr. Worms, Rhineland, Germany.

1778-88 FAÏENCE AND CREAMWARES. - - -

1778 GROSZBREITENBACH, Thuringia, Germany.

c.1778- HARD-PASTE PORCELAIN.
Major Anton Friedrich Wilhelm Erst von Hopfgarten.

1788- Gotthelf Greiner, Limbach mark-

1869- **Bühl & Söhne**

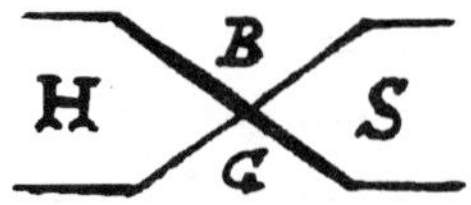

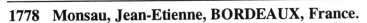

1778 Monsau, Jean-Etienne, BORDEAUX, France.

1778-83 FAÏENCE. - - - ***`F.P. Monsau`***

1779 (dated) - ***`Monsau fecit 1779`***

1783 (dated) - ***`Fait par Monsau 1783`***

1778 SWINTON, Yorkshire, England.

The individual factories and potters of SWINTON have been listed under their own dates and marks within this book.

1778 Bingley, England. - - - - see 1745 ROCKINGHAM
1778 Boulanger fils, (pastorals/children) France. - see 1745 SÈVRES.
1778 Bunel,Marie-Barbe, flowers, France. - - see 1745 SÈVRES.
1778 Le Gay, (figures/portraits) France. - - see 1745 SÈVRES.
1778 Le Guay, E-C, (figures) France. - - - see 1745 SÈVRES.
1778 Philippine aîné, (pastorals/children) France. - see 1745 SÈVRES.
1778 Weydinger, Joseph, (gilder) France. - - see 1745 SÈVRES.

1779 Barrière de Reuilly, PARIS, France.

1779-85 PORCELAIN.
Henri-Florentin Chanou.

1779 Féraud, Jean-Gaspard, MOUSTIERS, France.

1779-92 FAÏENCE.

Family continued until 1874.

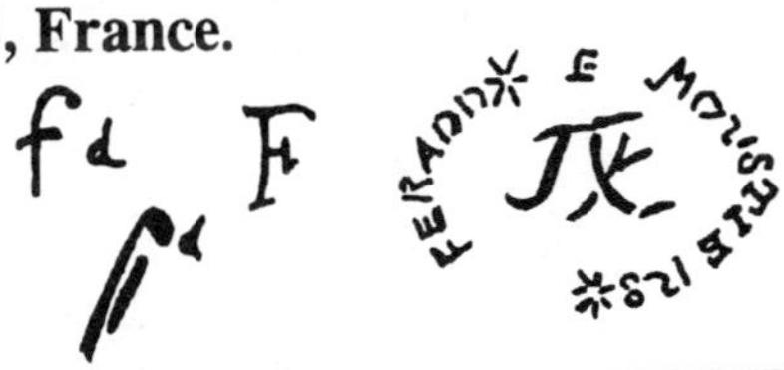

1779 PONTENX, Landes, France.

1779-90 HARD-PASTE PORCELAIN.
de Rosly. - - - -

1779/80

1779 Seligmann, (painter) NUREMBERG, Germany.
1779 (dated) - -

1779 Artois, Charles-Philippe, Comte d`, PARIS, France. see 1771 Faubourg Saint-Denis.
1779 Chanou, Dame, (gilder) France. - - - see 1745 SÈVRES.
1779 Léandre, (children/emblems) France. - - see 1745 SÈVRES.
1779 Massy, (flowers/birds) France. - - - see 1745 SÈVRES
1779 Stahn, PARIS, France. - - - - see 1771 Faubourg Saint-Denis.
1779 Teikichi, Honda, Japan. - - - - see 1650 KAGA.
1779 Vandé, P-J-B, (gilder) France. - - - see 1745 SÈVRES.

1780 Aynsley. John, LANE END, Staffordshire, England.

1780-1809 PRINTED EARTHENWARES.
Various printed marks with the name of the factory.

AYNSLEY
J. AYNSLEY
JOHN AYNSLEY
LANE END

1780 Haak, Arend de, (Delft Artist) DELFT, Holland.
TIN-GLAZED EARTHENWARE (DELFTWARE) -

1780 LANE DELPH, Staffordshire, England,
The individual factories and potters of LANE DELPH have been listed under their own dates and marks within this book.

1780 LE HAVRE, Seine-Infèrieure, France.
c.1780-1810 FAÏENCE AND CREAMWARES. impressed- **`DELAVIGNE AU HAVRE`**
`L.DELAVIGNE`
`AU HAVRE`

1780 NYON, nr. Geneva, Switzerland.
c.1780-1860 HARD-PASTE PORCELAIN, GEN. POTTERY.
blue-

c.1810 impressed- **`Dortu & Cie`**
c.1840 EARTHENWARE - - **`Poterie fine Bonnard et Gonin`**

c.1850- **Pfluger Bros. & Co.** -

1780 Plant, Benjamin, LANE END, Staffordshire, England.
c.1780-1820 EARTHENWARES. - incised- - - - -

1780 PORTOBELLO, nr. Edinburgh, Lothian, Scotland.

The individual factories and potters of PORTOBELLO have been listed under their own dates and marks within this book.

1780 Pratt, William, LANE DELPH, Staffordshire, England.

c.1780-99 EARTHENWARES. - - - **PRATT**

1780 rue de Bondy, PARIS, France.

1780-1829 HARD-PASTE PORCELAIN.
Dihl and Guerhard manufacturers

1780-c.93 **Duc d`Angoulême (patron)**
`Porcelaine d`Angoulême` gold-

1817-29 **Dihl.** mark on a can and saucer- blue-

c.1790 - **Guerhard & Dihl** mark on cup and saucer - - red-

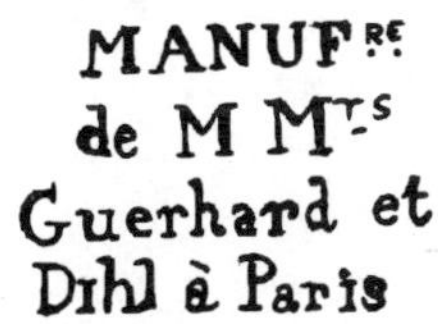

1780 St. Anthony`s Pottery, NEWCASTLE UPON TYNE, England.

c.1780-1878 EARTHENWARES ETC.,

1780-1820 Impressed- **ST. ANTHONY`S**

1804-c.28 **Sewell** Impressed or printed- **SEWELL**
ST. ANTHONY`S
SEWELL

1828-52 **Sewell & Donkin.** Impressed or printed- **SEWELL & DONKIN**

1852-78 **Sewell & Co.,** Impressed or printed- **SEWELL & CO.**

1780 SWANSEA, Glamorgan, Wales.

The individual factories and potters of SWANSEA have been listed under their own dates and marks within this book.

1780 Tittensor, Jacob, STOKE, Staffordshire, England.

1780-95 EARTHENWARES, FIGURES. Signature- - ***Jacob Tittensor`***

1780	Baccin, Giovanni Maria, Italy. - - -	see 1728 NOVE.
1780	Barre, (flowers) France. - - - -	see 1745 SÈVRES.
1780	Dutanda, (flowers) France. - - -	see 1745 SÈVRES.
1780	Filipuzzi & Co., Italy. - - - -	see 1776 TRIESTE.
1780	Gionetti, Dr, Italy. - - - -	see 1776 VINOVO.
1780	Ka, Japan. - - - - - - -	see 1583 CHIKUZEN.
1780	Keel, Abraham van der, DELFT, Holland. -	see 1759 de Lampet Kan.
1780	Kimura Uji, Japan. - - - -	see 1583 BIZEN.
1780	List, J.G.F., Germany. - - - -	see 1770 MOSBACH.
1780	Roland, Jean, France. - - - -	see 1722 LA ROCHELLE.
1780	Shun (for Shunzan) in Suo, Japan. - -	see 1583 CHIKUZEN.

1781 Abbott, Andrew, LANE END, Staffordshire, England.

c.1781-83 EARTHENWARES - Impressed- **ABBOTT POTTER**

1781 DOUAI, Nord, France.

1781- EARTHENWARES MADE IN ENGLISH STYLE. Impressed- ***Douai***

1781-84 **Leigh & Co.,(brothers)** - -

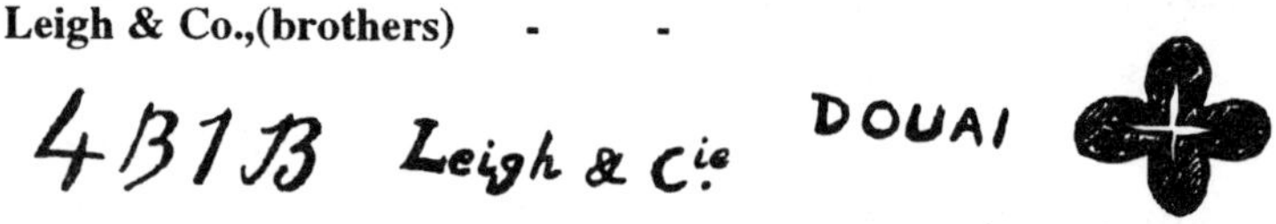

1784-c.88 **Houze de l`Aulnoit & Cie** - -

1788-c.1820 Halsfort, - - - **`HALSFORT`**

1799-1803 **Dammann, Martin,** - - ***Martin Dammann`***

1781 ESTE, Italy.

1781-c.1795 PORCELAIN. **Este**

Fiorina Fabris & Antonio Costa - - **G**

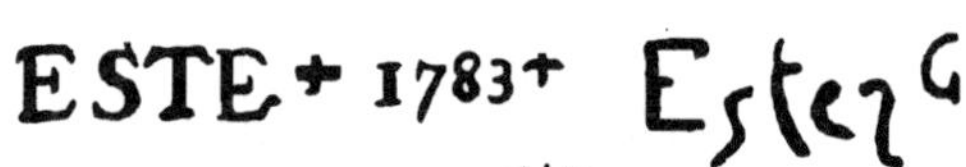

1785- **Gerolamo Franchini**

CREAMWARE - - -

1781 Letellier, Hubert, ROUEN, France.

1781- FAÏENCE. **From 1805** CREAMWARES -

1781 New Hall Porcelain Works, HANLEY, Staffordshire, England.

1781-1835 PORCELAIN.

c.1812-35 Bone China mark. printed- - - -

1781 Verneuilh, Pierre, BORDEAUX, France.
1781-87 HARD-PASTE PORCELAIN. gold or blue-

1781	Gérard,Dame (née.Vautrin) flowers, France. -	see 1745 SÈVRES.
1781	Mantzius, Jacob C.L., COPENHAGEN, Denmark.	see 1754 Kastrup.
1781	Parolini, Signor, Partnership, Italy. - -	see 1728 NOVE.
1781	Weydinger, Pierre, (painter/gilder) France. -	see 1745 SÈVRES.
1781	Wiengartner, Mathias Joseph, Germany. - -	see 1765 FLÖRSHEIM.
1781	Wood, Ralph, (grandson) BURSLEM, England.-	see 1715 Ralph Wood.

1782 rue Popincourt, PARIS, France.
1782-c.1850 HARD-PASTE PORCELAIN
Nast, J.N.H., Stencilled red-

1782	Hubaudière, Antoine de la, France. - -	see 1690 QUIMPER.
1782	Sailly, Noël, (son) France. - - - -	see 1750 TOURS.

1783 ANDENNES, Belgium.
1783- **A.D. Vander Waert** FAÏENCE. -

c.1794-1820 **B. Lammens & Co.,**
CREAMWARES - -

1783 Clowes, William, BURSLEM, Staffordshire, England.
c.1783-96 EARTHENWARES, ETC. Impressed- *W. CLOWES*

1783 PREMIÈRES, Cote-d`Or, France.
1783- FAÏENCE.
Dr. J. Lavelle
19th century marks

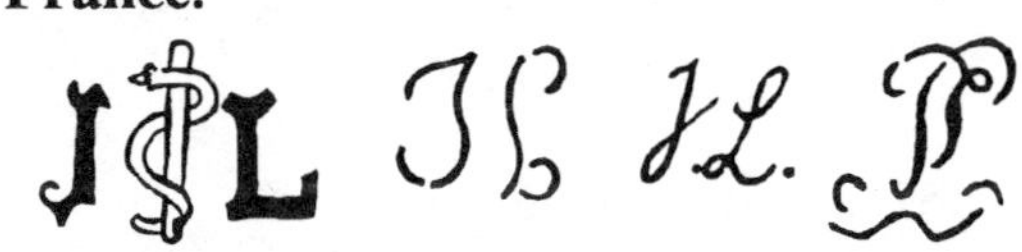

1783 RAUENSTEIN, Thuringia, Germany.
1783- HARD-PASTE PORCELAIN. Printed black- - -

c.1787 Printed blue-

19th century - - -

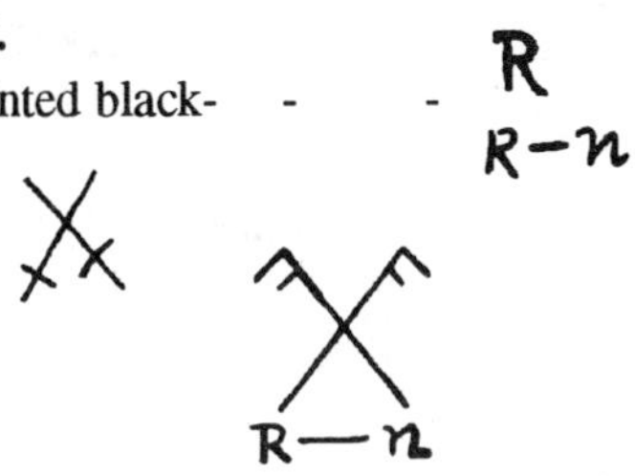

1783 SCHNEY, Bavaria, Germany.

c.1783-c.1910 HARD-PASTE PORCELAIN. Impressed- **SCHNEY**

Liebmann, E. - - - - - 

1783 Swansea Pottery, (Cambrian Pottery) SWANSEA, Wales.

c.1783-1870 EARTHENWARES AND CHINA. ***Early wares were not marked***

c.1783-c.1810 - - **SWANSEA**
CAMBRIA
CAMBRIAN
CAMBRIAN POTTERY

1802-17 **Dillwyn & Co.** - - - **DILLWYN & CO**
And 1824-50 **SWANSEA**
D. & CO.

1845-46 Etruscan Ware. - 

PORCELAIN MARKS

1814-24 **William Billingsley and George Walker. joined Mr Dillwyn to produce soft-paste porcelain as they did at Nantgarw**

Marks printed in red - **SWANSEA**
Swansea

Mark impressed - **DILLWYN**

Trident marks impressed- 

1823 Moulds etc. were purchased by Mr. Rose of Coalport. - - - see 1796 COALPORT.

c.1817-24 **Bevington & Co.** - Impressed- **BEVINGTON & CO. SWANSEA.**

c.1847-50 Impressed- **CYMRO STONE CHINA**

c.1850-62 **Evans, David & Glasson.**
POTTERY. Impressed or printed- 

Continued over -

1783 Swansea Pottery, Cambrian Pottery, SWANSEA, Wales. (Cont`)

c.1862-70 **Evans D. J. & Co.** - - **D.J. EVANS & CO.**

POTTERY. Factory`s name printed within marks of various designs- **EVANS & CO**

(For further information see `Jewitt`s Ceramic Art in Great Britain)

1783 Turner & Abbott, LANE END, Staffordshire, England.

c.1783-87 WEDGWOOD TYPE WARES. Impressed- **TURNER & ABBOTT**

1783 Couturier, gilder, France. - - - - - see 1745 SÈVRES.
1783 Flight period, England. - - - - - see 1751 WORCESTER.
1783 Fouque, Joseph, MOUSTIERS, France. - - see 1679 Clérissy, Pierre,
1783 Hartley, Green & Co., England. - - - see 1760 LEEDS POTTERY.
1783 Leopold period, Germany. - - - - see 1763 PROSKAU.
1783 Philippine, cadet, (flowers/animals) France - see 1745 SÈVRES.

1784 AMSTEL, nr. Amsterdam, Holland.

Transferred from Oude Loosdrecht.

1784-1820 HARD-PASTE PORCELAIN.
A. Dareuber (director)

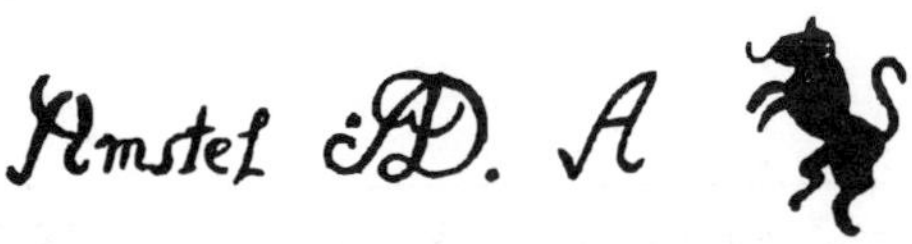

1784 Baddeley, John & Edward, SHELTON, Staffordshire, England.

1784-1806 EARTHENWARES **B** **I. E. B.**
I. E. B.
W

1806-22 **Hicks & Meigh.** Impressed or printed- **HICKS & MEIGH**
EARTHENWARE AND `IRONSTONE` (sometimes with Royal Arms)

1822-35 **Hicks, Meigh & Johnson.** Printed- **H M J**
EARTHENWARES AND IRONSTONE Printed- **H M & J**
(printed with Royal Arms)

Later became:- Ridgway, Morley, Wear & Co. see 1836 Ridgway.

1784 Booth, Hugh, STOKE, Staffordshire, England.

1784-89 EARTHENWARE AND CREAMWARE. impressed- **H. BOOTH**

1784 Cyples, Joseph, LANE END, Staffordshire, England.

c.1784-1840 EARTHENWARES - Impressed- **CYPLES**
I. CYPLES

1784

1784 Glass, John, HANLEY, Staffordshire, England.
c.1784-1838 EARTHENWARE AND STONEWARE. Impressed- **GLASS HANLEY**
J. GLASS HANLEY

1784 Hollins, Samuel, SHELTON, Staffordshire, England.
c.1784-1813 WEDGWOOD STYLE CERAMICS. Impressed- **S. HOLLINS**
HOLLINS

1784 LONGPORT, Staffordshire, England.
The individual factories and potters of LONGPORT have been listed under their own dates and marks within this book

---

1784 Menner, John, Womelsdorf, BERKS COUNTY, Pennsylvania, U.S.A.
c.1784- EARTHENWARES. SLIP-WARE.
Later taken over by Beck, Josiah,
1864- **Smith, Willoughby,** Impressed- **Willoughby Smith**
Wumelsdorf

1784 Neale & Wilson, HANLEY, Staffordshire, England.
c.1784-95 EARTHENWARES, WEDGWOOD STYLE.
Impressed- **NEALE & WILSON**
NEALE & CO.

1784 Rogers, John & George, LONGPORT, Staffordshire, England.
c.1784-1814 EARTHENWARES - - **ROGERS**
Impressed- **J. R.**
L.

Mark shown by `Jewitt` (Mars of Iron sign) - ♂ **ROGERS**

c.1814-36 **Rogers & Son, John,** - - **J.R.S.**
ROGER & SON

1784 rue Amelot, PARIS, France.
1784-1825 **M. Lefebvre Fabrique** - - *Lefebre a paris*

1784 Sarreguemines Vaisselle, PARIS, France.
c.1784- EARTHENWARE.
The origin of the faiencerie de Sarreguemines was founded around 1780 by two Strasburg natives, Jacobi & Fabry.

U&Cie

Continued over -

1784 Sarreguemines Vaisselle, PARIS, France. (Cont`)

c.1798- **Under the guidance of Paul Utzschneider the** factory made a considerable name for itself. Napoleon remarked on the quality of Sarreguemines products and conferred the Legion of Honour on this brilliant ceramist.
Under the second Empire, the railways and Sarres canal were opening up which allowed the earthenware plant to considerably expand its markets.

1876- **Following the Franco Prussian War, Sarreguemines director Paul de Geiger established a new factory in Digoin, France, producing earthenware, stoneware and porcelain.**

1960- **`Pyroblan`** china launched especially conceived for the catering industry.

1978- **The group, under the direction of Gilbert Fenal,** took control of the societe des faienceries of Sarreguemines, Digoin and Vitry-le-François. Digoin concentrates its entire production on `Pyroblan` china.

Some modern marks used by Sarraguemines today (1995) :-

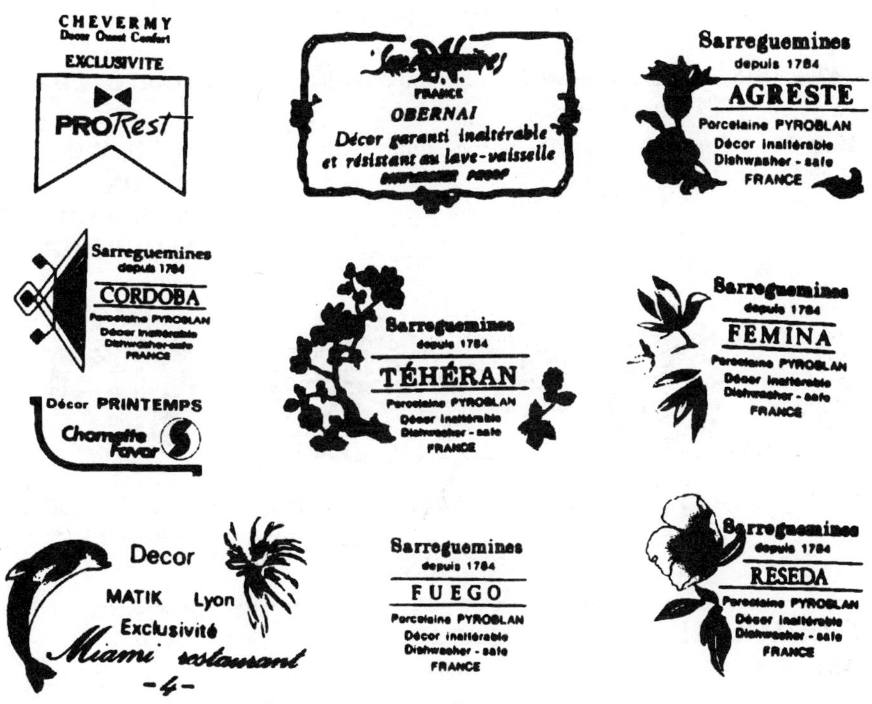

(By kind permission of Sarreguemines Vaisselle, PARIS, France.)

1784

1784 Smith & Co., Ambrose, BURSLEM, Staffordshire, England.

c.1784-86 EARTHENWARE. Impressed or printed- **A. S. & CO.**

1784 Taylor, George, HANLEY, Staffordshire, England.

c.1784-1811 EARTHENWARES. Impressed or incised- **G. TAYLOR**
GEO. TAYLOR

1784 Wolfe, Thomas, STOKE, Staffordshire, England.

c.1784-1800 EARTHENWARES. Impressed- **WOLFE**

c.1800-11 Wolfe & Hamilton.
Painted or impressed- **WOLFE & HAMILTON**
STOKE

c.1811-18 Wolfe, Thomas, - Impressed- **WOLFE W**

1784 Wood, Enoch, BURSLEM, Staffordshire, England.

c.1784-90 GENERAL CERAMICS. - - **WOOD E. WOOD**
E. W. W. W (***)

ENOCH WOOD SCULPSIT **E. WOOD SCULPSIT** **ENOCH WOOD**

c.1790-1818 Wood & Caldwell. EARTHENWARES. Impressed- **WOOD & CALDWELL**

1818-46 Enoch Wood & Sons. EARTHENWARES. Impressed- **ENOCH WOOD**
& SONS
BURSLEM
STAFFORDSHIRE

E. W. & S. **E. WOOD & SONS** **E. & E. WOOD**
BURSLEM

E. & E. WOOD **E. & E. W.**

1784 YARMOUTH, Norfolk, England.

1784-1815 Absolon, William, (ENAMELLER)
Painted brown- Absolon Yarm^a^

1784 Yates, John, HANLEY, Staffordshire, England.
c.1784-1835 EARTHENWARES. Printed or impressed- **J. Y.**

1784 Coccore, Carlo, NAPLES, Italy. - - - see 1771 Naples Royal Factory.
1784 Copeland, William, STOKE, England. - - see 1770 Spode, Josiah,
1784 Houze de l`Aulnoit & Cie., France. - - see 1781 DOUAI.
1784 Lamprecht, George, (figures/animals) France. - see 1745 SÈVRES.
1784 Leperre-Durot, France. - - - - see 1696 LILLE.
1784 Ring, Joseph, BRISTOL, England. - - see 1734 Franks, Richard,
1784 Sorgenthal period, Austria. - - - see 1719 VIENNA.

1785 Bristol Pottery, BRISTOL, England.
c.1785-1825 EARTHENWARE. - - - **BRISTOL POTTERY**

1785 CHOISY-LE-ROI, Seine, France.
c.1785- HARD-PASTE PORCELAIN.
M. Clément (founder)

1836- Hautin and Boulanger - **H B & Cie**
CHOISY
LE ROY

1785 Hubener, Goerg, MONTGOMERY COUNTY, Pennsylvania, U.S.A.
1785-98 EARTHENWARES, SGRAFFITO STYLE.
Sometimes with date-

1785 Johnson, Joseph, LIVERPOOL, England.
18th century ENGRAVER. - - - - - **I. JOHNSON**
LIVERPOOL

1785 Patience, Thomas, BRISTOL, England.
18th century STONEWARE. Impressed- **PATIENCE**

1785 Boulevard St. Antoine, PARIS, France.
1785- HARD-PASTE PORCELAIN - - **F.D.HONORÉ**
Honoré, François-Maurice, - **F.M. HONORÉ**
1812 Edward and Theodore (sons) became **R.F. DAGOTY**
partners and worked with Dagoty **DAGOTY ET HONORÉ**

1785 Ring, Joseph, (d.1788) BRISTOL, England,
1785-88 CREAMWARES Impressed- **RING & CO**
1788-1812 Continued by partners.

1785/86

1785 Thompson, James, MORGANTOWN, West Virginia, U.S.A.

c.1785- EARTHENWARES, LEAD-GLAZED.

Succeeded by Thompson, John W. (son)

c.1870-90 Thompson, Greenland, (grandson) — **MORGANTOWN**

SALT-GLAZED STONEWARES. — **Morgantown**

1785 Vecchio, Cherinto del, NAPLES, Italy.

1785-1855 Fabbrica del Vecchio Napoli -

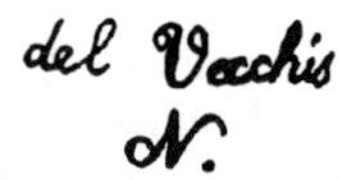

Gennaro del Vecchio Napoli. late mark - **G D V N**

Giustiniani - - -

1785	Bernard, François, France.- - - -	see 1737 LES ISLETTES.
1785	Boucot, P., (flowers/birds) France. - -	see 1745 SÈVRES.
1785	Bouillat, fils, (flowers/landscapes) France. -	see 1745 SÈVRES.
1785	Dannecker, J.H. Germany.- - - -	see 1756 LUDWIGSBURG.
1785	Drouet, (flowers/birds) France. - - -	see 1745 SÈVRES.
1785	Fauques, J-B, & Lamoninary, France. - -	see 1735 VALENCIENNES
1785	Franchini, Gerolamo, Italy. - - -	see 1781 ESTE.
1785	Moeller, Joachim, Germany. - - -	see 1750 KELLINGHUSEN.
1785	Scheffauer, P.J., Germany.- - - -	see 1756 LUDWIGSBURG.
1785	Volpate, Giovanni, Italy. - - - -	see 1600 ROME.

1786 Chamberlain`s, Diglis, WORCESTER, England.

c.1786-1852 SOFT-PASTE PORCELAIN.

c.1786-1810 Painted written marks-

c.1811-40 Written and printed marks -
under a crown -

Chamberlain`s
Worcester,
& 155
New Bond Street,
London,
Royal Porcelain Manufactory

Continued over -

1786 Chamberlain`s, Diglis, WORCESTER, England. (Cont`)

c.1811-20 `Regent` porcelain marks:-

c.1814-16 Written or printed mark:-

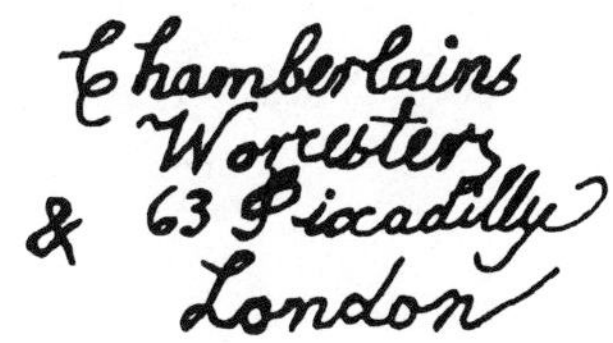

1840- Factory merged with Flight, Barr & Bar, under the name of Chamberlain & Co. see 1751 WORCESTER.

c.1840-45 Printed mark under crown `& Co.` added

CHAMBERLAIN & CO
WORCESTER
155 NEW BOND ST.
& No. 1
COVENTRY ST.
LONDON.

c.1846-50 Written or printed, sometimes with crown - **CHAMBERLAIN & CO. WORCESTER**

c.1847-50 impressed or printed- sometimes with `Worcester` - **CHAMBERLAINS**

c.1850-52 Printed mark - -

1852 Kerr & Binns took over the factory - see 1751 WORCESTER.

1786 Fletcher, Thomas, HANLEY, Staffordshire, England.

c.1786-1810 PRINTER AND DECORATOR. - **T. FLETCHER SHELTON**

1786/87

1786 GUSTAVSBERG, Sweden.

1786-1860 FAÏENCE AND SEMI-PORCELAIN.
1786-97 - -

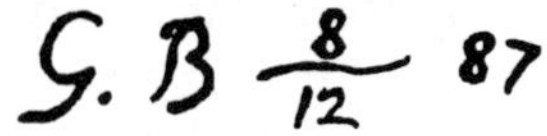

1820-60 **Godenius** EARTHENWARES.

1822- HARD-PASTE PORCELAIN

20th Century Gustavsbergs.

Fabriks-Interessenter-

1786 Pont-aux-Choux, PARIS, France.

1786- HARD-PASTE PORCELAIN.
J.B. Outrequin de Montarcy. monogram-
stencilled in red-

1786-93 **Louis Philippe, Duke of Orléans (Protector)** Underglaze blue marks-

Monogram `MJ` of Director-

1786 Scott Brothers, PORTOBELLO, Scotland.

c.1786-96 EARTHENWARES Impressed- **SCOTT BROTHERS**
SCOTT BROS. **SCOTT**
P.B.

1786	Buteux, Theodore, France.- - - -	see 1745 SÈVRES.
1786	Duesbury, William (son) England. - -	see 1749 DERBY
1786	Frederick William II. Germany. - - -	see 1751 BERLIN.
1786	Harlees, Dirck, DELFT, Holland. - - -	see 1653 De Porceleyne Fles.
1786	Schaerbeek, Belgium. - - - -	see 1705 BRUSSELS.
1786	Vliet, J.van der, Holland. - - - -	see 1630 ROTTERDAM.

1787 Abbott & Mist, LANE END, Staffordshire, England.

1787-1810 EARTHENWARES- Impressed or printed- **ABBOTT & MIST**

1787 Vanier, Michel, and Alluard, BORDEAUX, France.

1787-90 FAÏENCE Stencilled blue-

1787	Clair, Adam, (repairer) Germany. - - -	see 1755 FRANKENTHAL.
1787	Etterbeek, Belgium. - - - -	see 1705 BRUSSELS.
1787	Gauthier (figures/landscapes) France. - -	see 1745 SÈVRES.
1787	Greens, Bingley & Co., England. - - -	see 1745 ROCKINGHAM.
1787	Russinger, Laurent, PARIS, France. - -	see 1773 Porcelaine de Paris.

1788 Atkinson & Co., Southwick Pottery, SUNDERLAND, England.

1788-99 EARTHENWARE.. Impressed or printed - **ATKINSON & CO**

1788 Keller & Guerin, LUNÉVILLE, France.

1788-19th century - - -

Modern mark - -

1788 Southwick Pottery, SUNDERLAND, England.

EARTHENWARES, WHITE, COLOURED AND BROWN.

1788-1829	**Scott & Co.,Anthony, - -**	**A. SCOTT & CO.** **SCOTT, SOUTHWICK**
c.1829-44	**A. Scott & Sons. - - -**	**A. SCOTT & SONS** **S. & SONS**
c.1844-54	**Scott Brothers & Co. - -**	**S. B. & CO.** **SCOTT BROTHERS**
c.1854-97	**A. Scott & Sons. - - -**	**A. SCOTT & SONS** **S. & S.**

1788 VICENZA, Italy.

1788- CREAMWARES.

Vicentini del Giglio - - -

1791 PORCELAIN - - -

1788-90

1788 Adalbert III. von Harstall, Germany. - see 1741 FULDA.
1788 Alluaud, M., France, - - - see 1736 LIMOGES.
1788 Greiner, Gotthelf, Germany. - - see 1778 GROSZBREITENBACH.
1788 Halsfort, France.- - - - see 1781 DOUAI.
1788 Parpette, aînée,Dlle, (flowers) France. - see 1745 SÈVRES.
1788 Ring & Taylor, BRISTOL, England. - see 1734 Franks, Richard,

---

1789 rue de Crussol, PARIS, France.

1789- Christopher Potter.(founder)
HARD-PASTE PORCELAIN. -

Denuelle mark -

1792 E. Blancheron - - - -

Biscuit-ware in relief- - - **E. BLANCHERON**

1789 Greiner, Wilhelm Heinrich, Germany. - see 1760 KLOSTER-VEILSDORF.

1790 ANGARONO, nr. Bassano, Italy.
c.1790 CREAMWARE FIGURES ETC., - -

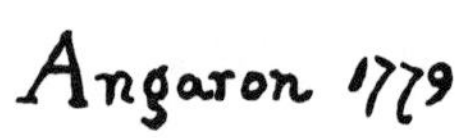

1790 Astbury, Richard Meir, SHELTON, Staffordshire, England.
c.1790- EARTHENWARE. - Impressed- **R. M. A.**

1790 Bourne, Edward, LONGPORT, Staffordshire, England.
1790-1811 EARTHENWARE. - Impressed- **E. BOURNE**

1790 CASTLEFORD, West Yorkshire, England.
The individual factories and potters of CASTLEFORD have been listed under their own dates and marks within this book.

1790 Don Pottery, SWINTON, Yorkshire, England.

1790-1893 EARTHENWARE, CREAM-COLOURED, BROWN, BLUE, ETC.
Impressed or printed- **DON POTTERY**

1800- **John Green. -** Impressed or printed- **GREEN DON POTTERY**

1807- **Greens, Clarke & Co.**
Other members of the Green family of Leeds joined the business, together with a Mr Clarke.

impressed or printed

1831- **Mr Green became sole proprietor.**

1834-93 **Barker, Samuel, of Mexborough Old Pottery purchased the business.**
1851 `& Sons` added.

1834-

1850-

1851-93

1790 Dunderdale & Co., David, CASTLEFORD, W. Yorkshire, England.

c.1790-1820 EARTHENWARES AND STONEWARES. **D. D. & CO.**
Castleford Pottery- Impressed- **D. D. & CO. CASTLEFORD POTTERY**

Characteristic Stoneware Teapots sometimes carry the impressed marked number '22' **'22'**

1790 Fasolt & Eichel, BLANKENHAIN, Thuringia, Germany.

1790- HARD-PASTE PORCELAIN. - -

1790 Garner, Robert, FENTON, Staffordshire, England.

Late 18th Century EARTHENWARE. Moulded - **R. G.**

1790 Greenwood, S., FENTON, Staffordshire, England.

c.1790- BASALT WARES. - Impressed- **S. GREENWOOD**

1790 Harrison, George, LANE DELPH, Staffordshire, England.

c.1790-95 EARTHENWARES. - Impressed- **G. HARRISON**

1790

1790 KORZEC, (Koretzki) Poland.

1790-97 HARD-PASTE PORCELAIN - blue -
c.1797-1870 Transferred to Gorodnitza

1817-31 in violet

19th century mark-

1790 LONGWY, Lorraine, France.

c.1790 FAIENCE AND EARTHENWARE
Incised or impressed-

1790 LORIENT, Morbihan, France.

1790-1808 HARD-PASTE PORCELAIN
`Porcelaine Lorientaise` - - **P L**

Sauvageau - - - - - ***`Fabrique dans le Dept du Morbihan par Sauvageau a Lorient`***

1790 Mayer, Elijah, HANLEY, Staffordshire, England.

c.1790-1804 WEDGWOOD TYPE WARES. Impressed- **E. MAYER**

1805-34 **Mayer & Son, Elijah,** Impressed or printed- **E. MAYER & SON.**

1790 MIRAGAYA, nr. Oporto, Portugal.

c.1790- FAÏENCE. - - - **MIRAGAYA. M.P.**

1790 Myatt, LANE DELPH, Staffordshire, England.

c.1790-c.1810 EARTHENWARES. - Impressed- **MYATT**

1790 Neale & Bailey, HANLEY, Staffordshire, England.

c.1790-1814 EARTHENWARES. Printed or impressed- **NEALE & BAILEY**

1790 Poole, Richard, HANLEY, Staffordshire, England.

1790-95 EARTHENWARES. - Impressed- **R. POOLE**

1790 PÖSSNECK, Saxony, Germany.

1790 HARD-PASTE PORCELAIN. Modern mark-
Conta & Boehme.

1790 Quai de la Cité, PARIS, France.

1790-1827 Duhamel PORCELAIN. - - Gold- ***Duhamel***

1790 ROUY, (Amigny-Rouy) France.

1790-1843 FAÏENCE, STRASBOURG TYPE.- - ***ROUY`***

1790 Smith, Theophilus, TUNSTALL, Staffordshire, England.

1790-c.97 EARTHENWARES. - Impressed- **T. SMITH**

1790 Steel, Daniel, BURSLEM, Staffordshire, England.

1790-1824 EARTHENWARES. WEDGWOOD TYPE. Impressed- **STEEL**

1790 TELECHANY, Poland.

c.1790- FAÏENCE - - -

Count Michael Oginski - -

C O
3

1790 Zillwood, W., AMESBURY, Wiltshire, England.

c.1790-c.1810 POTTERY. - Incised - - **W. Z.**

1790 Arnoux, Veuve, France. - - - see 1728 APT.
1790 Giordano (modeller) Italy. - - - see 1771 Naples Royal Porcelain.
1790 Giustiniani, Biagio,(son) NAPLES, Italy. see 1760 Giustiniani, Nicola.
1790 Guerhard & Dihl, PARIS, France. - see 1780 rue de Bondy.
1790 Launche, Pierre, and Perrier, France. - see 1730 CLERMONT-FERRAND.
1790 Moiron, (flowers) France. - - - see 1745 SÈVRES.
1790 Molier-Bardin, France. - - - see 1650 ORLÉANS.
1790 Wood & Caldwell, BURSLEM, England. see 1784 Wood, Enoch.

1791 Lakin & Poole, BURSLEM, Staffordshire, England.

c.1791-95 WEDGEWOOD-TYPE WARES, FIGURES, ETC. Impressed- **LAKIN & POOLE** / **L. & P.** / **BURSLEM**

1791 Villeroy, Nicolas, VAUDREVANGE, Saar, Germany.
(Now Wallerfangen)

1731- FAÏENCE FACTORY.

1797- **Nicolas Villeroy was the first to use hard coal to fire his kilns.**

1789-1836 Marks-

V.V N.V.

Vaudrevange

1836- **Villeroy & Boch Group created.**
(Merger with the Boch`s) see 1767 Villeroy & Boch.

Continued over -

1791/92

1791 Villeroy, Nicolas, VAUDREVANGE, Saar, Germany, (Cont`)

1836- Various marks-

1852- Bone-china produced by the factory.
(By kind permission of Villeroy & Boch AG., Germany.)

1791 Cretté, Louis, Belgium. - - - - - see 1705 BRUSSELS.
1791 Moitte, (modeller) PARIS, France. - - see 1771 Clignacourt.

1792 FERRYBRIDGE, Yorkshire, England.

The individual factories and potters of FERRYBRIDGE have been listed under their own dates and marks within this book.

1792 Nonne, Christian, ILMENAU, Germany.

1792-1808 HARD-PASTE PORCELAIN. - - **i**

1808- **Nonne & Roesch** - - - **N & R**

1792 Tomlinson & Co., FERRYBRIDGE, Yorkshire, England.

Knottingley Pottery, Tomlinson, William,
1792-c.1843 EARTHENWARES. CREAMWARES.
1792-96 and 1801-34 Printed or impressed- **TOMLINSON & CO.**

c.1796-1801 Ralph Wedgwood became partner.
Impressed- **WEDGWOOD & CO.**

1804-26 **Re-named `Ferrybridge Pottery`** Impressed- **FERRYBRIDGE**

c.1843-56 - - - see 1843 Reed & Taylor

1792 VALOGNES, Manche, France.

c.1792- **Factory opened to pruduce** FAÏENCE.
Le Tellier de la Bertiniere (from Bayeux)
c.1793-97 **Le Masson** HARD-PASTE PORCELAIN - **PORCELAINE DE VALOGNES**

c.1802-10 **Langlois, Joachim,** - - - **MANUFACTURE DE VALOGNES**

Continued over -

1792 VALOGNES, Manche, France. (Cont`)

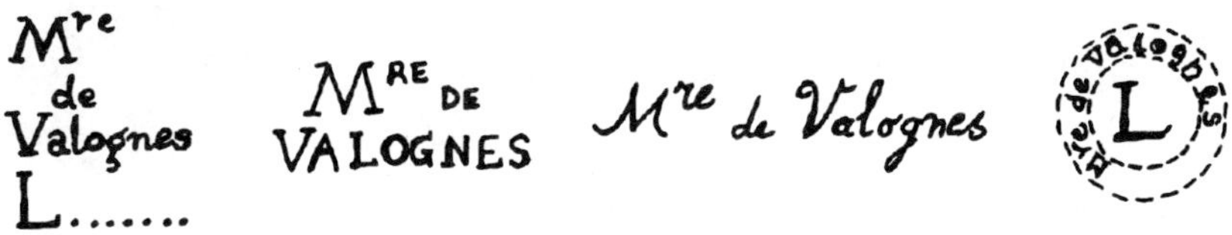

Transferred to Bayeux - - see 1810 BAYEUX

1792 Blancheron, E., PARIS, France. - - - see 1789 rue de Crussol.
1792 Fanciullacci, Pietro, Italy. - - - - see 1735 DOCCIA.
1792 First Republic, France. - - - - see 1745 SÈVRES.
1792 Flight & Barr, England. - - - - see 1751 WORCESTER.
1792 Godin, (gilder/painter) France. - - - see 1745 SÈVRES.

1793 Davenport & Co.,W., LONGPORT, Staffordshire, England.

c.1793-1887 GENERAL CERAMICS.

c.1793-c.1810 Lower-case mark -
Sometimes with anchor. impressed- **Davenport**
c.1805- Upper-case mark -
Sometimes with anchor. impressed- **DAVENPORT**

c.1805-20 STONE CHINA - -

c.1810-c.60 19th century mark which includes year of manufacture (i.e.38=1838)

c.1815- PORCELAIN. printed- - - **DAVENPORT LONGPORT**

c.1820-c.30 Anchor mark, impressed-

1820-60 Factory`s name printed within marks of various patterns and designs. **DAVENPORT**

c.1850-70 Porcelain plaques mark - - **DAVENPORT**
impressed- - - - **PATENT**

Continued over -

1793

1793 Davenport & Co., W., LONGPORT, Staffordshire, England. (Cont`)

c.1850-70 PORCELAIN. underglaze blue- - -

c.1850 (Mid 19th century) EARTHENWARES. Sometimes bear the date mark. (i.e. 6.72=June 1872)

DAVENPORT
LONGPORT
8.78

c.1860-87 **Wares sold by Minton`s Liverpool shop.** Printed-

c.1870-86 PORCELAIN. Printed- - - -

c.1881-87 EARTHENWARES. Printed- **DAVENPORT LTD.**

1793 Galeries du Louvre, PARIS, France.

1793-1800 **Lagrenée le jeune.** Painted maroon-

1793 GOINCOURT, Oise, France.

1793- FAÏENCE. - - - - - - **L`ITALIENNE**

Michel. Impressed-

1793 Herculaneum Pottery, LIVERPOOL, England.

c.1793-1841 EARTHENWARE AND PORCELAIN. Large and small impressed marks- **HERCULANEUM**

HERCULANEUM

1794-1806 **Worthington, Humble & Holland**
c.1796-1833 Impressed or printed-

1822-41 Impressed or printed- - **HERCULANEUM POTTERY**

1833-36 **Case, Thomas & Mort, John.** - Printed- -

Continued over -

1793 Herculaneum Pottery, LIVERPOOL, England. (Cont`)

c.1836-41 Mort & Simpson. `Liver` bird -
Printed or impressed-

1793 KLOSTERLE, Bohemia, Germany.

1793- EARTHENWARE AND PORCELAIN.

1794-1830- -

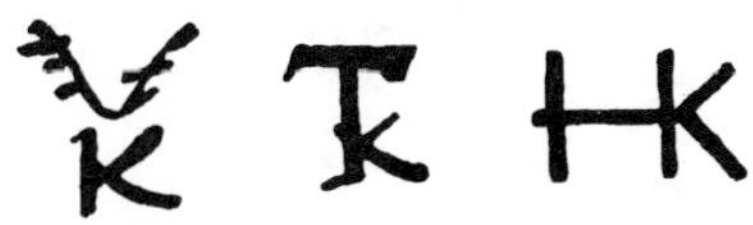

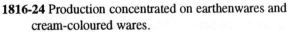

c.1895- Thun`sche Porzellanfabrik

1793 Minton, Thomas, STOKE, Staffordshire, England.

1793 Thomas Minton took Joseph Poulson into partnership and at a later date William Pownall joined the business. The early years concentrated on unmarked, blue printed, earthenwares.

1798-Cream-coloured earthenware and bone china introduced. By 1810 the range of production included printed and painted earthenwares, cream-coloured wares, stonewares, Egyptian black and printed and painted bone china.

c.1800- Many Minton patterns were very similar to their rivals i.e. Spode, Miles Mason, New Hall and Pinxton and can only be distinguished by the pattern numbers. Only some bone china tableware was marked with a painted `Sèvres` type mark.

c.1800-16 Sèvres-type mark on bone china-

1816-24 Production concentrated on earthenwares and cream-coloured wares.

1817-Thomas and Herbert Minton (2 sons) taken into partnership. Thomas soon left and Herbert eventually had joint control with his father. Through his drive and determination, Herbert changed the factory into the greatest Victorian pottery in Europe.

1824- Bone china reintroduced.

Continued over -

1793

1793 Minton, Thomas, STOKE, Staffordshire, England, (Cont`)

c.1824-36 Printed marks found on earthenware-

c.1830-60 Moulded mark found on stoneware
and earthenware.-

1836 **Thomas Minton died.**

1836-42 **Minton & Boyle. John Boyle taken into partnership.**
1836-41 (Minton & Boyle) Printed mark
found on earthenware.-

c.1841-50 Printed mark found on earthenware.

1842- **Michael Hollins and Colin Campbell (Herbert`s nephews) join the company.**

1842- Herbert Minton introduces parian ware.
1852- Parian catalogue published.

1845-68 (Minton & Hollins) Printed mark
found on earthenware. -

c.1845-65 (Ermine mark) Incised, painted or
printed on bone china and parian ware.

1846- **`Summerley Art Manufactures`** established by Sir Henry Cole to encourage well-known artists to design everyday goods for industrial production. The most notable being, the sculptor, John Bell.

c.1846-56 (Summerly mark) Moulded mark found
on wares designed by John Bell. -

1849- **Leon Arnoux (from Toulouse) became art director.** He encouraged other French artists to come to Stoke thus forming a strong link between Minton and France, which continued throughout the 19th century.

c.1850-70 Printed marks found on high-quality
earthenware and porcelain. -

1851 **The Great Exhibition. Arnoux introduced `majolica`**

Continued over -

1793 Minton, Thomas, STOKE, Staffordshire, England. (Cont`)

1858 **Herbert Minton died. Colin Minton Campbell takes control. At this stage Minton`s employed over 1500 people.**

1860s-70s **Majolica was produced with designs by Alfred Stevens and with painting by Continental artists such as Emile Lessore, Edouard Rischgitz and Louis Jahn.**

c.1860-1968 Impressed marks found on all types of ware
`S` was added in 1873 to make `MINTONS`

MINTON
MINTONS

c.1860-present day. Printed marks found on all wares -
1873 Name became `MINTONS` -
c.1880 A crown was added. -
1891 `England` was added.-
c.1912 Encircling wreaths and
`Made in England` added. -

MINTONS
MINTONS
MINTONS EST. 1793 MADE IN ENGLAND

1863- Acid Gold Process, a patented process by James Leigh Hughes was aquired by Minton.

1870- **Louis Marc Solon (from Sèvres) joined Minton** and intoduced the technique, pâte-sur-pâte decoration.

1871-75 Minton Art Pottery Studio, South Kensington, London, opened. Damaged by fire in 1875.

1871-75 Printed mark found on earthenware. - -

MINTONS
Art-Pottery
STUDIO
Kensington
Gore

1872- Antonin Boullemier (painter) joined Minton.
1874- Desire Leroy (enameller) joined Minton.

1878 Printed mark found on wares made for 1878 Exhibition.

PARIS EXHIBITION 1878
MINTONS

1885 Colin Minton Campbell died.
1892 Leon Arnoux retired.
1902 `Secessionist Ware` introduced.

c.1902-14 Printed mark found on Secessionist earthenware.

MINTONS LTD.

1904 Louis Marc Solon retired.

1909- **Leon Solon (son of Louis) became art director for a short while before emigrating to America.**

1935-55 **John W. Wadsworth was art director during this period.**

1939-45 World War II. Earthenware production discontinued. After the war Minton`s high quality bone china tableware was in considerable demand. Many new patterns were designed, including the best-selling `Haddon Hall`

MINTONS EST. 1793 ENGLAND
"Solano Ware"
DESIGNED BY
John Wadsworth

Continued over -

1793

1793 Minton, Thomas, STOKE, Staffordshire, England. (Cont`)

1953 Coronation of Her Majesty Queen Elizabeth II.
A commemorative vase was produced. The first copy was presented to Her Majesty and others were given to each member country of the Commonwealth.

1968- Minton became a member of the Royal Doulton Tableware Group. see 1815 Royal Doulton.

Present day printed mark (1995) - - -

MINTON 1793 BONE CHINA MADE IN ENGLAND

1842-1942

<u>Minton Year Cyphers.</u> <u>Impressed marks :-</u>

From 1943-68 the last two figures of the year were impressed.

1793 Norton Pottery, BENNINGTON, Vermont, U.S.A.

1793- EARTHENWARES.

c.1839-65 **Fenton, Christopher Weber,** STONEWARES.-

c.1865-82 **Norton, E. & L.P.,** SALT-GLAZED STONEWARES-

1793 rue des Récollets, PARIS, France.

1793-1825 HARD-PASTE PORCELAIN - - **DESPREZ**
Rue Des RÉCOLLETS
A PARIS

Desprez, WEDGWOOD-TYPE CAMEOS - **DESPREZ**

1793 SCHLAGGENWALD, Bohemia, Germany.

c.1793- HARD-PASTE PORCELAIN.

The individual factories and potters of SCHLAGGENWALD have been listed under their own dates and marks within this book.

1793 Lanfrey, Claude-François, France. - - see 1754 NIDERVILLER.
1793 Le Masson, France. - - - - see 1792 VALOGNES.
1793 Ludwig, Duke, Germany. - - - - see 1756 LUDWIGSBURG.

1794 CREIL, Oise, France.

c.1794-1895 EARTHENWARE. - Impressed- CREIL

1807-49 **Stone, Coquerel and Legros d'Anisy-**

Printed black-

1841-95 **Leboeuf and Milliet** Impressed- **L. M. & Cie.**

1794 RATIBOR, Silesia, Germany.

1794-1828 CREAMWARES AND STONEWARE - **R**
Beaumont, Joseph, - - - - **BEAUMONT**

1803-26 **Baruch, Salomon,** impressed- BARUCH

1794 Taney, Jacob or Isaac, BUCKS COUNTY, Pennsylvania, U.S.A.

1794 (dated) MOULDED RED POTTERY DISHES. - - **IT**

1794 Tettau GmbH., Königl. priv. Porzellanfabrik, TETTAU, Germany.

1794- HARD-PASTE PORCELAIN, COFFEE, TEA, CHOCOLATE AND TABLE SERVICES.

1794- **Greiner, Georg Christian Friedemann, and Schmidt, Johann Friedrich Paul, were the factory founders. This is the oldest porcelain factory in Bavaria.**
King Friedrich Wilhelm II. of Prussia reluctantly gave his approval or privilege for a `genuine porcelain factory` after persuasive reports by Alexander von Humboldt, the naturalist, and the Minister, Freiherr von Hardenberg. The proud title acquired which is still used in abbreviated form in the trademark today. `Royal privileged Porcelain Factory`

1852- **Klaus, Ferdinand, acquired factory.**
1866-79 **Sontag, William, and Birkner, Karl, acquired factory.**

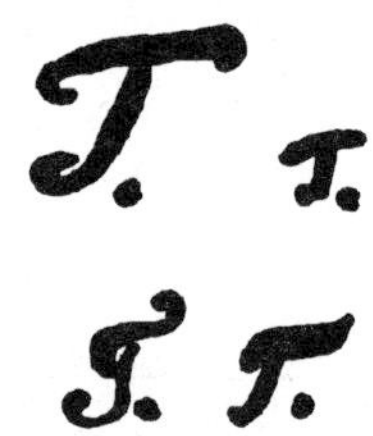

1794-1885 The famous `T` mark was used-

1794-1885
(in blue)

1879-1902 **Birkner, Karl, and Maisel, L., owned factory. The factory produced under the name of:- Sontag & Sons GmbH up to 1915.**

1885 Present marks used-

(in gold) (in various colours)

1915- **Factory changed its name to:- `Porzellanfabrik Tettau AG.`**
1957- **Seltmann Group of Weiden, acquired factory.** see 1910 Seltmann, Ch.,
1990 **German reunification.**
1990 **Aelteste Volkstedter Porzellanmanufaktur, acquired.** - - see 1762 Aelteste Volkstedter
1990 **Unterweissbacher Werstatten fur Porzellankunst, acquired.** - see 1882 Unterweissbacher, Werkstatten
1991 **Scheibe-Alsbach GmbH, Porzellanmanufactur, acquired.** - - see 1835 Scheibe-Alsbach

Modern mark (1995)- - -

(By kind permission of Porzellanfabriken Chr. Seltmann GmbH. Weiden, Germany.)

1794 Depèrais, C., (ornaments) France.- - - see 1745 SÈVRES.
1794 Lammens, B, & Co., Belgium. - - - see 1783 ANDENNES.
1794 Leboeuf & Housel, PARIS, France. - - see 1775 rue Thiroux.
1794 Parpette jeune Dlle, (flowers) France. - - see 1745 SÈVRES.
1794 Worthington, Humble & Holland, LIVERPOOL, Eng. see 1793 Herculaneum Pot.

1795 Booth & Son, Ephraim, STOKE, Staffordshire, England.

c.1795 EARTHENWARES. - Impressed- **E. B. & S.**

1795 Hollins, T. & J., SHELTON, Staffordshire, England.

c.1795-1820 EARTHENWARES. - Impressed- **T. & J. HOLLINS**

1795 Keeling, Anthony & Enoch, TUNSTALL, Staffordshire, England.

c.1795-1811 GENERAL CERAMICS. Painted **A. & E. KEELING**
A. E. KEELING

1795 MEXBOROUGH, S. Yorkshire, England.

The individual factories and potters of MEXBOROUGH have been listed under their own dates and marks within this book.

1795 PRAGUE, Czechoslovakia,

1795- EARTHENWARE.

1795-1810 - -

1810-62 - -

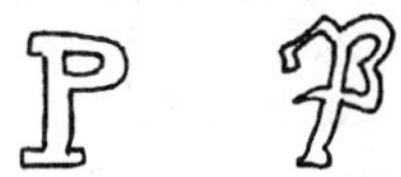

1810-35 **Hübel, Joseph Emanuel.** - -

1836-62 **Kriegel & Co.** Impressed- - - **K & C**
Prag

1795 rue de Charonne, PARIS, France.

1795- HARD-PASTE PORCELAIN. - - - **DARTE**
Darte frères (Bros) Stencilled red- **FRÈRES**
A PARIS

1795 SAINT-PAUL, Oise, France.

c.1795-Early 19th century. FAÏENCE. - - **St. Paul**
Michel.

1795/96

1795 Shorthose & Heath, HANLEY, Staffordshire, England.

c.1795-1815 EARTHENWARES. Impressed or printed- **SHORTHOSE & HEATH**

1795 Twemlow, John, SHELTON, Staffordshire, England.

1795-97 EARTHENWARE, BASALTS. - - - **J. T.**

1795 Warburton, Peter & Francis, COBRIDGE, Staffordshire, England.

1795-1802 EARTHENWARES, FIGURES, ETC. Impressed- **P. & F.W.** / **P. & F. WARBURTON**

c.1802-12 **Warburton, Peter, Gen. ceramics**
Printed or written under crown- **WARBURTON`S PATENT**

1795 Wilson, Robert, HANLEY, Staffordshire, England.

1795-1801 EARTHENWARES, CREAMWARES. Impressed- **WILSON**

Impressed- 

c.1802-18 **Wilson, David.** Impressed- **WILSON**
1815 `& Sons` added

1795	Auer, Anton, Germany. - - - - -	see 1753 NYMPHENBURG.
1795	Duesbury & Kean, England. - - -	see 1749 DERBY.
1795	Grauer, Dr. Sebastion, Germany. - - -	see 1750 KELLINGHUSEN.
1795	Michaud, Pierre-Louis, (painter/gilder) France. -	see 1745 SÈVRES.
1795	Recum, Peter van, Germany. - - -	see 1755 FRANKENTHAL.
1795	`Rockingham Ware` England. - - -	see 1745 ROCKINGHAM.
1795	Sagy, L., France. - - - -	see 1728 APT.
1795	Sandkuhl, Germany. - - - -	see 1720 ZERBST.
1795	Sinsson, J., (flowers) France. - - -	see 1745 SÈVRES.

1796 Birch & Whitehead, SHELTON, Staffordshire, England.

1796- BASALTS AND CREAMWARES. Impressed- **B. & W.**

1796-1814 **Birch, Edmund John,** Impressed- **BIRCH**
WEDGWOOD-TYPE WARES. **E. I. B.**

1796 Brunton, John, Wear Pottery, SUNDERLAND, England.

1796-1803 EARTHENWARES. - Printed - **J. BRUNTON**

1796 Chetham & Woolley, LANE END, Staffordshire, England.

1796-1810 EARTHENWARES. - Incised - **CHETHAM & WOOLLEY LANE END**

1796 COALPORT, Shropshire, (Salop) England.

c.1796- PORCELAIN.

c.1796- Known as `Coalbrook Dale` in the early days.

Early wares were rarely marked.

John Rose (founder) Apprenticed to Thomas Turner at Caughley.

Factory known as John Rose & Co.

1799- Acquired Caughley China Works.

see 1775 Caughley.

Some Caughley marks were still used after they moved to Coalport. -

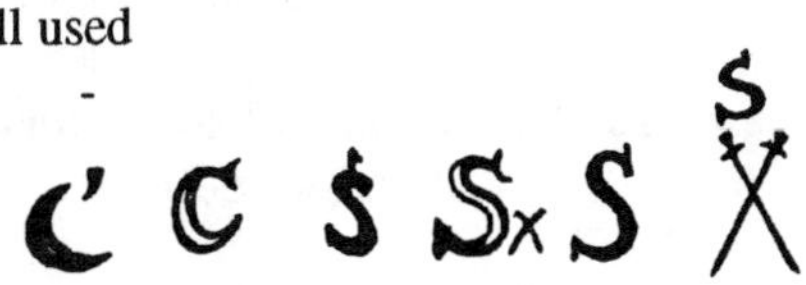

Early painted marks -

1805-20 During this period numerals between `1` and `8` are found impressed on the underside of dishes, platters, etc. from Coalport fine dinner services.

c.1810- Coalbrookdale marks. - -

1810-15 Mark used on blue printed items usually in Chinoserie manner - -

c.1815-25 Mark impressed - -

1820 Gold medal awarded by the Society of Arts for `Improved glaze for porcelain`

Continued over -

1796

1796 COALPORT, Shropshire (Salop) England. (Cont`)

1822-23 Swansea Porcelain Works discontinued. The moulds etc. were bought by Coalport. see 1783 Swansea.

Nantgarw merged into the Coalport works and the owners, Billingsley and Walker, worked for Coalport. see 1813 Nantgarw

Monogram of `C.S.` with initials `C.S.N.` Caughley, Swansea and Nantgarw. Factories absorbed by Coalport.

1830-50 Name of Factory found within marks of various designs. - - -

JOHN ROSE & CO
COALBROOKDALE
SHROPSHIRE

1841 John Rose died.

1841- William F. Rose (nephew) took over factory.

1860 mark for London dealer -

On blue printed ware. Imitation `Sèvres` mark and `Chelsea` mark

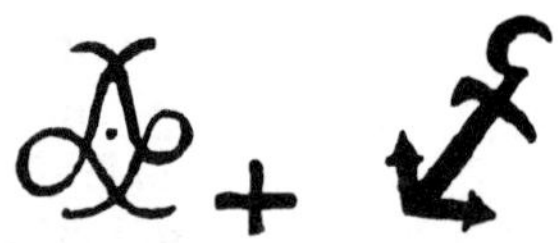

1862 William Rose retires and dies in 1864.

c.1881 Crown marks. Printed-
c.1891 `England` added
c.1920 `Made in England` added.

c.1926 Coalport Works moved to Stoke-on-Trent.

c.1950 Post-war marks. Printed-

1960- Revised mark Printed-

(Courtesy of Coalport China Ltd. (a member of the Wedgwood Group,Barlaston, England.)

1796 EISENBERG, Thuringia, Germany.
The individual factories and potters of EISENBERG have been listed under their own dates and marks within this book.

1796 Mason`s Ironstone, HANLEY, Staffordshire, England.

1796-1800 **Miles Mason, Thomas Wolfe and John Lucock at Islington China Manufactury, Liverpool.**

1796-1800 **Miles Mason and George Wolfe at Victoria Pottery, Lane Delph.**

1800-06 **Miles Mason at Victoria Pottery, Lane Delph.**
1804-13 Mark on porcelain- **M.MASON**
Impressed marks-
1807-13 Full name usually- **MILES MASON**

1806-13 **Miles Mason sets up the Minerva Works,** LANE DELPH. Producing porcelain and bone china in partnership with his son William. William also ran his own pot-works close by.

Transfer printed in blue -

1811-22 **William Mason at Sampson Bagnall`s Works, Lane Delph.** Transfer printed in blue - **W. MASON**

1813-16 **George & Charles Mason, Minerva Works,** Lane Delph. On the retirement of Miles, his sons, George Miles and Charles James carried on the business. Together, these two brothers were responsible for creating the colourful style of decoration that is typically known as `Mason`s`.
1813- Charles James took out his patent for `Improvements in the Manufacture of English Porcelain` `Ironstone Patent China` as it was called.

G. & C.J.M.
or
G.M. & C.J. MASON
Marks used 1813-26

MASON'S PATENT IRONSTONE CHINA
Earliest impressed marks

1815- **Fenton Stone Works acquired.**

1815-29 **George & Charles Mason.**
c.1824- Marks occurring on typical Ironstone patterns-

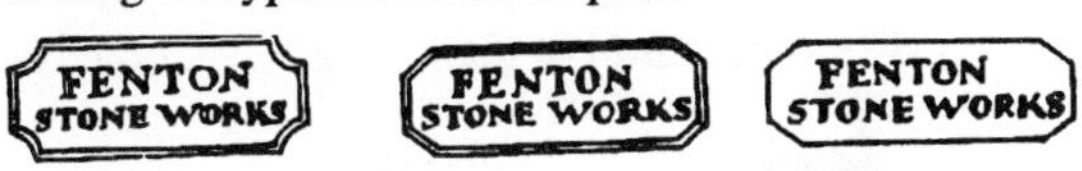

1815- Best known mark of Mason`s continued through to Geo. L. Ashworth until 1960`s when the word `china` was omitted. This mark is still in use.

Continued over -

1796

1796 Mason`s Ironstone, HANLEY, Staffordordshire, England. (Cont`)

Varients of the `crown` mark. The rounded crown is considered the earlier version. -

1822 Miles Mason died.

1822-25 Executors of Miles Mason at Sampson Bagnall`s Works, Lane Delph.

1822-24 **William Mason at John Smith`s Factory, Lane Delph.**

1825-26 **George & Charles Mason at Sampson Bagnall`s Works, Lane Delph.**

1819-21 Mason was buying Cambrian Welsh clay Earthenware impressed with this mark-

MASON'S
CAMBRIAN ARGIL

1829-45 **Charles J. Mason & Co.**

c.1829 Mark showing the Manufactory at Lane Delph- -

1841-44 **Mason & Faraday.**

1845-48 **Charles J. Mason.**

1848- **Francis Morley acquired the business and transferred the moulds and engravings to his works at Broad Street, Hanley.**

1850-58 **Francis Morley & Company.**

1855 Paris Exhibition. Morley awarded 1st class medal for Mason`s patterns.

1856 Charles J. Mason died.

1858- **Taylor Ashworth became Morley`s partner.**

1862-82 **Geo. L. Ashworth & Brothers.**

1862 A selection of marks used by Geo.L. Ashworth.

Continued over -

1796 Mason`s Ironstone, HANLEY, Staffordshire, England. (Cont`)

1882-1969 John Hackett Goddard bought the business for his son John Shaw, which was passed on to his son John Vivian Goddard, and later to the grandson, John Stringer Goddard. Name of Geo. L. Ashworth retained until 1969.

The above marks eventually replaced by -

1969- Mason`s Ironstone China Ltd. (name change)
1972- Mason`s Collectors Club, formed.
1973- Mason`s joins the Wedgwood Group.

1995- Current backstamp-

(By kind permission of Mason`s Ironstone (A Wedgwood Company) Hanley, England.)

1796 PINXTON, Derbyshire, England.

c.1796-1813 SOFT-PASTE PORCELAIN.
John Coke (founder) -

c.1796-99 William Billingsley, Painter and manager.
1801 Billingsley left Pinxton and moved to Mansfield where he decorated various wares. -

c.1803-13 John Cutts - - - - -

1796 Poole, J.E., BURSLEM, Staffordshire, England.

c.1796- EARTHENWARE. Impressed- **POOLE**

1796 Reinecke, F.A., EISENBERG, Germany.

1796- HARD-PASTE PORCELAIN. -

1796	Chia-ch`ing, China. - - - -	see 1644 CH`ING
1796	Grue, Saverio, Italy. - - - -	see 1679 CASTELLI.
1796	Melchior, Johann Peter, Germany. - -	see 1753 NYMPHENBURG.
1796	Maqueret, Dame, (flowers) France. - -	see 1745 SÈVRES.
1796	Paul 1., Russia, - - - - - -	see 1744 ST PETERSBURG.
1796	Wedgwood, Ralph, FERRYBRIDGE, England. -	see 1792 Tomlinson & Co.

1797 CAEN, Calvados, France.

1797- HARD-PASTE PORCELAIN Stencilled red- **caen**
M. D`Aigmont Desmares.

CAEN

M. Le François Stencilled red- ***Le François***
a`
Caen.

1797 LAIM, nr. Munich, Bavaria, Germany.

1797- EARTHENWARE. - Impressed- **Fab. Laim**

1797 Sowter & Co., Mexborough Old Pottery, YORKSHIRE, England.

c.1795-1804 EARTHENWARE, BLUE PRINTED, Impressed- **SOWTER & CO.**
MEXBRO
S. & CO.

1797	Amidayama, Japan. - - -	see 1630 HIGO
1797	Boitel, Charles-Marie-Pierre, France. -	see 1745 SÈVRES
1797	Fouque, J-J. & Arnoux, A., France. -	see 1650 TOULOUSE.
1797	Gejer, Bengt Rienhold, Sweden. - -	see 1725 RORSTRAND.
1797	Greiner Family, Germany. - - -	see 1760 KLOSTER-VEILSDORF.
1797	Guy & Housel, PARIS, France. - -	see 1775 rue Thiroux.
1797	Pouyat, François, PARIS, France. - -	see 1773 Porcelaine de Paris.
1797	Recum, Johann Nepomuk van, Germany.	see 1755 FRANKENTHAL.

1798 G.D.A. LIMOGES, France.

1798 TABLE PORCELAIN - - -
1960 **Merged with A Lanternier & Cie, Limoges and renamed Royal Limoges.**

GDA FRANCE

GDA LIMOGES

see 1960 Royal Limoges

1798 KIEV, Russia.

1798- FAÏENCE AND PORCELAIN. KIEBb KIEBZ

1799 Billingsley, William, MANSFIELD, Nottinghamshire, England.

1799-1802 PAINTER AND GILDER. Painted- **BILLINGSLEY**
MANSFIELD

1799 Cour-Mandar, PARIS, France.

1799- **Scheilheimer** - - Gold- *Schelheimer Cours Mandar*

1799 Dawson, John, SUNDERLAND, England.

c.1799-1864 South Hylton & Ford Potteries. EARTHENWARES — **DAWSON**, **I. DAWSON**

1800-64 Various printed marks incorporating the name - **DAWSON & CO**, **LOW FORD**, **FORD POTTERY**, **J. DAWSON**, **SOUTH HYLTON**

c.1837-48 Thomas Dawson & Co. - - **DAWSON & CO.**

1799 Greiner & Holzapfel, VOLKSTEDT, Germany

1799-c.1817 HARD-PASTE PORCELAIN.- - -

Älteste Volkstedter Porzellanfabrik

Modern marks-

see 1762 Alteste Volkstedter

1799	Dammann, Martin, France. - - -	see 1781 DOUAI.
1799	Fontebasso, Fratelli, Italy. - - - -	see 1775 TREVISO.
1799	Rose, John, Coalport, England. - - -	see 1775 CAUGHLEY.

1800 Adams, Benjamin, TUNSTALL, Staffordshire, England.

c.1800-20 EARTHENWARE, STONEWARES, Impressed- **B. ADAMS**

1800 Baddeley, Thomas, HANLEY, Staffordshire, England.

1800-34 ENGRAVER FOR TRANSFER PRINTS. Printed- **T. BADDELEY HANLEY**

1800 Barker, John, Richard and William, LANE END, England.

c.1800 EARTHENWARE. - Impressed- **BARKER**

1800 Bellanger, Jean-Nicolas, ROUEN, France.

1800- POTTER. - - -

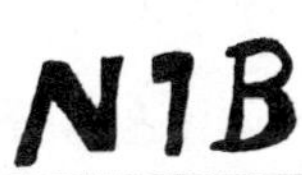

1800 Belper Pottery, BELPER, Derbyshire, England.

1800 **Bourne, William,** impressed marks- SALT-GLAZED STONEWARE bottles and some political type bottles of various `Reform leaders` — **BELPER**, **BELPER & DENBY**, **BOURNE**, **POTTERIES**, **DERBYSHIRE**

1812 **Bourne, Joseph, (son)** acquired the Denby Pottery and the two potteries were run together.

1834 **Belper Pottery closed and moved to Denby.** see 1809 Denby

1800

1800 Cartledge, John, COBRIDGE, Staffordshire, England.

c.1800 EARTHENWARE FIGURES. - - **JOHN CARTLEDGE**

1800 COLMAR, Alsace, France.

1800- PORCELAIN AND EARTHENWARE. - gold- *Colmar*

Anstett, Charles-Armand, - gold- *Anstett*

1800 Cour des Fontaines, PARIS, France.

1800-40 BONDEAU (DECORATOR) - Signature- ***Bondeux***

1800 Duban, rue Coquille`re, PARIS, France.

1800- - - - Printed red- **Duban**

1800 Dudson, Richard, Broad Street, HANLEY, Staffs. England.

1800-43 EARTHENWARE

Richard Dudson was one of the earlier potters of the Dudson family that still continue today under The Dudson Group.

Most wares were unmarked prior to 1880 but the following mark sometimes occurred.

1825-43 Moulded mark-

see 1809 Dudson, Thomas,

(By courtesy of The Dudson Group, Stoke-on-Trent, England)

1800 Fomin, MOSCOW, Russia.

c.1800 HARD-PASTE PORCELAIN. ПЕТРА ФОМИНА

1800 Halley-Lebon, PARIS, France.

1800-12 DECORATOR OF PORCELAIN - gold- *halley*

Signature- *Lebon-halley*

1800 Heath & Son, BURSLEM, Staffordshire, England.

c.1800 EARTHENWARE Impressed- **HEATH & SON**

1800 Kishere, Joseph, MORTLAKE, London, England.

c.1800-43 SALT-GLAZED STONEWARE. Impressed- **KISHERE**
I. K.

1800 Pierce & Co.,W.,BENTHALL, Salop, England.

c.1800-18 EARTHENWARES. - - **W. PIERCE & CO.**

1800 Popoff Factory, MOSCOW, Russia.

c.1800-72 HARD-PASTE PORCELAIN. - -

1800 Revil, PARIS, France.

1800- DECORATOR OF PORCELAIN. - - - - -

REVIL
Rue Neuve
des
Capucines

1800 SELB, Bavaria, Germany.

The individual factories and potters of SELB have been listed under their own dates and marks within this book.

1800 Shuhei, YAMASHIRO, Japan.

1800- ENAMELLED PORCELAIN AND GILT DESIGNS ON RED GROUND. - - -

1800 VENDRENNE, Vendée, France.

1800- **Marc Lozelet, decorator.**
HARD-PASTE PORCELAIN. - -

1800 Watson Potteries Ltd.,Henry, WATTISFIELD, Suffolk, England.

c.1800- EARTHENWARES, STONEWARES, **Early wares unmarked.**

c.1947 Impressed- **WATTISFIELD WARE**

c.1948 Printed or impressed-

see 1947 Watson`s Potteries.

1800 Wolfe & Hamilton, STOKE, Staffordshire, England.

c.1800-11 EARTHENWARES, CREAMWARES. Painted or impressed- **WOLFE & HAMILTON STOKE**

c.1811-18 **Wolfe, Thomas,.** Impressed- **WOLFE** **W**

see 1784 Thomas Wolfe.

1800/01

1800	Barlois and Dabot, France. - -	see 1650 ORLEANS
1800	Bettignies, Maximilien-Joseph, France. -	see 1718 SAINT-AMAND-LES-EAUX
1800	Clair, Adam, (repairer) Germany. - -	see 1753 NYMPHENBURG
1800	Green, John, SWINTON, England. -	see 1790 Don Pottery.
1800	Hozen, Zengoro, YAMASHIRO, Japan. -	see 1640 Zengoro Family.
1800	Kentei, YAMASHIRO, Japan. - -	see 1750 Kitei.
1800	Lachmann and Wolff, Germany. - -	see 1755 SCHLESWIG.
1800	Schoelcher, Marc, PARIS, France. -	see 1771 Faubourg Saint-Denis
1800	Yamaka, Japan. - - - -	see 1583 CHIKUZEN.

1801 BARANOVKA, Volhynia, Poland.

1801-95 **Mezer, Michael,** PORCELAIN.

Black, brown, etc. -

Blue-

1801 Grainger Wood & Co., New China Works, WORCESTER, England.

1801- **Founded by Thomas Grainger.**

c.1801-12 PORCELAINS - Written mark- **Grainger Wood & Co. Worcester, Warranted**

c.1812-c.39 Grainger, Lee & Co. Painted- *Grainger Lee & Co Worcester*

c.1812-39 - Painted- - **Royal China Works Worcester**

c.1820-39 - Painted- - **New China Works Worcester**

c.1839-1902 Grainger & Co., George,
Painted or printed marks of various designs - *George Grainger Royal China Works Worcester*

c.1839-60 - - - - **G. GRAINGER & CO. WORCESTER**
c.1850 `& Co.` added-

1848-55 - Printed- - **GRAINGER WORCESTER SEMI-PORCELAIN**
1849 Semi porcelain developed

1850s Retail shop opened at 39 Foregate St.
c.1850-70 Printed marks -

1851 Crystal Palace Exhibition.

c.1850-75 - Printed- **GRAINGER WORCESTER S. P. SEMI PORCELAIN**

1850-89 - Printed-- - -

1860-80 Initials printed on various marks - **G & CO. W.**

c.1860-80 - Printed- - - - -

c.1870-89 Printed or impressed- - -

1889 **Taken over by the Worcester Royal Porcelain Co. Ltd.**
c.1889-1902 Printed- - - -
1891 `England` added.

Continued over -

1801/02

1801 Grainger Wood & Co. New China W`ks, WORCESTER, Eng. (Cont`)

1891-1902 Year letters added:-

A 1891	D 1894	G 1897	J 1900
B 1892	E 1895	H 1898	K 1901
C 1893	F 1896	I 1899	L 1902

1902 Factory closed down by Worcester. see 1751 WORCESTER

(Information kindly supplied by The Dyson Perrins Museum Trust, Worcester)

1801 GRÜNSTADT, Rhineland, Germany.

1801- GENERAL POTTERY. GBG

1812-c.80 **Bordollo Family.** - -

1801 Hussl, Jos. Ant., SCHWAZ, Austria.

1801- EARTHENWARE - - **Schwaz**

1883- FAIENCE AND MAJOLIKA - - - - -

1801 TEINITZ, Bohemia, Germany.

1801-66 EARTHENWARE. - -

1801-39 **Count Wrtby.** - -

Impressed-

1839- **Welby, F.L.** - Impressed- - - -

1801 Alexander I., Russia. - - - - see 1744 ST PETERSBURG.

1801 Georget, (figures) France. - - - - - see 1745 SÈVRES.

1801 Troyon, (painter/gilder) France. - - - see 1745 SÈVRES.

1802 Baddeley, William, (Eastwood) HANLEY, Staffs. England.

1802-22 WEDGWOOD-TYPE WARES. Impressed- **EASTWOOD**

1802 Bagshaw & Meir, BURSLEM, Staffordshire, England.

1802-08 EARTHENWARE. Printed or impressed- **B. & M.**

1802 Clive, John Henry, TUNSTALL, Staffordshire, England.
1802-11 EARTHENWARES. - Impressed- **CLIVE**

1802 Clulow & Co., FENTON, Staffordshire, England. **CLULOW & CO.**
c.1802 EARTHENWARE. - - - **FENTON**

1802 FOECY, Cher, France.
1802- **Klien.** HARD-PASTE PORCELAIN.

1850-c1920 Pillivuyt & Co., C.H.. -

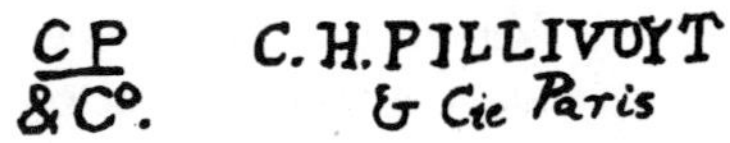

1886- **Lourioux, Louis,** - -

see 1886 Lourioux, Louis,

1802 Harley, Thomas, LANE END, Staffordshire, England.
1802-08 EARTHENWARES. - Impressed- **HARLEY**
T. HARLEY
Written or printed- **T. HARLEY**
LANE END

1802 Hölke, Friedrich, PIRKENHAMMER, Bohemia, Germany.
1802- HARD-PASTE PORCELAIN. - -
List, J.G.

1802 ITZEHOE, Holstein, Germany.
c.1802- FAÏENCE.
Stemmann, Heinrich, - -

1802 Keeling, Joseph, HANLEY, Staffordshire, England.
c.1802-08 EARTHENWARE, STONEWARE. Impressed- **JOSEPH KEELING**

1802 Lockett, J. & G., LANE END, Staffordshire, England.
c.1802-05 EARTHENWARES. - Impressed- **J.& G. LOCKETT**

1802 PIRKENHAMMER, Bohemia, Germany.
The individual factories and potters of PIRKENHAMMER have been listed under their own dates and marks within this book.

1802

1802 Ridgway, Job, HANLEY, Staffordshire, England.

c.1802-08 EARTHENWARE - Printed- **R J. R.**

c.1808-14 **Ridgway & Sons, Job,.** Impressed or printed- **RIDGWAY & SONS**

1814-c.30 **Ridgway, John & William,.** Impressed or printed- **J. W. R.** **J. & W. R.** **J. & W. RIDGWAY**

Various patterns included with the name and initials of the Factory.

1802 Riley, John & Richard, BURSLEM, Staffordshire, England.

1802-28 GENERAL CERAMICS. - - - **J. & R. RILEY**

Various painted, printed or impressed marks including the factory`s name `Riley` **RILEY`S SEMI-CHINA**

1814-26 impressed mark-

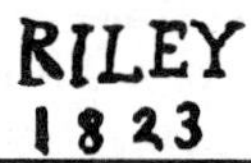

1802 Smith, James and Jeremiah, Myton, HULL, Yorkshire, England.

1802 EARTHENWARES.
The Smith Brothers were in partnership with Job Ridgway and Josiah Hipwood.

1804 **Job Ridgway sells to the remaining 3 partners.**
Josiah Hipwood left the business.
James Rose became partner with the Smiths.

1806 **Job & George Ridgway took over the business.**

1826-41 **William Bell became proprietor.**
Cream-coloured, green-glazed wares and blue and white wares.
Printed or impressed mark -
(Sometimes the bells appear without the words.)

1802 Stevenson, William, HANLEY, Staffordshire, England.

c.1802 EARTHENWARE. Rare mark impressed- **W. STEVENSON HANLEY**

1802 Union Pottery, SUNDERLAND, England.

c.1802 EARTHENWARES. Printed - **UNION POTTERY**

1802 VAL-SOUS-MEUDON, Seine-et-Oise, France.

1802-18 **Mittenhoff.** EARTHENWARE, White. **MITTENHOFF ET MOURON**

1806-18 **Mittenhoff & Mouron.** - -

1802 Warburton, John, COBRIDGE, Staffordshire, England.
c.1802-25 EARTHENWARES, STONEWARES. Impressed- **WARBURTON**

1802 Baroni, Giovanni, Italy. - - - - see 1728 NOVE.
1802 Bauer, A., Germany. - - - - see 1754 MAGDEBURG.
1802 Boullemier, Antoine-Gabriel, (gilder) France. - see 1745 SÈVRES.
1802 Dillwyn & Co., Wales. - - - - see 1783 Swansea Pottery.
1802 Durosey, C-C-M. (gilder) France.- - - see 1745 SÈVRES.
1802 Gotha, Prince August von, Germany. - - see 1757 GOTHA.
1802 Langlois, Joachim, France. - - - see 1792 VALOGNES.
1802 Swebach, (military subjects) France. - - see 1745 SÈVRES.
1802 Warburton, Peter, COBRIDGE, England. - see 1795 Warburton, P.& F.
1802 Wilson, David, HANLEY, England. - - see 1795 Wilson, Robert,.

1803 Fleury at rue du Faubourg Saint-Denis, PARIS, France.
1803-35 HARD-PASTE PORCELAIN. Printed gold-

1803 GIESSHÜBEL, nr. Carlsbad, Bohemia, Germany.
1803- EARTHENWARE AND HARD-PASTE PORCELAIN.
1803-28 - -

1828- **Knaute, Benedict,** - Impressed- **B K**

1846- **Neuberg-Gieshübl-Fabrik,** Impressed- **N.G.F.**

c.1850 - - **GIESSHÜBEL**

1803 Moore & Co.,Samuel, Wear Pottery, SUNDERLAND, England.
1803-74 EARTHENWARES. Impressed or printed- **MOORE & CO. SUNDERLAND**
Various marks which include name or initials.

S. MOORE & CO.
S. M. & CO.

1803 Baruch, Salomon, Germany. - - - see 1794 RATIBOR
1803 Bosch, H. van der, DELFT, Holland. - - see 1675 de Roos.
1803 Constant, (gilder) France. - - - - see 1745 SÈVRES.
1803 Consular period, France. - - - - see 1745 SÈVRES.
1803 Cutts, John, England. - - - - see 1796 PINXTON.
1803 Deutsch, (ornaments/flowers) France. - - see 1745 SÈVRES.
1803 Kameyama-Yaki, Japan. - - - - see 1580 HIZEN.
1803 Mandele, D. van der, DELFT, Holland. - - see 1675 de Roos.
1803 Pigory, Mayor of Chantilly, France. - - see 1725 CHANTILLY.

1804

1804 DALLWITZ, Bohemia, Germany.

1804- CREAMWARES.

1804-20 - - D DALWITZ

1832- Lorenz, W.W., - - W.W.L. DALWITZ

1850- Frant, Fischer, - - F.F. D.

1804 GUDUMLUND, Denmark.

1804-20 FAÏENCE AND EARTHENWARE. -

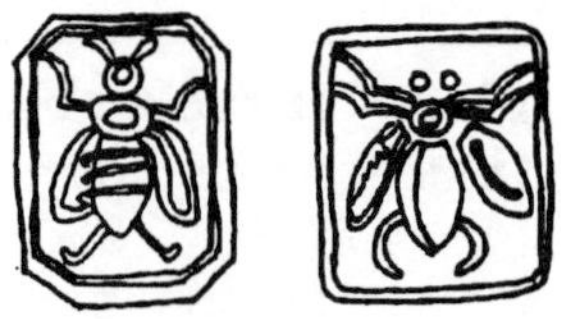

1805- Wolfsen & Sonne - -

1804 SARGADELOS, Spain.

1804-75 CREAM AND WHITE EARTHENWARES.

S

Various marks including the name `Sargadelos` - - -

SARGADELOS

1804 TILLOWITZ, Silesia, Germany.

1804- FAÏENCE AND EARTHENWARE.

Degotschon, Johann, - -

Tillowitz

1804	Barr, Flight & Barr, England. - - -	see 1751 WORCESTER.
1804	Delafosse, Denis, (figures) France. - -	see 1745 SÈVRES.
1804	Ferrybridge Pottery, FERRYBRIDGE, England.	see 1792 Tomlinson & Co.
1804	First Empire, France. - - - - -	see 1745 SÈVRES.
1804	Piccardt, Henricus Arnold, DELFT, Holland. -	see 1653 De Porceleyne Fles.
1804	Sewell, NEWCASTLE UPON TYNE, England.	see 1780 St. Anthony`s Pottery

1805 Breeze & Son, John, TUNSTALL, Staffordshire, England.

1805-12 POTTERY AND PORCELAIN. Incised or painted- **BREEZE**
Several other potters of this name operated in Staffordshire during the first half of the 19th century.

1805 Bridgewood & Son Ltd.,Sampson, LONGTON, Staffs. England.

c.1805- EARTHENWARE Impressed- **BRIDGEWOOD & SON**
c.1805-c.87 PORCELAIN
Impressed- **S. BRIDGEWOOD & SON**

c.1853- Various designs including Factory`s initials. Printed- **S. B. & S.**

1885 onwards produced various marks all of which included full name or initials of Factory.
1891 `England` added.
c.1933 `Ltd.` added.

1805 Keeling, Toft & Co.,HANLEY, Staffordshire, England.

1805-26 WEDGWOOD-TYPE STONEWARES. Impressed- **KEELING & TOFT**
KEELING, TOFT & CO.

1805 Meigh, Job (& Son) Old Hall Pottery, HANLEY, Staffs., England.

c.1805-34 EARTHENWARES. - Impressed- **MEIGH**
1805- Impressed or printed- **OLD HALL**
c.1812 `Son` added - - **J.M.& S.**

1835-49 **Meigh, Charles,** - Impressed- **CHARLES MEIGH**
EARTHENWARES, STONEWARES. - - **C. M.**
Factory`s name or initials within marks of various patterns and designs. - -

1850-51 **Meigh, C.,Son & Pankhurst,** Printed- **C.M.S. & P.**
EARTHENWARES.

1851-61 **Meigh & Son, Charles,** Printed- **C.M. & S.**
EARTHENWARES. - - **M. & S.**
Many marks include the Royal Arms which include Factory name or initials. **C. MEIGH & SON**

OPAQUE PORCELAIN **MEIGH`S CHINA**

Continued over -

1805/06

1805 Meigh, Job (& Son) Old Hall Pottery, HANLEY, England. (Cont`)

1861-86 **Old Hall Earthenware Co.Ltd.,**
EARTHENWARES. Printed- **O.H.E.C.**
Various printed marks including **O.H.E.C.(L)**
Factory initials.

Printed or impressed- -

1884 Trade mark Printed- - -

Continued by Old Hall Porcelain Works Ltd.

1886-1902 **Old Hall Porcelain Works Ltd.,**
PORCELAIN AND EARTHENWARES.

1805 Pearson & Co., CHESTERFIELD, England.

c.1805 EARTHENWARES, STONEWARES. Impressed- **P. & CO.**
1805-80 - Impressed- **PEARSON & CO. WHITTINGTON MOOR**

c.1880- Printed or impressed-

c.1925- **Pearson & Co. (Chesterfield) Ltd.,**
c.1928- Trade names- - - **KRUSTA**
PEANCO

1805 TOMASZÓW, Poland.

c.1805-10 HARD-PASTE PORCELAIN. - Red-
Mezer, Michael,

Incised-

1805 Mayer & Son, Elijah, HANLEY, England. - - see 1790 Mayer, Elijah.
1805 Wolfsen & Sonne, Denmark. - - - - see 1804 GUDUMLUND.

1806 Boulevard Montmartre, PARIS, France.

1806- **Person,** DECORATOR OF PORCELAIN gold- **Person**

1840- **Couderc,** DECORATOR - red-

1806 Geddes & Son, John, GLASGOW, Scotland.

c.1806-27 POTTERY AND PORCELAIN. Printed- **JOHN GEDDES**
1824 `& Son` added.- - **Verreville**
Pottery

1806 Vickers & Son, Thomas, DOWNINGTOWN, Pennsylvania, U.S.A.

c.1806- EARTHENWARES. SGRAFFITO, BLACK-GLAZED, ETC.
Incised - **T. V.**
1822- **Vickers & Son, John, LIONVILLE, PA.** - **J. V.**

1806 Benoist Le Brun, France. - - - see 1650 ORLEANS.
1806 Boullemier, François-Antoine,(figures) France. see 1745 SÈVRES.
1806 Brameld & Co., England. - - - see 1745 ROCKINGHAM.
1806 Hicks & Meigh, SHELTON, England. - see 1784 Baddeley, John & Edward,
1806 King Friedrich, Germany. - - - see 1756 LUDWIGSBURG.
1806 Mason, Miles, LANE DELPH, England. see 1796 Mason`s Ironstone.
1806 Mittenhoff & Mouron, France. - - see 1802 VAL-SOUS-MEUDON.
1806 Robert, J-F, (landscapes) France. - - see 1745 SÈVRES.
1806 Seto-Yaki, Japan. - - - - see 1573 OWARI.

1807 Cadborough Pottery, RYE, Sussex, England.

c.1807-40 **Smith, James,** EARTHENWARES -
Incised marks first used c.1850 (No connection with the Rye Pottery. see 1869) **OLD SUSSEX WARE**
RYE
c.1840-58 **Mitchell, William,** - - - **RYE POTTERY**

1859-69 **Mitchell, William & Sons.**- -
Incised - **MITCHELL**
1869-71 **Mitchell, F.& H.,** - - - **M**

1807 DESSAU, Thuringia, Germany.

1807- STONEWARE -
Hunold, Friedemann, Impressed- **HUNOLD**

20th century Waldkaterkeramik -

1807 Hackwood & Co., HANLEY, Staffordshire, England.

1807-27 EARTHENWARES, JASPERS. Impressed- **HACKWOOD & CO.**
H. & CO.
1827-43 **Hackwood, William,** Printed or impressed- **W. H.**
HACKWOOD

1807 RYE, Sussex, England.

The individual factories and potters of RYE have been listed under their own dates and marks within this book.

1807/08

1807 SCHAUBERG, Bavaria, Germany.

1807- HARD-PASTE PORCELAIN.
Greiner & Co., G., - - - 

1807 Shorthose, John, HANLEY, Staffordshire, England.

1807-23 EARTHENWARES - Impressed- **S SHORTHOSE**

1807 Sunderland or `Garrison` Pottery, SUNDERLAND, England.

c.1807-65 EARTHENWARES. PRINTED AND LUSTRE WARES.
Impressed marks of the names of the various partnerships at Sunderland.

c.1807-12 - - -	**J. PHILLIPS SUNDERLAND POTTERY**
c.1813-19 - - -	**PHILLIPS & CO DIXON & CO**
c.1820-26 - - -	**DIXON, AUSTIN & CO.**
c.1827-40 - - -	**DIXON, AUSTIN, PHILLIPS & CO. DIXON, AUSTIN & CO.**
c.1840-65 - - -	**DIXON PHILLIPS & CO.**

1807	Béranger, Antoine, (figures) France.	see 1745 SÈVRES.
1807	Davignon, Jean-François, (figures) France.	see 1745 SÈVRES.
1807	Greens, Clarke & Co., SWINTON, England.	see 1790 Don Pottery.
1807	Kinju, Japan.	see 1650 KAGA.
1807	Langlacé, (landscapes) France.	see 1745 SÈVRES.
1807	Moreau, D-J, (gilder) France.	see 1745 SÈVRES.
1807	Stone, Coquerel and Legros d`Anisy, France.	see 1794 CREIL.

1808 Donath, P., TIEFENFURT, Silesia, Germany.

1808- Hard-paste porcelain. - - 

1808 ELGERSBURG, Thuringia, Germany.

HARD-PASTE PORCELAIN.
1808- **Arnoldi, C.E. & F.**

1895- **Eichhorn & Bandorf.**
General pottery.

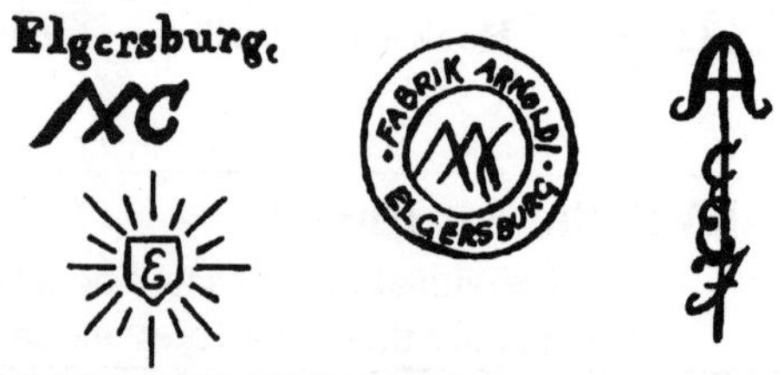

1808 Headman, Andrew, Rock Hill, BUCKS CO. Pennsylvania, U.S.A.

1808- EARTHENWARES, SGRAFFITO. - -

1808 Tuppack, Carl Hans, TIEFENFURT, Silesia, Germany.

1808- HARD-PASTE PORCELAIN. - -

1808 Degault, Jean-Marie, (figures) France. - - - see 1745 SÈVRES.
1808 Nonne & Roesch, ILMENAU, Germany. - - see 1792 Nonne, Christian.
1808 Ridgway & Sons, Job, HANLEY, England. - - see 1802 Ridgway, Job,.

1809 Cushman, Paul, ALBANY, New York, U.S.A.

1809 SALT-GLAZED STONEWARE. Incised (dated) **PAUL CUSHMAN**

1809 Drey, Johan, Eastern Pennsylvania, U.S.A.

1809 POTTERY. - - Pie plate (dated)-

1809 GIEY-SUR-AUJON, Haute-Marne, France.

1809-40 HARD-PASTE PORCELAIN - -
Guignet, F. - - -

1809 Godwin, Thomas & Benjamin, BURSLEM, Staffordshire, England.

c.1809-34 GENERAL CERAMICS. Printed- **T.& B.G.**
Various printed marks which include **T.B.G.**
the factory`s name or initials.
c.1809-34 Impressed- **T.& B. GODWIN**
NEW WHARF

1834-54 **Godwin, Thomas,** EARTHENWARES, - **T. G.**
Various marks with factory`s initials.
Printed or impressed- **THOS GODWIN**
BURSLEM
STONE CHINA

1809 Heath, John, BURSLEM, Staffordshire, England.

1809-23 GENERAL CERAMICS. Impressed- **HEATH**

1809 DENBY, Derbyshire, England.

1809 **Bourne, Joseph,** - Impressed- **BOURNES WARRENTED**
STONEWARES. - -

c.1846. **Bourne, Joseph & Son.**
(Joseph Harvey taken into the business) - **J. BOURNE & SON PATENTEES DENBY POTTERY NEAR DERBY**

c.1834 **Belper Pottery transferred to Denby** - see 1800 Belper Pottery.

c.1833-61 Marks including `CODNOR`- **BOURNES POTTERIES DENBY & CODNOR PARK DERBYSHIRE**
1861- Joseph Bourne died.
1869- Joseph Harvey Bourne died.
1869-98 **Sarah Elizabeth (widow) continued.**

c.1895 Impressed or printed in circle -
1910 - in square -

1898-1907 **Joseph Bourne-Wheeler and** - -
Joseph Henry Topham (nephews)
1907- **Joseph Bourne-Wheeler**
(became sole proprietor)
1916- **Limited Company formed.**
c.1930 marks - Impressed or printed- **BOURNE DENBY ENGLAND**
c.1934 Donald Gilbert (designer)
`EPIC` `MANOR GREEN`
`COTTAGE BLUE` (discontinued 1970)

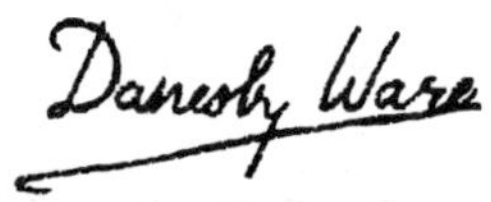

1942-Joseph Bourne-Wheeler died.
c.1950 mark - Impressed or printed-
Factory`s name `Denby` within marks
of various patterns and designs.

1950s Albert Colledge and son Glyn (designers)
`PEASANT` `GREENWHEAT` Etc.,

1959- **Acquired Langley Pottery.**
1960s Tableware patterns- `GYPSY` `COTSWOLD`
`TROUBADOUR` `POTTERS WHEEL` Etc.
1981- **Crown House PLC acquired Company.**
1987- **Coloroll Group PLC acquired Company.**
1990- **MBO team acquires Denby from Coloroll.**
1994- **The Denby Group plc launched on the London Stock Exchange.**
Denby Visitors Centre is open to the public most days.

(For further information see Denby Stonewares - A Collector`s Guide by G.& A.Key)
(By kind permission of The Denby Pottery Co.Ltd., Derbyshire, England.)

1809 Dudson, Thomas, Hope Street, HANLEY, Staffordshire, England.

1809- EARTHENWARE. DECORATIVE AND USEFUL WARES. (The Dudson dynasty of potters is today still headed by Mr Bruce Dudson who became Chairman of The Dudson Group in 1979)

Most wares were unmarked prior to 1880, but the following marks sometimes occur.

1830-45 Painted on base-

1845-82 **Dudson, James,**
EARTHENWARE. VITREOUS STONEWARE.
Impressed and incised marks that appear fairly regularly throughout 19th century. -

c.1825-82 Incised decoration numbers occur on the base of Jasperware. -

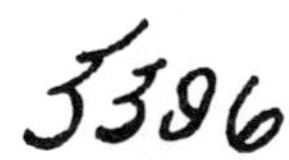

1845-82 Sometimes impressed on foot - especially on relief moulded stoneware and mosaic.

1845-82 Impressed inside stoneware lids -

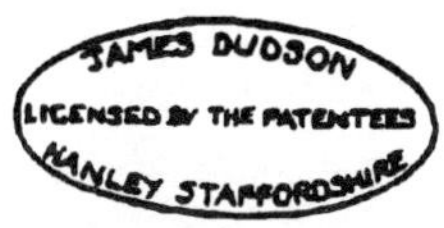

1855-65 Moulded registration diamonds mark-

1865-68 Moulded `Argyle` ware mark -

1868- Moulded circle mark-

1870-99 Impressed on base- - -

1870-80`s Wares were sometimes dated -

October 1878 -

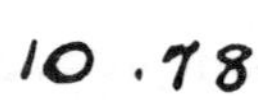

March 1880 -

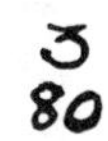

July 1882 -

Continued over -

1809

1809 Dudson, Thomas, Hope Street, HANLEY, Staff's, England. (Cont`)

1870-80`s Retailers names used but without the name of `Dudson`.

PAXTON
NORWOOD
MILLWARD
BRENT

1882-98 Dudson, J.T.,

EARTHENWARE, JASPERS.

1882-98 Impressed inside-stoneware lids

1882- Impressed on base-

1891-99 Impressed on foot-

1891 The Dudson factory concentrated exclusively on the production of tableware for the hotel trade.

1898- Dudson Bros Ltd.,

EARTHENWARE, STONEWARES, JASPERS.

1900-36 Impressed marks-

1930-36 Printed mark- -

1936-45 Printed mark-

1945-65 Printed mark specially designed for the American market - -

1945- Impressed or printed with year numbers. - -

The Dudson Group have the following companies within their Group:-

1950- Acquired The Albert Potteries, Burslem
Re-named J.E.Heath Ltd., see 1950 Heath Ltd., J.E.

1952- Acquired The Grindley Hotel Ware Co.Ltd.
(Now The Duraline Hotel Ware Co.Ltd.) see 1908 Grindley Hotel Ware.

Continued over -

1809 Dudson, Thomas, Hope Street, HANLEY, Staff's, England. (Cont`)

1995 Modern marks -

Further information can be found in *Dudson - A Family of Potters Since 1800*
By Dudson Publication 1985.
(By courtesy of The Dudson Group, Stoke-on-Trent, England.)

1809 METTLACH, Rhineland, Germany.

EARTHENWARE, GLAZED.

1809- **J.F. Boch & Buschmann.** - Blue - Impressed- **B B** **Boch Buschmann** **a` Mettlach**

1842- **Villeroy & Boch** -

see 1767 Villeroy & Boch AG.

1809 Pardoe, Thomas, BRISTOL, England.

c.1809-20 Decorator. - Painted- **Pardoe** **28 Bath Street,** **Bristol** **Warranted** **Pardoe, Bristol** **Pardoe, 1814**

Also painted at Derby, Worcester and Swansea.

1809 Woolley, Richard, LONGTON, Staffordshire, England.

1809-14 EARTHENWARE. - Impressed- **WOOLLEY**

1809 Yoshida Danemon (Kutani revival) Japan. - - see 1650 KAGA.

1810 ALTHALDENSLEBEN, Hanover, Germany.

Early 19th century CREAMWARES AND PORCELAIN.

1810- **Nathusius, Gottlob,** - Impressed- **N**

1810- EARTHENWARES
1826- PORCELAIN

c.1875 **Schmelzer & Gerike** - - - -

PORCELAIN.

1810

1810 BAYEUX, Calvados, France.

1810 Transferred from Valognes. - - **Bayeux**
HARD-PASTE PORCELAIN. **J. L.**

1810-30 **Langlois, Joachim** - -

1830-c.47 **Langlois, M. Frederic (son) and Joachim`s widow** -

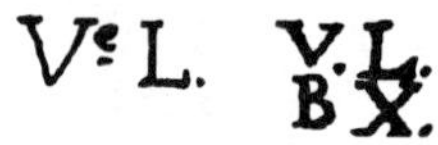

c.1847-78 **Gosse, François** - - -

1847-51 - -

1851-78 - -

1878-1945 **Morient,J.P., and Saintville, G.,** -

20th century marks - - -

1810 Bott & Co., LANE END, Staffordshire, England.

c.1810-11 EARTHENWARE. - Impressed- **BOTT & CO.**

1810 Chetham & Son, LONGTON, Staffordshire, England.

1810-34 EARTHENWARES. - Impressed- **CHETHAM**
1818 `& Son` added - **CHETHAM & SON**

1810 Chozo (potter) YAMASHIRO, Japan.

c.1810- **Makuzu** (blue and white porcelain)

c.1830 Chozo at Tokoname - -

1860 **Miyagana Kozan** (grandson) - - -
Makuzu Kozan tsukuru.

1810 Dale, John, BURSLEM, Staffordshire, England.

Early 19th century FIGURES. - Impressed- **J. DALE BURSLEM**
I. DALE BURSLEM

1810 Fifield, William, BRISTOL, England. - - **W. F.** **W. F. B.**

c.1810-55 PAINTER AT BRISTOL - - - **W. FIFIELD**

1810 Fischer & Reichenbach, PIRKENHAMMER, Germany.

1810-16 HARD-PASTE PORCELAIN. - - **F & R**

1810 Galloway & Graff, WEST PHILADELPHIA, Pennsylvania, U.S.A.

1810- TERRA-COTTA.- - - - - **Galloway & Graff**
Philadelphia

1810 Oldfield, Madin, Wright, Hewitt & Co., BRAMPTON, England.

1810-88 SALT-GLAZED BROWN EARTHENWARE.

1838-88 **Oldfield, John, became sole proprietor.** **J. OLDFIELD & CO.**
Factory`s name impressed within marks **OLDFIELD & CO.**
of various designs. **J. OLDFIELD**

(See `Jewitt`s` Ceramic Art in Great Britain.)

1810 Powell, John, LONDON, England. **Powell**

c.1810-30 PAINTER AND RETAILER - - - **91, Wimpole St.**

1810 Rantei, (studio name) YAMASHIRO, Japan.

c.1810 BLUE AND WHITE PORCELAIN AND CELADON.

Heian toko Rantei seizo - -
(carefully made by Rantei the Kioto potter)

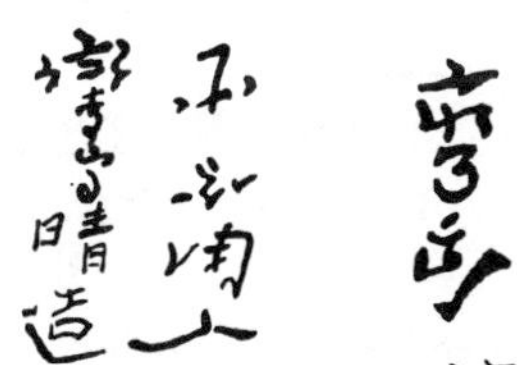

Rantei sei gwan (pure trinket of Rantei) -

c.1865 mark - -

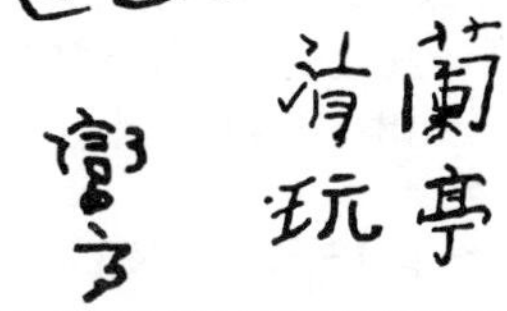

1810 Rathbone & Co., Thomas, PORTOBELLO, Scotland. **T. R. & CO.**

c.1810-45 EARTHENWARES. - Painted or impressed- **T. RATHBONE**
P

1810 Ray, George, LANE END, Staffordshire, England. **G. RAY**

Early 19th century MODELLER. - - - **Lane End**

1810 Stevenson, Ralph, COBRIDGE, Staffordshire, England.

c.1810-32 EARTHENWARES - Impressed-

R. STEVENSON

Factory`s initials painted within marks of
various patterns and designs. - - **R. S.**

1810/11

1810	Dortu & Cie, Switzerland. - - - - - -	see 1780 NYON.
1810	Hübel, Joseph Emanuel, Germany. - - -	see 1795 PRAGUE.
1810	Isawa, Japan. - - - - - - -	see 1736 ISE.
1810	`Shin-sei` Japan.- - - - - - -	see 1650 MINO.
1810	`Windmill Pottery` CHURCH GRESLEY, Derby, England.	see 1901 Mason Cash
1810	Yamamoto, Japan. - - - - - -	see 1650 KAGA.

1811 ALT-ROHLAU, Bohemia, Germany.

1811- CREAMWARES AND HARD-PASTE PORCELAIN.
The individual factories and potters of ALT-ROHLAU have been listed under their own dates and marks within this book.

1811 Ginder & Co., Samuel, FENTON, Staffordshire, England.

1811-43 EARTHENWARES - Printed- **S. Ginder & Co.**
Factory`s name found within marks of various patterns and designs.

1811 Hamilton, Robert, STOKE, Staffordshire, England.

1811-26 EARTHENWARES. - Impressed or printed- **HAMILTON STOKE**
Factory name found within marks of various designs and patterns.

1811 Musso, B. of Savona, MONDOVI, Piedmont, Italy.

1811-c.97 CREAMWARES - Impressed- MM. MA
Family continued until c.1897.

1811 Nassonoff, MOSCOW, Russia.

1811-c.13 HARD-PASTE PORCELAIN. - - AH Nasonow

1813-c.16 **Kiriakoff** - - - - - - AC

1811 Portheim & Sohn, CHODAU, Bohemia, Germany.

1811 HARD-PASTE PORCELAIN. - KODAU Chodau P&S

1845 `von Portheim` V.P. von Portheim

c.1875 **Haas & Czizek** - - -
(Also at Schlaggenwald)

1811 ROSCHÜTZ, Saxony, Germany.

1811- HARD-PASTE PORCELAIN.
Roschützer Porzellanfabrik Unger & Schilde.

1811 Roudebush, Henry, MONTGOMERY COUNTY, PA., U.S.A.

c.1811-16 EARTHENWARES - -

1811 (dated) on ornamental pie plate - -

1811 Bloor, Robert, England. - - - - see 1750 DERBY.
1811 Capronnier, François, (gilder) France. - - see 1745 SÈVRES.
1811 Huard, (ornaments) France. - - - see 1745 SÈVRES.
1811 Mason, William, LANE DELPH, England. - see 1796 Mason`s Ironstone.
1811 Rokubei Seisai (son) YAMASHIRO, Japan. - see 1759 Kyomizu.
1811 Wolfe, Thomas, STOKE, England. - - see 1784 Wolfe, Thomas,

---

1812 Batenin`s Factory, ST. PETERSBURG, Russia.

c.1812-20 HARD-PASTE PORCELAIN. С.З.К.Б Б

1812 Déroche, at rue Jean-Jacques Rousseau, PARIS, France.

1812- DECORATOR. - - - - - - - Deroche R.R Rousseau Paris

1812 GEIERSTHAL, nr. Wallendorf, Thuringia, Germany.

1812- **Sontag & Söhne** (DECORATERS OF PORCELAIN)

1812 Heath, Thomas, BURSLEM, Staffordshire, England. **T. HEATH**

1812-35 EARTHENWARES. Printed or impressed- **T. HEATH BURSLEM**

Various patterns are included within the marks

1812 Lockett & Co.,J., LANE END, Staffordshire, England.

c.1812-89 EARTHENWARES. Printed or impressed- **J. LOCKETT & CO.**

1882-1960 at LONGTON
1960- at BURSLEM

1812 Meir, John, TUNSTALL, Staffordshire, England.

c.1812-36 EARTHENWARES. Printed- **J. M.** **I. M.**

Factory`s name and initials are found within marks of various patterns and designs.

1837-97 **Meir & Son, John,** Printed or impressed- **J.M. & S.**

I. M. & S.

J.M. & SON

Dates included on some wares. - - **J. MEIR & SON**

10/74 (10 over 74) = Oct. 1874 - - **MEIR & SON**

c.1891 `England` added.

1812/13

1812 Bordollo Family, Germany. - - - see 1801 GRÜNSTADT.
1812 Grainger, Lee & Co.,WORCESTER, England. - see 1801 Grainger Wood & Co.

1813 Baker, Bevans & Irwin, Glamorgan Pottery, SWANSEA, Wales.

1813-38 EARTHENWARES. Printed or impressed- Factory`s name and initials are found within marks of various patterns and designs. — **B.B. & I.** / **BAKER BEVANS & IRWIN**

Glamorgan Pottery Co., - - - - - **G.P.& CO.**

1813 Gibson, John & Solomon, LIVERPOOL, England.
Early 19th century. EARTHENWARES - - — **JOHN GIBSON LIVERPOOL 1813**

1813 Hasslacher, Benedict, ALT-ROHLAU, Bohemia, Germany.

1813-23 CREAMWARES AND PORCELAIN

1823-84 **Nowotny, August,** - -

1813 NANTGARW, Glamorgan, Wales.

c.1813-14 **Nantgarw China Works.** PORCELAIN. Impressed- **Billingsley, William, and Walker, Samuel,** — **NANTGARW** / **NANT GARW**

Impressed- `C.W.` Stands for China Works.- — **NANT GARW C. W.**

1817-22 **Re-opened by Billingsley and Walker** - Painted or stencilled- — **NANTGARW**

1813 TANNOVA, Bohemia, Germany.

c.1813-80 FAÏENCE AND PORCELAIN.

1813-35 Mayer, J.,

1813 Vsevolojsky and Polivanoff, MOSCOW, Russia.

1813-55 HARD-PASTE PORCELAIN. Painted or incised-

F W **Fabrique de Wsevolojsky**

1813	Boullemier fils, (gilder) France. - - -	see 1745 SÈVRES.
1813	Develly, Jean-Charles, (animals) France. -	see 1745 SÈVRES.
1813	Dixon & Co., SUNDERLAND, England. -	see 1807 Sunderland Pottery.
1813	Flight, Barr & Barr Period, England. - -	see 1751 WORCESTER.
1813	Ganeau fils, (gilder) France. - - -	see 1745 SÈVRES.
1813	Henneberg, Egidius, Germany. - - -	see 1757 GOTHA.
1813	Mason, G.M.& C.J. LANE DELPH, England. -	see 1796 Mason`s Ironstone.
1813	Phillips & Co., SUNDERLAND, England. -	see 1807 Sunderland Pottery.
1813	Robert, P-R, (ornaments) France. - - -	see 1745 SÈVRES.

1814 ARKHANGELSKOIE, Russia.

1814-31 PORCELAIN - - - - **ARKHANGELSKOIE**

Prince Nicolas Yussupoff.

1814 Bailey & Batkin, LONGTON, Staffordshire, England.

1814-27 EARTHENWARES, LUSTRE. Impressed or moulded- **BAILEY & BATKIN**

B & B

1814 Hall & Sons, John, BURSLEM, Staffordshire, England.

I. HALL

1814-32 EARTHENWARES. Impressed or printed- **HALL**

Factory`s name printed within marks of various patterns and designs.

c.1822-32 Impressed or printed- **I. HALL & SONS**

1814 Hutschenreuther, Carl Magnus, HOHENBERG, Bavaria, Germany.

1814- HARD-PASTE PORCELAIN.

Carl Magnus Hutschenreuther (Founder) starts his first attempts at manufacturing porcelain.

1822- Finally granted licence to manufacture porcelain at Hohenberg.

1828 Marks printed green-

1843- **Partnership formed with his son, Lorenz, who secures a third of the business.**

Continued over -

1814

1814 Hutschenreuther, Carl Magnus, HOHENBERG, Germany. (Cont`)

1845- **Carl Magnus Hutschenreuther, dies and in his will his wife, Johanna takes over the Management supported by her sons, Lorenz and Christian.**
1855- Balduin Haag (lithograph modeller) is employed.

1856- **Lorenz Hutschenreuther leaves the business with a third share, amounting to 80,000 gulden.**

1860- **Johanna Hutschenreuther assigns management** to her son Christian and her two son-in-laws, Philipp Auvera and Heinrich Wolf. Green marks- Philipp Auvera in particular, shapes the firm for the next 20 years.

1860

1865

1877 **Christian Hutschenreuther dies. His son Albert enters management of the factory.**

1886 **Hugo Auvera Jr. enters as factory master.**
1866-1900 Marks printed black and blue-

16.12.1876

23.4.1878

4.12.1882

1878-1900

29.12.1893

1904 **Limited Company formed.**
Albert Hutschenreuther retires as the last of the Company bearing that name. The new directors are Hugo Auvera Sr. and Hugo Auvera Jr. Mark printed green-

1901-33

1914-33

1909- **Louis Schilling joins the firm and becomes Managing Director.**

1909- **Moritz Zdekauer, Altrohlau, Porcelain factory purchased by Company.** Marks printed green-

1918- **Three Dresden hand-painting firms:- Richard Klemm, Donath & Co. and Richard Wehsener are purchased by the Company. Hutschenruether starts Dresden hand-painting department.**

1914-33

1914-33

1919- **`Acker-Fabrik` Arzberg, taken over and is re-named C.M. Hutschenreuther Arzberg Porcelain Factory.** American mark-

1920-40

1921- The following companies now belong to C.M. Hutschenreuther AG. Hohenberg.
C.M. Hutschenreuther, Arzberg,
Altrohlau Porcelain Factory AG.
Tielsch and Co.AG Altwasser, Silesia.

Continued over -

1814 Hutschenreuther, Carl Magnus, HOHENBERG, Germany. **(Cont`)**

1921- The following companies etc. (Cont`)
Dresden Hand-painting Department.
Radeberg Dental Factory, nr. Dresden.

1922- Central Administration transferred to Dresden 1937- Werner Heckmann takes over management. Marks printed green-

1934-46

1939-45

1946- Resumption of production after the war. Large consignments to the American Headquarters, U.S. zone. Mark printed green-

1946-48

1946

1963- Hohenberg porcelain once again opens up their export markets,

1948-70 marks-

1969- Hohenberg Factory is bought out by Lorenz Hutschenreuther AG at Selb. see 1857 Hutschenreuther, Lorenz,

(Courtesy of Hutschenreuther AG. Selb, Germany.)

1814	Boullemier Dlle, (gilder) France. - - -	see 1745 SÈVRES.
1814	Charrin dlle, Fanny, (figures) France. - -	see 1745 SÈVRES.
1814	Frick, Christoph Georg, Germany. - -	see 1751 BERLIN.
1814	Louis XVIII, France. - - - - -	see 1745 SÈVRES.
1814	Ridgway, John & William, HANLEY, England.-	see 1802 Ridgway, Job.
1814	Roger & Son, John, LONGPORT, England. -	see 1784 Rogers,John & George.
1814	von Oppel, Germany. - - - - -	see 1710 MEISSEN.

1815 Bentley, Wear & Bourne, SHELTON, Staffordshire, England.

1815-23 PRINTERS AND ENAMELLERS - Printed- **BENTLEY, WEAR & BOURNE**

1815 Clyde Pottery Co. Ltd.,GREENOCK, Scotland.

c.1815-1903 EARTHENWARES - - - - **CLYDE**

c.1857-63 `Ltd` added - - - **G.C.P. CO.**

Impressed or printed- - **GREENOCK**

1815

1815 Dastin, rue de Bondy, PARIS, France.

1815-	DECORATOR AND MERCHANT.	Gold and red- Signature.	**DASTIN** **Dastin**

1815 Gaugain, PARIS, France.

1815-	DECORATOR OF HARD-PASTE PORCELAIN.	-	***Gaugain***

1815 Haidinger Brothers, ELBOGEN, Germany.

1815- EARTHENWARE AND HARD-PASTE PORCELAIN.
Wiener Porzella-Fabrick

1873- Springer & Oppenheimer
c.1900 Springer & Co. - -

Modern mark-

1815 Martin, Shaw & Cope, LONGTON, Staffordshire, England.

c.1815-24 EARTHENWARE, IRONSTONE AND CHINA.
Factory`s name printed within marks of various designs

MARTIN SHAW
& COPE
IMPROVED CHINA

1815 MONTREUIL, Seine, France.

1815-73 **Tinet.** HARD-PASTE PORCELAIN. - -

TINET
32
Rue du Bac

1885- **Marzolf & Cie.** - - - -

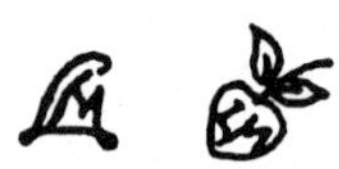

1815 PÁPA, Hungary.

c.1815- **Windschügel, K.A.,** -

20th century **Boskowitz, Samuel,**

1815 Royal Doulton plc., BURSLEM, Staffordshire, England.

1815- Jones, Watts & Doulton. Produced plain stoneware bottles and jugs and some finely-modelled brown mugs and jugs of Nelson, Wellington and Napoleon. After completing his apprenticeship at the Fulham Pottery, John Doulton found work at the Vauxhall Walk Pottery, Lambeth. Three years later, he became part-proprietor when in June 1815, Martha Jones (widow proprietor) took John Watts and John Doulton into partnership.

1820 Doulton & Watts. Mrs Jones withdrew from the business.

1826- Lambeth Pottery. Move to larger premises in Lambeth High Street.

c.1827-58 Impressed marks on stoneware and terracotta - **DOULTON & WATTS**
LAMBETH POTTERY
LONDON

1832 First Reform Act. Thousands of stoneware `Reform Bottles` and `Flasks` were made depicting King William IV. Lord Grey, Brougham and Russell, who were closely associated with the Bill.

1835- Henry Doulton, John`s second son joins the business. He eventually becomes the driving force, and was the first potter to appreciate the likely impact of the `sanitary revolution` and in 1846 Lambeth was the first factory in the world to produce stoneware drainpipes, conduits and related wares.

1853- John Watts retired.

c.1857- Doulton & Co., Lambeth. EARTHENWARES AND STONEWARES.

c.1857-1956 Impressed on Earthenwares and stonewares **DOULTON**
LAMBETH

c.1870-77 Impressed on decorated stonewares - -
1872-77 The date was added to the mark -

1867 Paris Exhibition. Some well-shaped vases and jugs were shown designed by George Tinworth and other students of the Lambeth School of Art.

1871 First International Exhibition, London. 70 pieces of craft pottery were exhibited which made a marked impression on the public. Queen Victoria ordered some to be sent to Windsor.

Continued over -

1815

1815 Royal Doulton plc., BURSLEM, Staffordshire, England. (Cont`)

From the outset of this new response, Henry Doulton resolved that each artist should be given the greatest possible scope for individual expression. Thus it was that George Tinworth, Arthur Barlow and his sisters Hannah and Florence, Mark Marshall, Frank Butler, to name but a few, were able to pursue their individual skills within a secure industrial environment.

c.1873-1914 Impressed or printed mark on Lambeth Faience. (1891 `England` added) - - -

c.1879-1902 Impressed or printed on decorated stonewares. (1891 `England` was added.)

c.1879-1910 Impressed or printed on `Impasto` ware. (1891 `England` added.) -

1878 Paris Exhibition. Doulton awarded Grand Prix. Henry Doulton made Chevalier of the Legion of Honour.

1877- Doulton acquired a major holding in Pinder, Bourne & Co.,Nile Street, Burslem.

c.1878 Earlier Pinder, Bourne mark on Burslem earthenware. -

1882 Mr.Pinder accepts settlement and retires.

c.1880-1932 Impressed on Lambeth `Silicon` stoneware- -

c.1882-1902 Marks on Burslem products. - - - - (1891 `England` added.)

1882- Doulton & Company, Burslem. (New company Name) John Slater (trained at Minton) was put in charge of design. John Cuthbert Bailey, a young man of 23 was chosen, with some scepticism by the locals, as General Manager. 1884 New wing built at Burslem producing fine bone china. A still larger group of designers, artists, gilders, etchers, engravers and modellers were recruited to cope with demand.

1885- Henry Doulton received the Albert Medal of the Society of Arts (now the Royal Society of Arts)

Continued over -

1815 Royal Doulton plc. BURSLEM, Staffordshire, England. (Cont`)

c.1886-1939 Mark on `chine` and `chine-gilt` wares. **DOULTON & SLATERS PATENT**

1887- Henry Doulton was knighted by Queen Victoria.

1886-1902 Marks impressed on Burslem wares.

1889- Charles Noke (designer) recruited.
1889 `Series Ware` introduced. The first series issued was the `Isthmian Games`

c.1891-1906 Impressed or printed on Lambeth `Marqueterie` ware -

c.1891-1924 Impressed or printed mark on `Carrara` ware. -

1893- Chicago Exhibition. Charles Noke introduces the large matt ivory-glazed models depicting jesters, minstrels and characters from Shakespeare and Gilbert and Sullivan.

c.1895-1915 Printed on Burslem `Holbien` wares. - -

1897 Sir Henry Doulton dies. Henry Lewis Doulton (son) **forms a Limited Company.**
1899- `Kingsware` introduced at Burslem.
1901- King Edward VII. presents a Royal Warrant on the company.

1902-32 Printed on Burslem and Lambeth products - - -
(Late 1920s `Made in England` added.)

1902-56 Mark on Lambeth and Burslem small objects -

1904- `Flambe` ware introduced.

1904-30 Printed mark on `Flambe` ware - - - -

c.1912-56 Impressed or printed on Lambeth slip-cast

Lambeth `Persian` ware - - -

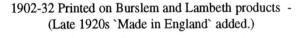

Continued over -

1815

1815 Royal Doulton plc., BURSLEM, Staffordshire, England. (Cont`)

1913- The famous `HN` Figures were launched, the first being the figure of a little boy in a nightgown which was named `Darling` and numbered HN1.

c.1914- C.J. Noke introduces the highly popular, animal figures.

1916-1929 Marks used on ` Titanian` ware -

1922-26 mark- - - -

1922-56 Impressed or printed on Lambeth products -

1925- `Chang` ware by C.F. Noke, goes into production.

c.1925-40 Marks on high-temparature `Chang` ware - -

1934 The first Royal Doulton character jug, `John Barleycorn Old Lad` was produced.

1932-59 Printed on Burslem earthenware and bone-china-

1934- `Bunnykins` childrens range introduced.

1956- Lambeth works and studios finally close down. Burslem became the principle centre of Royal Doulton production.

1959- Printed mark - - -

1968- Mintons of Stoke acquired. see 1793 Minton, Thomas,

1980- Royal Doulton International Collectors Club formed.

Present-day printed mark (1995) -

Continued over -

1815 Royal Doulton plc., BURSLEM, Staffordshire, England. (Cont`)

Below is a list, in date order, of some of the better known artists, together with their marks, who worked for Doultons, Lambeth. Many were ex-students of the Lambeth School of Art.

1866-1913	Tinworth, George, - -
1871-78	Barlow, Arthur B., - -
1871-1913	Barlow, Hannah B., - -
1872-1911	Butler, Frank A.,- - -
c.1873-90	Davis, Louisa J.,- - -
c.1873-90	Edwards, Louisa E., - -
1873-1909	Barlow, Florence E., - -
1873-1913	Simmance, Eliza, - -
c.1873-1910	Broad, John, - - -
1873-1930	Pearce, Arthur E., - -
c.1874-94	Butterton, Mary, - -
c.1875-80	Collins, F.M., - - -
c.1875-90	Lee, Francis E., - - -
c.1875-97	Lewis, Florence,- - -
c.1876-82	Atkins, Elizabeth, - -
c.1876-83	Capes, Mary, - - -
c.1876-83	Crawley, Minna L., - -
c.1876-84	Banks, Eliza, - - -
1876-87	Mitchell, Mary, - - -
c.1876-89	Lupton, Edith D., - -
c.1878-90	Tabor, George Hugo, - -

Continued over -

1815

1815 Royal Doulton plc., BURSLEM, Staffordshire, England. (Cont`)

Artists and Decorators at Doulton (Cont`)

1879-1912 Marshall, Mark V., - - 

c.1879-1930 Roberts, Florence C., - - 

c.1880-83 Sturgeon, Katie, - - - 

c.1880-85 Linnell, Florence M., - - 

c.1880-86 Watt, Linnie, - - - 

c.1880-90 Barnard, Harry, - - - 

c.1880-92 Rogers, Kate, - - - 

c.1880-1910 McLennan, John H., - - 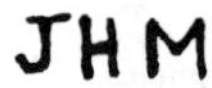

1880-1923 Pope, Frank C., - - - 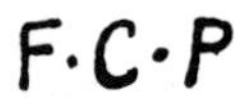

c.1883-95 Dunn, William E., - - 

1883-1939 Rowe, William, - - - 

c.1884-90 Eyre, John, - - - 

1894-1936 Simeon, Henry, - - - 

c.1900 Thompson, Margaret E., - - 

1902-15 Harradine, Leslie, - - 

Continue overleaf for Doulton, Burslem, artists.

Continued over -

1815 Royal Doulton plc., BURSLEM, Staffordshire, England. (Cont`)

Royal Doulton artists at Burslem:-

1879-1913 Hancock, Fred, - - -	
1880-1927 Hart, Charles, - - -	
1885-1954 Curnock, Percy, - - -	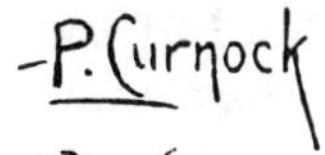
1885-1912 White, George, - - -	
1889-1919 Dewsberry, David, - -	
1889-1941 Noke, Charles, - - -	
1892-1919 Raby, Edward, - - -	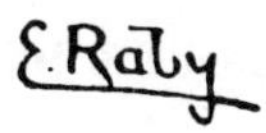
1893-1922 Hopkins, Charles B., - -	
1900-1950 Allen, Harry, - - -	
1900-1926 Birbeck, Joseph, - - -	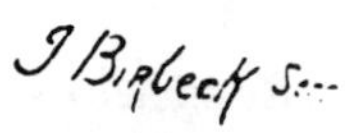
1900-1937 Johnson, Leslie, - - -	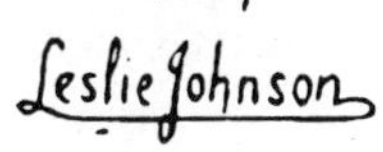
1900-1950 Nixon, Harry, - - -	
1900-1925 Tittensor, Harry. - -	
1903-1911 Brough, Charles, - -	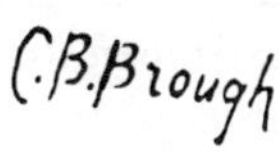
1920-1954 Noke, Cecil Jack, - -	
1927-1957 Moore, Fred, - - -	

1815/16

1815 Thompson, J., ASHBY-DE-LA-ZOUCH, England.

c.1815-56 GENERAL POTTERY. Impressed- **J. THOMPSON**

1818- Circular impressed mark- **JOSEPH THOMPSON WOODEN BOX POTTERY DERBYSHIRE**

1815 Tittensor, Charles, SHELTON, Staffordshire, England.

c.1815-23 EARTHENWARES, FIGURES. Printed or impressed- **TITTENSOR**

1815 VIERZON, Cher, France.

HARD-PASTE PORCELAIN.

1815- **Perrot and Delvincourt**
1825- **Dubois & Jamet**

Hache & Pépin-Le-Halleur - - **H & PL**
V

c.1875- **Hache & Julien** - - - **H. J. & Co.**
V

Late 19th century marks - - **A. H. & Co.**
V
FRANCE

1902- **Rondeleux et Cie** - - - -
HOTEL PORCELAIN WARES.

Jaquin et Cie - - - -

1815 Barbin, François-Hubert, (ornaments) France. - - see 1745 SÈVRES.
1815 Delahodde, France. - - - - - - see 1770 VRON.
1815 Phillips, John, SUNDERLAND, England. - - see 1762 Maling, William,
1815 Poupart, Achille, (landscapes) France. - - - see 1745 SÈVRES.

1816 Beerbower & Co., L.B., ELIZABETH, New Jersey, U.S.A.

c.1816- STONEWARE - - -
Later run by Mr. Pruden.
Yellow and Rockingham wares.

1816 Pountney & Allies, Bristol Pottery, BRISTOL, England.

c.1816-35 EARTHENWARES.

1835- Mr. Allies retired.

Printed, painted or impressed marks **P** **P. & A.**

P. A. **B. P.**

P. A.
BRISTOL POTTERY

Impressed mark

1836-49 **Pountney & Goldney.** Impressed mark - **BRISTOL POTTERY**
POUNTNEY & GOLDNEY

1849- **Pountney & Co, Ltd.,**
Bristol Victoria Pottery

1849-89 marks **P, & CO.**
POUNTNEY & CO.

c.1889 `Ltd` added

c.1889 From this date onwards Factory`s name or initials are found within marks of various patterns and designs:-

1962- **Acquired Cauldon Potteries Ltd.**

1968- **Cauldon Bristol Potteries Ltd.** - see 1856 Ridgway Bates & Co.

New Factory at Wilson Way, Redruth, Cornwall.

Fine tableware and advertising sundries.

(By kind permission of Cauldon Bristol Potteries Ltd., Ferrybridge, England)

1816 Stevenson, Andrew, COBRIDGE, Staffordshire, England.

c.1816-30 EARTHENWARES. Impressed- **STEVENSON**
A. STEVENSON

Ship mark is sometimes attributed to c.1810 Stevenson, Ralph, COBRIDGE, Painted or impressed-

1816/17

1816 Thomson, John & Sons, Annfield Pottery, GLASGOW, Scotland.

c.1816-84 EARTHENWARES. Printed or impressed- **J. T. ANNFIELD**
The Factory`s name or initials are found within marks of various patterns and designs.
1866 `& Sons` added. - **J. T. & SONS GLASGOW**
J. THOMSON & SONS GLASGOW

1816 Wilhelm, King, Germany. - - - see 1756 LUDWIGSBURG.

1817 BOULOGNE, Pas-de-Calais, France.

c.1817-59 HARD-PASTE PORCELAIN - Red- -
Haffreingue

1817 Bourne, Charles, FENTON, Staffordshire, England. **CB**

1817-30 PORCELAIN. Painted with pattern No.- **No.5**
CHARLES BOURNE

1817 Fell, Thomas, NEWCASTLE, England.

1817-90 EARTHENWARE, CREAMWARES.
1817-30 Impressed- **FELL**

c.1830-90 T. Fell & Co. Printed or impressed- - **F. & CO.**
The Factory`s name or initials are found within marks of various patterns and designs. **T. F. & CO.**
T. FELL & CO.

1817 LA MONCLOA, nr. Madrid, Spain.

1817-50 PORCELAIN. - Impressed-
Ferdinand VII.

Buen Retiro mark used. - -

1817 Maling, Robert, Ouseburn Bridge Pottery, Newcastle/Tyne, England.

1817- EARTHENWARES, PRINTED AND LUSTRES.

1817-59 Impressed mark - - **MALING**
M

1853- **Maling, C.T., (son)**

1859-90 **Ford Pottery built. Moved from Ouseburn.**

EARTHENWARES, SOME IN LUSTRE.

1859-90 Impressed - - **C. T. MALING**
C. T. M.

1875-c.1908 Impressed or printed mark-

1890-1963 **Maling & Sons Ltd.,**

EARTHENWARES. Printed marks:-

1890

c.1908-

c.1949-63

see 1762 Maling, William.

1817 Mayer & Newbold, LANE END, Staffordshire, England.

c.1817-33 EARTHENWARE AND PORCELAIN. Painted or printed- **M. & N.**

MAY^R^ & NEWB^D^
Mayer & Newbold

1817 PLAUE-ON-HAVEL, Thuringia, Germany.

1817- HARD-PASTE PORCELAIN. - -

Schierholz, C.G. & Sohn. - - -

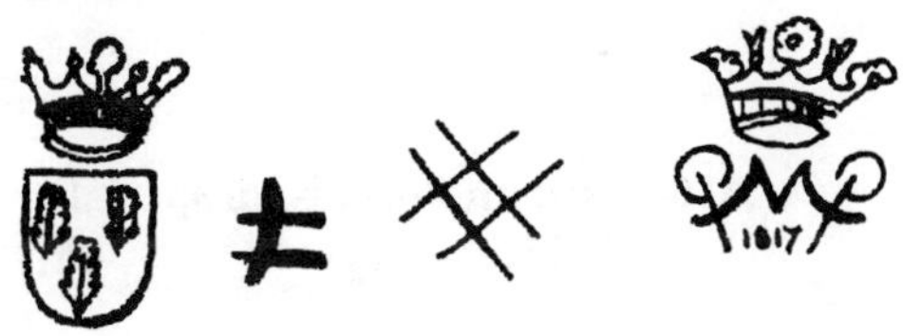

Plaue Porzellanmanufaktur (lithophanies) - **P.P.M.**

1817 Shorthose & Co., HANLEY, Staffordshire, England.

c.1817-22 EARTHENWARES. Impressed, written or printed- **SHORTHOSE & CO.**

1817 Bevington & Co., SWANSEA, Wales. - - see 1783 Swansea Pottery.

1817 Dihl, PARIS, France. - - - - see 1780 rue-de Bondy.

1818

1818 Bathwell & Goodfellow, BURSLEM, Staffordshire, England.

1818-23 EARTHENWARES. Impressed- **BATHWELL & GOODFELLOW**
1820-22 at TUNSTALL.

1818 Clews, James & Ralph, COBRIDGE, Staffordshire, England.

1818-34 EARTHENWARES AND PORCELAIN. - - **CLEWS WARRANTED STAFFORDSHIRE**
Impressed under crown-

On Blue printed wares. Impressed- - -

1818 Heathcote & Co., Charles, LANE END, Staffordshire, England.

1818-24 EARTHENWARES. Printed- -
The name of the Factory is included in various printed marks.

1818 Hollins, T.J. & R., HANLEY, Staffordshire, England.

c.1818-22 EARTHENWARE - Impressed- **T. J. & R. HOLLINS**

1818 Pattison, J., LONGTON, Staffordshire, England.

c.1818-30 EARTHENWARE FIGURES. Written- ***JOHN PATTISON***

1818 Pratt & Co.,Ltd. F.& R., FENTON, Staffordshire, England.

c.1818- EARTHENWARES. Printed- **F. & R. P. PRATT**
The name and initials of the Factory are included in various printed marks.

c.1840- \`& Co.\` added. - **F. & R. P. CO.**

c.1847-60 - Printed- **F. & R. PRATT & CO. FENTON MANUFACTURER\`S TO H.R.H. PRINCE ALBERT**

c.1850- Used on Pot-lids, (a speciality of this factory) Printed- -

c.1925 Taken over by Cauldon Potteries Ltd., who still use their marks. Printed- -

1818 Rivers, William, HANLEY, Staffordshire, England.
c.1818-22 EARTHENWARES, CREAMWARES. Impressed- **RIVERS**

1818 Thompson, Joseph, Hartshorne, ASHBY-DE-LA-ZOUCH, England.
c.1818-56 IRONSTONE-WARE, TERRA-COTTA, ETC.

Impressed marks-

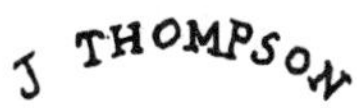

1818 Walton, John, BURSLEM, Staffordshire, England.
c.1818-35 EARTHENWARE FIGURES AND GROUPS.
Mark impressed on raised scroll-

1818	Bougon and Chalot, France. - - -	see 1725 CHANTILLY.
1818	Ducluzeau, Dame, (figures) France. - -	see 1745 SÈVRES.
1818	Schilt, Louis-Pierre, (flowers) France. - -	see 1745 SÈVRES.
1818	Sinsson, P. (flowers) France. - - -	see 1745 SÈVRES.
1818	Wood & Sons, Enoch, BURSLEM, England. -	see 1784 Wood, Enoch.
1819	Adams & Sons, W.,TUNSTALL, England. -	see 1769 Adams & Sons, W.
1819	Didier, Charles-Antoine, (ornaments) France. - -	see 1745 SÈVRES.

1820 Daniel, H.& R.,STOKE, Staffordshire, England.
1820-41 FINE PORCELAINS AND POTTERY. Written- ***H. & R. Daniel***
1829-41 - - ***H. Daniel & Sons***

1820 Doe and Rogers, WORCESTER, England.
c.1820-40 PORCELAIN DECORATORS - - **Doe & Rogers**
Worcester

1820 Folch, Stephen, STOKE, Staffordshire, England.
1820-30 EARTHENWARES, IRONSTONES, Impressed- **FOLCH`S GENUINE**
STONE CHINA

1820 Ford & Patterson, NEWCASTLE, England.
c.1820-c.30 EARTHENWARES. Impressed- **FORD & PATTERSON**
Sheriff Hill
Pottery

1820 Fowler, Thompson & Co., PRESTONPANS, Scotland.
c.1820-40 EARTHENWARES. Printed or impressed- **FOWLER THOMPSON**
& CO.

1820

1820 Green, Stephen, LAMBETH, London, England.

c.1820-58 STONEWARES. RELIEF, Impressed or incised- The name of the Factory is within marks of various designs and patterns.

**STEPHEN GREEN
IMPERIAL
POTTERIES
LAMBETH**

1820 Greenock Pottery, GREENOCK, Scotland.

c.1820-60 EARTHENWARES, CREAMWARES. - - The name of the factory is included in various impressed or printed marks.

**GREENOCK
POTTERY**

1820 HARIMA, Japan.

1820- **Maiko-Yaki. Mikuni Kyuhachi in the Akashi district.** BROWN STONEWARE. -

Suma - -

Asagiri Factory, Sohei.-

1820- **Tozan-Yaki. Made in the Himeji district.** PORCELAIN, MAINLY BLUE AND WHITE. -

Banyo Tozan (Tozan is the mountain where the materials were mined) - - - -

1820 Kozloff's Factory, MOSCOW, Russia.

c.1820-56 PORCELAIN, BISCUIT FIGURES. Incised-

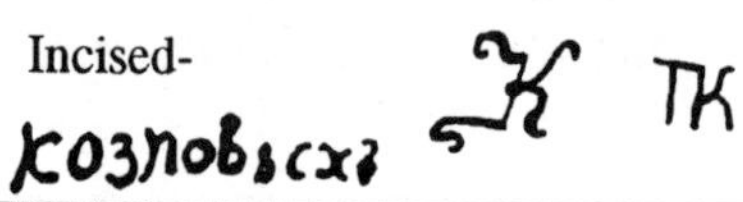

1820 Leplé, PARIS, France.

1820- DECORATOR OF HARD-PASTE PORCELAIN. -

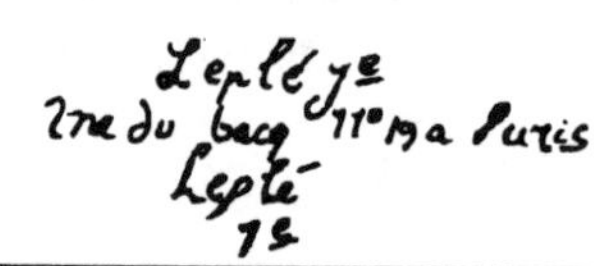

1820 LICHTE, Thuringia, Germany.

1820- HARD-PASTE PORCELAIN.
Heubach Bros., -

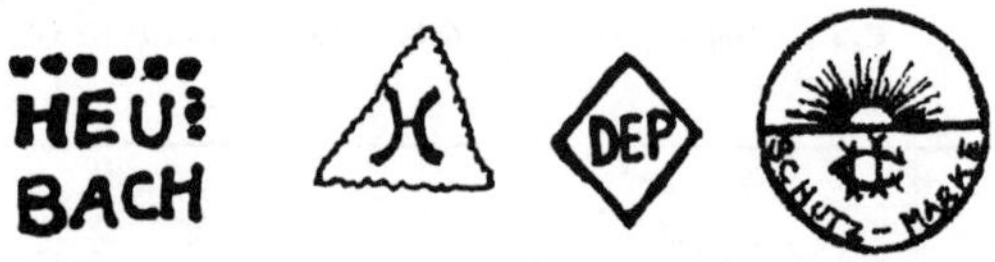

1820 Novyki Brothers, MOSCOW, Russia.

1820- HARD-PASTE PORCELAIN. - -

ВСИПЯТИНА Н БРАТЬЕВЪ НОВЫХЪ

1820 Pardoe, William Henry, BRISTOL, England.

c.1820-35 DECORATOR **(also at Cardiff, etc.)** - - **PARDOE, CARDIFF**
Son of Thomas Pardoe see c1809-20 BRISTOL.

1820 Pickman & Co. and M. Francesco de Aponte, SEVILLE, Spain.

19th century FAÏENCE -

1820 Renou, Rue Caumartin, PARIS, France.

1820- DECORATOR OF PORCELAIN. gold- Renou

1820 Rihouet, J., Rue de la Paix, PARIS, France.

1820- DECORATOR OF PORCELAIN. - gold- Rihouet

Lerosey - - - Lerosey 7 Rue de la paix

1820 Safronoff, MOSCOW, Russia.

c.1820- PORCELAIN - САФРОНОВА С САФРОНОВА 2

1820 Salt, Ralph, HANLEY, Staffordshire, England.

c.1820-46 EARTHENWARES. Impressed on scroll- **SALT**

1820 SCHRAMBERG, Wurtemberg, Germany.

1820- WHITE AND CREAM EARTHENWARES. Impressed- **SCHRAMBERG**

Villeroy & Boch - - - - -

c.1910- **Schramberger Majolika Fabrik** -

1912 Factory closed. - see 1767 Villeroy & Boch.

1820/21

1820 Taylor & Co. Tyne Pottery, NEWCASTLE, England.

c.1820-25 EARTHENWARES — Printed- **TAYLOR & CO.
TYNE POTTERY
NEWCASTLE**

or Tyler & Co. ?

1820 ZELL, Baden, Germany.

1820- HARD-PASTE PORCELAIN. - -

Schmider, Georg, - - -

1846-67 **Lenz, J.F.,** - - - **ZELL**

1820	\`Bizan\` Hasegawa Kumenosuke, Japan. - -	see 1655 Ninsei.
1820	Dixon, Austin & Co., SUNDERLAND, England.	see 1807 Sunderland Pottery.
1820	Hohei, Japan. - - - - - -	see 1596 SATSUMA.
1820	\`Kozan\` Awatafayence, YAMASHIRO, Japan. -	see 1655 Ninsei.
1820	Régnier, Ferdinand, (figures,etc.) France. -	see 1745 SÈVRES.
1820	Takatori Ki, Japan. - - - - -	see 1583 CHIKUZEN.
1820	Toyosuke-Yaki, Haraku Factory, Japan. - -	see 1573 OWARI.

1821 Burton, William, CODNOR PARK, Derbyshire, England.

c.1821-32 STONEWARES — Impressed- **W. BURTON
CODNOR PARK**

1821 GIEN, France.

1821- **Hall & Guyon (Founder Thomas Hulm)**
Faïence. utilitarian crockery and
decorated printed ware.

HALL
Mar. 1822- Aug. 26
moulded

GIEN ***GIEN***
1827-39
moulded

1839- **Paris Exhibition. Gien awarded a distinction.**

1834-44 printed marks as above

Continued over -

1821 GIEN, France. (Cont`)

1844-49 printed marks as above

1849-1914 A period of great developments in decorative and artistic techniques.

Mar. 1849-Oct. 51

1851-60

l`exposition de 1855
à Paris
1855-1860

1st mark with tower
1856-60

1860-71 printed marks as above

1860-71 Castle type marks

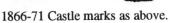

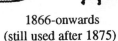

1866-71 Castle marks as above.

1866-onwards
(still used after 1875)

Continued over -

1821

1821 GIEN, France. (Cont`)

April 1871- Feb. 1875 as above

1871-75 Castle-type marks as above.

1875-1935 (`1923 `France` added) 1875 marks as above.

moulded
1880-83

1880-83 onwards. Various marks as above

1886-1938 Various marks

1886-?

Continued over -

1821 GIEN, France. (Cont`)

1914-39 **Modernisation of factory.** The longest kiln in Europe installed.

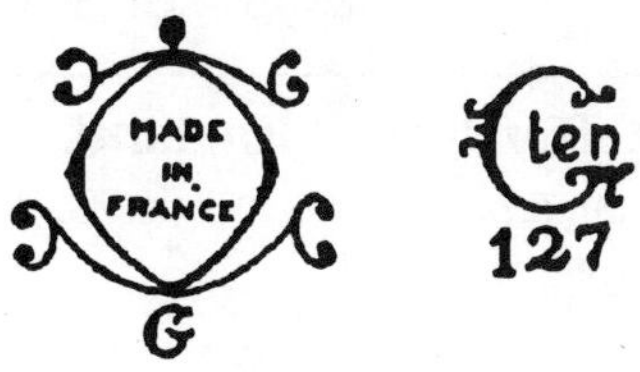

1920-onwards

1938-60

1941-50

1941-60

1945-80 **Foreign competition threatens orders. Vitroceramic and porcelain begin to take-over faïence in popularity.**

1956

1957-59

1960-71

1971

1984-89

1989-

1980 **Gien faced serious financial difficulties.**

1984 Liquidation of assets

1984 **Societe Nouvelle des Faïenceries de Gien is founded with a group of shareholders led by Mr Pierre Jeufroy. Known as `Gien France` it exhibits worldwide.**

(By kind permission of S.N. Faïenceries de Gien, France.)

1821/22

1821 Lockett, John, LANE END, Staffordshire, England.

1821-58 EARTHENWARES. - Impressed- **J. LOCKETT**

1821 Tao-kuang, China. - - - - see 1644 CH`ING.

1822 Baggerley & Ball, LONGTON, Staffordshire, England.

1822-36 EARTHENWARE. Printed blue- within oval form. **B. & B. L.**

1822 Chetham & Robinson, LONGTON, Staffordshire, England.

1822-37 EARTHENWARES - Printed- **C. & R.**
The Factory`s initials are printed within marks of various patterns and designs.

1822 Elkin, Knight & Co., FENTON, Staffordshire, England.

1822-26 EARTHENWARES. impressed or printed- **E. K. & CO.**
`The Factory`s name and initials are found within marks of various patterns and designs. **ELKIN KNIGHT & CO.**

c.1827-40 **Elkin, Knight & Bridgwood.** Printed- **E. K. B.**
CHINA AND EARTHENWARES.

1822 Hall, Ralph, TUNSTALL, Staffordshire, England.

1822-49 Earthenwares. - Printed- **R. HALL**
c.1836- - **R. HALL & SON**
1841-49 - - **R. HALL & CO.**
The name and initials of this Factory are printed within marks of various patterns and designs. **R. H. & CO.**

1822 Hilditch & Son, LANE END, Staffordshire, England.

1822-30 EARTHENWARES AND CHINA. Printed- **H & S**
The initials of the Factory are printed within marks of various patterns and designs.

1822 HOHENSTEIN, nr.Teplitz, Germany.

1822- EARTHENWARES. - - -
1822-34 **Hufsky, Carl,** - Impressed- - HOHENSTEIN b.TEPLITZ CH.

1834- **Hufsky, Vincent,** Impressed- - - - **V.H.**

1822- **Bloch, B.,** - - Impressed- - - - **B B**

1822 Keeling, Charles, SHELTON, Staffordshire, England.

1822-25	EARTHENWARES. - The initials of the Factory are printed within marks of various patterns and designs.	Printed-	**C. K.**

1822 Lockett & Hulme, LANE END, Staffordshire, England.

1822-26	EARTHENWARES. - The initials of the Factory are printed within marks of various patterns and designs. -	Printed-	**L & H** **L E**

1822 Mayer & Co.,Joseph, HANLEY, Staffordshire, England.

c.1822-33	EARTHENWARES. - - -		**JOSEPH MAYER & CO.** **HANLEY** **MAYER & CO.**

1822 Phillips, Edward & George, LONGPORT, Staffordshire, England.

1822-34	EARTHENWARES. The name and initials of this Factory are printed within marks of various patterns and designs.	Printed -	**PHILLIPS** **LONGPORT** **E. & G.P** **E. & G. PHILLIPS**
1834-48	**Phillips, George,**	Impressed or printed-	**PHILLIPS** **G. PHILLIPS**

The name of this Factory sometimes occurs with the Staffordshire knot and sometimes `LONGPORT`

1822 Pratt, Hassall & Gerrard, FENTON, Staffordshire, England.

1822-34	PORCELAIN AND EARTHENWARE The initials of the Factory are printed within marks of various patterns and designs.	Printed-	**P. H. G.** **P. H & G.**

1822 Stubbs, Joseph, Longport, BURSLEM, Staffordshire, England.

c.1822-35	EARTHENWARES -	Impressed-	**STUBBS**
	printed or impressed- - -		**JOSEPH STUBBS**
	in circular mark - -		**LONGPORT**

1822 Twigg, Joseph & Co.,SWINTON, Yorkshire, England.

c.1822-81	EARTHENWARES.	Impressed or printed- with pattern name.	**J. T.**
c.1822-66	**Newhill Pottery**	Impressed-	**TWIGG** **NEWHILL**
c.1839-81	**Kilnhurst Old Pottery**	Impressed-	**TWIGG** **K.P.**

1822-25

1822 Hicks, Meigh & Johnson, SHELTON, England.- see 1784 Baddeley, J.& E.
1822 Vickers & Son, John, DOWNINGTOWN, U.S.A. see 1806 Vickers & Son, Thom.

1823 Baxter, John Denton, HANLEY, Staffordshire, England.

1823-27 EARTHENWARES. Printed- **I.D.B.** **J.D.B.**

1823 Carey, Thomas & John, LANE END, Staffordshire, England.

c.1823-42 EARTHENWARES. Printed or impressed- **CAREYS**
The name of this Factory is found within marks of various designs especially an anchor.

1823 Troxel, Samuel, MONTGOMERY COUNTY, Pennsylvania, U.S.A.

c.1823-33 EARTHENWARE, SGRAFFITO. Incised -

1823 Borgano, Italy. - - - - - - see 1577 TURIN.
1823 Constantin, Figures, France. - - - - see 1745 SÈVRES.
1823 Nowotny, August, ALT-ROHLAU, Germany. - see 1813 Hasslacher,Benedict.

1824 VISTA ALEGRE, nr. Oporto, Portugal.

1824- HARD-PASTE PORCELAIN. -

.VA VA Portugal

1824 Charles X France. - - - - - see 1745 SÈVRES.
1824 Dillwyn, SWANSEA, Wales. - - - see 1783 Swansea Pottery.
1824 Lecomte and Dantier, France. - - - see 1733 SINCENY.

1825 Chesworth & Robinson, LANE END, Staffordshire, England.

1825-40 EARTHENWARES, printed with the Staffordshire knot- **C & R**
Could be Chetham & Robinson, see 1822.

1825 Daniell, A.B.& R.P., LONDON, England.

c.1825-1917 RETAILER. Printed on wares from various factories especially Coalport.

1825 Plant, Thomas, LANE END, Staffordshire, England. TP

1825-50 EARTHENWARE FIGURES, ETC., Printed-

1825 Raschkin Brothers, MOSCOW, Russia.

Early 19th century. HARD-PASTE PORCELAIN-

БРАТЬЕВЪ
РАУКИНЫХЬ

1825 rue de Jour, PARIS, France.

1825-28 **Allard.** HARD-PASTE PORCELAIN. - -

1825 Smith, William, Stafford Pottery, STOCKTON-ON-TEES, England.

1825- EARTHENWARE, QUEEN`S WARE, ETC.
The name and initials of this factory are found within marks of various designs. — **W. S. & CO. QUEEN`S WARE STOCKTON**

1826- **William Smith & Co.** (Partnership with John Whalley from Staffordshire)

1829- **George Skinner & Co.** (Partnership with George and William Skinner) — **G. S. & CO.**

1848- The partners in the business consisted of William Smith, John Whalley, George Skinner and Henry Cowap. An injunction was granted against them from using the marks `Wedgwood & Co.,` or `Wedgewood` — **W. S. & CO. WEDGEWOOD**

1870- **Skinner and Walker.** At this time the Company established a Company in Belgium called, `Capperman & Co., Genappes. — **S. & W. QUEEN`S WARE STOCKTON**

1825 Stevenson & Williams, COBRIDGE, Staffordshire, England.

c.1825 EARTHENWARES. Printed or impressed- **R. S. W.**
The name and initials of this Factory are found within various patterns and designs. **STEVENSON & WILLIAMS**

1825 Stevenson, Alcock & Williams, COBRIDGE, England.

c.1825 EARTHENWARES. Printed- **STEVENSON, ALCOCK & WILLIAMS**

1825 STOCKTON-ON-TEES, Cleveland, England.

The individual factories and potters of STOCKTON-ON-TEES have been listed under their own dates and marks within this book.

1825 Tucker, William Ellis, PHILADELPHIA, Pennsylvania, U.S.A.

c.1825- HARD-PASTE PORCELAIN. - -
1828 Dated mark on vase. Painted black- **William Ellis Tucker China Manufacturer Philadelphia 1828**

c.1828- **Tucker & Thomas Hulme partnership** - **Tucker & Hulme Philadelphia**

1832- **Tucker & Judge Joseph Hemphill partnership-**
1832 Mr Tucker died.

Continued over -

1825-27

1825 Tucker, William Ellis, PHILADELPHIA, PA. U.S.A. (Cont`)

1832-36 Hemphill, Judge Joseph - - **Manufactured by Jos. Hemphill Philad-**

Impressed marks of workmen are found on Tucker and Hemphill porcelain. Some of the workman are as follows:-

Walker, Andrew Craig (moulder) - 

Morgan, Joseph (moulder) - - 

Frederick, Charles (moulder) - - 

Hand, William, - - - - 

Vivian, a Frenchman, - - - 

Boulter, Charles J. (probably) - - 

1825 Antonibon, Giovanni Battista, Italy. - - see 1728 NOVE.
1825 Dubois & Jamet, France. - - - - see 1815 VIERZON.
1825 Fontaine, Jean-Joseph (flowers) France. - - see 1745 SÈVRES.
1825 Nicholas 1. Russia. - - - - see 1744 ST. PETERSBURG.
1825 Régnier, Hyacinthe (figures) France. - - see 1745 SÈVRES.
1825 Wainwright & Co., Samuel, England. - - see 1760 LEEDS POTTERY.
1825 Wessel, Ludwig, Germany. - - - see 1755 POPPELSDORF.

1826 HIRSCHAU, Bavaria, Germany.

1826- CREAMWARES. - Impressed- **HIRSCHAU**
c.1850-75 Dorfner & Cie, Ernst. - - **E.D. & Cie** 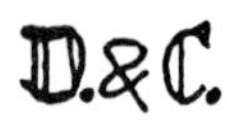
HARD-PASTE PORCELAIN AND EARTHENWARE. **Hirschau**

1826 Knight Elkin & Co., Foley Potteries, FENTON, Staff`s, England.

1826-46 EARTHENWARES. Factory`s name or initials printed within marks of various patterns and designs. **K. E. & CO. KNIGHT ELKIN & CO.**

1846-53 **Knight, John King,** Factory`s name printed within marks of various patterns and designs. **J. K. KNIGHT I. K. KNIGHT**

1826 Griffin-mark, Earl Fitzwilliam, England. - see 1745 ROCKINGHAM.

1827 DAMM, nr. Aschaffenburg, Germany.

1827- CREAMWARES.- - -
c.1840 `Höchst` moulds were used.

1827 Goodwin, Bridgwood & Orton, LANE END, Staffordshire, England.

1827-29 EARTHENWARES. - Printed- **G.B.O.**
The initials of this Factory are found within marks of various patterns and designs. - **G.B. & O.**

1829-31 **Goodwin, Bridgwood & Harris.** Printed- (under a lion) **G.B.H.**

c.1831-38 **Goodwins & Harris.** Impressed- **GOODWINS & HARRIS**

1827 Jeanne, Rue St-Louis, (Decorator) PARIS, France.

1827- DECORATOR OF HARD-PASTE PORCELAIN. Gold- *Jeanne*

1827	Dixon, Austin,Phillips & Co., England.	see 1807 Sunderland Pottery.
1827	Elkin, Knight & Bridgwood, FENTON, England.	see 1822 Elkin, Knight & Co.
1827	Gembei, Japan. - - - - -	see 1650 KAGA.
1827	Hackwood, William, HANLEY, England. -	see 1807 Hackwood & Co.
1827	Josiah Spode III (grandson) STOKE, England. -	see 1770 Josiah Spode.
1827	Soshichi at Hakata, Japan. - - - -	see 1583 CHIKUZEN.

1828 Alcock & Co., Samuel, COBRIDGE, Staffordshire, England.

c.1828-59 GENERAL CERAMICS. - -

c.1828-53 COBRIDGE. Printed or impressed- **SAML ALCOCK & CO. COBRIDGE**

c.1830-59 BURSLEM. Printed,impressed or moulded - - **SAML ALCOCK & CO. BURSLEM**

c.1830-59 The name and initials of this Factory are found within marks of various patterns and designs, including the Royal Arms or a bee-hive design. **S.A.& CO.** **S. ALCOCK & CO.** **SAML ALCOCK & CO.**

Continued by Sir James Duke & Nephews. see 1860.

1828 Bourne Nixon & Co., TUNSTALL, Staffordshire, England.

1828-30 EARTHENWARES. - Impressed- **BOURNE NIXON & CO.**

1828-30 The initials of this Factory are found within marks of various patterns and designs. Printed- **B.N.& Co.**

1828 Dimmock (Junr`) & Co.,Thomas, HANLEY, Staffordshire, England.

c.1828-59 EARTHENWARES - Printed- **D.**

The initial `D` of this Factory is found within various patterns and designs, some of which may be dated.

Monogram mark. Impressed or printed-

c.1830-50 Also at Shelton. see 1862 Dimmock & Co.

1828

1828 Godwin, Rowley & Co., BURSLEM, Staffordshire, England.

1828-31 EARTHENWARES. Printed- **G. R. & CO.**
The initials of this Factory are found within
marks of various patterns and designs.

1828 Goodfellow, Thomas, TUNSTALL, Staffordshire, England.

1828-59 EARTHENWARES. Printed- **T. GOODFELLOW**
The name of this Factory is found within
marks of various patterns and designs.

1828 Heath & Co., Joseph, TUNSTALL, Staffordshire, England.

1828-41 EARTHENWARES. - Printed- **J. HEATH & CO.**
The name and initials of this Factory are found
within marks of various patterns and designs. **J.H. & CO.**

1828 Hulme & Sons, John, LANE END, Staffordshire, England.

c.1828-30 EARTHENWARES. - Printed- **HULME & SONS**
The name of this Factory is found within
marks of various patterns and designs.

1828 Korniloff, S.W., Factory, PETERSBURG, Russia.

1827-c.85 PORCELAIN.- - - -

1828 Lahens and Rateau, BORDEAUX, France.

1828- FAÏENCE. - - -

1828 Lockett & Sons, John, LONGTON, Staffordshire, England.

1828-35 EARTHENWARES. - Impressed- **J. LOCKETT & SONS**

1828 Stubbs & Kent, BURSLEM, Staffordshire, England.

c.1828-30 EARTHENWARES.

Impressed or printed-

1828 Tunnicliff, Michael, TUNSTALL, Staffordshire, England.

1828-41 EARTHENWARE FIGURES, JUGS, ETC., **TUNNICLIFF**
Mark on raised scroll **TUNSTALL**

1828 Wood & Challinor, TUNSTALL, Staffordshire, England.

1828-43 EARTHENWARES. Printed- **W. & C.**

The initials of this Factory are found within marks of various patterns and designs.

1828	Bunsei Period, Kichizaemon, Japan. - -	see 1690 IZUMI.
1828	Knaute, Benedict, Germany, - - -	see 1803 GIESSHÜBEL.
1828	Sewell & Donkin, NEWCASTLE , England -	see 1780 St.Anthony`s Pottery.
1828	Tucker & Hulme, PHILADELPHIA, U.S.A. -	see 1825 Tucker, Wm. E.,

1829

1829 BODENBACH, Bohemia, Germany.

1829- STONEWARES.

Schiller & Gerbing - - **S & G.**

Gerbing, F. - - - **F. G.**

Gerbing & Stephen - - - G & St

Schiller, W. & Sons - - - -

20th century Dressler, Julius, - - -

1829 Booth & Co.,G.R., HANLEY, Staffordshire, England.

1829-44 EARTHENWARES. - Impressed- **PUBLISHED BY G.R. BOOTH & CO. HANLEY STAFFORDSHIRE**

c.1839 `& Co.` added.

1829 Henderson, D.& J., Jersey City Pottery, NEW JERSEY, U.S.A.

c.1829- EARTHENWARE, BROWN GLAZED WARE.

Impressed-

1829 Knight, Elkin & Bridgwood, FENTON, Staffordshire, England.

c.1829-40 EARTHENWARE. - Printed- - **K. E. & B.**

Various printed marks with these initials.

1829	Böck, Josef, (decorator) Austria. - - -	see 1719 VIENNA.
1829	Clauss, Jean-Marx, PARIS, France. - -	see 1773 Porcelaine de Paris.
1829	Fouque, François and Antoine with Arnoux, France.	see 1650 TOULOUSE.
1829	Goodwin,Bridgwood & Harris, England.	see 1827 Goodwin, Bridgewood
1829	Mason & Co.,Charles J., LANE DELPH, England.	see 1796 Mason`s Ironstone.
1829	Scott & Sons, Anthony, SUNDERLAND, England.	see 1788 Southwick Pottery.
1829	Skinner, George, STOCKTON, England. -	see 1825 Smith, William,

1830 AWAJI, Japan.

1830- **Kashiu Mimpei, at Igano Mura.**
1834 Ogata Shuhei.
1862 Mimpei retired, son continued.

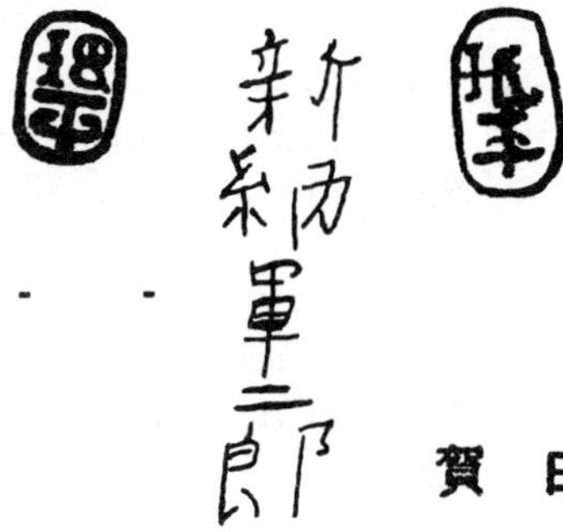

1850 **Nu-no Gun-Jiro** - - - - -

1875 **SAMPEI-YAKI, `Ni-pon Awaji Ka-shui Sampei`**
(Kashiu Sampei in the Island of Awaji)

日本淡路
賀集三平

1830 Booth & Sons, LANE END, Staffordshire, England.

1830-35 EARTHENWARES. - Impressed- **BOOTH & SONS**

1830 Boulevard des Italiens, PARIS, France.

1830- **Cassé-Mailard** (decorator) Red-

1845- Chapelle-Maillard Gold-

1830- **Montginot** (decorator) Gold-

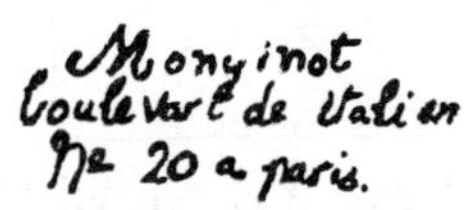

1830 Dunashoff, MOSCOW, Russia.

1830- HARD-PASTE PORCELAIN. -

1830 Edge & Grocott, TUNSTALL, Staffordshire, England.

c.1830 EARTHENWARE FIGURES. - - **EDGE & GROCOTT**

1830 Griffiths, Beardmore & Birks, LANE END, Staffordshire, England.

1830 EARTHENWARES. - Printed- **G. B. & B.**

1830 Jackson & Patterson, NEWCASTLE UPON TYNE, England.

1830-45 EARTHENWARES. - Printed- **J. & P.**

The initials of this Factory are found
within marks of various patterns and designs.

1830

1830 Mansard, PARIS, France.

1830- DECORATOR OF HARD-PASTE PORCELAIN. - -

1830 Methven & Sons, David, KIRKCALDY, Scotland.

Early 19th century-c.1930 EARTHENWARES. - - **D. M. & S.**

c.1875- - - **METHVEN**

D. METHVEN & SONS

1830 Milne Cornwall & Co., PORTOBELLO, Scotland.

c.1830-40 STONEWARES. - Impressed- **MILNE CORNWALL & CO.**

1830 Patterson & Co.,George, Sheriff Hill Pott., NEWCASTLE, England.

1830-1904 EARTHENWARES. printed or impressed- **PATTERSON & CO.**

The name of this Factory is found within marks of various patterns and designs.

1830 Pech, R.& E., KRONACH, Bavaria, Germany.

1830- PORCELAIN FIGURES. - - - - -

1830 Petit, Jacob and Mardochée, FONTAINEBLEAU, France.

1830-62 HARD-PASTE PORCELAIN. Incised or blue-

1830 Powell & Sons, William, Temple Gate Pottery, BRISTOL, England.

c.1830-1906 STONEWARES

Impressed-

c.1830- Impressed- **BRISTOL TEMPLE GATE POTTERY**

1830 Ridgway & Co., John, HANLEY, Staffordshire, England.

c.1830-55 EARTHENWARES AND PORCELAIN - - **J.R.**

Printed or impressed- **JOHN RIDGWAY**

JHN RIDGWAY

I. RIDGWAY

The name and initials of this Factory are found within marks of various patterns and designs

c.1841 `& Co.` added.

1830 Ridgway, William, SHELTON, Staffordshire, England.

c.1830-54 EARTHENWARES. Printed and impressed- **W. RIDGWAY**
c.1838-48 also at Hanley. **W. R.**
The name and initials of this Factory are found within marks of various patterns and designs. c.1834 `& Co.` added. **W. RIDGWAY & CO.** **W. R. & CO.**
1830-50 - - **QUARTZ CHINA**

1830 Scholl, Jacob, Tyler`s Port, MONTGOMERY COUNTY, Pa. U.S.A.

c.1830- EARTHENWARES SGRAFFITO Impressed-

1830 Smith, Fife & Co., PHILADELPHIA, Pa., U.S.A.

1830- PORCELAIN. (Exhibited at Franklin Institute)

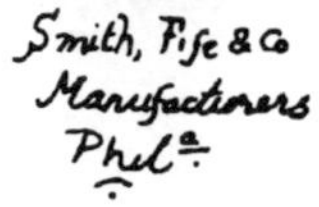

1830	Fell & Co., T., NEWCASTLE ON TYNE, England.	see 1817 Fell, Thomas.
1830	Fujina ware, Unyei, Japan. - - -	see 1677 IZUMO.
1830	Ichi-no-Kura Factory, Japan. - - -	see 1650 MINO
1830	Langlois, M. Frederic, France. - - -	see 1810 BAYEUX.
1830	Louis-Philippe, France. - - - -	see 1745 SÈVRES.
1830	Mittelstadt, Germany. - - - -	see 1753 GLIENITZ.
1830-	Moriot, (figures) France. - - - -	see 1745 SÈVRES.
1830	Putten & Cie, J. van, DELFT, Holland. - -	see 1671 de trie Klokken.
1830	Putten & Cie, J. van, DELFT, Holland. - -	see 1675 de Roos.
1830	Sei Kozan, Japan. - - - -	see 1596 SATSUMO.
1830	Sinsson,L., (flowers) France. - - -	see 1745 SÈVRES.
1830	Yusetsu, Mori, Japan. - - - -	see 1736 ISE.

1831 Jackson, Job & John, BURSLEM, Staffordshire, England.

1831-35 EARTHENWARES. Impressed or printed- **J.& J. JACKSON**
The Factory`s name is found within marks of various patterns and designs. **JACKSON`S** **WARRANTED**

1831 Jones, Elijah, COBRIDGE, Staffordshire, England.

1831-39 EARTHENWARE. Impressed with date- **PUBLISHED BY** **E. JONES** **COBRIDGE**
These initials are found within various printed patterns. **E. J.**

1831 Krister, Carl, WALDENBURG, Silesia, Germany.

1831- GENERAL POTTERY. -

1921 Acquired by Rosenthal & Co. see 1879 Rosenthal.

1831/32

1831 Machin & Thomas, BURSLEM, Staffordshire, England.

c.1831-32 EARTHENWARES. - Printed- **M. & T.**

1831 Middlesbrough Pottery Co.,MIDDLESBROUGH, York`s, England.

c.1831-44 EARTHENWARES AND CREAMWARES. - - **M. P. & Co.**
Impressed or printed- **MIDDLESBRO`**
The name and initials of this Factory **POTTERY CO.**
are found within marks of various patterns
and designs including an anchor.

1844-52 **Middlesbrough Earthenware Co.** - **M. E. & CO.**
Impressed or printed marks found within
various patterns and designs. **MIDDLESBROUGH**
With anchor **POTTERY**

1852-87 **Wilson & Co., Isaac,** Impressed or printed - **I. W. & CO.**
Printed marks of various patterns and designs
Impressed Crown and anchor mark with **MIDDLESBROUGH**
POTTERY

1831 Potts, William Wainwright, DERBY, England.

c.1831- EARTHENWARES. - - -
Decorators by special patent printing
processes. Exhibited at the 1851 Exhibition.
Dates of Patents 1831 & 1835.

1831 Ratcliffe, William, HANLEY, Staffordshire, England.

c.1831-40 EARTHENWARES. Printed or impressed- **R**
HACKWOOD

Printed in blue-

1831 Goodwins & Harris, LANE END, England. see 1827 Goodwin,Bridgwood & Orton.
1831 Richard, Joseph, France. - - - see 1745 SÈVRES.

1832 Buckau Porzellan Manufaktur, BUCKAU, Magdeburg, Germany.

1832- GENERAL POTTERY. - - - - - -

1832 Burton, Samuel & John, HANLEY, Staffordshire, England.

1832-45 EARTHENWARES. Impressed on raised pad- **S. & J. B.**

1832 Fouque, Arnoux & Cie, VALENTINE, France.

1832-60 FAÏENCE AND HARD-PASTE PORCELAIN.
Red-

1832 Léveillé, rue Thiroux, PARIS, France.

1832-50 HARD-PASTE PORCELAIN. - - **LÉVEILLÉ 12 Rue THIROUX**

1832 Lippert & Haas, SCHLAGGENWALD, Bohemia, Germany.

1832-46 HARD-PASTE PORCELAIN. - - **S SCHLAGGENWALD**

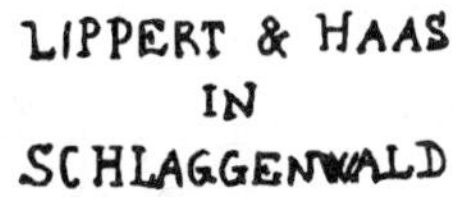

1832 Robinson & Wood, HANLEY, Staffordshire, England.

1832-36 EARTHENWARE. Printed- **R. & W.**

The initials of this Factory are found within marks of various patterns and designs.

1832 Stevenson & Son, Ralph, COBRIDGE, Staffordshire, England.

c.1832-35 EARTHENWARES. - Printed- **R. S. & S.**

The name and initials of this Factory are found within marks of various patterns and designs. **R. STEVENSON & SON**

1832 Wächtersbach Steingutfabrik, SCHLIERBACH, Germany.

1832- EARTHENWARES. - - -

1832	Girard, Abel, France. - - - - - -	see 1744 APREY.
1832	Hemphill, Judge Joseph, PHILADELPHIA, U.S.A. -	see 1825 Tucker, W.E.
1832	Lorenz, W.W., Germany. - - - - - -	see 1804 DALLWITZ.
1832	Richard, François, France. - - - - - -	see 1745 SÈVRES.
1832	Tucker & Hemphill, PHILADELPHIA, U.S.A. - -	see 1825 Tucker, W.E.

1833 American Pottery Man. Co., JERSEY CITY, N.J., U.S.A.

1833- **Henderson, David,** EARTHENWARES. -

Printed in black-

1840- English transfer printing introduced.
Marks printed on plates known as `CANOVA` design. Underglaze blue-

Continued over -

1833

1833 American Pottery Man. Co., JERSEY CITY, N.J., U.S.A. (Cont`)

1840 **American Pottery Co.,** Impressed-

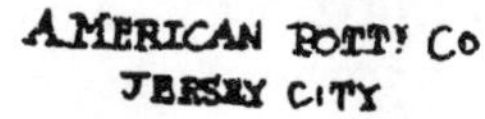

1840-45 Impressed- -

1850 **Rouse and Turner,** Used English type mark- -

1880- Mark on `ivory white ware` - -

1833 Davies & Co., R., NEWCASTLE UPON TYNE, England.

1833-51 EARTHENWARES. - Impressed- **DAVIES & CO.**

1833 Deakin & Son, LANE END, Staffordshire, England.

1833-41 EARTHENWARES. - Printed-

1833 Harvey, Bailey & Co., LANE END, Staffordshire, England.

1833-35 EARTHENWARES. - Printed- **H. B. & CO.**
These initials are found within marks of various patterns and designs.

1833 Machin & Potts, BURSLEM, Staffordshire, England.

1833-37 EARTHENWARES, ETC. - **MACHIN & POTTS**
The name of this partnership is found within marks ofvarious patterns and designs. Printed by Potts Patent Process.

MACHIN & POTTS
PATENT

1833 Manka, Franz, ALT-ROHLAU, Bohemia, Germany.

1833- HARD-PASTE PORCELAIN. - -

1833 Mayer, John, FOLEY, Staffordshire, England.

1833-41 EARTHENWARES. - Printed- **J M**
The initials of this Factory are found **F**
within marks of various patterns and designs.

1833 Read & Clementson, SHELTON, Staffordshire, England.

1833-35 EARTHENWARES, - Printed- **R. & C.**
The initials of this Factory are found within marks of various patterns and designs.

c.1836- **Read, Clementson & Anderson.** Printed- **R. C. & A.**

1833 Case, Thomas & Mort, John, LIVERPOOL, England. see 1793 Herculaneum Pottery.
1833 Copeland & Garrett, STOKE, England. - - see 1770 Spode, Josiah.
1833 Kuhn, Hienrich Gottlieb, Germany. - - see 1710 MEISSEN.
1833 Richard, Eugène, France. - - - - see 1745 SÈVRES.
1833 Richard & Co., Julius, Italy. - - - see 1725 MILAN.

1834 Bailey & Harvey, LONGTON, Staffordshire, England.

1834-35 EARTHENWARES (LUSTRE) Impressed- **BAILEY & HARVEY**

1834 Barker, Sutton & Till, BURSLEM, Staffordshire, England.

1834-43 EARTHENWARES. - Printed or impressed- **B. S. & T. BURSLEM**
The initials of this Factory are found within marks of various patterns and designs.

1834 Cutts, James, SHELTON, Staffordshire, England.

c.1834-70 ENGRAVER AND DESIGN ARTIST. - Signed- ***J. Cutts.***

1834 Dillon, Francis, COBRIDGE, Staffordshire, England.

1834-43 EARTHENWARES. - Impressed- **DILLON**
The initials of this Factory are found printed within marks of various designs. **F.D.**

1834 Godwin, Benjamin E.,COBRIDGE, Staffordshire, England.

1834-41 EARTHENWARES. - Printed- **B. G.**
The initials of this Factory are found within marks of various patterns and designs.

1834 Godwin, John & Robert, COBRIDGE, Staffordshire, England.

1834-66 EARTHENWARES. - Printed- **J. & R. G.**
The initials of this Factory are found within marks of various patterns and designs.

1834 Harding & Cockson, COBRIDGE, Staffordshire, England.

1834-60 EARTHENWARES. - Printed- **COBRIDGE H & C**
The initials of this Factory are found within marks of various patterns and designs.

1834 Ingleby & Co., Thomas, TUNSTALL, Staffordshire, England.

c.1834-35 EARTHENWARES. - Printed- **T. I. & CO.**
The initials of this Factory are found within marks of various patterns and designs.

1834 Johnston, David, BORDEAUX, France.

1834- CREAMWARES AND SOFT-PASTE PORCELAIN. -

1834/35

1834 Lloyd, John & Rebecca, Shelton, HANLEY, Staff's. England.
c.1834-52 EARTHENWARES AND CHINA FIGURES. Impressed- **LLOYD SHELTON.**

1834 Mellor, Venables & Co.,BURSLEM, Staffordshire, England.
1834-51 EARTHENWARES AND CHINA. Impressed or printed- **M.V. & CO.**
The name and initials of this Factory are found within marks of various patterns and designs. **MELLOR,VENABLES & CO.**

1834 Payne, SALISBURY, Wiltshire, England.
c.1834-41 RETAILER. - Printed- **PAYNE SARUM**

1834 Podmore, Walker & Co., TUNSTALL, Staffordshire, England.
1834-59 EARTHENWARES - Printed- **P.W. & CO.**
The initials of this Factory are found within marks of various patterns and designs.
1856-59 **Podmore, Walker & Wedgwood.** **P.W. & W.**
Enoch Wedgwood became partner- **WEDGWOOD**
WEDGWOOD & CO.
1860 **Wedgwood & Co. (Name change)**
No connection with the Josiah Wedgwood Co.
see 1862 Wedgwood & Co.Ltd.

1834 Barker & Sons, Samuel, SWINTON, England. - see 1790 Don Pottery.
1834 Godwin, Thomas, BURSLEM, England.- - see 1809 Godwin, T.& B.
1834 Hufsky, Vincent, Germany. - - - see 1822 HOHENSTEIN.
1834 Phillips, George, LONGTON, England. - - see 1822 Phillips, E.& G.

1835 Cooke & Hulse, LONGTON, Staffordshire, England.
1835-55 PORCELAIN. - Printed- **COOKE & HULSE**

1835 Edge, Barker & Co.,FENTON, Staffordshire, England.
1835-36 EARTHENWARES. - Printed- **E. B.& CO.**
1836-40 **Edge, Barker & Barker.** Printed- **E. B.& B.**
The initials of these Factories are found within marks of various patterns and designs.

1835 Hackwood & Keeling, HANLEY, Staffordshire, England.
1835-36 EARTHENWARES. - Printed- **H. & K.**
These initials are found within marks of various patterns and designs.

1835 Harvey, C.& W.K., LONGTON, Staffordshire, England.

1835-53 GENERAL CERAMICS. - Impressed- **HARVEY**

These initials are found within marks of various printed patterns and designs. - - **C. & W. K. H.**
Sometimes with Royal Arms.

1853-82 **Holland & Green. Earthenwares.** - **H. & G.**
LATE HARVEY

The name and initials of this Factory are printed or impressed within marks of various patterns and designs including the Royal Arms. **HOLLAND & GREEN**

1835 Knowles & Son, Matthew, BRAMPTON, Derbyshire, England.

c.1835-1911 EARTHENWARES, STONEWARES. - - **KNOWLES**

1835 Lowesby Pottery, LOWESBY, Leicestershire, England.

c.1835-40 EARTHENWARES. - Impressed- **LOWESBY**
Sir Frederick Fowke.

1835 Riddle & Bryan, LONGTON, Staffordshire, England.

c.1835-40 EARTHENWARES, LUSTRED. Printed- **RIDDLE & BRYAN,**
Longton.

1835 Ridgway & Abington, HANLEY, Staffordshire, England.

c.1835-60 EARTHENWARES. - Impressed- **E. RIDGWAY & ABINGTON**
Marks in assorted variations with dates **HANLEY**

1835 Scheibe-Alsbach GmbH, Porzellanmanufactur, Thuringia, Germany.

1835 **Oels, Louis, (Founder) decorator.**

1847- **Dressel & Kister**

Kister`s Porcelain Factory mark - **K. P. F.**

Quality porcelain figurines were being produced at this time with a high volume of sales. **K. P. M.**

1860`s brought a new subject in busts of composers and poets. The 80`s and 90`s continued with the lifesize bisque busts painted in muted, matt colours.

1873 **The Grand Prix Medal awarded** at the Vienna World Exhibition, was followed by many more at Melbourne, Chicago, Brussels, Turin, etc.

Continued over -

1835

1835 Scheibe-Alsbach GmbH. Porzellanmanu` Thuringia, Ger. (Cont`)

1890`s **August Kister (son)** reproduced well-known works of art in porcelain. Popular subjects were by David Watteau and other French painters and famous women such as Madame Pompadour and Marie Antoinette.

c.1900 **Felix Zeh (modeller)** (1869-1937) was a very busy artist in the early part of the 20th century. He specialized in Rococo and Biedermeier figures, especially `Napoleon`
Other significant artists were, Professors Reinhard Moller, Otto Poertzel, Carl Lysek, and Carl Fuchs and Heinz Schober.

1835

1990 **German reunification.**

1991- **Königlich priv. Porzellanfabrik Tettau, (part of Seltmann Group) acquired factory.** see 1794 Tettau GmbH

Modern Mark (1995) - -

1835
Porzellanmanufaktur
Scheibe-Alsbach
GmbH.

(By courtesy of Porzellanfabriken Chr. Seltmann GmbH., Weiden, Germany.)

1835 Søholm A/S, Rønne, Denmark.

1835- Stoneware and Faïence.
Early marks have the German ö. impressed- **Söholm**

Marks in capital Gothic script originate from the years before and around the turn of the century. Impressed- **SØHOLM**

This mark is probably contemporary with the Gothic backstamp above. - - **Søholm**

c.1878- **H. Wolffsen & Son and** Impressed- **H. Wolffsen & Son.**
1887-1902 **Chr. L. Wolffsen. (sole owner)** impressed- **Chr. L. Wolffsen**
These two marks were probably used simultaneously with the `Søholm` mark above.

1905-c.12 **A/S Wolffsen & Son** Impressed- **A/S Wolffsen & Son**
Aktieselskabet Wolffsen & Son

c.1908-30 **Carl Møller`s period.**
Marks printed in black-

SØHOLM BORNHOLM

SØHOLM BORNHOLM

Continued over -

1835 Søholm A/S, Rønne, Denmark. (Cont`)

1930s-	Production of earthenware introduced	- **Bornholms Stentojsfabrik**
c.1918-	Backstamp used between the two world wars. - Impressed-	**Bornholmsk Krukke**
c.1940-83	**Ship-type mark was used printed in Danish or English text `Søholm-Bornholm- Denmark` in a circle with blue ink.**	
1983-89	**Old trade-mark with ship was scrapped and a plain mark was used. - -**	**SØHOLM-DENMARK**
1989-	**Ship-type mark was reintroduced in a modernised version. - -**	

1989 mark- -

Throughout the period of the `Søholm` factory numbers are found impressed or printed on the wares; they refer to the plaster moulds, but unfortunately the records of the mould numbers have been lost.

1995 Modern mark -

(By kind permission of Søholm A/S, Rønne, Denmark.)

1835 Wilson & Proudman, Coleorton, ASHBY-DE-LA-ZOUCH, England.

1835-42 EARTHENWARES, STONEWARES. Impressed- **WILSON & PROUDMAN**

1835 WILHELMSBURG, Austria.

1835- **Wilhelmsburg Steingutfabrik.**
EARTHENWARE. - impressed-

WILHELMSBURG

1835 Meigh, Charles, HANLEY, England. - - see 1805 Meigh, Job.

1836 Belfield & Co., Prestonpans Pottery, PRESTONPANS, Scotland.

c.1836-1941 EARTHENWARES. - - - **BELFIELD & CO PRESTONPANS**
Name of the Factory is impressed or printed within marks of various designs - -

---

1836 Kling & Co.,C.F., OHRDRUF, Thuringia, Germany.

1836-1941 HARD-PASTE PORCELAIN. - - - -

1836-37

1836 Mayer, Thomas, John and Joshua, Dale Hall, BURSLEM, England.

1836 EARTHENWARE, STONEWARE, PARIAN.

According to `Jewitt` this firm produced not only ordinary earthenwares, but stoneware of a highly vitreous quality, and parian of an improved body, plus a fine caneware in which some remarkable good jugs (notably, the `oak` pattern) were made. Recognition was given through the Exhibitions of 1851, 1853-New York and 1855-Paris, where medals were awarded.

T. J.& J. MAYER

MAYER BROS.

The above marks were used within various patterns and designs

Afterwards, this firm traded under the following titles:-

Mayer Brothers and Elliot,
Liddle, Elliot & Co.,
Bates, Elliot & Co. - - see 1870 Bates, Elliot & Co.

(For further information see `Jewitts` Ceramic Art in Great Britain)

1836 Ridgway, Morley, Wear & Co.,HANLEY, Staff`s. England.

1836-42 EARTHENWARES. - Printed- **R.M.W.& CO.**
RIDGWAY, MORLEY WEAR & CO.

1842-44 **Ridgway & Morley,** Printed **R.& M.**
RIDGWAY & MORLEY

The name and initials of these Factories are found within marks of various patterns and designs.

see 1784 Baddeley, J & E.

1836 RUBELLES, nr. Melum, Seine-et-Marne, France.

c.1836-58 FAÏENCE. - Impressed- **Rubelles**
A.D.T.

M. le Baron de Tremblé (terre de pipe)
M. le Baron de Bourgoing (inventor)

1836 Sparks, George, WORCESTER, England.

Written- ***Sparks Worcester***

c.1836-54 Decorator of Worcester and Coalport porcelain. Various printed marks include the name `Sparks`

1836	Edge, Barker & Barker, FENTON, England. -	see 1835 Edge, Barker & Co.
1836-	Hautin and Boulanger, France. - - -	see 1785 CHOISY-LE-ROI.
1836	Kriegel & Co., Czechoslovakia, Germany. -	see 1795 PRAGUE.
1836	Minton & Boyle, STOKE, England. - -	see 1793 Minton.
1836	Mort & Simpson, LIVERPOOL, England. -	see 1793 Herculaneum Pottery.
1836	Pountney & Goldney, BRISTOL, England. -	see 1816 Pountney & Allies.
1836	Read, Clementson & Anderson, SHELTON, England.	see 1833 Read & Clementson.

1837 Alberti, Carl, UHLSTÄDT, Thuringia, Germany.

1837- HARD-PASTE PORCELAIN. - - - - -

1837 Emery, James, MEXBOROUGH, Yorkshire, England.

1837-61 EARTHENWARES. - Incised - **J. EMERY MEXBRO**

1837 Mayer & Maudesley, TUNSTALL, Staffordshire, England.

1837-38 EARTHENWARES. - Printed- **M. & M.**

1837 Ridgway & Robey, HANLEY, Staffordshire, England.

c.1837-39 PORCELAIN FIGURES. - Printed- **RIDGWAY & ROBEY HANLEY STAFFORDSHIRE POTTERIES**

Rare character figures with date.

1837 Rousseau, F., Boulevard St-Martin, PARIS, France.

1837-70 Hard-paste porcelain. - - ***Rousseau 43 Rue Coquillere***

ROUSSEAU
Boul^d St Martin
49
Fournisseur du Roi

1837 Dawson & Co.,Thomas, SUNDERLAND, England. - see 1799 Dawson, John,

1837 Meir & Son, John, TUNSTALL, England. - - see 1812 Meir, John.

1838 Ridgway, Son & Co., William, HANLEY, Staffs. England.

c.1838-48 EARTHENWARES. printed with various dates- **PUBLISHED BY W. RIDGWAY, SON & CO. HANLEY**

These initial are found within marks of various patterns and designs.- Printed- **W. R. S. & CO.**

1838 Robinson, Wood & Brownfield, COBRIDGE, Staff's. England.

1838-41 EARTHENWARES. - Printed- **R. W. & B.**

This mark is found within various patterns and designs.

1838 Tirschenreuth Porcelain Factory, BAVARIA, Germany.

1838 HARD-PASTE PORCELAIN
Founder: Heinrich Eichhorn (manufacturers) Schney, nr. Lichtenfels.

1880 Heinrich Eichhorn died.
Edmund Tittel Friedrich Muther and August Bauscher purchase shares of the factory.
August Bauscher sells his title deeds to Karl Gotthold Mezger and with the proceeds finances the porcelain factory at Weiden.

1927 **Lorenz Hutschenreuther AG Selb acquires Factory.** see1857 Hutschenreuther, Lorenz

Continued over -

1838/39

1838 Tirschenreuth Porcelain Factory, BAVARIA, Germany. (Cont`)

1927 Lorenz Hutschenreuther AG, Selb. (Cont`)

1969 mark -

1995 modern mark - - -

(By kind permission of Hutschenreuther AG. Germany)

1838 Wallace & Co.,J., NEWCASTLE UPON TYNE, England.

1838-93 EARTHENWARES. - Impressed- **WALLACE & CO.**

1838 Wood & Brownfield, COBRIDGE, Staffordshire, England.

c.1838-50 EARTHENWARES. - Impressed or printed- **W. & B.**
These initials are found within marks of various patterns and designs.

1838 Oldfield, John, BRAMPTON, England. - - see 1810 Oldfield, Madin, etc.

1839 Acker-Fabrik porcelain factory, ARZBERG, Bavaria, Germany.

1839 HARD-PASTE PORCELAIN.

1918 **Incorporated into C.M. Hutschenreuther AG. Arzberg.** - - Marks:-

1995 Modern mark- -

(By kind permission of Hutschenreuther AG. Germany)

1839 Alcock, John & George, COBRIDGE, Staffordshire, England.

1839-46 EARTHENWARES. - Impressed- **J. & G. ALCOCK COBRIDGE**

These initials are found within marks of various patterns and designs. Printed or impressed- **J. & G. A.**

1839 ARBORAS, Rhône, France.

1839- HARD-PASTE PORCELAIN - - - - 

1839 Baker & Co.Ltd.,W., FENTON, Staffordshire, England.

1839-1932 EARTHENWARES. - Impressed or printed- **W. BAKER & CO.**
Factory`s name found within marks of various **BAKER & CO.**
patterns and designs. 1893 `Ltd` added.

1839 Clementson, Joseph, HANLEY, Staffordshire, England.

c.1839-64 EARTHENWARES. - printed- **J.C.**
These marks are found within various **J. CLEMENTSON**
patterns and designs.

1865-1916 **Clementson Bros. Ltd.,** - **CLEMENTSON BROS.**

1867-80 Printed marks of various designs

1901-16 - Printed-
1910 `Ltd` added.

1839 Edwards, James & Thomas, BURSLEM, Staffordshire, England.

1839-41 EARTHENWARES. - Printed or impressed- **J. & T. E.**
These marks are found within various **J. & T. EDWARDS**
patterns and designs. **B.**

1839 Fischer, Moritz, HEREND, Hungary.

1839- HARD-PASTE PORCELAIN. - -

1839 ISIGNY, Calvados, France.

1839-45 **Langlois, Frédéric,** HARD-PASTE PORCELAIN.

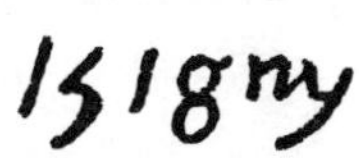

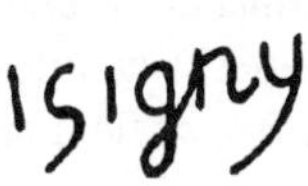

1839

1839 Kahler, Herman J., NAESTVED, Denmark.

1839-75 EARTHENWARE AND STONEWARE.
In 1839 Herman J Kahler took over an old workshop in Naestved and produced earthenware and heating stoves.

1875-1917 **Herman A. Kahler (son) Especially known for his red lustre glazes.**
1917-40 **Herman H.C. Kahler (third generation)**
1940- Herman H.C. Kahler died.
1940-74 **Herman and Nils Kahler (sons) take over management.**
Ceramics are still hand-made.

(by kind permission of Herman A. Kahler, Naestved, Denmark.)

1839 Maddock & Seddon, BURSLEM, Staffordshire, England.

c.1839-42 EARTHENWARES. - Printed- **M. & S.**
These initials are found within marks of various patterns and designs.
see 1842 Maddock, John,

1839 Reed, James, Rock Pottery, MEXBOROUGH, Yorkshire, England.

c.1839-49 EARTHENWARE. - Impressed- **REED**
1849-73 **Reed, John, (son) Re-named Mexbro Pottery.**
1873- **Woolf & Co., Sidney,** owners of the Australian Pottery, Ferrybridge, acquired the factory.

1839 South Wales Pottery, LLANELLY, Dyfed, Wales.

c.1839-58 EARTHENWARES. - Printed or impressed-
c.1839-54 **Chambers & Co.** - - **CHAMBERS, LLANELLY**
These marks are found within various patterns and designs.
c.1854-58 **Coombs & Holland** - - **SOUTH WALES POTTERY**
S. W. P.

1839 VOISINLIEU, nr. Beauvais, France.

1839- **Ziegler, Jules-Claude** - -
SALT-GLAZE STONEWARE.

1839 Wood & Bowers, BURSLEM, Staffordshire, England.

1839 EARTHENWARES. - Printed- **W. & B.**
These initials are found within marks of various patterns and designs.
(Wood & Brownfield and Wood & Baggaley also used these initials.)

1839 Fenton, Christopher Weber, BENNINGTON, U.S.A. see 1793 Norton Pottery.
1839 Grainger, George & Co., WORCESTER, England. see 1801 Grainger Wood & Co.
1839 Kilnhurst Old Pottery, SWINTON, England. - see 1822 Twigg, Joseph & Co.
1839 Welby, F.L., Germany. - - - - see 1801 TEINITZ.

1840 Batkin, Walker & Broadhurst,LANE END, Staffordshire, England.

1840-45 EARTHENWARES. - Printed- **B. W. & B.**
These initials are found within marks of various patterns and designs.

1840 Gailliard, Passage de l`Opéra, PARIS, France.

c.1840 DECORATOR OF PORCELAIN. Gold- - -

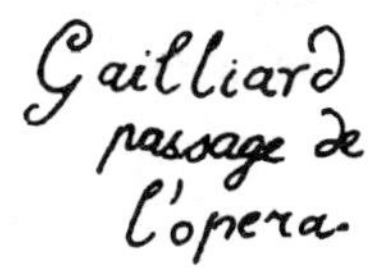

1840 Hall, Samuel, HANLEY, Staffordshire, England.

c.1840-56 EARTHENWARES. - Impressed- **HALL**

1840 Harker, Benjamin, Sr., EAST LIVERPOOL, Ohio, U.S.A.

1840- **Harker Pottery.** YELLOW AND ROCKINGHAM WARES.

c.1847-50 Harker, Taylor & Co.
Embossed or impressed- -

c.1855- Harker & Co., George S., -

1890- Harker Pottery Co. (incorporated) - -

1840 Keeling & Co.,Samuel, HANLEY, Staffordshire, England.

1840-50 EARTHENWARES. - Printed- **S. K. & CO.**
These marks are found within various patterns and designs. **S. KEELING & CO.**

1840 Millar, John, EDINBURGH, Lothian, Scotland.

1840-82 RETAILER. - - Printed- **JOHN MILLAR**
Name printed within marks of various designs.

1840 PASSAU, Bavaria, Germany.

1840- HARD-PASTE PORCELAIN.
c.1860 **Lenck family-** - -

1840/41

1840 Shirley & Co., Thomas, GREENOCK, Scotland.

c.1840-57 EARTHENWARES. - Impressed- **T. S. & COY.**
T. S. & C.

1840 Stiff, James, LAMBETH, London, England.

c.1840-63 STONEWARES. - Impressed- **J. STIFF**
Name found within marks of various patterns and designs.

c.1863-1913 Stiff & Sons, James. Impressed- **J. STIFF & SONS**
Taken over by Doultons.

1840 Swift & Elkin, LONGTON, Staffordshire, England.

1840-43 EARTHENWARES. - Printed- **S. & E.**
These initials are found within marks of various patterns and designs, sometimes written.

1840 TAMBA, Japan.

17th century. TAMBA WARE was produced at Onohara and Tachikui.
1840- Naosaku (potter) of Sasayama-

NAOSAKU

1840 Vernon, FISMES, Marne, France.

1840- HARD-PASTE PORCELAIN. - -

1840 Yates, William, (Retailer) LEEDS, England.

c.1840-76 RETAILER Printed or painted- **YATES**
LEEDS

1840	American Pottery Co., JERSEY CITY, U.S.A. -	see 1833 American Man. Co.
1840	Bonnard et Gonin, Switzerland. - - -	see 1780 NYON.
1840	Chappell, Stephen & James, England. - -	see 1760 LEEDS POTTERY.
1840-	Couderc,(decorator) PARIS, France. - -	see 1806 Boulevard Montmartre.
1840	Dixon Phillips & Co.,SUNDERLAND, England.	see 1807 Sunderland Pottery.
1840-	Hachiroemon, lida, Japan. - - - - -	see 1650 KAGA.
1840	Mitchell, William, RYE, Sussex, England. -	see 1807 Cadborough Pottery.
1840-	Raku Tanniu, YAMASHIRO, Japan. - -	see 1528 Raku Ware.
1840	\`Shodai\` Japan. - - - - - -	see 1630 HIGO.
1840	Weigel and Messerschmidt, Germany. - -	see 1770 HUBERTUSBURG.
1840	Yoshida tsukuru, Japan. - - - - -	see 1583 BIZEN.

1841 Chetham, Jonathan Lowe, LONGTON, Staffordshire, England.

1841-62 EARTHENWARES. - Printed- **J. L. C.**

1841 Edge, William & Samuel, LANE DELPH, Staffordshire, England.

1841-48 EARTHENWARES. - Printed- **W. & S. E.**
These initials are found within marks of various patterns and designs.

1841 Guérin-Pouyat-Elite Ltd., LIMOGES, France.

1841- PORCELAIN - - -

1841 Jones & Walley, COBRIDGE, Staffordshire, England.

1841-43 EARTHENWARES, ETC., Impressed or relief- **BY JONES & WALLEY COBRIDGE**
`Published by` mark with date. - -
These initials are found within marks of various printed patterns and designs. **J. & W.**

1845-56 **Walley, Edward,** - Printed- **EDWARD WALLEY COBRIDGE STAFFORDSHIRE**
This mark is found within various patterns and designs.

Impressed- **IRONSTONE CHINA E. WALLEY**

This printed mark is found within various - patterns and designs. **W**

1841 Knight, Elkin & Knight, FENTON, Staffordshire, England.

1841-44 EARTHENWARES. - Printed- **K. E. & K.**
These initials are found within marks of various patterns and designs.

1841 Wood, John Wedge, BURSLEM, Staffordshire, England.

1841-44 EARTHENWARES. - Impressed- **W. W.**
1845-60 at Tunstall Printed- **J. WEDGWOOD**
This mark is found within various patterns and designs. Sometimes mistaken for Josiah Wedgwood. who, however never used the initial `J`

1841 Yale & Barker, LONGTON, Staffordshire, England.

1841-53 EARTHENWARES. - Printed- **Y. & B.**
These initials are found within marks of various patterns and designs.

1841	Leboeuf and Milliet, France. - - - -	see 1794 CREIL.
1841	Mason & Faraday, LANE DELPH, England. -	see 1796 Mason`s Ironstone.
1841	Trager, J., (Flowers) France, - - - -	see 1745 SÈVRES.

1842

1842 Bell & Co. Ltd., J.& M.P., Glasgow Pottery, GLASGOW, Scotland.

1842-1928 EARTHENWARES, PARIAN,

Factory`s initials printed or impressed within marks of various designs.
1881 `Ltd` added

1840- **J. B.**
1850-70 **J. & M. P. B.**
J. & M.P. BELL & Co.

1842 Boote,Ltd., T.& R. BURSLEM, Staffordshire, England.

1842- EARTHENWARES, TILES. printed or impressed- These Factory marks are found within marks of various patterns and designs.

T. & R. B.
T. & R. BOOTE
T. B. & S.

1890-1906 - - Printed-
1891-`England` added.

1906- Tiles only produced.

1842 Bovey Tracey Pottery Co. BOVEY TRACEY, England.

1842-94 EARTHENWARES. Printed or impressed- **B.T.P. CO.**
These initials are found within marks of various patterns and designs.

1894-1957 **Bovey Pottery Co.Ltd.,**
c.1937-54 - Printed or impressed-

c.1954-57 **Blue Waters Pottery**
Name printed within marks of various designs.

1842 Bowers & Co.,G.F. TUNSTALL, Staffordshire, England.

1842-68 EARTHENWARES AND PORCELAIN. Printed- These initials are found within marks of various patterns and designs.

G. F .B.
G. F. B. B. T.

Printed or impressed- **G.F. BOWERS**

1842 Challinor, Edward, TUNSTALL, Staffordshire, England.

1842-67 EARTHENWARES. - printed- **E. C.**
The factory`s name is found within marks of various patterns and designs. **E. CHALLINOR**

1842 Hawley & Co., FOLEY, Staffordshire, England.

1842-87 EARTHENWARES. - Impressed- **HAWLEY**
HAWLEY & CO.

1842 Maddock, John, BURSLEM, Staffordshire, England.

1842-55 EARTHENWARES. - Printed- **M.**

This initial is found within printed mark-

This mark is found within various patterns and designs. **MADDOCK**

1855- **Maddock & Sons Ltd.,John, Earthenwares**

1896 `Ltd` added

Printed- **JOHN MADDOCK & SONS LTD.**

This mark is found within various patterns and designs. 1945- Modern marks

1842 Schmidt, H.,FREIWALDAU, Bohemia, Germany.

1842- HARD-PASTE PORCELAIN. - -

1842 Avisseau, Charles, France.- - - - see 1750 TOURS.
1842 Baguley, Alfred & Isaac, England. - - see 1745 ROCKINGHAM.
1842 Ridgway & Morley, HANLEY, England.- - see 1836 Ridgway,Morley,Wear.
1842 Villeroy & Boch, Germany. - - - see 1809 METTLACH.

1843 Clark, Uriah & Nephews, LOWER DICKER, Sussex, England.

1843-1946 EARTHENWARES. - Incised- **DICKER**
Impressed- **U. C. & N.**
THE DICKER
SUSSEX

1933-59 Trade name - **DICKER WARE**

1946-59 **Dicker Potteries Ltd.,**

1843 Floyd, Benjamin, LANE END, Staffordshire, England.

c.1843 EARTHENWARES. - Printed- **B. F.**

These initials are printed within marks of various patterns and designs.

1843

1843 Furnival, Jacob & Thomas, HANLEY, Staffordshire, England.

c.1843 EARTHENWARE. printed under Royal Arms- **J. & T. F.**

c.1844-46 **Furnival & Co.,Thomas,** Printed- **T. F. & CO.**

These initials are printed within marks of various patterns and designs.

1843 KAHLA/Thuringen Porzellan GmbH, THURINGIA, Germany.

1843- HARD-PASTE PORCELAIN.
Eckhardt, Christian Jacob (Founder)

1856 **Koch, Friedrich August acquired factory by a compulsory auction.**

1872 **Koch, Friedrich August Hermann, (son) bought factory from his father.**
1876- Bunzli, Johann, joined company.

1883 Beyersche Wiesenmuhle (mill) acquired.

1888 Joint-stock company established by banking house of Strupp, Meiningen.

1889 `Old Lehmann Factory` acquired.

1890 Newly built porcelain factory in Hermsdorf starts production.
Zwickau Porcelain Factory acquired.

1900 Jagersdorf mill acquired.

P. F. K.
c.1900

1901 Station factory is built.

1904-06 Freiberg Porcelain Factory established.

1907 Kemmlitz Kaolin Factory acquired.

1914 Some production switched to war goods (insulators)

1921-22 `Old Lehmann Factory` demolished, new administration building constructed. (now medical building)

c.1924

1927 **Merger with porcelain factories, H. Schomburg & Sons AG., E.& A. Müller AG. and Schonwald AG. Affiliation of factories at Schonwald, Arzberg, Margarthenhutte, Freiberg and Roslau.**

1925-32 (USA)

1926

1931

1931

1939

1940-44 **Production switched to war goods (insulators/condensers)**

1946 **Dissolution of the AG. and establishment of the Soviet Electronic Joint-Stock Company (SAG)**

Continued over -

1843 KAHLA/Thuringen Porcelain GmbH, THURINGIA, Ger. (Cont`)

1952 **Transferred into national ownership.**

1957

1961 **Official opening of newly built porcelain factory.**

1964 **Merger with VEB Porcelain Factory of Konitz to form VEB United Porcelain Factories of Kahla-Kohnitz.**

1968 **Merger of nationalised factories at Triptis, Gera-Roschutz, Rudolstadt-Volkstedt, Uhlstadt, Kahla-Konitz to form the Kahla VEB Porcelain Combine (4321 employees)**

1969 Addition of the VEB porcelain factories at Reichenbach and Konigsee.

1979 Kahla VEB Porcelain Combine renamed Kahla VEB United Porcelain Factories.

1981 The factories at Eisenberg, Gera-Roschutz, Konigsee, Konitz, Reichenbach, Rudolstadt-Volkstedt and Triptis are subordinated to the Kahla VEB United Porcelain Factories.

1987 **Triptis VEB Porcelain Factory becomes independent.**

1989 **Reichenbach VEB Porcelain Factory becomes independent.**

1990 Kahla VEB Fine Ceramics Combine is changed to Kahla Porcelain GmbH with the closure of all divisions except Konitz.

1991 Privatisation through Berlin Trust Agency, Florian J. Hofmann is majority shareholder.

1991

1993 **Bankruptcy application.**

1994 **KAHLA/Thuringia Porcelain GmbH established. Gunther Raithel is majority shareholder.**

Modern mark -

1994

(By kind permission of KAHLA/Thuringen, Kahla, Thuringia, Germany.)

1843 Kennedy, William Sadler, BURSLEM, Staffordshire, England.

1843-54 EARTHENWARES. - Impressed or printed- **W.S. KENNEDY**

1854-60 **Kennedy & Macintyre** Impressed or printed- **W.S. KENNEDY & J. MACINTYRE**

These names are found within marks of various patterns and designs.

c.1860-1928 Macintyre & Co.Ltd. James. **MACINTYRE**

Impressed or printed marks found within various patterns and designs. 1867 `& Co.` added c.1894 `Ltd` added

J. MACINTYRE

J. M. & CO.

1843 Mayer, Thomas, John & Joseph, BURSLEM, Staffordshire, England.
1843-55 EARTHENWARES, PARIAN, ETC. - Printed- **T. J. & J. MAYER**
This Factory`s name is printed within marks
of various patterns and designs.

1843 Procter, John, LONGTON, Staffordshire, England. **J. P.**
1843-46 EARTHENWARES. - Impressed or printed- **L.**

1843 Pulham, J., BROXBOURNE, Hertfordshire, England. **J. P.**
c.1843-1918 TERRA-COTTA, ARCHITECTURAL AND GENERAL. impressed

---

1843 Reed & Taylor, FERRYBRIDGE, Yorkshire, England.
c.1843-56 EARTHENWARES. - - Printed- **R. & T.**
1856-83 **Woolf & Sons, L.,** - - **L. W.** **L. W. & S.**
1884-97 **Poulson Bros. Ltd.** Printed or impressed- **P. B.** **P. BROS.**
c.1897-1919 **Sefton & Brown** Printed or impressed- **S. & B.**
Most of these initials are found within marks **F. B.**
of various patterns and designs.
1919- **Brown & Sons, T.,** Impressed- **T. B. & S.**
F.B.
1985- **Cauldon Potteries Ltd. acquired this Factory.**
EARTHENWARES.
Printed mark-

(By kind permission of Cauldon Potteries Ltd., Ferrybridge, W.Yorkshire, England.)

1843 Wolfsohn, Helena, DRESDEN, Germany.
1843- DECORATOR. **Meissen type designs.**
K.P.M. Meissen took legal proceedings
against the use of the A.R. mark.

1843 André, Jules, (Landscapes) France. - - see 1745 SÈVRES.

1844 Bradbury Anderson & Bettanny, LONGTON, Staffordshire, England.
1844-52 EARTHENWARES, PARIAN, ETC. printed- **B A & B**
These initials are printed within marks
of various patterns and designs.

1844 Clementson, Young & Jameson, HANLEY, Staffordshire, England.
1844 EARTHENWARES. - Printed- **C Y & J**
1845-47 **Clementson & Young.** - **CLEMENTSON & YOUNG**
Impressed or printed-
This factory`s name is found within marks
of various patterns and designs.

1844 Elkin & Newbon, LONGTON, Staffordshire, England.

c.1844-45 EARTHENWARES. - Printed- **E. & N.**

These initials are printed within marks of various patterns and designs.

1844 Goodwin, John, EAST LIVERPOOL, Ohio, U.S.A.

1844- YELLOW AND ROCKINGHAM WARES.

1876- Mr. Goodwin died and was succeeded by his three sons. - -

1893- **Goodwin Pottery Co. (Incorporated) -**

PEARL WHITE CREAM-COLOURED WARES, SEMI-PORCELAIN AND IRONSTONE CHINA.

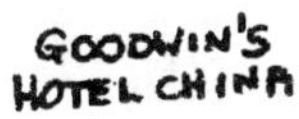

1844 Moriot, N. SÈVRES, France.

1844-52 DECORATOR IN SÈVRES STYLE. - -

1844 Seifu Yohei (potter) YAMASHIRO, Japan.

1844-61 IMITATED CHINESE BLUE AND WHITE PORCELAIN.

1861 succeeded by son

1878 grandson (a renowned Kioto potter)

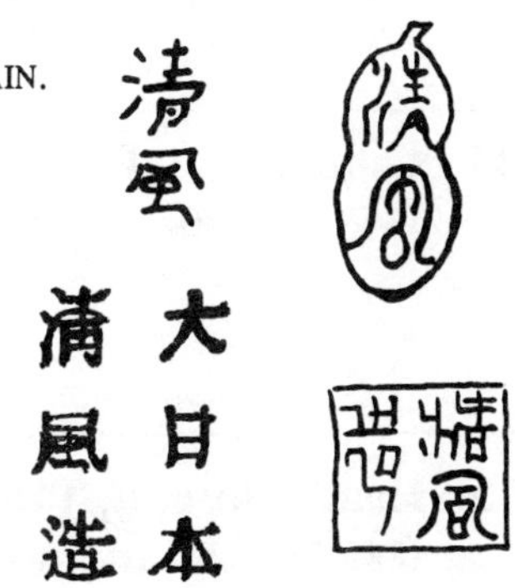

1844 Williamson, John, Wellington Pottery, GLASGOW, Scotland.

1844-94 TERRA-COTTA, ETC. Impressed or printed-

WELLINGTON POTTERY

WILLIAMSON WELLINGTON POTTERY

1844 Worthington & Green, SHELTON, Staffordshire, England.

1844-64 EARTHENWARES, PARIAN, ETC. - -

Impressed mark on applied pad-

WORTHINGTON & GREEN

1844/45

1844	Barre, Louis Desiré, (flowers) France. - -	see 1745 SÈVRES.
1844	David, Alexandre, (ornaments) France. - -	see 1745 SÈVRES.
1844	Furnival & Co.,Thomas, HANLEY, England. -	see 1843 Furnival, J. & T.
1844	Middlesbrough Earthenware Co., England. -	see 1831 Middlesbrough Pottery.
1844	Scott Brothers & Co., SUNDERLAND, England.	see 1788 Southwick Pottery.

1845 Aaron, Michel-Isaac, CHANTILLY, Oise, France.

1845-70 PORCELAIN, BISCUIT FIGURES

Underglaze blue-

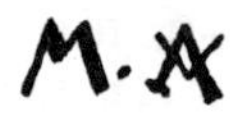

1845 Beech, Ralph Bagnell, Kensington, PHILADELPHIA, Pa. U.S.A.

1845-c.57 EARTHENWARE. - - -

1851- Patented `Ornamenting baked Earthenware` - **RALPH B. BEECH**
PATENTED
JUNE 3, 1851
KENSINGTON, PA.

1845 Carr, John, Low Light Pottery, NORTH SHIELDS, England.

c.1845-1900 EARTHENWARES. - - - **J. CARR & CO.**

1845 Furnival & Co.,Jacob, COBRIDGE, Staffordshire, England.

c.1845-70 EARTHENWARES. - Printed- **J F & CO.**

These initials are printed within marks
of various patterns and designs.

1845 Gille, jeune, Rue de Paradis-Poissonniere, PARIS, France.

1845- BISCUIT-WARE - - -

1845 Heath, Joseph, TUNSTALL, Staffordshire, England.

1845-53 EARTHENWARES. - Printed- **J. HEATH**

The Factory`s name is found within marks
of various patterns and designs.

1845 Housset, Rue de Faubourg St-Honore, PARIS, France.

1845-74 DECORATOR OF HARD-PASTE PORCELAIN.

Red-

1845 Morley & Co.,Francis, HANLEY, Staffordshire, England.

1845-58 EARTHENWARES, IRONSTONES, ETC. - **F. M.**
Factory`s name and initials are found within **F. M. & CO.**
marks of various patterns and designs. **F. MORLEY & CO.**
Impressed or printed-

1859-62 **Morley & Ashworth.** - - **M. & A.**
Marks of various patterns and designs. **MORLEY & ASHWORTH HANLEY**

see 1796 Mason`s Ironstone.

1845 Phillips & Son, Thomas, BURSLEM, Staffordshire, England.

c.1845-46 EARTHENWARES. printed or impressed- **T. PHILLIPS & SON BURSLEM**

1845 Reinhold Merkelbach Pottery, HOHR-GRENZHAUSEN, Germany.

1845- STONEWARE FOR HOUSEHOLD AND TECHNICAL USE.

1882-1933 mark - -

1882- **First Art Pottery produced and first artistically designed stein, (Merkelbach mould No.1.)**

c.1900- mark - - - -

1901- **Riemerschmid, Richard,** (Art nouveau artist) designed beer-steins and wine-jugs.

c.1903- mark - - **R.MERKELBACH GRENZHAUSEN**

Other artists:-
Velde, H. van der (Weimar)
Behrens, P., and Ehmcke, F.H. (Dusseldorf)
Wynand, Paul, (Hohr)

REINHOLD MERKELBACH HOHR-GRENZHAUSEN 1936

c.1909

c.1911

c.1916

1916-45

Continued over -

1845

1845 Reinhold Merkelbach, HOHR-GRENZHAUSEN,Germany. (Cont`)

1945-64

1964-68

1968-71

1970-78

1972 **Goebel Group acquired factory**
1977- Welling, Hanns, (designer)

1978-88

1980-88

1989

(By courtesy of Merkelbach Manufaktur GmbH, Hohr-Grenzhausen, Germany.)

1845 Samson & Co.,PARIS, France.

1845-REPRODUCTIONS OF CHINESE AND JAPANESE WARES and almost all of the famous European factories, including Meissen porcelain, French faïence, Dutch delft, Strasbourg porcelain, etc. Copies of English soft-paste porcelain figures were made in hard-paste by Samson and can be fairly easily detected.

Samson insisted that all their reproductions were marked with the letter `S` But sometimes this mark was ground out.

Some marks found on `Samson` reproductions-

Chinese and Japanese - - 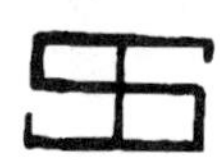

Sèvres porcelain. - - - - - 

Meissen - - - - - 

French, Italian, Spanish and English porcelain - - - 

1845 Smith, William (Junr) North Shore, STOCKTON-ON-TEES, Eng.

c.1845-84 EARTHENWARES. - Impressed or printed- **W. S. JUNR. & CO.**
These initials are found within marks **W. S.**
of various patterns and designs. **STOCKTON**

1845 Sneyd & Hill, HANLEY, Staffordshire, England.

c.1845 EARTHENWARES. - Printed- **SNEYD & HILL**
HANLEY
STAFFORDSHIRE
POTTERIES

1846-47 **Sneyd, Thomas,** - Impressed- **T. SNEYD**
HANLEY

1845 Tielsch, C. & Co.,ALTWASSER, Silesia, Germany.

1845- HARD-PASTE PORCELAIN. - -
The initials C.T. are incorporated within
most marks.

1845 Toy, W.E., Rue de la Chausee-d`Antin, PARIS, France.

1845- PORCELAIN DEALER. - - -
Violet-

1845 Vieillard, J., BORDEAUX, France.

1845- PORCELAIN -
Impressed-

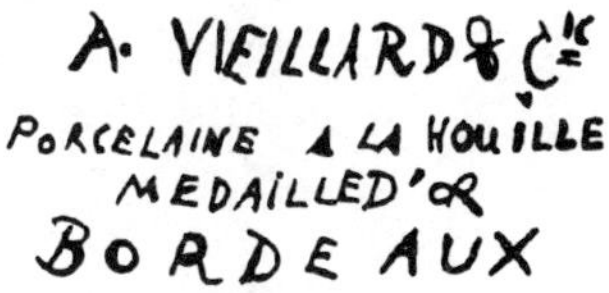

1845 Walker, Thomas, TUNSTALL, Staffordshire, England.

1845-51 EARTHENWARES. - Printed- **T. WALKER**
THOS. WALKER

1845	Aaron, Michel-Isaac, France. - - -	see 1725 CHANTILLY.
1845	Chapelle-Maillard, PARIS, France. - -	see 1830 Boulevard des Italiens.
1845	Clementson & Young, HANLEY, England. -	see 1844 Clementson,Young & Jameson.
1845	Dudson, James, HANLEY, England. - -	see 1809 Dudson, Thomas,
1845	Mason, Charles James, LANE DELPH, England.	see 1796 Mason`s Ironstone.
1845	Minton & Hollins, STOKE, England. - -	see 1793 Minton.
1845	Walley, Edward, COBRIDGE, England. - -	see 1841 Jones & Walley.

1846

1846 Bennett, Edwin, BALTIMORE, Maryland, U.S.A.

1846- STONEWARE.

1848 William Bennett (brother) joined Firm.

E. & W. BENNETT
CANTON AVENUE
BALTIMORE MD.

1850- Coxon, Charles, (modeller)

1856- William Bennett withdrew from Firm.

1875- Mark on white granite ware -

1880-84 -

1884 Marks on Parian plaques-

1886- -

1890-96 **Bennett Pottery Co.** - -
Miss De Witt Berg, Kate, (decorator)
Miss Brinton, Annie Haslam, (decorator)

The Factory`s name and initials are found within marks of various patterns and designs.

1897 Coronet mark for cream-coloured wares-

1846 Chetham, J.R.& F., LONGTON, Staffordshire, England.

1846-69 EARTHENWARES. - Printed- **J. R. & F. C.**
These initials are printed within marks of various patterns and designs.

1846 Cochran & Co.,R., GLASGOW, Scotland.

1846-1918 GENERAL CERAMICS. - Impressed- **R. C. & CO.**
The Factory`s name is found within **R. COCHRAN & CO.**
marks of various patterns and designs. **GLASGOW**

1846 Cork & Edge, Newport Pottery, BURSLEM, Staffordshire, England.

1846-60 EARTHENWARES. - Printed- **C. & E.**
The Factory`s initials are printed within
marks of various patterns and designs.

1860-71 **Cork, Edge & Malkin,** Printed- **C. E. & M.**
within marks of various patterns and designs,
see 1871 Edge Malkin & Co.

1846 Cyples & Barker, LONGTON, Staffordshire, England.

1846-47 EARTHENWARES. - Impressed- **CYPLES & BARKER**

1846 Fischer, Christian, PIRKENHAMMER, Bohemia, Germany.

1846-57 HARD-PASTE PORCELAIN. - -

CF HK C.F F&R

1857- **Fischer & Mieg** - - - F&M

1846 Hackwood & Son, William,SHELTON, Staffordshire, England.

1846-49 EARTHENWARES. - Printed-
These initials are printed within marks **W. H. & S.**
of various patterns and designs.

1846 Holdcroft & Co.,Peter, BURSLEM, Staffordshire, England.

1846-52 EARTHENWARES. - Printed- **P. H. & CO.**
These initials are printed within marks of
various patterns and designs.

1846 Möller & Dippe, UNTERKÖDITZ, Thuringia, Germany.

1846- GENERAL POTTERY. - - -
Dolls and porcelain figures. - -

1846/47

1846 Reinl, H., LUBENZ, Bohemia, Germany.

1846- PORCELAIN - - -

1846 Smith, Sampson, Ltd.,LONGTON, Staffordshire, England.

c.1846-1963 EARTHENWARE, FIGURES, ETC., Impressed- **S. S.**

c.1851-90 mark (but sometimes used in the 20th century on original moulds) — SAMPSON SMITH 1851 LONGTON

20th century China.
c.1918 `Ltd` added.
`S.S.` monogram is printed within marks of various patterns and designs during 20th century.

1846	Clauss, Alphonse-Marx, PARIS, France. - -	see 1773 Porcelaine de Paris.
1846	Knight, John King, FENTON, England. - -	see 1826 Knight Elkin & Co.
1846	Lenz, J.F., Germany. - - - -	see 1820 ZELL.
1846	Luigi, Richard, Italy. - - - -	see 1577 TURIN.
1846	Neuberg-Gieshübl-Fabrik, Germany. - -	see 1803 GIESSHÜBEL.
1846	Sneyd, Thomas, HANLEY, England. - -	see 1845 Sneyd & Hill.
1846	Summerley Art Manufacturer, STOKE, England.	see 1793 Minton, Thomas,

1847 Devers, Joseph, PARIS, France.

c.1847- EARLY TYPE FAÏENCE. - - Black-

1847 Edwards, John, & Co.,FENTON, Staffordshire, England.

1847-1900 GENERAL CERAMICS. impressed or printed- **J. E.** **J. E. & Co.**
The name and initials of this Factory is found within marks of various patterns and designs.
c.1873 `& Co.` added
c.1880-1900- Printed in various marks incorporating the name etc. **JOHN EDWARDS** ***Porcelaine De Terre*** ***Warrented Ironstone China***

1847 Everard, Glover & Colclough, LANE END, Staffordshire, England.

c.1847 CHINA AND EARTHENWARES Printed- within marks of various patterns and designs. **E. G. & C.**

1847 Green, Thomas, FENTON, Staffordshire, England.

1847-59 EARTHENWARES AND CHINA. - Printed- within marks of various design. **T. GREEN FENTON POTTERIES**

1859-76 **Green & Co.,M.,** - Printed- within marks of various designs, **M. GREEN & Co.**

1876-89 **Green, T.A.& S.** - - Printed- within marks of various designs. **T. A. & S. G.**

1889 **Crown Staffordshire Porcelain Co.** see 1889 Crown Staffordshire Co.

1847 Hampson & Broadhurst, LONGTON, Staffordshire, England.

1847-53 EARTHENWARES. - Printed- **H. & B.**
These initials are printed within marks of various patterns and designs.

1847 Krüger, Edmund, BLANKENHAIN, Thuringia, Germany.

1847- HARD-PASTE PORCELAIN. - -

1847 Northern & Co.,W. Lambeth, LONDON, England.

1847-92 STONEWARES. Impressed- **W. NORTHERN POTTER VAUXHALL LAMBETH**
1887 `& Co.` added.

1847 Revol, Gustave, Père & Fils, SAINT-UZE, Drôme, France.

1847- HARD-PASTE PORCELAIN. - -

1847 Cabau, Eugène-Charles, (flowers) France. - see 1745 SÈVRES.
1847 Copeland & Sons Ltd.,W.T. STOKE, England. - see 1770 Spode, Josiah.
1847 Dressel & Kister, Germany. - - - see 1835 Scheibe-Alsbach,
1847 Gosse, François, France. - - - - see 1810 BAYEUX.
1847 Harker, Taylor & Co., EAST LIVERPOOL, U.S.A. see 1840 Harker Pottery Co.

1848 Alcock Junior, John & Samuel, COBRIDGE, England.

c.1848-50 EARTHENWARES. - Impressed or printed- **J. & S. ALCOCK JR.**

1848

1848 Cartlidge & Co., Charles, GREENPOINT, N.Y. U.S.A.

1848-56 BONE CHINA, ETC.
Table ware, Parian busts, buttons, ornamental figures, etc., were produced and decorated by the best painters and decorators.
A collection of Cartlidge porcelain may be seen in the Pennsylvania Museum.

NO FACTORY MARKS HAVE BEEN FOUND ON THESE WARES.

1848 Collier Ltd.,S.& E., READING, Berkshire, England.

c.1848-1957 TERRA-COTTA

Impressed or printed -

1848 Lyman, Fenton & Co., BENNINGTON, Vermont, U.S.A.

c.1848- STONEWARE IN ROCKINGHAM STYLE.
1849 `Patent Flint Enamelled` Impressed-

1849 **United States Pottery Co.**
PARIAN WARE. - - -

1848 Moritz, Carl, TAUBENBACH, Thuringia, Germany.

1848- HARD-PASTE PORCELAIN. - -

1848 Salamander Works, NEW YORK, N.Y., U.S.A.

1848- EARTHENWARES. -

Impressed-

1848 Woodward & Vodrey, EAST LIVERPOOL, Ohio, U.S.A.

1848- EARTHENWARES, WHITE GRANITE, SEMI-PORCELAIN.
1849- **Woodward, Blakeley & Co.,**
1857- **Vodrey & Brother,**
WHITE GRANITE AND SEMI-PORCELAIN.
1896- **Vodrey Pottery Co.,**
1879- Factory`s name or monogram found within marks of various patterns and designs:-

1848	Mérigot, (decorator) France. - - -	see 1745 SÈVRES.
1848	Morley, Francis, LANE DELPH, England. -	see 1796 Mason`s Ironstone.
1848	Second Republic, France. - - - -	see 1745 SÈVRES.

1849 Barlow, Thomas, LONGTON, Staffordshire, England.

1849-82 GENERAL CERAMICS. - Impressed- **B.**

1849 BOLOGNA, Italy.

15th to 18th Century LEAD-GLAZED EARTHENWARE (SGCRAFFIATO)

1849- **Minghetti & Son, Angelo.**

Reproductions of Italian Renaissance Maiolica.

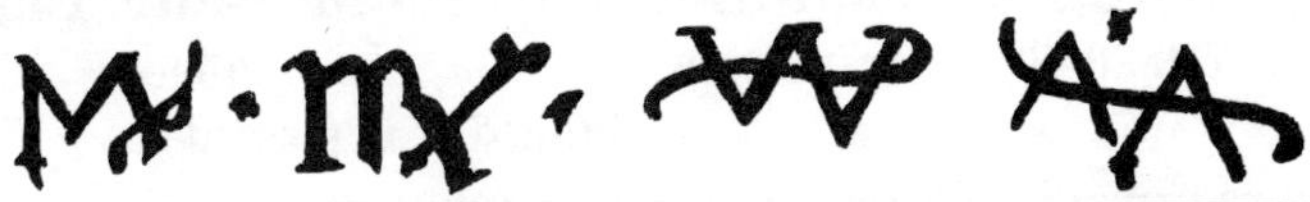

1849 Harwood, J., Clarence Pottery, STOCKTON-ON-TEES, England.

c.1849-77 EARTHENWARES - Impressed- **HARWOOD STOCKTON**

1849 Myatt Pottery Co., BILSTON, Staffordshire, England.

c.1849-94 EARTHENWARES.

1880 Trade mark- - MYATT

1849 Pinder, Thomas, Nile Street Works, BURSLEM, Staff`, England.

1849-51 EARTHENWARES. Printed or impressed- **PINDER BURSLEM**

1851-62 **Pinder, Bourne & Hope,** - Printed-
marks of various patterns and designs - **P. B. & H.**
PINDER, BOURNE & CO.

1862-82 **Pinder, Bourne & Co.,** Printed-
marks of various patterns and designs **P. B. & CO.**
PINDER, BOURNE & CO.
Impressed date marks sometimes occur i.e. 9.80 = Sept. 1880.
1878 purchased by Doultons.
1882 became Doulton & Co.,Ltd.,

see 1815 Royal Doulton plc.

1849 Zoroku, (potter) YAMASHIRO, Japan.

1849-78 FAÏENCE AND CELADON PORCELAIN. -

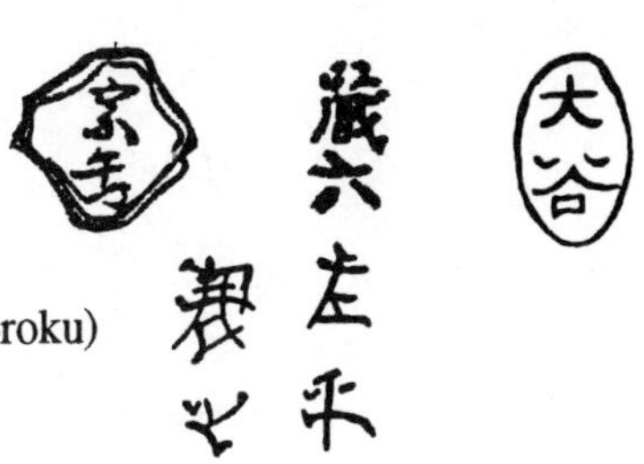

Sahei seizo (made by Sahei mark of Zoroku)

1849/50

1849	Gobert, (figures) France. - - - - -	see 1745 SÈVRES.
1849	Locker & Co., England. - - - - -	see 1749 DERBY.
1849	Pountney & Co.,Ltd., BRISTOL, England. -	see 1816 Pountney & Allies.
1849	Piccardt, Geertruida, DELFT, Holland. - -	see 1653 De Porceleyne Fles.
1849	Reed, John (son) MEXBOROUGH, England. -	see 1839 Reed, James.
1849	United States Pottery Co., BENNINGTON, U.S.A.	see 1848 Lyman, Fenton & Co.
1849	Woodward, Blakeley & Co., E. LIVERPOOL, U.S.A.	see 1848 Woodward & Vodrey.

1850 Adams & Cooper, LONGTON, Staffordshire, England.

1850-77 PORCELAIN. - Printed- **A. & C.**

1850 Barker & Son, BURSLEM, Staffordshire, England.

c.1850-60 EARTHENWARES. - Printed- **B. & S.**

Printed or impressed- **BARKER & SON**

1850 Brownfield & Sons, William, COBRIDGE, Staffordshire, England.

1850-91 EARTHENWARES AND PORCELAIN. **W. B.**

1850-71 These initials are sometimes printed, impressed or moulded within marks of various patterns and designs.
1871 Porcelain, especially parian jugs.

1860- Impressed mark- **BROWNFIELDS**

Also printed with crown- **BROWNFIELD**

1871 `& S` or `& Sons` added. Printed- **W. B. & S.**

1876- `Son` became `Sons` **W. B. & SON**

1871-91 Printed with two globes.

1891-1900 **Brownfields Guild Pottery Society Ltd.**

Impressed- **B. G. P. CO.**

1891-98 - Printed marks-

1850 Brunt, Wm., Son & Co., EAST LIVERPOOL, Ohio, U.S.A.

c.1850- EARTHENWARE, IRONSTONE CHINA. - -

1894 Brunt, William, Pottery Co., (Phoenix Pottery)

1850 Campbellfield Pottery Co.Ltd., Springburn, GLASGOW, Scotland.

1850-1905 EARTHENWARES.

1850-84 - - **CAMPBELLFIELD**
C. P. CO.

1884 `Ltd` added - **C. P. CO. LTD.**

Factory`s name or initials printed or impressed within marks of various designs.

c.1884-c.1905- -

1850 Cotton & Barlow, LONGTON, Staffordshire, England.

1850-55 EARTHENWARES. - - Printed **C. & B.**

Printed within marks of various patterns and designs.

1850 GÄVLE, Sweden.

1850-1910 EARTHENWARES - - -

1910- HARD-PASTE PORCELAIN - - -

Gefle-Porslin- - -

1850 Gerrier, le, PARIS, France.

1850 HARD-PASTE PORCELAIN DECORATOR.

LE GERRIEZ
20 Rᵉ DE LA HARPE
paris

1850 Harding, Joseph, BURSLEM, Staffordshire, England.

1850-51 EARTHENWARES. - Factory`s name printed **J. HARDING**

within marks of various patterns and designs.

1850 Heron & Son, Robert, KIRKCALDY, Scotland.

c.1850-1929 EARTHENWARES. - Printed- **R. H. & S.**

Printed marks of various patterns and designs.

1920-29 **WEMYSS WARE** -

Printed mark - -

1850

1850 Keys & Mountford, STOKE, Staffordshire, England.

1850-57 PARIAN WARES. - Impressed- **K. & M.**
S. KEYS
& MOUNTFORD

1857-59 **Mountford, John,** Incised signature mark- ***J. MOUNTFORD***
STOKE

1850 Maw & Co. Ltd., Benthall Works, BROSELEY, Shropshire, England.

1850 ENCAUSTIC TILES, MOSAICS AND MAJOLICA. **MAW & CO**
The factory was initiated at Worcester. **MAW & CO**
c.1875 Art pottery produced. **BENTHALL**
WORKS
Factory`s name impressed or printed **BROSELEY**
within marks of various designs. **SALOP**

FLOREAT MAW
SALOPIA

1850 Menard, C.H., PARIS, France.

c.1850- HARD-PASTE PORCELAIN.

1850 Pankhurst & Co.,J.W., HANLEY, Staffordshire, England.

1850-82 EARTHENWARES,IRONSTONE,ETC. Printed- **J. W. P.**
The Factory`s name and initials are printed **J.W. PANKHURST**
within marks of various patterns and designs.
1852- `& Co.` added-

1850 Port Dundas Pottery Co. Ltd., GLASGOW, Scotland.

c.1850-1932 STONEWARES. Impressed or printed- **PORT DUNDAS**
GLASGOW POTTERY

1850 Primavesi & Sons, F., CARDIFF & SWANSEA, Wales.

c.1850-1915 RETAILERS OF EARTHENWARES. - **F. PRIMAVESI & SON**
Printed marks of various patterns and **CARDIFF**
designs.
c.1860 `& Son` added.

1850 Robrecht, G., MILDENEICHEN, Austria.

1850- HARD-PASTE PORCELAIN. - - - -

1850 Stanley & Lambert, LONGTON, Staffordshire, England.

c.1850-54 EARTHENWARES. - Printed- **S. & L.**
These initials are printed within marks
of various patterns and designs.

1850 Till & Sons, Thomas, BURSLEM, Staffordshire, England.

c.1850-1928 EARTHENWARES. Printed marks of various patterns and designs.- - **TILL** **TILL & SON**

1855 Paris Exhibition. Awarded `Certificate of Merit`

c.1861-c.1880 Printed- - -

c.1919-c.1928 Printed-

1850 Townsend, George, LONGTON, Staffordshire, England.

c.1850-64 EARTHENWARES. Factory`s name is printed within marks of various patterns and designs. **G. TOWNSEND**

1850 Voigt, Alfred, SITZENDORF, Thuringia, Germany.

1850- HARD-PASTE PORCELAIN. - -

Sitzendorfer Porzellan-Manufaktur. -

1850 Walley, John, BURSLEM, Staffordshire, England.

1850-67 EARTHENWARES. - Printed or impressed- **J. WALLEY** **J. WALLEY`S WARE**

1850 Woods, Richard, MALVERN, Worcestershire, England.

c.1850- RETAILER. Printed- **R. WOODS**

1850 Ynysmedw Pottery, YNYSMEDW, nr. Swansea, Wales.

c.1850-70 EARTHENWARES. - Impressed- **Y.M.P.** **Y.P.**

1850	Akoji, Japan. - - - - - -	see 1736 ISE.
1850	Boch frères, Belgium. - - - - -	see 1751 TOURNAY.
1850	Coxon, Charles, (modeller) BALTIMORE, U.S.A.	see 1846 Bennett, Edwin,
1850	Dorfner & Cie, Ernst.,Germany. - - -	see 1826 HIRSCHAU.
1850	Evans & Glasson, SWANSEA, England.- -	see 1783 Swansea Pottery.
1850	Frant, Fischer, Germany. - - - - -	see 1804 DALLWITZ.
1850	Hennebergsche Porzellan Manufaktur, Germany.	see 1757 GOTHA.
1850	Kiyo-chika, Japan. - - - - -	see 1583 BIZEN.
1850	Lessore, Emile, (painter) France. - - -	see 1745 SÈVRES.
1850	Marcenaro, Italy. - - - - -	see 1550 SAVONA.
1850	Meigh, Son, C., & Pankhurst, HANLEY, England.	see 1805 Meigh, Job & Son.
1850	Pfluger Bros. & Co., Switzerland, - -	see 1780 NYON.

Continued over -

1850/51

1850	Pillivuyt & Co., C.H., France. - -	see 1802 FOECY.
1850	Rouse & Turner, JERSEY CITY, U.S.A. -	see 1833 American Pottery Man. Co.
1850	Roussel, (figures) France. - - -	see 1745 SÈVRES.
1850	Sanrakuyen-Yaki, Japan. - - -	see 1750 KII or KISHIU.
1850	Teiten, Japan. - - - -	see 1583 CHIKUZEN.
1850	Terami, Japan. - - - -	see 1583 BIZEN.
1850	Warburton and Britton, England. - -	see 1760 LEEDS POTTERY.

1851 Collinson & Co.,Charles, BURSLEM, Staffordshire, England.

1851-73 EARTHENWARES. Factory`s name is printed within marks of various patterns and designs. — **C. COLLINSON & CO.**

1851 Edwards & Son, James, Dale Hall, BURSLEM, Staffs. England.

1851-82 EARTHENWARES, IRONSTONES, ETC. Printed or impressed marks of various patterns and designs. - -

J. E. & S.
JAMES EDWARDS & SON, DALE HALL
EDWARDS
D. H.

1851 Emberton, William, TUNSTALL, Staffordshire, England.

1851-69 EARTHENWARES. Printed marks of various patterns and designs. — **W. E.**

1869-82 **Emberton, T. I. & J.** Printed mark- **T. I. & J. E.**

1851 Godwin, B. C., BURSLEM, Staffordshire, England.

c.1851 EARTHENWARES. Printed marks of various patterns and designs. — **B. C. G.**

1851 Kurlbaum & Schwartz, Kensington, PHILADELPHIA, PA. U.S.A.

1851- HARD-PASTE PORCELAIN. - - **K & S**

Incised mark (probably decorator)-

1851 Livesley Powell & Co., HANLEY, Staffordshire, England.

1851-66 EARTHENWARES AND CHINA. Impressed or printed marks of various patterns and designs.

LIVESLEY POWELL & CO.
L. P. & CO.

1867-78 **Powell & Bishop.** Impressed or printed marks of various patterns and designs.

P. & B.
POWELL & BISHOP

1876 Caduceus mark -

Continued over -

1851 Livesley Powell & Co.,HANLEY, Staffordshire, England. (Cont`)

1878-91 **Powell, Bishop & Stonier.** Impressed or printed marks of various patterns and designs. **P. B. & S.**

1880 Oriental type marks-

1891-1939 **Bishop & Stonier Ltd.** Impressed or printed marks of various patterns and designs. **B. & S.**

1936-39 - - - **BISHOP ENGLAND**

1851 J. & G. Meakin Ltd., Eagle Potteries, HANLEY, Staff`, England.

1851- Earthenwares, stonewares, etc.
James and George Meakin were 19th Century pioneers of the modern practice of production of high quality goods, in quantity, for the export markets.
Name of Factory printed or impressed within marks of various patterns and designs - **J. & G. MEAKIN**

1887- **Acquired Eastwood Pottery** which belonged to Charles Meakin a member of the Meakin family.
c.1890-onwards various printed marks:- - see 1883 Meakin,Charles.

1891- **George Meakin died. George Elliot Meakin (son) became chairman of the company.**
c.1912-onwards printed marks:- -

Continued over -

1851/52

1851 J.& G. Meakin Ltd., HANLEY, Staffordshire, England. (Cont`)

c.1939-onwards printed marks:- -

Modern marks printed underglaze- -

1970- **Became part of the Wedgwood Group.**

(By kind permission of J.& G. Meakin Ltd., (A Wedgwood Company,) Stoke-on-Trent, England.)

1851 Shaw, Anthony, TUNSTALL, Staffordshire, England.

1851-1900	EARTHENWARES. Impressed or printed	**ANTHONY SHAW**
c.1851-56	marks of various patterns and designs.	**A. SHAW**
(Burslem)	c.1882-98 `& Son` added	**BURSLEM**
	c.1898 `& Co.` replaced `& Son`	**SHAWS**
	1900 Factory acquired by A.J.Wilkinson Ltd.	**BURSLEM**

1851 Venables & Baines, BURSLEM, Staffordshire, England.

c.1851-53	EARTHENWARES. Impressed or printed marks-	**VENABLES & BAINES**
c.1853-55	**Venables & Co.,John,** Impressed or printed-	**J. VENABLES & CO.**

1851 Wooliscroft, George, TUNSTALL, Staffordshire, England.

1851-53 and 1860-64 EARTHENWARES. Impressed or printed marks of various patterns etc. — **G. WOOLISCROFT** or **G. WOOLLISCROFT**

1851	Gély, J.,(pâte-sur-pâte) France. - - -	see 1745 SÈVRES.
1851	Hsien-fêng, China. - - - -	see 1644 CH`ING.
1851	Humbert, (figures) France.- - - -	see 1745 SÈVRES.
1851	Meigh & Son, Charles, HANLEY, England. -	see 1805 Meigh & Son, Job.
1851	Pinder, Bourne & Hope, BURSLEM, England. -	see 1849 Pinder, Thomas.

1852 Calland & Co.,John F.,Landore Pottery, SWANSEA, Wales.

1852-56	EARTHENWARES. Impressed or printed- Marks of various patterns and designs.	**CALLAND SWANSEA** **CALLAND & CO.** **LANDORE, SWANSEA** **J. F. CALLAND & CO** **LANDORE POTTERY**

1852 Holland, John, TUNSTALL, Staffordshire, England.

1852-54 EARTHENWARES. - Printed- **J. HOLLAND**

1852	Barriat, Charles, (figures) France.- - -	see 1745 SÈVRES.
1852	Charpentier (gilder) France. - - -	see 1745 SÈVRES.
1852	Chobei (potter) YAMASHIRO, Japan. - -	see 1644 Asahi.
1852	Dammouse, Pierre-Adolphe (models) France. -	see 1745 SÈVRES.
1852	Ferro, Francesco, Italy. - - - - -	see 1550 SAVONA.
1852	Kerr & Binns, England. - - - -	see 1751 WORCESTER.
1852	Klaus, Ferdinand, TETTAU, Germany. - -	see 1794 Tettau GmbH.
1852	Renard, Emile,(decorator) France. - -	see 1745 SÈVRES.
1852	Second Empire, France. - - - - -	see 1745 SÈVRES.
1852	Sewell & Co., NEWCASTLE, England. - -	see 1780 St. Anthony`s Pottery.
1852	Wilson & Co., Issac, England. - - -	see 1831 Middlesbrough Pottery.

1853 Alcock, John, COBRIDGE, Staffordshire, England.

1853-61 EARTHENWARES. - Printed- **JOHN ALCOCK COBRIDGE**
Marks of various patterns and designs.

1861-1910 **Alcock & Co.,Ltd.,Henry,** - Printed- **H. A. & Co.**
Marks of various patterns and designs.
1880-1910 Printed Coat of Arms with- **HENRY ALCOCK & Co. COBRIDGE**
1891 `England` added
1900 `Ltd` added

1910-35 **The Henry Alcock Pottery,**
Printed with Coat of Arms - - **HENRY ALCOCK POTTERY**

1853 Beyer & Boch, VOLKSTEDT, Thuringia, Germany.

1853- Decorating - - -
1890- Manufacturing - - -

1853 Brougtham & Mayer, TUNSTALL, Staffordshire, England.

1853-55 EARTHENWARES. The Factory`s name is printed within marks of various patterns and designs. **BROUGHAM & MAYER**

1853 CALDAS DA RAINHA, Portugal.

1853- PALISSY TYPE WARE - -
Mafra & Son Impressed-

1853

1853 Challinor & Co.,E., FENTON, Staffordshire, England.

1853-62 EARTHENWARES. - Printed- **E. CHALLINOR & CO.**
Marks of various patterns and designs.

1862-91 **Challinor E.& C.** - Printed- **E. & C. C.**
Marks of various patterns and designs, including Royal Arms and Staffordshire knot. **E. & C. CHALLINOR FENTON**

1892-96 **Challinor & Co.,C.** Printed- **C. CHALLINOR & CO. ENGLAND**
Marks of various patterns and designs.

1853 Elsmore & Forster, TUNSTALL, Staffordshire, England.

1853-71 EARTHENWARES, PARIAN, ETC. Printed- **ELSMORE & FORSTER**
The Factory`s name is printed within marks of various patterns and designs.

1872-87 **Elsmore & Son, T.** Earthenwares- **ELSMORE & SON ENGLAND**

1853 Haviland & Co., LIMOGES, Haute-Vienne, France.

1853-Haviland, David, (Founder) HARD-PASTE PORCELAIN.

There were eight brothers of the Haviland family seven of them were in the tableware trade In 1821 Edmund Haviland retailed imported English faience from his New York shop. In 1829 he took his brother David into the business. In 1838 David left Edmund and with his elder brother Daniel created a table-ware import company. in 1852 Robert, a further brother joined the company which was to become Haviland Brothers & Co. New York. 1853 David Haviland opens factory in Limoges to mainly supply the American market. Other members of the family opened up other companies mainly in the south of America.

1863 Haviland Brothers closes down due to the collapse of the American market because of the Civil War.
Haviland & Co., Limoges became the major business.

1865 David Haviland`s sons, Charles and Theodore were brought into the business. Theodore was sent to promote Haviland in America.
Eventually Charles took over the running of the company.

1867 Silver medal at the Paris Universal Exhibition.

1870 War with Germany declared.

1853
whiteware mark

HAVILAND

H&Co

1865
whiteware marks

pre 1876

Continued over -

1853 Haviland & Co., LIMOGES, Haute-Vienne, France. (Cont`)

1872 Bracquemond, Felix, (etcher) Head of painter`s workshop at Sèvres joins Charle`s new studio at 115 rue Michel-Ange, Paris.

1875-85 Haviland & Co. opened a decorating workshop in Auteuil. Marks were as follows:-

H & Co / L	HAVILAND & Co / Limoges		H & Co / L	HAVILAND	
1875-82	1875-82	1883-85	1876-89 green	1883-85	1883-89 sepia

Marks on whiteware in chrome green -

H & Co	H & Co / L	H & Co
1876-79	1876-79	1876-86

1876 Philadelphia Centennial Exhibition. and Paris Union Centrale Exhibition.

	HAVILAND & Co / Limoges	H & Co
1876-78	1876-78	1877
Marks on decorated wares in red		Marks on whiteware

1878 World Fair. Haviland won Gold Medal.
1879 David Haviland (founder) dies.
1879 Theodore Haviland returns to Limoges from America and takes charge of manufacturing.

Marks on decorated ware-

H & Co ELITE	HAVILAND & Co	H & Co SPECIAL	
1878-83	1879-83	1879-89	1879-89

Marks on whiteware -

H & Co DEPOSE	H & Co L FRANCE
1887	1888-96

1891 Deterioration of relations beween Charles and Theodore. On the 31st December Haviland & Co., is closed down and re-opened the next day when Charles and his son Georges establishes a new company under the old name. Theodore buys a piece of land to build his own workshop.

see 1892 Haviland, Theodore

Continued over -

1853

1853 Haviland & Co.,LIMOGES, Haute-Vienne, France. (Cont`)

1892 Haviland & Co. (new company)

Mark on decorated ware - Décoré par HAVILAND & Co Limoges
1893-95

Mark on whiteware - Haviland France
1894-1931

Mark on decorated ware - Haviland & Co Limoges "Feu de Four"
1905-30 American
1926-31 French.

1931 Company closed. see 1892 Haviland, Theodore,
(Courtesy of Haviland S.A. Limoges, France)
(For further information see HAVILAND by Jean d`Albis.)

1853 Hughes & Co.,Elijah, COBRIDGE, Staffordshire, England.

1853-67 EARTHENWARES. - Impressed- **E. HUGHES & CO.**

1853 Hulse, Nixon & Adderley, LONGTON, Staffordshire, England.

1853-68 EARTHENWARES. These initials are printed within marks of various patterns and designs. **H. N. & A.**

1869-75 **Hulse & Adderley.** CHINA AND EARTHENWARES.

H. & A.

1876-1905 **Adderley & Co.,William Alsager,** **W. A. A.**
1876-85 Printed marks of various patterns and designs.
1886-1905 `& Co.` added. - - - **W. A. A. & Co.**

1876-1905 Trade mark Printed-

Continued over -

1853 Hulse, Nixon & Adderley, LONGTON, Staff`, England. (Cont`)

1906- **Adderleys Ltd.,**

1906-26 Trade mark - Printed- *Mark as above*

1912- Name of Factory printed within marks of various patterns and designs. **ADDERLEYS LTD.**

1947 **Ridgway Potteries Ltd acquired the Factory but kept the name of `Adderleys`**

1853 Millington & Astbury, TRENTON, N.J., U.S.A.

1853- EARTHENWARES.

1859- **Millington, Astbury & Poulson.** Impressed-

Mark on white granite ware-

1853 Morrison & Carr, New York City, N.Y., U.S.A.

1853-71 POTTERY. - - impressed-

1871 Partnership ended. Mr Carr continued alone. Mark on white granite ware - -

1871 Mark used on sanitary ware and interior car fittings for James L. Howard & Co.

1879 **Lincoln Pottery Co.** Mr Carr purchased old Speeler Pottery, Trenton and took on a new partner, Edward Clark of Burslem, England and named it Lincoln Pottery Co.

Mr Carr left Trenton after a few months, but continued at the New York City Pottery using these same marks.

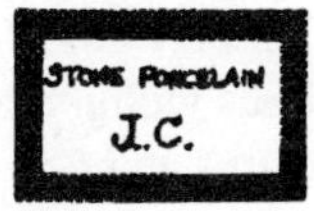

1888- **Factory at Trenton closed**

1853/54

1853 Pillivuyt & Cie, MEHUN-SUR-YÈVRE, Cher, France.

1853- HARD-PASTE PORCELAIN. - -

1853 Young & Sons, William, TRENTON, N.J., U.S.A.

1853-57 EARTHENWARE, CHINA.

1857-79 **Excelsior Pottery Works,**
William Young & Sons
(William, Jr., Edward and John)
1866-79 Continued by sons.
1858 Mark of an eagle and English Arms used

1853 Maling, C.T., England. - - - - see 1817 Maling, Robert,
1853 Venables & Co.,John, BURSLEM, England. - see 1851 Venables & Baines

1854 American Porcelain Man. Co., GLOUCESTER, N.J., U.S.A.

1854-57 SOFT-PASTE PORCELAIN impressed- **A.P.M. Co.**

1854 Bing & Gröndahl, COPENHAGEN, Demark.

1854- PORCELAIN, EARTHENWARE. - - -

1854 Bohne, Ernst, RUDOLSTADT, Thuringia, Germany.

1854- HARD-PASTE PORCELAIN. - -

1854 Butterfield, William & James, TUNSTALL, Staffordshire, England.

1854-61 EARTHENWARES. These initials are printed - **W. & J. B.**
within marks of various patterns and designs.

1854 Ford, T. & C., HANLEY, Staffordshire, England.

1854-71 EARTHENWARES. Initials are printed or - **T. & C. F.**
impressed within marks of various
patterns and designs.

1871-74 **Ford, Thomas,** CHINA. Printed or impressed initials within marks of various patterns and designs. **T. F.**

Continued over -

1854 Ford, T.& C., HANLEY, Staffordshire, England. (Cont`)

Registration type marks. Impressed or Printed

Dated numerals 5/73 =May 1873. etc.

1874-1904 **Ford, Charles,** CHINA. Impressed or Printed monogram-

c.1900-04 Impressed or printed-

1904 **Robinson & Sons Ltd.,J.A. acquired Factory.**

1854 Knowles, Isaac W., & Harvey, Isaac A., E.LIVERPOOL, Ohio, U.S.A.

1854-70 EARTHENWARES. - - -

1870- **Knowles, Taylor & Knowles.**
WHITE GRANITE WARE. Bison mark-

1891- **Knowles, Taylor & Knowles (Incorporated)**

1893 Fine Art porcelain `Lotus` ware -
Crescent and Star - -

Trade marks used on table and toilet services-

Other marks contained the following place names-
`MONTANA, DAKOTA, IOWA, WASHINGTON, HARVARD, VIRGINIA, STANFORD, PRINCETON, CORNELL, ST.PAUL, FLORIDA, TACOMA, MAINE, UTAH`

1854 Marshall & Co., Ltd., John, BO`NESS, Scotland.

1854-99 EARTHENWARES. - Printed- **JOHN MARSHALL & CO.**
1897 `Ltd` added.

1854/55

1854 Meagher, Frederick, EAST BOSTON, Mass., U.S.A.

1854-75 WHITE WARE.
1875- **New England Pottery Co.**
Thomas Gray and L.W. Clark partnership.
IRONSTONE CHINA, WHITE GRANITE WARE.

1883-86
Stone china

1887
Cream ware

1886-92
White granite ware

1886-89 Semi-porcelain

1889-95 Printed red

1897 `Paris White`

1854 Nicholas & Co.,Thomas, CASTLEFORD, W.Yorkshire, England.

c.1854-71 EARTHENWARES. These initials are printed or impressed within marks of various patterns and designs.

T. N. & CO.

1854 Nichols & Alford, BURLINGTON, VT., U.S.A.

1854- EARTHENWARES, ROCKINGHAM, STONEWARE.

Nichols & Alford
Manufacturers
1854
Burlington, Vt.

1854 Ristori, T. H., MARZY, Nièvre, France.

1854- FAÏENCE IN THE STYLE OF ROUEN AND NEVERS.

1854 Swaine & Co., HÜTTENSTEINACH, Thuringia, Germany.

1854- HARD-PASTE PORCELAIN. - -

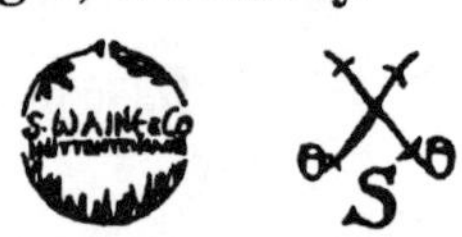

1854	Coombs & Holland, LLANELLY, Wales. -	see 1839 South Wales Pottery.
1854	Kennedy & Macintyre, BURSLEM, England. -	see 1843 Kennedy, W. S.
1854	Merigot (ornaments) France. - - -	see 1745 SÈVRES.
1854	Napoleon III. Emperor, France. - - -	see 1745 SÈVRES.
1854	Pline, (decorator) France. - - - -	see 1745 SÈVRES.
1854	Scott, A., SUNDERLAND, England. - -	see 1788 Southwick Pottery.

1855 Bailey, W.& J.A., Alloa Pottery, ALLOA, Scotland.

1855-1908 EARTHENWARES. Various patterns within this mark

BAILEY

1855 Close & Co., STOKE, Staffordshire, England. **CLOSE & CO. LATE W. ADAMS & SONS STOKE-UPON-TRENT**

1855-64 EARTHENWARES. Printed or impressed within marks of various patterns and designs.

1855 Lockett, Baguley & Cooper, HANLEY, Staffordshire, England.

1855-60 PORCELAIN. - **LOCKETT BAGULEY & COOPER**

1855 Lockhart & Arthur, GLASGOW, Scotland. **L. & A.** **LOCKHART & ARTHUR**

1855-64 EARTHENWARES. Printed or impressed within marks of various patterns and designs.

1865-98 **Lockhart & Co., David,** Marks of various patterns and designs with- **D. L. & CO.**

1898-1953 **Lockhart & Sons Ltd., David.** Printed or impressed marks with various patterns and designs, with- - - **D. L. & SONS**

1855 Phillips, Edward, SHELTON, Staffordshire, England.

1855-62 EARTHENWARES. - Printed- **EDWARD PHILLIPS SHELTON STAFFORDSHIRE**

1855 Smith, George F., STOCKTON-ON-TEES, England.

c.1855-60 EARTHENWARES. These initials are printed- or impressed within marks of various patterns and designs. **G. F. S.**

1855 Uffrecht & Co.,J., NEUHALDENSLEBEN, Saxony, Germany.

1855- EARTHENWARE. - - -

1855 Zsolnay, W., (and Family) PECS, Hungary.

c.1855- GENERAL CERAMICS. - -

1855 Alexander II, Russia. - - - - - see 1744 ST. PETERSBURG.
1855 Bulot, Eugène, (flowers) France. - - - see 1745 SÈVRES.
1855 Harker & Co., George S., E.LIVERPOOL, U.S.A. see 1840 Harker, B., Snr.
1855- Maddock & Sons Ltd., John, BURSLEM, England. see 1842 Maddock, John.

1856 Beardmore & Edwards, LONGTON, Staffordshire, England.

1856-58 EARTHENWARES. Printed marks of various designs- **B. & E.**

1856

1856 Cockson & Harding, SHELTON, Staffordshire, England. C. & H.

1856-62 EARTHENWARES. Printed or impressed marks with various patterns and designs — **C. & H. LATE HACKWOOD**

1862-72 **Harding, W. & J.,** Printed marks with various patterns and designs. - — **W. & J. H.**

1856 Elkin, Samuel, LONGTON, Staffordshire, England.

1856-64 EARTHENWARES. These initials are printed within marks of various patterns and designs. — **S. E.**

1856 Evans & Booth, BURSLEM, Staffordshire, England.

1856-69 EARTHENWARES. These initials are printed within marks of various patterns and designs. — **E. & B.**

1856 LAVENO, Italy.

1856- EARTHENWARES AND PORCELAIN

1856 Plymouth Pottery Co. Ltd., PLYMOUTH, Devon, England.

1856-63 EARTHENWARES. - - - — **P. P. COY. L. STONE CHINA**

1856 Ridgway Bates & Co., John, HANLEY, Staffordshire, England.

1856-58 EARTHENWARES AND PORCELAIN. Printed marks with various patterns and designs, with- — **J. R. B. & CO. JOHN RIDGWAY BATES & CO.**

1859-61 **Bates, Brown-Westhead & Moore.** These initials are printed or impressed within marks of various patterns and designs- — **B. B. W. & M.**

1862-1904 **Brown-Westhead, Moore & Co.** Printed or impressed marks within various patterns and designs.- - — **B. W. M. B. W. M. & CO.**

1862- Impressed mark- - — **T. C. BROWN-WESTHEAD MOORE & CO.**

Continued over -

1856 Ridgway Bates & Co., John, HANLEY, Staff , England, (Cont`)

1884-91 Printed or impressed -

1905-20 **Cauldon Ltd.** Printed marks with various patterns and designs included - -

CAULDON
ENGLAND

1920-62 **Cauldon Potteries Ltd.**
Same marks as used by Brown-Westhead, Moore & Co, but with the name `Cauldon`

1930-50 Printed mark - -

1950-62 Printed mark - -

1962 **Factory acquired by Pountney & Co.,Ltd., Bristol.**
1968 **Cauldon Bristol Potteries Ltd.** see 1816 Pountney & Allies
New Factory at Wilson Way, Redruth, Cornwall.
FINE TABLEWARE AND ADVERTISING SUNDRIES.
(By kind permission of Cauldon Bristol Potteries Ltd.,Ferrybridge, W.Yorkshire, England.)

1856 Southern Porcelain Co., KAOLIN, South Carolina, U.S.A.

1856-62 PARIAN, WHITE CHINA, BROWN STONEWARE
TELEGRAPH INSULATORS. Impressed-

1856 Villeroy & Boch, DRESDEN, Germany.

1856- GENERAL CERAMICS. -

see 1767 Villeroy & Boch.

1856/57

1856 Worthington & Harrop, HANLEY, Staffordshire, England.

1856-73 EARTHENWARES. These initials are found within marks of various patterns and designs. **W. & H.**

1856 Faraquet, (figures) France.- - - - - see 1745 SÈVRES.
1856 Folco, Antonio, (creamware) Italy. - - see 1550 SAVONA.
1856 Podmore, Walker & Wedgwood, TUNSTALL, Eng. see 1834 Podmore,Walker & Co.
1856 Woolf & Sons, L., FERRYBRIDGE, England. - see 1843 Reed & Taylor.

1857 Ball, William, Deptford Pottery, SUNDERLAND, England.

1857-1918 EARTHENWARES. - Printed- **COPYRIGHT BALL**
1884- Ball Bros. - - - **BROS**
SUNDERLAND

1857 Beech & Hancock, Churchbank, TUNSTALL, Staffordshire, England.

And Swan Bank Works, BURSLEM.

1857-76 EARTHENWARES. Printed within marks of various patterns and designs. **BEECH & HANCOCK**
B. & H.
1877-89 **Beech, James** printed **J. B.**
Printed initials under design of a swan.

1889-99 **Boulton, Machin & Tennant.** printed or impressed mark -

B. M. & T.

1857 Belleek Pottery Ltd., BELLEEK, Co. Fermanagh, Ireland.

1857-In the early years earthenware was the principal product. In 1863 a small amount of parian was produced. By 1869 after a praiseworthy report in the Journal, orders of tremendous prestige were coming in which included orders from Queen Victoria and the Prince of Wales.

Large and small
First Marks, 1863-90
mainly black but sometimes
red,blue,green or brown

McBirney, David and Armstrong, Robert W. founded the factory with the enthusiastic aid of John Caldwell Bloomfield who owned the Castlecaldwell estate, which encompassed the village of Belleek.

Continued over -

1857 Belleek Pottery Ltd., BELLEEK, Co. Fermanagh, Ireland. (Cont`)

Armstrong brought 14 craftsmen from Stoke-on-Trent, who trained the local workers and apprentices. Two of the craftsmen were William Bromley and William Gallimore, forman and chief modeller from Goss Pottery. 1865 Henshall, William, from Stoke-on-Trent, is credited with introducing the Basketware and Flowers that gained Belleek world recognition.

BELLEEK
BELLEEK POTTERY
BELLEEK.
CO. FERMANAGH
First marks. impressed. Sometimes used with the printed mark above.

The `Harp` and `Crown Harp` marks were usually impressed but sometimes printed. They were used to designate the composition of earthenware bodies during Armstrong`s era, and not as many collectors concluded, the early marks of Belleek`s history.

1872 Dublin Exposition.
1880 Melbourne International Exposition. Belleek wins 2nd. Gold medal.
1882 David Mcbirney dies.
1884 Robert William Armstrong dies.
1884 Belleek Pottery was to be sold by auction.
1884 A group of local investors purchased the factory and traded as Belleek Pottery Works Co. Ltd.,

Second Mark. 1891–1926

Mr Poole from Staffordshire, had a short stay as manager. The Cleary brothers had a longer stay as managers:-
1884-90 James Cleary.
1900-19 Edward Cleary.

Third Mark. 1926–1946

1887 International Exhibition in Adelaide, Australia. Belleek wins yet another Gold medal.
1893 Frederick Slater joins Belleek from England.
1900 Paris Exhibition. Belleek wins Gold medal for 28 inch tall Centre Piece believed to be modelled by Frederick Slater and now stands in the Foyer of the Visitors Complex at Belleek.

Fourth Mark. 1946–1955

1914-18 1st World War. Belleek struggles and once more is offered for sale.
1920 Bernard O`Rourke becomes main shareholder Belleek Pottery Ltd., (new name)
1939-45 2nd World War. Belleek struggled through by making basic utility earthenware.
1945 Belleek concentrates all its production on parian, and could barely keep up with orders.

Fifth Mark. 1955–1965

Continued over -

1857

1857 Belleek Pottery Ltd., BELLEEK, Co. Fermanagh, Ireland. (Cont`)

1982 Recession puts Belleek in financial difficulties.
I.D.B. restructures the company and appoints Mr Roger Troughton as Managing Director.
1984 Mr Roger Troughton buys 70% of the company. 30% being owned by the Allied Irish Banks Ltd.
1988 Powerscreen International Plc buys Belleek. Modern Visitors Complex built which now attracts over 70,000 tourist per year.
1990 Erne Heritage investments, owned by George Moore of Dundalk, buys Belleek Pottery Ltd.

Sixth Mark, 1965–March 31, 1980

Seventh Mark, April 1, 1980–December 22, 1992

Eighth Mark, January, 1993–

1971 The use of trademark designs exclusive to a particular piece or series, began with the 1971 Christmas plate. Below are some of those special trademarks:-

Continued over -

1857 Belleek Pottery Ltd., BELLEEK, Co.Fermanagh, Ireland. (Cont`)

`Basketware` is one of Belleek`s major successes in skill and design and some of the most desirable pieces to collect. Below are the dates of various marks used on Belleek baskets.

How to Date a Belleek Basket

	DATE	WEAVING ON BASE	WORDING ON STRIPS
	Post 1865 (circa) - 1889	Three Strand Weaving	Belleek
	or		
2.	1865 - 1889	Three Strand Weaving	Belleek / Co. Fermanagh
3.	1890 - 1920	Three Strand Weaving	Belleek / Co. Fermanagh / Ireland
4.	1921 - 1954	Four Strand Weaving	Belleek / Co. Fermanagh / Ireland
5.	1955 - 1979	Four Strand Weaving	Belleek ® / Co. Fermanagh
6.	1980 - 1989	Four Strand Weaving	Belleek ® / Ireland
7.	1989	Four Strand Weaving	® Belleek Ireland — Brown-gold Stamp
9.	1990	Four Strand Weaving	Brown-gold Stamp — ® Belleek Ireland

1992 Baskets from 1992 - to present (1995)

The mark is returned to a square on every type of basket, except for the Degenhardts Special Basket, which was introduced in 1995 and has a special mark which is triangular and has the Blue Current Stamp, with a number and `Richards` signature.

(By kind permission of Belleek Pottery Ltd., Co. Fermanagh, Ireland.)

1857 Bridgwood & Clarke, BURSLEM, Staffordshire, England.

1857-64 EARTHENWARES. - Impressed- **BRIDGWOOD & CLARKE**

(Also at TUNSTALL)

These initials are printed within marks of various patterns and designs. - **B & C** / **B & C BURSLEM**

Continued over -

1857

1857 Bridgwood & Clarke, BURSLEM, Staffordshire, England. (Cont`)

c.1865-77 **Clarke & Co., Edward,** Printed within marks of various patterns and designs. With name of Factory location included- As below:-

EDWARD CLARK
EDWARD CLARK & CO.

c.1865-77 TUNSTALL
c.1878-80 LONGPORT
1880-87 BURSLEM

1857 Cartwright & Edwards Ltd., LONGTON, Staffordshire, England.

c.1857- GENERAL CERAMICS. These initials are printed or impressed within marks of various patterns and designs.

C & E

c.1912- Crown mark, printed- -

c.1926 `Ltd.` added `Boronian` ware -

c.1929-c.36 Printed marks-

1955- **Factory became part of Alfred Clough Ltd.**

1857 Flacket, Toft & Robinson, LONGTON, Staffordshire, England.

1857-58 EARTHENWARES. These initials are printed within marks of various patterns and designs. **F. T. & R.**

1857 Gillet and Brianchon, Rue de Lafayette, PARIS, France.

1857 PATENTED LUSTRE FINISH. Black-

1857 Gray & Sons, Ltd., W.A., PORTOBELLO, Lothian, Scotland.

c.1857-1931 EARTHENWARES AND STONEWARES. Printed- **W. A. GRAY**

1870- `& Sons` added.
1926- `Ltd` added.

1857 Hutschenreuther AG, Lorenz, SELB, Bavaria, Germany.

1857- HARD-PASTE PORCELAIN.
Lorenz Hutschenreuther leaves the firm at Hohenberg. Granted a licence to build a porcelain factory at Selb.

Early wares were not marked

1859- New factory put into operation.

1864- Hans Pabst, Father-in-law of Lorenz becomes a partner in the factory.

1865-72 Impressed marks - -

1873-90 mark - - - -

1877- Lorenz Hutschenreuther retires.
1880- Leopold Gmelin (artist) join the Firm.

1886- Lorenz Hutschenreuther dies.

1890-1902 mark in green -

1902-20 mark in green -

1906- Jager, Werner & Co., porcelain factory at Selb, is purchased and known as Department `B` within the Company.

1917- Paul Müller, porcelain factory at Selb, is purchased.
Lorenz Hutschenreuther Art department is founded. Professor Fritz Klee (manager)

1925-39 marks in green -

1927- Tirschenreuth Porcelain Factory and Bauscher Factory, Weiden are purchased.

1929- Gran Premio award at Barcelona Exibition.

1934- Max Adolf Pfeiffer (former general manager at Meissen) is artistic and technical adviser.
Paul Scheurich, Max Esser and Professor Borner, brought into factory.
Sculptors, Karl Tutter, Carl Werner and decoration designer, Arthur Jahreis work in art department.

1937- Gold medal at the Paris World Fair.

1939-64 mark in green - - -

Continued over -

1857

1857 Hutschenreuther AG, Lorenz, SELB, Bavaria, Germany. (Con`t)

1946- **Resumption of production, large consignment for American headquarters in U.S. zone.**

1957- Centenary celebrations.

1965-67 mark in green -

1966- 50th anniversary of Art department.

1968-69 mark in green -

1969- **Purchase of the majority of shares of C.M. Hutschenreuther, Hohenberg.**
Hutschenreuther AG. new name of Company.

1970 mark - -

1972- **Merger with Kahla AG, which contributes its works at Arzberg, Schonwald, Wiesau and Schwandorf to Hutschenreuther AG.**

1979- **Companies taken over from were:-**
1979 Groh & Co., Hof.
1981 Naila Porcelain Factory Albin Klober KG.
1982 Theresienthal Crystal Glass Manufactory.
1984 Eugen Wagner, Neustadt/Coburg.

1995 modern mark - -

(Courtesy of Hutschenreuther AG. Germany.)

1857 Lanternier & Cie, A., LIMOGES, France.

1857- PORCELAIN.

1960- **Merged with G.D.A. Porcelaines, Limoges.**
Re-named `Royal Limoges`

see 1960 Royal Limoges.

1857 Mason, Holt & Co., LONGTON, Staffordshire, England.

1857-84 PORCELAIN. Printed or impressed initials within marks of various patterns and designs. **M. H. & CO.**

1857 Proctor & Co., J.H., LONGTON, Staffordshire, England.

1857-84 EARTHENWARES. Printed or impressed-

WARRANTED
P.

1857 Schmidt, Sebastian, SCHMIEDEFELD, Saxony, Germany.

1857- HARD-PASTE PORCELAIN. - -

1857 Doulton & Co. LAMBETH, England. - - see 1815 Royal Doulton plc.
1857 Excelsior Pottery Works, TRENTON, U.S.A. - see 1853 Young & Son, Wm.
1857 Fischer & Mieg, PIRKENHAMMER, Germany. see 1846 Fischer, Christian.
1857 Mountford, John, STOKE, England. - - see 1850 Keys & Mountford.
1857 Spinaci, Giovanni, Italy. - - - - see 1495 GUBBIO.
1857 Vodrey & Brothers, E.LIVERPOOL, U.S.A. - see 1848 Woodward & Vodrey.

1858 Baensch, Heinrich, LETTIN, Saxony, Germany.

1858- Hard-paste porcelain. - -

1945- V.V.B. Keramik-Zweigbetrieb Factory.

1858 Blashfield, J.M., STAMFORD, England.

1858-75 TERRA-COTTA. ARCHITECHTURAL. impressed marks- **J.M. BLASHFIELD**
Many famous public buildings were
enriched by this factory`s art works. **BLASHFIELD**
1874- Stamford Terra-cotta Company. **STAMFORD**
1875- Company was wound up **STAMFORD**
TERRA COTTA CO.LTD.

1858 Goss Ltd., William Henry, STOKE, Staffordshire, England.

c.1858-1944 PORCELAIN, PARIAN AND POTTERY. Impressed or printed- **W. H. G.**
W. H. GOSS

c.1862- Printed-
1891- `England` added.

c.1934- **Goss China Co.,Ltd.,**
c.1934- **Acquired by Cauldon Potteries Ltd.**
Now Royal Doulton Group.

1858 Hancock & Sons, Sampson, STOKE, Staffordshire, England.

1858-1937 EARTHENWARES. These initials are printed **S. H.**
within marks of various patterns and designs-
Printed- **S. HANCOCK**
1891-1935 These initials are printed within **S. H. & S.**
marks of various patterns and designs- **S. H. & SONS**
1900-12 Printed marks-

1911- Registered mark- **THE DUCHESS CHINA**

1935-37 **S. Hancock & Sons (Potters) Ltd.,**

1858/59

1858 Malkin, Walker & Hulse, LONGTON, Staffordshire, England.

1858-64 EARTHENWARES. These initials are printed within marks of various patterns and designs-

M. W. & H.

1858 Mann & Co., HANLEY, Staffordshire, England.

1858-60 EARTHENWARES AND CHINA. Printed within marks of various patterns and designs-

MANN & CO.
HANLEY

1858 Mayer & Elliott, LONGPORT, Staffordshire, England.

1858-61 EARTHENWARES. These initials are printed within marks of various patterns and designs-
Impressed date marks: 3/60 = March 1860
(Month over Year)

1858 Sältzer, August, EISENACH, Saxony, Germany.

1858- POTTERY AND REPRODUCTIONS. - -

1858	Bonnuit, Achile, (decorator) France. - -	see 1745 SÈVRES.
1858	Derischsweiler, J-C-G., (gilder) France. - -	see 1745 SÈVRES.
1858	Lessore, Emile, (decorator) BURSLEM, England.	see 1759 Wedgwood, Josiah.
1858	Meyer (Figures) France. - - - - -	see 1745 SÈVRES.
1858	Réjoux, Emile, (decorator) France. - -	see 1745 SÈVRES.
1858	Taylor Ashworth, LANE DELPH, England. -	see 1796 Mason`s Ironstone.
1858	Wazen, Zengora, (son) Japan. - - -	see 1650 KAGA.

1859 Allerton & Sons, Charles, LONGTON, Staffordshire, England.

1859-1942 EARTHENWARES, CHINA. Name and initials of Factory are printed or impressed within marks of various patterns and designs.

CHAS ALLERTON &
SONS
ENGLAND

C. A. & SONS

1890-1912 Printed marks-

1912-42 **Allertons Ltd.,**
1912- Acquired by Cauldon Potteries Ltd.

1912-42 Printed marks-

1859 Deck, Théodore (b.1823, d.91) PARIS, France.

c.1859- EARLY STUDIO POTTER - -
Impressed, incised or printed- -

1887-91 Director of SÈVRES.

1859 Heath & Blackhurst & Co., BURSLEM, Staffordshire, England.

1859-77 EARTHENWARES. The Factory`s initials are printed within marks of various patterns and designs, especially garter type. - **H. & B.** **H. B. & CO.**

1859 Hudden, John Thomas, LONGTON, Staffordshire, England.

1859-85 EARTHENWARES. Name and initials printed within marks of various patterns and designs- - **J. T. H.** **J. T. HUDDEN**

1859 Rhodes & Yates, City Pottery, TRENTON, U.S.A.

1859- EARTHENWARE, GRANITE WARE.
1865-71 **Yates & Titus**
1871-75 **Yates, Bennett & Allan** - - **Y.B.A.**
1875- **City Pottery Co. (Incorporated)** - **C.P.& Co.**
Initials incorporated into English type marks.

1876- New mark introduced -

1859 Trenton China Co., TRENTON, N.J., U.S.A.

1859-91 EARTHENWARES, VITRIFIED CHINA. Impressed- **TRENTON CHINA Co. TRENTON, N.J.**

1859 Wardle & Ash, HANLEY, Staffordshire, England.

1859-62 EARTHENWARES, MAJOLICA, FIGURES, ETC., Impressed- **W. & A.**

1859 Woodward Ltd., James, BURTON-ON-TRENT, England.

1859-88 **Swadlincote Pottery.**
EARTHENWARES, MAJOLICA, ETC.,
Impressed or printed mark-

1859	Bates, Brown-Westhead & Moore, HANLEY, England.	see 1856 Ridgway Bates & Co.J.
1859	Green & Co.,M.,FENTON, England. - -	see 1847 Green, Thomas.
1859	Maling, C.T., Ford Pottery, England. - -	see 1817 Maling, Robert,
1859	Millington, Astbury & Poulson, TRENTON, U.S.A.	see 1853 Millington & Astbury.
1859	Mitchell & Sons, William, RYE, England. -	see 1807 Cadborough Pottery.
1859	Morley & Ashworth, HANLEY, England. -	see 1845 Morley & Co.,F.
1859	Stevenson Sharp & Co., England.- - -	see 1749 DERBY.

1860

1860 Davenport, Banks & Co., HANLEY, Staffordshire, England.

1860-73 EARTHENWARES, MAJOLICA, ETC., These initials are printed within marks of various patterns and designs. **D. B. & CO.**

Printed or impressed mark- **DAVENPORT BANKS & CO ETRURIA**

1873-80 **Davenport Beck & Co.** Printed- **D. B. & CO.**

1860 Dornheim, Koch & Fischer, GRÄFENRODA, Thuringia, Germany.

1860- HARD-PASTE PORCELAIN AND EARTHENWARE- Dolls and Dolls` Heads.

1860 Duke & Nephews, Sir James, BURSLEM, Staffordshire, England.

c.1860-63 PORCELAINS, PARIANS, ETC. Impressed-

1860 Dunmore Pottery, AIRTH, Scotland.

c.1860-1903 **Gardner, Peter,** EARTHENWARE. Impressed- within a circle **PETER GARDNER DUNMORE POTTERY**

1903-11 **Dunmore Pottery Co.** - Impressed- **DUNMORE.**

1860 Eichler, E., DUX, Bohemia, Germany.

1860- **Duxer Porzellan-Manufaktur**

1860 Ellis, Unwin & Mountford, HANLEY, Staffordshire, England.

1860-61 EARTHENWARES. Printed with name of pattern- **E. U. & M.**

1860 Goode & Co.,Ltd., Thomas, LONDON, W.1., England.

c.1860- RETAILER. The name of this firm are within marks of various well-known factories- -

1860 Hammersley & Son, Ralph, BURSLEM, Staffordshire, England.

1860-1905 EARTHENWARES. Initials are printed within marks of various patterns and designs. 1884 `& Son` added. **R. H.** **R. H. & S.**

1860 Holdcroft, Hill & Mellor, BURSLEM, Staffordshire, England.

1860-70 EARTHENWARES. Initials are printed within marks of various patterns and designs. **H. H. & M.**

1860 Hughes, Thomas, BURSLEM, Staffordshire, England.

1860-94 EARTHENWARES. - Impressed- **THOMAS HUGHES IRONSTONE CHINA**

1895-1957 **Hughes & Son Ltd.,Thomas.** **THOS. HUGHES & SON ENGLAND**
Printed or impressed within marks of various patterns and designs.
1910 `Ltd` added.

1930-57 printed marks-

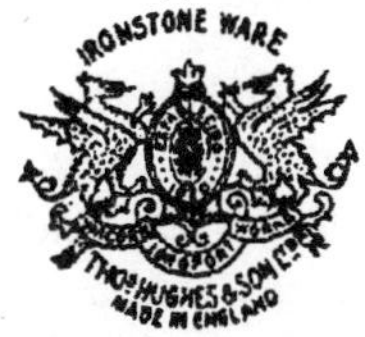

1860 Königszelt, Porzellanfabrik, KÖNIGSZELT, Silesia, Germany.

1860- HARD-PASTE PORCELAIN
August Rappsilber.

1860 Morgan, Wood & Co., BURSLEM, Staffordshire, England.

1860-70 EARTHENWARES. Initials printed within marks of various patterns and designs. Sometimes with bee. **M. W. & CO.**

1860 Speeler, Henry & Sons, International Pottery, TRENTON, U.S.A.

1860-79 EARTHENWARES, YELLOW AND ROCKINGHAM WARE.
1876 Exhibited at Philadelphia Exposition.

1879- **Carr & Clark (International Pottery Co.)**

c.1880- **Burgess & Campbell**
Factory`s name and initials found within marks of various patterns and designs.

`Royal Blue` marks on semi-porcelain

c.1903- **Burgess & Co.** - - **B-C WILTON**

`Royal Blue` ware -

`Rugby` pattern, `Flint China` - - - -

International Pottery Co. - -

1860/61

1860 Turner & Tomkinson, TUNSTALL, Staffordshire, England.

1860-72	EARTHENWARES. Name or initials printed within marks of various patterns and designs Initials sometimes printed in elaborate form-	**TURNER & TOMKINSON** **T. & T.**
1873-95	**Turner & Sons, G. W.,** Impressed-	**TURNERS** **G. W. T. & SONS.**
	Initials printed within marks of various patterns and designs, sometimes Royal Arms. 1891 `England` added.	**G. W. T. S.** **G. W. T. & S.** **G. T. & S.**

1860 Twyford, Thomas, HANLEY, Staffordshire, England.

1860-98	EARTHENWARES. Factory`s initials found within marks of various designs.	**T. T.**

1860 Vernon & Son, James, BURSLEM, Staffordshire, England.

1860-80	EARTHENWARES. Initials printed within marks of various patterns and designs.	**J. V.**
	c.1875-80 Within various patterns and designs-	**J. V. & S.** **J. V. & SON.** **J. V. junr.**

1860 Wood, Challinor & Co., TUNSTALL, Staffordshire, England.

c.1860-64	EARTHENWARES. These initials are printed within marks of various patterns and designs.	**W. C. & CO.**

1860	Cork, Edge & Malkin, BURSLEM, England. -	see 1846 Cork & Edge.
1860	Imbe Pottery, Japan. - - - -	see 1583 BIZEN.
1860	Lenck Family, Germany. - - - - -	see 1840 PASSAU.
1860	Macintyre & Co.,Lt.,James, BURSLEM, England.	see 1843 Kennedy, W.S.
1860	Maussion, (figures) France. - - -	see 1745 SÈVRES.
1860	Ricci, Sebastiano, Italy. - - - -	see 1550 SAVONA.
1860	Riemann, Albert, Germany. - - -	see 1738 COBERG.
1860	Ristori, T., France. - - - -	see 1589 NEVERS.
1860	Wedgwood & Co.,TUNSTALL, England. -	see 1834 Podmore,Walker & Co.

1861 Allman, Broughton & Co., BURSLEM, Staffordshire, England.

1861-68	EARTHENWARES. Initials printed or impressed within marks of various patterns and designs	**A. B. & CO.** **WEDGWOOD PLACE** **BURSLEM**

1861 Fishley, Edwin Beer, FREMINGTON, Devon, England.

1861-1906	EARTHENWARES. Incised mark-	**E.B. FISHLEY** **FREMINGTON** **N. DEVON**

1861 Hill Pottery Co. Ltd., BURSLEM, Staffordshire, England.

c.1861-67 GENERAL CERAMICS. Initials (sometimes monogram) printed within marks of various patterns and designs. - **J. S. H.**

1861 Jones & Sons Ltd., George, Trent Pottery, STOKE, Staffs, England.

1861-1951 GENERAL CERAMICS. Monogram in relief, impressed or printed-

1867 Awarded a medal at the Paris Exhibition.

1873 `& Sons` added - - - - -

c.1874-1924 Printed or impressed- -

1891 `England` added - -

c.1924-51 Printed or impressed-

1861 Lycett, Edward, (decorator) ATLANTA, Georgia, U.S.A.

Regarded as one of the formost decorators in the U.S.A.

1861-	Green Street, New York.
1884-90	Joined New York Faience Manufacturing Co.
1890-	Atlanta, with his son, William. (Lustre glazes)

1861 Schlegelmilch, Erdmann, SUHL, Prussia, Germany.

1861- HARD-PASTE PORCELAIN. - -

1861 Stephens, Tams & Co., TRENTON, New Jersey, U.S.A.

1861-68 EARTHENWARES. - - -

1868-75 **Greenwood Pottery Co.**

Arms of the State of New Jersey mark -

For ironstone china or white granite -

Table porcelain mark stamped- **G.P. Co.**

1886 Table and Toilet wares mark.

Impressed- **GREENWOOD CHINA TRENTON, N.J.**

Continued over -

1861/62

1861 Stephens, Tams & Co., TRENTON, New Jersey, U.S.A. (Cont`)

1883-86 Art wares mark. Printed purple-

1886 mark Printed purple-
Similar mark used for
special orders from
Messrs Ovington Bros.,
Brooklyn, New York.

Mark used sometimes on Royal Worcester
type wares - - -

1861 Tempest, Brockmann & Co., CINCINNATI, Ohio, U.S.A.

1862-81 POTTERY. - - -

1881- **Tempest, Brockmann & Sampson Pottery Co.**
1887- **Brockmann Pottery Co.**
Cream coloured and white granite wares.
Coat of Arms mark as above but with- **B. P. CO.**

WARRANTED BEST
IRONSTONE CHINA

1861 Unger, Schneider & Hutschenreuther, GRÄFENTHAL, Germany.

1861- HARD-PASTE PORCELAIN. - -

c.1885 **Schneider & Hutschenreuther.**

1861 Alcock & Co. Ltd., Henry, COBRIDGE, England. see 1853 Alcock, John.
1861 Ens, Karl, RUDOLSTADT, Germany. - - see 1762 Aelteste Volkstedter.
1861 Old Hall Earthenware Co. Ltd., HANLEY, England. see 1805 Meigh, Job, & Son.

1862 Bodley & Co.,E. F., Scotia Pottery, BURSLEM, Staffs, England.

1862-81 EARTHENWARES. Initials are printed within marks of various patterns and designs. **E.F.B.& CO.** **E.F.B.**

Printed mark within Staffordshire knot- **SCOTIA POTTERY**

1881-98 **Bodley & Son, E.F., (LONGTON)** - **E.F.B.& SON**
New Bridge Pottery.
Initials printed or impressed within marks of various patterns and designs. **E.F.B.& S.**
1883-98 Printed mark - -

1862 Broadhurst & Sons Ltd., James, FENTON, Staffordshire, England.

c.1862- EARTHENWARES.

1862-70- Initials are printed within marks of various patterns and designs. — **J. B.**

1870-1922 - - - — **J. B. & S.**

1922- `Ltd` added -

1957- Printed marks with the name of `Broadhurst` included. — **BROADHURST**

1862 Burgess, Leigh & Co., Central Pottery, BURSLEM, Staffs, England.

1862- EARTHENWARES.

1862 Monogram, impressed or printed-

Factory`s initials printed or impressed - within marks of various patterns and designs. — **B. & L.**

1867- Hill Pottery opened.

1862 Beehive mark, printed within various designs-

1877- **Burgess & Leigh.** name adopted

1880-1912 Printed mark- - -

1889- Middleport Pottery opened.

1906- Printed marks- -
1919 `Ltd` added

c.1919 Printed mark- -

c.1930 `Burleigh Ware` printed marks-
Various patterns and designs- -

c.1940 Printed mark - -

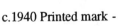

Continued over -

1862

1862 Burgess, Leigh & Co., BURSLEM, Staffordshire, England. (Cont`)

c.1960 Ironstone printed mark -
Second mark is modern

(By kind permission of Burgess & Leigh Ltd. England.)

1862 Dimmock & Co., J, Albion Works, J. HANLEY, Staffs, England.

1862-1904 EARTHENWARES. Initials or monogram-printed within marks of various patterns and designs. - - **J. D. & CO.**

c.1878-1904 Cliff, W.D., acquired Factory.
c.1878-90 Impressed mark- **CLIFF ALBION CHINA**

c.1878-1904 Name printed within marks of various patterns and designs

see 1828 Dimmock & Co., T.

1862 Eardley & Hammersley, TUNSTALL, Staffordshire, England.

1862-66 EARTHENWARES. Initials within marks - of various patterns and designs. **E. & H.**

1862 Hope & Carter, BURSLEM, Staffordshire, England.

1862-80 EARTHENWARES. Initials printed within - marks of various patterns and designs especially in garter form. **H. & C.**

1862 Jacquemin, E., FONTAINEBLEAU, France.

1862 HARD-PASTE PORCELAIN. - -

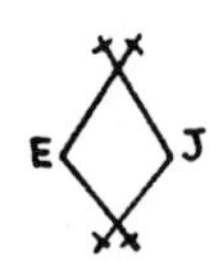

1862 Kirkham, William, STOKE, Staffordshire, England.

1862-92 EARTHENWARES, TERRA-COTTA, ETC., Impressed- **W. KIRKHAM**

1862 Maudsley & Co.,J., TUNSTALL, Staffs, England.

1862-64 **Earthenwares.** **Printed mark-** **STONE WARE J. M. & CO.**
(These initials are used by other Factories)

1862 Skey, George, Wilncote Works, nr.Tamworth, Staffordshire, England.

1862-1900 TERRA-COTTA, STONEWARES.

Mark impressed in an oval form — **GEORGE SKEY WILNCOTE WORKS NR. TAMWORTH**

1864 Limited company formed.
George Skey & Co.Ltd.

1862 Wathen & Lichfield, FENTON, Staffordshire, England.

1862-64 EARTHENWARES. Initials are printed within marks of various patterns and designs. — **W & L FENTON**

1864-69 **Wathen, James B.,** Within printed marks of various patterns and designs. — **J. B. W. F.**

see 1870 Reeves, James.

1862 Wedgwood & Co.,Ltd., TUNSTALL, Staffordshire, England.

1862- EARTHENWARES, STONE-CHINA, ETC., Impressed- **WEDGWOOD & CO.**

1862 Printed Trade mark- -

c.1890-1906 Printed mark- -
1900 `Ltd` added

1900 Impressed mark- **WEDGWOOD & CO. LTD.**

c.1906-57 The Factory`s name is printed within marks of various patterns and designs — **WEDGWOOD & CO.,LTD.**

Some design names used:- **WACOLWARE**
WACOL
EVERWARE
ROYAL TUNSTALL

1962 Trade-name - - **VITRILAIN**

(Josiah Wedgwood & Sons Ltd., is sometimes mistaken for this Factory but has no connection)

1862/63

1862	Ashworth & Bros., Geo. L., LANE DELPH, England.	see 1796 Mason`s Ironstone.
1862	Avisseau, M.E.(son) France. - - -	see 1750 TOURS.
1862	Benard, V., France. - - - -	see 1735 VALENCIENNES.
1862	Brown-Westhead, Moore & Co., HANLEY, England.	see 1856 Ridgway, Bates & Co.
1862	Carocci, Fabbri & Co., Italy. - - -	see 1495 GUBBIO.
1862	Challinor, E. & C. FENTON, England. - -	see 1853 Challinor E.& Co.
1862	Evans & Co.,D.J., SWANSEA, England.- -	see 1783 Swansea Pottery.
1862	Harding, W.& J., SHELTON, England. - -	see 1856 Cockson & Harding.
1862	Milet, Optat, (decorator) France. - - -	see 1745 SÈVRES.
1862	Pinder, Bourne & Co.,BURSLEM, England. -	see 1849 Pinder, Thomas.
1862	Tùng-chih, China. - - - -	see 1644 CH`ING.
1862	Worcester Royal Porcelain Co.,Ltd., England. -	see 1751 WORCESTER.

1863 Bernardaud & Cie.,L., LIMOGES, France. **B. & CO.**

1863- PORCELAIN - - - **LIMOGES**

FRANCE

1863 Bloor, Ott & Booth, Etruria Pottery, TRENTON, N.J., U.S.A.

1863-65 WHITE GRANITE

1865- **Ott & Brewer** British Coat of Arms mark- - -

1876 Centennial Exposition Fair.
Exhibited Parian portrait busts and figures vases modelled by Prof. Isaac Broome.

1882 Irish Belleek ware introduced, believed to be the first in the U.S.A. - -

O. & B.

c.1901- **Cook Pottery Co. acquired Factory.** see 1894 Cook Pottery Co.

1863 Bodley & Harrold, Scotia Pottery, BURSLEM, Staff`s.,England.

1863-65 EARTHENWARES. The Factory`s name and - initials are printed within marks of various patterns and designs.- -

B & H

BODLEY & HARROLD

Within `Staffordshire Knot` **SCOTIA POTTERY**

see 1865 Bodley & Co.

1863 Coxon & Co., TRENTON, New Jersey, U.S.A.

1863-84 **Coxon, Charles, and Thompson, J.F.,**
CREAM-COLOURED AND WHITE GRANITE WARES.

Mark printed black - -

1868 Mr. Coxon died. Widow and four sons continued business.
1884 Sold to Alpaugh & Magown (Empire Pottery)

1863 Glasgow Pottery, TRENTON, New Jersey, U.S.A.

1863- **Moses, John,** WHITE GRANITE AND CREAM-WARE

1876-93 -

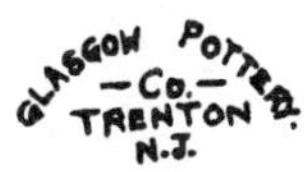

1895- Initials of Factory found within marks of the British Coat of Arms on white granite.

IRONSTONE CHINA
J. M. & Co.

Vitrified China mark on toilet and table services

GLASGOW CHINA
VITRIFIED
TRENTON, N.J.

John Moses & Sons Co.
Factory`s initials printed within marks of various patterns and designs.

J. M. & S. Co.

1899- United States Government ordered crockery for The National Home for Disabled Volunteer Soldiers.

Orders were placed for other departments of Government. i.e. Quartermasters Department
Stamped mark-

Q.M.D.

United States Marine Corps. Stamped mark-
And many other departments.

U.S.M.C.

Special marks are also found on wares made for dealers throughout the U.S.A.

1863 Hancock, Whittingham & Co., Swan Bank, BURSLEM, England.

1863-72 EARTHENWARES. Factory`s initials printed within marks of various patterns and designs. **H. W. & CO.**

1873-79 **Hancock & Whittingham, Bridge Works, STOKE.** Printed marks within various patterns and designs. **H. & W.**

1863 Hawley, W.& G., Northfield Pottery, ROTHERHAM, England.

1863-68 EARTHENWARES. Factory`s name printed or impressed within marks of various patterns and designs.- - **W. & G. HAWLEY**

1868-1903 **Hawley Bros.,Ltd.,** Printed- **H. B.**
1897 `Ltd` added **HAWLEY BROS.**

1903-19 **Northfield Hawley Pottery Co.Ltd.,** Impressed or printed-

1863 Malkin, Ralph, Park Works, FENTON, Staffordshire, England.

1863-81 EARTHENWARES. Factory`s initials printed within marks of various patterns and designs- **R. M.**

1882-92 **Malkin & Sons, Ralph,** Various printed marks with- **R. M. & S.**

1863 McNicol Pottery Co., EAST LIVERPOOL, Ohio, U.S.A.

1863- **Goodwin, John, (Novelty Pottery Works)**
CREAM-COLOURED AND WHITE GRANITE WARES.

1863 Goupil, (figures) France. - - - - - - see 1745 SÈVRES.
1863 Stiff & Sons, James, LAMBETH, England. - - see 1840 Stiff, James.

1864 Adams & Co.,John, Victoria Works, HANLEY, Staffs, England.

1864-73 EARTHENWARES, STONEWARES, MAJOLICA.
Impressed- **J. ADAMS & CO.**
ADAMS & CO.

1873-86 **Adams & Bromley,**
Printed or impressed- **A. & B.**
A. & B.
SHELTON
ADAMS & BROMLEY

1864 Aynsley & Sons Ltd., John, LONGTON, Staffordshire, England.

1864- PORCELAIN. - - **Early wares unmarked.**

1875- Impressed- **AYNSLEY**

1875-90 Printed-

1891- Factory`s name printed within marks of various patterns and designs. **AYNSLEY**

1891 `England` added

1864 Baddeley, William, Drury Court Works, LONGTON, Staffs. England.

1864-75 TERRA-COTTA, ETC., - Impressed- **W. BADDELEY**

1864 Bailey, C.I.C., Fulham Pottery,LONDON,England.

1864-89 STONEWARES, TERRA-COTTA AND CHINA.

These works originally belonged to John Dwight, the renowned potter of Fulham who was the first person to make stoneware successfully in England. see 1671 Dwight, John,

Marks used, sometimes with year of production.

I. H. C. BAILEY FULHAM	**BAILEY FULHAM**	**C.I.C. BAILEY FULHAM POTTERY LONDON**

This factory supplied industry with its stonewares, including shippers, brewers and chemists.

In addition to industrial products, works of art are latterly included from artists such as M.Cazin, late Director of the School of Arts, Tours, France. ***CAZIN, 1872, STUDY***

1872 Dublin Exhibition. Medal for stoneware and Terra-Cotta.

Mr. R.W. Martin (sculptor) student of the Royal Academy engaged as modeller and designer. ***R.W. MARTIN fecit***

1889- **Fulham Pottery & Cheavin Filter Co. Ltd.,**

STONEWARES.

1948 Impressed marks **FULHAM POTTERY
LONDON**

Continued over -

1864

1864 Bailey, C.I.C., Fulham Pottery, LONDON, England. (Cont`)

Present name: The Fulham Pottery Ltd.

HAND-TURNED RED-WARE POTTERY.
Current impressed marks

FULHAM • Est 1671 • POTTERY

MADE IN ENGLAND

FULHAM POTTERY

FULHAM POTTERY Est 1671

FULHAM POTTERY LONDON SW8

(Information by courtesy of Fulham Pottery Ltd., London, England.)

1864 Bingham, Edward, Art Pottery, CASTLE HEDINGHAM, England.

1864-1901 EARTHENWARES IN EARLY ENGLISH STYLES.

Pad in relief-

Incised signature- **E. BINGHAM**
CASTLE HEDINGHAM
ESSEX

c.1902 **Essex Art Pottery.** Incised mark- **ROYAL ESSEX ART POTTERY WORKS**

1864 Burgess, Henry, BURSLEM, Staffordshire, England.

1864-92 EARTHENWARES. Printed or impressed- under Royal Arms. **H. B.** **HENRY BURGESS**

1864 Corn, W.& E., LONGPORT, Staffordshire, England.

1864-1904 (Also at BURSLEM) Early wares are rarely marked.
EARTHENWARES. Factory`s initials are printed within marks of various patterns and designs.
1891 `England` added

W. & E. C.
W. E. C.

1864 Green, T.G., & Co.Ltd., CHURCH GRESLEY, Derbyshire, England.

A Mr. Leedham originally built this pottery in 1790 manufacturing coarse ware pans. Since then there has been a number of owners Mr T.G. Green taking over in 1864

c.1864 EARTHENWARES, STONEWARES. *No Record of early marks*

1888 Churh mark printed:

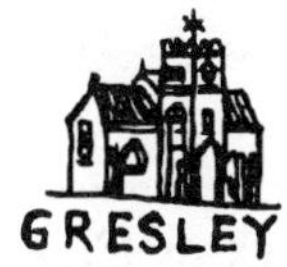

c.1892 Factory`s initials printed within `church` type marks - - **T. G. G. & Co. Ltd.**

20th Century. Factory`s name printed within marks of various patterns and designs. - - **T. G. GREEN & Co. Ltd.**

1968 **Freeman, P.H. acquired the factory from a London Finance Partnership after receivership in 1967.**

1987 **The Clover Leaf Group acquired the Company.**

(By kind permission of T.G. Green Ltd.,Member of The Clover Leaf Group England.)

1864 Robinson & Leadbeater, Ltd., STOKE, Staffordshire, England.

1864-1924 CHINA, PARIAN FIGURES, ETC., Impressed-
c.1905 `Ltd` added

c.1905-24 Printed mark with head of an elephant. - - -

1864 Selman, J.& W., TUNSTALL, Staffordshire, England.

c.1864-65 EARTHENWARE FIGURES, ETC., Impressed- **SELMAN**

1864 Shepherd & Co.,Alfred, LONGTON, Staffordshire, England.

1864-70 EARTHENWARES. Factory`s name printed within marks of various patterns and designs. **A. SHEPHERD & CO.**

1864

1864 Unwin, Mountford & Taylor, HANLEY, Staffordshire, England.

c.1864. EARTHENWARES. Factory's initials printed within marks of various patterns and designs. — **U. M. & T.**

c.1865-68 **Unwin, Holmes & Worthington.** Printed within marks of various patterns etc., — **U. H. & W.** / **UNWIN, HOLMES & WORTHINGTON.**

1864 Wayte & Ridge, LONGTON, Staffordshire, England.

c.1864 GENERAL CERAMICS, FIGURES, ETC., — **W. & R.** / **L.**

1864 Wileman, James & Charles, Foley China Works, FENTON, England.

1864-69 GENERAL CERAMICS. Factory's initials printed within marks of various patterns and designs. - - - — **J. & C. W.** / **J. F. & C. W.**

Charles J. Wileman mark- **C. J. W.**

J. Wileman & Co. mark- **J. W. & CO.**

1869-92 **Wileman, James F.,** printed within marks of various patterns and designs- — **J. F. W.** / **J. F. WILEMAN**

1892-1925 **Wileman & Co.,**

1925 Shelley Potteries - - see 1925 Shelley Potteries.

1864 Wilkinson & Wardle, Denaby Pottery, MEXBOROUGH, England.

1864-66 EARTHENWARES.

Printed or impressed-

1866-70 **Wardle & Co.,John,**

Printed-

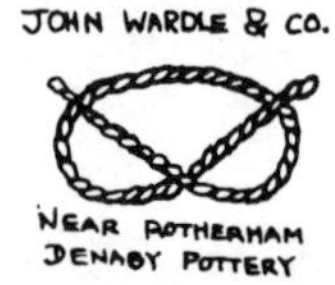

1864	Ficquenet, Charles, (flowers/pâte-sur-pâte) France.	see 1745 SÈVRES.
1864	Guillemain, (decorator) France. - - -	see 1745 SÈVRES.
1864	Hertwig & Co.,Germany. - - - - -	see 1762 KATZHÜTTE.
1864	Lambert, (flowers) France. - - -	see 1745 SÈVRES.
1864	Smith, Willoughby, WOMELSDORF, U.S.A. -	see 1784 Menner, J.,
1864	Watham, James B., FENTON, England. - -	see 1862 Watham & Lichfield.

1865 Ainsworth, W.H.& J.A., STOCKTON-ON-TEES, England.

1865-1901 EARTHENWARES.

Impressed mark- 

1865 Bevington,James & Thomas, HANLEY, Staffordshire, England.

1865-78 PORCELAIN. Impressed- **J. & T. B.**

1877-91 **Bevington, Thomas,** GENERAL CERAMICS. **T. B.**
Factory`s initials printed on marks of
various patterns and designs. - -

1892-99 **Hanley Porcelain Co.,** CHINA.
Printed- 

1899-1901 **Hanley China Co.,** - Printed- - - - 

1865 Bodley & Co.,Scotia Pottery, BURSLEM, Staffordshire, England.

1865 EARTHENWARES. - Printed- 

see 1863 Bodley & Harrold.

1865 Ford, Challinor & Co., Lion Works, TUNSTALL, Staffs, England.

1865-80 EARTHENWARES. Factory`s initials printed **F. C. & CO.**
within marks of various patterns and designs. **F. & C.**

1865 FRAUREUTH, Werdau, Saxony, Germany.

1865- **Fraureuth, Porzellanfabrik-** - -

1865 Hobson & Son, Charles, BURSLEM, Staffordshire, England.

1865-80 EARTHENWARES. Factory`s initials printed **C. H.**
or impressed within marks of various
patterns and designs.
c.1873-75 `& S` added - - **C. H. & S.**

1865

1865 Holdcroft, Joseph, LONGTON, Staffordshire, England.

1865-1939 GENERAL CERAMICS.

1865-1906 Printed or impressed -

1890-1931 Printed monogram on globe

c.1906 **Holdcroft Ltd.,**
Later-1940 **Cartwright & Edwards.**

1865 Jones & Co., Frederick, LONGTON, Staffordshire, England.

1865-86 EARTHENWARES. Factory's name is printed or impressed within marks of various patterns and designs. - **F. JONES LONGTON**

1865 Sutherland & Sons, Daniel, LONGTON, Staffordshire, England.

1865-75 MAJOLICA, PARIAN, STONEWARES.
Factory's initials impressed or printed- - **S. & S.**

1865 Tams & Lowe, LONGTON, Staffordshire, England.

1865-74 EARTHENWARES. Factory's initials printed - **T. & L.**
within marks of various patterns and designs.

1874-1930 **Lowe, William,** CHINA,
1874-1912 Printed or impressed, sometimes with crown -

1912-30 Factory's name or initials printed within marks of various patterns and designs.

W. L.
L.
W. LOWE
LONGTON

1865 Trenton Pottery Co., TRENTON, New Jersey, U.S.A.

1865- WHITE GRANITE. - Printed black- **T. P. Co.**
CHINA

1870- **Taylor, Goodwin & Co.**

1865 Turner, Hassall & Peake, STOKE, Staffordshire, England.

1865-69 EARTHENWARES, PARIAN, ETC., Factory's name or initials printed within marks of various patterns and designs. - **TURNER, HASSALL & PEAKE**
T. H. & P.

1865 Wood & Sons, Ltd., BURSLEM, Staffordshire, England.

1865- EARTHENWARES, IRONSTONES, ETC.,

Early wares unmarked.

1891-1907 - Printed-

WOOD & SONS

1907- Factory`s name printed within marks of various patterns and designs.
c.1907 `& Son(s) added
c.1910 `Ltd` added sometimes.

1930 - onwards marks-

1865	Archelais, France. - - - -	see 1745 SÈVRES.
1865	Célos, (decorator of pâte-sur-pâte) France. -	see 1745 SÈVRES.
1865	Clarke & Co.,Edward, BURSLEM, England. -	see 1857 Bridgwood & Clarke.
1865	Clementson Bros.,Ltd., HANLEY, England. -	see 1839 Clementson, Joseph.
1865	Lockhart & Co.,David, GLASGOW, Scotland. -	see 1855 Lockhart & Arthur.
1865	Norton, E.& L.P., BENNIGTON, U.S.A.- -	see 1793 Norton Pottery.
1865	Ott & Brewer, TRENTON, U.S.A. - -	see 1863 Bloor, Ott & Booth.
1865	Unwin,Holmes & Worthington, HANLEY, England.	see 1864 Unwin,Mountford & Taylor.
1865	Yates & Titus, TRENTON, U.S.A. - -	see 1859 Rhodes & Yates.

1866 Adams, William & Thomas, TUNSTALL, Staffordshire, England.

1866-92 EARTHENWARES. The Factory`s name printed within marks containing the Royal Arms and other emblems. - **W. & T. ADAMS. TUNSTALL**

1866 Bareuther & Co., WALDSASSEN, Bavaria, Germany.

1866- HARD-PASTE PORCELAIN. - -

1866

1866 Bishops Waltham Pottery, Hampshire, England.

1866-67 TERRA-COTTA. - Printed- **BISHOPS WALTHAM**

1867 Exhibited pottery and terra-cotta at the Paris Exhibition.

1866 Fischer, Emil, BUDAPEST, Hungary.

1866- HARD-PASTE PORCELAIN - -

1866 Hamann, Adolf, DRESDEN, Germany.

1866 DECORATOR IN MEISSEN STYLE. -

1866 Jackson & Gosling Ltd., LONGTON, Staffordshire, England.

1866- CHINA. The Factory`s initials are printed or impressed within marks of various patterns and designs. - - **J. & G.**

J. & G.
L.

1912+ - **GROSVENOR CHINA**

1866 Kennedy & Sons Ltd., Henry, GLASGOW, Scotland.

1866-1929 STONEWARES. - Trade mark-

1866 Milet & Fils, Paul, SÈVRES, France.

1866- ARTIST POTTERS,

1941- Céramique d`Art Milet. - -

1866 Pearce, Alfred B., Ludgate Hill, LONDON, England.

1866-1940 RETAILERS. - - Printed-

ALFRED B. PEARCE
39 LUDGATE HILL
LONDON

1866 Robertson, Alexander W., CHELSEA, Mass., U.S.A.

1866- **Chelsea Keramic Art Works.** C K A W

ANTIQUE AND ORIENTAL REPRODUCTIONS

1875-89 Impressed- **CHELSEA KERAMIC ART WORKS ROBERTSON & SONS.**

1891- **Chelsea Pottery U.S. (Incorporated)**

1891- Impressed-

1893- Impressed- - - -

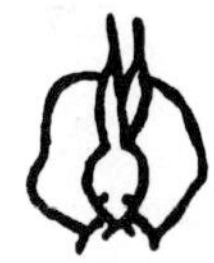

c.1896- **Factory moved to Dedham, Mass.**

Dedham Pottery, Printed or impressed-

1866 Walker & Carter, LONGTON, Staffordshire, England.

1866-72 EARTHENWARES. The Factory`s initials are printed within marks of various patterns and designs. Sometimes an Anchor. **W. & C.**

1872-89 Factory based at STOKE.

1866	Hallion, François, (gilder/decorator) France. -	see 1745 SÈVRES.
1866	Legay, (pâte-sur-pâte) France. - - -	see 1745 SÈVRES.
1866	Morgenroth & Co., Germany. - - -	see 1757 GOTHA.
1866	Tinworth, George, LAMBETH, England. -	see 1815 Royal Doulton.
1866	Wardle & Co.,John, MEXBOROUGH, England.	see 1864 Wilkinson & Wardle.

1867 Buchan, A.W., & Co.Ltd., PORTOBELLO, Scotland.

1867 STONEWARE

c.1920-39 Pattern names - **PORTOVASE CENOLITH**

1949 Thistle Pottery. Trade mark -

1972 Moved to Muthill Road, CRIEFF.

(By kind permission of A.W.Buchan & Co.Ltd., Comrie St., Crieff, Scotland.)

1867

1867 Cockson & Chetwynd, COBRIDGE, Staffordshire, England.

1867-75 EARTHENWARE. The Factory's name or initials are printed within marks of various patterns and designs.- - - **COCKSON & CHETWYND**
C. C. & CO.

1875-77 **Cockson & Seddon.** Printed with Royal Arms- **IMPERIAL IRONSTONE CHINA**
COCKSON & SEDDON

1877-86 **Birks Brothers & Seddon.** IRONSTONES. Printed with Royal Arms- **IMPERIAL IRONSTONE CHINA**
BIRKS BROS. & SEDDON

1867 Daniel & Cork, BURSLEM, Staffordshire, England.

1867-69 EARTHENWARES. - Printed- **DANIEL & CORK**

1867 Gelson Bros., HANLEY, Staffordshire, England.

1867-76 EARTHENWARES. Factory's name printed within marks of various patterns and designs. **GELSON BROS.**
HANLEY

1867 Haas & Czjzek, SCHLAGGENWALD, Bohemia, Germany.

1867-88 HARD-PASTE PORCELAIN. - -

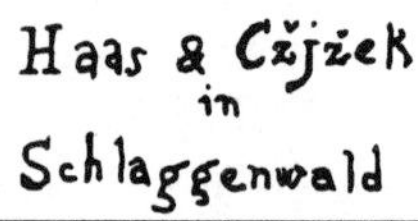

1867 Jäger, Wilhelm, EISENBERG, Thuringia, Germany.

1867- HARD-PASTE PORCELAIN. - -

1867 Jones Shepherd & Co., LONGTON, Staffordshire, England.

1867-68 EARTHENWARES. Factory's initials printed - within marks of various patterns and designs. **J. S. & Co.**

1868-72 **Jones, Josiah Ellis,** Printed- **J. E. J.**
JOSIAH ELLIS JONES

1867 Knapper & Blackhurst, TUNSTALL, Staffordshire, England.

1867-71 EARTHENWARES. The Factory's name and initials are printed or impressed within marks of various patterns and designs. 1883-88 Also at BURSLEM. **KNAPPER AND BLACKHURST**
K. & B.

1867 Phoenix Pottery, PHOENIXVILLE, PA. U.S.A.

Kaolin and Fire Brick Co.,

1867-72 FIREBRICK, YELLOW AND ROCKINGHAM WARES

1872-77 **Schreiber, W.A.H., and Betz, J.F.** - WALL DECORATION AND PARIAN WARE.

1877-79 **Beerbower, L.B., and Griffen, H.R.,** - WHITE GRANITE WARE.

Phoenix Pottery

1879-94 **Griffin, Smith & Hill, `Etruscan Majolica`**

Impressed monogram-

Impressed- **ETRUSCAN**

Other factory marks were used to identify the products. They were sometimes found alone on the pieces. The letter indicates the shape and the number indicates the decoration. i.e. -
A1, A2, etc. were impressed on butter plates with leaf or flower shapes.

The letter run from A to O :-

A1 B13 C4 D15 E14
F11 G2 H9 I3 J10
K8 L6 M5 N7 O12

1894- **Buckwalter, E.L., and Brownback, H.I., Chester Pottery Co., PA.**

1895-96 Printed black-

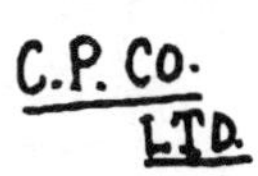

1902- **Tuxedo Pottery Co.** (No marks used)
1902- Closed.

1867

1867 Taylor & Kent Ltd., LONGTON, Staffordshire, England.

1867- PORCELAINS. Factory`s initials printed or impressed within marks of various patterns and designs.- -

T. & K.
L.

1939- Printed marks within various designs.
`KENT CHINA` `Elizabethan Fine Bone China`

TAYLOR & KENT

1867 Turner, Goddard & Co., TUNSTALL, Staffordshire, England.

1867-74 EARTHENWARES. Factory`s name printed within marks of various patterns and designs.

TURNER, GODDARD & CO.

1867 Wade Group of Potteries, BURSLEM, Staffordshire, England.

CERAMIC GIFTWARE AND COLLECTABLES.
The first Wade Company was founded in 1810 and over the years has developed into the progressive Company it is today.

1867 Wade Pottery, George,

EARTHENWARES. Manufacturing for the textile trade.

c.1900 **Hallen Pottery absorbed by this factory.**

1919- **George Wade & Son Ltd., (Private limited Co.)**

Various marks used by George Wade & Son Ltd:-

Mark Type 21
Circa Early 1930's-Late 1930's
Ink Stamp

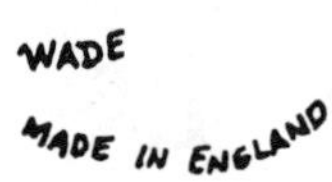

Mark Type 22
Circa Early 1930's-Late 1930's
Hand Painted Ink

Mark Type 21A
Late 1930's
Ink Stamp

Mark Type 20A
1931 - Mid 1930's
Ink Stamp

Mark Type 23
Circa 1939
Ink Stamp

Mark Type 23A
1947+
Ink Stamp

Mark Type 25
1957-1981
Molded

Mark Type 24
1958+
Molded

Mark Type 26
1959+
Molded

Mark Type 27A
Mid 1980's
Transfer

Continued over -

1867 Wade Group of Potteries, BURSLEM, Staffs, England. (Cont`)

1927- **Wade Ltd., Albert J., (George Wade`s brother.) incorporated as a Private limited Co.**

Wades'
England

Mark Type 0
Late 1900's - Mid 1920's
Ink Stamp

WADES
ENGLAND

Mark Type 1
Mid 1920's-1927
Ink Stamp

WADES
ORCADIA
WARE
BRITISH MADE

Mark Type 1A
Mid 1920's-1927
Ink Stamp

1927- **Wade Heath & Co.Ltd., formed.**
EARTHENWARES.

WADEHEATH
ENGLAND

Mark Type 2
1928-1937
Ink Stamp

WADEHEATH
ORCADIA
WARE
BRITISH MADE

Mark Type 2A
1928-1934
Ink Stamp

WADEHEATH
BY PERMISSION
WALT DISNEY
ENGLAND

Mark Type 2C
Mid 1930's - Late 1930's
Ink Stamp

WADEHEATH WARE
BY PERMISSION
WALT DISNEY
MICKEYMOUSE
LTD
MADE IN ENGLAND

Mark Type 2D
1934 - Late 1930's
Ink Stamp

Flaxman Ware
Hand Made Pottery
BY WADEHEATH
ENGLAND

Mark Type 4
Circa 1936
Ink Stamp

Wadeheath
Ware
England

Mark Type 5
Circa 1937
Ink Stamp

FLAXMAN
WADE
HEATH
ENGLAND

Mark Type 6
Circa 1937-1938
Ink Stamp

WADEHEATH
B
ENGLAND

Mark Type 3
1939-1942
Ink Stamp

WADE
HEATH
ENGLAND

Mark Type 7
Circa 1938-1950
Ink Stamp

WADE
HEATH
ENGLAND

Mark Type 8
Circa 1938-1950
Ink Stamp

c.1950 **Wade Heath & Co.Ltd., and Reginald Corfield (Sales) Ltd.,**

7/8"
3/4"
WADE
Regicor
LONDON
ENGLAND

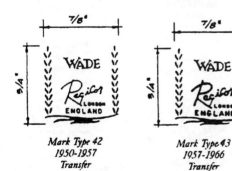

Mark Type 42
1950-1957
Transfer

7/8"
3/4"
WADE
Regicor
LONDON
ENGLAND

Mark Type 43
1957-1966
Transfer

(NOTE: MARK 43 SIMILAR TO MARK 42 BUT HEAVIER LETTERING.)

WADE
Regicor
HAND PAINTED
IN STAFFORDSHIRE
ENGLAND

Mark Type 43A
Circa Early - Mid 1960's
Transfer

5/8"
3/8"
WADE
Regicor
LONDON
ENGLAND

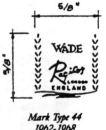

Mark Type 44
1962-1968
Transfer

REGINALD CORFIELD LIMITED
REDHILL · SURREY
WADE
Regicor
ENGLAND

Mark Type 45
1968-1970
Transfer

Continued over -

1867

1867 Wade Group of Potteries, BURSLEM, Staffs, England. (Cont`)

1935- Colonel G.A.Wade (George Wade`s son) later to become Sir George Wade, inherits control of A.J. Wade Ltd., and Wade Heath & Co.Ltd., forming a public company:- Wade Potteries Plc.

WADE
ENGLAND

Mark Type 10
Circa Late 1940's
Ink Stamp

WADE
ENGLAND

Mark Type 15
Circa 1947-1953
Ink Stamp

"HARVEST" WARE
WADE
ENGLAND

Mark Type 13
Circa 1947-Early 1950's
Ink Stamp

WADE
Bramble
ENGLAND

Mark Type 12
Circa 1950-1955
Ink Stamp

WADE
MADE IN
ENGLAND
HAND PAINTED

Mark Type 16
Circa 1953+
Transfer

ROYAL VICTORIA
WADE
ENGLAND
POTTERY

Mark Type 17
Circa 1953+
Transfer

WADE
"FESTIVAL"
ENGLAND

Mark Type 18
Circa 1953+
Transfer

WADE
ENGLAND

Mark Type 19
Circa 1953+
Transfer
(George Wade & Son Ltd. Also Used This Mark From Circa 1953 On.

1935- George Wade & Son Ltd., remain autonomous.

1950- Wade (Ulster) Ltd., Portadown, N.Ireland. founded.

Mark Type 27C
Circa 1950+
Ink Stamp

Irish Porcelain
MADE IN IRELAND

Mark Type 28
1953+
Impressed

Shamrock Pottery
made in Ireland

Mark Type 31
Mid 1950's+
Molded

Irish Porcelain
T
MADE IN IRELAND

Mark Type 32
1955
Impressed

Celtic
Porcelain
by Wade
Ireland

Mark Type 34
Mid 1960's
Molded

Irish
Porcelain
by Wade
Ireland
DESIGN BY

Mark Type 33
1962
Molded

MADE IN
A.S.Cooper
IRELAND

Mark Type 39
1965-1968
Impressed

AN RK PRODUCT
WADE
OF IRELAND

Mark Type 32A
Circa - Early 1960's - 1967
Transfer

Continued over -

1867 Wade Group of Potteries, BURSLEM, Staffs, England. (Cont`)

1958- **A.J.Wade Ltd., Wade Heath & Co.Ltd., George Wade and Son Ltd. and Wade (Ulster) Ltd., combined to form the public company, The Wade Group of Potteries, which is still controlled by the Wade family.**

Mark Type 27B
1990+
Transfer

Mark Type 20
1985+
Transfer

Wade Potteries produce special advertising ceramics for many varied companies, below are just a few backstamps:-

1966- **Wade (Ireland) Ltd., changed from Wade (Ulster) Ltd.**

Mark Type 35
1970
Impressed

Mark Type 36
1973
Impressed

Mark Type 40
1977+
Molded

Mark Type 41
1980+
Molded
&
Transfer

Mark Type 41A
1991
Ink Stamp

1969- **Wade (P.D.M.) Ltd., P.D.M. means Point of sale,** Design and Marketing. specializing to the drinks and tobacco industry.

Mark Type 46
1970-1980
Transfer

Mark Type 47
1980+
Transfer

Mark Type 49
1990+
Transfer

1990- **Beauford Plc. acquird The Wade Group of Potteries.**

1990- **Seagoe Ltd., changed from Wade (Ireland) Ltd.,**

(By Courtesy of The Wade Group of Potteries Plc., England.
and the Wade Collectors Club, Royal Victoria Pottery, Westport Rd. Burslem, ST6 4AG)

1867/68

1867 Watcombe Pottery Co., ST.MARY CHURCH, Sth. Devon, England.

1867-1901 EARTHENWARES AND GENERAL POTTERY. - **WATCOMBE TORQUAY**

1867- Impressed marks- **WATCOMBE POTTERY**

1875-1901 Printed-

1901 **Merged with Royal Aller Vale** see 1868 Phillips & Co., John,

---

1867 Powell & Bishop, HANLEY, England. - - see 1851 Livesley Powell & Co.

1868 Bates & Bennett, COBRIDGE, Staffordshire, England.

1868-95 EARTHENWARES. The Factory`s initials are printed or impressed within marks of various patterns and designs. - **B. & B.**

1868 Booth & Co.,Thomas, BURSLEM, Staffordshire, England.

1868-72 EARTHENWARES. Factory`s initials are printed within marks of various patterns and designs. - - **T. B. & CO.**

1872-76 **Booth & Son, Thomas, TUNSTALL.** Marks within various patterns and designs. **T. B. & S.**

1876-83 **Booth, Thomas G.,** - Printed-

1883-91 **Booth, T.G.& F.** Printed within marks of various patterns and designs. - **T. G. & F. B.**

1891-1948 **Booths Limited.**

1891-1906 - Printed mark- -

1905- Earthenware reproductions of old Worcester porcelain. Painted or printed-

c.1906 Printed mark, sometimes with `England` -

Continued over -

1868 Booth & Co., Thomas, BURSLEM, Staffordshire, England. (Cont`)

1912 Printed mark-

1930-48 Marks with full name or initials -

1868 Jeffords & Co., J.E., PHILADELPHIA, PA, U.S.A.

1868 EARTHENWARES. Much of this Factory`s wares are unmarked and are reproductions of earlier antique pieces.

1876 Philadelphia Exhibition.
Exhibited yellow, Rockingham, majolica and lava wares.

1868 KÖRMÖCZBANYA (Kremnice) Hungary.

Mid-19th century. GENERAL EARTHENWARE -

20th Century. Kossuch, János. -

1868 Mercer Pottery Co., TRENTON, New Jersey, U.S.A.

1868- **Moses, James,** SEMI-PORCELAIN.

MERCER POTTERY
TRENTON, N.J.

The Double Shield mark was also used by:-
Carr & Clark, and Burgess & Campbell.

1868

1868 Phillips & Co., John, Aller Pottery, NEWTON ABBOT, England.

1868-87 EARTHENWARES. Printed or impressed-

1887-1901 **Aller Vale Art Potteries,** Impressed- **ALLER VALE**

c.1901-62 **Royal Aller Vale & Watcombe Pottery Co.**
Torquay, Devon. Printed or impressed-

ROYAL ALLER VALE
DEVON MOTTO
WARE
ROYAL
TORQUAY
POTTERY

see 1867 Watcombe Pottery Co.

1868 Rieber & Co., Josef, MITTERTEICH, Bavaria, Germany.

1868- HARD-PASTE PORCELAIN.

1868 Steinmann, K., TIEFENFURT, Silesia, Germany.

1868-1932 HARD-PASTE PORCELAIN.

1868 Taylor, Tunnicliffe & Co.,Ltd., HANLEY, Staffordshire, England.

1868- GENERAL CERAMICS. Factory`s initials are printed within marks of various patterns and designs.- - **T. T.**
T. T. & CO.

Monogram included in some marks- -

1868 Thompson & Co., C.C., EAST LIVERPOOL, Ohio, U.S.A.

1868 POTTERY.
1876 Centennial Pottery
1889 **Thompson Pottery Co., C.C.**
CREAM-COLOURED AND DECORATED ROCKINGHAM AND YELLOW WARES.

Toilet services pattern marks - -

SYDNEY
LELAND
OREGON

Dinner ware pattern marks. - -

MELROSE
DREXEL

1868 Tomkinson & Billington, LONGTON, Staffordshire, England.

1868-70 EARTHENWARES. Factory`s initials printed - within marks of various patterns and designs. **T. & B.**

1868 Whittingham, Ford & Co., BURSLEM, Staffordshire, England.

1868-73 EARTHENWARES. Factory`s initials printed - within marks of various patterns and designs. **W. F. & CO.**

1868	Greenwood Pottery Co., TRENTON, U.S.A. -	see 1861 Stephens, Tams & Co.
1868	Hawley Bros.,Ltd., ROTHERHAM, England. -	see 1863 Hawley, W.& G.
1868	Jones, Josiah Ellis, LONGTON, England. -	see 1867 Jones, Shepherd & Co.

1869 Bevington & Co., John, HANLEY, Staffordshire, England.

1869-71 EARTHENWARES. Initials are printed within marks of various patterns and designs. **J. B. & Co.**
H.

1869 Clark, Henry, CHEAM, Surrey, England. **HENRY CLARK**

1869-80 EARTHENWARES. Impressed or incised- **CHEAM POTTERY**

1869 Grosvenor & Son, F.,GLASGOW, Scotland.

c.1869-1926 EARTHENWARES.

1879-1926 Printed Eagle trade-mark- -

c.1899- `& Son` added - - **GROSVENOR & SON**

1869 Heintschel, J. E., FRIEDLAND, Bohemia, Germany. **J. E. H.**

1869- HARD-PASTE PORCELAIN. **F.**

1869 Klemm, Karl R., DRESDEN, Germany.

1869- DECORATOR IN THE STYLE OF MEISSEN. Marks printed black usually -

1869 Maddock, Thomas, TRENTON, New Jersey, U.S.A.

1869- EARTHENWARE. - - -
1876- **Astbury & Maddock.**
c.1879- **Maddock & Sons, Thomas,**

Dinner ware mark -

Sanitary ware mark - - -

1869

1869 New Jersey Pottery Co., TRENTON, New Jersey, U.S.A.

1869- CREAM-COLOURED AND WHITE GRANITE WARES.

Printed black-

1883- **Union Pottery Co.**

1869 North British Pottery, James Miller & Co,, GLASGOW, Scotland.

1869-75 EARTHENWARES. Factory`s initials are printed within marks of various patterns and designs. - - - **J. M. & CO.** **I. M. & CO.** **J. M. CO.**

1869 Rye Pottery, Bellevue Pottery, RYE, Sussex, England.

1869- POTTERY. ***Early wares unmarked.***

c.1885-c.1910 - **SUSSEX WARE**

c.1869-c.1920 **`Sussex Rustic Ware`** mark - -

c.1920-39 **`Sussex Art Ware`** mark - - -

1939-45 **Closed during war years.**

1947- **Cole, J.C., and Cole, W.V.,** - -

1957 Walter V. Cole mark - -

(Rye Pottery, Ferry Road, Rye, are still producing pottery today [1995])

1869 Wood & Pigott, TUNSTALL, Staffordshire, England.

1869-71 EARTHENWARES. Initials printed within marks of various patterns and designs. - **W. & P.**

1869 Wood, Son & Co., COBRIDGE, Staffordshire, England.

1869-79 EARTHENWARES, IRONSTONES. Printed under Royal Arms. **WOOD, SON & CO.**

1869	Bühl & Söhne, Thuringia, Germany. -	see 1778 GOSZBREITENBACH.
1869	Clauss, Eugène-Marx, PARIS, France. -	see 1773 Porcelain de Paris.
1869	Emberton, T.I. & J., TUNSTALL, England.	see 1851 Emberton. Wm.
1869	Hulse & Adderley, LONGTON, England.	see 1853 Hulse, Nixon & Adderley.
1869	Mitchell, F.& H., RYE, England.- -	see 1807 Cadborough Pottery.
1869	Wileman, James F., FENTON, England. -	see 1864 Wileman, J.& C.

1870 Adams & Co., Harvey, LONGTON, Staffordshire, England.

1870-85 CHINA AND EARTHENWARES. - Printed- **H. A. & Co.**

1870 Bates Elliott & Co., Dale Hall, BURSLEM, Staffordshire, England.

1870-75 GENERAL CERAMICS. Factory`s initials are printed within marks of various patterns. - **B. E. & Co.**

Factory`s Trade mark -

1875-78 **Bates Walker & Co.,** - - **B. W. & Co.**
Printed within various patterns and designs- **BATES WALKER & CO.**

1878-81 **Bates, Gildea & Walker** - - **B. G. & W.**
Printed within various patterns and designs.

1881-85 **Gildea & Walker,** EARTHENWARES. - **G. & W.**
Printed within various patterns and designs.
Mark with month and year. Impressed- - **GILDEA & WALKER**
4
83

Factory`s Trade mark

1885-88 **Gildea, James,** EARTHENWARES.
Initials printed within marks of various patterns and designs including Trade-mark - **J. G.**

1870 Balaam, W., Rope Lane Pottery, IPSWICH, Suffolk, England.

1870-81 SLIPWARES. Impressed- **W. BALAAM**
ROPE LANE POTTERY
IPSWICH

1870

1870 Collingwood & Greatbatch, LONGTON, Staffordshire, England.

1870-87 PORCELAIN.

Printed or impressed-

C & G

1887-1957 Collingwood Bros. Ltd.

1887-1900 Impressed- **COLLINGWOOD**

1887-1900 Printed with Crown **C. B. L**

COLLINGWOOD
MADE IN
ENGLAND

1912-24 Factory`s name or initials printed within marks of various designs -

1924-57 Various marks printed with the name, `COLLINGWOOD` **COLLINGWOOD**

1870 Crocker, W.H., BIDEFORD, Devonshire, England.

1870- EARTHENWARES - impressed- **W.H. CROCKER BIDEFORD**

1870 Hollinshead & Kirkham Ltd., TUNSTALL, Staffordshire, England.

1870-1956 EARTHENWARES. Factory`s initials are printed or impressed within various designs. - **H. & K.** / **H. & K. TUNSTALL**

c.1890 Wedgwood & Co.,Unicorn Pottery taken over. - **H. & K. LATE WEDGWOOD**

1900-24 - Printed- - - -

1924-56 - Printed-

1933-56 - Printed- - -

1956 Johnson Bros. (Hanley) Ltd. acquired Factory.

1870 Jackson & Co.,J., ROTHERHAM, Yorkshire, England.

1870-87 EARTHENWARES. Factory`s initials are printed within marks of various patterns and designs. - - - **J. J. & CO.** **J. & CO.**

1887-1948 **Shaw & Sons Ltd., George,** Printed- **G. S. & S.**
Within various patterns and designs.

1870 Matthews, John, WESTON-SUPER-MARE, Avon, England.

1870-88 TERRA-COTTA. Impressed mark under Royal Arms. -

JOHN MATTHEWS
LATE PHILLIPS
ROYAL POTTERY
WESTON-SUPER-MARE

1870 Moehling, M. J., AICH, nr. Karlsbad, Bohemia, Germany.

c.1870 HARD-PASTE PORCELAIN. -

1870 Murray & Co. Ltd., W.F., Caledonian Pottery, GLASGOW, Scotland.

1870-98 GENERAL CERAMICS. - - -

Lion rampant, Impressed or printed-

1870 Okazaki, YAMASHIRO, Japan.

1870- RAKU WARE. Usually marked `Kagura`- -
Made by Bunzaburo.

1870 Pearson Ltd., James, BRAMPTON, Derbyshire, England.

19th century-1939 STONEWARES, ETC., ***Early wares not marked.***

1907- Impressed or printed- **J. P. LTD.**

1920- Trade name, written- **Bramfield Ware.**

1939 **Merged with Pearson & Co. (Chesterfield) Ltd.** see 1805 Pearson & Co.

1870 Pellatt & Wood, Baker St., LONDON, England.

c.1870-90 RETAILERS. Printed- **PELLATT & WOOD**

1870 Reeves, James, FENTON, Staffordshire, England.

1870-1948 EARTHENWARES. Factory`s name and initials printed or impressed within marks of various patterns and designs. -

J. R.

J. R.
F.

J, REEVES

see 1862 Wathen & Lichfield.

1870/71

1870 Risler & Cie., FREIBERG, Germany.

c.1870- HARD-PASTE PORCELAIN (BUTTONS) - - R & C

1870 Scrivener & Co.,R.G., HANLEY, Staffordshire, England.

1870-83 GENERAL CERAMICS. Factory's initials printed or impressed within marks of various patterns and designs. - **R. G. S.** / **R. G. S. & CO.**

1883-1916 Pointon & Co.,Ltd. Printed mark- 1891 'England' added. - -

Impressed mark- **POINTON**

1870 VALLAURIS, France.

c.1870 **Massier, Clement & Jerome, at Golfe Juan**
ARTIST POTTERS.

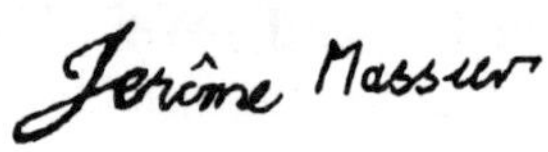

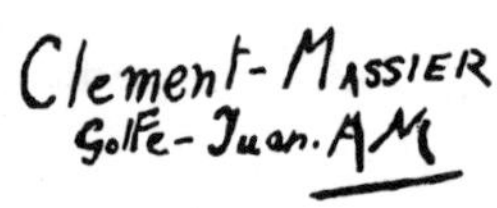

Levy, Lucien, ARTIST AND DESIGNER. - - - L LEVY

1870 Wood & Baggaley, BURSLEM, Staffordshire, England.

1870-80 EARTHENWARES. Factory's initials printed - within marks of various patterns and designs. Sometimes with bee-hive mark. **W. & B.**

1880-86 **Baggaley, Jacob,** Impressed- **J. B.**

1870 Hallion, Eugène (landscapes) France. - - see 1745 SÈVRES.
1870 Knowles, Taylor & Knowles, U.S.A. - - see 1854 Knowles & Harvey.
1870 Magrini & Co., Italy. - - - - see 1520 PESARO.
1870 Signoret, France. - - - - see 1589 NEVERS.
1870 Skinner & Walker, STOCKTON-ON-TEES, England. see 1825 Smith, William,
1870 Solon, Marc Louis, (Pâte-sur-pâte) STOKE, England. see 1793 Minton.
1870 Taylor, Goodwin & Co., TRENTON, U.S.A. - see 1865 Trenton Pottery Co.
1870 Thompson, Greenland, MORGANTOWN, U.S.A. see 1785 Thompson, James,

1871 Baehr & Proeschild, OHRDRUF, Thuringia, Germany.

1871- HARD-PASTE PORCELAIN, - -
Dolls and dolls' heads, etc.

1871 Bloch, B., EICHWALD, Bohemia, Germany.

1871- GENERAL CERAMICS. - - - **Eichwald**

1871 Cazin, Charles, FULHAM, London, England.

1871-74 STONEWARES. - -
Designer for C.I.C. Bailey`s at Fulham.

see 1864 Bailey, C.I.C.,

1871 Edge, Malkin & Co. Ltd., BURSLEM, Staffordshire, England.

1871-1903 EARTHENWARES. - Impressed- **EDGE, MALKIN & CO.**

Factory`s initials are printed within marks of various patterns and designs. - **E. M. & CO. B.**
1899 `Ltd` added.

1904-10 **Dean, S.W.** - Printed -

1910-19 **Deans (1910) Ltd.,** Printed - **DEANS (1910) LTD. BURSLEM ENGLAND**

see 1846 Cork & Edge

1871 Furnival & Sons, Thomas, COBRIDGE, Staffordshire, England.

1871-90 EARTHENWARES. Monogram marks, Printed-

1890- **Furnivals Ltd.,**
1890-95 Factory`s name is found within - marks of various patterns and designs. **FURNIVALS ENGLAND**

1871

1871 Furnival & Sons, Thomas, COBRIDGE, England. (Cont`)

1890-1910 Anchor and dagger trade-mark

1895 `Ltd` added.

1895-1913 Factory`s name within marks of various designs. — **FURNIVALS, LTD. ENGLAND**

1913- `1913` added to mark- **FURNIVALS (1913) LTD.**

1967 Barratt`s of Staffordshire acquired Factory.
1968 Closed Factory.

1871 Goebel, W., Porzellanfabrik, RODENTAL, Germany.

1871- CERAMIC FIGURES. (`M.I. HUMMEL` & COLLECTABLES)
Founders: Franz Detleff Goebel and son William. Originally, the company produced slates, slate pencils and toy marbles, but soon expanded into ceramics. In the early 20th century F.& W. Goebel Company introduced porcelain figurines.

1909-Franz Detleff Goebel died. William (son) took over and expanded the Company through export markets.

1929 Franz Goebel, his mother Frida, and brother-in-law Dr. Eugen Stocke. took direction of the Company. Great strides were taken to improve the production facilities of the Company.

1968 Wilhelm Goebel and Ulrich Stocke head the company as general partners.

1995 General partners: Wilhelm Goebel, Ulrich Stocke, Christian Goebel, Detlev Stocke, who represent the 5th and 6th family generation.

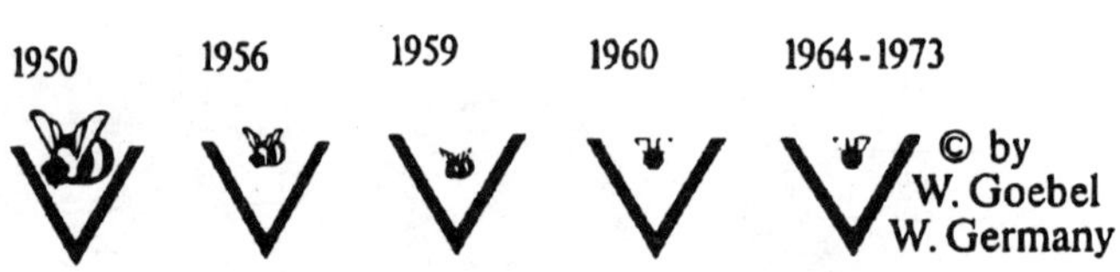

The above marks are for all Goebel products

Continued over -

1871 Goebel, W., Porzellanfabrik, RODENTAL, Germany. (Cont`)

1935 **Sister M.I. Hummel`s sketches were introduced to make figurines.**
The marks below are for `M.I. Hummel` products and in general bear one of the following trademarks.

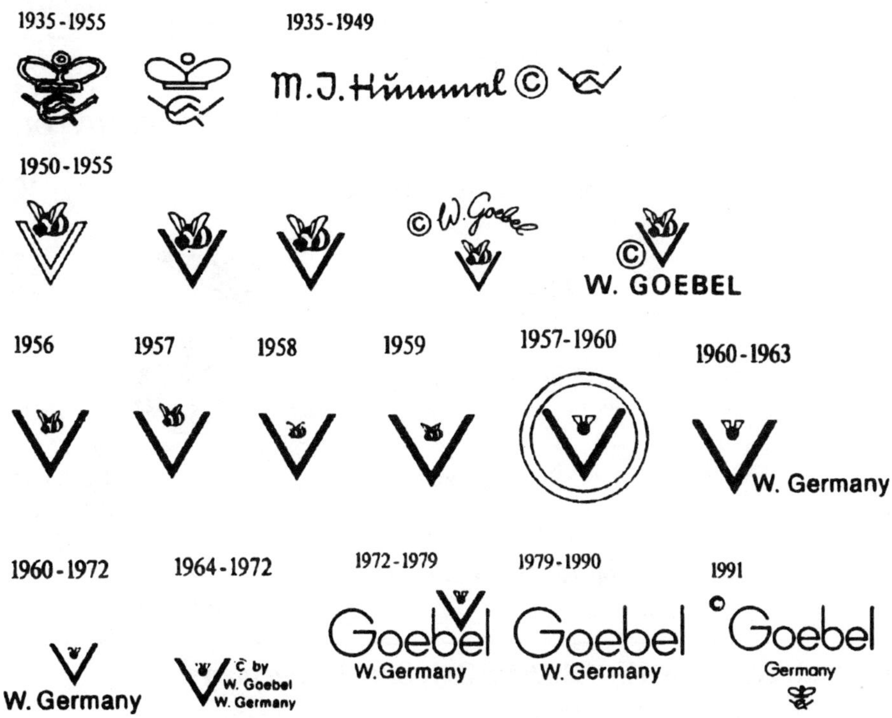

(Courtesy of W. Goebel Porzellanfabrik, Germany.)

1871 Grove & Stark, LONGTON, Staffordshire, England.

1871-85 EARTHENWARES. Factory`s initials are printed within marks of various patterns and designs. - - - G. & S.

Printed and impressed- **GROVE & STARK LONGTON**

c.1880-c.85 Monogram impressed- - -

1871 Krug, Fritz, LAUF-PEGNITZ, Frankonia, Bavaria, Germany.

1871- TERRA-COTTA, PORCELAIN. - -

1871

1871 Onondaga Pottery Co., SYRACUSE, New York, U.S.A.

1871- WHITE GRANITE WARE.

1874-93 New York State Arms mark - -

1886-98 `Semi-Vitreous` mark - -

O. P. CO.
CHINA
SEMI-VITREOUS

1890-93 `Imperial Geddo` mark on china - - -

1893-95 - -

1895-97 Globe mark -

1897- `Syracuse China`-

O. P. CO.
SYRACUSE
CHINA

c.1900- Mrs Alsop-Robineau, Adelaide.
(decorator) - - - - - **A-R**

1871 Pohl, Gebr., SCHMIEDEBERG, Silesia, Germany.

1871- HARD-PASTE PORCELAIN. - -

1871 Poole & Unwin, LONGTON, Staffordshire, England.

1871-76 EARTHENWARES, ETC. Printed or impressed- **P. & U.**
Sometimes in diamond shape.

1877-1926 **Unwin & Co., Joseph,** Moulded in relief- **UNWIN**
1891 `& Co.` added.

1871 Taft & Co., J.S., Hampshire Pottery, KEENE, N. Hampshire, U.S.A.

1871- EARTHENWARE, MAJOLICA.
Mainly souvenir pieces for summer resorts.
Usually printed red-

1871 Wardle & Co. Ltd., HANLEY, Staffordshire, England.

1871-1910 EARTHENWARES, PARIAN, MAJOLICA, ETC.

1871- Impressed mark- WARDLE
1891 `England` added.

c.1885-90 Printed mark- -

c.1890-1935 Printed mark- -

1910-24 **Wardle Art Pottery Co. Ltd.** - - WARDLE ART POTTERY CO. LTD.
Branch of A.J. Robinson. STOKE.
1924-35 Branch of Cauldon Potteries Ltd. SHELTON.

1871 Wood & Clarke, BURSLEM, Staffordshire, England.

c.1871-72 EARTHENWARES. Printed within pattern-

W. & C.

1873-78 **Withinshaw, W. E.** Factory`s initials or name are printed or impressed within marks of various patterns and designs. W. E. W. / W.E. WITHINSHAW

1871	Barlow, Arthur B., LAMBETH, England. - -	see 1815 Royal Doulton
1871	Barlow, Hannah B., LAMBETH, England. - -	see 1815 Royal Doulton
1871	Ford, Thomas, HANLEY, England. - - -	see 1854 Ford, T.& C.,
1871	Third Republic, France. - - - - - -	see 1745 SÈVRES.
1871	Yates, Bennett & Allen, TRENTON, U.S.A. - -	see 1859 Rhodes & Yates.

1872 Alboth & Kaiser GmbH & Co. KG., STAFFELSTEIN, Germany.

PORCELAIN IN TABLEWARE, GIFTWARE AND FIGURINES.

1872- **Alboth, August, COBURG,**
Designer and decorator.

1899- **Alboth, Ernst, (son) KRONACH, Bavaria.**
Founded a small factory.
1908- August Alboth dies.

1922- **Kaiser, Georg, marries Erna Alboth**
Georg Kaiser becomes partner.

Continued over -

1872

1872 Alboth & Kaiser GmbH & Co. KG. Germany. (Cont`)

1925- **Willy Alboth (son of Ernst) joins the company.**
1927- Ernst Alboth dies.

1927 **`Alka-Kunst`** new trade-mark introduced. `Al` for Alboth, `ka` for Kaiser, `Kunst` means `art` in German.

1935-38 marks -

1935

1938

1938- **Silbermann Bros. (founded in 1804 by Felix Peter Silbermann) acquired.**

1940-47 marks -

1940

1947

1945- **Hubertus Kaiser (son of Georg) joins the company.**

1948-55 marks -

1948

1955

1953- **New modern factory built in Staffelstein.**
1964- Georg Kaiser dies.

1958-60 marks

1958

1960

1964 **Ernst Alboth (son of Willy) joins the company.**

1967-70 marks -

1967

1970

1970- **`Alka` trade-mark changed to `Kaiser Porcelain`**
1991- Willy Alboth dies.

1993- **Hubertus Alboth (son of Ernst) joins the company.**
Modern mark (1995)-

(By kind permission of Alboth & Kaiser GmbH & Co. KG. Staffelstein. Germany.)

1872 Bevington, John, HANLEY, Staffordshire, England.

1872-92 PORCELAIN. Painted mark-

Printed marks above `Royal Arms` - Reproductions of old Dresden, Derby, etc.,

JOHN BEVINGTON
KENSINGTON WORKS
HANLEY, STAFFS

1872 Blackhurst, Jabez, TUNSTALL, Staffordshire, England.

1872-83 EARTHENWARES. Factory`s name printed - **JABEZ BLACKHURST**
within marks of various patterns and designs.

1872 Britton & Son, Richard, LEEDS, W. Yorkshire, England.

1872-78 EARTHENWARES. Factory`s initials are - **R. B. & S**
printed within marks of various patterns and designs. - -

1872 Brough & Blackhurst, LONGTON, Staffordshire, England.

1872-95 EARTHENWARES. Factory`s name is printed or impressed within marks of various patterns and designs. 1891 `England` added sometimes.

BROUGH &
BLACKHURST

1872 Brownhills Pottery Co., TUNSTALL, Staffordshire, England.

1872-96 EARTHENWARES. Factory`s initials printed or impressed within marks of various patterns and designs. 1891 `England` added

B. P. CO.

c.1880-96 Printed-

1897-1904 Salt Bros. Impressed or printed-

SALT BROS.
TUNSTALL
ENGLAND

Acquired by T. Till & Sons.

1872 CANNETO, Mantova, Italy.

1872- **Ceramica Furga.** HARD-PASTE PORCELAIN.

1872

1872 Clokie & Masterman, CASTLEFORD, W.Yorkshire, England.

1872-87 EARTHENWARES. Factory`s initials and name are printed or impressed within marks of various patterns and designs.

C. & M.
CLOKIE & MASTERMAN

1888-1961 Clokie & Co. Ltd., Printed- **CLOKIE & CO.**

1872 Craven, Dunhill & Co, JACKFIELD, Shropshire, England.

1872-1951 ENCAUSTIC AND GEOMETRICAL TILES
Formerly owned by Hargreaves & Craven.

HARGREAVES
&
CRAVEN

According to `Jewitt` `The quality of the tiles is remarkably good - Many of the patterns are of extreme beauty and excellence`

CRAVEN
& CO

Marks impressed on the back of the tiles:-

CRAVEN DUNHILL & CO	**CRAVEN**	**HARGREAVES CRAVEN**
LIMITED	**DUNHILL & CO**	**DUNHILL & CO**
JACKFIELD	**JACKFIELD**	**JACKFIELD**
Nr. IRONBRIDGE, SALOP	**SALOP**	**Nr. IRONBRIDGE SALOP**

1872 De Morgan, William, FULHAM, London, England.

c.1872-1907 EARTHENWARES. DECORATOR.
Early wares were decorated from blanks from other potters.

c.1880-82 Impressed mark-

c.1882- Impressed mark-
1888 `& Co.` added.

1882-88 Merton Abbey mark
Impressed or painted-

1888-97 Sands End Pottery Partnership with Halsey Ricardo.

Continued over -

1872 De Morgan, William, FULHAM, London, England. (Cont`)

1898-1907 **Partnership with Frank Iles, Charles and Fred Passenger at Fulham.**

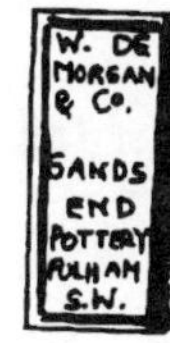

Initial marks used by individual decorators-

Fred Passenger -	-	**F. P.**
Charles Passenger-	-	**C. P.**
Joe Juster-	-	**J. J.**
J. Hersey-	-	**J. H.**

1907-11 **Passenger, Charles and Fred continued decorating after De Morgan retired in 1907.**

1872 Donath & Co., DRESDEN, Germany.

1872- DECORATOR IN MEISSEN STYLE.

1872 Hammersley & Asbury, LONGTON, Staffordshire, England.

1872-75 EARTHENWARES. Factory`s initials are printed within marks of various patterns and designs, sometimes with the Prince of Wales crest. - **H. & A.**

1875-1925 **Asbury & Co.,Edward,** Printed Trade mark-

ASBURY
LONGTON

1875-1925 Factory`s initials are printed - within marks of various patterns and designs- **A & CO.**

1872 Jaeger & Co., MARKTREDWITZ, Bavaria, Germany.

1872- HARD-PASTE PORCELAIN. - -

1872 Lake & Son Ltd.,W.H., Chapel Hill Pottery, TRURO, England.

1872- EARTHENWARES. Printed or impressed- **LAKE`S CORNISH POTTERY TRURO**

1872

1872 Moore & Co., FENTON, Staffordshire, England.

1872-92 EARTHENWARES. Initials printed or impressed within marks of various patterns and designs. - - **M. & CO.**

1892-96 **Moore, Leason & Co.** Impressed or printed within various marks. - - **M. L. & CO.**

1872 Moore Bros., LONGTON, Staffordshire, England.

1872-1905 PORCELAINS. Printed or impressed- **MOORE**

Impressed- **MOORE BROS.**

c.1880- Printed-
c.1891 `England` added

1891-1905 Impressed- **MOORE BROTHERS ENGLAND**

1902-05 Printed-

1905- **Continued by Bernard Moore.** - - see 1905 Moore, Bernard,

1872 Pratt & Co. Ltd.,John, FENTON, Staffordshire, England.

1872-78 EARTHENWARES. Printed within various patterns- **J. P. & CO. (L)**

1872 Vodrey`s Pottery, DUBLIN, Ireland.

1872-c.85 EARTHENWARES. Impressed- **VODREY DUBLIN POTTERY**

1872 Voigt, Hermann, SCHAALA, Thuringia, Germany.

1872- HARD AND SOFT-PASTE PORCELAIN. - -

1872	Booth & Son, Thomas, TUNSTALL, England. -	see 1868 Booth & Co.,T.
1872	Bracquemond, Felix, LIMOGES, France. -	see 1853 Haviland & Co.
1872	Britton & Sons, Richard, England. - -	see 1760 LEEDS POTTERY.
1872	Butler, Frank A., LAMBETH, England. - -	see 1815 Royal Doulton
1872	Elsmore & Son,T., TUNSTALL, England. -	see 1853 Elsmore & Forster.
1872	Fougeray, France. - - - - -	see 1690 QUIMPER.
1872	Schreiber, W.A.H., and Betz, J.F., PHOENIX, U.S.A.	see 1867 Phoenix Pottery.

1873 Aynsley, H, & Co.Ltd., LONGTON, Staffordshire, England.

1873 EARTHENWARES. Factory's name or initials printed within marks of various patterns and designs.
1891 'England' added sometimes.
1932 'Ltd' added.

H. AYNSLEY & CO.
LONGTON
H. A. & CO.
L.

Staffordshire knot mark-

1946-54 marks

VOGUE MODERNE BY H. AYNSLEY & CO. ENGLAND

1873 Carter & Co. Ltd., POOLE, Dorset, England.

1873-1921 EARTHENWARES, ART POTTERY, ETC.
Factory's name either printed, impressed or incised within marks of various designs.

1921- **Carter, Stabler & Adams.**
1924 Became a Limited Company.

1963- **Name changed to Poole Pottery Ltd.**

Below are the marks from 1900 to the present day (1995) by kind permission of Poole Pottery Ltd., Poole Pottery Collectors Club, and Leslie Hayward, author of <u>Poole Pottery.</u>

Mark No.1
Moulded, about 1900. Found on teapot stands.

Mark No.2
Incised, 1900-1908. Found on lustre wares.

Mark No.3
Incised, 1900-1908. Found on lustre wares.

Mark No.4
Impressed, 1900-1908. Found on lustre wares

Mark No.5
Impressed, 1908-1921. Found on lustre, tin glazed and unglazed wares.

Mark No.6
Moulded 1914-1915

KERAMIC COPY OF BASSANO'S PORTRAIT OF LORD KITCHENER BY CARTERS OF POOLE NOV-1914 -

Mark No.7
Impressed, 1915-1921. Found on lustre and tin glazed wares.

MADE FOR LIBERTY & C°

Mark No.8
Impressed, 1915-1921. Found on lustre and tin glazed wares.

Mark No.9
Incised, 1915-1921. Found on modelled lustre wares.

Mark No.10
Impressed, 1921-1922. Found on grey semi-stonewares.

Mark No.11
Impressed, 1921-1934. Found throughout the red eathenware period

Mark No.12
Moulded, 1921-1924. Found on garden and other moulded wares

Mark No.13
Impressed, 1921-1924. Found on slip trailed and other wares

Continued over -

1873

1873 Carter & Co., Ltd., POOLE, Dorset, England. (Cont`)

Marks continued.

Mark No.14
Impressed. 1922-1934.
Raised frame and letters
POOLE ENGLAND

Mark No.15
Impressed, 1922-1934.
Raised frame and letters
POOLE ENGLAND

Mark No.16
Painted, 1922-1935
Found on John Adams stonewaress
Poole

Mark No.17
Painted, 1922-1935
Found on John Adams stonewares
Poole

Mark No.18
Impressed, 1924-1950
POOLE ENGLAND

Mark No.19
Impressed, 1924-1950
POOLE ENGLAND

Mark No.20
Impressed, 1925-1927
CARTER STABLER ADAMS L^D POOLE ENGLAND

Mark No.21
Impressed, 1925-1934
CARTER STABLER ADAMS L^D POOLE ENGLAND

Mark No.22
Moulded, 1925-1930. Found on 'The Ship' model
CSA POOLE ENGLAND

Mark No.23
Impressed, 1925-1926
POOLE ENGLAND

Mark No.24
Impressed, c1930
MADE IN ENGLAND EXPRESSLY FOR B. ALTMAN & C^O

Mark No.25
Moulded, about 1930. Found on bookends
CARTER STABLER & ADAMS L^D POOLE ENGLAND

Mark No.26
Stencilled, 1930-1931
PLANE WARE

Mark No.27
Impressed, 1930-1935.
Found on sugar sifters
CSA POOLE ENGLAND

Mark No.28
Impressed, 1930-present
POOLE ENGLAND

Mark No.29
Impressed, 1930-present
POOLE ENGLAND

Mark No.30
Stencilled, 1931-1935
EVEREST

Mark No.31
Stencilled, 1934-1937
POOLE ENGLAND

Mark No.32
Stencilled, 1934-1937
SYLVAN WARE

Mark No.33
Stamped, 1935-1949 and 1985-present
POOLE ENGLAND

Mark No.34
Stamped, 1935-present
POOLE ENGLAND

Mark No.35
Stamped, 1946-1950
Found on Utility wares
A POOLE DORSET

Mark No.36
Stamped, 1951-1955
POOLE ENGLAND

Mark No.37
Stamped, 1952-1955
HAND MADE POOLE ENGLAND HAND DECORATED

Mark No.38
Stamped, 1955-1956
Found only on Ann Read painted plaques
POOLE POTTERY STUDIO

Mark No.39
Stamped, 1955-1959
POOLE ENGLAND

Mark No.40
Painted 1956-1959
Found only on black glazed wares
POOLE ENGLAND

Mark No.41
Stamped 1959-1967
POOLE ENGLAND

Mark No.42
Stamped 1960-1969
OVEN POOLE ENGLAND TABLEWARE

Continued over -

1873 Carter & Co. Ltd., POOLE, Dorset, England. (Cont`)

Marks continued.

Mark No.43
Stamped or impressed.
1962-1964

Mark No.44
Impressed, 1963-1964

Mark No.45
Stamped, 1964

Mark No.46
Stamped 1964-1966

Mark No.47
Stamped, 1966-1980

Mark No.48
Stamped, 1967-1972

Mark No.49
Stamped, 1969

Mark No.50
Stamped, 1970-1972

Mark No.51
Stamped, 1970-1980

Mark No.52
Stamped, 1972
Found on a stoneware coffee set by Tony Morris

Mark No.53
Impressed, 1973-1976

Mark No.54
Screen printed, 1974

Mark No.55
Screen printed, 1973

Mark No.56
Screen printed, 1977

Mark No.57
Stamped, 1973-1974

Mark No.58
Impressed, 1973-1980

Mark No.59
Stamped, 1973-1974

Mark No.60
Screen printed, 1973

Mark No.61
Stamped, 1974

Mark No.62
Stamped, 1974-present

Mark No.63
Stamped, 1974-1976

Mark No.64
Stamped, 1974-present

Mark No.65
Stamped, 1976

Mark No.66
Stamped, 1976-1977

Mark No.67
Stamped, 1977-1980

Mark No.68
Screen printed, 1978

Continued over -

1873

1873 Carter & Co. Ltd., POOLE, Dorset, England. (Cont`)

Marks continued

Mark No.69
Transfer printed, 1978
Found on Camelot plates

Mark No.70
Impressed, 1978
Found on Olympus wares

Mark No.71
Stamped, 1978-present

Mark No.72
Transfer printed, 1979

Mark No.73
Transfer printed, 1979-1992

Mark No.74
Transfer printed, 1979-present

Mark No.75
Transfer printed, 1979

Mark No.76
Transfer printed, 1983-1986
Found on Flair tableware

Mark No.77
Transfer printed, 1983-1994
Found on Scenic plates

Mark No.78
Transfer printed, 1983-1987

Mark No.79
Transfer printed, 1979-present

Mark No.80
Stamped 1985-1989
Found on Concert Harmonies tableware

Mark No.81
Stamped, 1986
Found on sponge decorated tableware by Hinchcliffe & Barber

Mark No.82
Stamped, 1987-present

Mark No.83
Stamped, 1988-1991
Found on Bradford Exchange plates

Mark No.84
Stamped, 1989-1990
Found on Astral tableware.

Mark No.85
Transfer printed, 1989-1991

Mark No.86
Stamped, 1990-1991

Mark No.87
Stamped, 1991

Mark No.88
Stamped, 1992-1993

Mark No.89
Impressed, 1993-present

Mark No.90
Stamped, 1993-1995
Transfer printed 1994-present

Mark No.91
Transfer printed 1994-present

Mark No.92
Transfer printed, 1994-present

Mark No.93
Transfer printed, 1994-present

(By kind permission of Poole Pottery Ltd., Poole, Dorset, England. Poole Pottery Collectors Club and Leslie Hayward author of Poole Pottery)

1873 Martin Brothers, FULHAM & SOUTHALL, London, England.

1873-1914 Robert Wallace, Walter, Edwin and Charles.

STUDIO-POTTERS, STONEWARE.

1873-75 Incised, signed- **R.W. Martin fecit.**

1873-74 Incised (Fulham) — R W Martin 84 Fulham

1874-78 Incised (London) — R W Martin 9

1878-79 Incised (Southall) — R W Martin 21 Southall

Impressed marks- **SOUTHALL MARTIN POTTERY** — **MARTIN SOUTHALL POTTERY**

1879-82 (London and Southall) — R W Martin London & Southall

1882-1914 `Bros` or `Brothers` added. - - R W Martin & Brothers London & Southall

(Martin Brothers marks are either incised or impressed, and most of the time, include the month and year)

1873 Meakin, Henry, COBRIDGE, Staffordshire, England.

1873-76 EARTHENWARES. Printed with Royal Arms- **IRONSTONE CHINA H. MEAKIN**

1873 Peoria Pottery Co., PEORIA, ILL., U.S.A.

1873- STONEWARES. - - - **PEORIA ILLINOIS**

1888-90 Cream-coloured ware marks - -

1889-90 Hotel wares -

1890-99 Monogram marks - -

1873 Ridgway, Sparks & Ridgway, HANLEY, Staffordshire, England.

1873-79 Earthenwares. Factory`s initials printed within marks of various patterns and designs including `staffordshire knot` — **R. S. R.**

1879-1920 Ridgways, Bedford Works.

1880 Trade-mark -

c.1905-c.1912 Factory`s name within marks of various patterns and designs — **RIDGWAYS ENGLAND**

1920-52 Ridgways (Bedford Works) Ltd.
Marks within various patterns and designs — **RIDGWAYS BEDFORD WARE**

c.1930-c.56 Printed marks incorporating:- - **JONROTH**
For wares made for an American firm John R. Roth & Co. — **J. H. R. & CO.**

1962 Marks used by Ridgway Potteries Ltd. and its sister companies.

1952	**Acquired by Allied English Potteries Ltd but kept as**
1952-55	**Ridgway & Adderley Ltd.and Booths & Colcloughs Ltd.**
1955	**Ridgways Potteries Ltd.**
Now	**Royal Doulton Group.**

see 1955 Ridgways Potteries Ltd.

1873 Pfeiffer & Löwenstein, SCHLACKENWERTH, Bohemia, Germany.

1873-1945 HARD-PASTE PORCELAIN. - -

PLS

1873 Striegauer Porzellanfabrik, STANOWITZ, Silesia, Germany.

1873- (Formerly C. Walter & Co.) - -

1873 Tundley, Rhodes & Proctor, BURSLEM, Staffordshire, England.

1873-83 EARTHENWARES. Factory's initials printed - within marks of various patterns and designs. **T. R. & P.**

1883-85 **Rhodes & Proctor.** Printed marks - of various patterns and designs. **R. & P.**

1873 Wood & Co.,W., BURSLEM, Staffordshire, England.

1873-1932 EARTHENWARES Factory's initials - - printed or impressed within marks of various patterns and designs. **W. W. & CO.**

1880-1915 Staffordshire knot mark. printed-

1915-32 Printed mark with crown- -

1873	Adams & Bromley, HANLEY, England. -	see 1864 Adams & Co.,John.
1873	Barlow, Florence E., LAMBETH, England.	see 1815 Royal Doulton
1873	Broad, John, LAMBETH, England. -	see 1815 Royal Doulton
1873	Davenpot Beck & Co. HANLEY, England.	see 1860 Davenport Banks & Co.
1873	Davis, Louisa J., LAMBETH, England. -	see 1815 Royal Doulton
1873	Edwards, Louisa E., LAMBETH, England.	see 1815 Royal Doulton.
1873	Hancock & Whittingham, STOKE, England.	see 1863 Hancock, Whittingham & Co.
1873	Merkelbach & Wick, Germany. - -	see 1597 GRENZHAUSEN., Hohr,
1873	Pearce, Arthur E., LAMBETH, England.-	see 1815 Royal Doulton.
1873	Richard-Ginori Società Ceramica, Italy. -	see 1725 MILAN.

Continued over -

1873/74

1873 Simmance, Eliza, LAMBETH, England. - - see 1815 Royal Doulton.
1873 Springer & Oppenheimer, Germany. - - see 1815 Haidinger Brothers.
1873 Turner & Sons, G.W., TUNSTALL, England. - see 1860 Turner & Tomkinson.
1873 Withinshaw, W.E.,BURSLEM, England. - - see 1871 Wood & Clarke.
1873 Woolf & Co., Sidney, MEXBOROUGH, England. see 1839 Reed, James,

---

1874 Bodley & Son, BURSLEM, Staffordshire, England.

1874-75 BONE-CHINA. Initials printed within Staffordshire knot. - **B. & SON**

1875-92 **Bodley, E.J.D.** Impressed mark - **E.J.D. BODLEY**

Factory`s initials printed within marks of various patterns and designs. Sometimes in monogram form. - **E.J.D.B.**

1874 Laughlin Bros., EAST LIVERPOOL, Ohio, U.S.A.

1874- WHITE GRANITE, SEMI-VITREOUS CHINA

1879-97 **Homer Laughlin China Co.**

Factory`s name found within marks of various patterns and designs - **HOMER LAUGHLIN** **LAUGHLIN**

Marks on White granite. American Eagle over the British Lion- -

Mark on semi-vitreous china - -
With pattern names- `COLONIAL` `GOLDEN GATE` `AN AMERICAN BEAUTY`

1874 Martin Bros., LUBAU, Bohemia, Germany.

1874- HARD-PASTE PORCELAIN. - -
Porzellan Fabrik and Kaolinschlammerie Alp GmbH.

1874 Tams, John, & Son Ltd., Crown Pottery, LONGTON, Staffs, England.

John Tams (Great-grandfather of the present Chairman, Gerald R. Tams) had previously been in partnership since 1864 with a Mr Lowe, under the name of Tams & Lowe. -

1874 EARTHENWARES. Factory`s name and initials printed within marks of various patterns and designs. Sometimes in monogram form.
1903-12 `& Son` added.

J. T.
J. Tams

J. T. & S.

1912- `Ltd` added.
c.1913- Various trade and brand names were printed within the marks -

NANKIN WARE
TAMS WARE
ELEPHANT BRAND
TAMS REGENT
CHININE
TAMS ENGLAND

(By kind permission of John Tams Group Plc., Longton, England.)

1874	Butterton, Mary, LAMBETH, England. - -	see 1815 Royal Doulton.
1874	Escallier, Mme, (Decorator) France. - -	see 1745 SÈVRES.
1874	Ford, Charles, HANLEY, England. - -	see 1854 Ford, T. & C.

1875 Bayley, Murray & Co., Saracen Pottery, GLASGOW, Scotland.

1875-84 EARTHENWARES. Factory`s initials printed or impressed within marks of various designs.
c.1884 Saracen Pottery Co.

B. M. & Co.
SARECEN POTTERY.

1875

1875 Bridgett, Bates & Beech, LONGTON, Staffordshire, England.

1875-82 CHINA. - - -

Printed or impressed-

1882-1915 **Bridgett & Bates.** Impressed- or printed within other patterns. **B. & B.**

c.1912- Printed mark-

1916-30 **Beswick & Son.** Factory's initials printed or impressed within marks of various patterns and designs. **B. & S.**

Trade name- **ALDWICH CHINA**

1875 Buckley Wood & Co., BURSLEM, Staffordshire, England.

1875-85 EARTHENWARES. Factory's initials are printed or impressed within marks of various patterns and designs. - - - **B. W. & CO.**

1875 Cardigan Potteries, Woodward & Co.,CARDIGAN, Dyfed, Wales.

c.1875-90 EARTHENWARES. Printed marks of various patterns and designs.

CARDIGAN
POTTERIES
WOODWARD & CO.
CARDIGAN

1875 Clive, Stephen, TUNSTALL, Staffordshire, England.

1875-80 EARTHENWARES. Factory's initials are printed within marks of various patterns and designs. **S. C.**
1876 '& Co.' added. **S. C. & CO.**

1875 Davis, Isaac, TRENTON, New Jersey, U.S.A.

c.1875-80 **Prospect Hill Pottery.** - -
WHITE GRANITE WARE,
OPAQUE PORCELAIN.

1880-94 **Dale & Davis.** - - -

D—D

1875 Dunn Bennett & Co. Ltd., BURSLEM, Staffordshire, England.

1875- EARTHENWARES. Factory`s initials printed within marks of various patterns and designs. 1875-1907. **D. B. & CO.**

Beehive mark-

1937- Printed-

1955- Design mark includes- **VITREOUS IRONSTONE**

1875 Hubbe Bros. NEUHALDENSLEBEN, Saxony, Germany.

1875- GENERAL CERAMICS. - - -

1875 Martin, Charles, & Duché, LIMOGES, France.

1875 PORCELAIN - - -

1875 Meakin Ltd., Alfred, TUNSTALL, Staffordshire, England.

1875- EARTHENWARES. Factory`s name printed or impressed within marks of various patterns and designs. **ALFRED MEAKIN**
ALFRED MEAKIN LTD.

1891 `England` added.
1897 `Ltd.` added. -
Printed-

c1913 **Alfred Meakin (Tunstall) Ltd. (Re-named)**

Printed-

c.1930-c.37 `Ltd.` excluded from the marks from 1930-

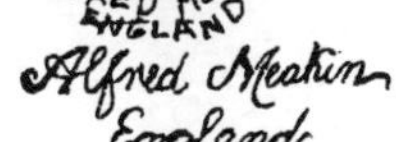

Continued over -

1875

1875 Meakin Ltd., Alfred, TUNSTALL, Staffordshire, England. (Cont`)

Modern marks-

1875 Metzler Bros. & Ortloff, ILMENAU, Thuringia, Germany.

1875- HARD-PASTE PORCELAIN. - -

1875 Neale, Harrison & Co., HANLEY, Staffordshire, England.

1875-85 GENERAL CERAMICS. Factory`s initials are printed within marks of various patterns and designs. **N. H. & CO.**

1875 Steele & Wood, STOKE, Staffordshire, England.

1875-92 TILES, ETC. Printed or impressed-

1875 TOKIO, Musashi, Japan.

In the Middle Ages Miura-Kenya from Kioto opened a factory at Asakusa producing RAKU-YAKI.

1875 `Ni-pon To-kio Hyo-chi-yen gua` Painted at the Hyochi garden, Tokio, Japan.

1885 `Ni-pon Tokio Kinshosha sei tsukuru` - - - Carefully made by the Kinsho Company at Tokio, Japan.

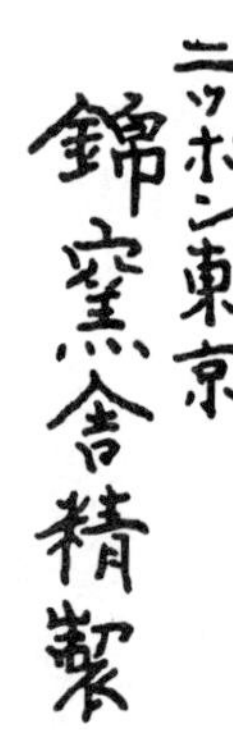

1875 Torquay Terra-Cotta Co. Ltd., Dr. Gillow, TORQUAY, England.

1875-1909 FIGURES, PLAQUES, ETC., Impressed mark- **TORQUAY**

Factory`s name impressed or printed within marks of various patterns and designs - - - **TORQUAY TERRA-COTTA CO. LIMITED**

Impressed or printed- 

1900-09 Impressed or printed- - 

1875	Asbury & Co.,Edward, LONGTON, England. -	see 1872 Hammersley & Asbury.
1875	Bates, Walker & Co., BURSLEM, England. -	see 1870 Bates, Elliott & Co.
1875	Bodley, E.J.D., BURSLEM, England. - -	see 1874 Bodley & Son.
1875	City Pottery Co., TRENTON, N.J., U.S.A. -	see 1859 Rhodes & Yates.
1875	Cockson & Seddon, COBRIDGE, England. -	see 1867 Cockson & Chetwynd.
1875	Collins, F.M., LAMBETH, England. - -	see 1815 Royal Doulton plc.
1875	Hache & Julien, France. - - - -	see 1815 VIERZON.
1875	Ise-Banko-Yaki, Japan. - - - -	see 1736 ISE.
1875	Jakuzan, Japan. - - - - -	see 1677 IZUMO.
1875	Kato Gosuke of Tajimimura, Japan. - -	see 1650 MINO.
1875	Kuang-hsü, China. - - - -	see 1644 CH`ING DYNASTY.
1875	Lee, Francis E., LAMBETH, England. - -	see 1815 Royal Doulton plc.
1875	Lewis, Florence, LAMBETH, England. - -	see 1815 Royal Doulton plc.
1875	Naka-jima, Japan. - - - -	see 1596 SATSUMA.
1875	New England Pottery Co., U.S.A. - -	see 1854 Meagher, F.,
1875	Sampei-Yaki, Japan. - - - -	see 1830 AWAJI.
1875	Uchiumi, Kichizo, Japan. - - - -	see 1650 KAGA.

1876 American Crockery Co., TRENTON, New Jersey, U.S.A.

1876- BISQUE, WHITE GRANITE WARE.

printed- 

Eagle and monogram mark- - - - 

1890 mark printed black- **AMERICAN CHINA A. C. Co.**

1876

1876 Barker Bros. Ltd., Meir Works, LONGTON, Staffordshire, England.

1876- CHINA AND EARTHENWARES. Impressed- **B. B.**

c.1880- Printed-

1901 `Ltd` added.

1912-30 Factory`s name or initials printed within marks of various patterns and designs- **B. B.** **BARKER BROS Ltd.** **MEIR CHINA**

1930-37 Printed-

1937- Factory`s name printed within marks of various patterns and designs - **BARKER BROS Ltd.** **TUDOR WARE**

1876 Bradley, F.D., LONGTON, Staffordshire, England.

1876-96 PORCELAIN. Impressed- **BRADLEY**

1876 Brown & Co., Robert, PAISLEY, Scotland.

1876-1933 EARTHENWARE.

Printed or impressed- BROWN PAISLEY

1876 Cooper & Dethick, LONGTON, Staffordshire, England.

1876-88 EARTHENWARES. Factory`s initials printed within marks of various patterns and designs. **C. & D.**

1876 Gallé Emile, NANCY, Meuthe-et-Moselle, France.

c.1876-c.1900 (b.1846, d. 1904) ARTIST POTTER. Renowned for his l`art nouveau glass. **GALLÉ** **NANCY**

1876 Hancock, B. & S., STOKE, Staffordshire, England.

1876-81 EARTHENWARES. Factory`s initials printed within marks of various patterns and designs. **B. & S. H.**

1876 Holmes, Plant & Maydew, BURSLEM, Staffordshire, England.

1876-85 EARTHENWARES. Factory`s initials printed within marks of various patterns and designs. **H. P. & M.**

1876 Jones, Alfred B., Grafton China Works, LONGTON, Staffs, England.

1876-1900 China.

1900- **W.B. and A.B. Jones (sons) became partners.**

A.B. Jones & Sons. — **A. B. J. & S.**

China tea and breakfast sets etc. — **A. B. J. & SONS**

1900- Factory`s name and initials found within marks of various designs. — **A. B. JONES & SONS**

1906 Introduced miniature crested wares.

1900-13 printed mark - -

1913-60 printed marks all carried the word `GRAFTON` or `ROYAL GRAFTON`

1955- **A.B. Jones & Sons Limited.** (incorporated company) Produced bone china dinnerware and giftware.

1968- **Ceramco (New Zealand based company) acquired the business.**

1985- **John Bullock headed a syndicate of investors including Tony Boulton and Stan Nicholls and brought the company back to private ownership as RGC Ltd.**

1989 modern printed mark- -

(By kind permission of RGC Ltd., Grafton Works, Longton, Staffs., England.)

1876 McLaughlin, Miss M. Louise, CINCINNATI, Ohio, U.S.A.

1876- Experimented in porcelain within the grounds adjoining her residence.

Impressed or painted in blue- Losanti

1876 Pittsburgh Encaustic Tile Co., PITTSBURGH, PA., U.S.A.

1876-82 Unglazed tiles

1882- **Star Encaustic Tile Co.** Impressed- **S.E.T.**
CO.

1876

1876 Potters` Co-Operative Co., EAST LIVERPOOL, Ohio, U.S.A.

1876- **Brunt, Bloor, Martin & Co.,(Dresden Works)**

WHITE GRANITE, VITREOUS AND HOTEL CHINA.

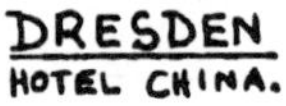

Printed pattern names used within marks- **DRESDEN**
CALIFORNIA
MADRID
YALE

Hotel china mark. Impressed- **DRESDEN**
HOTEL CHINA
WARRANTED

1876 Robinson, Joseph, BURSLEM, Staffordshire, England.

1876-98 EARTHENWARES. Factory`s name or initials printed or impressed within marks of various patterns and designs. - - -

J. R.
B.
J. ROBINSON
BURSLEM

1876 Union Porcelain Works, GREENPOINT, N.Y. U.S.A.

Smith, Thomas C., HARD-PASTE PORCELAIN.

Impressed-

Smith, C.H.L. (son)

1877 Printed mark in green-

1879 Printed in red -
(sometimes with date)

1891 Semi-circular mark- -

1876 Whittingham, Ford & Riley, BURSLEM, Staffordshire, England.

1876-82 EARTHENWARES. Factory`s initials printed within marks of various patterns and designs. — **W. F. & R.**

1882-93 **Ford & Riley.** Within printed marks of various patterns and designs. - **F & R**
B

1893-1938 **Ford & Sons Ltd.,** Within printed marks of of various patterns and designs. — **F & S**
F & S
B

1908 `Ltd` added. - **F & SONS LTD.**

1930- Printed marks including- - **Crown Ware**
NEWCRAFT WARE

1938- **Ford & Sons (Crownford) Ltd.** Printed-

c.1961 -

1876	Adderley & Co.,William Alsager, England. -	see 1853 Hulse, Nixon & Adderley.
1876	Astbury & Maddock, TRENTON, U.S.A. -	see 1869 Maddock & Sons, T.,
1876	Atkins, Elizabeth, LAMBETH, England.- -	see 1815 Royal Doulton plc.
1876	Banks, Eliza, LAMBETH, England. - -	see 1815 Royal Doulton plc.
1876	Booth, Thomas G., BURSLEM, England. -	see 1868 Booth & Co.,Thomas.
1876	Capes, Mary, LAMBETH, England. - -	see 1815 Royal Doulton plc.
1876	Crawley, Minna L., LAMBETH, England. -	see 1815 Royal Doulton plc.
1876	De Porceleyne Fles, (re-established) DELFT, Holland.	see 1653 De Porceleyne Fles.
1876	Green T.A.& S., FENTON, England. - -	see 1847 Green, Thomas.
1876	Hansuke, Japan. - - - - -	see 1573 OWARI.
1876	Lupton, Edith D., LAMBETH, England.- -	see 1815 Royal Doulton plc.
1876	Mitchell, Mary, LAMBETH, England. - -	see 1815 Royal Doulton plc.
1876	Nagoya-Yaki, Shippo Kuwaisha, Japan. - -	see 1573 OWARI.
1876	Philadelphia Exhibition, Pennsylvania, U.S.A. -	

1877/78

1877 Guest & Dewsbury, South Wales Pottery, LLANELLY, Wales.

1877-1927 EARTHENWARES. Factory`s initials printed within marks of various patterns and designs. — **G. & D. L.** / **G. D.**
`L` for Llanelly. — **L.**

1877 Hammersley, J. & R., HANLEY, Staffordshire, England.

1877-1917 GENERAL CERAMICS. Factory`s initials printed within marks of various patterns and designs. — **J. R. H.**

1877 Lear, Samuel, HANLEY, Staffordshire, England.

1877-86 GENERAL CERAMICS. Impressed- **LEAR**

1877 Sherwin & Cotton, HANLEY, Staffordshire, England.

1877-1930 TILES. Impressed or incised- **SHERWIN & COTTON**

Impressed mark-

1877 Wagner & Apel, LIPPELSDORF, Thuringia, Germany.

1877- HARD-PASTE PORCELAIN, FIGURES, GIFTS, ETC. -

1877	Auvillain (Ground colour) France. - -	see 1745 SÈVRES.
1877	Beech, James, TUNSTALL, England. - -	see 1857 Beech & Hancock.
1877	Beerbower & Griffen, PHOENIXVILLE, U.S.A.	see 1867 Phoenix Pottery.
1877	Bevington, Thomas, HANLEY, England. -	see 1865 Bevington, J.& T.
1877	Bieuville (Decorator) France. - - -	see 1745 SÈVRES.
1877	Birks Brothers & Seddon, COBRIDGE, England.	see 1867 Cockson & Chetwynd.
1877	Derby Crown Porcelain Co., England. - -	see 1749 Derby.
1877	Unwin & Co., Joseph, LONGTON, England. -	see 1871 Poole & Unwin.

1878 Emery, Francis J., BURSLEM, Staffordshire, England.

c.1878-93 EARTHENWARES. Factory`s name printed - within marks of various patterns and designs. c.1891 ` England` added. — **F. J. EMERY**

1878 Haviland, Charles Field, LIMOGES, Haute-Vienne, France.

1878-83 EXPORTER. — **C F H / G D M / FRANCE**

1883-1901 **Morel & Duffraisseix.**

1878 New Wharf Pottery Co., BURSLEM, Staffordshire, England.

1878-94 EARTHENWARES. Factory`s initials printed - within marks of various patterns and designs.

N. W. P. & CO.
B.
N. W. P. & CO.
BURSLEM

c.1890-94 Printed-

1878 Pohl, Theodor, SCHATZLAR, Bohemia, Germany.

1878- **Porzellanfabrik Schatzlar,** HARD-PASTE PORCELAIN.

1878 Pratt & Simpson, FENTON, Staffordshire, England.

1878-83 EARTHENWARES. Factory`s initials printed within a circular mark. - **P. & S.**

1878 Reinecke, Otto, HOF-MOSCHENDORF, Bavaria, Germany.

1878- HARD-PASTE PORCELAIN.

1894- **Kühnert & Tischer -**

1878	Bates, Gildea & Walker, BURSLEM, England. -	see 1870 Bates Elliott & Co.
1878	Belet, E., (Flowers, etc.) France. - - -	see 1745 SÈVRES.
1878	Blanchard, Alexandre, (decorator) France. -	see 1745 SÈVRES.
1878	Cantagalli, Ulysse, Italy. - - - - -	see 1575 FLORENCE.
1878	Cliff, W.D., HANLEY, England. - - -	see 1862 Dimmock & Co.
1878	Doat, T-M, (Sculptor, Pâte-sur-Pâte) France. -	see 1745 SÈVRES.
1878	Morient, J.P. and Saintville, G., France. - -	see 1810 BAYEUX.
1878	`Portland Vase` mark, BURSLEM, England. -	see 1759 Wedgwood, J. & Sons.
1878	Powell, Bishop & Stonier, HANLEY, England. -	see 1851 Livesley Powell & Co.
1878	Seger, Hermann, Germany. - - -	see 1751 BERLIN.
1878	Tabor, George Hugo, LAMBETH, England. -	see 1815 Royal Doulton plc.
1878	Wolffsen & Son, W., Roenne, Denmark. - -	see 1835 Søholm A/S.

1879 Bednall & Heath, HANLEY, Staffordshire, England.

1879-99 EARTHENWARES. Factory`s initials printed- within marks of various patterns and designs 1891 `England` added. **B. & H.**

1899-1901 **Wellington Pottery Co.,**Printed or impressed-

Continued over -

1879

1879 Bednall & Heath, HANLEY, Staffordshire, England. (Cont`)

1901-19 **Lockitt, William H.,** Printed monogram - ***W. H. L.***
H

1913-19 Printed mark with rampant lion - **DURA - WARE**
WILLIAM H. LOCKIT

1879 Blackhurst & Tunnicliffe, BURSLEM, Staffordshire, England.

c.1879 EARTHENWARES. Factory`s initials printed- within marks of various patterns and designs. **B. & T.**

1880-92 **Blackhurst & Bourne,** Printed- **B. & B.**

1879 Brannam Ltd., C.H., Litchdon Pottery, BARNSTAPLE, England.

1879- EARTHENWARES. Incised in written letters **C. H. BRANNAM**
BARUM

1879-1913 Impressed- **C. H. BRANNAM**
1913- Impressed- `Ltd` added. **C. H. BRANNAM LTD.**
BARNSTAPLE

1929- Printed or impressed-

1930- Impressed- `Made in England` sometimes. **C. H. BRANNAM**
BARUM DEVON

1879 Burroughs & Mountford Co., TRENTON, New Jersey, U.S.A.

1879-c.95 EARTHENWARES, WHITE GRANITE, ART WARES.

B—M

1879 Cincinnati Art Pottery Co., CINCINNATI, Ohio, U.S.A.

1879-91 FAÏENCE, POTTERY ART WARE. - - - - -

1886 Indian name for a turtle.
impressed- KEZONTA

1890 Impressed mark - - - - - -

1879 Dean & Sons Ltd., Thomas, TUNSTALL, Staffordshire, England.

1879-1947 EARTHENWARES.

1896-1947 Printed-

1937-47 Printed- -

1879 Elton, Sir Edmund, CLEVEDON, Somerset, England.

1879-1930 EARTHENWARES.

1879-1920 Painted or incised-

1920- A `cross` was added to the mark after Sir Edmund Elton`s death.

1879 Fielding & Co. Ltd., S., STOKE, Staffordshire, England.

1879- EARTHENWARES. MAJOLICA, ETC., Impressed- **FIELDING**

1880-1917 Factory`s initials printed - **S. F. & CO.**
within marks of various patterns and designs.

1913-30 Marks printed with crown **CROWN DEVON**
S. F. & Co.
FIELDINGS

c.1930 `Crown Devon` Trade mark printed-

1953 Date mark. impressed- **FIELDING**
26th February 1953 **26 F 53**

(Part of Crown Devon Group.)

1879 Hamill & Bullock, BALTIMORE, Maryland, U.S.A.

1879- **Maryland Queensware Factory.**
WHITE GRANITE WARE.

1880- **Hamill, Brown & Co.**

1888- **Maryland Pottery Co.**

Continued over -

1879

1879 Hamill & Bullock, BALTIMORE, Maryland, U.S.A. (Cont`)

Messrs. D.F. Haynes & Co., Baltimore. -
were agents and wholesalers for
Maryland Pottery Co.
1881-83 Marks on white-granite

1880-92 Mark on cream-coloured wares -

1883-91 Mark on white granite or ironstone
China.(Seal of the State of Maryland) -

1885-87 Printed in black on toilet sets. - - **ETRUSCAN**

1891- Sanitary earthenware mark - -

1879 Kirkby & Co., William, FENTON, Staffordshire, England.

1879-85 GENERAL CERAMICS. Factory`s initials printed or impressed within marks of various patterns and designs. Sometimes in monogram. **W. K. & CO.** **K. & CO.**

1879 Linthorpe Pottery, John Harrison, MIDDLESBROUGH, England.

1879-89 EARTHENWARES, ART POTTERY. Impressed- **LINTHORPE**

c.1879-89 Dresser, Christopher (designer)
Incised, impressed or painted signature- **Chr. Dresser**

1879-82 **Tooth, Henry,** Monogram marks-

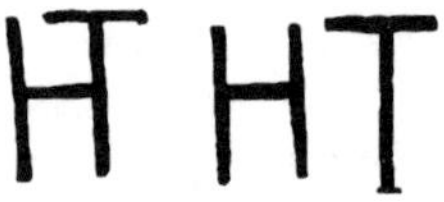

1879 Morley & Co., WELLSVILLE, Ohio, U.S.A.

1879-85 WHITE GRANITE, MAJOLICA. - -

Continued over -

1879 Morley & Co., WELLSVILLE, Ohio, U.S.A. (Cont`)

1885-96 **Pioneer Pottery Co.,** - -

Mark on `Imperial China`

Mark on porcelain -

1896- **Wellsville Pioneer Pottery Co.** - **W. P. P. Co.**
SEMI-PORCELAIN

Wellsville China Co. - - -

1879 Radford Ltd., Samuel, FENTON, Staffordshire, England.

1879-1957 PORCELAIN. Printed monogam mark S.R. within various patterns and designs. **S R**

c.1880-91 printed-
1891 `England` added.

c1913-24 printed-

c.1928-57 printed-

1879 Rookwood Pottery Co., CINCINNATI, Ohio, U.S.A.

1879- **Taylor, William W.,** ART POTTERY.

1879-82 painted or incised mark -

Maria Longworth Nichols mark -
(Rookwood Pottery, Cincinnati, Ohio,
Maria Longworth Nichols) - - -

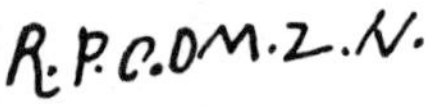

1880-82 Pottery kiln and two rooks mark in black -

Rare Anchor mark, stamped or in relief - -

1882- Mark on beer tankard made for Cincinnati Cooperage Co. - - -

1882-86 Regular mark with date - - - **ROOKWOOD 1884**

1882 Dated mark - -

1883 Impressed marks-

1886 Monogram mark- - - -

1887- Flame point added- - - -
Then each year another
point was added.

1900 with 14 flame points- - -

1901 Same mark was used plus a roman numeral to indicate the first year of the century. -

1897 Date mark Mrs Maria Longworth Storer (Founder) Incised or printed- -

Continued over -

1879 Rookwood Pottery Co., CINCINNATI, Ohio, U.S.A. (Cont`)

Clay marks consist of six different letters indicating colour of body:-

G. indicates	**Ginger**	**S. indicates**	**Sage Green**
O. "	**Olive**	**W. "**	**White**
R. "	**Red**	**Y "**	**Yellow**

__Decorators marks incised on wares (in alphabetical order) :-__

A.B. Alfred Brennan.

A.B.S. Amelia B. Sprague

A.D.S. Adeliza D. Sehon,

A.G. Arthur Goetting -

A.H. Albert Humphreys.

A.M.B. A.M.Bookprinter,Miss.

A.M.V. Anna M. Valentien.

A.R.V. Albert R. Valentien.

A.V.B. Artus Van Briggle.

B.- Bruce Horsfall. - -

C.A.B. Constance A. Baker.

C.C. Cora Crofton. - -

C.C.L. Clara L. Lindeman.

C.F.B. Caroline Bonsall. -

C.J.D. Charles John Dibowski.

C.N. Clara Chipman Newton.

C.S. Carrie Steinle

C.S. Charles Schmidt.

D.C. Daniel Cook.

E.A. Edward Abel. -

E.B.I.C. E. Bertha I. Cranch.

E.C.L. Eliza C. Lawrence. -

E.D. E.D. Diers.

E.D.F. Emma D. Foertmeyer.

E.P.C. Edward P. Cranch.

E.R.F. Edith R. Felten. -

E.T.H. E.T. Hurley.

E.W.B. Elizabeth W. Brain. -

F.A. Fannie Auckland.

F.R. Fred Rothenbusch. -

F.V. F.W. Vreeland.

G.H. Grace M. Hall. -

G.Y. Grace Young.

H.A. Howard Altman. -

H.E.W. Harriet E. Willcox.

H.H. Hattie Horton. -

H.P.S. H. Pabodie Stuntz.

H.R.S. Harriet R. Strafer -

Continued over -

1879

1879 Rookwood Pottery Co., CINCINNATI, Ohio, U.S.A. (Cont`)

Decorators marks incised on wares (in alphabetical order):- (Cont`)

H.W. Harriet Wenderoth.	I.B. Irene Bishop. -
J.D.W. J.Dee Wareham.	J.E.Z. Josephine E. Zettel.
J.S. Jeannette Swing.	K.C.M. Kate C. Machette.
K/F.D.K. F.D.Koehler, Mrs.,	K.H. Katharine Hickman. -
L.A. Leonore Asbury.	L.A.F. Laura A. Fry. - -
L.E.H. Lena E. Hanscom.	L.E.L. Laura E. Lindeman
L.N.L. Lizzie N. Lingenfelter.	L.V.B. Leona Van Briggle.
M.A.D. Matt A. Daly.	M.F. Mattie Foglesong. -
M.H.S. Marion H. Smalley.	M.L.P. Mary L.Perkins
M.L.S. Maria Longworth Storer.	M.N. Mary Nourse. -
M.R. Marie Rauchfuss	M.R. Martin Rettig. -
M.T./M.A.T. Mary Taylor.	N.J.H. N.J. Hirschfield. -
O.G.R. O.Geneva Reed.	P.P. Pauline Peters. -
R.F. Rose Fechheimer.	S.E.C. Sallie Coyne. -
Shirayamadani, Kataro. Japan.	S.L. Sturgis Lawrence. -
S.M. Sadie Markland.	S.S. Sara Sax. -
S.T. Sallie Toohey.	T.O.M. Tom Lunt. -
V.B.D. Virginia B. Demarest.	W.H.B. W.H. Breuer. -
W.K. William Klemm.	W.P.McD. W.P. McDonald.

1879 Rosenthal & Co., Philipp, Erkersreuth, nr. Selb, Bavaria, Germany.

1879-PORCELAIN. **(Founded by Philipp Rosenthal)**

Throughout the history of Rosenthal they have produced some of the finest household and luxury porcelain in the world and yet at the same time have been in the forefront of technical porcelain products for industry.

Marks of Rosenthal & Co. -

1886- Branch opened at Asch/Böhmen (closed 1898)

1890- Decorating work-shop moved from Erkersreuth to Selb.

1891- White porcelain factory established at Selb.

1897- Porzellanfabrik Ph. Rosenthal & Co. AG. (Company change)

1897 Bauer, Rosenthal & Co. KG, Kronach/Ofr. established. see 1897 Rosenthal & Co.

Marks of Bauer, Rosenthal Co.

1908- Thomas, F. & Co., Sophienthal, acquired.
PORCELAIN TABLEWARE (Founded 1904)

Marks of F.Thomas & Co. -

1910- Founded artistic department and central laboratory in Selb.

1917- Zeidler & Co., Jakob, Plössberg, nr. Selb, acquired (Founded 1866) closed 1971.
TABLEWARE AND ARTISTIC PORCELAIN.

1918- Specialized and artistic porcelain was being produced from this time.

1921- AEG-Rosenthal established, producing technical/ electrical porcelain AEG in Hennigsdorf nr. Berlin.

1921- Krister Porzellan-Manufactur AG. Waldenburg/ Schlesien, acquired. (Founded 1831) see 1831 Krister, Carl

1921- Weber & Co., Adam, Nuremberg, acquired.
CERAMIC SPARK-PLUGS AND GAS-LIGHT BURNERS.

1922- Bohemia-Werkin, Neu-Rohlau, Bohemia, merged to make tableware.

Marks of Bohemia-Werkin -

1923- Koalin and sand foundry established by AEG. and Rosenthal (KATO) GmbH at Halle/Saale.

1923- Weber & Co.,Adam, sold to Steatit-Magnesia AG.

Continued over -

1879

1879 Rosenthal & Co.,Philipp, Erkersreuth, nr.Selb, Germany. (Cont`)

1924- Rosenthal and Società Italiana, establish the factory, Società Cerámica del Verbano, Laveno, Italy.

1926- Keramik department moved to Plössburg.

1928- Zollfrank, Porzellanfabrik, Erkersreuth, acquired.
Founded 1923. Electrical products.

1932- Zöllner, Rudi, Porzellanwerkstatten, Munich, acquired. (Founded 1921, closed 1963)
Workshop for hand-painted decorators.

1934- Philipp Rosenthal resigns from the Board.

1936- Rosenthal-Isolatoren GmbH (RIG) established
Producing technical ceramics at Selb, Erkersreuth and Hennigsdorf, nr.Berlin.

1937- Waldershof, Porzellanfabrik, AG acquired.
(Formerly Johann Haviland. Bought by Società Cerámica Richard Ginori in 1924) see 1907 Haviland, Johann

1939- Rosenthal Porzellan AG, Selb. (Company change)

1942- Cristallerie Saint Louis, Münztal, acquired.
DRINKING GLASSES AND GIFTWARE.

1950- Philipp Rosenthal rejoined the Board.

1952- New porcelain factory built at Landstuhl. (Krister Porzellan-Manufactur AG, Landstuhl.)

1956- Financial interest in Porcelana Renner S.A. Porto, Brasil.

1957- Financial interest in Explotaciones Ceramicas Espanolas S.A. Burela, Spain. (Mining of Kaolin)

1958- Design studio built in Selb for central production of porcelain, glass and cutlery.

1959- Financial interest in Continental China Ltd. South Africa. (Sold 1963)

1965- Rosenthal Aktiengesellschaft, Selb. (Company change)

1965- Rosenthal Technical Components Ltd., England. established.

1967- Established new factory at Rothbuhl, Selb. Producing tableware.

1967- Celtic Ceramics Ltd., Kilrush, Ireland. acquired. Producing tableware and giftware.

1969- Factory established in Sandiago, Chile. Porcelanas Rosenthal Chile S.A.

1977- Established Rosenthal Metceram Corporation in Providence, U.S.A. producing technical ceramics.

1979- 100 years anniversary.

Modern mark - Rosenthal

(By kind permission of Rosenthal Aktiengesellschaft AG, Selb, Germany.)

1879 Schönwald, Porzellanfabrik, SCHÖNWALD, Germany.

1879- HARD-PASTE PORCELAIN. HOTEL WARE.
Founder Johann Nikol Müller.

1891-94 Partnership with his two sons, Friedrich and Michael.

1896- Transformation to `Aktiengesellschaft Porzellanfabrik Schönwald` and incorporated into the Strupp combine.

1898- Muller, Friedrich, retires.

1927- Porcelain Factory Schönwald AG together with Factory E.& A. Müller AG.into the ownership of Kahla AG, Thuringia.
The Schönwald Factory continues as `Porzellanfabrik Schönwald, Zweigniederlassung der Porzellanfabrik Kahla`

1949- Transfer of Kahla AG headquarters to Schönwald.

1954- Silver medal awarded for tableware series Schönwald 411 at X Triennial, Milan. Designed by Heinrich Loffelhardt.

1957- Gold medal awarded tableware series 511 at X1 Triennial.

1959-61 `Premio internazionale Vicenza` awarded for tableware series 1011 and 498.

1972- Merger of Kahla AG, with Lorenz Hutschenreuther AG.

1976- Hutschenreuther AG, makes large scale investment into the Schönwald factory.

Todays modern mark (1995)-

(Courtesy of Hutschenreuther AG, Germany)

1879

1879 Smith & Co., Thomas, Old Kent Road, LONDON, England.

1879-93 STONEWARES.

Impressed or incised- **T. .SMITH & CO. OLD KENT RD. LONDON**

1879 Steubenville Pottery Co., STEUBENVILLE, Ohio, U.S.A.

1879 EARTHENWARE AND PORCELAIN.

Marks on white granite and `Canton` china:-

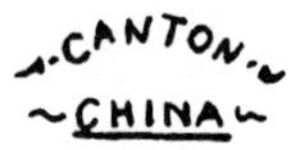

1890-95 Marks on toilet wares and dinner services.
With various pattern names.- -

Mr Day`s mark. (Secretary of the Company)

1879 Volkmar, Charles, GREENPOINT, N.Y., U.S.A.

1879-95 POTTERY AND TILES.

1879-88 Monogram mark- -

1895 **Volkmar Keramic Co.,Brooklyn, N.Y.**

Impressed with raised letters-

1895 **Volkmar & Cory, Corona, N.Y.**

Partnership with Miss Kate Cory - - **VOLKMAR & CORY**

1896 Plain coloured glazes.

Mark incised or in relief - -

1903 **Volkmar & Sons, Charles, Metuchen, N.J.**

ART WARE IN MATT ENAMELS

1879 Wheeling Pottery Co., WHEELING, W. VA., U.S.A.

1879-87 WHITE GRANITE WARES. - -

1880-86 - -

1887- **La Belle Pottery Co.,**
`Adamantine` China.- -

c.1889- **Both Companies were consolidated**

1893 Marks on `La Belle` china-

1894 Marks on cream-coloured ware
Souvenir ware related to Spanish/
American war. - -

Other marks used during this period -

1879 Willets Manufacturing Co., TRENTON, New Jersey, U.S.A.

1879- STONE CHINA.

\- - - -

1884 Monogram mark adopted - -
impressed or printed -

Other marks with Factory`s name or initials-
found within various patterns and designs i.e.
`ARNO` `DUCHESS` `FORGET-ME-NOT`
`ADELAIDE` `SARATOGA` `BELLEEK` etc.

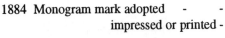

W. M. CO.
WILLETS

1879 Williamson & Sons, H. M., LONGTON, Staffordshire, England.

c.1879-1941 PORCELAIN. Factory`s initials and name printed within marks of various patterns and designs. **W. & SONS WILLIAMSONS**

c.1879 Printed-

c.1903-12- Printed-

1879	Belet, L. (Decorator) France. - - -	see 1745 SÈVRES.
1879	Birkner and Maisel, TETTAU, Germany. -	see 1794 Tettau GmbH.
1879	Carr & Clark, TRENTON, U.S.A. - -	see 1860 Speeler, Henry,
1879	Drouet (Decorator) France. - - -	see 1745 SÈVRES.
1879	Griffen, Smith & Hill, PHOENIXVILLE, U.S.A.	see 1867 Phoenix Pottery Co.
1879	Laughlin China Co., Homer, E. LIVERPOOL, U.S.A.	see 1874 Laughlin Bros.
1879	Lincoln Pottery Co., NEW YORK CITY, U.S.A.	see 1853 Morrison & Carr.
1879	Maddock & Sons, Thomas, TRENTON, U.S.A.-	see 1869 Maddock, Thomas,
1879	Marshall, Mark V., LAMBETH, England. -	see 1815 Royal Doulton plc.
1879	Ouint, Ch. (Decorator) France. - - -	see 1745 SÈVRES.
1879	Ridgways, Bedford Works, HANLEY, England.-	see 1873 Ridgway, Sparks & Ridgway.
1879	Roberts, Florence C., LAMBETH, England. -	see 1815 Royal Doulton plc.
1879	Tristan (Decorator) France. - - -	see 1745 SÈVRES.

1880 Blair & Co., LONGTON, Staffordshire, England.

c.1880-1911 PORCELAIN, Impressed or printed- **B**

1900-Impressed or printed- **BLAIRS CHINA ENGLAND**

1900- Printed-

c.1912-23 Blairs Ltd.

1914-30 Printed-

1923-30 Blairs (Longton) Ltd.

1880 **Boseck & Co., Carl Fr., HAIDA, Bohemia, Germany.**

1880- DECORATORS OF PORCELAIN. - - -

1880 **Broome, Prof. Isaac, TRENTON, New Jersey, U.S.A.**

Worked as a modeller for Ott & Brewer, but produced some of his own wares in very small quantities in a vitrified porcelain body. These are regarded as very collectable and of high value.

Incised below glaze - -

Modelled for Providential Tile Works and Trent Tile Co., TRENTON, and later for Beaver Falls Art Tile Co.

Usually marked on face with monogram - -

or impressed with surname- ***BROOME***

1880 **Cotton Ltd., Elijah, Nelson Pottery, HANLEY, Staffs. England.**

1880- EARTHENWARES. ***Early wares unmarked.***

Factory's name printed within marks of various designs. **ELIJAH COTTON Ltd.**

c.1913- Printed-

Trade names - **NELSON WARE**
LORD NELSON WARE

1880 **Enterprise Pottery Co., TRENTON, New Jersey, U.S.A.**

c.1880-92 SANITARY WARE. - - - **Enterprise Pottery Co.**

1892 Incorporated within the Trenton Potteries Co.

see 1892 Trenton Potteries Co.

1880 **Faience Manufacturing Co., GREENPOINT, N.Y., U.S.A.**

1880-92 FAÏENCE AND PORCELAIN ART POTTERY.

Early mark incised - **F M G**

Mark on 'Royal Crown' ware. Printed- - -

1886-92 Mark on decorated faïence -

1880

1880 Gill & Sons, William, CASTLEFORD, Yorkshire, England.

1880-1932 EARTHENWARES. Printed-
1891 `England` added.

1880 Grindley & Co. Ltd., W. H., TUNSTALL, Staffordshire, England.

1880- EARTHENWARES, IRONSTONE, ETC.

1880-1914 Printed-
1891 `England` added.

c.1914-25 Factory`s name printed within marks of various patterns and designs.

W.H.GRINDLEY & Co.
GRINDLEY`S

1925- Printed marks of various types including- `Ltd` added.

W.H. GRINDLEY
& Co. Ltd.

c.1936-54 Printed-

c.1954- Printed-

1960 Factory acquired by Alfred Clough Ltd. see 1961 Clough`s Royal Art Pottery.

1880 Hallam & Day, LONGTON, Staffordshire, England.

1880-85 EARTHENWARES. Factory`s initials printed within various patterns and designs, including `Royal Arms` at times.

H. & D.

1880 Haines, Batchelor & Co., LONDON, England.

1880-90 RETAILER. Initials on china and earthenware made on their behalf.

H. B.

1880 Kratzer & Söhne, Josef, HAINDORF, Bohemia, Germany.

1880- HARD-PASTE PORCELAIN. - -

1880 Mellor, Taylor & Co., BURSLEM, Staffordshire, England.

1880-1904 EARTHENWARES. Factory`s name printed or impressed within marks of various patterns.

MELLOR, TAYLOR & Co.
`ROYAL IRONSTONE CHINA`
`SEMI PORCELAIN`

1880 Pearson, James, Ltd., Oldfield Pottery, CHESTERFIELD, England.

c.1880-1939 EARTHENWARES, ETC.

Impressed or printed- **J. P. LTD.**

1920 -

1930 -

1939 Merged with Pearson & Co.(Chesterfield) Ltd.

1880 Poole, Thomas, LONGTON, Staffordshire, England.

1880-1952 EARTHENWARE AND CHINA, Impressed or printed-

1912- Printed marks-

c.1929-52 Printed-

1948- Merged with Gladstone China Ltd.

Name changed see 1952 Royal Stafford China.

1880 Star Pottery, Johnstone Wardlaw, GLASGOW, Scotland.

1880-1907 EARTHENWARES, STONEWARES. Impressed or printed-

1880/81

1880 Turner & Wood, STOKE, Staffordshire, England.

1880-88 GENERAL CERAMICS. Impressed- **TURNER & WOOD STOKE.**

1880 Wagstaff & Brunt, LONGTON, Staffordshire, England.

1880-1927 EARTHENWARES AND CHINA. Factory`s name and initials printed within marks of various patterns and designs. **WAGSTAFF & BRUNT W. & B. LONGTON**

1880 Zeh, Scherzer & Co., REHAU, Bavaria, Germany.

1880- HARD-PASTE PORCELAIN. - - **Z. S. & CO. BAVARIA**

1880	Baggaley, Jacob, BURSLEM, England.	see 1870 Wood & Baggaley.
1880	Barnard, Harry, LAMBETH, England.	see 1815 Royal Doulton plc.
1880	Blackhurst & Bourne, BURSLEM, England,	see 1879 Blackhurst & T`cliffe.
1880	Brécy (Decorator) France.	see 1745 SÈVRES.
1880	Burgess & Campbell, TRENTON, U.S.A.	see 1860 Speeler, H. & Sons.
1880	Dale & Davis, TRENTON, U.S.A.	see 1875 Davis, Isaac,
1800	Devicq (Decorator) France.	see 1745 SÈVRES.
1880	Dörfl, Franz, (Decorator) Austria.	see 1719 VIENNA.
1880	Hamill, Brown & Co., BALTIMORE, U.S.A.	see 1879 Hamill & Bullock.
1880	Linnell, Florence, LAMBETH, England.	see 1815 Royal Doulton plc.
1880	Mclennan, John H., LAMBETH, England.	see 1815 Royal Doulton plc.
1880	Peluche (Decorator) France.	see 1745 SÈVRES.
1880	Pope, Frank C., LAMBETH, England.	see 1815 Royal Doulton plc.
1880	Rogers, Kate, LAMBETH, England.	see 1815 Royal Doulton plc.
1880	Schiffer, Hubert, Germany.	see 1565 RAEREN.
1880	Sturgeon, Katie, LAMBETH, England.	see 1815 Royal Doulton plc.
1880	Watt, Linnie, LAMBETH, England.	see 1815 Royal Doulton plc.

1881 Bauscher Brothers, WEIDEN, Upper Palatine, Germany.

1881- HARD-PASTE PORCELAIN for Hotels, railway and maritime companies, etc.,

1882- mark-

1881 Bauscher Brothers, WEIDEN, Upper Palatine, Germany. (Cont`)

1892- Norddeutsche Lloyd Shipping Line equipped with Hotel porcelain from the house of `Bauscher`

1895- New York Sales Agency established.

1911- mark-

1917- August Bauscher dies.
1918- Due to the war, Factory sold to `Bank fur Thuringen`

1919- mark-

1920- Bauscher supplies 98% of all American catering imports of porcelain.

1921- mark AS BELOW.

1927- Merger with Lorenz Hutschenreuther, Selb, as a subsidiary company. see 1857 Hutschenreuther, L.,
1946- Production resumes after the war.
1960- Heinz H. Engler. Designer of system B 1100, still the best selling table ware in the world.
1978- First shipment to the USSR. Pan Am is equipped with Bauscher tableware.

Modern and present mark-

(Courtesy of Hutschenreuther AG, Germany)

1881 Booth, Frederick, BRADFORD, W. Yorkshire, England.

c.1881 EARTHENWARES.

Mark with shield and a potters wheel- **F. B.**

1881 Crescent Pottery Co., TRENTON, New Jersey, U.S.A.

1881 **Cook, C.H., and Hancock, W.S.,**
EARTHENWARE, WHITE GRANITE.
1885 State of New Jersey Coat of Arms

1890-96 Printed marks- -

Continued over -

1881

1881 Crescent Pottery Co., TRENTON, New Jersey, U.S.A. (Cont`)

Pattern marks - **`Dainty` and `Melloria`**

1896-98 Printed marks-

1899-

1881 Davis, John Heath, HANLEY, Staffordshire, England.

1881-91 EARTHENWARES. Printed with pattern mark- **J. H. DAVIS HANLEY**

1881 Frederick, Shenkle, Allen & Co., E. LIVERPOOL, Ohio, U.S.A.

1881- EARTHENWARES.
1888- **The Globe Pottery Co.** Semi-porcelain.

1896 marks - -

Made by
Globe Pottery Co
E.L.,O.

HOTEL
GP CO

Incorporated- see 1900 East Liverpool Potteries Co.

1881 Honiton Art Potteries Ltd., HONITON, Devon, England.

Pottery started its life in Honiton before 1763 when Samuel Ford was a master potter. The Fords were still there at the end of the 18th Century with two other known potters, Flood and Hussey, who had separate businesses. Earthenware was basic and rarely decorated.

Pieces were rarely marked

1881-c.95 **Webber, James,** DECORATED EARTHENWARE. Honiton`s first notable potter sold his wares in the streets of Exeter.

Marks not known.

c.1895- **Foster & Hunt.** EARTHENWARE.

Forster & Hunt Honiton	F H Honiton	Gee Crediton Devon
pre 1915 Rare impressed mark	pre 1915 Incised normal mark	c.1912 F. & H. outlet

Continued over -

1881 Honiton Art Potteries Ltd., HONITON, Devon, England. (Cont`)

1918-47 **Collard, C.,**

HONITON ENGLAND	HONITON	C Collard 1938	MADE IN ENGLAND
c.1920-29 Impressed	1920-47 Incised or black paint	1920-47 incised signature	c.1925 Impressed (rare)

COLLARD HONITON ENGLAND	HONITON POTTERIES.	COLLARD HONITON ENGLAND C	COLLARD HONITON ENGLAND HANDMADE	CC H England
c.1927-47 Impressed	c.1937 Stamp,black ink on Barton Pottery	c.1940-47 Impressed very rare	c.1940-47 Very rare	c.1940 Very rare in Collard`s hand.

1947-56 **<u>Collard in Retirement.</u>**

CC TORQUAY	H	COLLARD TORQUAY
c.1948-56 Stamp with black ink (rare)	c.1947 black paint (very rare)	c.1950 Impressed (very rare)

1947-55 **Hull, Norman, T.S.**
Also managed Norman Hull Pottery, Honiton.

HONITON ENGLAND	HONITON DEVON
1947-49 1920-29 revival Collard mark.	1948 Black painted mark

H HONITON DEVON J.B.	NORMAN HULL	MADE IN HONITON DEVON POTTERY ENGLAND
1948-55 Black painted mark often with decorators initials	c.1950 Black painted mark	1957 onwards Black stamped mark.

Continued over -

1881

1881 Honiton Art Potteries Ltd., HONITON, Devon, England. (Cont`)

Various marks from 1950 onwards:-

1950-60

1956

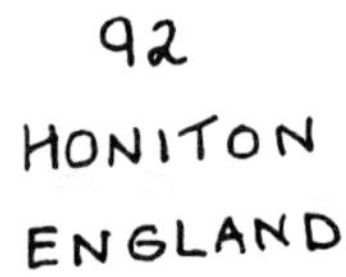

1956

1958-65

1965-67

1965-67

1994 **Dartmouth Pottery acquired business.**

see 1948 Dartmouth Pottery

(Courtesy of Mr P. Redvers (M.Dir.) Honiton Pottery Ltd.)
Marks by kind permission of Mr Carl Rosen, Chairman of Honiton Pottery Collectors Society, 112 Sylvan Ave., London, N22 5JB.

1881 Karlsbader Kaolin-Industrie-Gesellschaft, MERKELSGRÜN, Ger.

1881- HARD-PASTE PORCELAIN. - -

1881 Kindler, Bernard, AUSSIG, Bohemia, Germany.

1881- GENERAL POTTERY. - - - **P. K.**

Kindler, Paul, **A.**

1881 Mayer Pottery Co. Ltd., BEAVER FALLS, PA. U.S.A.

1881- **J.& E. Mayer.** WHITE GRANITE WARES.
1881-91 Marks on white granite wares - - -

Semi-vitreous china -

State of Pennsylvania mark- -

Continued over -

1881 Mayer Pottery Co. Ltd., BEAVER FALLS, PA. U.S.A. (Cont`)

`Nile` and `Amazon` marks for toilet ware -

Factory`s name printed within marks of various patterns and designs. - **J. & E. MAYER**

1896- Pattern marks used on special services- **`DIANA`**
`POTOMAC`
`WINDSOR`

1881 Plant & Co., R.H., LONGTON, Staffordshire, England.

1881-98 PORCELAIN.

Printed- -

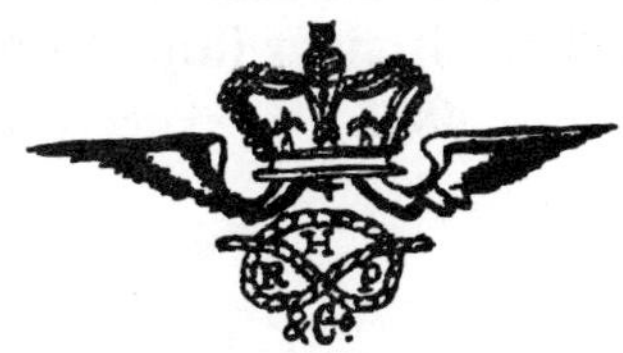

c.1898- Plant Ltd., R.H. & S.L., Tuscan Works.
Factory`s name or trade-mark `Tuscan` are printed within marks of various patterns and designs.
Numerals added indicate the year,
i.e. 74 = 1974

R.H. & S.L. PLANT
PLANT
TUSCAN CHINA

TUSCAN CHINA
METALLISED
MADE IN ENGLAND

1881 Robinson & Son, Foley China Works, LONGTON, Staffs. England.

1881-1903 PORCELAIN. Factory`s initials printed or impressed within marks of various patterns and designs.

R. & S.
L.
FOLEY CHINA

1903- Brain & Co. Ltd., E., FENTON. Trade name- **HARJIAN**
ENGLAND

Impressed mark- **E. B. & CO.**
F.

Printed mark- -

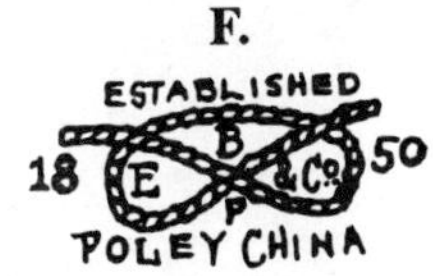

1905-48 Printed marks -

FOLEY
ENGLISH BONE CHINA
PAINTED BY HAND

1948- Printed mark- -

1958 Now Coalport a division of the Wedgwood Group.

1881/82

1881 Schertler, Fr. PILSEN, Bohemia, Germany. **F. S**

1881- HARD-PASTE PORCELAIN. - - **P**

1881 Schumann, Carl, ARZBERG, Bavaria, Germany.

1881- HARD-PASTE PORCELAIN. - -

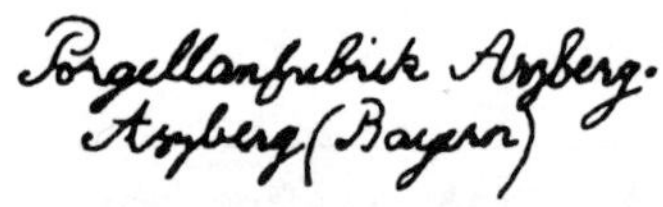

1881 Strnact jun., Josef, TURN, Bohemia, Germany.

1881- PORCELAIN DECORATOR. - -

1881	Alexander III. Russia, - - - -	see 1744 ST. PETERSBURG.
1881	Bodley & Son, E.F., LONGTON, England. -	see 1862 Bodley & Co. E.F.
1881	Gildea & Walker, BURSLEM, England. - -	see 1870 Bates Elliott & Co.
1881	Mangendre, (Sculptor) France. - - -	see 1745 SÈVRES.
1881	Renard, H. (Decorator) France. - - -	see 1745 SÈVRES.
1881	Tempest,Brockmann & Sampson, U.S.A. -	see 1861 Tempest, Brockmann,

---

1882 Baxter, Rowley & Tams, LONGTON, Staffordshire, England.

1882-85 PORCELAIN. Impressed- **B. R. & T.**

1882 Beck, A.M., Crown Pottery, EVANSVILLE, IND., U.S.A.

1882-84 MAJOLICA.
1884- **Bennighof, Uhl & Co., White ware.**
1891- **Crown Pottery Co.,**

Factory`s initials found with pattern marks usually with a `crown` on dinner ware:- **`REX` `REGINA` `ROYAL` JEWEL`** **C. P. Co.**

Mark on semi-porcelain-

Pattern marks on toilet ware:- **`ALMA` `HELEN` `HOBSON` `RENA`**

Mark on Hotel ware- **CROWN HOTEL WARE**

c.1903 **Crown Pottery Co. and Peoria Pottery Co. merged to make the Crown Potteries Co.**

1882 Bennett (Hanley) Ltd., William, HANLEY, Staffordshire, England.

1882-1937 Earthenwares. Factory`s name and initials printed or impressed within marks of various patterns and designs.

W. B.
H.
WILLIAM BENNETT
HANLEY

1882 Burmantofts, Wilcox & Co. Ltd., LEEDS, W. Yorkshire, England.

1882-1904 Art-pottery. Impressed- **BURMANTOFTS FAIENCE**

Impressed-

1904-14 **Leeds Fireclay Co. Ltd.,**
Earthenwares, Terra-cotta.

L.
F. C.

Trade-names- **LEFICO**
GRANITOFTS

1914 Utilitarian wares only after this date.

1882 Candy &Co. Ltd., Great Western Pot`s. NEWTON ABBOT, England.

1882- Earthenwares. Factory`s initials printed or impressed within marks of differing designs. - - -

C
N A

20th Century Trade-mark - - **CANDY WARE**

1882 Crystal Porcelain Pottery Co.Ltd., COBRIDGE, Staff`s, England.

1882-86 Porcelain and pottery. Factory`s initials printed or impressed within marks of various patterns and designs. especially a dove mark.

C. P. P. CO.

1882 Day, George, LONGTON, Staffordshire, England.

1882-89 Earthenwares.

Printed-

STAFFORDSHIRE

1882 Dressler, Julius, BIELA, Bohemia, Germany.

1882- General pottery. - - -

1882

1882 Edwards & Brown, LONGTON, Staffordshire, England.

1882-1933 PORCELAIN. Factory`s initials printed or impressed within marks of varoius patterns and designs. **E. & B. L.**

1910-33 Printed-

1882 Lang, Jean, VILLEDIEU-SUR-INDRE, France.

1882- PORCELAIN. - - -

J L
V
FRANCE

1882 Lowe, Ratcliffe & Co., LONGTON, Staffordshire, England.

1882-92 EARTHENWARES. Printed or impressed-

1882 Morimura Brothers & Co., Tokyo, Japan.

1882-90 WHOLESALERS AND CHINA DECORATORS.
Forerunner of Noritake Co. Ltd.
Some of the individual artists signatures:-

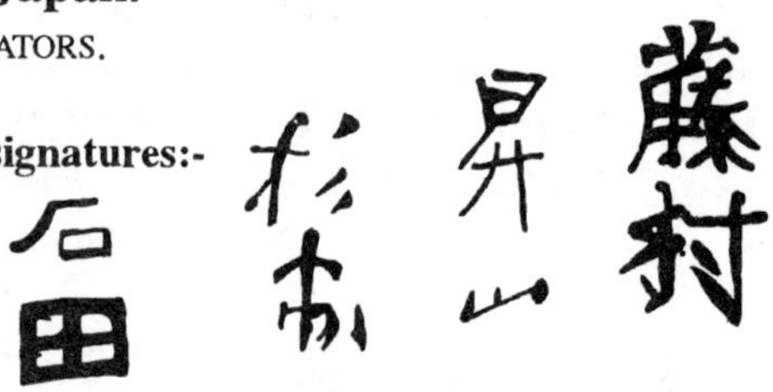

1904- **Noritake Co. Ltd.** see 1904 Noritake Co.Ltd.

1882 Ohme, Hermann, NIEDER-SALZBRUNN, Silesia, Germany.

1882- HARD-PASTE PORCELAIN.

1882 Salopian Art Pottery Co., BENTHALL, Shropshire, England.

1882-c.1912 EARTHENWARES. Impressed- **SALOPIAN**

1882 Schaller, Oscar, & Co. SCHWARZENBACH, Germany.

1882- HARD-PASTE PORCELAIN HOUSEHOLD WARE ETC.
1882-1917 Printed marks

1917- **Winterling Porzellan acquired the Company.** see 1907 Winterling OHG.

1882 Unterweissbacher Werkstatten fur Porzellankunst GmbH., Germany.

1882- HARD-PASTE PORCELAIN. Specializing in figurines decorated in true lace, hunting scenes and richly decorated carriages.

1882- **Hermann Jost (founder) Traded under the name of Mann & Porzelius Porcelain Factory.**

1909- **Max Adolph Pfeiffer acquired the factory** and started an ambitious artistic programme that was part of the reform efforts in applied arts at the beginning of the century. He created the brand Schwarzburger Werkstatten fur Porzellankunst and marked the sculptures with the prowling fox. - -

Renowned sculptors were commissioned to create models that became master works of European art. Among those were:- Ernst Barlach, Max Esser, Gerhard Marcks, Paul Scheurich, Etha Richter, etc.

1910- Gold Medal at World Exhibition in Brussels.

1910- Silver Medal at the International Hunting Exhibition in Vienna.

1911- Special Award at Turin Exhibition.

1913- Gold Medals in Leipzig and Geneva.

1915- Medal at the Baltic Exibition.

c.1927 **Schaubach, Heinz, acquired the factory.**

1990 **German reunification.**

1990- **Königlich priv. Porzellanfabrik Tettau,(part of the SELTMANN Group) acquired factory.** see 1794 Tettau GmbH.

1995- Thuringian porcelain figurines are still modelled, designed and painted exclusively by hand, as they have always been.

Modern mark (1995) -

(By courtesy of Porzellanfabriken Chr. Seltmann GmbH., Weiden, Germany)

1882 Wolfinger, R., WEINGARTEN, Baden, Germany.

1882- **Porzellanfabrik Weingarten.** HARD-PASTE. - **P. W.**

1882/83

1882 Wood & Hawthorne, COBRIDGE, Staffordshire, England.

1882-87 EARTHENWARES. Printed with `Royal Arms` — **WOOD & HAWTHORNE ENGLAND**

1887-93 **Sant & Vodrey.** Printed or impressed- **S. & V. COBRIDGE**

1882 Wood & Hulme, BURSLEM, Staffordshire, England. **W. & H.**

1882-1905 EARTHENWARES. - Printed or impressed- **B.**

1906-32 **Hulme & Sons, Henry,** Mark as above.

1882	Bridgett & Bates, LONGTON, England. -	see 1875 Bridgett,Bates & Beech.
1882	Doulton & Co.Ltd., BURSLEM, England.	see 1815 Royal Doulton plc.
1882	Dudson, J.T., HANLEY, England. -	see 1809 Dudson, Thomas,
1882	Ford & Riley, BURSLEM, England. -	see 1876 Whittingham, Ford & Riley.
1882	Malkin & Sons, Ralph, FENTON, England.	see 1863 Malkin, Ralph.
1882	Paillet, (Figures) France. - - -	see 1745 SÈVRES.
1882	Star Encaustic Tile Co., U.S.A. - -	see 1876 Pittsburgh Encaustic Tile Co.

1883 Bretby Art Pottery, Tooth & Co. Ltd., BURTON-ON-TRENT, Eng.

1883-87 **Tooth & Ault, Earthenwares.**
Printed or impressed- -

c.1883-1900 Tooth, Henry, Initials - - HT

1887- **Tooth & Co.**
1891 `England` added

c.1914- - **CLANTA WARE**

(By kind permission of Bretby Art Pottery, Tooth & Co.Ltd. England.)

1883 Forester & Sons Ltd., Thomas, FENTON, Staffordshire, England.

1883-1959 PORCELAIN AND EARTHENWARES. Factory`s initials found within marks of various patterns and designs. **T. F. & S.**

1891-1912 Printed-
`Ltd` or `Ld` added

1910-59 Found on marks of various patterns and designs. **PHOENIX WARE** **PHOENIX CHINA**

1883 Hall & Read, HANLEY, Staffordshire, England.

1883-88 EARTHENWARES. Printed with pattern name- Sometimes in the form of a horse-shoe.

HALL & READ
HANLEY

1883 Hobson, G. & J., BURSLEM, Staffordshire, England.

1883-1901 EARTHENWARES. Printed- **HOBSON'S**

1901-23 Hobson, George,

1883 Jacobus, Pauline, Mrs., CHICAGO, U.S.A.

1883- ART WARES. Early marks were impressed - Later ones printed black - 'C' stands for CHICAGO

1888-c.94 Pauline Pottery Co., EDGERTON, WIS.

1883 Johnson Brothers Ltd., HANLEY, Staffordshire, England.

1883-EARTHENWARES, SEMI-PORCELAIN, ETC.

Henry and Alfred Johnson joined forces and set up in business to manufacture semi-porcelain at a factory in Hanley. The brothers expanded their manufacturing activity and they built three factories in Stoke-on-Trent:-

1883- Name of Factory printed or impressed within marks of various patterns and designs, including 'Coat of Arms' -

JOHNSON BROS.
ENGLAND

1888- **Hanley Pottery.**

1889- **Alexandra Pottery.**

1891- **Imperial Pottery.**
All these factories were specially adapted for large-scale production of their fine earthenware tableware for world-wide markets.

1896- **The Trent Pottery was built.**

c.1900 Printed mark-

c.1913 Printed marks -

Continued over -

1883

1883 Johnson Brothers Ltd., HANLEY, Staffordshire, England. (Cont`)

1960- **Eastwood Pottery acquired.**
Various patterns and designs of recent marks:-

1968- **Joined the Wedgwood Group.**

Modern mark with `Bull Logo` -

(By kind permission of Johnson Brothers Ltd., A Wedgwood Company, Stoke-on-Trent,England.)

1883 Kaestner, Friedrich, OBERHOHNDORF, Saxony, Germany.

1883- HARD-PASTE PORCELAIN. - -

1883 Matthes & Ebel, MÄBENDORF, Saxony, Germany.

1883- HARD-PASTE PORCELAIN. - -

1883 Meakin, Charles, HANLEY, Staffordshire, England.

1883-89 EARTHENWARES. Printed-

see 1851 J. & G. Meakin.

1883 Morgan Art Pottery Co., Matt, CINCINNATI, Ohio, U.S.A.

1883- ART WARES. Impressed-

Company failed after a short period of manufacture but during that time it produced pieces of the highest quality from its very competent decorators and artists.

Hirschfeld, N.J., (decorator) - - **N. J. H.**

1883 Mosa, Koninklijke, B.V., MAASTRICHT, Holland.

PORCELAIN, TABLEWARE AND CERAMIC TILES.

1883- **Regout, Hubertus Gerardus Louis, (Founder)** **LOUIS REGOUT MAASTRICHT**

Specialized in chinese type wares.

1883-c.1900- marks--

c.1900-c.1914- marks- -

1914- **World War 1. Louis Regout II was director of the company.**

c.1918-1930 marks:-

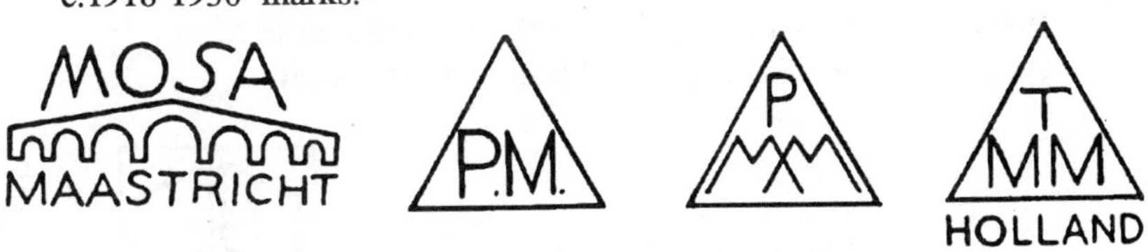

1925- English-type tea services were being produced, such as `Stuart` `Grimsby` `Dover` and `Bristol`

1932- **Earthenware introduced.**

1939-45 **Second World War.** Factory fared badly and only got back to normal in 1945, after which there was the post-war boom.

c.1941-47 marks- -

1950- **Bellefroid, Edmond, (designer) joins company.**

c.1950-66-marks-

Continued over -

1883

1883 Mosa, Koninklijke, B.V., MAASTRICHT, Holland. (Cont`)

1957- **`Golden Badge` awarded in Brussels for `Noblesse` tea service.**

1966-77 marks-

1972- **Last Regout descendent resigned as director and Mosa became part of Thyssen Bornemisza Group.**

1975- **DSM Building division acquire Mosa.**

1977-83 mark- - - -

1983- **`Royal` status granted to Mosa for its 100 years of continuous existence.**

1983-87 mark- - - -

1984- **Redland and Bredero acquire Mosa.**

1985- **Redland acquire 100% shareholding in Mosa.**

1991- **France Alfa buys Mosa from Redland.**

Modern marks (1995) -

1987 1993

(By kind permission of Koninklijke Mosa B.V. Maastricht, Holland.)

1883 Rathbone, Smith & Co.,Soho Pottery, TUNSTALL, Staffs, England.

1883-97 EARTHENWARES. Factoy`s initials printed within marks of various patterns and designs. **R. S. & CO.**

1897-1900 **Smith & Binnall,** - Printed-

1901-06 **Soho Pottery Ltd.** - Printed-

1906-44 at COBRIDGE. Factory`s name printed within various marks. **SOHO POTTERY LTD. COBRIDGE**

Continued over -

1883 Rathbone, Smith & Co., Soho Pottery, England. (Cont`)

1901-06 **Soho Pottery Ltd. (Cont`)**

Pattern names- **SEMI-PORCELAIN**, **SOLIAN WARE**, **AMBASSADOR**, **QUEENS GREEN**, **HOMESTEAD**, **CHANTICLEER**

1944- **Simpsons (Potters) Ltd.** Factory`s name printed within marks of various patterns and designs.

SIMPSONS (POTTERS) LTD.

1883 Schmidt & Co. Porzellanfabrik Viktoria, ALT-ROHLAU, Germany.

1883- HARD-PASTE PORCELAIN. (Victoria) - -

1883	Booth, T.G.& F., TUNSTALL, England. -	see 1868 Booth & Co., T.
1883	Dunn, William E., LAMBETH, England.	see 1815 Doulton & Watts.
1883	Ligné, (Decorator) France.- - -	see 1745 SÈVRES.
1883	Pointon & Co.Ltd., HANLEY, England. -	see 1870 Scrivener & Co. R.G.
1883	Rhodes & Proctor, BURSLEM, England.	see 1873 Tundley,Rhodes & Proctor.
1883	Rowe, William, LAMBETH, England. -	see 1815 Doulton & Watts.
1883	Sieffert, (Decorator) France. - -	see 1745 SÈVRES.
1883	Simard, (Decorator) France. - -	see 1745 SÈVRES.
1883	Simson, Gebr, Germany. - - -	see 1757 GOTHA.
1883	Union Pottery Co., TRENTON, U.S.A. -	see 1869 New Jersey Pottery Co.

1884 Auvera, Carl, ARZBERG, Bavaria, Germany.

1884- HARD-PASTE PORCELAIN. - -

1884 British Anchor Pottery Co. Ltd., LONGTON, Staffordshire, England.

1884- EARTHENWARES.

1884-1913 Printed or impressed-
1891 `England` added.

Continued over -

1884

1884 British Anchor Pottery Co.Ltd., LONGTON, England. (Cont`)

1910-40 Printed or impressed-

BRITISH ANCHOR
POTTERY
ENGLAND

1940-45 Factory closed.

1945- Factory`s name printed within marks of various patterns and designs. Sometimes with crown and with various trade-names -

BRITISH ANCHOR

REGENCY
MONTMARTRE
RICHMOND
HOSTESS
TRIANON

1971- Hostess Tableware Ltd.

1884 Gimson & Co., Wallis, FENTON, Staffordshire, England.

1884-90 EARTHENWARES. Printed with beehive - **WALLIS GIMSON & CO.**

1884 Günthersfeld, Porzellanfabrik, GEHREN, Thuringia, Germany.

1884- HARD-PASTE PORCELAIN. -

1884 Krautheim & Adelberg, SELB, Bavaria, Germany.

1884- DECORATORS. - -

1884 Oliphant & Co., Delaware Pottery, TRENTON, New Jersey, U.S.A.

c.1884- EARTHENWARE, Some Belleek porcelain.

Impressed or printed black-

see 1892 Trenton Potteries Co.

1884 Wood Ltd., H.J., BURSLEM, Staffordshire, England.

1884- EARTHENWARES. - -

c.1884- - - - -

c.1930- Charlotte Rhead mark - -

c.1935- E. Radford mark -

c.1948-c.62- Factory`s name printed within marks of various patterns and designs

H. J. WOOD LTD.
ENGLAND

1884	Alpaugh & Magowan, TRENTON, U.S.A. -	see 1863 Coxon & Co.
1884	Bennighof, Uhl & Co., EVANSVILLE, U.S.A. -	see 1882 Beck, A.M.,
1884	Cleary, James, Ireland. - - - -	see 1857 Belleek Pottery.
1884	Eyre, John, LAMBETH, England. - -	see 1815 Royal Doulton plc.
1884	Hallion, E. (Landscapes) France. - - -	see 1745 SÈVRES.
1884	Poulson Bros. Ltd., FERRYBRIDGE, England. -	see 1843 Reed & Taylor.

1885 Buckley, Heath & Co., BURSLEM, Staffordshire, England.

1885-90 EARTHENWARES. Printed or impressed-

1885 Gater & Co.,Thomas, BURSLEM, Staffordshire, England.

1885-94 EARTHENWARES.

1895-1943 **Gater, Hall & Co. TUNSTALL.**
1907 moved to BURSLEM.
Factory`s initials found within marks of various patterns and designs.

G. H.& CO.

1914- Printed-

1936-43 Printed- -

1943- **Barratt`s of Staffordshire Ltd.** Acquired the Factory. see 1943 Barratt`s

1885

1885 Gibson & Sons Ltd. BURSLEM, Staffordshire, England.

1885- EARTHENWARES.

c.1904-09 Printed- - - -
Harvey Pottery

1905 Printed- within marks of various patterns and designs. **G. & S. LTD. B.**

c.1909-1930 Printed- within marks of various patterns and designs. **G. & S. LTD. GIBSON & SONS Ltd.**

c.1940- - **GIBSONS**

c.1950- Printed-

1885 Goldscheidersche Factory, VIENNA, Austria.

1885-1954 Porcelain, Majolica, Terracotta and Artistic stoneware, etc.
1910- Faïences made only

(See W. Neuwirth's *Wiener Keramic* *for further information)*

1885 ÖSPAG, WIEN, Austria.

1885-CHINA HOTELWARE AND SANITARY WARE.

Originally the pottery was founded in 1795 by a **Martin Leinwather,** a textile manufacturer, who went into partnership with an Englishman.

1883-Lichtenstern, Heinrich, acquired the factory in a Real Estate transaction, and placed his son, Richard (who had failed at school) into the pottery at Wilhelmsburg.

porcelain
Before 1900

c.1900- marks - - -

porcelain

sanitary

Continued over -

1885 ÖSPAG, WIEN, Austria. (Cont`)

1886-Richard Lichtenstern took over the factory and from a one kiln plant advanced the factory to 17 kilns with a workforce of over 450. By 1912 the factory had become the largest earthenware company in the Austro-Hungarian Empire.

c.1910-14 marks -

porcelain

sanitary

1912-Maravia sanitary factory acquired.
1914-Northern Bohemia sanitary factory acquired.
c.1918 These two factories above became known as Ditmar-Urbach AG. in the new independent Czechoslavakia.

c.1918-22 marks -

porcelain

sanitary

1923-Wilhemsburg factory added sanitary ware to its production.

c.1938-45 marks -

sanitary

porcelain

1937- Richard Lichtenstern died.
1948-Controlling stock of the Austrian Corporation was returned to Conrad Lester (son of Richard Lichtenstern) who had changed his name during his war-time stay in the U.S.A. army.
1948-The factories in Czechoslovakia were taken over by the Communist Regime.

c.1945-60 marks -

sanitary

From 1956

From 1958

1968- ÖSPAG joined the Laufen Group.

c.1967- marks

LAUFEN

sanitary

porcelain
From 1993

1990sPaul C. Lester (4th generation of the Lichtenstern-Lester family) is still active in the company as superintendent of the Gmunden plant.

(By kind permission of ÖSPAG, Wien, Austria.)

1885 Porsgrunds Porselaensfabrik A/S, PORSGRUNN, Norway.

1887- PORCELAIN TABLEWARE AND DECORATIVE OBJECTS.

(By courtesy of Porsgrunds Porselaensfabrik A/S, Norway.) 1995

1885 Sutcliffe & Co.Ltd.,MANCHESTER, Lancashire, England.

c.1885-1901 TILES. Printed or impressed-

1885 Wilkinson Ltd., Arthur J.,Staffordshire BURSLEM, England.

Royal Staffordshire Pottery,

1885- EARTHENWARES.

c.1891-1909 Printed within marks of various patterns and designs including Coat of Arms.
c.1896 `Ltd` added

WILKINSON`S
A.J. WILKINSON Ltd.
ROYAL STAFFORDSHIRE
POTTERY

c.1910- Printed-

c.1930- Printed-
`Clarice Cliff` marks

c.1930-47 Printed-

1964 **Merged with Midwinter Ltd.,W.R.**

1885 Winkle & Wood, HANLEY, Staffordshire, England.

1885-90 EARTHENWARES.

Printed- 

1890-1931 **Winkle & Co.Ltd., F., STOKE.**

1890-1910 Printed or impressed within marks of various patterns and designs. **F. W.& Co. ENGLAND**

1890-1910 **F. WINKLE & CO**
1911 `Ltd` added.

1890-1925 Printed- - - - 

1908-25 Printed or impressed- - 

1925-31 Printed- - - - - - - 

1885 Wood & Co.,Thomas, BURSLEM, Staffordshire, England.

1885-96 EARTHENWARES. Printed or impressed- **T. W. & CO.**

1896-97 **Wood & Sons, Thomas,** Printed- **T. W. & S.**
within marks of various patterns and designs,

1897-1903 **Wood & Barker Ltd.** Printed- - 

1885	Gildea, James, BURSLEM, England. -	see 1870 Bates,Elliott & Co.
1885	Kinsho Company, Japan. - - -	see 1875 TOKIO.
1885	Marzolf & Cie, France. - - -	see 1815 MONTREUIL.
1885	Pioneer Pottery Co.,WELLSVILLE, U.S.A.	see 1879 Morley & Co.
1885	Rozenburg Factory, Holland, - -	see 1766 HAGUE, THE,.
1885	Schneider & Hutschenreuther, Germany.-	see 1861 Unger, Schneider & Hutsch`.
1885	Vater, Josef, Austria. - - -	see 1719 VIENNA.

1886

1886 Avon Pottery, CINCINNATI, Ohio, U.S.A.

1886-c.87 EARTHENWARES. - - - **AVON**

1886 Cumberlidge & Humphreys, TUNSTALL, Staffordshire, England.

1886-89 and 1893-95 EARTHENWARES. Printed or impressed marks within various patterns and designs. **C. & M.** / **C. & M. TUNSTALL**

1886 Grimwades Bros., Winton Pottery, HANLEY, Staffordshire, England

1886-1900 EARTHENWARES, CHINA.

Printed- -

1900- **Grimwades Ltd., HANLEY & STOKE.**

Printed- -

c.1906- Various printed marks usually with Factory`s name and trade-marks as follows-
WINTON, RUBIAN ART,

c.1930-34 **VITRO HOTEL WARE, ROYAL WINTON.**

1930 `Royal` added

c.1951- Printed- -

1964 **Howard Pottery Co. acquired the Company.**
1976 **Taunton Vale Industries " " "**
1979 **Staffordshire Potteries " " "**
Now part of Coloroll Group.

Modern mark - -

By kind permission of Royal Winton Pottery, Stoke-on-Trent.)

1886 Hines Brothers, FENTON, Staffordshire, England.

1886-1907 EARTHENWARES. Impressed- **H. B.**

Printed-

1907- **Grimwades Ltd. acquired Factory.**

1886 Hutschenreuther, H., PROBSTZELLA, Thuringia, Germany.

1886- HARD-PASTE PORCELAIN. - -

1886 Keeling & Co.Ltd., BURSLEM, Staffordshire, England.

1886-1936 EARTHENWARES. Printed within marks of various patterns and designs. - **K. & CO.** **K. & CO. B.**

Trade-mark - -
1891 `England` added
1909 `Ltd` added -

c.1912-36 Trade-name- **LOSOL WARE**
see 1870 Bates, Elliott & Co.

1886 Lourioux, Louis, FOECY, Cher, France.

1886- PORCELAIN, LUXURY AND UTILITY WARES.

Early marks - - -

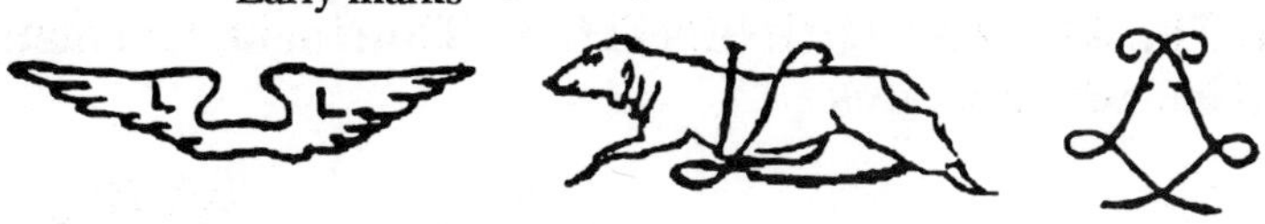

c.1925 -

1930-49 Madam Lourioux mark -

1942-80 **Société Française de Porcelaine.**

1942-80 marks

1980 **Porcelaine Phillipe Deshoulieres.**
TABLE AND HOTEL WARES.
1980 mark - - PHILIPPE DESHOULIERES PORCELAINE · FRANCE

(By kind permission of Philippe Deshoulieres, Limoges, France.)

1886

1886 Meyer, Siegm. Paul, BAYREUTH, Bavaria, Germany.

1886- HARD-PASTE PORCELAIN. - -

1886 New Milford Pottery Co., CONNECTICUT, U.S.A.

1886 EARTHENWARES - -

Re-named The Wannopee Pottery Co. -

Lang & Schafer (New York agents) - -

1886 Recknagel, Th., ALEXANDRINENTHAL, Thuringia, Germany.

1886- HARD-PASTE PORCELAIN. - -

1886 Whittaker & Co.,HANLEY, Staffordshire, England.

1886-92	EARTHENWARES.	Printed within marks of various patterns.	**W. & Co.**
1892-98	**Whittaker, Heath & Co.** Printed within marks of various designs- -		**W. H. & CO.**

1886	Hugo Auvera Jr., HONENBERG, Germany. -	see 1814 Hutschenreuther, C.M.,
1886	Jardel (Decorator) France. - - - -	see 1745 SÈVRES.
1886	Old Hall Porcelain Works Ltd.,HANLEY, England.	see 1805 Meigh,Job,

1887 Ault, William, SWADLINCOTE, Sth. Derbyshire, England.

1887-1923 EARTHENWARES.

Printed-

1887- Printed or impressed monogram - -

1891-96 Christopher Dresser designed for this factory and some wares bear his signature.

1923-37 **Ault & Tunnicliffe Ltd.**

Printed or impressed-

1937- **Ault Potteries Ltd.** Printed or impressed-

1887 Barker Pottery Co.,CHESTERFIELD, Derbyshire, England.

1887-1957 STONEWARES.

1928-57 Printed or impressed-

1887 Colclough & Co.,Stanley Pottery, LONGTON, Staff's, England.

1887-1928 CHINA AND EARTHENWARES.

1903-19 Printed- -

1919-28 Printed- -

1928-31 **Stanley Pottery Ltd.** Same marks continued.

1887

1887 Cope & Co.Ltd.,J.H. Wellington Works, LONGTON, Staffs, England.

1887-1947 PORCELAIN. Printed or impressed- **C. & CO.**

c.1900- Printed mark within various patterns and designs. - **J. H. C. & CO.**

c.1906-47- Printed- within various designs. **WELLINGTON CHINA**

1887 Day & Pratt, LONGTON, Staffordshire, England.

1887-88 CHINA. Printed or impressed- **DAY & PRATT**

1887 Delaherche, Auguste, PARIS, France.

c.1887- STUDIO POTTER IN STONEWARE.

Incised or impressed-

1887 Fenton & Sons, Alfred, HANLEY, Staffordshire, England.

1887-1901 GENERAL CERAMICS. Printed or impressed marks within various patterns and designs. **A.F. & S.**

1887 Forester & Hulme, FENTON, Staffordshire, England.

1887-93 EARTHENWARES.

Printed-

c.1891 `England` added.

1893-1902 **Hulme & Christie,** Printed-

1902-03 **Christie & Beardmore.** Printed marks- within various patterns and designs. **C. B.** **C. B. F.**

1903-14 **Beardmore & Co.,Frank,** Printed or impressed- marks within various patterns and designs. **F. B. & CO.** **FRANK BEARDMORE & CO.**

1887 Hammersley & Co.,LONGTON, Staffordshire, England.

1887-1932 PORCELAIN. Printed or impressed- marks within various designs including a crown. — **H. & C.** / **H. & CO.**

1912-39 Printed- **HAMMERSLEY & CO.** with crown. - - -

1932- **Hammersley & Co.(Longton) Ltd.**

1939 Printed- BONE CHINA - -

1887 Heubach, Ernst, and Marseille,Armand, KÖPPELSDORF, Germany.

1887- HARD-PASTE PORCELAIN. - -

1919- Dolls` heads. porcelain and biscuit.

Vereinigte Köppelsdorfer Porzellanfabriken.

1930 - - -

1887 Johnson Ltd.,Samuel, BURSLEM, Staffordshire, England.

1887-1931 EARTHENWARES. Printed marks- within various patterns and designs. - 1912 `Ltd` added. — **S. J.** / **S. J. B.** / **S. J. LTD.**

1916-31 **Britannia Pottery** Printed-

1887 Knoch Bros., NEUSTADT, Coburg, Germany.

1887- PORCELAIN DOLLS AND DOLLS` HEADS. -

1887

1887 Lamm, A., DRESDEN, Germany.

1887- DECORATOR IN MEISSEN STYLE. -

1887 Massey Wildblood & Co., LONGTON, Staffordshire, England.

1887-89 CHINA. Printed marks of various designs - **M. W. & CO.**

1887 McNay & Sons, Charles W., BO`NESS, Central Region, Scotland.

1887-1958 EARTHENWARES.

c.1946-58 Stick-on labels-

1887 Schumann, Christoph, ARZBERG, Bavaria, Germany.

1887- HARD-PASTE PORCELAIN.
Founder Christoph Schumann.

1891- Theodor Lehmann acquired factory.

1892- Registration of porcelain factory, `Lehmann & Oberg`

1903- Sale of factory to `Porzellanfabrik Schönwald AG` for 650,000 RM.

1906- Factory renamed `Porzellanfabrik Schönwald Abteilung Arzberg`

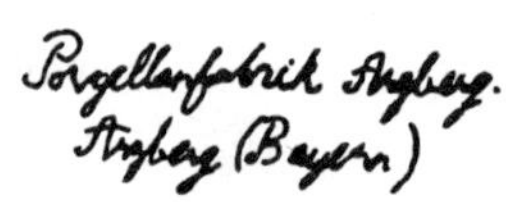

1908- Theodor Lehmann dies.

1927- Porcelain factories Schönwald and Arzberg are intergrated into the Kahla-Corporation of Thuringia.

1936/37 Gold medal award for Arzberg tableware 1382 VI Triennial, Milan. and World Fair, Paris.

1954- Gold medal award for Arzberg tableware 2000 (designer Heinrich Loffelhardt) at X Triennial.

1972- Merger of Kahla AG, Schönwald, with Hutschenreuther AG, Selb.

1987- Elected `Good Design Product` for `Arzberg city modern art` in Japan.

see 1857 Hutschenreuther AG.

(Courtesy of Huschenreuther AG, Germany)

1887 Sebring Pottery Co., EAST LIVERPOOL, Ohio, U.S.A.

1887- WHITE GRANITE

1887 Shore & Co.,J. LONGTON, Staffordshire, England.

1887-1905 CHINA. Printed marks- within various patterns and designs. — **J. S. & CO.**

1905-10 **Shore, Coggins & Holt.** CHINA AND EARTHENWARES. Printed-

1911- **Shore & Coggins.** Printed marks- within various patterns and designs. — **BELL CHINA**
SHORE & COGGINS
S. & C.

1949-59 Printed- within various marks. — **QUEEN ANNE**
FINE BONE CHINA

1887 Warrilow & Sons Ltd.,George, LONGTON, Staffordshire, England.

1887-1940 PORCELAIN. Printed marks- within various patterns and designs. 1928 `S` `Sons` & `Ltd` added - — **G. W.**
G. W. & S.
G. W. & SONS

1941- **Rosina China Co. Ltd.,** Printed marks within various designs including a crown.

1946- -

1887 Warwick China Co., WHEELING, West Virginia, U.S.A.

1887 Semi-porcelain

c.1892- - -

1893-98 - - — **WARWICK**
SEMI PORCELAIN

1898- - - - — **WARWICK**
CHINA

1887/88

1887 Wildblood, Richard Vernon, LONGTON, Staffordshire, England.

1887-88 CHINA.

Printed-

1889-99 **Wildblood & Heath,** Printed with crown - **W & H**

1899-1927 **Wildblood, Heath & Sons Ltd.** Printed - with crown **W.H.& S. L**

c.1908 Printed-
c.1915 `Ltd` added.

1887 Aller Vale Art Potteries, NEWTON ABBOT, England. see 1868 Phillips & Co.,John.
1887 Bloch, Achille, and Bourdois, Leon, PARIS, France. see 1773 Porcelains de Paris.
1887 Brockmann Pottery Co. CINCINNATI, U.S.A. - see 1861 Tempest,Brockmann & Co.
1887 Collingwood Bros.Ltd.,LONGTON, England. - see 1870 Collingwood & Greatbatch.
1887 La Belle Pottery Co. WHEELING, U.S.A. - see 1879 Wheeling Pottery Co.
1887 Sant & Vodrey, COBRIDGE, England. - - see 1882 Wood & Hawthorne.
1887 Shaw & Sons Ltd.,George, ROTHERHAM, England. see 1870 Jackson & Co. J.
1887 Tooth & Co.,BURTON-ON-TRENT, England. - see 1883 Bretby Art Pottery.
1887 Trager, H. (Decorator) France. - - - see 1745 SÈVRES.
1887 Wolffsen, Chr. L., ROENNE, Denmark. - - see 1835 Søholm A/S.

1888 East Trenton Pottery Co., TRENTON, New Jersey, U.S.A.

1888- CHINA OR WHITE GRANITE bearing portraits of the Presidential candidates.

1888 Forester & Co.,Thomas, LONGTON, Staffordshire, England.

c.1888 EARTHENWARES. Printed-

1888 Galluba & Hofmann, ILMENAU, Thuringia, Germany.

1888- HARD-PASTE PORCELAIN.

1888 Green & Clay, LONGTON, Staffordshire, England.

1888-91 EARTHENWARES. - - -

Printed or impressed- -

1888 Mountford, G.T., STOKE, Staffordshire, England.

1888-98 EARTHENWARES. -

Printed-

1898- **Myott, Son & Co. Ltd.,** Factory`s name or initials printed within marks of various patterns and designs.- -

1898-1902 STOKE
1902-46 COBRIDGE
c.1947- HANLEY

M S & Co.
STOKE
MYOTT, SON & Co.

MYOTTS

c.1959 - **"China-Lyke" WARE**
c.1961 - **Olde Chelsea**
"Safari"

1888 Sorau, Porzellanfabrik, SORAU, Brandenburg, Germany.

1888 HARD-PASTE PORCELAIN. - - - -

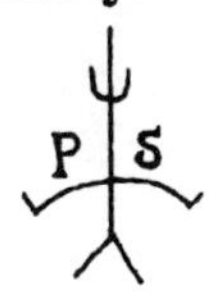

1888 Thomas & Co., Uriah, HANLEY, Staffordshire, England.

1888-1905 EARTHENWARES, MAJOLICA, ETC.

Printed or impressed- - -
1891 `England` added.

1888	Clokie & Co.Ltd., CASTLEFORD, England.	see 1872 Clokie & Masterman.
1888	Globe Pottery Co.,E, LIVERPOOL, U.S.A.	see 1881 Frederick,Shenkle,Allen & Co.
1888	Maryland Pottery Co., BALTIMORE, U.S.A.	see 1879 Hamill & Bullock.
1888	Morin (Gilder) France. - - -	see 1745 SÈVRES.
1888	Pihan (Decorator) France. - - -	see 1745 SÈVRES.
1888	Ouint, E. (Coloured grounds) France. -	see 1745 SÈVRES.
1888	Pauline Pottery Co., EDGERTON, U.S.A.	see 1883 Jacobus, Mrs Pauline.
1888	Sands End Pottery, FULHAM, England. -	see 1872 De Morgan, Wm.
1888	Trager L., (Decorator) France. - -	see 1745 SÈVRES.

1889

1889 Amison & Co. Ltd.,Ch. Stanley China, LONGTON, Staffs. England.

1889-1962 Porcelain. - Impressed- **C A**
L

1906-30 Printed-
1916 `& Co.` added.
1930 `& Co.Ltd.` added

1930-41 Printed-

1949-53 Printed-

1951-62 Printed marks of
various designs containing-

STAFFORDSHIRE
FLORAL
BONE CHINA
STANLEY FINE
BONE CHINA

1889 Barkers & Kent Ltd., FENTON, Staffordshire, England.

1889-1941 EARTHENWARES. Initials of Factory printed or impressed within marks of various patterns and designs, -
1898 `L` or `Ltd` added.

B. & K.
B. & K. L.

1889 Cartlidge & Co.,F., LONGTON, Staffordshire, England.

1889-1904 CHINA. Initials of Factory printed or impressed within marks of various patterns and designs.
c.1892 `& Co` added.

F. C.
F. C. & CO.

1889 Ceramic Art Co., TRENTON, New Jersey, U.S.A.

Jonathan Coxon and Walter D. Lenox.

1889- FINE WARES IN BELLEEK ETC.

Mark printed on undecorated wares-

Before 1895 - -

After 1897 -

1889 Chapman & Sons, David, LONGTON, Staffordshire, England.

1889-1906 PORCELAIN. - Printed-

1904 Chapman & Sons (Stoke-on-Trent)

1889 Crown Staffordshire Porcelain Co.Ltd., FENTON, Staffs, England.

1889- CHINA.

1889-1912 Printed-

1906- Printed-
Bone-china reproductions
of `Chelsea` porcelains.

1930- Pan design. Printed- **CROWN STAFFORDSHIRE**

1948 **Crown Staffordshire China Co. Ltd.**

c.1962- Tableware marks

Printed- **QUEENSBERRY**

1973 **Wedgwood China Division acquired the company.**

see 1847 Green, Thomas

1889

1889 Godwin & Hewitt, HEREFORD, England.
1889-1910 TILES. Printed or impressed-

1889 Hibbert & Boughey, LONGTON, Staffordshire, England.
1889 GENERAL CERAMICS. Printed-

H & B

1889 Hudson, William, LONGTON, Staffordshire, England.
1889-1941 PORCELAIN. Initials printed within marks of various patterns and designs. **W. H.**

1892-1912 Printed-

1912-41 Printed- -

1941- Hudson & Middleton Ltd. Printed-

1947- Printed- - -

1889 Hughes & Co.,E., FENTON, Staffordshire, England.
1889-1953 PORCELAIN.

1889-98 Impressed- **H**

1898-1905 Impressed or printed-

1905-12 Printed-

1912-41 Globe mark. Printed within marks of various patterns and designs.

i.e. `ROYAL CHINA` PALADIN` `EUSANCOS`

1940- Hughes (Fenton) Ltd. Renamed.

1889 Middleton & Co.,J.H., Delphine Pottery, LONGTON, Staffs, England.

1889-1941 PORCELAIN. -

Printed-

Various marks with `DELPHINE` incorporated.

1889 Plant Bros., Crown Pottery, BURSLEM, Staffordshire, England.

1889-1906 PORCELAIN. Printed-

1898 at LONGTON.

1889 Stadtlengsfeld Porzellanfabrik, STADTLENGSFELD, Germany.

1889- HARD-PASTE PORCELAIN. - -

1889	Boulton, Machin & Tennant, TUNSTALL, England.	see 1857 Beech & Hancock.
1889	Dewsberry, David, LAMBETH, England. -	see 1815 Royal Doulton plc.
1889	Noke, Charles,(designer) BURSLEM, England.-	see 1815 Royal Doulton plc.
1889	Thompson Pottery Co.,C.C., E. LIVERPOOL, U.S.A.	see 1868 Thompson & Co.,C.C.
1889	Ulrich (Decorator) France.- - - -	see 1745 SÈVRES.
1889	Wildblood & Heath, LONGTON, England. -	see 1887 Wildblood, R.V.

1890 Blackhurst & Hulme, Belgrave Works, LONGTON, Staffs, England.

1890-1932 CHINA.

1890-1914 Initials printed within marks of various patterns and designs.

B. & H.

c.1914- Printed-

**THE BELGRAVE
CHINA
B. & H.
L.
ENGLAND**

1890 Hollinshead & Griffiths, Chelsea Works, BURSLEM, Staffs England.

1890-1909 EARTHENWARES. - -

Printed mark with lion -

**CHELSEA ART POTTERY
H & G
BURSLEM, ENGLAND**

1890

1890 Longbottom, Samuel, HULL, Yorkshire, England.

Late 19th century-1899 EARTHENWARES. Impressed- **S. L.**

1890 Mansfield Bros.,Ltd., WOODVILLE, Derbyshire, England.

Art Pottery Works.

c.1890-1957 EARTHENWARES AND TILES. Impressed- **M. B.**

1890 Müller, E.& A., SCHWARZA-SAALBAHN, Thuringia, Germany.

1890- HARD-PASTE PORCELAIN. - -

1890 Müller, Paul, SELB, Bavaria, Germany.

1890- HARD-PASTE PORCELAIN. - - **P. M. S.**

1917 acquired by Hutschenreuther, Lorenz. see 1857 Hutschenreuther, C.M.

1890 Ohnemüller & Ulrich, KÜPS, Bavaria, Germany.

1890- HARD-PASTE PORCELAIN. - -

1890 Schäfer & Vater, VOLKSTEDT, Thuringia, Germany.

1890- DECORATORS, HARD-PASTE PORCELAIN. -

1890 Wiltshaw & Robinson Ltd., Carlton Works, STOKE, Staffs, England.

1890-1957 EARTHENWARES AND CHINA Printed-

1890-1906

1914- - - - -

1925-57

1958 **Carlton Ware Ltd. (Renamed)**

1890	Bennett Pottery Co.,BALTIMORE, Maryland, U.S.A.	see 1846 Bennett, Edwin.
1890	Furnivals Ltd., COBRIDGE, England. - -	see 1871 Furnival & Sons, T.
1890	Harker Pottery Co., EAST LIVERPOOL, U.S.A.	see 1840 Harker, Benjamin.
1890	Kaempfe & Heubach, Germany. - - -	see 1764 WALLENDORF.
1890	Kister, August, Germany. - - - - -	see 1835 Scheibe-Alsbach GmbH.
1890	Maling & Sons Ltd. C.T., NEWCASTLE, England.	see 1817 Maling, Robert,
1890	Montagnon, M., France. - - - - -	see 1589 NEVERS.
1890	Royal Crown Derby Porcelain Co.Ltd., England.	see 1749 DERBY.
1890	Sandoz (Decorator) France. - - -	see 1745 SÈVRES.
1890	Winkle & Co.Ltd.,F., STOKE, England. - -	see 1885 Winkle & Wood.

1891 American Art China Works, TRENTON, New Jersey, U.S.A.

Rittenhouse, Evans & Co.

1891- CHINA (CALLED AMERICAN CHINA) - - -

1891 Dresser, Christopher, SWADLINCOTE, Sth. Derbyshire, England.

1891-96 Designer with the Factory of William Ault. see 1887 Ault, William,
Some wares bear his signature - - **Chr. Dresser**
c.1879-89 Also with Linthorpe Pottery,
MIDDLESBROUGH. see 1879 Linthorpe Pot.
Also designed for Minton and Wedgwood.

1891 Heath & Greatbatch, BURSLEM, Staffordshire, England.

1891-93 EARTHENWARES. Printed or impressed- **H & G**
B

1891 Heufel & Co., DRESDEN, Germany.

1891- HARD-PASTE PORCELAIN. - - -

1891 Hulme, William, BURSLEM, Staffordshire, England.

1891-1941 EARTHENWARES.

1891-1936 Printed- -

1925 **Hulme (Burslem) Ltd., William,** (re-named)

1936-41 Printed or impressed- **ALPHA WARE**
H
ENGLAND

1891

1891 Malkin, Frederick, Belle Works, BURSLEM, Staffordshire, England.

1891-1905 EARTHENWARES.

c.1900-05 Printed-

1891 Procter, George, & Co. Ltd., Gladstone Pottery, LONGTON, Eng.

1891-1940 BONE-CHINA TABLEWARES Factory`s initials are printed within marks of various patterns and designs. 1891-1940

G. P. & CO

G. P. & CO
L

1924-40 printed

1939-52 **Gladstone China (Longton) Ltd.**

1946-61 printed
(Gladstone China continued with this mark until 1961)

1952-67 **Gladstone China.**
Thomas Poole & Gladstone China Ltd.

1952-67 printed

1967- **Gladstone Pottery Museum.**
Museum preserved from the old Gladstone China works.

see 1974 Gladstone Pottery Museum

1891 Ratcliffe & Co., LONGTON, Staffordshire, England.

1891-1914 EARTHENWARES. Printed-

1891 Triptis, Porzellanfabrik, TRIPTIS, Thuringia, Germany.

1891- HARD-PASTE PORCELAIN

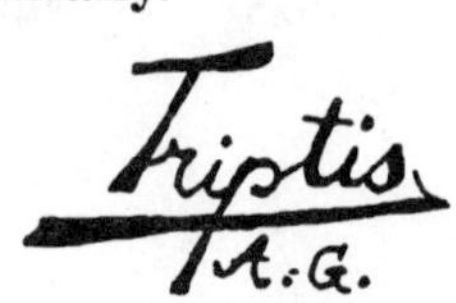

1891 Waine & Co. Ltd.,Charles, LONGTON, Staffordshire, England.

1891-1920 PORCELAIN Printed initials found on various patterns and designs. - - **C. W.**

1913 `Ltd` added.

1891-1913 Monogram mark-

c.1913-20 Crown mark- - -

1891 Weatherby, J.H., & Sons Ltd., Falcon Pottery, HANLEY, England.

1891- EARTHENWARE, DINNER AND TEA WARE, TOILET WARE, TRINKETS, ETC.

Family records of J.H. Weatherby go back to 1600 and show that John Weatherby, a potter, left Burslem in about 1726 and became a potter and glass maker in London and eventually part-owner of the Bow Pottery in 1750.

1891- Factory`s initials printed within marks of various patterns and designs.- **J. H. W. & SONS**

1892- Printed mark -

1920s **John Stuart Weatherby and John Lucas Weatherby (grandsons of the Founder) joined the business and became Joint-Managing Directors.**

1920 Hotelware introduced and is today (1995) the principal output of the factory.

1928- Printed mark -

1933 J.H. Weatherby Snr. died.
1938 S.M. Weatherby died.
1954 J.H. Weatherby Jnr. died.

1936- Printed marks -
The `Flag` mark is still in use today (1995)

1970s **C.H. Weatherby and J.R. Weatherby (great-grandsons of the founder) joined the business.**

(By kind permission of J.H.Weatherby & Sons Ltd., Hanley, England.)

1891/92

1891 Weiss, Kühnert & Co., GRÄFENTHAL, Thuringia, Germany.

1891- HARD-PASTE PORCELAIN. - -

1891	Bishop & Stonier Ltd.,HANLEY, England. -	see 1851 Livesley Powell & Co.
1891	Booths Ltd., BURSLEM, England. - -	see 1868 Booth & Co.,Thom.
1891	Brownfields Guild Pottery Soc.,Ltd., England. -	see 1850 Brownfield & Son Wm.
1891	Chelsea Pottery,U.S., CHELSEA, Mass. U.S.A.-	see 1866 Robertson, A.W.
1891	Crown Pottery Co., EVANSVILLE, Ind., U.S.A.	see 1882 Beck, A.M.
1891	Knowles, Taylor & Knowles Co., U.S.A. -	see 1854 Knowles & Harvey.
1891	Lehmann, Theodor, ARZBERG, Germany. -	see 1887 Schumann, Christoph,

1892 Boulton & Co., LONGTON, Staffordshire, England.

1892-1902 PORCELAIN. Printed initials found within- marks of various patterns and designs. **B. & Co.**

1900-02 Printed or impressed-

1892 Ceramic Art Co.Ltd., HANLEY, Staffordshire, England.

1892-1903 DECORATORS. Printed with shape of vase-

**THE CERAMIC ART
CO. LTD. HANLEY
STAFFORDSHIRE
ENGLAND**

1892 Coggins & Hill, LONGTON, Staffordshire, England.

1892-98 PORCELAIN. Initials printed or impressed - within marks of various patterns and designs. **C. & H.**

1892 Cone Ltd., Thomas, Alma Works, LONGTON, Staffs, England.

1892- EARTHENWARES.

1892-1912 Initials printed or impressed- within marks of various patterns and designs.

**T. C.
L.
T. C.
LONGTON**

1912-35 Monogram mark

1935- Crown mark with- **ALMA WARE ENGLAND**

1946- Crown mark with- **ROYAL ALMA MADE IN ENGLAND**

1892 Kensington Fine Art Pottery Co., HANLEY, Staffordshire, England.

1892-99 EARTHENWARES. Printed or impressed-

1892 Haviland, Theodore, LIMOGES, Haute-Vienne, France.

Theodore leaves Haviland & Co to start his own Hard-paste porcelain factory. - see 1853 Haviland & Co.

A special new paste was developed which was whiter and thinner ware; it was sold under the name of `porcelaine mousseline`

Marks on whiteware in underglaze green:-

1892

1892

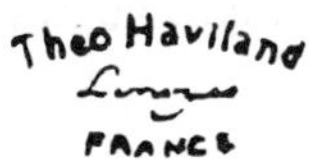

1893

1894-1957

Marks on decorated wares:-

1894

1894

1895

1895

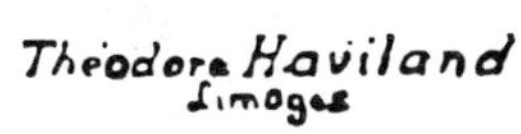

1897

1903 **William Haviland (eldest son) joins the company as a director.**

Marks on decorated wares:-

1903

1907 American embargo on French porcelain, American Potters Association accuse French of dumping practices. Limousin factories had to lay-off people and reduce output.

Marks on whiteware in underglaze blue-

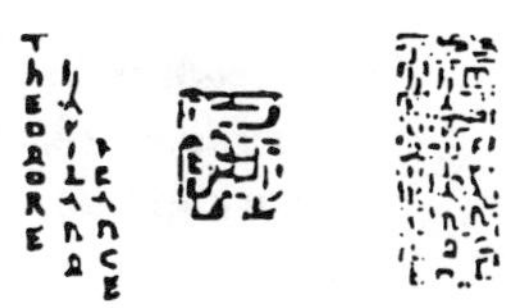

1912

1914-18 First World War caused difficulties and output was reduced significantly.

Continued over -

1892

1892 Haviland, Theodore, LIMOGES, Haute-Vienne, France. (Cont`)

1919 Theodore Haviland dies.
William Haviland takes over the chairmanship and was assisted by his two brothers-in-law H.de Luze and L.d`Albis and his brother Guy.

Marks on whiteware in underglaze blue:-

1920-36

1925 Arts Decoratifs, Exhibition, Paris.
Art Deco revolution.
Wall Street Crash almost cripples the Limoges Porcelain industry.

Marks on decorated ware- - -

Théodore Haviland
Limoges
FRANCE

1925

Marks on whiteware in underglaze blue- -

1936-45

U.S.A. marks -

THEODORE HAVILAND
NEW YORK

1936
green or black

Theodore Haviland
New York
MADE IN AMERICA

1937-56
red or black

HAVILAND
U. S. A.

1957
red

1939-45 World War II. Factory just barely survives. William Haviland and his sisters buy back all the designs, trademarks and rights of the Company created 100 years earlier by their grandfather.

Mark on whiteware-

Haviland
France

1946-62

1957 William Haviland and his two brothers-in-law retire. Harold Haviland (son) takes over.

Marks on decorated ware-

HAVILAND
LIMOGES
FRANCE

1958

Haviland
LIMOGES
FRANCE

1967

1959 The availability of natural gas gave Haviland the opportunity for major improvements. Haviland invested heavily in technology to improve output and quality.

1961 Theodore becomes chairman, and with his brother Frederick they managed the New York office. Mark on whiteware- -

Haviland
France
Limoges

1962

(Courtesy of Haviland S.A., Limoges, France)
For further information see HAVILAND *by Jean d`Albis.*

1892 Kirkland & Co., ETRURIA, TUNSTALL, Staffordshire, England.

1892- EARTHENWARES. Initials printed within- marks of various patterns and designs **K & Co.** **K & Co.** **E**

1892- Mark with crown, printed-

1928- Printed mark with- **KIRALPO WARE** -

c.1938 **Kirklands (Etruria) Ltd.** Printed mark-

1947 **Kirklands (Staffordshire) Ltd.**

1892 Kloster Vessra, Porzellanfabrik, KLOSTER VESSRA, Germany.

1892- HARD-PASTE PORCELAIN. - -

1892 Lawrence (Longton) Ltd. Thomas, Falcon Works, LONGTON, Eng.

1892- EARTHENWARES. Early wares not marked.

1936- Printed or impressed marks with the word `FALCON`

1944- Trade-name used- **FALCON WARE**

1947- `Made in England` added.

1892 Longton Porcelain Co. Ltd., LONGTON, Staffordshire, England.

1892-1908 PORCELAIN. - -

Printed monogram mark - -

1892

1892 Lonhuda Pottery, STEUBENVILLE, Ohio, U.S.A.

Messrs. Long, Hunter and Day (name derives from the first syllables)

1892- SLIP-PAINTED WARES -

1892-96 Impressed-

1896- Impressed - -

<u>Marks of decorators who worked for the Company-</u>

Fry, Miss Laura A. - -

McLaughlin, Miss Sarah R. -

Harper, Miss Helen M. -

Long, Mr. W.A. - -

Spaulding, Miss Jessie R. -

1892 Mackee, Andrew, LONGTON, Staffordshire, England.

1892-1906 GENERAL CERAMICS. Initials found printed or-impressed within marks of various patterns and designs. **A. M. L.**

1892 Mannl, W., KRUMMENNAAB, Bavaria, Germany.

1892- HARD-PASTE PORCELAIN.

1892 Mills, Henry, HANLEY, Staffordshire, England.

c.1892 EARTHENWARES. Printed within designs- **H. MILLS**

1892 Morris, Thomas, Regent Works, LONGTON, Staffordshire, England.

1892-1941 PORCELAIN. Printed

c.1892- Crown mark with Trade-name - **CROWN CHELSEA CHINA**

1892 Redfern & Drakeford Ltd., LONGTON, Staffordshire, England.

1892-1933 PORCELAIN. Printed or impressed-

1909-33 `BALMORAL CHINA` and `England` added.

1933 Acquired by Royal Albion China. see 1921 Royal Albion China

---

1892 Schlegelmilch, Oscar, LANGEWIESEN, Thuringia, Germany.

1892- HARD-PASTE PORCELAIN. - -

1892 Trenton Potteries Co., TRENTON, New Jersey, U.S.A.

Five sanitary ware factorys intergrated to make this Company The Crescent, The Delaware, The Empire, The Enterprise and The Equitable. Later the Ideal Pottery was included.

T.P.Co.
CHINA

1892-GENERAL CERAMICS. - - -

Star mark with numeral indicates the factory it was made at. i.e. 1. Crescent, 2. Delaware, 3. Empire, 4. Enterprise, 5. Equitable and 6. Ideal.

1900 Paris Exposition (awarded two gold medals)

TRENTON POTTERIES CO
TRENTON, NEW JERSEY
U.S.A.

1892	Challinor & Co.,C., FENTON, England. - -	see 1853 Challinor & Co. E.
1892	Hanley Porcelain Co., HANLEY, England. -	see 1865 Bevington, J.& T.
1892	Moore, Leason & Co., FENTON, England. -	see 1872 Moore & Co.
1892	Pfeffer, Fr., Germany. - - - -	see 1757 GOTHA.
1892	Raby, Edward, LAMBETH, England. - -	see 1815 Royal Doulton plc.
1892	Whittaker, Heath & Co., HANLEY, England. -	see 1886 Whittaker & Co.
1892	Wileman & Co., FENTON, England. - -	see 1864 Wileman, J.& C.

1893

1893 American Encaustic Tiling Co., ZANESVILLE, Ohio, U.S.A.

c.1893- EMBOSSED TILES.

Pre 1893 Mueller, Herman C. Monogram-

1893- Stamped mark- **A.E.T. Co.**

1893 Bellmark Pottery Co., TRENTON, New Jersey, U.S.A.

1893- EARTHENWARES FOR PLUMBERS` AND DRUGGISTS`

1893 Hering & Sohn, Julius, KÖPPELSDORF, Thuringia, Germany.

1893- HARD-PASTE PORCELAIN. - -

1893 Low Art Tile Co., CHELSEA, Mass., U.S.A.

c.1893 TILES.

Pre 1893 Osborne, Arthur (Chief modeller)- **A**

1893 Maddock Pottery Co., Lamberton Works, TRENTON, U.S.A.

1893- SEMI-PORCELAIN WARES. -

M
CHINA
L

1893 Plant & Co.,J., STOKE, Staffordshire, England.

1893-1900 EARTHENWARES. - Printed-

1900 **Acquired by Grimwade Bros.** **STOKE POTTERY**

1893 Sudlow & Sons Ltd.,R., BURSLEM, Staffordshire, England.

1893- EARTHENWARES.

c.1920- Printed or impressed marks with the name `SUDLOW/S` included.

1965- **Aquired by Howard Pottery Co., SHELTON.**

1893 Taylor, Nicholas, DENHOLME, W.Yorkshire, England.

1893-1909 EARTHENWARES. Incised- **N. Taylor Denholme**

1893 Thewalt, Albert Jacob, (Founder) HOEHR-GRENZHAUSEN, Ger.

1893- STONEWARE. SPECIALIZING IN BEERSTEINS.
Kamp, Wilhelm Anton, (modeller) designed the first stein.

1893-1900 Incised mark-

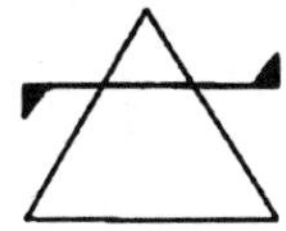

1900-20 Incised mark-

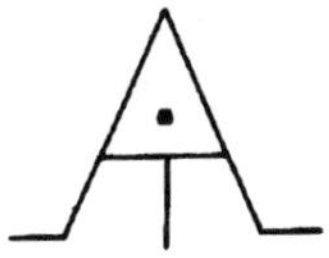

1920-30 Incised mark- (without dot)

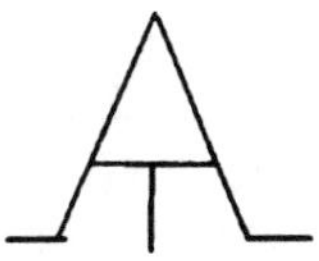

1930-present day(1995)

1939- **Albert Jacob Thewalt (Founder) dies. Albert Johann Thewalt (son) assumed control of the company.**

Paper label mark,used- where mark cannot be incised.

1957- **Albert Johann Thewalt dies. Albert Jakob Thewalt (grandson) takes control**

(By courtesy of Albert Jac.Thewalt GmbH, Hoehr-Grenzhausen, Germany)

1893 West End Pottery Co., EAST LIVERPOOL, Ohio, U.S.A.

1893- IRONSTONE CHINA. - - - **W.E.P. Co. CHINA**

1893 Ford & Sons Ltd., BURSLEM, England.- see 1876 Whittingham, Ford & Riley.
1893 Hulme & Christie, FENTON, England. - see 1887 Forester & Hulme.
1893 Goodwin Pottery Co., E. LIVERPOOL, U.S.A. see 1844 Goodwin, John.

1894 Ahrenfeldt, Charles, LIMOGES, Haute-Vienne, France.

1894- HARD-PASTE PORCELAIN. - -

1894

1894 Anchor Pottery, James E. Norris, TRENTON, New Jersey, U.S.A.

c.1894 SEMI-PORCELAIN WARE. - -

1898- marks -

1894 Bennett & Co.,George, STOKE, Staffordshire, England.

1894-1902 EARTHENWARES. Impressed or printed- **G. B. & CO.**

1894 Burslem Pottery Co.Ltd., BURSLEM, Staffordshire, England.

1894-1933 EARTHENWARES. - Printed-

1894 Cook Pottery Co., TRENTON, New Jersey, U.S.A.

1894- General ceramics. - - -
Mellor & Co. mark used to avoid confusion with the`Cook & Hancock` mark of Crescent Pottery. see 1863 Bloor, Ott & Booth.

1894 Della Robbia Co.Ltd., BIRKENHEAD, Merseyside, England.

c.1894-1901 EARTHENWARES. Impressed or incised- **DELLA ROBBIA**

Incised-
Initials above the mark refer to the decorator-

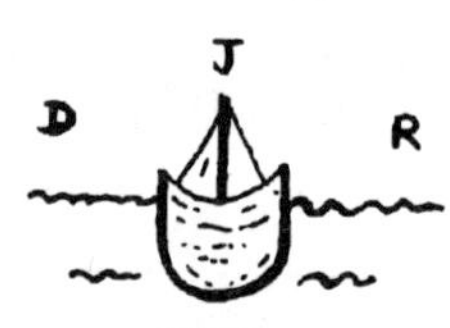

1894 Dewes & Copestake, LONGTON, Staffordshire, England.

1894-1915 EARTHENWARES. Factory`s initials printed- **D. & C.**
within marks of various patterns and designs. **L**

1894 Harrop & Burgess, HANLEY, Staffordshire, England.

1894-1903 EARTHENWARES. - Printed-

1903-17 **Burgess, Thomas,** Printed or impressed-
(as above)

1894 Maddock & Sons, John, Coalport Works, TRENTON, U.S.A.

1894- EARTHENWARES. - - -

1894 McNeal & Co.Ltd., LONGTON, Staffordshire, England.

1894-1906 EARTHENWARES. - Printed-

1894 Meigh, W. & R., STOKE, Staffordshire, England.

1894-99 EARTHENWARES. Printed-

1894 Pearl Pottery Co.Ltd., HANLEY, Staffordshire, England.

1894-1936 EARTHENWARES.

1894-1912 Printed or impressed-

1912-36 Printed initials within marks of various patterns and designs. **P.P.Co.Ltd.**

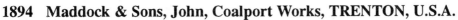

1894

1894 Riessner, Stellmacher & Kessel, Amphora Porzell`, TURN, Germany.

1894- GENERAL CERAMICS. - - -

1903- **Riessner & Kessel.**

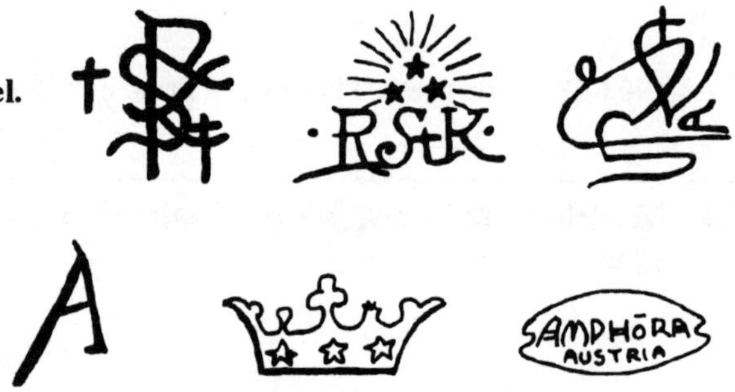

1894 Rigby & Stevenson, HANLEY, Staffordshire, England.

1894-1954 EARTHENWARES. Factory`s initials printed- **R. & S.**
within marks of various patterns and designs.

1894 Wahliss, Ernst, Alexandra Porcelain Works, TURN, Germany.

1894- GENERAL CERAMICS. - - -

1894	Bovey Pottery Co.Ltd.,BOVEY TRACEY, England.	see 1842 Bovey Tracey Co.
1894	Buckwalter and Brownback, U.S.A. - -	see 1867 Phoenix Pottery.
1894	Brunt Pottery Co.,William, E. LIVERPOOL, U.S.A.	see 1850 Brunt Son & Co.,W.
1894	Chester Pottery Co. PHOENIXVILLE, U.S.A. -	see 1867 Phoenix Pottery.
1894	Nicholas II., Russia. - - - -	see 1744 ST. PETERSBURG.
1894	Simeon, Henry, LAMBETH, England. - -	see 1815 Royal Doulton plc.

1895 Britannia China Company, Longton, Staffordshire, England.

1895-1906 CHINA. Impressed- **B. C. Co.**

1900-04 Printed mark within a circle- **BRITANNIA CHINA Co.**
LONGTON
ENGLAND

1904-06 Printed or impressed-

1895 Bremer & Schmidt, EISENBERG, Thuringia, Germany.

1895- HARD-PASTE PORCELAIN. - -

1895 Bullock & Co.,A., HANLEY, Staffordshire, England.

1895-1915 EARTHENWARES. Printed or impressed- **A. B.& CO. H.**
Initials of Factory found within marks of **A. B.& CO.**
various patterns and designs.

1895 Capper & Wood, Bradwell Wks. LONGTON, Staffordshire, England.

1895-1904 EARTHENWARES. Initials printed or impressed- **C & W**
within marks of various patterns and designs.

1904-28 **Wood, Arthur,** Impressed or printed- **A. W.**
`England` added sometimes. **L.**

1928- **Wood & Son (Longport) Ltd., Arthur,**
Factory`s name printed within marks of various patterns and designs.

ARTHUR WOOD & SON
ARTHUR WOOD
ROYAL BRADWELL
ART WARE
WOOD

1895 Eckert & Co., Richard, VOLKSTEDT, Thuringia, Germany.

1895- HARD-PASTE PORCELAIN. - -

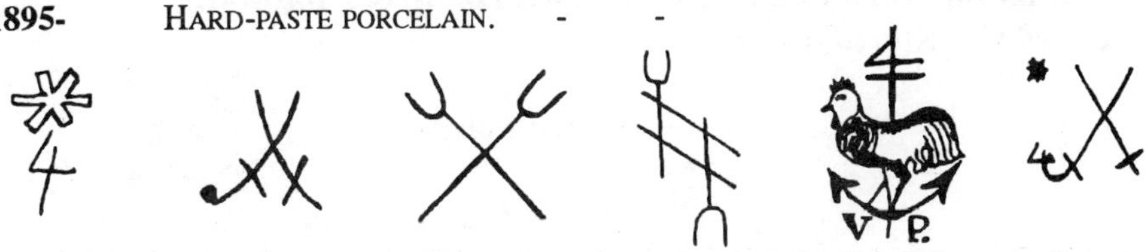

1895

1895 Hawley, Webberley & Co., LONGTON, Staffordshire, England.

1895-1902 EARTHENWARES.

Printed- - 

1895 Locke & Co., WORCESTER, England.

1895-1904 PORCELAIN. - Written- **LOCKE & CO. WORCESTER**

c.1895-1900 Printed- - 

c.1900-94 Printed- - 

1895 Lovatt & Lovatt, LANGLEY MILL, Nottingham, England.

1895- EARTHENWARES, STONEWARES. Impressed- **LANGLEY WARE**

1895- Printed or impressed- 

c.1900- Printed or impressed- 

1931- **Lovatt`s Potteries Ltd.** - -
c.1931-62 Trade-mark -
Various other marks occur with
`LANGLEY` incorporated in them.

1959- **Aquired by J. Bourne & Son Ltd.**

1895 Manzoni, Carlo, HANLEY, Staffordshire, England.

c.1895-98 STUDIO POTTER.

Incised with date- 

1895 Meyer & Sohn, DRESDEN, Germany.
Late 19th century. MEISSEN STYLE DECORATOR.

1895 Pitcairns Ltd., TUNSTALL, Staffordshire, England.
1895-1901 EARTHENWARES.

Printed-

1895 Plant & Sons, R., LONGTON, Staffordshire, England.
1895-1901 EARTHENWARES. - Printed- **P. & S.**
L.

1895 Schweig, August, WEISSWASSER, Silesia, Germany.
1895- HARD-PASTE PORCELAIN. - -

1895 Smith & Ford, BURSLEM, Staffordshire, England.
1895-98 EARTHENWARES. - -

Printed- -

1898-1939 Ford & Co., Samuel, Iniitials printed as-
per mark above- **S. & F**
F. & Co.
c.1936-39 Printed- **Samford**
Ware

1895 Upper Hanley Pottery Co.Ltd., HANLEY, Staffordshire, England.
1895-1910 EARTHENWARES. Impressed or printed initials- **U.H.P. CO.**
found within marks of various patterns and designs. **ENGLAND**

1895-1910 Printed- -

1900 Moved to Cobridge. `Ltd` added.

1895/96

1895	Cory, Miss Kate, GREENPOINT, N.Y., U.S.A. -	see 1879 Volkmar, Charles.
1895	Eichhorn & Bandorf, Thuringia, Germany. -	see 1808 ELGERSBURG.
1895	Foster & Hunt, HONITON, England. - -	see 1881 Honiton Art Potteries.
1895	Gater, Hall & Co. TUNSTALL, England. -	see 1885 Gater & Co.,Thom.
1895	Hughes & Son Ltd.,Thomas, BURSLEM, England.	see 1860 Hughes, Thomas.
1895	Lombarda, Società Ceramica, Italy. - -	see 1725 MILAN.
1895	Thun`sche Porzellanfabrik, Bohemia, Germany.-	see 1793 KLOSTERLE.
1895	Volkmar Keramic Co., NEW YORK, U.S.A. -	see 1879 Volkmar, Charles.

1896 Bennett & Co., J., HANLEY, Staffordshire, England.

1896-1900 EARTHENWARES. Initials printed or impressed within marks of various patterns and designs. **J. B. & Co.**

1896 Birks & Co. L. A., Vine Pottery, STOKE, Staffordshire, England.

1896-1900 GENERAL CERAMICS. Impressed- **BIRKS**

Printed initials found within marks of various patterns and designs.- - **B. & Co.**

1900-33 **Birks, Rawlins & Co. Ltd.,** Factory`s name or initials printed within marks of various patterns and designs. **B. R. & CO.** **BIRKS, RAWLINS & CO.**

c.1930- Trade-names **SAVOY CHINA** **CARLTON CHINA**

1896 Cochran & Fleming, Britannia Pottery, GLASGOW, Scotland.

1896-1920 EARTHENWARES. Factory`s name or initials printed or impressed within marks of various patterns and designs including a seated Britannia. **C. & F.** **C. & F. G.**

COCHRAN & FLEMING

1900-20 Printed- -

Continued over -

1896 Cochran & Fleming, Britannia Pot., GLASGOW, Scotland. (Cont`)

Impressed- **FLEMING**

Printed with Crown- **PORCELAIN OPAQUE**
GLASGOW, BRITAIN
FLEMING

1920-35 **Britannia Pottery Co. Ltd.** Printed-

c.1925- Trade-name - **HIAWATHA**

1896 Delaherche, Auguste, LA CHAPPELLE-AUX-POTS, France.

1896- ARTIST-POTTER. CHINESE-TYPE GLAZES ON STONEWARE.

1896 Dresden Porcelain Co., Blyth Works, LONGTON, Staffs, England.

1896-1904 PORCELAIN. Initials printed or impressed within marks of various patterns and designs. **D. P. CO**
L.

1905-35 **Blyth Porcelain Co. Ltd.**, Printed initials within various patterns and designs. **B. P. CO. LTD.**
`Diamond China` printed mark.

c.1925-35 Printed or impressed-

1896 East Liverpool Pottery Co., E. LIVERPOOL, Ohio, U.S.A.

c.1896- `WACO` CHINA (WHITE GRANITE BODY) -

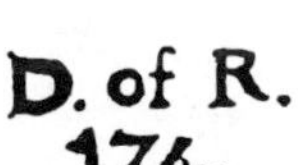

c.1897-1900 Printed- **WACO CHINA**
E.L.P.Co.
`Daughters of Rebecca` **D.of R.**
174

see 1900 East Liverpool Potteries Co.

1896

1896 Empire Porcelain Co. Ltd., STOKE, Staffordshire, England.

1896- EARTHENWARES.

1896-1912 Printed-

1912-28 Printed-

1928-39 Printed with month and year-

1930- Printed marks of various designs with trade-name **EMPIRE WARE SHELTON IVORY**

1940- Printed or impressed marks with the words- **EMPIRE WARE EMPIRE ENGLAND**

1960- Printed marks of various designs with **EMPIRE PORCELAIN CO.**

1896 Hadley & Sons Ltd., James, WORCESTER, England.

1896-1905 PORCELAIN, EARTHENWARES. - -

c.1875-94 James Hadley mark on figures etc., for the Worcester Royal Porcelain Co. Incised or impressed- - Hadley

1896-97 Printed or impressed-

1897-1900 Printed-
1900-02 Without the word `Faience` - -

c.1897-1902 Impressed- - **FINE ART HADLEY`S TERRA-COTTA**

1902-05 Printed- -

1905 Acquired by Royal Worcester Co. see 1751 WORCESTER

1896 Nautilus Porcelain Co., GLASGOW, Scotland.

1896-1913 CHINA. Printed- -

1896 Newcomb Pottery, Newcomb College, NEW ORLEANS, U.S.A.

1896-POTTERY. The art department of this college was run by a Prof. Ellsworth Woodward and his assistant, Miss Mary G. Sheerer. Under their supervision, the young lady pupils designed and decorated artistic pieces in original underglaze designs.

NEWCOMB COLLEGE

Each piece was marked with one of the college marks plus the monogram of the decorator.

List of decorators and their personal marks:

Leoni Nicholson -

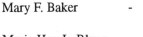

Bessie A. Ficklen -

Sarah Henderson -

Hattie Joor -

Gertrude R. Smith -

Katherine Kopman -

Frances H. Cocke - FHC

Roberta Kennon - RK·99

Mary Sheerer - M S

Mary W. Butler - **M.W.B.**

Emily Huger -

Amalie Roman -

Mazie T. Ryan - MTR

Elizabeth G. Rogers -

Frances Jones - - F. J

Desiree Roman - DR

Mary F. Baker -

Marie Hoe-LeBlane - M.H.L

Irene B. Keep - - I.B.K.

Selina E.B. Gregory - S.E.B.G.

Raymond A. Scudder -

Beverly Randolph - BR

Esther Huger Elliott -

Francis E. Lines -

Mary W. Richardson -

Olive W. Dodd -

Joseph Meyers, the potter -

Other Marks:-

Mixtures of clays - R - U - Q - etc.

Registration mark - A1 - A2 - etc.

One scratch through Pottery Mark denotes a second.

The Mark obliterated, denotes the piece is unindorsed by the Pottery.

1896

1896 Price Brothers, Crown Works, BURSLEM, Staffordshire, England.

1896-1903 EARTHENWARES.

Printed mark -

1903-61 **Price Bros. (Burslem) Ltd.**

1903-10 Mark as above continued.

c.1925-30 Printed marks of various patterns and designs with Factory`s name or initials.

PRICE
PRICE BROS. Ltd.
P.B.B.

Trade-names - **PALM ATHLO**
ATHLO WARE -
MATTONA WARE

c.1934-61 Printed-

1962- **Price & Kensington Potteries Ltd. LONGPORT,**

1962-63 Mark as above continued.

1963- - Printed-

(By kind permission of Price & Kensington Potteries Ltd, Longport, Staffordshire.,England.)

1896 Rowley & Newton Ltd., LONGTON, Staffordshire, England.

1896-1901 GENERAL CERAMICS. Initials printed or impressed within marks of various patterns and designs which sometimes include a lion mark. **R. & N.**

1896 Scheidig, Carl, REICHMANNSDORF, Thuringia, Germany.

1896- HARD-PASTE PORCELAIN. - -

1896 Spitz, Carl, BRÜX, Bohemia, Germany.

1896- EARTHENWARES. - - -

1896 Wild & Co., Thomas C., Albert Works, LONGTON, Staffs. England.

1896-1904 CHINA. Printed or impressed- T. W. & CO.

1905-17 **Wild, Thomas C., St. Mary`s Works,**

Printed-

1917- **Wild & Sons Ltd., Thomas C.**

c.1917-45 Printed mark with Crown.

ROYAL ALBERT
CROWN CHINA
BONE CHINA

Royal Albert Ltd.

Printed mark- -

Now Royal Doulton Group.

1896 Dedham Pottery, CHELSEA, Mass. U.S.A. - see 1866 Robertson, A.W.,
1896 Lasserre, (Decorator) France. - - - - see 1745 SÈVRES.
1896 Vodrey Pottery Co., EAST LIVERPOOL, U.S.A. see 1848 Woodward & Vodrey.
1896 Wellsville Pioneer Pottery Co., WELLSVILLE, U.S.A. see 1879 Morley & Co.
1896 Wood & Sons, Thomas, BURSLEM, England. - see 1885 Wood & Co.,T.

1897 American China Co. TORONTO, Ohio, U.S.A.

1897- SEMI-PORCELAIN, WHITE GRANITE WARE.

Trade-names- **BILTMORE**
EUGENIA

1897 Baum, J.H., WELLSVILLE, Ohio, U.S.A.

Late 19th century - 1897 SEMI-GRANITE WARE. -

1897

1897 Chittenango Pottery Co., CHITTENANGO, New York, U.S.A.

1897- CHINA.
Made the souvenir china for the Buffalo Exhibition.

C. P. Co.
C.P. Co.
CHITTENANGO, N.Y.
CHINA

1897 Colclough, H.J., Vale Works, LONGTON, Staffordshire, England.

1897-1937 CHINA, EARTHENWARES. Factory`s initials printed within marks of various patterns and designs. **H. J. C.** **L.**

1908-28 Printed- -

1928-37 Printed-

1935-37 Printed- - **COLCLOUGH**
LONGTON
ENGLAND
BONE CHINA

1937-48 **Colclough China Ltd.**

1939- Printed-

c.1945-48 Printed marks of various designs including-

1948—54 **Booths & Colcloughs Ltd. HANLEY.** Printed marks with trade-marks **Blue Mist**
Malvern
Royal Swan

see 1955 Ridgway Potteries Ltd.

1897 Grueby Faience Co., BOSTON, Mass. U.S.A.

Messrs. Grueby, Graves and Kendrick.

GRUEBY
GRUEBY POTTERY

1897- SEMI-PORCELAIN IN ANCIENT EGYPTIAN STYLE.

Impressed marks

Modelled and decorated by hand, mainly by young women artists whose monograms are shown below in alphabetical order:

Erickson, Miss Ruth -
Farrington, Miss Ellen R. - E R.F.
Liley, Miss Florence S. -
Lingley, Miss Annie V. -
Newman, Miss Lillian, -
Pierce, Miss Norma, -
Post, Miss Wilhelmina, - W.P.
Priest, Miss Gertrude, -
Seaman, Miss Marie A. - S M.S
Stanwood, Miss Gertrude -
Yamada, Mr. Kiichi,

1897 Heinz & Co., GRÄFENTHAL-MEERNACH, Thuringia, Germany.

1897- HARD-PASTE PORCELAIN.

1897 Kent Ltd. James, Old Foley Pottery, LONGTON, Staffs., England.

1897- CHINA, EARTHENWARES. - -

1897-1915 Printed with Royal Arms-

ROYAL SEMI CHINA
JAMES KENT
ENGLAND

c.1897-c.1910 Factory`s initials and name found printed within marks containing shield or globe. - - - -
1913 `Ltd` added.

c.1936-50 Printed-

c.1955- Printed- -

Old Foley
JAMES KENT LTD.
STAFFORDSHIRE
MADE IN ENGLAND

1981 Bayer U.K. Ltd., acquired business.
1989 M.R.Hadida Ltd., acquired business. James Kent (1989)
(By kind permission of James Kent (1989) Fenton, Staffordshire, England.)

1897

1897 Menzl, Jos.T., JOKES, Bohemia, Germany.

1897- HARD-PASTE PORCELAIN. - -

1897 Merrimac Ceramic Co., NEWBURYPORT, Mass. U.S.A.

1897- TERRA-COTTA AND ENAMELLED POTTERY.
T.S. Nickerson (Member Society of Arts and Crafts, Boston)

1900-01 Paper label printed-
1901- Mark is impressed-

1902 **Merrimac Pottery Co.**

1897 Mountford, Arthur J., BURSLEM, Staffordshire, England.

1897-1901 EARTHENWARES. Printed-

1897 Pilkington Tile & Pottery Co.Ltd., CLIFTON JUNCTION, England.

c.1897-1938 and 1948-57 EARTHENWARES AND TILES, LUSTRE EFFECTS.

c.1897-1904 Incised- **P**

Trade-mark- 1904-05 Printed-
1905-14 Impressed-
Roman numeral denotes date. (i.e. VII = 1907)

c.1914-38 Impressed-
c.1920 `England` added.
c.1920-38 `Made in England` added.

ROYAL LANCASTRIAN

Continued over -

1897 Pilkington Tile & Pott. Co.Ltd., CLIFTON JUNCTION, Eng. (Cont`)

Monograms of artists and designers in alphabetical order:

Burton, Annie -

Crane, Walter -

Cundall, C.E. -

Dacre, Dorothy, -

Day, Lewis F.

Forsyth, G.M. -

Jones, Jessie. -

Joyce, R. -

Mycock, W. -

Rodgers, Gladys.-

1948-57 Re-opened pottery section of factory. -

1897 Robinson Brothers, CASTLEFORD, Yorkshire,England.

1897-1904 STONEWARES. Factory`s initials printed or impressed within marks of various patterns and designs. **R. B.**

1905-33 **Robinson & Son, John,** Impressed- **J. R. & S.**

1897 Rosenthal & Co.,Porzellanfabrik Ph., KRONACH, Germany.

1897- EARTHENWARES. - -

Rosenthal Porzellan, Selb. is the parent company. see 1879 Rosenthal, Selb.

1897/98

1897 Wood & Co. J.B., LONGTON, Staffordshire, England.

1897-1926 EARTHENWARES.

1910-26 Printed or impressed- -

1897 Salt Bros., TUNSTALL, England. - - see 1872 Brownhills Pottery.
1897 Sefton & Brown, FERRYBRIDGE, England. - see 1843 Reed & Taylor.
1897 Smith & Binnall, TUNSTALL, England.- - see 1883 Rathbone, Smith & Co.
1897 Storer, Mrs Maria Longworth, CINCINNATI, U.S.A. see 1879 Rookwood Pottery.
1897 Wood & Barker Ltd., BURSLEM, England. - see 1885 Wood & Co. Thom.

1898 Bentley & Co. Ltd.,G.L., LONGTON, Staffordshire, England.

1898-1912 PORCELAIN. Factory`s initials found printed - within marks of various patterns and designs **G. L. B. & Co. LONGTON**

1904 `Ltd` added.

1898 Davison & Son Ltd., BURSLEM, Staffordshire, England.

1898-1952 EARTHENWARES.

c.1948-52 Printed Trade-mark-

1898 Greiner & Herda, OBERKOTZAU, Bavaria, Germany.

1898-1944 HARD-PASTE PORCELAIN. - -

1898 Hartley`s (Castleford) Ltd., CASTLEFORD, Yorkshire, England.

c.1898-1960 STONEWARES, EARTHENWARES. Trade-name-

1953 Art-wares - **HARTROX**

1898 Hill & Co., LONGTON, Staffordshire, England.

1898-1920 PORCELAIN. Factory`s initials found printed or impressed within marks of various designs. **H. & CO.**

1898 Holmes & Son, LONGTON, Staffordshire, England.

1898-1903 EARTHENWARES. Impressed or printed- **H. & S. LONGTON**

Printed within circle- **HOLMES & SON LONGTON**

1898 King & Barratt Ltd., BURSLEM, Staffordshire, England.

1898-1940 EARTHENWARES, ETC. Factory`s initials printed- or impressed within marks of various designs. **K. & B.**

1898 Moore & Co., HANLEY, Staffordshire, England.

1898-1903 EARTHENWARES. Printed with various patterns- `England` sometimes added.

1898 Plant, Enoch, Crown Pottery, BURSLEM, Staffordshire, England.

1898-1905 EARTHENWARES. Printed or impressed- (Mark is also used by other factories)

1898 Possil Pottery Co., GLASGOW, Scotland.

1898-1901 EARTHENWARES, CHINA. Printed-

1898 Rathbone & Co., T., TUNSTALL, Staffordshire, England.

1898-1923 EARTHENWARES. Factory`s initials found within marks of various designs.

T. R. & Co.
TUNSTALL

c.1919-23 Printed-

1898 Ruskin Pottery, (W. Howson Taylor) SMETHWICK, England.

1898-1935 EARTHENWARES.

1898- Impressed- **TAYLOR**

1898- Painted or incised-

c.1904- Impressed, usually with date. -

c.1904- Impressed with- **RUSKIN**
c.1920 `Made in England` added.
c.1920- Printed or incised- **W. HOWSON TAYLOR**
RUSKIN

1898/99

1898 Smith, James, Glebe Pottery, STOKE, Staffordshire, England.
1898-1924 GENERAL CERAMICS. - - **JAMES SMITH**

c.1898-1922 Printed-

c.1922-24 Smith & Partners Ltd., James,
Printed or impressed-

1898 Smith Ltd., W.T.H., LONGPORT, Staffordshire, England.
1898-1905 EARTHENWARES. Printed around globe- **W.T.H.SMITH & CO. LONGPORT**

1898 Wilson & Sons, J., FENTON, Staffordshire, England.
1898-1926 CHINA. - Printed-

1898 Wingender & Bro. Charles, HADDONFIELD, New Jersey, U.S.A.
c.1898- STONEWARE WITH COBALT BLUE DECORATIONS.
Sometimes impressed- **C.W. & BRO.**

1898 Wooldridge & Walley, BURSLEM, Staffordshire, England.
1898-1901 EARTHENWARES. Factory`s initials printed- **W. & W.**
within marks of various patterns and designs. **B.**

1898 Dudson Bros. Ltd., HANLEY, England. - - see 1809 Dudson, Thomas,
1898 Ford & Co.,Samuel, BURSLEM, England. - see 1895 Smith & Ford.
1898 Iles, Frank & Passenger C.& F., FULHAM, England. see 1872 De Morgan, Wm.
1898 Lockhart & Sons Ltd.,David, GLASGOW, Scotland. see 1855 Lockhart & Arthur.
1898 Myott, Son & Co., STOKE, England. - - see 1888 Mountford, G.T.
1898 Plant Ltd., R.H.& S.L., LONGTON, England. - see 1881 Plant & Co.,R.H.

1899 Baron, W.L., Rolle Quay Pottery, BARNSTAPLE, Devon, England.
1899-1939 EARTHENWARES. Incised in writing- **BARON. BARNSTAPLE**

1899 Decoeur, Emile, PARIS, France. - - **Decoeur**
Late 19th century STUDIO POTTER IN STONEWARE. - **E. Decoeur**

1899 Forster & Co., VIENNA, Austria.
1899-1906 STUDIO CERAMICS.
Director: Alexander Forster.- -

1899 Gareis, Kühnl & Cie, WALDSASSEN, Bavaria, Germany.

1899- HARD-PASTE PORCELAIN. - -

1899 Geijsbeek Pottery Co., DENVER, Colorado, U.S.A.

1899- WHITE AND VITRIFIED COLOURED WARE. -

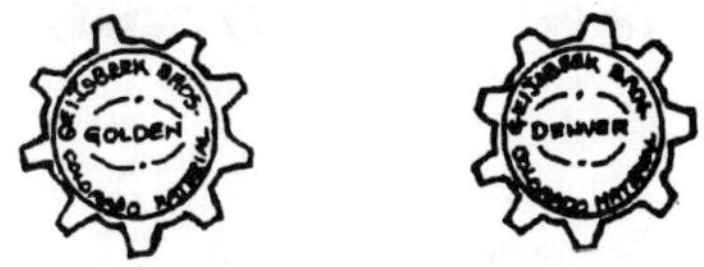

1899 Gutherz, Oscar & Edgar, ALT-ROHLAU, Bohemia, Germany.

1899- HARD-PASTE PORCELAIN. Printed Green-

1918- Incorporated into EPIAG.

1899 Hancock & Co.,F., STOKE, Staffordshire, England.

1899-1900 EARTHENWARES. - Printed-

1899 Irelan, Mrs. Linna, SAN FRANCISCO, California, U.S.A.

c.1899- ART POTTERY. All pieces are thrown on the wheel. Mr. Alexander W. Robertson assists in the processes.
`Roblin` mark, made from `Rob` of Robertson and `lin` from Linna. Impressed-

1899 Kalk, Porzellanfabrik, EISENBERG, Thuringia, Germany.

1899- HARD-PASTE PORCELAIN. -

1899 Lehmann & Sohn, C.A., KAHLA, Thuringia, Germany.

1899- HARD-PASTE PORCELAIN. - -

1899

1899 New Hall Pottery Co.Ltd., HANLEY, Staffordshire, England.

1899-1956 EARTHENWARES. - - -

c.1930-51 Printed- -

1899 Oliver China Co., SEBRING, Ohio, U.S.A.

1899- POTTERY, `VERUS` PORCELAIN. - -

THE OLIVER
CHINA CO.
SEBRING, OHIO
V E R U S
PORCELAIN

1899 Physick & Cooper, HANLEY, Staffordshire, England.

1899-1900 EARTHENWARES.

Printed-

1900-11 **Art Pottery Co.** Printed- - -

c.1912-58 **Coopers Art Pottery Co.** Printed mark as above.

1899 Sadler & Sons Ltd., James, BURSLEM, Staffordshire, England.

c.1899- EARTHENWARES. TEAPOT SPECIALISTS. -
This Factory was first established in 1882 by James Sadler, and after a century of production it still remains in the Sadler family.

1899-1937 Impressed-

ENGLAND
J. S. S. B.

1937- Impressed or printed-

SADLER
BURSLEM
ENGLAND

c.1947 to today. Printed-

Current mark -

(By kind permission of James Sadler & Sons Ltd., Burslem, England.)

1899 Stubbs Bros., FENTON, Staffordshire, England.

1899-1904 BONE-CHINA. - Printed-

1899 Taylor, Lee & Smith Co., EAST LIVERPOOL, Ohio, U.S.A.

1899- SEMI-VITREOUS PORCELAIN. - - **TAYLOR LEE & SMITH**

1901 Taylor, Smith & Taylor Co. - -

1899 United States Pottery Co., WELLSVILLE, Ohio, U.S.A.

1899- SEMI-VITREOUS PORCELAIN. - -

1899	Fourmaintraux, Gabriel, France. - -	see 1732 DESVRES.
1899	Hanley China Co., HANLEY, England. -	see 1865 Bevington, James & Thomas.
1899	Wellington Pottery Co., HANLEY, England.	see 1879 Bednall & Heath.
1899	Wildblood, Heath & Sons Ltd., England.	see 1887 Wildblood, R.V.

1900 Anger, A.C.J., AICH, nr. Karlsbad, Bohemia, Germany.

c.1900- HARD-PASTE PORCELAIN. Impressed-

1900 Barnard, Harry, BURSLEM, Staffordshire, England.

c.1900- Decorator at Wedgwood & Sons Ltd., BURSLEM.

1900

1900 Biltons Ltd., London Road, STOKE, Staffordshire, England.

1900- EARTHENWARES. Impressed marks - **BILTON**
BILTONS

1912- **Biltons (1912) Ltd.**
Joseph Tellwright purchased the business.
BROWN TEAPOTS, RED FLOOR TILES, ROCKINGHAM WARE.
1952- Peter Tellwright (son) joined the business.
1963- Tile factory closed and all production converted to domestic tableware.

1960s-70s Various printed marks - -

1986- **Coloroll Group plc. acquired business.**

BILTONS
TABLEWARE
ENGLAND

1990- **Management buyout after the collapse of the Coloroll Group. The company became part of Staffordshire Tableware Ltd.** see 1916 Keele St. Pottery.

1995 **Biltons Tableware Ltd. was sold to management team.**

(Information by courtesy of Biltons Tableware Ltd., Staffordshire Tableware Ltd.)

1900 Brown & Steventon Ltd., BURSLEM, Staffordshire, England.

1900-23 EARTHENWARES. Factory`s initials printed within marks of various patterns and designs. **B. & S.**

1920-23 Printed-

1923- **Steventon & Sons Ltd.,John,**
1923-36 Printed with crown-

ROYAL
VENTON WARE
JOHN STEVENTON
& SONS LTD.
BURSLEM ENGLAND

1936- Factory now produces tiles and sanitary ware.

1900 Carstens, C.& E., REICHENBACH, Thuringia, Germany.

1900- HARD-PASTE PORCELAIN.

Also at BLANKENHAIN, - -

1900 Dalton, William B., LONDON, England.

1900- STUDIO POTTER IN STONEWARE AND PORCELAIN

Incised or painted-

1941- In U.S.A.

1900 East Liverpool Potteries Co., EAST LIVERPOOL, Ohio, U.S.A.

Early 20th century Company incorporating the following factories:-

The Globe Pottery, - - see 1881 Frederick, Shenkle, Allen,

The Wallace & Chetwynd Pottery, -

SEMI-VITREOUS OPAQUE CHINA. - -

The United States Pottery,-

The East Liverpool Pottery Co. - see 1896

The George C. Murphy Pottery, -

The East End Pottery. - -

c.1900- Since their incorporation, all of them use the same mark as shown here. - -

1900

1900 Ens, Karl, VOLKSTEDT, Thuringia, Germany.

1900- HARD-PASTE PORCELAIN. - -

1900 Heber & Co., NEUSTADT, Gotha, Germany.

1900- HARD-PASTE PORCELAIN. - -

1900 Kretschmann, Heinrich, ELBOGEN, Bohemia, Germany.

c.1900- HARD-PASTE PORCELAIN. - -

1900 Lancaster & Sons Ltd., Dresden Works, HANLEY, Staffs. England.

1900-44 EARTHENWARES. Factory`s initials printed within marks of various designs. - **L. S.**

1906- Printed-
1906- `& Sons` `& S` added
1906- `Ltd` added

1920- - -

1930- Printed Trade-mark- **Royall & Lansan**

c.1935- Printed-

c.1938-44 Printed with crown- **LANCASTERS Ltd. HANLEY ENGLAND**

Continued over -

1900 Lancaster & Sons Ltd., Dresden Works, HANLEY, England. (Cont`)

1944- **Lancaster & Sandland Ltd.**

Marks as per c.1935 above- **BRITISH CROWN WARE CROWN DRESDEN WARE**

1944-52 Factory`s name printed within marks of various designs. **LANCASTER & SANDLAND LTD.**

1952- Printed marks with- **SANDLAND WARE**

1900 Lingard Webster & Co. Ltd., TUNSTALL, Staffordshire, England.

1900- EARTHENWARES. - - -

1946- Impressed or printed-

1900 Ledgar, Thomas P., LONGTON, Staffordshire, England.

1900-05 GENERAL CERAMICS. Factory`s initials printed or impressed within marks of various designs. **T. P. L.**

1900 Owens Pottery Co., J.B., ZANESVILLE, Ohio, U.S.A.

Turn of the century company manufacturing art wares.

Pattern & Trade-marks **OWENS UTOPIAN**

OWENS FEROZA

HENRI DEUX

Vases, lamps, jardinieres, etc. Special underglaze decorations painted by a team of fine decorators of which a list of their names and marks are given below in alphabetical order:-

Beardsley, Estelle,		Bell, Edith, -	EB
Bell, Fanny, -	FB	Best, A.F. -	
Bloomer, Cecilia,-		Bloomer, Lillian,-	LB.
Davis, Cora, -	C.D.	Denny, W. -	WD
Eberlein, Harrie, -	HE	Eberlein, Hattie,-	HE

Continued over -

1900

1900 Owens Pottery Co.,J.B., ZANESVILLE, Ohio, U.S.A. (Cont`)

Excel, Cecil, -
Gray, Charles, -
Gray, Martha E. -
Harvey, Delores, -
Haubrich, Albert,-
Hook, Roy, - -
Hoskins, H. -
Larzelere, Harry, -
Lewis, A.V. -
McCandless, Cora, -
McDonald, Carrie,-
Oshe, Miss, - -
Pierce, Mary L. -
Robinson, Harry, -
Ross, Hattie M. -
Shoemaker, R. Lillian,-
Steele, Ida, -
Stemm, Will H. -
Stevens, Mary Fauntleroy, -
Timberlake, Mae, -
Timberlake, Sarah,-
Williams, Arthur, -

1900 Rheinische Porzellanfabrik, MANNHEIM, Baden, Germany.

1900- HARD-PASTE PORCELAIN. - -

1900 Sèvres China Co., EAST LIVERPOOL, Ohio, U.S.A.

1900- CHINA. Mark taken from Sèvres Factory, France.

1900 Stabler, Harold & Phoebe, LONDON, England.

Early 20th century. DESIGNERS IN EARTHENWARES -
Harold Stabler was formerly with Carter, Stabler & Adams of Poole. Incised or painted signatures with date-

Phoebe Stabler
(date)
Stabler
(date)

1900 Star China Co., LONGTON, Staffordshire, England.

1900-19 CHINA. Factory`s initials printed within marks of various designs. **S. C. Co.**

c.1904- Printed Trade-mark **PARAGON CHINA ENGLAND**

1920- **Paragon China Co. Ltd.** PORCELAIN. Factory`s name printed within marks of various designs, especially the `Royal Arms` and the word `Paragon`

Acquired by Allied English Potteries Ltd.
Now Royal Doulton Group.

1900 Zdekauer, Moritz, ALT-ROHLAU, Bohemia, Germany.

1900 HARD-PASTE PORCELAIN.

1909 **C.M. Hutschenreuther, Hohenberg acquired the Factory and renamed it `Altroulauer Porcelain Factory AG`** see 1814 Hutschenreuther,C.M.

1920-38 marks - -

1938-45 mark - - -

1945 **Renamed `Starolsk`y Porcelan Narodni Podnik Stara Role`**

1945 mark - - -

(Courtesy of Hutschenreuther AG., Germany.)

1900/01

1900	Alsop-Robineau, Adelaide, SYRACUSE, U.S.A.	see 1871 Onondaga Pottery Co.
1900	Art Pottery Co., HANLEY, England. - -	see 1899 Physick & Cooper.
1900	Birks, Rawlins & Co.Ltd., STOKE, England. -	see 1896 Birks & Co.,L.A.
1900	Cleary, Edward, Ireland. - - - - -	see 1857 Belleek Pottery.
1900	Grimwades Ltd., HANLEY, England. - -	see 1886 Grimwade Bros.
1900	Hallen Pottery, BURSLEM, England. - -	see 1867 Wade Group.
1900	Jones & Sons, A.B., LONGTON, England. -	see 1876 Jones, Alfred B.,
1900	Kieler Kunst-Keramik, Germany. - - -	see 1762 KIEL.
1900	Springer & Co., ELBOGEN, Germany. - -	see 1815 Haidinger, R.E.
1900	Thompson, Margaret E., LAMBETH, England. -	see 1815 Royal Doulton plc.
1900	Zeh, Felix, (modeller) Germany. - - -	see 1835 Scheibe-Alsbach GmbH.

1901 Adderley, J. Fellows, LONGTON, Staffordshire, England.

1901-05 PORCELAIN. Factory`s initials printed within marks of various patterns and designs. **J. F. A.**

Printed Trade-mark-

1901 American Art Ceramic Co., CORONA, New York, U.S.A.

1901- POTTERY AND TERRA-COTTA. - -

`Ungaren` means Hungary in German. -

1901 Anchor Porcelain Co. Ltd., LONGTON, Staffordshire, England.

1901-18 PORCELAIN. - - Impressed- **A. P. CO.**
A. P. CO. L.

1901-15 Impressed or printed-

1915-18 Printed-

1901 Elton & Co. Ltd.,J.F., BURSLEM, Staffordshire, England.

1901-10 EARTHENWARES. Factory`s initials or monogram found within printed or impressed marks of various designs. **J. F. E. CO. LTD.**
BURSLEM

1901 Hüttl, Theodor, BUDAPEST, Hungary.

1901- HARD-PASTE PORCELAIN. - -
Name of Factory found within marks of various designs. - - -

1901 Johnson Tiles Ltd., H.& R. TUNSTALL, Staffordshire, England.

1901- **H.& R. Johnson, COBRIDGE.** CERAMIC TILES.
Impressed or printed - **H. & R. J. ENGLAND**

1916- Registered trademark -
(Not used for some considerable time)

1911- Acquired Alfred Meakin Ltd., TUNSTALL,
1919- Acquired Sherwin & Cotton, HANLEY,
1919- and Longport Mills,
1952- Acquired Thomas Peake Ltd.,
1958- Acquired Jeffrey Tiles Ltd.,
1958- and Trent Tiles Ltd.,
1964- Malkin Tiles (Burslem) Ltd.,

1968- **H.& R. Johnson - Richards Tiles Ltd.,**
1979- **Taken over by Norcros plc.**
becomes H.& R. Johnson Tiles Ltd.,
The largest UK manufacturer of ceramic tiles.

(By kind permission of H.& R. Johnson Tiles Ltd., England.)

1901 KARLSRUHE, Baden, Germany.

1901- EARTHENWARES. - - -
Grossherzogliche Keramische Manufaktur-

Staatliche Majolika-Manufaktur - -

Kunst,D. und Sebald, Handwerk Friedrich -

1901

1901 Knowles China Co., Edwin M., EAST LIVERPOOL, Ohio, U.S.A.

1901- SEMI-PORCELAIN, WHITE GRANITE.

Semi-porcelain mark-

EDWIN M. KNOWLES
CHINA CO.

White granite mark- **E.M.K.
C. CO**

1901 Mason Cash & Co.Ltd., Pool Pottery, CHURCH GRESLEY, Eng.

1901-EARTHENWARE. ESPECIALLY NOTED FOR `MEASHAM` OR `BARGE WARE` AND `MOTTO` WARE.

There appears to have been a pottery on this site for many years prior to 1901, the Title Deeds indicate a `Windmill Pottery` early in the 19th Century, and before that it was called `Baths Pottery`

WINDMILL POTTERY
c.1810-

In the late 19th century, the pottery was owned by a Mr William Mason who by all accounts was known as `Bossy` Mason and could be found most mornings in either the Bird in Hand or the Gresley Arms public houses. Manufacture of these wares continued into the 20th. century.

MASON
c.1860-1900

MASON CASH & CO
1901-

c.1870- Rockingham teapots were first produced in various shapes and sizes. All were of the same walnut brown glaze with brightly coloured designs and usually bore a legend such as `Bless this House`.

c.1918-39 Inter-war-years Company produced decorated bulb bowls, vases and kitchen ware.

MASON CASH & CO. LTD
1941-

1979- Mr.John Perks became Managing Director, and holds that position today (1995) Company mainly produces traditional cane coloured kitchen pottery, pet feeding bowls and ceramic bird feeders.

MASON CASH OF ENGLAND
1993-

All the above marks are impressed.

(By kind permission of Mason Cash & Co.Ltd., Church Gresley, England.)

1901 Middle Lane Pottery, EAST and WEST HAMPTON, N. York, U.S.A.

c.1901- EARTHENWARES IN METALIC LUSTRES
Factory established by Mr. T.A. Brouwer, Jr.

Impressed-

Pieces produced at West Hampton bear the signature of the maker. - -

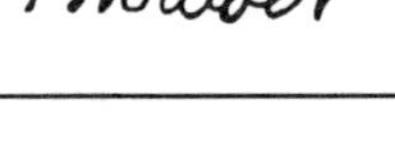

1901 Robinson, W.H., LONGTON, Staffordshire, England.

1901-04 PORCELAIN. Printed within a circle under a crown- **W.H. ROBINSON LONGTON BALTIMORE CHINA**

1901 Salt & Nixon Ltd., LONGTON, Staffordshire, England.

1901-34 PORCELAIN.

c.1901-21 Printed-

c.1914-21 Printed-

c.1921-34 Printed within a shield. - **SALON CHINA S. & N. ENGLAND**

1901 Schoenau & Hoffmeister, BURGGRUB, Bavaria, Germany.

1901- DOLLS` HEADS AND DOLLS.

Porzellanfabrik Burggrub - -

1901 Seltmann, Johann, VOHENSTRAUSS, Bavaria, Germany.

1901- HARD-PASTE PORCELAIN. - -

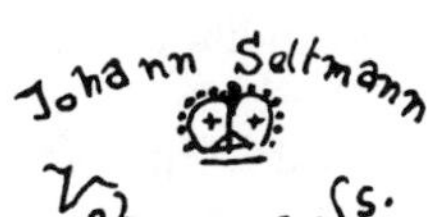

1901 Shaw & Copestake, LONGTON, Staffordshire, England.

1901- EARTHENWARES. - - -

c.1925-36 Printed or impressed-

c.1936-40 Trade-mark used in various forms. **SYLVAC WARE**

1901

1901 Stockton Art Pottery Co., STOCKTON, Cal. U.S.A.

c.1901- EARTHENWARES. - - -

1901 Van Briggle Pottery Co., COLORADO SPRINGS, Colorado, U.S.A.

1901- ART POTTERY established by Artus Van Briggle.

Dated incised mark-

1904 Mr. Van Briggle died

1901 Weller, S.A., ZANESVILLE, Ohio, U.S.A.

c.1901 ART POTTERY WITH UNDERGLAZE DECORATIONS.

Eosian WELLER	**Aurelian WELLER**	**LOUWELSA WELLER**	**TURADA WELLER**

`Dickens` ware had a matt finish- **DICKENS WARE WELLER**

Mr. J. Sicard from Clement Massier of Golfe Juan, France, joined the Company and perfected metalic lustre ware on an iridescent background. - - - **SICARDO WELLER.**

<u>A list of decorators and their marks found on the wares of this factory:-</u>

Adams, Virginia, -	VA.	Ayers, Elizabeth, -	EA
Blake, Lizabeth, -	L:B	Burgess, Levi J., -	L.J.B.
Dautherty, Anna, -	A.D.	Dunlavy, Anthony, -	AD.
Ferrell, Frank, -	F.F.	Gillie, Mary, - -	MG
Haubrich, Albert,-	A.H.	Hurst, Madge, -	MH
Imlay, Josephine,-	J.I.	Kappes, Karl, -	K.K.
McLaughlin, S. Reid,-		Mitchell, Hattie, -	HM

Continued over -

1901 Weller, S.A., ZANESVILLE, Ohio, U.S.A. (Cont`)

Mitchell, Lily, -	LM	Mitchell, Minnie, -	M.M.
Mull, Gordon, -	GM	Pickens, Edwin, -	ELP
Pillsbury, Hester W.-	HP	Roberts, Eugene, -	ER
Steele, Tot, -	TS.	Terry, C. Minnie, -	TF.
Windle, Helen B.-	H.W.		

1901 Zenari, Oscar, LEIPZIG, Saxony, Germany.

1901- Decorator of hard-paste porcelain.

1901	Hobson, George, BURSLEM, England. - -	see 1883 Hobson, G.& J.
1901	Lockitt, William H., HANLEY, England. -	see 1879 Bednall & Heath.
1901	Riemerschmid, Richard, Germany. - -	see 1845 Reinhold Merkelbash.
1901	Royal Aller Vale & Watcombe Pot. Co. England.	see 1868 Phillips & Co. John.
1901	Soho Pottery Ltd., TUNSTALL, England. -	see 1883 Rathbone, Smith & Co.
1901	Taylor, Smith & Taylor Co., E. LIVERPOOL, U.S.A.	see 1899 Taylor, Lee & Smith Co.

1902 Dudson, Wilcox & Till Ltd., Britannic Works, HANLEY, Staffs, Eng.

1902-26 Earthenwares. - - -

Printed or impressed-

1902 Matthews & Clark, LONGTON, Staffordshire, England.

c.1902-06 General ceramics. - - -

Found within printed mark- **M & C**
L

1902 Persch, Adolf, ELBOGEN, Bohemia, Germany.

1902- Hard-paste porcelain.

1902 Reichel, Lorenz, SCHIRNDING, Bavaria, Germany.

1902- Hard-paste porcelain decorator.

1902 Selle, Ferdinand, BURGAU-GÖSCHWITZ, Thuringia, Germany.

1902- **Porzellan-Manufaktur-Burgau.** - -

1902	Ballanger (Decorator) France. - - -	see 1745 SÈVRES.
1902	Bocquet (Decorator) France. - - -	see 1745 SÈVRES.
1902	Catteau (Decorator) France. - - -	see 1745 SÈVRES.
1902	Christie & Beardmore, FENTON, England. -	see 1887 Forester & Hulme.
1902	Essex Art Pottery. CASTLE HEDINGHAM, England.	see 1864 Bingham, Edward.
1902	Gobled (Decorator) France. - - -	see 1745 SÈVRES.
1902	Harradine, Leslie, LAMBETH, England.- -	see 1815 Royal Doulton plc.
1902	Merrimac Pottery Co., NEWBURYPORT, U.S.A.	see 1897 Merrimac Ceramic Co.
1902	Quennoy (Decorator) France. - - -	see 1745 SÈVRES.
1902	Richard, L., (Decorator) France. - - -	see 1745 SÈVRES.
1902	Rondeleux et Cie, France. - - - -	see 1815 VIERZON.
1902	Tuxedo Pottery Co., PHOENIXVILLE, U.S.A. -	see 1867 Phoenix Pottery Co.

1903 American Terra-cotta Co., CHICAGO, ILL. U.S.A.

c.1903- TECO WARE (TERRA-COTTA) - -

1903 Chew, John, LONGTON, Staffordshire, England.

J. C.

1903-04 PORCELAIN. Impressed- **L.**

1903 Coronation Pottery Co.Ltd., STOKE, Staffordshire, England.

1903-54 EARTHENWARES. Early wares not marked.

c1947-54 Printed or impressed- `Ltd` added.

1903 Fasolt & Stauch, BOCK-WALLENDORF, Thuringia, Germany.

1903- HARD-PASTE PORCELAIN. FIGURES ETC. -

1903 Kranichfelder Porzellan-Manufactur, KRANICHFELD, Germany.

1903- HARD-PASTE PORCELAIN. - -

1903 Pennsylvania Museum and School of Industrial Art. Phila., U.S.A.

1903- Pottery introduced to School .
Mr. Leon Volkmar (Head of department)
Earthenwares carved and decorated in relief.

1903 Poillon, C.L.& H.A., WOODBRIDGE, New Jersey, U.S.A.

c.1903 EARTHENWARE ART POTTERY. - -

Monogram of Clara L. Poillon -

1903 Wheeling Potteries Co., WHEELING, West Virginia, U.S.A.

1903- An organization consisting of Wheeling, La Belle, Riverside and Avon potteries, of which Mr Charles W. Franzheim was its first president and general manager.

Mark used by the Avon on their art ware -

see 1879 Wheeling Pottery Co.
see 1886 Avon Pottery.

1903 Winterling, Heinrich, MARKLEUTHEN, Bavaria, Germany.

1903- HARD-PASTE PORCELAIN. -

1903	Beardmore & Co., Frank, FENTON, England. -	see 1887 Forester & Hulme.
1903	Brain & Co. Ltd.,E., LONGTON, England. -	see 1881 Robinson & Son.
1903	Burgess, Thomas, HANLEY, England. - -	see 1894 Harrop & Burgess.
1903	Burgess & Co., TRENTON, N.J., U.S.A. -	see 1860 Speeler & Sons, H.
1903	Dunmore Pottery Co., AIRTH, Scotland.- -	see 1860 Dunmore Pottery.
1903	Fournerie (Decorator) France. - - -	see 1745 SÈVRES.
1903	Northfield Hawley Pottery Co.Ltd., England. -	see 1863 Hawley, W.& G.
1903	Price Bros. (Burslem) Ltd., England. - -	see 1896 Price Bros.
1903	Volkmar & Son, Charles, METUCHEN, N.J. U.S.A.	see 1879 Volkmar, Charles,

1904

1904 Arkinstall & Sons Ltd., STOKE, Staffordshire, England.

1904-24 BONE-CHINA Factory`s initials printed within marks of various patterns and designs. **A & S**

1904-24 Souvenir wares- **ARCADIAN**
ARCADIAN CHINA

1908 **Robinson & Leadbeater acquired Factory.**
Robinson & Sons, A.J.
1925- **Cauldon Ltd.**

1904 Dachsel, Paul, TURN, Bohemia, Germany.

1904- ART-WARE POTTERY. - - -
Monogram within mark-

1904 Heinrich & Co., SELB, Bavaria, Germany.

1904- PORCELAIN AND DECORATORS. - -

1929- **Gräf & Krippner (Branch)**
PORCELAIN.

1904 Kronester & Co.,J., SCHWARZENBACH, Bavaria, Germany.

1904- HARD-PASTE PORCELAIN. - -

1904 Noritake Co. Ltd., Japan.

1904- **The Nippon Toki Kaisha Ltd.**

Founders:- Ichizaemon Morimura, Magobei Okura,
Jitsuei Hirose, Yasukata Murai,
Kazuchika Okura and Kotaro Asukai.

Note

In general the name `Noritake` is printed on most marks. The name `Nippon` dates back to the earlier period.

The letter `M` (Morimura) was first used in c.1911 until 1953 when the letter `N` (Nippon Toki) was used

1891- Printed mark -
Green indicates first grade wares-
Blue indicates second grade -

c.1908- Domestic market -
`R.C.` means Royal Crockery
Symbol design (Yajirobe) means
`Toy of Balance` symbolising the
balance of management.

Centre symbol is Chinese character
`Komaru` meaning `difficulty` Known
as `spider mark` - -

c.1908- U.K. Market - -
Spider symbol with arrows means
`difficulty` Unacustomed dealings
in the export market was the
reason behind this mark.
(Sometimes with Design No.)

c.1911- U.S.A. Market `M` means Morimura-

The Nippon Toki Kaisha Ltd.

1911 Additional marks registered in Japan.-

Continued over -

1904

1904 Noritake Co. Ltd., Japan. (Cont`)

1914- Pattern name `SEDAN` No.D1441.
First dinner set produced by Noritake.

1918- India and Southeast Asia market. - -

c.1918- U.S.A. Market. (`M` means Morimura) -
Because of the McKinley Tariff Act (1890)
`Nippon` was changed to `Made in Japan`

1933 - -

1946- `Rose China` mark used during the period just after the war, where the quality of the chinaware was not so good.

1947- `Made in Occupied Japan` mark - -

1950- The name `Noritake` finally registered as Trade name.

The Nippon Toki Kaisha Ltd.
1947- Noritake Co.Incorporated, established.
New York City, U.S.A.

1953- Letter `N` first used
`N` means Nippon Toki.

Continued over -

1904 Noritake Co. Ltd., Japan. (Cont`)

1958- **Noritake (Australia) Pty.,Ltd. Sidney. established.**

1964-

1975- **Noritake Ireland Ltd., established.**

Some modern marks:

(Courtesy of Noritake Co. Ltd., Japan.)

1904 Müller, E.& A., SCHÖNWALD, Bavaria, Germany.

1904- HARD-PASTE PORCELAIN. - - M. P. M.

1927- **Merged into Kahla AG with Porzellanfabrik Schönwald.** see 1879 Porzellanfabrik Schönwald

---

1904 Powell, Alfred & Louise, LONDON, England.

c.1904-39 DECORATORS OF WEDGWOOD WARES.

1904

1904 Reinhardt & Aurnhammer, BRAMBACH, Saxony, Germany.

1904- HARD-PASTE PORCELAIN. - -

1904 Schneider & Co., ALT-ROHLAU, Bohemia, Germany.

1904- Hard-paste porcelain - -

1904 Schomburg & Co., TELTOW, Prussia, Germany.

1904- HARD-PASTE PORCELAIN. - -
Teltow, Porzellan Fabrik GmbH.
Berliner Porzellan-Manufactur

1904 SCHORNDORF, Bavaria, Germany.

1904- Bauer & Pfeiffer. HARD-PASTE PORCELAIN -
Württembergische Porzellan-manufactur -

1904 Sommer & Matschak, SCHLAGGENWALD, Bohemia, Germany.

1904- HARD-PASTE PORCELAIN. - -

1904 Wild Bros., LONGTON, Staffordshire, England.

1904-27 PORCELAIN. Factory`s initials found within marks of various designs. - -

J. S. W.
W. BROS.

Printed or impressed- - -

c.1922-27 Printed-

1904 Wittelsberger & Co., DUISDORF, Bonn, Rhineland, Germany.

1904- Porzellan-Fabrik Rhenania. - - - - -

Westdeutsche Porzellanfabrik GmbH. -

1904	Dean, S.W., BURSLEM, England. -	see 1871 Edge, Malkin & Co.
1904	Eaubonne,d` (Decorator) France. - -	see 1745 SÈVRES.
1904	Leeds Fireclay Co.Ltd., LEEDS, England.	see 1882 Burmantofts, Wilcox & Co.
1904	Wood, Arthur, LONGPORT, England. -	see 1895 Capper & Wood.

1905 Ceramic Art Co.(1905) Ltd. STOKE, Staffordshire, England.

1905-19 EARTHENWARES. Factory`s initials printed or impressed within marks of various patterns and designs. **C. A. & CO. LTD.**

1905 Hirsch, F., DRESDEN, Germany.

Early 20th century. MEISSEN STYLE DECORATOR. -

1905 Jones (Longton) Ltd. A.E. LONGTON, Staffordshire, England.

1905-46 EARTHENWARES.

c.1908-36 Printed or impressed- - -

c.1936-41 Printed-

c.1937-46 Printed-

1946- **Palissy Pottery Ltd.** Marks used as above

c.1948- Various marks used with the Factory`s name included- **PALISSY**

Now part of Royal Worcester Ltd. see 1751 WORCESTER.

1905

1905 Moore, Bernard, STOKE, Staffordshire, England.

1905-15 ART POTTERY AND PORCELAIN WITH SPECIAL GLAZES.

Painted monogram-

Monograms of decorators were also marked on these wares.
Painted or printed sometimes with year-

see 1872 Moore Bros. and 1912 Billington, Dora,

1905 Richter, Felkl, & Hahn, CHODAU, Bohemia, Germany.

1905- HARD-PASTE PORCELAIN. **R. F. & H.**

1905 Schumann & Schreider, SCHWARZENHAMMER, Germany.

1905- HARD-PASTE PORCELAIN. - -

1905 Shorter & Son Ltd. STOKE, Staffordshire, England.

1905- EARTHENWARES. Printed within marks of various patterns i.e. - - **SHORTER & SON STOKE-ON-TRENT**
c.1914-36 - - **BATAVIA WARE**
c.1936-40 - - **SUNRAY POTTERY**

Printed-

1905 Wehinger & Co., H., HORN, Bohemia, Germany.

1905- HARD-PASTE PORCELAIN, DECORATORS. -

1905	Blyth Porcelain Co.Ltd. LONGTON, England. -	see 1896 Dresden Porc. Co.
1905	Cauldon Ltd., HANLEY, England. - -	see 1856 Ridgway Bates & Co.
1905	Robinson & Son, John, CASTLEFORD, England.	see 1897 Robinson Bros.
1905	Shore, Coggins & Holt, LONGTON, England. -	see 1887 Shore & Co. J.
1905	Wild, Thomas C. LONGTON, England. - -	see 1896 Wild & Co. T.C.
1905	Wolffsen & Son A/S. ROENNE, Denmark. -	see 1835 Søholm A/S.

1906 Clews & Co. Ltd., George, TUNSTALL, Staffordshire, England.

1906-61 EARTHENWARES. Factory`s name printed within marks of a globe. - -

G. CLEWS & Co.

1906- Trade-name printed or impressed- **CHAMELON WARE**

1935-61 Various marks,all of which include the full name of the Factory. -

G. CLEWS & Co. Ltd.
George
Clews & Co. Ld.

1906 Gallimore & Co. Ltd., LONGTON, Staffordshire, England.

1906-34 EARTHENWARES. - - -

Impressed or printed-

1906 Porzellanfabrik Creidlitz, CREIDLITZ, Bavaria, Germany.

1906- HARD-PASTE PORCELAIN.

1906 Hertel, Jakob & Co., REHAU, Bavaria, Germany.

1906- HARD-PASTE PORCELAIN. - -

1906 Mayer & Sherratt, LONGTON, Staffordshire, England.

1906-41 CHINA. - - -

1906 with crown-

M & S
L

1921-41 with crown-

MELBA BONE CHINA

1906 Langenthal Swiss China Works Ltd., LANGENTHAL, Switzerland.

1906- HOTEL AND HOUSEHOLD CHINA.
1988 **Keramik Holding AG Laufen. acquired this Company.**

ERSTE LANGENTHAL-PRODUKTE WURDEN ZUM TEIL OHNE STEMPEL GEFERTIGT

1916

1931

1947-59

1906

1920

1932/33

1960-63

1911

1923

1934-46

1964-

(By kind permission of Langenthal Swiss China Works Ltd.)

1906 Morley Fox & Co. Ltd., FENTON, Staffordshire, England.

1906-44 EARTHENWARES. Factory`s initials printed within marks of various designs. **M. F. & Co.**

c.1906-

c.1920- **MORLEY FOX & COMPANY Ltd.**

c.1929- Trade-name- **HOMELEIGH WARE**

c.1938-

1944-57 **Morley & Co.Ltd.,William,**
Continued marks as above c.1938.
c.1944 Trade-name- used within various marks, plus month and year. i.e. III/V=March 1945. - **MORLEY WARE**

1906 Rubian Art Pottery Ltd., FENTON, Staffordshire, England.

1906-33 EARTHENWARES. Printed or impressed- **L. S. & G.**

c.1926-33 Trade-name- **RUBAY ART WARE**

c.1913 **Grimwades Ltd., acquired Factory.**

1906 Scheidig, Carl, GRÄFENTHAL, Thuringia, Germany.

1906- HARD-PASTE PORCELAIN. - -

1906 Schwarzwalder Steingutfabik, HORNBERG, Baden, Germany.

1906- EARTHENWARE. - - -

1906 Swinnertons Ltd., HANLEY, Staffordshire, England.

1906- EARTHENWARES. - - -

c.1906-17 Printed-

c.1917-46 Printed:-

c.1946- Printed marks all include Factory`s name - **SWINNERTONS**

Acquired by Allied English Potteries Ltd.

Now Royal Doulton Group.

1906 Adderleys Ltd., LONGTON, England. - see 1853 Hulse,Nixon & Adderley.
1906 Holdcroft Ltd., LONGTON, England. - see 1865 Holdcroft, Joseph.
1906 Hulme & Son, Henry, BURSLEM, England. see 1882 Wood & Hulme.

1907 Fischer, Arno, ILMENAU, Thuringia, Germany.

1907- HARD-PASTE PORCELAIN. - -

1907

1907 Floyd & Sons R., STOKE, Staffordshire, England.

1907-30 EARTHENWARES. - - -

Printed or impressed-

1907 Haviland, Johann, WALDERSHOF, Bavaria. Germany.

1907- HARD-PASTE PORCELAIN. - - **J H W. Bavaria**

1936- Merged with Rosenthal-Porzellan Aktiengesellschaft, SELB.

1907 Hewitt & Leadbeater, Willow Pottery, LONGTON, Staffs, England.

1907-19 CHINA, PARIAN WARES.

Printed- -

1919-26 **Hewitt Bros.** Used same mark. - -

1907 Jones, A.G. Harley, FENTON, Staffordshire, England.

1907-34 EARTHENWARES, CHINA. Factory`s initials printed within marks of various patterns and designs. - - - **H. J.** **A.G.H.J.**

c.1907 - -

c.1920 Pattern name - **FENTONIA WARE**

c.1921 - -

c.1923-34 in various designs-

1907 Kestner & Co., OHRDRUF, Thuringia, Germany.

1907 HARD-PASTE PORCELAIN. - -

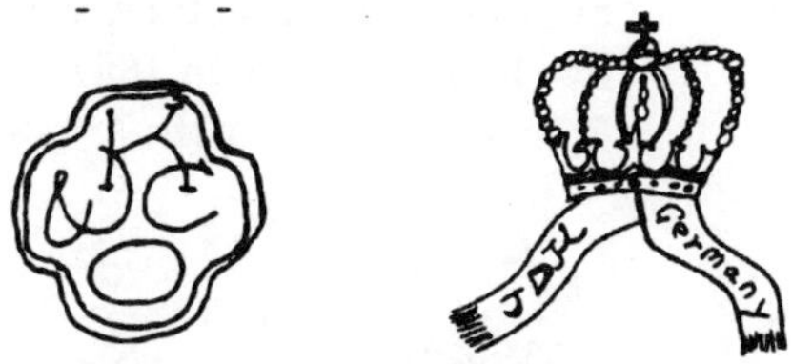

1907 Müller & Co., VOLKSTEDT, Thuringia, Germany.

1907- HARD-PASTE PORCELAIN.

1907 Sandlands & Colley Ltd., HANLEY, Staffordshire, England.

1907-10 EARTHENWARES, CHINA. - -

Printed- -

1907 SESTO FIORENTINO, Italy.

1907- Ceramics Artistica Ciulli.

Fantani, Bruno, Maiolica reproduction -

1907 Winterling Bros. OHG. RÖSLAU, Bavaria, Germany.

1907- HARD-PASTE PORCELAIN.

Gebr. Winterling OHG. was founded by the Winterling family of seven sisters and brothers in ROSLAU, Bavaria.

Printed marks from 1907 to the present day-

Continued over -

1907/08

1907 Winterling Bros. OHG. ROSLAU, Bavaria, Germany. (Cont`)

1917- **Schwarzenbach factory, which was founded by Oscar Schaller in 1882, acquired.**
Printed marks from 1917 to the present day:-

see 1882 Schaller & Co.,Oscar,

1920- **Kirchenlamitz factory acquired.**

1964- 1986-

1928- **Haberlander porcelain factory, Windischeschenbach, acquired (founded 1913)**
Printed marks from 1929 to the present day:-

1929 1929 1945-47 1948 1986-

1954- **Bruchmuhlbach (5th production plant) built in the Rhine Palatinate area.**
1972- Earthenware produced here under the brand name **`Pfalzkeramik`.**

1992- **Winterling Porzellan AG. (limited share company) formed with headquarters in Kirchenlamitz.**

(By kind permission of Winterling Porzellan AG., Germany.)

1907 Passenger, Charles and Fred, FULHAM, England. - see 1872 De Morgan, Wm.

1908 Ackermann & Fritze, VOLKSTEDT, Thuringia, Germany.

1908- HARD-PASTE PORCELAIN.

1908 Cowlishaw, William H., LETCHWORTH, Hertfordshire, England.
1908-14 EARTHENWARES. Impressed- **ICENI WARE**

1908 Diamond Pottery Co. Ltd., HANLEY, Staffordshire, England.
1908-35 EARTHENWARES. Factory`s initials printed within marks of various patterns and designs. **D. P. CO.** **D. P. CO. LTD.**

1908 Grindley Hotel Ware Co.Ltd., TUNSTALL, Staffordshire, England.
1908- EARTHENWARES. HOTEL WARES.

1946- printed marks

1952- **The Dudson Group acquired the company.**
1979- **Duraline Hotelware Co.Ltd.,**
(Change of name)

Subsidiary of The Dudson Group. see 1809 Dudson, Thomas,
(By courtesy of The Dudson Group, Stoke-on-Trent, England)

1908 Mavaleix & Co., LIMOGES, France.
1908-14 PORCELAIN.

1920- **Mavaleix & Granger** - -
1922-50 **Granger & Co.**

1908 PLANKENHAMMER, Bavaria, Germany.
1908- HARD-PASTE PORCELAIN. - -
Porzellanfabrik Plankenhammer -

1908 Union Limousine, LIMOGES, France.
1908- PORCELAIN. - - -

1908 Möller, Carl, ROENNE, Denmark. - - - see 1835 Søholm A/S.
1908 Thomas & Co., F., SOPHIENTHALL, Germany. - see 1879 Rosenthal & Co.

1909

1909 Colley & Co. Ltd., Alfred, TUNSTALL, Staffordshire, England.

1909-14 EARTHENWARES. Printed or impressed- with crown.

1909 Metzel Bros., KÖNITZ, Thuringia, Germany.

1909- HARD-PASTE PORCELAIN. - -

1909 Osborne China Co. Ltd., LONGTON, Staffordshire, England.

1909-40 CHINA. - Printed-

1909 Schrembs, J., ERBENDORF, Bavaria, Germany.

Early 20th century. - - -

1909 Wells, Reginald, WROTHAM, Kent, England.

c.1909-51 STUDIO-POTTERY. - - -

c.1909 Slip-ware - **COLDRUM WROTHAM**

c.1910-24 Chelsea, London-
Impressed or incised - **COLDRUM CHELSEA**

c.1910- Incised-

c.1910- Incised or painted- **R. F. WELLS**
c.1918-51 Impressed or incised- **SOON**
c.1925-51 Storrington, Sussex. **S**

1909 Wild & Adams Ltd., LONGTON, Staffordshire, England.

1909-27 EARTHENWARES. Printed or impressed- **W. & A.**

c.1923-27 `Ltd` added Printed- -

1909 Hsüan-t`ung, China. - - - - see 1644 CH`ING.
1909 Pfeiffer, Max Adolph, Germany. - - - see 1882 Unterweissbacher.

1910 Andersson & Johansson, HÖGANÄS, Sweden.

1910- EARTHENWARE PRODUCTS.

1910 1920 1935 1956

1970- **Höganäs Keramik AB** Name changed, and in the same year commenced production of stoneware which is free from lead.

1967 1976

1988- **BodaNova International AB acquired the Company.** Name changed to BodaNova-Höganäs Keramik AB.

1990- **Pomonagruppen AB acquired the Company (100%)**

Modern mark (1995)-

(By kind permission of BodaNova-Höganäs Keramik AB, Sweden.)

1910 Braunton Pottery Co. Ltd., BRAUNTON, Nth. Devon, England.

1910- EARTHENWARES. Early wares not marked.

c.1947- Printed or impressed-

1910

1910 Carstens, C.& E., ZEVEN, Hanover, Germany.

Early 20th century.

Zevener Porzellanfabrik-

1910 Emanuel, Max, & Co., MITTERTEICH, Bavaria, Germany.

Early 20th century. HARD-PASTE PORCELAIN. MOSAIC POTTERY.

1910 Fischer, Carl, BÜRGEL, Thuringia, Germany.

Early 20th century. ARTIST POTTER - -

1910 Haviland, Frank, LIMOGES, Haute-Vienne, France.

1910-31 HARD-PASTE PORCELAIN. Decorators for Haviland & Co. see 1853 Haviland & Co.

Marks in underglaze green:-

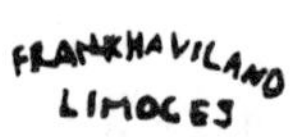

1910-14

1914-25

1825-31

(Courtesy of Haviland S.A., Limoges, France.)

For further information see *HAVILAND* *by Jean d`Albis.*

1910 Junkersdorf, Franz, DRESDEN, Germany.

Early 20th century. Decorator. - -

1910 Midwinter Ltd., W.R., BURSLEM, Staffordshire, England.

c.1910- EARTHENWARES. Factory`s name found within marks of various designs c.1932-41

c.1946 With crown - **MIDWINTER**

c.1953 Trade-name - **Stylecraft**

1910 Seltmann GmbH, Christian, WEIDEN, Bavaria, Germany.

1910- HARD-PASTE PORCELAIN. DINNERWARE, HOTELWARE, ETC.,
1910 Christian Seltmann (Founder)

1910-14 marks-

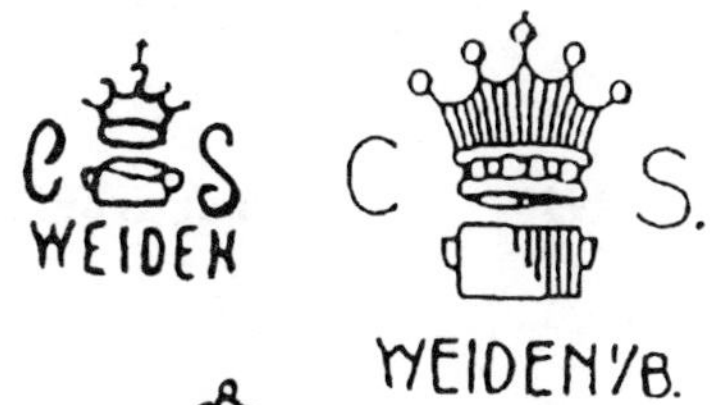

1914-45 marks-

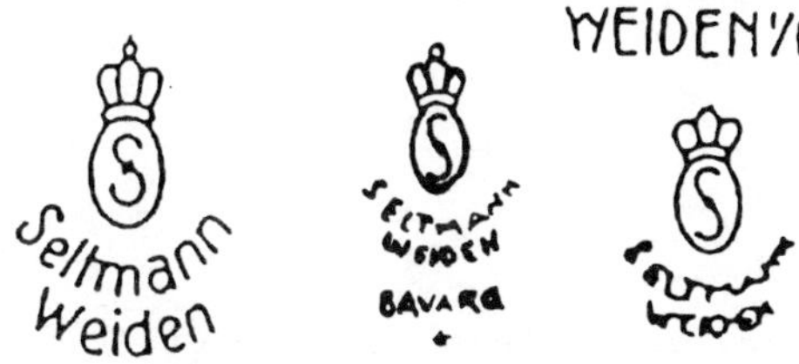

1939- **Acquired Hermann Lange`s Factory, Krummennaab.** see 1934 Hermann Lange.

1940- **Acquired Erbendorf Porcelain Factory, Erbendorf.**

1940-45 marks-

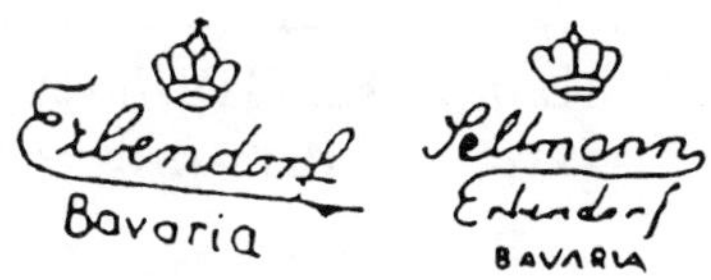

Special Trade marks before 1945-

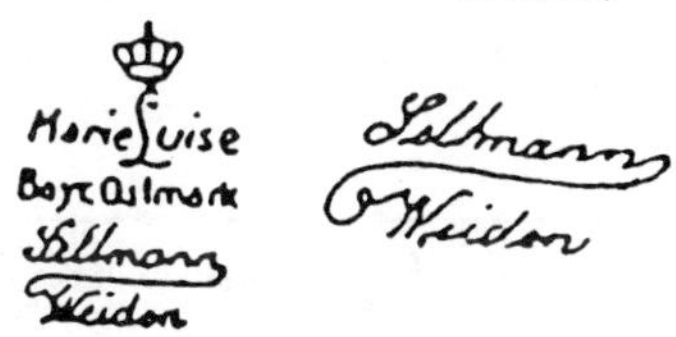

1945-48 mark-

1948- mark- -

Continued over -

1910-12

1910 Seltmann GmbH, Christian, WEIDEN, Bavaria, Germany. (Cont`)

1954- mark- -

1957- Acquired Königlich privilegierte Porzellanfabrik Tettau. see 1794 Tettau, Porzellanfabrik,

1979 `Gift items` special trade mark-

1983- mark- - - -

1990- German reunification.

1991- mark-

1995 Modern mark- -

(By courtesy of Porzellanfabriken Chr. Seltmann GmbH. Weiden)

1910 Alcock Pottery, Henry, COBRIDGE, England. - see 1853 Alcock, John,
1910 Deans (1910) Ltd., BURSLEM, England. - see 1871 Edge, Malkin & Co.
1910 Schramberger Majolika Fabrik, Germany. - see 1820 SCHRAMBERG.
1910 Wardle Art Pottery Co.Ltd., HANLEY, England. see 1871 Wardle & Co.Ltd.,

---

1911 Kampf, R., GRÜNLAS, Bohemia, Germany.

1911- HARD-PASTE PORCELAIN. - -

1911 Shore & Coggins, LONGTON, England.- - see 1887 Shore & Co.,J.

1912 Bailey & Sons, William, Gordon Pottery, LONGTON, Staff, England.

1912-14 EARTHENWARES. - Printed-

1912 Billington, Dora, LONDON, England.

1912- STUDIO POTTERY. - - -

1912-15 Mark of Bernard Moore wares. -

1920- incised or painted - -

see 1905 Moore, Bernard,

1912 Gray & Co. Ltd., A.E., HANLEY, Staffordshire, England.

1912-33 HANLEY, 1934-61 STOKE,

1912-30 Printed mark with sailing ship

A. E. GRAY & Co.Ltd.
HANLEY ENGLAND

1930-33 Printed mark with sailing ship

1934-61 `England` added-

GRAY`S POTTERY

1960 Retitled Portmeirion Pottery.

see 1960 Portmeiron Pottery.

1912 Mogridge & Underhay Ltd., Holborn, LONDON, E.C.4. England.

c.1912- RETAILER. - - -

TRADE MARK
M&U
"EMUNDU"

1912 Walton, J.H., LONGTON, Staffordshire, England.

1912-21 CHINA. Factory`s initials printed or impressed within marks of various designs. -

J. H. W.
LONGTON

1912 Warrington Pottery Co.Ltd., STOKE, Staffordshire, England.

1912-30 EARTHENWARES, ETC.

STOKE STAFFS
Reg.
TRADE MARK
BERYL
ENGLAND
FIREPROOF

1912/13

1912	Allertons Ltd., LONGTON, England. - -	see 1859 Allerton & Sons, C.
1912	Biltons (1912) Ltd., STOKE, England. - -	see 1900 Biltons Ltd.
1912	Blairs Ltd., LONGTON, England. - -	see 1880 Blairs & Co.
1912	Coopers Art Pottery Co., HANLEY, England. -	see 1899 Physick & Cooper.

1913 Fry, Roger, Omega Workshops, LONDON, England.

c.1913-19 STUDIO POTTERY. - - -

Impressed or incised-

1913 Govancroft Potteries Ltd., GLASGOW, Scotland.

1913- EARTHENWARES, STONEWARES. - -

1913-49 - Printed or impressed-

1949- Printed marks with `GOVANCROFT`

HIGHLAND WARE
GOVANCROFT
MADE IN
SCOTLAND

1962 Trade-name - - **CHIEFTAIN WARE**

1913 Moorcroft Ltd., W., BURSLEM, Staffordshire, England.

1913- EARTHENWARES, STUDIO POTTERY.

Signature of William Moorcroft -
Before 1918 Usually green -
Thereafter usually blue - -

Initials sometimes used - -

1914- Impressed backstamp introduced
(From February 1914)

MOORCROFT
BURSLEM
1914
M46

Impressed Shape Numbers. Some prefixed with an `M`
1915-16 Date was deleted.

1916-17 `ENGLAND` added. `BURSLEM` was eventually withdrawn.

1918-26 `MADE IN ENGLAND` was added to comply with U.S.A. import regulations.

MADE IN
ENGLAND

1926-28 Shape numbers were withdrawn.

Continued over -

1913 Moorcroft Ltd., W., BURSLEM, Staffordshire, England. (Cont`)

1928- Following the granting of the Royal Appointment, signature of William Moorcroft with `Potter to H.M. The Queen` in place of `MOORCROFT`

POTTER TO
H.M. THE QUEEN

Round paper label also affixed -

1936- On George V`s death the paper label was changed to. - -

BY APPOINTMENT
W. MOORCROFT
POTTER TO
H.M.QUEEN MARY

1945- **William Moorcroft died. Walter took over.**
Walter`s signature mark painted blue, later changed to green; with impressed marks unaltered. - - -

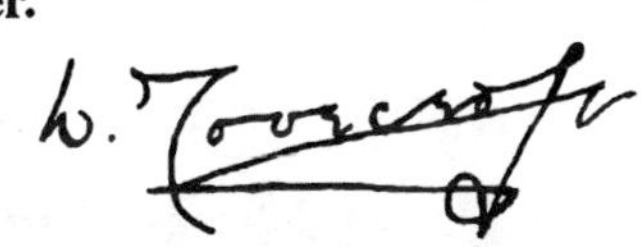

Walter`s initials shown on pieces over 5 inches high.- - -

1949- Backstamp reintroduced- -

MOORCROFT
MADE IN
ENGLAND

1953-78 Paper label changed to `BY APPOINTMENT TO THE LATE QUEEN MARY` until the right expired after 25 years.

1970- Backstamp used on miniature vases-

1980`s Backstamp used on vases measuring 9.5 to 14.5 inches and bowls 8 to 10 inches. to indicate particular shapes, sizes and year.

NO. 25
OF
100 PIECES
393/12"
MADE IN
1982

1987- **Walter Moorcroft retired.**
William John Moorcroft used stylised initials-
Impressed backstamp was unchanged.

Continued over -

1913

1913 Moorcroft Ltd., W., BURSLEM, Staffordshire, England. (Cont`)

William John Moorcroft (Cont`)

Very large pieces are signed in full using his initial `J` - - -

1987- Sally Tuffin became designer and on large special vases put her mark - **`ST des`**

<u>1990-</u> <u>Date marks were introduced as follows:-</u>

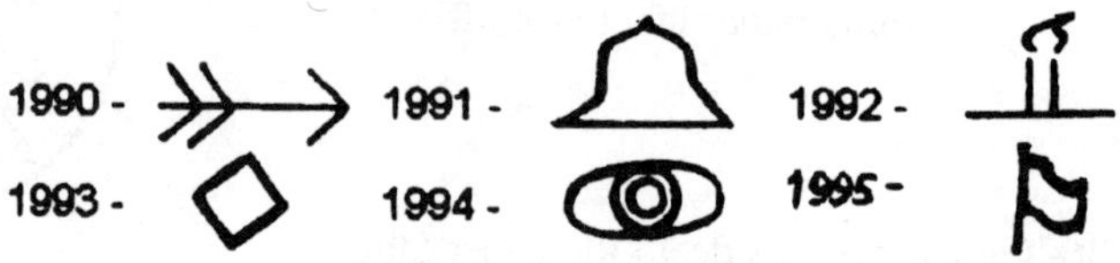

1993- Rachel Bishop appointed designer.
Large special vases marked - - **`RJB des`**

<u>SOME RETAILERS MARKS used on MOORCROFT wares:-</u>

(By kind permission of W. Moorcroft Ltd. Further information can be found in <u>Moorcroft Pottery</u> by Dennis & Edwards.)

1913 New Chelsea Porcelain Co.Ltd., LONGTON, Staffordshire, England.

c.1913-51 CHINA. Factory's name or initials printed within marks of various designs. -

c.1913-43 Marks with 'Anchor'

1951-61 **New Chelsea China Co.Ltd.** Printed-

1961- **Grosvenor China Ltd.** BONE CHINA. Printed-

1913 Reid & Co., Park Place Works, LONGTON, Staffordshire, England.

1913-46 CHINA. Factory's name and initials printed within marks of various designs. -

REID'S
PARK PLACE CHINA
ENGLAND

1924-46 Trade-name- **ROSLYN CHINA**

1946-63 **Roslyn China.** BONE CHINA - -

1946-50 - -

1913 Roper & Meredith, LONGTON, Staffordshire, England.

1913-24 EARTHENWARES. Initials printed within mark plus a 'crown'

R & M
LONGTON

1913-15

1913 Sunderland Pottery Co. Ltd., SUNDERLAND, England.

c.1913-27 EARTHENWARES. - - - **SUNDREX**

1913 Upchurch Pottery, (W.& J. Baker) RAINHAM, Kent, England.

1913-61 EARTHENWARES. - Impressed- **UPCHURCH**

1945-61 Seeby of Reading- was agent - **UPCHURCH SEEBY**

Sometimes painted- **SEEBY**

1913 Meakin (Tunstall) Ltd., Alfred, TUNSTALL, England. see 1875 Meakin Ltd., Alfred,

---

1914 Globe Pottery Co. Ltd., COBRIDGE, Staffordshire, England.

1914- EARTHENWARES. Factory`s name printed within marks of various designs including a `globe` - - - **GLOBE POTTERY Co. SEMI PORCELAIN**

1930-40 Trade-names- **STANLEY HOTEL WARE**

c.1934- Moved to SHELTON.

1947-54 Printed marks- -

Now owned by Royal Doulton Group.

1914 Harrison & Phillips, BURSLEM, Staffordshire, England.

1914-15 EARTHENWARES. Factory`s initials printed within marks of various designs. **H. & P. BURSLEM**

1915 Richardson & Co. Ltd., A.G., TUNSTALL, Staffordshire, England.

1915-34 EARTHENWARES. - - -

c.1916- Printed trade-mark- -

c.1925-30 Printed- **CROWN DUCAL WARE**

c.1934- Printed- **OLD HALL Ivory Ware**

1934 Moved to COBRIDGE.

1916 Chapmans Longton Ltd., LONGTON, Staffordshire, England.

1916- CHINA. - - -

1916-30 Printed-

c.1930-49 Printed marks-

Taken over by Paragon China Ltd.
Now part of Royal Doulton Group.

1916 Dixon & Co., R.F., Ruby Works, LONGTON, Staffordshire, England.

1916-29 CHINA AND EARTHENWARES, retailers and importers in LONDON. Printed-

1916 Keele Street Pottery Co.Ltd., TUNSTALL, Staffordshire, England.

1916- EARTHENWARES. Mainly egg cups. Founder, Alderman Charles Hall Bowers.

Early wares were not marked

1920- **Incorporated Company formed.**

1939-45 Closed during World War II.

1945- **Charles Griffith Bowers (son) re-opened the factory.**

c.1945 Factory`s initial mark- **K. S. P.**

1946- **Paramount Pottery Co. formed.**

1946- **Piccadilly Pottery Co.Ltd., Tunstall, formed as a wholesale business.**
Conway Pottery Co.Ltd., Fenton, acquired.

1949- **South Weston Industrial Corp.Ltd., took over the whole group. Mr. Bowers becoming a Director.**

1950- **Staffordshire Potteries Ltd., Meir. New company formed with the latest machinery installed.**

1955- Staffordshire Potteries (Holdings) Ltd., with Mr. C.G. Bowers as Managing Director was segregated from the main body of South Western Industrial Corp.

Continued over -

1916

1916 Keele Street Pottery Co.Ltd., TUNSTALL, Staffs., England. (Cont`)

Some Early 1980s printed marks:-

1986- **Coloroll Group plc., acquired control.**

1990- **Management buyout after the collapse of the Coloroll Group.**
Staffordshire Tableware Ltd., included the Meir Park site and the Biltons factory, London Road, Stoke-on-Trent.

see 1900 Biltons Ltd.

(Information by courtesy of Staffordshire Tableware Ltd., Stoke-on-Trent, England.)

1916 Neukirchner, Franz, MARKTREDWITZ, Bavaria, Germany.

1916- HARD-PASTE PORCELAIN.

1916 Parnell, Miss Gwendolen, Chelsea, LONDON, England.

1916-36 STUDIO-POTTER. FIGURES, ETC. Incised-

CHELSEA CHEYNE
date

Personal mark with drawing of a rabbit - **G. P.**

1916 Stanyer, A., BURSLEM, Staffordshire, England.

c.1916-41 EARTHENWARE. Impressed-

A. S. B. ENG.	**A. S. ENG B.**

1916 Beswick & Son, LONGTON, England. - - see 1875 Bridgett,Bates & Beech.
1916 Britannia Pottery, BURSLEM, England. - - see 1887 Johnson Ltd.,Sam.
1916 Hung-hsien, (Yüan Shih-kai) China. - - see 1644 CH`ING.

1917 Ford & Pointon Ltd., HANLEY, Staffordshire, England.

1917-36 CHINA. - Printed-

1921- **Became part of the Cauldon Group.**

1917 Mitterteich Porcelain Factory, MITTERTEICH, Bavaria, Ger.

1917- PORCELAIN.

1917 Soviet regime, Russia. - - - - see 1744 ST.PETERSBURG.
1917 Wild & Sons Ltd.,Thomas C., LONGTON, England. see 1896 Wild & Co.,T.C.
1917 Zeidler & Co.,Jakob. Plossberg, Germany. - see 1879 Rosenthal & Co.

1918 Carstens, C.& E., SORAU, Brandenburg, Germany.

1918- HARD-PASTE PORCELAIN. - -

1918 Gaston, Sailly, CHÂTRES, sur Cher, France.

1918- HARD-PASTE PORCELAIN. - -

1918 Collard, C., HONITON, Devon, England. see 1881 Honiton Art Potteries Ltd.
1918 `Soon` WROTHAM, England. - - see 1909 Wells, Reginald.

1919

1919 Alcock, Lindley & Bloore Ltd., HANLEY, Staffordshire, England.

1919- EARTHENWARES. - Printed or impressed-

1919 Aldridge & Co., LONGTON, Staffordshire, England.

1919-49 EARTHENWARES. Impressed **ALDRIDGE & CO LONGTON**

1919 Dura Porcelain Co.Ltd., HANLEY, Staffordshire, England.

1919-21 PORCELAIN.

Printed-

SILVAN CHINA

1919 Hoods Ltd., FENTON, Staffordshire, England.

1919- EARTHENWARES. Printed-

H. LTD.

1919 Murray, William Staite, LONDON, England.

c.1919-40 STUDIO POTTERY. Incised or painted- with date - **W.S. MURRAY date LONDON**

1940- Southern Rhodesia.

Seal mark-

1919 Okura Art China, TOKYO, Japan.

1919 Founders:- Magobei Okura and son Kazuchika. Also founder members of Noritake Co.

款

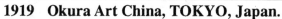

Marks with dates-

Modern mark - -

Parent company of Noritake Co. Ltd.

1919 Oxshott Pottery, OXSHOTT, Surrey, England.

1919- STUDIO POTTERY. - - - **OXSHOTT**

c.1919-47 Henry Wren. Incised-

c.1919 Denise K. Wren, Mrs. -

1945 Rosemary Wren, Miss. Impressed-
1950 `Oxshott` added.

1919 Parr, Harry, Chelsea, LONDON, England.

c.1919-45 STUDIO POTTERY. Incised or impressed- **HY PARR**
With date - - **CHELSEA (date)**

1919 Raynaud & Cie, LIMOGES, Haute-Vienne, France.

1919- PORCELAIN.

1919 Serres, George, (b.1889, d.1956) PARIS, France.

c.1919- STUDIO POTTERY. - - -

1919 Tharaud, C. LIMOGES, Haute-Vienne, France.

1919- PORCELAIN. - - -

1919 Vyse, Charles, Chelsea, LONDON, England.

1919-63 STUDIO POTTERY. Incised or impressed- **C. V.**
With date - - **CHELSEA**

Signature with year- **Charles Vyse**

Painted with year -

Incised or painted - - **VYSE** **C.VYSE**
With year - -

1919/20

1919 Brown & Sons, T., FERRYBRIDGE, England. - see 1843 Reed & Taylor.
1919 Haviland, William, LIMOGES, France. - - see 1892 Haviland, Theodore,
1919 Hewitt Bros., LONGTON, England. - - see 1907 Hewitt & Leadbeater.
1919 Wade, George, & Son Ltd., BURSLEM, England. see 1867 Wade Group.

1920 Barlows (Longton) Ltd., LONGTON, Staffordshire, England.

1920-52 EARTHENWARES. - Impressed- **B. LTD.**

1920-52 Printed within - various designs. - **MELBAR WARE**

1920 British Art Pottery Ltd., Rialto Works, FENTON, Staffs., England.

1920-26 PORCELAIN.

Printed or impressed-

1920 British Pottery Ltd., TUNSTALL, Staffordshire, England.

1920-26 EARTHENWARES. - - -

Printed-

1920 Creyke & Sons, G.M., HANLEY, Staffordshire, England.

1920-48 EARTHENWARES. Factory`s initials printed or impressed within marks of various designs. **G. M. C.**

1930-48 Printed-

1920 Leach, Bernard Howell, ST. IVES, Cornwall, England.

1920- STUDIO POTTERY - Personal marks-
Many students of handmade studio pottery passed through Bernard Leach`s capable hands, and many of them eventually went on to open their own potteries.

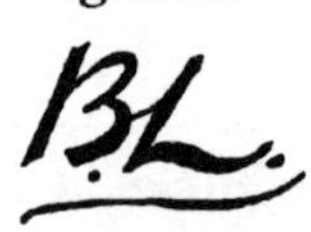

St. Ives seal impressed mark-

c.1920-23 and 1929-30 Hamada, Shoji, (Also worked in Japan) Impressed-

Continued over -

1920 Leach, Bernard Howell, ST. IVES, Cornwall, England. (Cont`)

1930-56 **Leach, David, (son) -** -
1946-55 Became partner in the Pottery.

1956- Lowerdown Pottery, Bovey Tracey, Devon. see 1956 Leach, David,

1945-63 **Quick, Kenneth,** - (Apprentice) Incised-

c.1955-60 Tregenna Hill Pottery
Incised or impressed- **TREGENNA HILL**

1950-52 **McKenzie, Warren,** Incised or seal mark- **M W**

1963- Dartington, Devon. Impressed- -

1954-56 **Marshall, William,** Incised- -

1956- Impressed- -

1956- **Leach, Janet,** (Wife of Bernard) Impressed-
Continues to run the Leach Pottery today (1996) but does not take in students. - -

1960-63 **Leach, John, (grandson)** -
Impressed-

1964- Muchelney Pottery, Somerset. see 1964 Leach,John,

1961 **Lewis, Glenn,** Impressed- - -

(Courtesy of Janet Leach, St. Ives Pottery, Cornwall, England.)

1920 Leadbeater, Edwin, LONGTON, Staffordshire, England.

1920-24 China.
Printed or impressed- -

1920 Neumann, Ludwig, FRAUENTHAL, Austria.

1920- Hard-paste porcelain.

1920

1920 Newport Pottery Co.Ltd., BURSLEM, Staffordshire, England.

1920- EARTHENWARES. - - -

c.1920- Printed- -

c.1938-66 `Clarice Cliff` printed mark- -

c.1945- Printed- - - **VITRIFIED**

1920 Richardson, Albert G., Regal Pottery, COBRIDGE, Staffs., England.

c.1920-21 EARTHENWARES.

Printed- -

1921-25 **Richardsons (Cobridge) Ltd.,**

Printed- - -

1920 Ruscoe, William, STOKE, Staffordshire, England.

c.1920-44 EARTHENWARE FIGURES, ETC.- -

1920- Incised or painted-

c.1925 Monogram with year-

1944- at Exeter.

c.1925-50 Signature- **Wm. Ruscoe**

c.1950- Signature in full- **William Ruscoe**

1920 Wächter, Rudolf, KIRCHENLAMITZ, Bavaria, Germany.

Early 20th century- HARD-PASTE PORCELAIN.

1920	Britannia Pottery Co.Ltd., GLASGOW, Scotland.	see 1896 Cochran & Fleming.
1920	Cauldon Potteries Ltd., HANLEY, England. -	see 1856 Ridgway Bates & Co.
1920	Paragon China Co.Ltd., LONGTON, England. -	see 1900 Star China Co.
1920	Ridgways (Bedford Works) Ltd. HANLEY, England.	see 1873 Ridgway,Sparks etc.
1920	Sussex Art Ware, RYE, England. - - -	see 1869 Rye Pottery.

1921 Ellgreave Pottery Co.Ltd., BURSLEM, Staffordshire, England.

1921- EARTHENWARES. Early wares not marked.

1947 Factory`s name printed within various designs- - **ELLGREAVE POTTERY CO. LTD.**

Lottie Rhead Ware

Heatmaster mark -

1921 Holland, William Fishley, The Pottery, CLEVEDON, England.

c.1921- STUDIO POTTERY, EARTHENWARES. - -

Incised-

1929-42 **Holland, Isabel Fishley (daughter)** Signature- **I. HOLLAND**

1955- **Holland, George Fishley.** - -

1959 Dunster Pottery, Somerset.

Printed, painted or impressed-

1959 `Dunster` added- **DUNSTER**

1921 Parrott & Co. Ltd., BURSLEM, Staffordshire, England.

1921-62 EARTHENWARES. - - -

Printed Trade-mark-

1921 Perrin, Mrs Ida, Bushey Heath, LONDON, England.

1921-33 EARTHENWARE DECORATORS - -

Mark of Fred Passenger sometimes occurs- - **F. P.**

1921/22

1921 Podmore China Co., Sylvan Works, HANLEY, Staffs., England.

1921-41 CHINA. - - -

Printed-

see 1946 Sylvan Pottery Ltd.

1921 Royal Albion China Co., LONGTON, Staffordshire, England.

1921-48 CHINA. Factory`s name printed within - marks of various designs usually with crown.

1921 Watson, Dorothy, Bridge Pottery, ROLVENDEN, Kent, England.

1921- EARTHENWARES.

Impressed or printed-

1921	Carter,Stabler & Adams Ltd., POOLE, England.	-	see 1873 Carter & Co.Ltd.
1921	Richardson (Cobridge) Ltd., COBRIDGE, England.	-	see 1920 Richardson, A.G.

1922 Budapester Zsolnaysche, BUDAPEST, Hungary.

c1922- GENERAL CERAMICS. - - -

see 1855 Zsolnay, W.

1922 Bradleys (Longton) Ltd., Crown Clarence Works, LONGTON, Eng.

1922-41 CHINA.

Printed with crown - -

c.1928-41 printed with- - -

1922 Burgess Bros., LONGTON, Staffordshire, England.

1922-39 EARTHENWARES. Factory`s name printed within marks of various designs - -

BURGESS WARE
BURCRAFT
BURGESS BROS.

1922 Cooper & Co., J., Ducal Works, BURSLEM, Staffordshire, England.

1922-25 EARTHENWARES. - - -

Printed or impressed in circle- **J. COOPER & Co. ENGLAND DUCAL WORKS**

1922 Co-operative Wholesale Society Ltd., LONGTON, Staffs., England.

1922- CHINA. - - -

c.1946- Printed -

1950- Printed within marks of various patterns and designs **BONE WINDSOR CHINA**
CLARENCE BONE CHINA

1946- **Crown Clarence Pottery, LONGTON.**
EARTHENWARES. `Crown Clarence` printed within marks of various patterns and designs. i.e.
1946- Printed -

1946/50/62- Printed with- **CROWN CLARENCE BALMORAL**

1922 Hales, Hancock & Godwin Ltd., LONDON, E.C.1. England.

1922-60 RETAILERS.

1922 Kensington Pottery Ltd., HANLEY, Staffordshire, England.

c.1922-37 EARTHENWARES. Printed -

c.1937- BURSLEM. - -

1962 **Amalgamated with Price Bros.(Burslem) Ltd.**

see 1896 Price Brothers.

1922 Moira Pottery Co. Ltd., Nr. BURTON-ON-TRENT, England.

c.1922 STONEWARES.

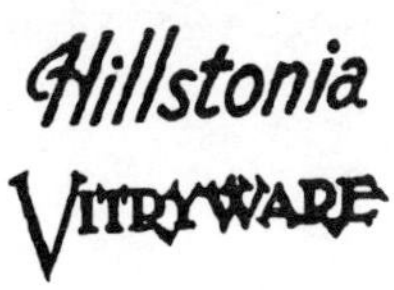

1922 Richards, Frances E., Highgate, LONDON, England.

1922-31 STUDIO POTTERY - - -

Incised with year -

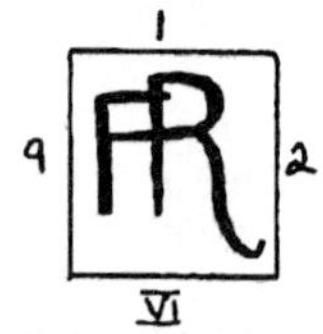

1922 Sibley Pottery Ltd., WAREHAM, Dorset, England.

1922-62 EARTHEN AND STONEWARES. - -

Incised - Sibley

1946-52 Impressed -

1952-62 Printed or impressed- **SIBLEY POTTERY Ltd. DORSET. ENGLAND.**

1922 Bohemia-Werkin, New-Rohlau, Germany. - see 1879 Rosenthal & Co.
1922 Smith & Partners Ltd.,J., STOKE, England. - see 1898 Smith, James.

1923 Fell & Co., J.T., Cyples Old Pottery, LONGTON, Staffs., England.

1923-57 EARTHENWARES. Printed or impressed- **EMBOSA WARE**

Printed or impressed- **MADE BY CYPLES OLD POTTERY**

Original date of the first Cyples Pottery- **1793**

1923 Ault & Tunnicliffe Ltd., SWADLINCOTE, England. see 1887 Ault, William,
1923 Blairs (Longton) Ltd., LONGTON, England. - see 1880 Blair & Co.
1923 Steventon & Sons Ltd.,John, BURSLEM, England. see 1900 Brown & Steventon Ltd.

1924 Braden, Miss Norah, Leach Pottery, ST. IVES, Cornwall, England.

1924-28 Studio potter at ST. IVES.
1928-36 At COLESHILL, Wiltshire.
Impressed and incised-

see 1920 Leach, Bernard H.

1924 Dunn, Mrs Constance, (Miss Wade) BILLINGHAM, England.

1924- STUDIO POTTERIES at various addresses.

Incised-

1924 Elektra Porcelain Co.Ltd., LONGTON, Staffordshire, England.
1924- EARTHENWARES

Printed- 

c.1940- Printed- 

1924 Pfeiffer, Max Adolf, Germany. - - - see 1710 MEISSEN.
1924 Staatliche Porcelain Factory, LENINGRAD, Russia. see 1744 ST. PETERSBURG.

1925 Bensinger, Fritz, MANNHEIM, Baden, Germany.
c.1925- DECORATOR OF PORCELAIN. - -

1925 Dahl-Jensens, COPENHAGEN, Denmark.
1925- HARD-PASTE PORCELAIN. - -

1925 Fontanille & Marraud, LIMOGES, Haute-Vienne, France.
1925- PORCELAIN. - - - **PORCELAINE ARTISTIQUE**
F. M.
In a half circle - **LIMOGES**
FRANCE

1925 Howard Pottery Co.Ltd., SHELTON, Staffordshire, England.
1925- EARTHENWARES. Various marks incorporating
the trade name `Brentleigh` **BRENTLEIGH WARE**

1925 Pleydell-Bouverie, Katharine, KILMINGTON MANOR, England.
1925- STUDIO POTTERY, STONEWARES.

Incised or stamped- 

1925 Regal Pottery Co.Ltd., COBRIDGE, Staffordshire, England.
1925-31 EARTHENWARES. - - -

Printed- 

1925-26

1925 Roddy & Co., E., BURSLEM, Staffordshire, England.

1925-28 EARTHENWARES. Printed with a circle - **STAFFORDSHIRE RODDY WARE ENGLAND.**

1925 Shelley Potteries Ltd., LONGTON, Staffordshire, England.

1925- CHINA. - - -

This business was founded in 1864 by J.& C. Wileman.

c.1925-40 Printed -

c.1945- Printed - -

Now Royal Doulton Group. see 1864 Wileman, J.& C.

1925 Pearson & Co.(Chesterfield) Ltd., England. - see 1805 Pearson & Co.

1926 Ashstead Potters Ltd., ASHSTEAD, Surrey, England.

1926-36 EARTHENWARES.

Printed -

1926 Winchcombe Pottery, WINCHCOMBE, Gloucestershire, England.

c.1926-42 and 1946-70 STUDIO POTTERY. impressed-

c.1926-40 **Cardew, Michael,** - impressed- - -

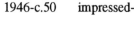

c.1927-40 **Tustin, Sidney,** - - - -
and 1946-78 - - - - impressed-

1936- **Finch, Raymond,** 1936-42 impressed- - -

1946-c.50 impressed-

c.1970-95 impressed- - -

c.1970-95 **General Pottery seal** - impressed-

(Courtesy of Raymond Finch, Winchcombe Pottery) see 1939 Wenford Bridge Pottery.

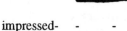

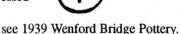

1927 Bakewell Bros. Ltd., HANLEY, Staffordshire, England.

1927-43 EARTHENWARES. Factory`s name printed within marks of various designs. **BAKEWELL BROS. LTD.**

1927 Salisbury Crown China Co., LONGTON, Staffordshire, England.

c.1927-61 CHINA. Factory`s name printed within marks of various patterns and designs.

c.1937/46 -

1949 **Salisbury China Co.**

1927 Winterton Pottery (Longton) Ltd., LONGTON, Staffs., England.

1927-54 EARTHENWARES. Printed marks with crown-

c.1939-41 Trade-mark - **Bluestone Ware**

1927	Schaubach, Heinz, Germany. - - -	see 1882 Unterweissbacher.
1927	Wade, Heath & Co.Ltd., BURSLEM, England. -	see 1867 Wade Group,
1927	Wade, Albert J., Ltd., BURSLEM, England. -	see 1867 Wade Group.

1928 Carrigaline Pottery Ltd., CARRIGALINE, Co. Cork, Ireland.

c.1928-79 EARTHENWARES. - printed- **CARRIG WARE CARRIGALINE POTTERY**

1968 Awarded `Irish Exporter of the year`

Company taken over by Herr Lutz Kiel.

1979-83 **Cork Art Pottery Ltd.**

1984-89 **Workers Co-operative.**
Carrigdhoun Pottery.
Company taken over by Oxford SA Brazil Ltd.

1990- **Oxford (Ireland) Ltd.** (subsidiary)

(Courtesy of Oxford (Ireland) Ltd., Carrigaline, Ireland.)

1928/29

1928 Slack & Brownlow, TONBRIDGE, Kent, England.

c.1928-34 EARTHENWARES. - - - **TONBRIDGE WARE**

Printed or impressed - -

1928 Wearside Pottery Co., Millfield, SUNDERLAND, England.

1928-57 EARTHENWEARS - - -

Printed or impressed -

1928 Weithase, C.K., RUDOLSTADT, Thuringia, Germany.

c.1928- DECORATOR ON PORCELAIN AND GLASS. -

1928	Stanley Pottery Ltd., LONGTON, England. - -	see 1887 Colclough & Co.
1928	Wood & Son (Longport) Ltd., Arthur, LONGTON, England.	see 1895 Capper & Wood.
1928	Zollfrank Porzellanfabrik, Erkersreuth, Germany. -	see 1879 Rosenthal & Co.

1929 Lindner Porzellanfabrik, KÜPS, Bavaria, Germany.

1929- **Ernst Lindner (Founder)**

HARD-PASTE PORCELAIN. SPECIALISING IN FINE CLASSICAL STYLES ETC. Pre 1950 mark-

1977 Dr. Hans Lindner (son) died.

pre 1975

pre 1982

pre 1982

Post 1982 marks-

(By courtesy of Lindner Porzellan KG. Küps, Germany.)

1929 Nilson, J.O., HACKEFORS, Sweden.

1929- HARD-PASTE PORCELAIN. - -

1929 Holland, Miss Isabel Fishley, CLEVEDON, England. - see 1921 Holland, Wm. F.

1930 Avon Art Pottery Ltd., LONGTON, Staffordshire, England.

1930- EARTHENWARES. - - -

1930-39 Printed or impressed-

1939-47 Printed within various designs - **Avon Ware**

1930 British Pottery Ltd., LONGTON, Staffordshire, England.

c.1930- AGENTS FOR MANUFACTURERS. - -
Sometimes initials incorporated in Factory`s marks. **B. P. LTD.**

1930 Conway Pottery Co.Ltd., FENTON, Staffordshire, England.

1930- EARTHENWARES. - - -

1945 Printed within marks of various patterns and designs- **CONWAY POTTERY ENGLAND**

1945 Pattern name - **Lavender Blue**
1960 " " - **Rose Pink**

1930 Cooper Pottery, Susie, BURSLEM, Staffordshire, England.

c.1930- GENERAL CERAMICS. -

Printed - -

c.1950-59 **at LONGTON.** BONE CHINA. Printed

c.1961 **Susie Cooper Ltd.**

1930/31

1930 Era Art Pottery Co., STOKE, Staffordshire, England.

1930-47 EARTHENWARES. Factory`s name printed within marks of various designs. **ERA**

1930 Isle of Wight Pottery, (Saunders, S.E.) Whippingham, I.o.W. England.

c.1930-40 EARTHENWARES. - - -

Printed or impressed -

1930 Rhead, Charlotte, BURSLEM, England. - - see 1884 Wood Ltd.,H.J.

1931 Dinky Art Pottery Co.Ltd., LONGTON, Staffordshire, England.

1931-47 EARTHENWARES. Printed -

1931 Illinger & Co., KRUMMENNAAB, Bavaria, Germany.

HARD-PASTE PORCELAIN.

1931 Naturecraft Ltd., CONGLETON, Cheshire, England.

1931- CERAMIC AND RESIN FIGURINES AND COLLECTABLES.
Brand names;- **`MEMORY LANE COTTAGES`**
`TIMELESS CHARACTERS`

1947- **Factory re-launched after WW2.**
Now operates from two factories:-
Albion Factory and Dane Valley Factory,
which are both in Havannah Street.

(By courtesy of Naturecraft Ltd., England.)

1931 Rainbow Pottery Co., FENTON, Staffordshire, England.

1931-41 EARTHENWARES. Printed or impressed

RAINBOW POTTERY
FENTON
MADE IN ENGLAND

1931 Shaw & Sons (Longton) Ltd., LONGTON, Staffordshire, England.

1931-63 GENERAL CERAMICS. Printed -

1931-49 -

1959-63 - **Burlington Ware**

1931 Lovatt`s Potteries Ltd., LANGLEY MILL, England. - see 1895 Lovatt & Lovatt.

1932 Edelstein Porzellanfabrik, KÜPS, Bavaria, Germany.

1932- HARD-PASTE PORCELAIN. - - **Edelstein BAVARIA**

1932 Longton New Art Pottery Co.Ltd., LONGTON, Staffs., England.

1932-65 EARTHENWARES. Printed in various designs- **Kelsboro` Ware MADE IN ENGLAND**

1932 Hammersley & Co.(Longton) Ltd., LONGTON, England. see 1887 Hammersley & Co.

1932 Zöllner, Rudi, Munich, Germany. - - - - see 1879 Rosenthal & Co.

1933 Decoro Pottery Co., Tuscan Works, LONGTON, Staffs., England.

1933-49 EARTHENWARES. Printed in various designs- **Decoro Pottery Tuscan Decoro**

1933 Eduard Bay GmbH & Co. KG. RANSBACH-BAUMBACH, Ger.

1933- DECORATIVE AND HOUSEHOLD CERAMICS.
1933- Founder Eduard Bay.

1936 mark -

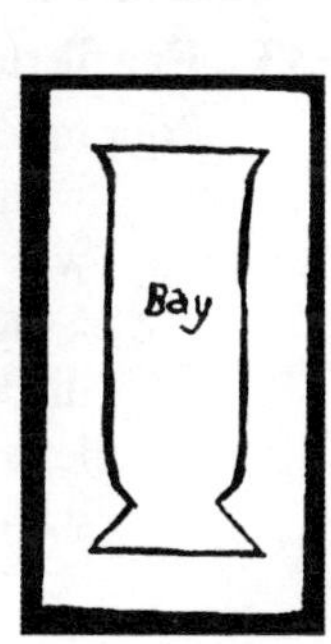

1938- **EBERA Associated Company founded.**

1938 Change of trade-mark

Continued over -

1933

1933 Eduard Bay GmbH & Co. KG., Germany. (Cont`)

1947- Production resumed after the war with priority on table ware. - - - -

1954- Production changed to decorative ceramics, especially with gold painting.
Change of trade-mark - -

1966- New trade-mark -

1968- Production of `ROMERTOPF` started. More than 25 million pieces sold to date.

1974- New trade-mark -

1992- The Bay family, unfortunately, had no successors, so they sold the company to:- Mr Boris Levin and Dr Thomas Heidecker.

1994- New modern trade-mark-

(By kind permission of Bay Keramik, Rannsbach-Baumbach. Germany.)

1933 Frankoma Pottery, SAPULPA, Oklahoma, U.S.A.

Prior to 1933 John Frank signed all his early pioeces, along with the date. After the ceramic department was established at the University of Oklahoma a logo was designed for marking the pottery made on the campas. An India tepee with the letters `OU`. John Frank used the logo together with his initials and date. Incised-

JOHN FRANK or JNF

Continued over -

1933 Frankoma Pottery, SAPULPA, Oklahoma, U.S.A. (Cont`)

c.1933 **John Frank began producing and selling pottery in small quantities under the name of, FRANK POTTERIES.**

1933-34 The mark was applied in black by rubber stamp- **FRANK POTTERIES NORMAN, OKLAHOMA**

1934-35 **Francoma Potteries Incorporated.**

1934-35 The `O` in FRANKOMA was the shape of a circle **FRANKOMA**
1940`s The `0` was an oblong (skinny) shape.

1936-38 Incised leopard mark -

Early 1950`s Larger incised mark - **FRANKOMA**
After 1955 mark in mould - **FRANKOMA**

1960 Joniece Frank. Personal mark- -

Mark on small objects- -

(By kind permission of Frankoma Pottery, Sapulpa, Oklahoma, U.S.A.)

1933 Nehmzow GmbH, Karl, ALTENKUNSTADT, Germany.

1933- HARD-PASTE PORCELAIN.

1933 Radford Handcraft Pottery, BURSLEM, Staffordshire, England.

1933-48 EARTHENWARES. Printed signature- ***G. Radford*** **Burslem**

1934 Hammond, Henry, FARNHAM, Surrey, England.

1934 STUDIO POTTERY. -

Incised - - -

Impressed- -

1934-36

1934 Lange, Hermann, KRUMMENNAAD, Bavaria, Germany.

1934- HARD-PASTE PORCELAIN. - -

see 1910 Seltmann.

1934 Goss China Co. Ltd., STOKE, English. - - see 1858 Goss Ltd., W.H.

1935 Bailey Potteries Ltd., FENTON, Staffordshire, England.

1935-40 EARTHENWARES. Name printed within marks of various patterns and designs.

BEWLEY POTTERY
MADE IN ENGLAND

1935 Burslem School of Art, BURSLEM, Staffordshire, England.

1935-41 EARTHENWARE FIGURES, ETC. Impressed-
Sometimes marks are impressed with the name of the instructor, William Ruscoe, or the pupils and date.

1935 New Park Potteries Ltd., LONGTON, Staffordshire, England.

1935-57 EARTHENWARES. Factory`s name or initials printed within marks of various patterns and designs. - - -

N. P. P. LTD.
NEW PARK
POTTERIES
LONGTON
NEW PARK

1935 Hancock & Sons (Potters) Ltd., S., STOKE, England. see 1858 Hancock & Sons, S.
1935 Hummel, Sister M.I., RODENTAL, Germany. - see 1871 Goebel, W.,
1935 Radford, E., BURSLEM, England. - - see 1884 Wood Ltd., H.J.

1936 Beswick Ltd., John, LONGTON, Staffordshire, England.

1936- EARTHENWARES. - Printed -
This business was originally founded by James Wright Beswick in 1894.

1973- **Acquired by Royal Doulton Group.**

1936 Haile, T.S., DARTINGTON, Devon, England.

c.1936-43 STUDIO POTTERY - Impressed-
and 1945-48 - - -

1936 New Pearl Pottery Co.Ltd., HANLEY, Staffordshire, England.

1936-41 EARTHENWARES. Printed **NEW PEARL POTTERY CO. LTD.**
HANLEY

ROYAL BOURBON WARE

1937 Coalbrook Potteries, SHELTON, Staffordshire, England.

1937- FLORAL AND DECORATIVE WARES. Printed **COALBROOK**
MADE IN ENGLAND

1937 Bullers Ltd., HANLEY, Staffordshire, England.

1937-55 EARTHENWARES, Painted - **BULLERS MADE**
IN ENGLAND

BY BULLERS.

1937 Dietrich, Philipp, PASSAU, Bavaria, Germany.

1937-42 Porzellanfabrik Passau - -

1937 Sunfield Pottery, STOURBRIDGE, Worcestershire, England.

1937- EARTHENWARES. Impressed or printed -
1952- STONEWARES. - - -

1937 Ault Potteries Ltd., SWADLINCOTE, England.- - see 1887 Ault, William.
1937 Colclough China Ltd., LONGTON, England. - - see 1897 Colclough, H.J.

1938 Greta Pottery, STOKE, Staffordshire, England.

1938-41 EARTHENWARES. Printed or painted - **G**
P

1938 Rie, Mrs Lucie, Albion Mews, LONDON, England.

1938- STUDIO POTTERY. Impressed-

1938 EBERA, Ransbach-Baumbach, Germany. see 1933 Eduard Bay GmbH.
1938 Ford & Sons (Crownford) Ltd., England. see 1876 Whittingham,Ford & Riley.
1938 Kirklands (Etruria) Ltd., England. - see 1892 Kirkland & Co.

1939/40

1939 Blue John Pottery Ltd., HANLEY, Staffordshire, England.

1939- EARTHENWARES. Factory`s name printed within marks of various designs.

1939 Goddard Ltd., Elaine, BRUTON, Somerset, England.

1939- EARTHENWARES. Printed label - **elaine goddard ltd.**

1939 Kemp, Dorothy, FELIXSTOWE, Suffolk, England.

1939- STUDIO POTTERY. Incised or impressed - Student of Bernard Leach.

see 1920 Leach, Bernard,

1939 Wenford Bridge Pottery, BODMIN, Cornwall, England.

1939- STUDIO STONEWARE POTTERY. impressed- Wenford Bridge Pottery seal. Often seen with initials of students and `Cardew` marks. -

1939-83 **Michael Cardew (Founder)** built a pottery at `The Wenford Inn` impressed- Backstamp also used at Winchcombe Pottery and on Abuja work, Nigeria, Africa.1950-65.

1975- **Seth Cardew (son)** impressed- 1983- Michael Cardew died. and son, Seth, took over pottery.

1982 **Ara Cardew (Grandson)** In partnership with father, Seth. - impressed-

(Courtesy of Seth Cardew, Wenford Bridge Pottery.) see 1926 Winchcombe Pottery.

1939 Gladstone China (Longton) Ltd., England. - see 1891 Procter & Co. Ltd., G.
1939 Thewalt, Albert Johann, HOEHR Germany. - see 1893 Thewalt, Albert J.

1940 Floral China Co.Ltd., LONGTON, Staffordshire, England.

1940-51 CHINA. - - -

Printed with variations -

1940 Leighton Pottery Ltd., BURSLEM, Staffordshire, England.

1940-54 EARTHENWARES. -

c.1946-54 Printed -

PRODUCED AT THE LEIGHTON POTTERIES BURSLEM, ENGLAND

ROYAL LEIGHTON WARE

1940 North Staffordshire Pottery Co.Ltd., COBRIDGE, Staffs., England.

1940-52 EARTHENWARES.

1944 Registered Trade-mark-

1952 **Acquired by Ridgway Potteries Ltd.**

1940 Thorley China Ltd., LONGTON, Staffordshire, England.

1940-70 DECORATIVE AND JEWELLERY CHINA. -

1950 Printed mark -

1940 Wulstan Pottery Co.Ltd., HANLEY, Staffordshire, England.

c.1940-58 (Closed 1941-46) EARTHENWARES.

Printed -

1940	Cartwright & Edwards, LONGTON, England. -	see 1865 Holdcroft, Joseph,.
1940	Erbendorf Porcelain Factory, Germany. - -	see 1910 Seltmann, Christian,
1940	Hughes (Fenton) Ltd., FENTON, England. -	see 1889 Hughes & Co.,E.,
1941	Hispania, Ceramicas, Valencia, Spain. - -	see 1610 MANISES.
1941	Hudson & Middleton Ltd., LONGTON, England.	see 1889 Hudson, William.
1941	Milet, Ceramique d`Art, SÈVRES, France. -	see 1866 Milet & Fils, Paul.
1941	Rosina China Co.Ltd., LONGTON, England. -	see 1887 Warrilow & Sons Ltd.
1942	Société Française de Porcelaine, FOECY, France.	see 1886 Lourioux, Louis,

---

1943 Neuerer K.G.,Porzellanfabrik, OBERKOTZAU, Bavaria, Germany.

1943- HARD-PASTE PORCELAIN. - -

1943-45

1943 Barratt`s of Staffordshire Ltd., BURSLEM, Staffordshire, England.

1943- EARTHENWARES.

Gater Hall & Co. Marks-continued- -

1945- Printed -

1961- Printed -

see 1885 Gater & Co.,Thom.

1944 Kent (Porcelains) Ltd., William, BURSLEM, Staffordshire, England.

1944-62 EARTHENWARES. - - -

Printed -

c.1944-62 19th century moulds used for for modern figures. - **W B K**

1944 Lancaster & Sandland Ltd., HANLEY, England. see 1900 Lancaster & Sons Ltd.
1944 Morley & Co.Ltd., Wm., FENTON, England. - see 1906 Morley, Fox & Co.
1944 Simpsons (Potters) Ltd., COBRIDGE, England.- see 1883 Rathbone, Smith & Co.

1945 Adderley Floral China, LONGTON, Staffordshire, England.

1945- CHINA FIGURES AND ORNAMENTS. Printed -

1973- **Acquired by Royal Doulton Group.**

1945 Baggaley Ltd., E., Branksome China Wks, FORDINGBRIDGE, Eng.

1945 FINE CHINA TABLEWARE.

1966- Moved from Branksome to Fordingbridge.

Branksome
China
England

(Courtesy of E. Baggaley Ltd., Branksome China Works, England.)

1945 Bournemouth Pottery Co., HANLEY, Staffordshire, England.

1945-51 at Bournemouth EARTHENWARES. Printed or impressed - **BOURNEMOUTH POTTERY ENGLAND**

1952-57 at HANLEY Printed or impressed- BOURNEMOUTH HANLEY POTTERY CO.

1945 Cara China Co., LONGTON, Staffordshire, England.

1945- CHINA FIGURES AND ORNAMENTS. Printed- **CARA CHINA**

1945 Denton China (Longton) Ltd., LONGTON, Staffordshire, England.

1945- CHINA FIGURES AND JEWELLERY. Printed script mark- **BEST BONE DENTON CHINA ENGLAND**

1945 Dresden Floral Porcelain Co.Ltd., LONGTON, Staffs., England.

1945-56 CHINA FIGURES AND ORNAMENTS, Printed - DRESDEN FLORAL FINE BONE CHINA ENGLAND

1945 Holdsworth, Peter, RAMSBURY, Wiltshire, England.

1945- EARTHENWARES. Printed or impressed - PH PH P J H RAMSBURY

1945 Marshall, Ray, STEDHAM, Sussex, England.

1945- STUDIO POTTERY. - - -

Impressed-

Signature- **Ray Marshall** (date)

1945 Prinknash Pottery, Prinknash Abbey, CRANHAM, Gloucester, Eng.

c.1945 EARTHENWARES.

1945-76 marks. Printed or impressed

The pottery was established by a group of monks, Dom Asaph Harris, Dom Basil Robinson and Brother Thomas Morey, basically to help the building fund of the new abbey. The clay was found during the dig of the Abbey foundations.

1976 to early 80`s - -

Current marks (1995) -

(Courtesy of Prinknash Pottery, Gloucester, England.)

1945 Walters, Miss Helen, Hornsey, LONDON, England.

1945- STUDIO POTTERY.

1945-53 on Doulton wares. Incised -

1953-Painted or incised with last two figures of year

Now Helen Swain, **H W S**

1945	Bloch, Robert, PARIS, France. - - -	see 1773 Porcelaine de Paris.
1945	Molho, Paul, PARIS, France. - - -	see 1773 Porcelaine de Paris.
1945	Moorcroft, William, BURSLEM, England. -	see 1913 Moorcroft Ltd., W.,
1945	Quick, Kenneth, ST. IVES, England. - -	see 1920 Leach, Bernard.
1945	Starolsk`y Porcelan Narodni Podnik Stara Role, Ger.	see 1900 Zdekauer, Moritz,
1945	Wren, Rosemary, OXSHOTT, England. - -	see 1919 Oxshott Pottery.

1946 Albert Potteries Ltd., BURSLEM, Staffordshire, England.

1946-54 EARTHENWARES. Printed or impressed -

1946 Crowan Pottery, (H.& M. Davis) PRAZE, Cornwall, England.

1946-62 STUDIO POTTERY.

Impressed seal mark -

1946 Crown China Crafts Ltd., STOKE, Staffordshire, England.

1946-58 CHINA AND EARTHENWARE. Printed -

1946 Ehlers, A.W.G., Lowerdown Cross, Bovey Tracey, Devon, England.

1946-55 STUDIO-POTTER.

Incised or painted -

1946 Fancies Fayre Pottery, HANLEY, Staffordshire, England.

c.1946-51 EARTHENWARES.

1946 Printed or impressed-

1949 - - - - - -

1950 - - - -

STAFFORDSHIRE
F. F.
ENGLAND

c.1951- **Mount Pleasant, SHELTON.**

c.1953 - - - -

1954- **Bairstow & Co., P.E.**, BONE CHINA - **Mark as above**

Printed - - -

1946

1946 Goldscheider (Staffordshire) Pottery Ltd., HANLEY, England.

1946-59 EARTHENWARE AND CHINA FIGURES.

Printed signature -

1946 Grenville Pottery Ltd., TUNSTALL, Staffordshire, England.

1946- EARTHENWARES. Printed -

1946 Jersey Pottery Ltd., Gorey Village, JERSEY, C.I., England.

1946 EARTHENWARES AND PORCELAIN.

1946 Painted mark -

Impressed or printed marks

1946

1951

1954- **The Jones Family acquired the pottery.**

Printed marks used.

Visitors are welcome to see the Pottery, Monday to Friday.
(Information by courtesy of The Jersey Pottery Ltd., C.I.)

1946 Kirkhams Ltd., STOKE, Staffordshire, England.

1946-61 EARTHENWARES.

Printed -

c.1952-61 Printed -

Kirkhams Ltd.
STOKE ON TRENT
ENGLAND

1961- **Now Portmeiron Potteries Ltd.** see 1960 Portmeirion Potteries.

1946 Leach, Miss Margaret, Taena Community, AYLBURTON, England.

1943-45 Worked at Bernard Leach`s Pottery St. Ives, Cornwall. (No relation) see 1920 Leach, Bernard,

1946-56 Studio-potter.

1946-51 **Barnhouse Pottery, Brockweir, Monmouth.**

1951-56 **Taena Community, Aylburton and Upton St. Leonards.** Taena seal mark -

Partner with L.A. Groves.

1946 Longton Pottery Co. Ltd., Bluebell Works, LONGTON, Staff., Eng.

1946-55 EARTHENWARES. Factory`s initials printed within marks of various designs. **L. P. CO. LTD.** **Blue Bell Ware**

1946 Melba-Wain (England) Ltd., Melba Works, LONGTON, England.

1946- **H.A. Wain & Sons Ltd.**

EARTHENWARES.

Printed mark-

1982- **Melba-Wain (England) Ltd. (name change)**

EARTHENWARES. GIFTWARE AND KITCHENWARE

Printed marks-

(By courtesy of Melba-Wain (England) Ltd., Longton, England.)

1946 Mills, Donald, LONDON, S.E.1. England.

1946-55 STUDIO-POTTER, STONEWARES.

Printed - **D. M.**

Signature, sometimes with year added -

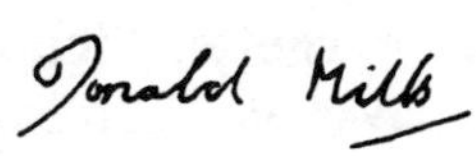

1946 Nowell, C.D., Prestbury and Disley, CHESHIRE, England.

1946-59 STUDIO POTTERY.

c.1946-51 Disley signature mark -
Sometimes with `house`

c.1951-59 Prestbury signature mark -

1946 Portland Pottery Ltd., COBRIDGE, Staffordshire, England.

1946-53 EARTHENWARES. - - -

Trade monogram -

Factory`s name found within marks of various patterns and designs. - - **PORTLAND POTTERY LTD**

1953- **Acquired by Ridgways** Printed -

1946 Ramié Suzanne & Georges, Madoura, VALLAURIS, France.

1946- STUDIO-POTTERS.

1946 Picasso, Pablo, worked with these potters.

1946 Sylvan Pottery Ltd., HANLEY, Staffordshire, England.

1946- EARTHENWARES. Printed -

1946-48 `B` was included in marks.

see 1921 Podmore China Co.

1946 Vergette, Nicholas, LONDON, England.

1946-58 STUDIO-POTTER, TILES, ETC. Printed or incised-

At the Camberwell School of Art for a time.

c.1946- Signature mark- ***Vergette***

1946 Walton Pottery Co.Ltd., W. Gordon, WHITTINGHAM, England.

1946-56 SALT-GLAZED STONEWARES. - -

Incised or impressed -

1946 Washington Pottery Ltd., SHELTON, Staffordshire, England.

1946- EARTHENWARES. Factory`s name printed within marks of various patterns and designs.

1946	Crown Clarence Pottery, LONGTON, England. -	see 1922 Co-op Wholesale Ltd.
1946	Dicker Potteries Ltd., LOWER DICKER, England.	see 1843 Clark, Uriah,
1946	Palissy Pottery Ltd., LONGTON, England. -	see 1905 Jones Ltd.,A.E.
1946	Roslyn China, LONGTON, England. - -	see 1913 Reid & Co.

1947 Balfour China Co.Ltd., LONGTON, Staffordshire, England.

1947-52 BONE CHINA. Printed in circle with crown- **BALFOUR ROYAL CROWN POTTERY**

1952-57 **Trentham Bone China Ltd.** **Trentham ROYAL CROWN POTTERY**

1947 Coper, Hans, WELWYN GARDEN CITY, Herts., England.

1947- STUDIO POTTERY, STONEWARES.
Impressed or incised -

1947 Creigiau Pottery (R.G.Southcliffe & Co.Ltd) CREIGIAU, Wales.

c.1947- LUSTRE EARTHENWARES. Factory`s name is printed or impressed within various marks. `CREIGIAU` is usually in the mark. - **CREIGIAU POTTERY WALES**

SOUTHCLIFFE POTTERY CREIGIAU

1947 Devonshire Potteries Ltd., BOVEY TRACY, Devon, England.

1947- EARTHENWARES. -

Printed -

1956- Printed - -

1959- Trentham Art Wares. Printed -

1947

1947 Durham China Co. Ltd., GATESHEAD, Co. Durham, England.

1947-57 EARTHENWARE AND CHINA.

Printed or impressed -

1947 Finney & Sons Ltd., A.T., Duchess China Wks, LONGTON, England.

1947- PORCELAIN. Factory`s trade name `DUCHESS` printed within marks of various designs.

DUCHESS
BONE CHINA
MADE IN ENGLAND

1947 Futura Art Pottery Ltd., HANLEY, Staffordshire, England.

1947-56 EARTHENWARES. - Printed -

1947 Hall Bros (Longton) Ltd., LONGTON, Staffordshire, England.

1947- CHINA FIGURES ETC.

Printed-

1947 Langdale Pottery Co.Ltd., HANLEY, Staffordshire, England.

1947-58 EARTHENWARES. - Printed -

<u>Langdale</u>
MADE IN ENGLAND

1947 Sterling Pottery Ltd., FENTON, Staffordshire, England.

1947-53 EARTHENWARES. -

Printed - - -

c.1949-53 Printed

1947 Trey, Marianne De, Shinner`s Bridge, DARTINGTON, England.

1947- STUDIO POTTERY. (With Sam Haile)

Incised or painted, sometimes within triangls- -

Impressed within a circle or square-

1984- **Dart Pottery.**

Peter Cook, Stephen Course, Peter Hazell. - -

Janice Tchalenko (designer)

(By kind permission of Dart Pottery, England.)

1947 Watson`s Potteries Ltd.,Henry, WATTISFIELD, Suffolk, England.

1947- TERRACOTTA AND EARTHENWARE.
The Watson family have been producing quality earthenware since 1800. Founded by Thomas Watson and continued by his great great grandson Michael Watson the present day Chairman (1995)

1995- New red-clay tableware mark-

Registered Trade Mark- -

(Courtesy of Henry Watson`s Potteries Ltd., England.)

1947 Hull, Norman, T.S., HONITON, England. - see 1881 Honiton Art Potteries.
1947 Kirklands (Staffordshire) Ltd., England. - see 1892 Kirkland & Co.

1948 Barron, Paul, FARNHAM, Surrey, England.

1948- STUDIO POTTERY. Impressed-

1948 Bowker, Arthur, FENTON, Staffordshire, England.

1948-58 PORCELAIN FIGURES, ETC. Printed -

1950-58 - - STAFFORDSHIRE
FINE BONE CHINA
OF
ARTHUR BOWKER

1948 Briglin Pottery Ltd., LONDON, W.1., England.

1948- EARTHENWARES. - Impressed- **BRIGLIN**

Barson, Anthony, (decorator) Painted mark- **A. B.**

1948 Fine Arts Porcelain Ltd., Charlton, LONDON, S.E.7. England.

1948-52 EARTHENWARES. - Printed -

1948 Dartmouth Pottery Ltd., Warfleet, DARTMOUTH, Devon, England.

1948- EARTHENWARE. - - - -

1948-60 impressed marks -

DP LTD
c. 1948-50

DARTMOUTH POTTERY
HAND MADE
IN ENGLAND
c. 1948-60

c. 1948-53

1950`s Rubber stamp marks-

Moulded wares had the mark incorporated -

DARMOUTH
DEVON
ENGLAND

DARTMOUTH
ENGLAND

Elaine Goddard mark -

1960`s- Paper labels used-

1992- Current paper label mark-

For further information see <u>Dartmouth Pottery</u> by Virginia Brisco.
(Courtesy of Dartmouth Pottery Ltd. Subsidiary of Samuel Heath & Sons plc.England.)

1948 Hulme, William, COBRIDGE, Staffordshire, England.

1948-54 EARTHENWARE.

Printed -

1948 Newland, William, PRESTWOOD, Buckinghamshire, England.

1948- STUDIO POTTERY, SCULPTURE, ETC. - -

Painted or incised with date - - WN 51

Signature with date - - **William Newland 55**

Painted with date - - W 6 1 N

1948 Ollivant Potteries Ltd., STOKE, Staffordshire, England.

1948-54 EARTHENWARES. Factory`s name and initials printed within marks of various patterns and designs.- -

O. P.
O. P. L.
OLLIVANT

1948 SIC Ceramiche Srl., CASALE MONFERRATO, Italy.

1948- CERAMICS, EARTHENWARE DINNER, TEA AND COFFEEWARE. Founded by Liliana Coppo (designer) and his two brothers.

Trade patterns:- **Mosaico, Portici, Vittoria, Sweet Home, Mirtillo, Pesci, Girasole, Bamboo, California and Scozia.**

ceramiche s.r.l.

(Courtesy of SIC Ceramiche Srl., Casale Monferrato.)

1948 Stevenson, Spencer & Co. Ltd., LONGTON, Staffordshire, England.

1948-60 CHINA.- Printed

SPENCER STEVENSON ENGLAND BONE CHINA.

ROYAL STUART BONE CHINA SPENCER STEVENSON ENGLAND

1948 Sykes, Steven, RICHMOND, Surrey, England.

1948-55 STUDIO POTTERY. - Signature- ***Steven Sykes***

1948 Walford, J.F., REDHILL, Surrey, and CROWBOROUGH, England.

1948- STUDIO POTTERY. - Impressed- WJ

1948 Westminster Pottery Ltd., HANLEY, Staffordshire, England.

1948-56 EARTHENWARES. - Printed -

1952- Trade-name - **CASTLECLIFFE WARE**

1948 Booths & Colcloughs Ltd., HANLEY, England. see 1897 Colclough, H.J.
1948 Crown Staffordshire China Co.Ltd., England. see 1889 Crown Staff. Porc. Co.Ltd.

1949 Babbacombe Pottery, TORQUAY, Devon, England.

1949-67 MOTTO, POLKADOT AND SEAGULL WARE FROM TERRACOTTA CLAY.

1967- **Sold to Toni-Raymond Pottery Ltd.** (see 1951) CERAMIC GIFTWARE.

1987- **Incorporated with Philip Laureston Designs.**

Information by kind permission of Philip Laureston Designs, Babbacombe Pottery, from The Old Torquay Potteries by D.& E. Lloyd Thomas.

1949 Blackman, Mrs Audrey, OXFORD, England.

1949- FIGURES AND GROUPS (Astbury type) Signature- ***A. Blackman***

1949 Featherstone Potteries, STOKE, Staffordshire, England.

1949-50 EARTHENWARES. Factory`s initials printed **F. P.**
or impressed within marks of various designs **F. N. P.**

1949 Foster`s Pottery Co., REDRUTH, Cornwall, England.

1949- EARTHENWARES. Impressed- **FOSTER`S POTTERY REDRUTH**

1949 King Werk Wuerfel & Mueller GmbH, HOEHR-GREN`, Germany.

1949- CERAMICS. Mainly BEER STEINS.

1949-95 mark- - **King**

(Courtesy of King Werk Wuerfel & Mueller GmbH, Germany.)

1949 Pendley Pottery,(Murray Fieldhouse) TRING, Herts., England.

1949- STUDIO POTTERY, STONEWARES.

Incised or printed-

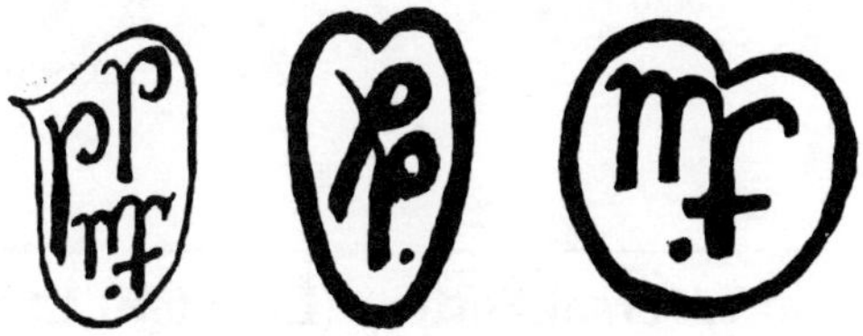

1949 Hornsea Pottery Ltd., HORNSEA, Humberside, England.

1949-CERAMIC GIFTWARE AND `FANCIES` AND LATER TABLEWARE AND KITCHEN STORAGE ACCESSORIES.
Rawson, Desmond and Colin (founders)
1954-Moved to 29 acre site in Hornsea developed into a Retail and Leisure Park which attracts over 1 million visitors a year.
1984 Steinburg Group acquired factory.
1987 Peter Black Holdings plc acquired factory, and injected needed capital into the company.
1991 The company is now privately held.

HORNSEA
c.1949-52
impressed or moulded

c.1951-52
impressed or printed

c.1952-53

c.1955

c.1956-62

1960-62

1960-62

1960

1962-64

1962-c73

HORNSEA
ENGLAND
moulded
impressed

c.1963-65

1973-77

1974-77

1977-80
and 1984-

HORNSEA
••••••••••••
ENGLAND
••••••••••••

1980-83

1987-95 Modern Marks -

(By kind permission of Hornsey Pottery Ltd, Humberside. England.)

1949/50

1949 Samuel, Miss Audrey, Kensington, LONDON, W.8., England.

1949- STUDIO POTTERY.

Incised or painted -

1949 Universal Pottery (Longton) Ltd., LONGTON, Staffs., England.

1949-62 CHINA AND EARTHENWARES.

Printed -

1949 Victoria Porcelain (Fenton) Ltd., FENTON, Staffordshire, England.

1949-57 EARTHENWARES. Factory`s name printed within marks of various designs.

1957-60 **Victoria & Trentham Potteries Ltd.**
CHINA AND EARTHENWARES. Printed with Lion-

VICTORIA
& TRENTHAM
POTTERIES LTD.

1949 Bloit, Michel, PARIS, France. - - - see 1773 Porcelaine de Paris.
1949 Salisbury China Co., LONGTON, England. - see 1927 Salisbury Crown China.
1949 Thistle Pottery, PORTOBELLO, Scotland. - see 1867 Buchan & Co.Ltd.

1950 Alton China Co. Ltd., LONGTON, Staffordshire, England.

1950-57 BONE CHINA FIGURES, ETC., Printed -

ALTON
BONE CHINA

BONE CHINA
ALTON ENGLAND

1950 Collyer, Ernest and Pamela, STANMORE, Middlesex, England.

1950- STUDIO POTTERY, TILES, ETC.

Ernest Collyer`s initials, incised or painted- ***E. C./ (date)***

Mrs Collyer (Pamela Nash) " " ***P. N.***

Name mark on panels - - **COLLYER-NASH**

1950 Faiencerie Lallier, MOUSTIERS, Ste-Marie, France.

c.1950 Faïence was first made in Moustiers in the 17th Century by Pierre Clerissy and his family.
Unfortunately, the last kiln closed down at the end of the 19th Century, but now in the 20th Century the faïence has been revived by this Company.

(Courtesy of Faiencerei Lallier, Moustiers, France.)

1950 Heath Ltd., J.E., Albert Potteries, BURSLEM, Staffs., England.

1950- FINE CHINA, SUPER VITRIFIED HOTELWARE.
Dudson (Holdings) Ltd., purchased factory from **Parrot & Company**.
see 1809 Dudson, Thomas,
Trade names: **`ERICA` and `ARMORLITE`** mainly used for the export trade.

Printed -

(By courtesy of The Dudson Group, Stoke-on-Trent, England.)

1950 Pincombe, Helen, The Forge, OXSHOTT, Surrey, England.

1950- STUDIO POTTERY. Impressed-

1950 Thompson, Pauline, EAST HENDRED, Berkshire, England.

1950- STUDIO POTTERY. Incised or painted -

1950 Viking Pottery Co., COBRIDGE, Staffordshire, England.

1950- CHINA AND EARTHENWARES. Printed -

1950/51

1950 Bellefroid, Edmund, (designer) MAASTRICHT, Holland. see 1883 Mosa,Koninklijke
1950 `Calyx Ware` TUNSTALL, England. - - see 1769 Adams Ltd., Wm.
1950 Corfield, Reginald, (Sales) Ltd., BURSLEM, England.- see 1867 Wade Group.
1950 Mckenzie, Warren, ST. IVES, England. - - see 1920 Leach, Bernard.
1950 Wade (Ulster) Ltd., BURSLEM, England. - - see 1867 Wade Group.

1951 Blackhurst & Co. Ltd., John, COBRIDGE, Staffordshire, England.

1951-59 EARTHENWARES. Printed - **J. BLACKHURST**
ENGLAND
JOHN
BLACKHURST

1951 Clare China Co. Ltd., LONGTON, Staffordshire, England.

1951- DECORATORS OF BONE-CHINA. Printed with crown- **BONE CHINA**
CLARE
MADE IN ENGLAND

1951 Holkham Studio Pottery, HOLKHAM, Norfolk, England.

1951-61 EARTHENWARES.

1961- **Holkham Pottery Ltd.**

1951 Moorland Pottery Ltd., Chelsea Works, BURSLEM, Staffs., England.

1951-86 **Studio Szeiler Ltd.,**
Joseph Szeiler (founder) came to England from his native Hungary in 1947.
Printed or impressed mark-

1951-55 Lichfield Road, HANLEY.
1955- 74 Moorland Road, BURSLEM.
EARTHENWARE, MAINLY ANIMAL FIGURES.

1986 **Moorland Pottery Ltd.** (change of ownership)
Giftware is still being manufactured, but the Company has now added modelling and design facilities. Printed or impressed mark-

(Courtesy of Moorland Pottery Ltd., Chelsea Works, Burslem, England.)

1951 Toni-Raymond Pottery Ltd., TORQUAY, Devon, England.

1951- EARTHENWARE, WHITE CLAY PRODUCTS.

Impressed or printed -

1967 **Bought Babbacombe Pottery** - see 1949 Babbacombe Pottery.
(By kind permission of Toni-Raymond Pottery Ltd. England.)

1951 New Chelsea China Co. Ltd., LONGTON, England. see 1913 New Chelsea Por.
1951 Taena Community, AYLBURTON, England. - - see 1946 Leach, Margarate.

1952 Avoncroft Pottery, (Geoffrey Whiting) HAMPTON LOVETT, Eng.

1952- STUDIO POTTERY, STONEWARES, ETC.

Impressed within circle- -

1952- Geoffrey Whiting mark

1952 Chelsea Pottery, LONDON, S.W.3. England.

1952- EARTHENWARES. Incised - **CHELSEA POTTERY**

1952- impressed or incised- -

1952 Groves, Lavender, Kings Road, LONDON, S.W.3. England.

1952- STUDIO POTTERY.

Incised or painted -

1952 Maund, Geoffrey, Pottery Ltd., CROYDON, Surrey, England.

1952- EARTHENWARES.

1952 Royal Stafford China, LONGTON, Staffordshire, England.

Amalgamation of Thomas Poole and Gladstone China Ltd.

1952- PORCELAIN. Factory`s name printed within marks of various patterns and designs.

ROYAL STAFFORD
BONE CHINA

see 1880 Poole, Thomas,

1952 Summerbank Pottery Ltd., TUNSTALL, England.

1952- EARTHENWARES. Factory`s name printed within marks of various designs.

SUMMERBANK

1954- Peter Scott (Bird pieces) Printed -

SUMMERBANK POTTERY
STAFFORDSHIRE
ENGLAND

1970- **Summerbank Pottery (1970) Ltd.**

1952-55

1952 Gladstone China, LONGTON, England. - see 1891 Procter, George & Co.
1952 Trentham Bone China Ltd., LONGTON, England. see 1947 Balfour China Co. Ltd.

1953 Alton Towers Handcraft Pottery (Staffs) Ltd., STOKE, England.

1953- EARTHENWARES. Printed or impressed - Usually within a circle.

ALTON TOWERS
HANDCRAFT
STAFFS
ENGLAND

TOWERS CRAFT WARE

1953 Green Dene Pottery, EAST HORSLEY, Surrey, England.

Denis Moore and Michael Buckland.

1953- STUDIO POTTERY. Impressed-

1953 Denis Moore monogram - -

1953 Michael Buckland monogram -

1953 O`Malley, Peter, Chelsea, LONDON, S.W.3., England.

1953- STUDIO POTTERY. - Impressed-

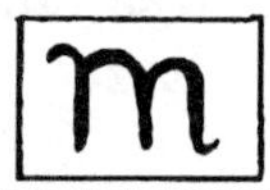

1953 Regency China Ltd., LONGTON, Staffordshire, England.

1953- CHINA.

Printed Trade-mark -

1954 Ceramicas Benlloch SA, Manises, VALENCIA, Spain.

1954- CERAMICS, TABLE LAMPS.
Ceramicas Benlloch,SA. have won many prizes of industrial and quality design within the Valencia region.

(Courtesy of Manuel Benlloch Marroco, Ceramicas Benlloch SA. Spain.)

1954 Leaper, E.T., Newlyn, Nr. PENZANCE, Cornwall, England.

1954- Studio Pottery.

1954 Wedgwood & Co.Ltd., H.F., Islington Works, LONGTON, England.

c.1954-59 EARTHENWARES AND CHINA. Factory`s initials printed within marks of various designs.

**H.F.W.& CO. LTD.
ISLINGTON**

1954 Bairstow & Co.,P.E., SHELTON, England. - see 1946 Fancies Fayre Pottery.
1954 Blue Waters Pottery, BOVEY TRACEY, England. see 1842 Bovey Tracey Pottery.
1954 Marshall, William, ST. IVES, England. - - see 1920 Leach, Bernard, H.

1955 Eastgate Potteries Ltd., WITHERNSEA, E. Yorkshire, England.

1955- EARTHENWARES. -

Printed -

1955 Eeles, David, Shepherds Well Pottery, LONDON, N.W.3., England.

1955-62 STUDIO POTTERY, TILES, ETC.

1955- Incised, painted or impressed - **D. E.**

c.1955- Shepherd`s Well Pottery, impressed-

1962- **Mosterton, Dorset.**

1955 Lladro Comercial SA., Tavernes Blanques, VALENCIA, Spain.

c.1955- PORCELAIN FIGURINES, GIFTWARES AND FANCIES.

Founded by the Lladro brothers, Juan, Jose, and Vicente,
From a small family business Lladro`s grew to be the large scale enterprise it is today. The workshop at Tavernes Blanques was enlarged seven times and in 1969 employed 1,600 people.
Lladro products are highly acclaimed, and have found their place in a number of museums and private collections.

1988- **Lladro Museum, New York, opened.**

1953

1956

1956

1957

1960

1960

Continued over -

1955

1955 Lladro Comercial SA, VALENCIA, Spain. (Cont`)

1963

1963

1970

1975

1990

(By kind permission of Lladro Comercial SA, VALENCIA, Spain.)

1955 Ridgway Potteries Ltd., STOKE, Staffordshire, England.

1955- EARTHENWARES. General mark printed with variations, sometimes including the different factories that belong to the Ridgway Group. i.e.
Adderley Floral China Works, LONGTON.
Bedford Works, SHELTON.
Booths, TUNSTALL.
Colcloughs, LONGTON.
Gainsborough Works, LONGTON.
North Staffordshire Pottery, COBRIDGE.
Paladin Works, FENTON.
Portland Pottery, COBRIDGE.

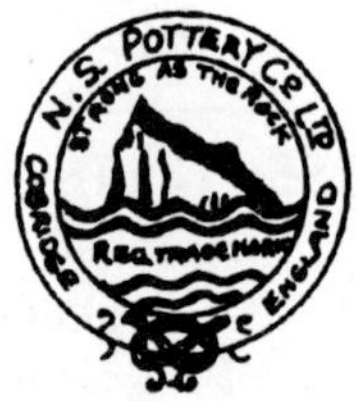

1962- Ridgway modern marks -

Taken over by Allied English Potteries Ltd.
Now part of the Royal Doulton Group.

see 1897 Colclough, H.J.
see 1873 Ridgway, Sparks & Ridgway.

1955 Holland, George Fishley, CLEVEDON, England. see 1921 Holland, Wm., Fishley.

1956 Arbeid, Dan, Abbey Art Centre, NEW BARNET, Herts., England.

1956- STUDIO POTTERY. - - -

Painted or impressed on small pieces - **D. A.**

on large pieces - **ARBEID**

1956 Duckworth, Ruth, KEW, Surrey, England.

1956- STUDIO POTTERY.

Painted or incised -

1956 Island Pottery Studio (Seaview) Ltd., ISLE OF WIGHT, England.

1956- Lester, Joe, EARTHENWARES.

Printed or impressed **J. O.**
I. O. W.

SEAVIEW

1956 Leach, David, Lowerdown Pottery, Bovey Tracey, Devon, England.

1956- STUDIO POTTERY

1930- Started his career at his father`s work-shop (Bernard Leach) at St. Ives, Cornwall. see 1920 Leach, Bernard

1946-55 **Became partner to Bernard Leach.**

Exhibits regularly in various parts of the world and his work is on show in many European museums. He has contributed much towards the process of pottery within education. David Leach trained his three sons in the trade and they are now all potters in their own right.

Impressed seal marks -

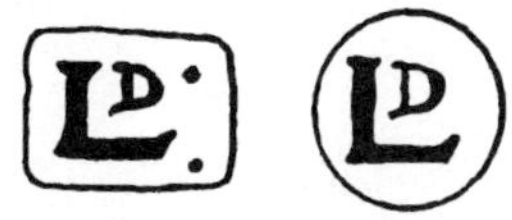

1956 mark (This seal represents the `Lowerdown Cross`) - -

(Courtesy of David Leach, Lowerdown Pottery, Devon. England.)

1956 Leach, Michael, Yelland Manor Pottery, FREMINGTON, Devon.

1956- STUDIO-TYPE POTTERY.

Apprentice to Bernard Leach (Father) at St. Ives Pottery, Cornwall.

see 1920 Leach, Bernard H.,

1956 Surrey Ceramic Co.Ltd., KINGWOOD, nr.Godalming, England.

1956- EARTHENWARE, STONEWARE.
This company was formed from the old Compton Pottery, established by Mrs Mary Watts in the early 20th century.
Pre 1956 underglaze- -

1956-77 marks:-

Cast Ware embossed in mould

Stamped onglaze

Stamped onglaze and waterslide transfer

Stamped on thrown ware (Kingwood Pottery)

1967- **Grayshott Pottery bought.**
1978-88 marks:-

Embossed into mould on cast ware.

Embossed into mould on cast ware. Also onglaze waterslide transfers.

1978 to date. Stamped onto thrown ware when wet with brass stamp:- - -

1978- Sometimes used in conjunction with above mark: - -

Michael Dixon (potter)

Joy Real (decorator)

1988-90 Onglaze waterslide transfer-

1990-to date (1995) Onglaze waterslide transfer and underglaze back stamp.-

(By kind permission of Surrey Ceramic Co.Ltd.,Grayshott Pottery, England.)

1956 Leach, Janet, ST IVES, England. - - - see 1920 Leach, Bernard H.,

1957 Five Towns China Co.Ltd., MIDDLEPORT, Staffordshire, England.

1957- FLORAL PORCELAIN. Factory`s name printed- within marks of various patterns and designs. **FIVE TOWNS CHINA CO. LTD. ENGLAND**

1957 Lotus Pottery, Stoke Gabriel, South Devon, England.

1957 EARTHENWARES

LP

STOKE GABRIEL LOTUS S. DEVON

1957 New Devon Pottery Ltd., NEWTON ABBOT, Devon, England.

1957 EARTHENWARES.

Printed

1957 Cole, Walter V., RYE, England. - - - see 1869 Rye Pottery.
1957 Haviland, William, LIMOGES, France. - - see 1892 Haviland, Theodore,
1957 Thewalt, Albert Jakob, Germany. - - see 1893 Thewalt, A.J.
1957 Victoria & Trentham Potteries Ltd., England. - see 1949 Victoria Porcelain Ltd.

1958 Aristocrat Florals & Fancies, LONGTON, Staffordshire, England.

1958- CHINA DECORATIVE WARES.

Printed -

ENGLISH
Aristocrat
Florals
BONE
CHINA

1958 Benham, Tony, Kensington Church St., LONDON, W.8., England.

1958- STUDIO POTTERY.

Incised or painted signature- **TONY BENHAM**

1958 Britannia Designs Ltd., DARTMOUTH, Devon, England.

c.1958 EARTHENWARE. DECORATORS. - -

c.1958-64
Rubber stamp

c.1965-70s
Rubber stamp

1985-87
Paper label

(For further information see Dartmouth Pottery by Virginia Brisco)

1958 Cambrian Pottery Co.Ltd., LLANDUDNO, Gwynedd, Wales.

1958- STUDIO POTTERY. Impressed or printed - **CAMBRIAN STUDIO WARE MADE IN WALES**

1958 Norfolk Pottery Co.Ltd., SHELTON, Staffordshire, England.

1958 EARTHENWARES

Printed- Royal Norfolk STAFFORDSHIRE ENGLAND

ROYAL NORFOLK POTTERY MADE IN ENGLAND

1958 Carlton Ware Ltd., STOKE, England. - - see 1890 Wiltshaw & Robinson.

1959 Auld, Ian, Wimbish, SAFFRON WALDEN, Essex, England.

1959- STUDIO POTTERY.

Impressed seal mark - **I A**

Painted - IA

1959 Leach, Jeremy, Craft Pottery, LONDON, S.E.1., England.

c.1959- STUDIO POTTERY - Impressed- **J. L. D. S.**

Was taught at Bernard Leach`s Pottery, Cornwall, from an early age.

Incised - **J. L.**

1962-63 Impressed- **J. L. C. P.**

1963- Incised - **J. L.**

see 1920 Leach, Bernard H.,

1959 Lewenstein, Eileen, LONDON, N.W.3., England.

1959- STUDIO POTTERY. - - -

E·L

1959 Trentham Art Wares, BOVEY TRACEY, England. see 1947 Devonshire Potteries.

1960 Ceramica de Conimbriga, Faia, CONDEIXA, Portugal.

1960- EARTHENWARE hand-made and hand-painted.
in the tradition of Brioso and Vandelli, earlier masters of Coimbra`s ceramics.
17th and 18th century reproductions with strong influences of Arabic designs.

(By kind permission of Ceramica de Conimbriga, Condeixa, Portugal.)

1960 Portmeirion Potteries Ltd., STOKE, Staffordshire, England.

1960 EARTHENWARES AND PORCELAIN.
Factory`s name printed within marks of various patterns and designs.
Susan Williams-Ellis (designer) uses a variety of botanical designs which features, plants, butterflies, bees, birds, etc.

Below are a selection of the marks used on Portmeirion wares-

North American mark

(Courtesy of Portmeirion Potteries Ltd. Staffordshire, England.) see 1912 Gray & Co., A.E.

1960 Royal Limoges, rue Donzelot, LIMOGES, France.

1960- PORCELAIN.

1995- Delaygue, Jean-Claude, (Man. Director)

The Limoges factories of GDA, (1797) and A. Lanternier & Cie, (1857) were incorporated and re-named `Royal Limoges.`

see 1798 GDA. Limoges.
see 1857 A. Lanternier & Cie.

(By kind permission of Royal Limoges, Limoges, France.)

1961/62

1961 Clough`s Royal Art Pottery, LONGTON, Staffordshire, England.

1961- EARTHENWARES. - Printed -

(1951-61) Mark
Formerly by Royal Art Pottery
(Alfred Clough Ltd.)

1968- **Barker Bros. Ltd.** see 1880 Grindley & Co.

1961 Diane Pottery Co., LONGTON, Staffordshire, England.

1961- PORCELAIN ORNAMENTS. Factory`s name printed within marks of various designs.

DIANE
POTTERY
LONGTON
STAFFORDSHIRE

1961 Gem Pottery Ltd., TUNSTALL, Staffordshire, England.

1961- EARTHENWARES. - Printed -

1961 Heatherley Fine China & Glass Co.Ltd., Chessington, Surrey, Eng.

1961- DECORATORS. Printed -

1961 Iden Pottery, (D. Townsend and J.H.Wood) RYE, Sussex, England.

1961- STUDIO POTTERY. - Printed

1961 Grosvenor China Ltd., LONGTON, England. - see 1913 New Chelsea Porc` Co.
1961 Lewis, Glenn, ST. IVES, England. - - see 1920 Leach, Bernard.
1961 Susie Cooper Ltd., LONGTON, England. - see 1930 Cooper Pottery, Susie,

---

1962 Cerasarda S.p.A., OLBIA, Sardinia, Italy

1962 POTTERY, HAND-PAINTED IN GRAFFITO STYLES. Promoted by the Consortium of the Costa Smeralda. Started by His Highness The Prince Karim Aga Khan, now owned by MERIDIANA Airlines.

(By kind permission of Cerasarda S.p.A., Olbia, Sardinia, Italy.)

1962 Haverfordwest Pottery, HAVERFORDWEST, Pembrokeshire, Eng.

1962- STUDIO POTTERY.

1962 Springfield China Ltd., LONGTON, Staffordshire, England.

1962- BONE CHINA.

(Courtesy of Springfield China Ltd., Longton, Staffs., England.)

1962 Price & Kensington Potteries Ltd., LONGPORT, England. see 1896 Price Brothers.

1963 Coquet, Jean-Louis, Saint Leonard de Noblat, LIMOGES, France.

1824 **Originally founded in 1824,** this factory has witnessed the coming and going of several generations of porcelain manufacturing families, the most famous being the Pouyat family in 1835.

Jusqui en (Before) 1960

1963- **Pierre Coquet (father) purchased the factory.** Jean-Louis Coquet (son) who had served his apprenticeship in his father`s factory in Paris, was made head of the business.

Various printed marks:-

1960-64

1964-73

1973

1983
Trademark

1991- **Lalique, the renowned French crystal House purchaced the business.**

(Courtesy of Jean-Louis Coquet, Limoges, France.)

1963/64

1963 Everett, Raymond R., RYE, Sussex, England.

1963- STUDIO POTTERY. -

Painted -

Printed or impressed - -

1963 Isle of Man Potteries Ltd., ISLE OF MAN, England.

1963- EARTHENWARES.

1963 Troika Pottery, St. Ives, Cornwall, England.

1963-83 STUDIO POTTERS. Various marks with the name of the Pottery included.
Founded by Leslie Illsley (sculptor) Benny Sirota (potter) and Jan Thompson (architect)
Troika pottery was individually made in contemporary styles by artists who were not afraid to experiment with shapes and colours.

TROIKA

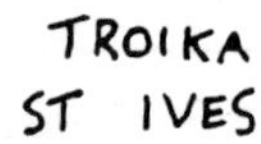

1963	\`Micratex\` TUNSTALL, England.	- -	see 1769 Adams Ltd., Wm.
1963	Poole Pottery Ltd., Poole, England.	- -	see 1873 Carter & Co.Ltd.

1964 Desirée, Porcelaensfabrikken A/S, RINGSTED, Denmark.

1964- TABLEWARE, COMMEMORATIVES AND GIFT ARTICLES.
Torbol, Hans Christian, (Founder)

Tableware mark - - -

Known for the Hans Christian Andersen Wallplates, decorated in blue with motifs from the famous fairytales.

1995 edition mark - -

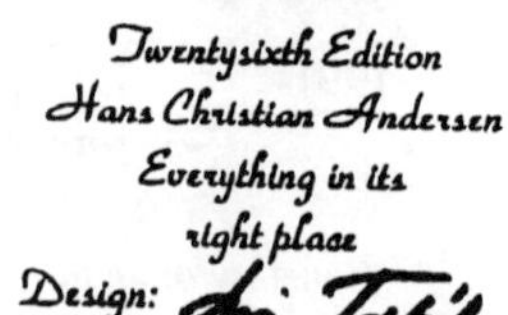

Twentysixth Edition
Hans Christian Andersen
Everything in its
right place
Design:

(Courtesy of Mr Knud Lars Torbol, Porcelaensfabrikken Desiree A/S, Denmark.)

1964 Leach, John, Muchelney Pottery, nr. Langport, Somerset, England.

1964- STUDIO POTTERY.

1957- Worked with his father David Leach Bovey Tracey, Devon. see 1956 Leach, David.

1960-63 Worked with his grand-father Bernard Leach. see 1920 Leach, Bernard,

1964 John Leach establishes the Muchelney Pottery with the help of his wife, Lizzie and family. 1972 Nick Rees joined the firm and contributed to the repeat stoneware production and the day-to-day running of the pottery.

MUCHELNEY

(Courtesy of John Leach, Muchelney Pottery, Somerset. England.)

1964 Howard Pottery Co., TUNSTALL, England. - - see 1886 Grimwade Bros.

1966 Purbeck Pottery Ltd., Westbourne, BOURNEMOUTH, England.

1966- STONEWARES.

1966-75 Printed mark-

The Company says that very little of its tableware has ever been back-stamped. Only the decorated giftware is stamped in the main.

1975 to present (1995) - -

(Courtesy of Purbeck Pottery Ltd., England.)

1967 Marioni Paolo s.r.l., Calenzano, FIRENZE, Italy.

1967 CERAMIC FIGURES, DECORATIVE ITEMS AND ARTISTIC REPRODUCTIONS.

1967-91 | 1967-91 | 1991-present (95)

(By kind permission of Marioni Paolo s.r.l., Italy.)

1967 Celtic Ceramics Ltd., KILRUSH, Ireland. - see 1879 Rosenthal & Co.

1967 Grayshot Pottery, Surrey, England. - - see 1956 Surrey Ceramic Co.

1967 Toni-Raymond Pottery Ltd., DEVON, England.- see 1949 Babbacombe Pottery

1968/69

1968 Aston, Christopher, ELKESLEY, Nottinghamshire, England.

1968- STONEWARE.

Applied label - 

1968 Blakeney Art Pottery, STOKE, Staffordshire, England.

1968- EARTHENWARES. STAFFORDSHIRE FIGURES, ETC.
Bailey, M.J. & S.K.

\`Flow Blue Victoria\`
Printed in blue- 

Printed in brown with
\`M.J.B.\`(M.J.Bailey) 

\`Romantic\` - 

1968 Freeman, P.H., CHURCH GRESLEY, England. - see 1864 Green & Co.Ltd., T.G.
1968 \`Romertopf\` RANSBACH-BAUMBACH, Germany. see 1933 Eduard Bay GmbH.

1969 Kellam, Colin, The Lion Brewery, TOTNES, Devonshire, England.

1969- STUDIO STONEWARE, Mainly Planters, lamp bases, umbrella stands and tiles.

1969- marks -  

1962-68 Trained at Shinners Bridge Pottery by Marianne de Trey. 1962-68 marks -  

Colin Kellam and Diana Cater work with a team of four.

(Courtesy of Colin Kellam, The Lion Brewery , England.)

1970 S. C. Apulum S.A., Alba lulia, Romania.

1970- HOUSEHOLD AND DECORATIVE PORCELAIN AND STONEWARE.
50% of this factory`s production is exported throughout the world.

1992- **Private Company established.**

1972-92

1984-94

1984-Today (1995)

(Courtesy of S.C. Apulum S.A.., Alba lulia, Romania.)

1971 Anton Potteries, Jon, LONGTON, Staffordshire, England.

1971-74 BONE-CHINA. - - -

1974- **Anton Potteries Ltd., Jon,** IRONSTONE -

1971 Hostess Tableware Ltd., LONGTON, Staffordshire, England.

1971- BONE-CHINA, IRONSTONE. - -
Factory`s name within marks of various patterns and designs.

Hostess Tableware
FINE BONE CHINA
STAFFS, ENGLAND
Royal Stafford

1971 Porcelanas Nou C.B., Ctra. Cheste, VILLAMARCHANTE, Spain.

1971- PORCELAIN FIGURINES, GIFT-WARES AND FANCIES.

(By kind permission of Porcelanas Nou C.B. Valencia, Spain.)

1972 Ceramic Workshops, Crossgar, DOWNPATRICK, Co. Down, Ireland.

1972 **Proprietor: Donald Nelson**
CERAMICS, PORCELAIN, ETC.

1972- **Little Orchard Pottery, Co. Armagh.**

1974- **Little Orchard Ceramics Ltd.,**

1975- **Little Orchard Porcelain Ltd.**

1978- **Ceramic Workshops, Co. Down.**

(By kind permission of Ceramic Workshops, Co.Down, Ireland.)

1972 Monaco, Manufacture De Porcelaine, Principaute De Monaco.

1972- HARD-PASTE PORCELAIN, FINE QUALITY TABLEWARE.
Founded by Erich Rozewicz with the help and encouragement of the Prince`s Family of Monaco.
Erich Rozewicz has devoted his working life to the art of ceramics. Through a series of creative posts in the ceramic industry Erich Rozewicz eventually established the Manufacture De Porcelaine De Monaco in 1972.

Fournisseur Breveté de
S.A.S. le Prince de Monaco

1986- Awarded the Prix De Promotion Internationale Art-Porcelain-Ceramique by Institut International de Promotion et de Prestige. UNESCO affiliated.

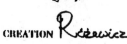

PORCELAINE DE MONACO
CREATION Rozewicz

1972-88 mark

MANUFACTURE DE MONACO

1988-95 mark

Fournisseur breveté de S.A.S. le Prince de Monaco
MANUFACTURE DE MONACO
- Porcelaine -
La porcelaine made in Monaco

1995- mark

(By kind permission of Manufacture De Porcelaine De Monaco S.A.M.)

1974 Castlewynd Studios Ltd., INVERDRUIE, Scotland.

1974- EARTHENWARES, STONEWARES.

Printed -

Trade-names -**Castlewynd and Aviemore**

1974 Gladstone Pottery Museum, LONGTON, Staffordshire, England.

1974- Complete Victorian pottery factory preserved from the era of coal-fired bottle kilns. Still producing pottery which is sold through their museum shop.

GLADSTONE POTTERY MUSEUM

c.1974-86
terracotta and earthenwares

GLADSTONE POTTERY MUSEUM STOKE-ON-TRENT ENGLAND

c.1986-94

DECORATED & SUPPLIED BY GLADSTONE POTTERY MUSEUM LONGTON, STOKE-ON-TRENT

c.1986-94
decorated items

GLADSTONE STOKE-ON-TRENT

1995-onwards

(By kind permission of Gladstone Pottery Museum)

see 1891 Proctor, George,

1974 Anton Potteries Ltd., Jon., LONGTON, England. - see 1971 Anton Potteries, J

1975 Clayholes Pottery & Fine Art, MAGHERAFELT, Co., N. Ireland.

1975 Proprietors: Ivor & Pat Coburn.
Stonewares. Decorative and oven-to-table, some decorated with signs of the zodiac, and flowers, etc.

Mark on small items

(Courtesy of Clayholes Pottery & Fine Art, Co. Derry, N.Ireland.)

1975 Crich Pottery, CRICH, Derbyshire, England.

1975- HIGH QUALITY STONEWARE STUDIO POTTERY.
Diana and David Worthy export most of their production, with over 50% going to Japan.
Winner of Supreme Gift Award Int. Spring Fair at National Exhibition Centre.

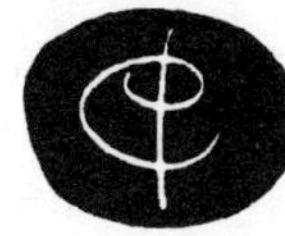

(By kind permission of Diana Worthy, Crich Pottery, England.)

1975 Porcellane Principe, VICENZA, Italy.

1975- PORCELAIN FIGURES IN THE TRADITIONAL CAPODIMONTE STYLE.
Founded by Luciano Cazzola (sculptor) Sergio Traforetti (painter) and Lino Gobbi (mould maker)

1975-94

1994-

1975-94 Signature mark of Luciano Cazzola-

1994-present (1995) mark of Luciano Cazzola-

(By kind permission of Porcellane Principe, Italy.)

1975 Pordamsa - Porcelanas del Ampurdan SA, GERONA, Spain.

1975- PORCELAIN. FANTASY PORCELAIN PRODUCTS, FLOWER VASES, BOXES, BATHROOM SETS, ETC.

(Courtesy of Pordamsa-Porcelanas del Ampurdan SA Spain.)

1975 Cardew, Seth, BODMIN, England. - - see 1939 Wenford Bridge Pottery

---

1976 Cockram, Roger John, Chittlehampton Pottery, Nth. Devon, England.

1976- STUDIO POTTER. Mark used on personal individual pieces and all larger pieces of standard ware. - Impressed-

1976-79 **Dell Cottage Pottery, Muddiford. Nth. Devon.** First pottery, making stoneware pottery mainly for kitchen use.

1979-86 **Northcott Pottery, Ashreigney, North Devon.** Domestic pottery, large plant pots and some `individual` pieces.

1986- **Chittlehampton Pottery, Chittlehampton.** Domestic ware, `individual` pieces. and decorative figures and candlesticks made by Ros Cockram.

(By kind permission of Roger J. Cockram, Chittlehampton Pottery ,England.)

1976 Taunton Vale Industries, HANLEY, England. - - see 1886 Grimwade Bros.

1977 Chessell Pottery (I.O.W.) Ltd.,Yarmouth, ISLE OF WIGHT, England.

1977- PORCELAIN GIFTWARE, FIGURES ETC
Founded by John and Sheila Francis.

Impressed marks -

The pottery is open to the public all year round.

(By kind permission of Chessell Pottery (I.O.W.) Ltd., England)

1977 Eigen Arts, JERSEY CITY, New Jersey, U.S.A.

1977- **Barbara Eigen** founded the pottery from a artist-in-residence loft in Soho, NYC. Earthenware in vegetable and fruit shapes etc., was made.

Printed marks- -

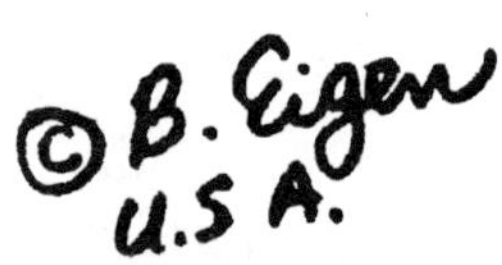

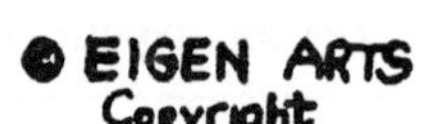

1989- **Eigen Arts incorporated,** moved to a larger workshop in Jersey City, NJ. They continue to add new models to their nature inspired pieces.
Their lidded pears were used at a White House luncheon when President Carter was in office.

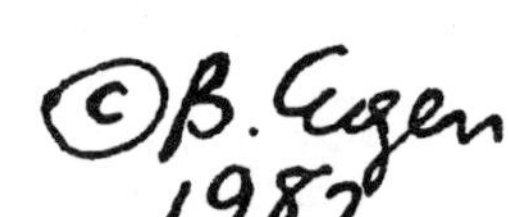

(By kind permission of Eigen Arts, Jersey City, NJ. U.S.A.)

1977 FAIART, Faianças e Porcelanas, S.A. BATALHA, Portugal.

1977- **FAIART 1.** First factory built producing decorative earthenware.

1987- **PORCELANAS DA BATALHA** was established.

1988 Backstamp-

1990- **FAIART 2** Second earthenware factory built.

1995- **FAIART - FAIANÇAS E PORCELANAS S.A.** Became an economic group producing earthenware, porcelain and terracotta.

1996- **FAIART ARGENTINA.** Acquired Porcelanus Verbano (a company established 50 years)

1990

1990 used for the Italian and spanish markets

1992

1994

Tody (1996) this company produces Porcelain, Earthenware and Terracotta and is one of the most modern ceramic factories in Portugal.

(Courtesy of FAIART, Faiançes Porcelanas, S.A., Portugal.)

1977 Lindner, Dr. Hans, KUPS, Germany. - - see 1929 Lindner Porzellanfabrik.

1978 Ceramadad, Old Bank Mill, LEEK, Staffordshire, England.

1978- POTTERY. -

Printed -

(By kind permission of Ceramadad, England.)

1978 Putnam, John, Heritage Houses, Blackawton, TOTNES, England.

1978- REPLICA CERAMIC HOUSES.

From his original 17 miniature houses, there are now (1995) a collection of 167 based on British buildings and 38 on U.S.A. buildings. John Putnam`s houses are exported throughout most of the world.

(Courtesy of John Putnam, Wood Farm, Blackawton,Totnes, Devon, England.)

1979

1979 Connoisseur Ltd., LEDBURY, Herefordshire, England.

1979- **Tunbridge Mill Studio.**
FIGURES IN FINE BONE CHINA. (Mainly limited editions)
1980- Moved to Malvern Wells, Worcester.
1986- Moved to Ledbury Studio

Connoisseur have a dating system with letters of the alphabet, starting with the year, 1979 with the LETTER `A`
Then- 1980-B, 81-C, 82-D, 83-E, 84-F, 85-G, 86-H, 87-I, 88-J, 89-K, 90-L, 91-M, 92-N, 93-O, 94-P
AND SO ON.

Connoisseur states that every model bears the name of the designer and the symbols of the craftsmen who have helped to create it, which are reproduced below:- (By kind permission of Connoisseur Ltd.)

<u>Craftsmen`s Marks:-</u>

Diane Lewis. Director, Designer & Flowermaker. - 

Chris Ashenden. Designer.

Richard Sefton. Designer.

Stephen Dalley. Mouldmaker. - - - - 

Darren Encock. Mouldmaker. - - - - D

Aileen Burton. Flowermaker. - - - - A

Wendy Green. Flowermaker. - - - - W

Jane Collins. Flowermaker. - - - - J

Joyce Calvesbert. Flowermaker. - - - - J

Sue Terry. Flowermaker. - - - - - S

Tracey Walmsley. Flowermaker. - - - - 

Terry Lewis. Director, Caster & Assembler. - - 

Peter Waltham. Caster & Assembler. - - - 

Mark Farmer. Caster & Assembler. - - - 

Henry Taylor. Caster & Assembler. - - - H

Continued over -

1979 Connoisseur Ltd., LEDBURY, Herefordshire, England. (Cont`)

Craftsmen`s Marks (Cont`)

Richard Jones. Caster & Assembler. - - - 

Nigel Evans. Ceramic Technician. - - - 

Marc Hodgkiss. Kiln Technician. - - - - 

Anthony Tomson. Director & Painter. - - - 

Freda Griffiths. Painter. - - - - - 

Sandy Griffiths. Painter. - - - - - 

Fay Stephens. Painter. - - - - - 

Lorraine Smith. Painter. - - - - - 

Sue Redding. Painter. - - - - - 

Tracey Arrowsmith. Painter. - - - - 

(Courtesy of Connoisseur Ltd., Lower Road, Ledbury, Herefordshire, HR8 2DJ. England)

1979 Crochendy Crefftau`r Cantref Tywyn Pottery, GWYNEDD, Wales.

1959- BONE CHINA. COMMEMORATIVES AND CELTIC DESIGNS. Printed -
Principal: Peter Roberts.

(Courtesy of Peter Roberts, Crochendy Crefftau`r Tywyn Pottery, Wales.)

1979 Cruse & Co., HARROWGATE, North Yorkshire, England.

1979- CERAMIC GIFTWARE AND WALL PLATES
manufactured by outside factories.
Printed mark -

(By kind permission of Cruse & Co. England.)

1979 Cork Art Pottery Ltd., CARRIGALINE, Ireland. see 1928 Carrigaline Pottery Ltd.,
1979 Duraline Hotelware Co. Ltd., TUNSTALL, England. see 1908 Grindley Hotel Ware
1979 Northcott Pottery, Nth. Devon, England. - - see 1976 Cockram, R.J.,

1980 Crown Trent China Ltd., LONGTON, Staffordshire, England.

1980- BONE CHINA BEAKERS AND TEAWARE.

Printed- Fine Bone China CROWN TRENT Staffordshire England

(Courtesy of Crown Trent China Ltd., Longton, England.)

1980	Molho, Patrick, PARIS, France. - - -	see 1773 Porcelaine de Paris.
1980	Porcelaine Philippe Deshouliers, FOECY, France.	see 1886 Lourioux, Louis,
1982	Cardew, Ara, BODMIN, England. - -	see 1939 Wenford Bridge Pottery.
1982	Melba-Wain (England) Ltd., LONGTON, England.	see 1946 Melba-Wain.

1983 Steelite International plc. Stoke-on-Trent, Staffordshire, England.

1983 CERAMIC TABLEWARE FOR HOTELS AND CATERERS.
David E.D. Johnson acquired the company from Royal Doulton 16th March 1983.
Trade names: **STEELITE and ALBALITE.**

STEELITE INTERNATIONAL ENGLAND

(Courtesy of Steelite International plc., Stoke-on-Trent. England.)

1984 Park Rose Ltd., BRIDLINGTON, Yorkshire, England.

1984 CERAMIC GIFTWARE, TABLEWARE AND INTERIOR LIGHTING.
The factory is situated within a Pottery Leisure Park where visitors can see the pieces taking shape from mould-making, glazing and firing, through to the finished product.

PARK ROSE BRIDLINGTON ENGLAND

(By kind permission of Park Rose Ltd., Yorkshire, England.)

1984	Carrigdhoun Pottery, CARRIGALINE, Ireland. -	see 1928 Carrigaline Pottery Ltd.,
1984	Dart Pottery, DARTINGTON, England. - -	see 1947 Trey, Marianne De,

1985 Donegal Parian China, BALLYSHANNON, Co. Donegal, Ireland.

1985- PARIAN CHINA GIFTWARE, TABLEWARE AND BASKETWARE.
Founders: Daniel J. Breslin, Sean O`Loughlin,
Benny Carty, Philip Cleary and Cyril Barrett.

1986-88 (Black)
Mark for larger pieces

1986-95 (Black)
Smaller pieces
(e.g. Thimbles)

1988-95 (Black)
Larger pieces

1992-95 (Black)
Smaller pieces
(e.g. Thimbles)

1996 (Gold)

The Company now operates from two large pottery complexes, which includes a state of the arts Visitors Centre, open, at present, from Monday to Saturday.

(By kind permission of Donegal Parian China, Ballyshannon, Ireland)

1986	Chittlehampton Pottery, Nth. Devon, England. -	see 1976 Cockram, R.J.,
1986	Moorland Pottery Ltd., BURSLEM, England. -	see 1951 Moorland Pottery.
1987	Clover Leaf Group, CHURCH GRESLEY, England.	see 1864 Green T.G., & Co.Ltd.
1987	Moorcroft, William John, BURSLEM, England.	see 1913 Moorcroft Ltd., W.
1987	Philip Laureston Designs, TORQUAY, England.	see 1949 Babbacombe Pottery.
1987	Tuffin, Sally, BURSLEM, England. - -	see 1913 Moorcroft Ltd., W.
1988	Keramik Holding AG Laufen, Switzerland. -	see 1906 Langenthal Swiss Ltd.
1990	Oxford (Ireland) Ltd., Ireland. - - -	see 1928 Carrigaline Pottery Ltd.
1991	Luc Doublet, PARIS, France. - - -	see 1773 Porcelaine de Paris.

1992 Amberglade Limited, RIPLEY, Derby, England.

1992- EARTHENWARE
Printed backstamps-

1992-
printed red

1994-
green

1995-
black

(Courtesy of Amberglade Ltd. England.)

1992 Rossware, Lower Eggleton, LEDBURY, Herefordshire, England.

1992- EARTHENWARE AND BONE CHINA.

Company was started in a small way under the name of `Rosspots` in 1988 by Tony and Manda Orton.Marks not used at this stage.
1992- Sold to parent company, Bosmere Products Ltd.

Marks 1992 to present (1995)

(By kind permission of Rossware, Ledbury, England.)

1992	Winterling Porzellan AG. KIRCHENLAMITZ, Germany.	see 1907 Winterling Gebr.
1993	Bishop, Rachel, BURSLEM, England. - -	see 1913 Moorcroft Ltd., W.,

Bibliography

Auscher, E.S.	History and Description of French Porcelain -	1905
Barber, E.A.	Artificial Soft-Paste Porcelain. - -	1907
Barber, E.A.	Marks of American Potters. - -	1904
Barrett, F.A.	Caughley and Coalport Porcelain. - -	1951
Binns, R.W.	Worcester China, 1852-97. - -	1897
Bowes, James Lord,	Japanese Marks and Seals - -	1882
Burton and Hobson,	Marks on Pottery and Porcelain. - -	1909
Chaffers, William,	Marks and Monograms of European and Oriental Pottery and Porcelain. - - -	1965
Clark, Garth,	American Ceramics, 1876 to the Present. -	1987
Cooper E. & Lewenstein, E.	POTTERS. Directory of Craft Potters Association. -	1992
Cushion, John,	Continental Porcelain. - - -	1974
Cushion, J.P.,	Handbook of Pottery and Porcelain Marks. -	1980
d'Albis, Jean,	HAVILAND. - - - -	1988
Danckert, L.,	Directory of European Porcelain. - -	1981
Delenne, Rene Louis,	Dictionaire des Marques de l'ancienne Faïence de Delft. - - -	1947
Fleming, J.A.,	Scottish Pottery. - - -	1923
Fortnum, (C.Drury E.)	Maiolica, a Historical Treatise. - -	1896
Gasnault, Paul, and Garnier, Eduard,	French Pottery. - - -	1884
Godden, G.A.,	Encyclopedia of British Pottery and Porcelain Marks.	1988
Godden, G.A.,	The Handbook of British Pottery & Porcelain Marks.	1972
Godden, G.A.,	Godden's Guide to English Porcelain. - -	1992
Godden, G.,	Godden's Guide to European Porcelain. -	1993
Graesse, J.G. Theodore,	Guide de l'amateur de Porcelaines et de Poteries. -	1872
Graesse, J.G. Theodore, and Jaennicke, E.,	Führer Für Sammier von Porzellan und Fayence. -	1867
Graesse - Jaennicke,	Guide de l'amateur de Porcelaines et de Faïences. -	1901
Greslou, Jules,	Recherches sur la Ceremique Suivies De Marques et Monogrammes Des Différentes Fabriques. - -	1863
Hayden, Arthur,	Chats on English China. - - -	1952
Hayden, A.,	Spode and his Successors. - -	1925
Hillier, Bevis,	Pottery and Porcelain. 1700-1914 - -	1968
Hooper, W.H. and Phillips, W.C.,	Manual of Marks on Pottery and Porcelain. -	1898
Hurlbutt, F.,	Bristol Porcelain. - - -	1928
Jewitt, Llewellynn,	Ceramic Art of Great Britain. - -	1878
Justice, J.,	Dictionary of Marks and Monograms of Delft Pottery.	1930
Knudsen, Ann Vibeke,	Die Keramikfabrik SØHOLM. (Bornholms Museum)	1993
Kybalova, Jana,	Guide to Ceramic Marks of the World. -	1981
Kovel, R.M. & T.H.,	A Dictionary of Marks, Pottery & Porcelain. -	1953
Leach, B.,	A Potter's Book. - - -	1940
Lewenstein, Eileen and Cooper, Emmanuel	New Ceramics. - - -	1974
Litchfield, Frederick,	Pottery & Porcelain (A Guide to Collectors) -	1892

Bibliography (Cont')

Mankowitz, W.,	Wedgwood.- - - -	1953
Mankowitz, Wolf, and Haggar, Reg. G.,	The Concise Encyclopedia of English Pottery and Porcelain -	1968
Mareschal, A.A.,	Les Faïences Anciennes et Modermes Marques and Décors (2 Volumes) -	1874
Nance, E.M.,	The Pottery and Porcelain of Swansea and Nantgarw. -	1942
Ormsbee, Thomas, H.,	English China and its Marks. - -	1962
Patten, Joan Van,	The Collector's Encyclopedia of Noritake. -	1984
Poche, Emanuel,	Porcelain Marks of the World. - -	1974
Prime, William C.,	Pottery and Porcelain of all Times and Nations.- -	1878
Ramsey, John,	American Potters and Pottery. - -	1939
Rontgen, Robert E.,	Marks on German, Bohemian and Austrian Porcelain. 1710 - present. -	1981
Rontgen, Robert E.,	The Book of Meissen. - - -	1984
Rose, M.,	Artist Potters in England. - -	1955
Schiffer N.N.,	Japanese Porcelain 1800 - 1950 - - -	1986
Solon, L.,	A History & Description of Italian Majolica. -	1907
Spargo, John,	Early American Pottery and China. - -	1926
Towner, D.,	The Leeds Pottery. - - -	1963

REGARDING THIS INDEX

The index of a book is vitally important, the major criteria is that it includes as much information as space allows. It must be succinct, and each entry should take the reader directly to where the information they are seeking lies.
This index has both the page number and the date of the mark or factory. In some cases,however, the factory you are looking for may be entered under the date of the original business name which has subsequently changed ; under these circumstances the factory or mark that you are engaged in finding will be best found under the page number and you should look in subsidiary parts of the page to find it.
Each letter of the alphabet has been compiled like a telephone directory. All the initials are entered first in alphabetical order; after which the names follow.
Each mark entry is shown by the abbreviation, 'mk'. Sometimes a mark might have to be described. i.e. Anchor mk or crown mk. Where these types of mark occur with the addition of initials they will be cross referenced as shown below:-

Anchor + R.H.mk. WORCESTER, Eng. (1751) 129.

R.H.+ Anchor mk. WORCESTER, Eng. (1751) 129.

Abbreviations:-

Mark -	mk.	Italy.	Ita.
Plus-	+	Japan.	Jap.
Austria	Aus.	Portugal	Por.
Belgium	Bel.	Russia.	Rus.
China.	Chi. or China.	Scotland.	Sco.
Denmark.	Den.	Spain.	Spa.
England.	Eng.	Sweden.	Swe.
France.	Fra.	Switzerland.	Swi.
Germany.	Ger.	U.S.A.	USA.
Holland.	Hol.	Wales.	Wal.
Ireland.	Ire.		

We have endeavoured to produce this index as comprehensively as we possibly can. If it does not come up to your expectations we apologise and would gratefully accept any suggestions that would improve it for the next revised edition.

E.G.P.

B

C

D

E

F

G

H

I

J

K

L

M

N

P

Q

R

T

U

V

W

X

Y

Z

MISCELLANEOUS MARKS

****